Benchmark Series

Level 1

Microsoft® Excel® 2010

Nita Rutkosky
Pierce College at Puyallup
Puyallup, Washington

Audrey Rutkosky
Pierce College at Puyallup
Puyallup, Washington

St. Paul • Indianapolis

Managing Editor	Sonja Brown
Senior Developmental Editor	Christine Hurney
Production Editor	Donna Mears
Copy Editor	Susan Capecchi
Cover and Text Designer	Leslie Anderson
Desktop Production	Ryan Hamner, Julie Johnston, Jack Ross
Proofreader	Laura Nelson
Indexer	Sandi Schroeder

Acknowledgements: The authors, editors, and publisher thank the following instructors for their helpful suggestions during the planning and development of the books in the Benchmark Office 2010 Series: Somasheker Akkaladevi, Virginia State University, Petersburg, VA; Ed Baker, Community College of Philadelphia, Philadelphia, PA; Lynn Baldwin, Madison Area Technical College, Madison, WI; Letty Barnes, Lake Washington Technical College, Kirkland, WA; Richard Bell, Coastal Carolina Community College, Jacksonville, NC; Perry Callas, Clatsop Community College, Astoria, OR; Carol DesJardins, St. Clair County Community College, Port Huron, MI; Stacy Gee Hollins, St. Louis Community College--Florissant Valley, St. Louis, MO Sally Haywood, Prairie State College, Chicago Heights, IL; Dr. Penny Johnson, Madison Technical College, Madison, WI; Jan Kehm, Spartanburg Community College, Spartanburg, SC; Jacqueline Larsen, Asheville Buncombe Tech, Asheville, NC; Sherry Lenhart, Terra Community College, Fremont, OH; Andrea Robinson Hinsey, Ivy Tech Community College NE, Fort Wayne, IN; Bari Siddique, University of Texas at Brownsville, Brownsville, TX; Joan Splawski, Northeast Wisconsin Technical College, Green Bay, WI; Diane Stark, Phoenix College, Phoenix, AZ; Mary Van Haute, Northeast Wisconsin Technical College, Green Bay, WI; Rosalie Westerberg, Clover Park Technical College, Lakewood, WA.

The publishing team also thanks the following individuals for their contributions to this project: checking the accuracy of the instruction and exercises—Robertt (Rob) W. Neilly, Traci Post, and Lindsay Ryan; developing lesson plans, supplemental assessments, and supplemental case studies—Jan Davidson, Lambton College, Sarnia, Ontario; writing rubrics to support end-of-chapter and end-of-unit activities—Robertt (Rob) W. Neilly, Seneca College, Toronto, Ontario; writing test item banks—Jeff Johnson; writing online quiz item banks—Trudy Muller; and developing PowerPoint presentations—Janet Blum, Fanshawe College, London, Ontario.

ISBN 978-0-76384-311-3 (Text)
ISBN 978-0-76384-314-4 (Text + CD)

875 Montreal Way
St. Paul, MN 55102
Email: educate@emcp.com
Website: www.emcp.com

Printed in the United States of America

19 18 17 16 15 14 13 12 11 4 5 6 7 8 9 10

Contents

Preface

Benchmark Microsoft Excel 2010 is designed for students who want to learn how to use this powerful spreadsheet program to manipulate numerical data in resolving issues related to finances or other numbers-based information. No prior knowledge of spreadsheets is required. After successfully completing a course using this textbook, students will be able to

- Create and edit spreadsheets of varying complexity
- Format cells, columns, and rows as well as entire workbooks in a uniform, attractive style
- Analyze numerical data and project outcomes to make informed decisions
- Plan, research, create, revise, and publish worksheets and workbooks to meet specific communication needs
- Given a workplace scenario requiring a numbers-based solution, assess the information requirements and then prepare the materials that achieve the goal efficiently and effectively

In addition to mastering Excel skills, students will learn the essential features and functions of computer hardware, the Windows 7 operating system, and Internet Explorer 8.0. Upon completing the text, they can expect to be proficient in using Excel to organize, analyze, and present information.

Achieving Proficiency in Excel 2010

Since its inception several Office versions ago, the Benchmark Series has served as a standard of excellence in software instruction. Elements of the book function individually and collectively to create an inviting, comprehensive learning environment that produces successful computer users. The following visual tour highlights the text's features.

UNIT OPENERS **display the unit's four chapter titles. Each level has two units, which conclude with a comprehensive unit performance assessment.**

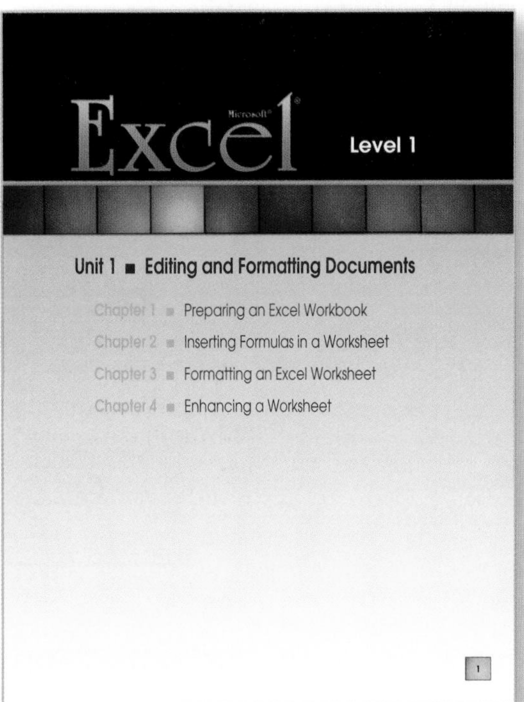

Microsoft Excel
Level 1
Unit 1 ■ Editing and Formatting Documents
Chapter 1 ■ Preparing an Excel Workbook
Chapter 2 ■ Inserting Formulas in a Worksheet
Chapter 3 ■ Formatting an Excel Worksheet
Chapter 4 ■ Enhancing a Worksheet
1

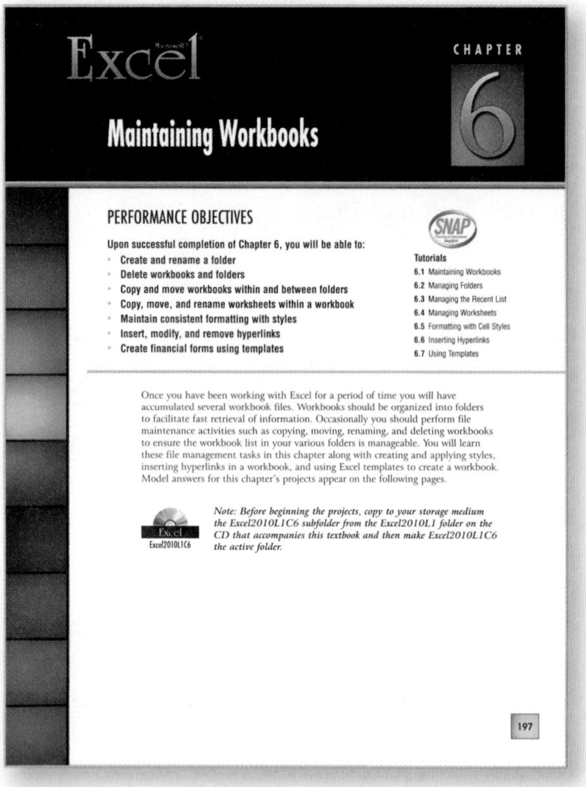
Microsoft® Excel

CHAPTER 6

Maintaining Workbooks

PERFORMANCE OBJECTIVES

Upon successful completion of Chapter 6, you will be able to:
- Create and rename a folder
- Delete workbooks and folders
- Copy and move workbooks within and between folders
- Copy, move, and rename worksheets within a workbook
- Maintain consistent formatting with styles
- Insert, modify, and remove hyperlinks
- Create financial forms using templates

SNAP

Tutorials
6.1 Maintaining Workbooks
6.2 Managing Folders
6.3 Managing the Recent List
6.4 Managing Worksheets
6.5 Formatting with Cell Styles
6.6 Inserting Hyperlinks
6.7 Using Templates

Once you have been working with Excel for a period of time you will have accumulated several workbook files. Workbooks should be organized into folders to facilitate fast retrieval of information. Occasionally you should perform file maintenance activities such as copying, moving, renaming, and deleting workbooks to ensure the workbook list in your various folders is manageable. You will learn these file management tasks in this chapter along with creating and applying styles, inserting hyperlinks in a workbook, and using Excel templates to create a workbook. Model answers for this chapter's projects appear on the following pages.

Excel2010L1C6

Note: Before beginning the projects, copy to your storage medium the Excel2010L1C6 subfolder from the Excel2010L1 folder on the CD that accompanies this textbook and then make Excel2010L1C6 the active folder.

197

CHAPTER OPENERS present the performance objectives and an overview of the skills taught.

SNAP interactive tutorials are available to support chapter-specific skills at www.snap2010.emcp.com.

DATA FILES are provided for each chapter. A prominent note reminds students to copy the appropriate chapter data folder and make it active.

PROJECT APPROACH: Builds Skill Mastery within Realistic Context

MODEL ANSWERS provide a preview of the finished chapter projects and allow students to confirm they have created the materials accurately.

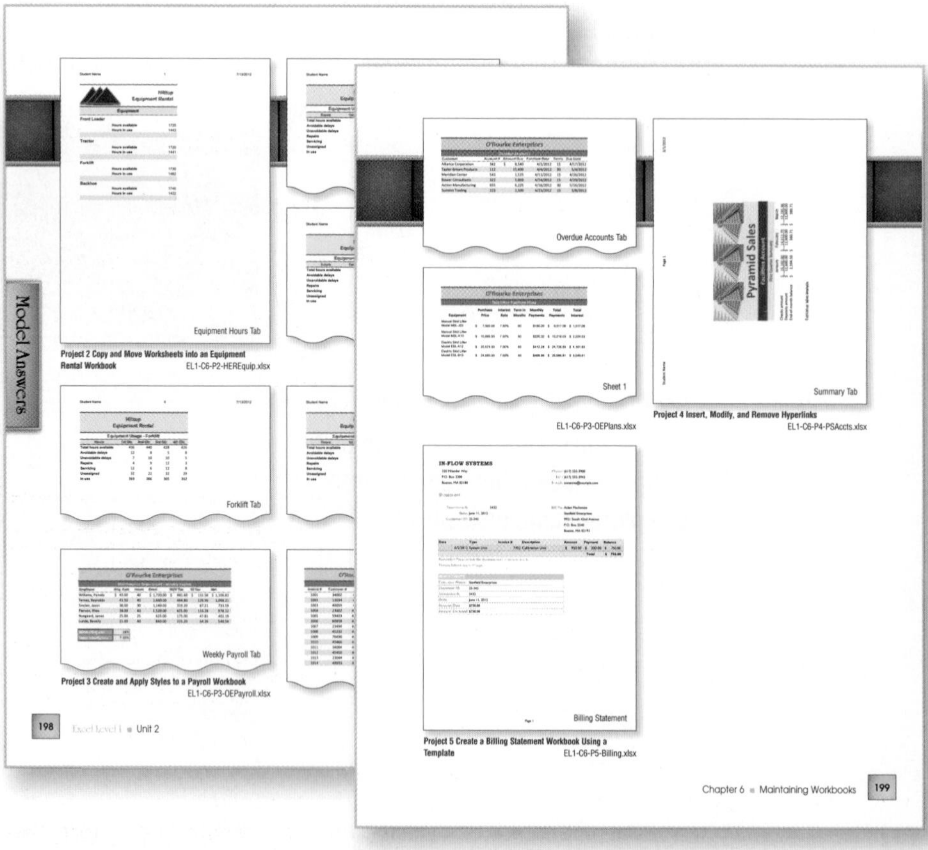

Model Answers
Equipment Hours Tab
Project 2 Copy and Move Worksheets into an Equipment Rental Workbook
EL1-C6-P2-HEREquip.xlsx
Forklift Tab
Weekly Payroll Tab
Project 3 Create and Apply Styles to a Payroll Workbook
EL1-C6-P3-OEPayroll.xlsx
198 Excel Level 1 ■ Unit 2
Overdue Accounts Tab
Sheet 1
EL1-C6-P3-OEPlans.xlsx
Pyramid Sales
Summary Tab
Project 4 Insert, Modify, and Remove Hyperlinks
EL1-C6-P4-PSAccts.xlsx
Billing Statement
Project 5 Create a Billing Statement Workbook Using a Template
EL1-C6-P5-Billing.xlsx
Chapter 6 ■ Maintaining Workbooks 199

Project 1 Format a Product Pricing Worksheet 7 Parts

You will open a workbook containing a worksheet with product pricing data, and then format the worksheet by changing column widths and row heights, inserting and deleting rows and columns, deleting rows and columns, and clearing data in cells. You will also apply font and alignment formatting to data in cells and then preview the worksheet.

Changing Column Width

Columns in a worksheet are the same width by default. In some worksheets you may want to change column widths to accommodate more or less data. You can change column width using the mouse on column boundaries or at a dialog box.

Changing Column Width Using Column Boundaries

As you learned in Chapter 1, you can adjust the width of a column by dragging the column boundary line or adjust a column width to the longest entry by double-clicking the boundary line. When you drag a column boundary, the column width displays in a box above the mouse pointer. The column width number that displays represents the average number of characters in the standard font that can fit in a cell.

You can change the width of selected adjacent columns at the same time. To do this, select the columns and then drag one of the column boundaries within the selected columns. As you drag the boundary the column width changes for all selected columns. To select adjacent columns, position the cell pointer on the first desired column header (the mouse pointer turns into a black, down-pointing arrow), hold down the left mouse button, drag the cell pointer to the last desired column header, and then release the mouse button.

HINT
To change the width of all columns in a worksheet, click the Select All button and then drag a column boundary to the desired position.

Project 1a Changing Column Width Using a Column Boundary Part 1 of 7

1. Open **CMProducts.xlsx**.
2. Save the workbook with Save As and name it **EL1-C3-P1-CMProducts**.
3. Insert a formula in cell D2 that multiplies the price in cell B2 with the number in cell C2. Copy the formula in cell D2 down to cells D3 through D14.
4. Change the width of column D by completing the following steps:
   a. Position the mouse pointer on the column boundary in the column header between columns D and E until it turns into a double-headed arrow pointing left and right.
   b. Hold down the left mouse button, drag the column boundary to the right until *Width: 11.00 (82 pixels)* displays in the box, and then release the mouse button.
5. Make cell D15 active and then insert the sum of cells D2 through D14.
6. Change the width of columns A and B by completing the following steps:
   a. Select columns A and B. To do this, position the cell pointer on the column A header, hold down the left mouse button, drag the cell pointer to the column B head[er, and then] release the mouse button.

Step 4b

MULTIPART PROJECTS provide a framework for the instruction and practice on software features. A project overview identifies tasks to accomplish and key features to use in completing the work.

STEP-BY-STEP INSTRUCTIONS guide students to the desired outcome for each project part. Screen captures illustrate what the student's screen should look like at key points.

   b. Position the cell pointer on the column boundary between columns A and B until it turns into a double-headed arrow pointing left and right.
   c. Hold down the left mouse button, drag the column boundary to the right until *Width: 10.14 (76 pixels)* displays in the box, and then release the mouse button.
7. Adjust the width of column C to accommodate the longest entry by double-clicking on the column boundary between columns C and D.
8. Save **EL1-C3-P1-CMProducts.xlsx**.

Step 6c

Between project parts, the text presents instruction on the features and skills necessary to accomplish the next section of the project.

Quick Steps
Change Column Width
Drag column boundary line.
OR
Double-click column boundary.
OR
1. Click Format button.
2. Click *Column Width* at drop-down list.
3. Type desired width.
4. Click OK.

Format

Changing Column Width at the Column Width Dialog Box

At the Column Width dialog box shown in Figure 3.1, you can specify a column width number. Increase the column width number to make the column wider or decrease the column width number to make the column narrower.

To display the Column Width dialog box, click the Format button in the Cells group in the Home tab and then click *Column Width* at the drop-down list. At the Column Width dialog box, type the number representing the average number of characters in the standard font that you want to fit in the column and then press Enter or click OK.

Figure 3.1 Column Width Dialog Box

Type the column width in this text box.

Project 1b Changing Column Width at the Column Width Dialog Box Part 2 of 7

1. With **EL1-C3-P1-CMProducts.xlsx** open, change the width of column A by completing the following steps:
   a. Make any cell in column A active.
   b. Click the Format button in the Cells group in the Home tab and then click *Column Width* at the drop-down list.
   c. At the Column Width dialog box, type 12.75 in the *Column width* text box.
   d. Click OK to close the dialog box.
2. Make any cell in column B active and then change the width of column B to *12.75* by completing steps similar to those in Step 1.
3. Make any cell in column C active and then change the width of column C to *8* by completing steps similar to those in Step 1.
4. Save **EL1-C3-P1-CMProducts.xlsx**.

Step 1c

Step 1d

Typically, a file remains open throughout all parts of the project. Students save their work incrementally.

QUICK STEPS provide feature summaries for reference and review.

HINTS provide useful tips on how to use features efficiently and effectively.

MAGENTA TEXT identifies material to type.

At the end of the project, students save, print, and then close the file.

Working with Ranges

A selected group of cells is referred to as a ***range***. A range of cells can be formatted, moved, copied, or deleted. You can also name a range of cells and then move the insertion point to the range or use a named range as part of a formula.

To name a range, select the cells and then click in the Name Box located at the left of the Formula bar. Type a name for the range (do not use a space) and then press Enter. To move the insertion point to a specific range and select the range, click the down-pointing arrow at the right side of the Name Box and then click the range name.

You can also name a range using the Define Name button in the Formulas tab. To do this, click the Formulas tab and then click the Define Name button in the Defined Names group. At the New Name dialog box, type a name for the range and then click OK.

You can use a range name in a formula. For example, if a range is named *Profit* and you want to insert the average of all cells in the *Profit* range, you would make the desired cell active and then type *=AVERAGE(Profit)*. You can use a named range in the current worksheet or in another worksheet within the workbook.

Quick Steps

Name a Range
1. Select cells.
2. Click in Name Box.
3. Type range name.
4. Press Enter.

HINT

Another method for moving to a range is to click the Find & Select button in the Editing group in the Home tab and then click *Go To*. At the Go To dialog box, double-click the range name.

Define Name

Project 2b **Naming a Range and Using a Range in a Formula** Part 2 of 2

1. With **EL1-C5-P2-HCEqpRpt.xlsx** open, click the Sheet2 tab and then type the following text in the specified cells:
   A1 = EQUIPMENT USAGE REPORT
   A2 = Yearly hours
   A3 = Avoidable delays
   A4 = Unavoidable delays
   A5 = Total delay hours
   A6 = (leave blank)
   A7 = Repairs
   A8 = Servicing
   A9 = Total repair/servicing hours
2. Make the following formatting changes to the worksheet:
   a. Automatically adjust the width of column A.
   b. Center and bold the text in cells A1 and A2.
3. Select a range of cells in worksheet 1, name the range, and use it in a formula in worksheet 2 by completing the following steps:
   a. Click the Sheet1 tab.
   b. Select cells B5 through M5.
   c. Click in the Name Box located to the left of the Formula bar.
   d. Type adhours (for Avoidable Delays Hours) and then press Enter.
   e. Click the Sheet2 tab.
   f. Make cell B3 active.
   g. Type the equation =SUM(adhours) and then press Enter.

Step 1

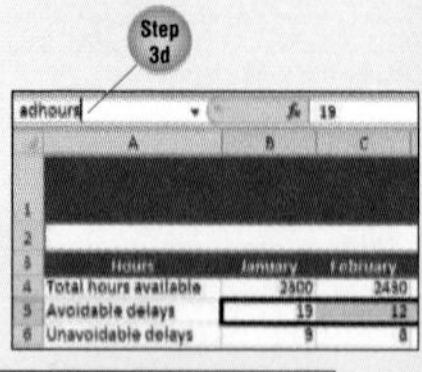

Step 3d

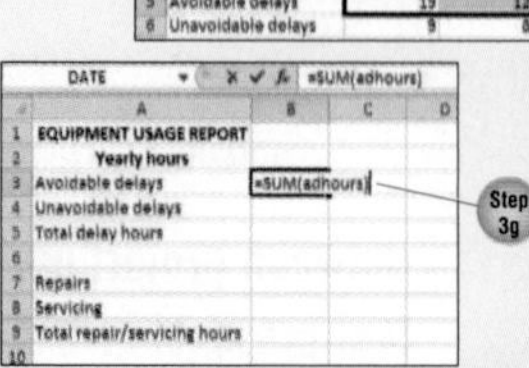

Step 3g

Chapter 5 ■ Moving Data within and between Workbooks 177

CHAPTER REVIEW ACTIVITIES: A Hierarchy of Learning Assessments

Chapter Summary

- The Page Setup group in the Page Layout tab contains buttons for changing margins, page orientation and size, and buttons for establishing a print area, inserting a page break, applying a picture background, and printing titles.
- The default left and right margins are 0.7 inch and the default top and bottom margins are 0.75 inch. Change these default margins with the Margins button in the Page Setup group in the Page Layout tab.
- Display the Page Setup dialog box with the Margins tab selected by clicking the Margins button and then clicking *Custom Margins* at the drop-down list.
- Center a worksheet on the page with the *Horizontally* and *Vertically* options at the Page Setup dialog box with the Margins tab selected.
- Click the Orientation button in the Page Setup group in the Page Layout tab to display the two orientation choices — *Portrait* and *Landscape*.
- Insert a page break by selecting the column or row, clicking the Breaks button in the Page Setup group in the Page Layout tab, and then clicking *Insert Page Break* at the drop-down list.
- To insert both a horizontal and vertical page break at the same time, make a cell active, click the Br down list.
- Display a worksheet in button in the view area clicking the Page Break
- Use options at the Page that you want column box by clicking the Pri Layout tab.
- Use options in the Sca on a specific number o
- Use the Background bu insert a worksheet bac screen but does not pri
- Use options in the She want gridlines and hea
- Specify a print area by in the Page Setup grou at the drop-down list. clicking the Print Area down list.
- Create a header and/or group in the Insert tab dialog box with the He
- Customize print jobs w
- To check spelling in a Spelling button.

138 Excel Level 1 ■ Unit 1

CHAPTER SUMMARY **captures the purpose and execution of key features.**

- Click the Undo button on the Quick Access toolbar to reverse the most recent action and click the Redo button to redo a previously reversed action.
- Use options at the Find and Replace dialog box with the Find tab selected to find specific data and/or formatting in a worksheet.
- Use options at the Find and Replace dialog box with the Replace tab selected to find specific data and/or formatting and replace with other data and/or formatting.
- Sort data in a worksheet with options from the Sort & Filter button in the Editing group in the Home tab.
- Create a custom sort with options at the Sort dialog box. Display this dialog box by clicking the Sort & Filter button and then clicking *Custom Sort* at the drop-down list.
- Use the filter feature to temporarily isolate specific data. Turn on the filter feature by clicking the Sort & Filter button in the Editing group in the Home tab and then clicking *Filter* at the drop-down list. This inserts filter arrows in each column label. Click a filter arrow and then use options at the drop-down list that displays to specify the filter data.

Commands Review

FEATURE	RIBBON TAB, GROUP	BUTTON, OPTION	KEYBOARD SHORTCUT
Margins	Page Layout		
Page Setup dialog box with Margins tab selected	Page Layout		
Orientation	Page Layout		
Size	Page Layout		
Insert page break	Page Layout		
Remove page break	Page Layout		
Page Break Preview	View, Workb		
Page Setup dialog box with Sheet tab selected	Page Layout		
Scale width	Page Layout		
Scale height	Page Layout		
Scale	Page Layout		
Background picture	Page Layout		

COMMANDS REVIEW **summarizes visually the major features and alternative methods of access.**

FEATURE	RIBBON TAB, GROUP	BUTTON, OPTION	KEYBOARD SHORTCUT
Print Area	Page Layout, Page Setup		
Header and footer	Insert, Text		
Page Layout view	View, Workbook Views		
Spelling	Review, Proofing		F7
Find and Replace dialog box with Find tab selected	Home, Editing	Find	Ctrl + F
Find and Replace dialog box with Replace tab selected	Home, Editing	Replace	Ctrl + H
Sort data	Home, Editing		
Filter data	Home, Editing		

Concepts Check Test Your Knowledge

Completion: In the space provided at the right, indicate the correct term, symbol, or command.

1. This is the default left and right margin measurement. ____________
2. This is the default top and bottom margin measurement. ____________
3. The Margins button is located in this tab. ____________
4. By default, a worksheet prints in this orientation on a page. ____________
5. Click the Print Titles button in the Page Setup group in the Page Layout tab and the Page Setup dialog box displays with this tab selected. ____________
6. Use options in this group in the Page Layout tab to adjust the printed output by a percentage to fit the number of pages specified. ____________
7. Use this button in the Page Setup group in the Page Layout tab to select and print specific areas in a worksheet. ____________
8. Click the Header & Footer button in the Text group in the Insert tab and the worksheet displays in this view. ____________

140 Excel Level 1 ■ Unit 1

CONCEPTS CHECK **questions assess knowledge recall.**

Skills Check Assess Your Performance

Assessment

1 INSERT AVERAGE, MAX, AND MIN FUNCTIONS

1. Open **DISalesAnalysis.xlsx**.
2. Save the workbook with Save As and name it **EL1-C2-A1-DISalesAnalysis**.
3. Use the AVERAGE function to determine the monthly sales (cells H4 through H9).
4. Format cell H4 with the Accounting Number Format with no decimal places.
5. Total each monthly column including the Average column (cells B10 through H10).
6. Use the MAX through G10)
7. Use the MIN through G10)
8. Save, print, ar

Assessment

2 INSERT PMT FUNCT

1. Open **CMRef**
2. Save the work
3. The manager either $125,0 total payment specifications:
   a. Make cell E
   b. Use the Ins using the Pl
      Rate =
      Nper =
      Pv =
   c. Copy the fo
4. Insert a formul
5. Copy the form
6. Insert a formu in F5. (The fo
7. Copy the form
8. Save, print, ar

Assessment

3 INSERT FV FUNCTI

1. Open **RPInve**
2. Save the work
3. Make the follo
   a. Change the

SKILLS CHECK **exercises ask students to create a variety of documents using multiple features without how-to directions.**

Assessment

5 APPLY CONDITIONAL FORMATTING TO A SALES WORKBOOK

Help

1. Use Excel Help files or experiment with the options at the Conditional Formatting button drop-down gallery to learn about conditional formatting.
2. Open **PSSales.xlsx** and then save the workbook with Save As and name it **EL1-C6-A5-PSSales**.
3. Select cells D5 through D19 and then use conditional formatting to display the amounts as data bars.
4. Insert a header that prints your name, a page number, and the current date.
5. Save, print, and then close **EL1-C6-A5-PSSales.xlsx**.

Visual Benchmark Demonstrate Your Proficiency

FILL IN AN EXPENSE REPORT FORM

1. Display the New tab Backstage view, click the Sample templates button, and then double-click the *Expense Report* template.
2. With the expense report open, apply the Paper theme.
3. Select cells J1 through L1 and then apply the Note cell style.
4. Type the information in the cells as indicated in Figure 6.9.
5. Make cell L18 active and apply the Bad cell style.
6. Save the completed workbook and name it **EL1-C6-VB-OEExpRpt**.
7. Print and then close **EL1-C6-VB-OEExpRpt.xlsx**.

Figure 6.9 Visual Benchmark

O'Rourke Enterprises

Expense Report

For Office Use Only

PURPOSE: Advertising Media Conference

EMPLOYEE INFORMATION:

Name Sophia Constanza

Department Advertising

APPROVED: Approved by Seth Morgenstern on 10/31/2012

VISUAL BENCHMARK **assessments test students' problem-solving skills and mastery of program features.**

Case Study Apply Your Skills

Part 1

You are a loan officer for Dollar Wise Financial Services and work in the department that specializes in home loans. You have decided to prepare a sample home mortgage worksheet to show prospective clients. This sample home mortgage worksheet will show the monthly payments on variously priced homes with varying interest rates. Open the **DWMortgages.xlsx** worksheet and then complete the home mortgage worksheet by inserting the following formulas:

- Since many homes in your area sell for at least $400,000, you decide to add that amount to the worksheet with a 5%, 10%, 15%, and 20% down payment.
- In column C, insert a formula that determines the down payment amount.
- In column D, insert a formula that determines the loan amount.
- In column G, insert a formula using the PMT function. (The monthly payment will display as a negative number.)

Save the worksheet and name it **EL1-C2-CS-DWMortgages**.

Part 2

If home buyers put down less than 20 percent of the home's purchase price, mortgage insurance is required. With **EL1-C2-CS-DWMortgages.xlsx** open, insert an IF statement in the cells in column H that inserts the word "No" if the percentage in column B is equal to or greater than 20% or inserts the word "Yes" if the percentage in column B is less than 20%. Save and then print **EL1-C2-CS-DWMortgages.xlsx**.

Part 3

Interest rates fluctuate on a regular basis. Using the resources available to you, determine a current interest rate in your area. Delete the interest rate of 7% in the Dollar Wise worksheet and insert the interest rate for your area. Save and then print **EL1-C2-CS-DWMortgages.xlsx**.

Part 4

When a client is required to purchase mortgage insurance, you would like to provide information to the client concerning this insurance. Use the Help feature to learn about creating hyperlinks in Excel. Locate a helpful website that specializes in private mortgage insurance. Create a hyperlink in the worksheet that will display the website. Save, print, and then close **EL1-C2-CS-DWMortage.xlsx**.

Help

Chapter 2 ■ Inserting Formulas in a Worksheet 67

CASE STUDY **requires analyzing a workplace scenario and then planning and executing multipart projects.**

Students search the Web and/or use the program's Help feature to locate additional information required to complete the Case Study.

UNIT PERFORMANCE ASSESSMENT: Cross-Disciplinary, Comprehensive Evaluation

Excel

UNIT 2

Performance Assessment

Note: Before beginning unit assessments, copy to your storage medium the Excel2010L1U2 subfolder from the Excel2010L1 folder on the CD that accompanies this textbook and then make Excel2010L1U2 the active folder.

Assessing Proficiency

In this unit, you have learned how to work with multiple windows; move, copy, link, and paste data between workbooks and applications; create and customize charts with data in a worksheet; save a workbook as a web page; insert hyperlinks; and insert and customize pictures, clip art images, shapes, SmartArt diagrams, and WordArt.

Assessment 1 Copy and Paste Data and Insert WordArt in a Training Scores Workbook

1. Open **RLTraining.xlsx** and then save the workbook with Save As and name it **EL1-U2-A1-RLTraining**.
2. Delete row 15 (the row for *Kwieciak, Kathleen*).
3. Insert a formula in cell D4 that averages the percentages in cells B4 and C4.
4. Copy the formula in cell D4 down to cells D5 through D20.
5. Make cell A22 active, turn on bold, and then type Highest Averages.
6. Display the Clipboard task pane and make sure it is empty.
7. Select and then copy each of the following rows (individually): row 7, 10, 14, 16, and 18.
8. Make cell A23 active and then paste row 14 (the row for *Jewett, Troy*).
9. Make cell A24 active and then paste row 7 (the row for *Cumpston, Kurt*).
10. Make cell A25 active and then paste row 10 (the row for *Fisher-Edwards, Theresa*).
11. Make cell A26 active and then paste row 16 (the row for *Mathias, Caleb*).
12. Make cell A27 active and then paste row 18 (the row for *Nyegaard, Curtis*).
13. Click the Clear All button in the Clipboard task pane and then close the task pane.
14. Insert in cell A1 the text *Roseland* as WordArt. Format the WordArt text to add visual appeal to the worksheet.
15. Save, print, and then close **EL1-U2-A1-RLTraining.xlsx**.

ASSESSING PROFICIENCY checks mastery of features.

WRITING ACTIVITIES involve applying program skills in a communication context.

	...display	4,...	4,500.00	...
9	Payroll taxes	2,430.00	2,200.00	91%
10	Telephone	1,450.00	1,500.00	103%
11				

Writing Activities

The following activities give you the opportunity to practice your writing skills along with demonstrating an understanding of some of the important Excel features you have mastered in this unit. Use correct grammar, appropriate word choices, and clear sentence constructions.

Activity 1 Prepare a Projected Budget

You are the accounting assistant in the financial department of McCormack Funds and you have been asked to prepare a yearly proposed department budget. The total amount for the department is $1,450,000. You are given the percentages for the proposed budget items, which are: Salaries, 45%; Benefits, 12%; Training, 14%; Administrative Costs, 10%; Equipment, 11%; and Supplies, 8%. Create a worksheet with this information that shows the projected yearly budget, the budget items in the department, the percentage of the budget, and the amount for each item. After the worksheet is completed, save the workbook and name it **EL1-U2-Act1-MFBudget**. Print and then close the workbook.

Optional: Using Word 2010, write a memo to the McCormack Funds Finance Department explaining that the proposed annual department budget is attached for their review. Comments and suggestions are to be sent to you within one week. Save the file and name it **EL1-U2-Act1-MFMemo**. Print and then close the file.

310 Excel Level 1 ■ Unit 2 Performance Assessment

- Include the following information somewhere in the workshee...
  - Book your vacation today at special discount prices.
  - Two-for-one discount at many of the local ski resorts.

Save the workbook and name it **EL1-U2-Act3-CTSkiTrips**. Print an... **EL1-U2-Act3-CTSkiTrips.xlsx**.

Internet Research

Find Information on Excel Books and Present the Data in a Worksheet

Locate two companies on the Internet that sell new books. At the first new book company site, locate three books on Microsoft Excel. Record the title, author, and price for each book. At the second new book company site, locate the same three books and record the prices. Create an Excel worksheet that includes the following information:

- Name of each new book company
- Title and author of the three books
- Prices for each book from the two book company sites

Create a hyperlink for each book company to the website on the Internet. Then save the completed workbook and name it **EL1-U2-DR-Books**. Print and then close the workbook.

Excel Level 1 ■ Unit

INTERNET RESEARCH project reinforces research and spreadsheet development skills.

Job Study

Create a Customized Time Card for a Landscaping Company

You are the manager of a landscaping company and are responsible for employee time cards. Locate the time card template that is available with *Sample templates* selected at the New tab Backstage view. Use the template to create a customized time card for your company. With the template open, insert additional blank rows to increase the spacing above the Employee row. Insert a clip art image related to landscaping or gardening and position and size it attractively in the form. Include a text box with the text Lawn and Landscaping Specialists inside the box. Format, size, and position the text attractively in the form. Fill in the form for the current week with the following employee information:

Employee = Jonathan Holder
Address = 12332 South 152nd Street, Baton Rouge, LA 70804
Manager = (Your name)
Employee phone = (225) 555-3092
Employee email = None
Regular hours = 8 hours for Monday, Tuesday, Wednesday, and Thursday
Overtime = 2 hours on Wednesday
Sick hours = None
Vacation = 8 hours on Friday
Rate per hour = $20.00
Overtime pay = $30.00

Save the completed form and name it **EL1-U2-JS-TimeCard**. Print and then close **EL1-U2-JS-TimeCard.xlsx**.

JOB STUDY at the end of Unit 2 presents a capstone assessment requiring critical thinking and problem solving.

Student Courseware

Student Resources CD Each Benchmark Series textbook is packaged with a Student Resources CD containing the data files required for completing the projects and assessments. A CD icon and folder name displayed on the opening page of chapters reminds students to copy a folder of files from the CD to the desired storage medium before beginning the project exercises. Directions for copying folders are printed on the inside back cover.

Internet Resource Center Additional learning tools and reference materials are available at the book-specific website at www.emcp.net/BenchmarkExcel10. Students can access the same files that are on the Student Resources CD along with study aids, web links, and tips for using computers effectively in academic and workplace settings.

SNAP Training and Assessment SNAP is a web-based program offering an interactive venue for learning Microsoft Office 2010, Windows 7, and Internet Explorer 8.0. Along with a web-based learning management system, SNAP provides multimedia tutorials, performance skill items, document-based assessments, a concepts test bank, an online grade book, and a set of course planning tools. A CD of tutorials teaching the basics of Office, Windows, and Internet Explorer is also available if instructors wish to assign additional SNAP tutorial work without using the web-based SNAP program.

eBook For students who prefer studying with an eBook, the texts in the Benchmark Series are available in an electronic form. The web-based, password-protected eBooks feature dynamic navigation tools, including bookmarking, a linked table of contents, and the ability to jump to a specific page. The eBook format also supports helpful study tools, such as highlighting and note taking.

Instructor Resources

Instructor's Guide and Disc Instructor support for the Benchmark Series includes an *Instructor's Guide and Instructor Resources Disc* package. This resource includes planning information, such as Lesson Blueprints, teaching hints, and sample course syllabi; presentation resources, such as PowerPoint slide shows with lecture notes and audio support; and assessment resources, including an overview of available assessment venues, live model answers for chapter activities, and live and PDF model answers for end-of-chapter exercises. Contents of the *Instructor's Guide and Instructor Resources Disc* package are also available on the password-protected section of the Internet Resource Center for this title at www.emcp.net/BenchmarkExcel10.

Computerized Test Generator Instructors can use the EXAMVIEW® Assessment Suite and test banks of multiple-choice items to create customized web-based or print tests.

Blackboard Cartridge This set of files allows instructors to create a personalized Blackboard website for their course and provides course content, tests, and the mechanisms for establishing communication via e-discussions and online group conferences. Available content includes a syllabus, test banks, PowerPoint presentations with audio support, and supplementary course materials. Upon request, the files can be available within 24–48 hours. Hosting the site is the responsibility of the educational institution.

System Requirements

This text is designed for the student to complete projects and assessments on a computer running a standard installation of Microsoft Office 2010, Professional Edition, and the Microsoft Windows 7 operating system. To effectively run this suite and operating system, your computer should be outfitted with the following:

- 1 gigahertz (GHz) processor or higher; 1 gigabyte (GB) of RAM
- DVD drive
- 15 GB of available hard-disk space
- Computer mouse or compatible pointing device

Office 2010 will also operate on computers running the Windows XP Service Pack 3 or the Windows Vista operating system.

Screen captures in this book were created using a screen resolution display setting of 1280 × 800. Refer to the *Customizing Settings* section of *Getting Started in Office 2010* following this preface for instructions on changing your monitor's resolution. Figure G.10 on page 10 shows the Microsoft Office Word ribbon at three resolutions for comparison purposes. Choose the resolution that best matches your computer; however, be aware that using a resolution other than 1280 × 800 means that your screens may not match the illustrations in this book.

About the Authors

Nita Rutkosky began teaching business education courses at Pierce College in Puyallup, Washington, in 1978. Since then she has taught a variety of software applications to students in postsecondary Information Technology certificate and degree programs. In addition to *Benchmark Office 2010,* she has co-authored *Marquee Series: Microsoft Office 2010, 2007,* and *2003; Signature Series: Microsoft Word 2010, 2007,* and *2003;* and *Using Computers in the Medical Office: Microsoft Word, Excel, and PowerPoint 2007* and *2003*. She has also authored textbooks on keyboarding, WordPerfect, desktop publishing, and voice recognition for Paradigm Publishing, Inc.

Audrey Rutkosky Roggenkamp has been teaching courses in the Business Information Technology department at Pierce College in Puyallup since 2005. Her courses have included keyboarding, skill building, and Microsoft Office programs. In addition to this title, she has co-authored *Marquee Series: Microsoft Office 2010* and *2007; Signature Series: Microsoft Word 2010* and *2007;* and *Using Computers in the Medical Office 2007* and *2003* for Paradigm Publishing, Inc.

Getting Started in Office 2010

In this textbook, you will learn to operate several computer application programs that combine to make an application "suite." This suite of programs is called Microsoft Office 2010. The programs you will learn to operate are the software, which includes instructions telling the computer what to do. Some of the application programs in the suite include a word processing program named Word, a spreadsheet program named Excel, a database program named Access, and a presentation program named PowerPoint.

Identifying Computer Hardware

The computer equipment you will use to operate the suite of programs is referred to as hardware. You will need access to a microcomputer system that should consist of the CPU, monitor, keyboard, printer, drives, and mouse. If you are not sure what equipment you will be operating, check with your instructor. The computer system shown in Figure G.1 consists of six components. Each component is discussed separately in the material that follows.

Figure G.1 Microcomputer System

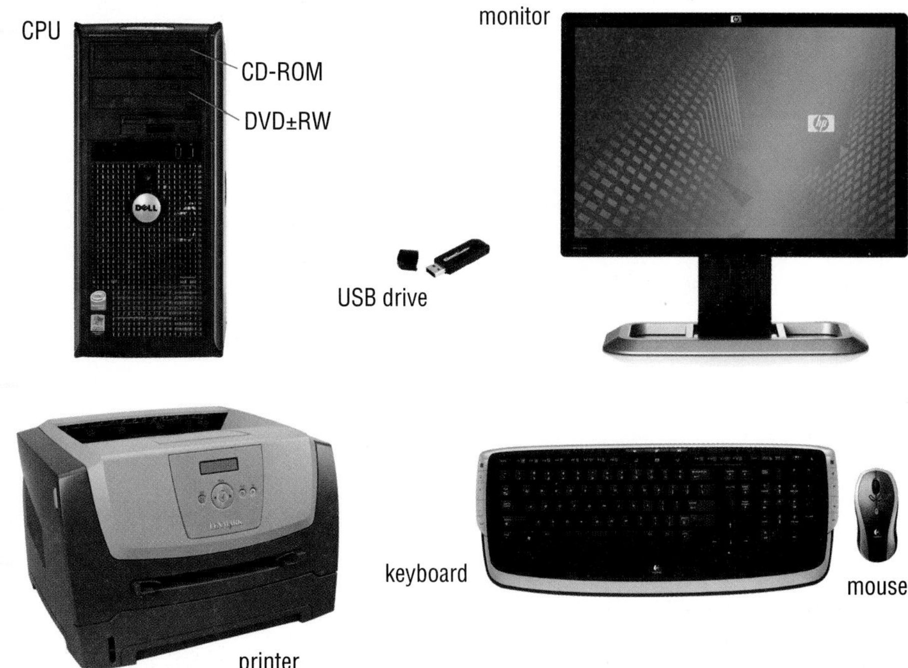

CPU

CPU stands for Central Processing Unit and it is the intelligence of the computer. All the processing occurs in the CPU. Silicon chips, which contain miniaturized circuitry, are placed on boards that are plugged into slots within the CPU. Whenever an instruction is given to the computer, that instruction is processed through circuitry in the CPU.

Monitor

The monitor is a piece of equipment that looks like a television screen. It displays the information of a program and the text being input at the keyboard. The quality of display for monitors varies depending on the type of monitor and the level of resolution. Monitors can also vary in size—generally from 15-inch size up to 26-inch size or larger.

Keyboard

The keyboard is used to input information into the computer. Keyboards for microcomputers vary in the number and location of the keys. Microcomputers have the alphabetic and numeric keys in the same location as the keys on a typewriter. The symbol keys, however, may be placed in a variety of locations, depending on the manufacturer. In addition to letters, numbers, and symbols, most microcomputer keyboards contain function keys, arrow keys, and a numeric keypad. Figure G.2 shows an enhanced keyboard.

Figure G.2 Keyboard

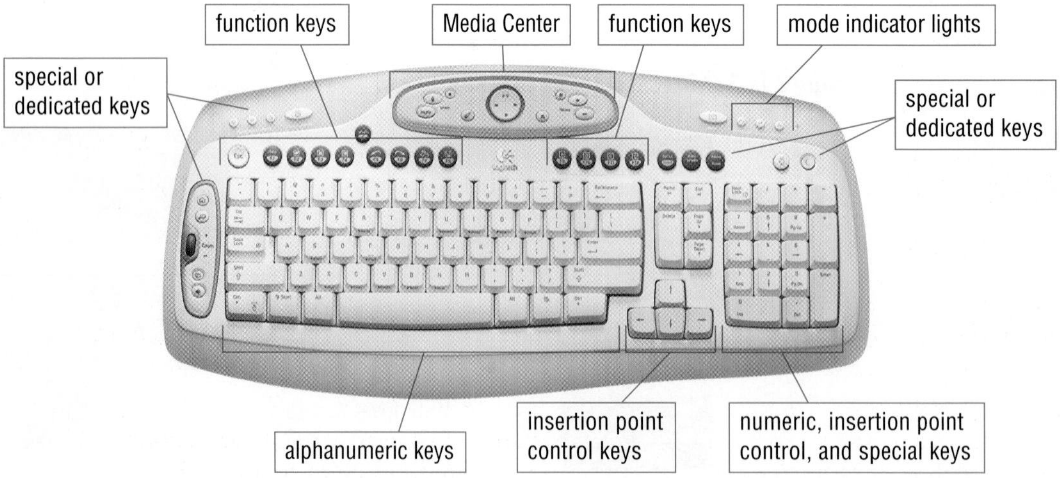

The 12 keys at the top of the keyboard, labeled with the letter F followed by a number, are called ***function keys***. Use these keys to perform functions within each of the suite programs. To the right of the regular keys is a group of ***special*** or ***dedicated keys***. These keys are labeled with specific functions that will be performed when you press the key. Below the special keys are arrow keys. Use these keys to move the insertion point in the document screen.

A keyboard generally includes three mode indicator lights. When you select certain modes, a light appears on the keyboard. For example, if you press the Caps Lock key, which disables the lowercase alphabet, a light appears next to Caps Lock. Similarly, pressing the Num Lock key will disable the special functions on the numeric keypad, which is located at the right side of the keyboard.

Disk Drives

Depending on the computer system you are using, Microsoft Office 2010 is installed on a hard drive or as part of a network system. Whether you are using Office on a hard drive or network system, you will need to have available a DVD or CD drive and a USB drive or other storage medium. You will insert the CD (compact disc) that accompanies this textbook in the DVD or CD drive and then copy folders from the CD to your storage medium. You will also save documents you complete at the computer to folders on your storage medium.

Printer

A document you create in Word is considered soft copy. If you want a hard copy of a document, you need to print it. To print documents you will need to access a printer, which will probably be either a laser printer or an ink-jet printer. A laser printer uses a laser beam combined with heat and pressure to print documents, while an ink-jet printer prints a document by spraying a fine mist of ink on the page.

Mouse

Many functions in the suite of programs are designed to operate more efficiently with a mouse. A mouse is an input device that sits on a flat surface next to the computer. You can operate a mouse with the left or the right hand. Moving the mouse on the flat surface causes a corresponding mouse pointer to move on the screen. Figure G.1 shows an illustration of a mouse.

Using the Mouse

The programs in the Microsoft Office suite can be operated with the keyboard and a mouse. The mouse may have two or three buttons on top, which are tapped to execute specific functions and commands. To use the mouse, rest it on a flat surface or a mouse pad. Put your hand over it with your palm resting on top of the mouse and your wrist resting on the table surface. As you move the mouse on the flat surface, a corresponding pointer moves on the screen.

When using the mouse, you should understand four terms — point, click, double-click, and drag. When operating the mouse, you may need to point to a specific command, button, or icon. Point means to position the mouse pointer on the desired item. With the mouse pointer positioned on the desired item, you may need to click a button on the mouse. Click means quickly tapping a button on the mouse once. To complete two steps at one time, such as choosing and then executing a function, double-click a mouse button. Double-click means to tap the left mouse button twice in quick succession. The term drag means to press and hold the left mouse button, move the mouse pointer to a specific location, and then release the button.

Using the Mouse Pointer

The mouse pointer will change appearance depending on the function being performed or where the pointer is positioned. The mouse pointer may appear as one of the following images:

- The mouse pointer appears as an I-beam (called the I-beam pointer) in the document screen and can be used to move the insertion point or select text.

- The mouse pointer appears as an arrow pointing up and to the left (called the arrow pointer) when it is moved to the Title bar, Quick Access toolbar, ribbon, or an option in a dialog box.

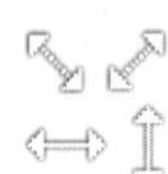

- The mouse pointer becomes a double-headed arrow (either pointing left and right, pointing up and down, or pointing diagonally) when performing certain functions such as changing the size of an object.

- In certain situations, such as moving an object or image, the mouse pointer displays with a four-headed arrow attached. The four-headed arrow means that you can move the object left, right, up, or down.

- When a request is being processed or when a program is being loaded, the mouse pointer may appear with a circle beside it. The moving circle means "please wait." When the process is completed, the circle is removed.

- The mouse pointer displays as a hand with a pointing index finger in certain functions such as Help and indicates that more information is available about the item. The mouse pointer also displays as a hand when you hover the mouse over a hyperlink.

Choosing Commands

Once a program is open, you can use several methods in the program to choose commands. A command is an instruction that tells the program to do something. You can choose a command using the mouse or the keyboard. When a program such as Word or PowerPoint is open, the ribbon contains buttons for completing tasks and contains tabs you click to display additional buttons. To choose a button on the Quick Access toolbar or in the ribbon, position the tip of the mouse arrow pointer on a button and then click the left mouse button.

The Office suite provides access keys you can press to use a command in a program. Press the Alt key on the keyboard to display KeyTips that identify the access key you need to press to execute a command. For example, press the Alt key in a Word document with the Home tab active and KeyTips display as shown in Figure G.3. Continue pressing access keys until you execute the desired command. For example, if you want to begin spell checking a document, you would press the Alt key, press the R key on the keyboard to display the Review tab, and then press the letter S on the keyboard.

Choosing Commands from Drop-Down Lists

To choose a command from a drop-down list with the mouse, position the mouse pointer on the desired option and then click the left mouse button. To make a selection from a drop-down list with the keyboard, type the underlined letter in the desired option.

Figure G.3 Word Home Tab KeyTips

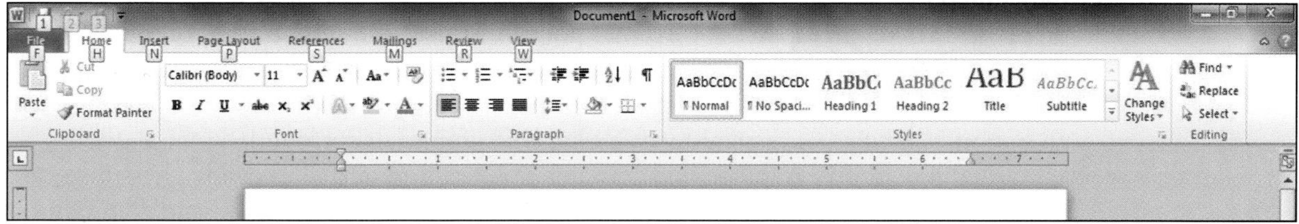

Some options at a drop-down list may be gray-shaded (dimmed), indicating that the option is currently unavailable. If an option at a drop-down list displays preceded by a check mark, that indicates that the option is currently active. If an option at a drop-down list displays followed by an ellipsis (...), a dialog box will display when that option is chosen.

Choosing Options from a Dialog Box

A dialog box contains options for applying formatting to a file or data within a file. Some dialog boxes display with tabs along the top providing additional options. For example, the Font dialog box shown in Figure G.4 contains two tabs — the Font tab and the Advanced tab. The tab that displays in the front is the active tab. To make a tab active using the mouse, position the arrow pointer on the desired tab and then click the left mouse button. If you are using the keyboard, press Ctrl + Tab or press Alt + the underlined letter on the desired tab.

Figure G.4 Word Font Dialog Box

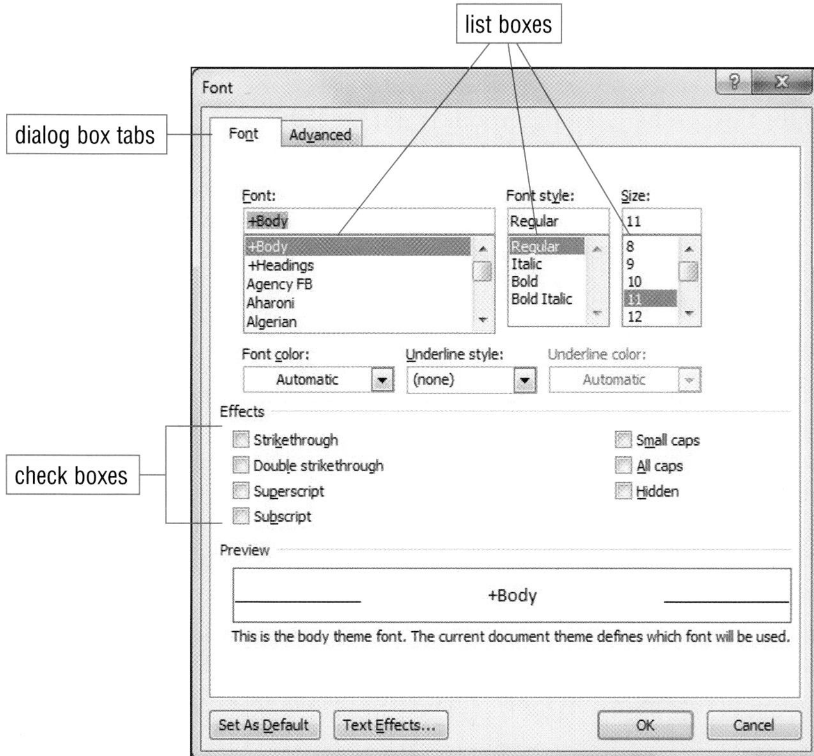

To choose options from a dialog box with the mouse, position the arrow pointer on the desired option and then click the left mouse button. If you are using the keyboard, press the Tab key to move the insertion point forward from option to option. Press Shift + Tab to move the insertion point backward from option to option. You can also hold down the Alt key and then press the underlined letter of the desired option. When an option is selected, it displays with a blue background or surrounded by a dashed box called a marquee. A dialog box contains one or more of the following elements: text boxes, list boxes, check boxes, option buttons, measurement boxes, and command buttons.

List Boxes

Some dialog boxes such as the Word Font dialog box shown in Figure G.4 may contain a list box. The list of fonts below the *Font* option is contained in a list box. To make a selection from a list box with the mouse, move the arrow pointer to the desired option and then click the left mouse button.

Some list boxes may contain a scroll bar. This scroll bar will display at the right side of the list box (a vertical scroll bar) or at the bottom of the list box (a horizontal scroll bar). You can use a vertical scroll bar or a horizontal scroll bar to move through the list if the list is longer than the box. To move down through a list on a vertical scroll bar, position the arrow pointer on the down-pointing arrow and hold down the left mouse button. To scroll up through the list in a vertical scroll bar, position the arrow pointer on the up-pointing arrow and hold down the left mouse button. You can also move the arrow pointer above the scroll box and click the left mouse button to scroll up the list or move the arrow pointer below the scroll box and click the left mouse button to move down the list. To move through a list with a horizontal scroll bar, click the left-pointing arrow to scroll to the left of the list or click the right-pointing arrow to scroll to the right of the list.

To make a selection from a list using the keyboard, move the insertion point into the box by holding down the Alt key and pressing the underlined letter of the desired option. Press the Up and/or Down Arrow keys on the keyboard to move through the list.

In some dialog boxes where enough room is not available for a list box, lists of options are inserted in a drop-down list box. Options that contain a drop-down list box display with a down-pointing arrow. For example, the *Underline style* option at the Word Font dialog box shown in Figure G.4 contains a drop-down list. To display the list, click the down-pointing arrow to the right of the *Underline style* option box. If you are using the keyboard, press Alt + U.

Check Boxes

Some dialog boxes contain options preceded by a box. A check mark may or may not appear in the box. The Word Font dialog box shown in Figure G.4 displays a variety of check boxes within the *Effects* section. If a check mark appears in the box, the option is active (turned on). If the check box does not contain a check mark, the option is inactive (turned off). Any number of check boxes can be active. For example, in the Word Font dialog box, you can insert a check mark in any or all of the boxes in the *Effects* section and these options will be active.

To make a check box active or inactive with the mouse, position the tip of the arrow pointer in the check box and then click the left mouse button. If you are using the keyboard, press Alt + the underlined letter of the desired option.

Text Boxes

Some options in a dialog box require you to enter text. For example, the boxes below the *Find what* and *Replace with* options at the Excel Find and Replace dialog box shown in Figure G.5 are text boxes. In a text box, you type text or edit existing text. Edit text in a text box in the same manner as normal text. Use the Left and Right Arrow keys on the keyboard to move the insertion point without deleting text and use the Delete key or Backspace key to delete text.

Option Buttons

The Word Insert Table dialog box shown in Figure G.6 contains options in the *AutoFit behavior* section preceded by option buttons. Only one option button can be selected at any time. When an option button is selected, a blue circle displays in the button. To select an option button with the mouse, position the tip of the arrow pointer inside the option button and then click the left mouse button. To make a selection with the keyboard, hold down the Alt key and then press the underlined letter of the desired option.

Measurement Boxes

Some options in a dialog box contain measurements or numbers you can increase or decrease. These options are generally located in a measurement box. For example, the Word Paragraph dialog box shown in Figure G.7 contains the *Left*, *Right*, *Before*, and *After* measurement boxes. To increase a number in a measurement box, position the tip of the arrow pointer on the up-pointing arrow to the right of the desired option and then click the left mouse button. To decrease the number, click the down-pointing arrow. If you are using the keyboard, press Alt + the underlined letter of the desired option and then press the Up Arrow key to increase the number or the Down Arrow key to decrease the number.

Command Buttons

In the Excel Find and Replace dialog box shown in Figure G.5, the boxes along the bottom of the dialog box are called command buttons. Use a command button to execute or cancel a command. Some command buttons display with an ellipsis (...). A command button that displays with an ellipsis will open another dialog box. To choose a command button with the mouse, position the arrow pointer on the desired button and then click the left mouse button. To choose a command button with the keyboard, press the Tab key until the desired command button contains the marquee and then press the Enter key.

Figure G.5 Excel Find and Replace Dialog Box

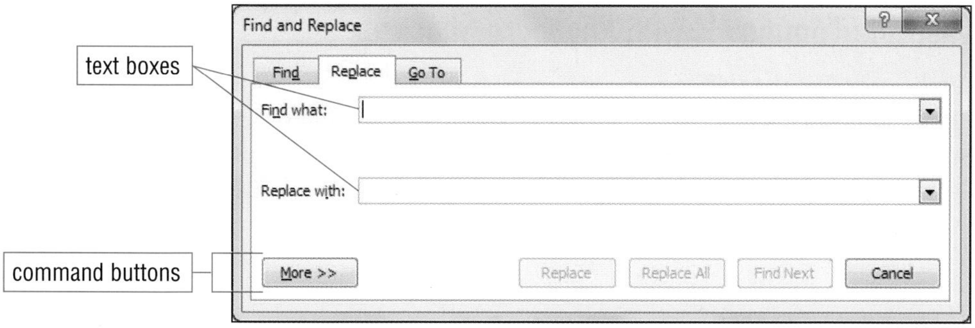

Figure G.6 Word Insert Table Dialog Box

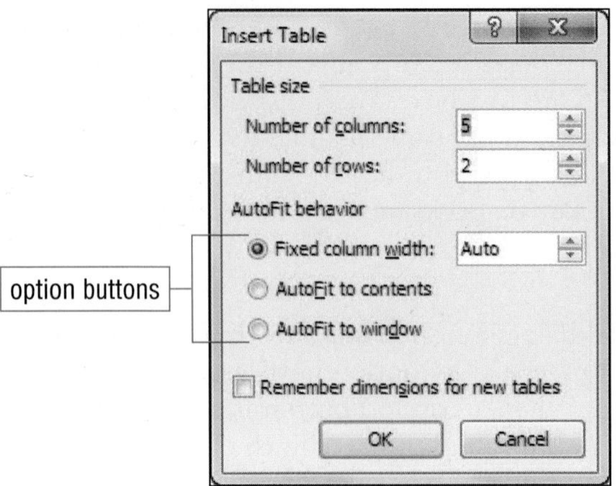

Figure G.7 Word Paragraph Dialog Box

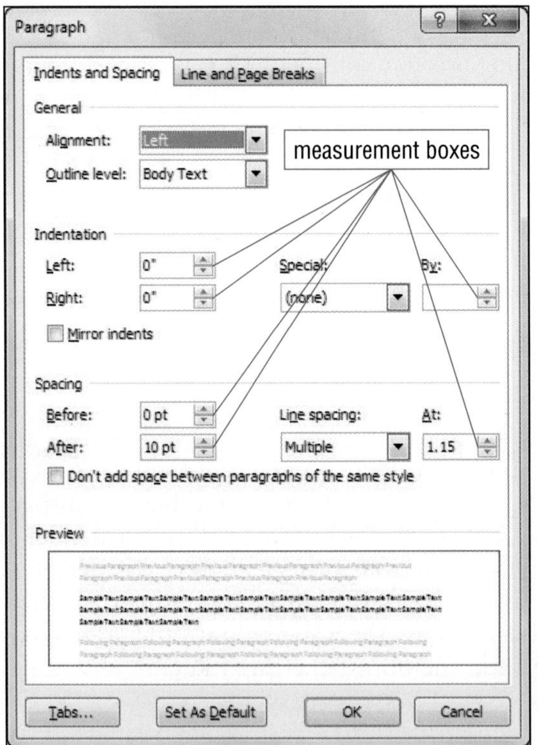

Choosing Commands with Keyboard Shortcuts

Applications in the Office suite offer a variety of keyboard shortcuts you can use to execute specific commands. Keyboard shortcuts generally require two or more keys. For example, the keyboard shortcut to display the Open dialog box in an application is Ctrl + O. To use this keyboard shortcut, hold down the Ctrl key, type the letter O on the keyboard, and then release the Ctrl key. For a list of keyboard shortcuts, refer to the Help files.

Choosing Commands with Shortcut Menus

The software programs in the suite include menus that contain commands related to the item with which you are working. A shortcut menu appears in the file in the location where you are working. To display a shortcut menu, click the right mouse button or press Shift + F10. For example, if the insertion point is positioned in a paragraph of text in a Word document, clicking the right mouse button or pressing Shift + F10 will cause the shortcut menu shown in Figure G.8 to display in the document screen (along with the Mini toolbar).

To select an option from a shortcut menu with the mouse, click the desired option. If you are using the keyboard, press the Up or Down Arrow key until the desired option is selected and then press the Enter key. To close a shortcut menu without choosing an option, click anywhere outside the shortcut menu or press the Esc key.

Working with Multiple Programs

As you learn the various programs in the Microsoft Office suite, you will notice how executing commands in each is very similar. For example, the steps to save, close, and print are virtually the same whether you are working in Word, Excel, or PowerPoint. This consistency between programs greatly enhances a user's ability to transfer knowledge learned in one program to another within the suite. Another appeal of Microsoft Office is the ability to have more than one program open at the same time. For example, you can open Word, create a document, and then open Excel, create a spreadsheet, and copy the spreadsheet into Word.

Figure G.8 Word Shortcut Menu

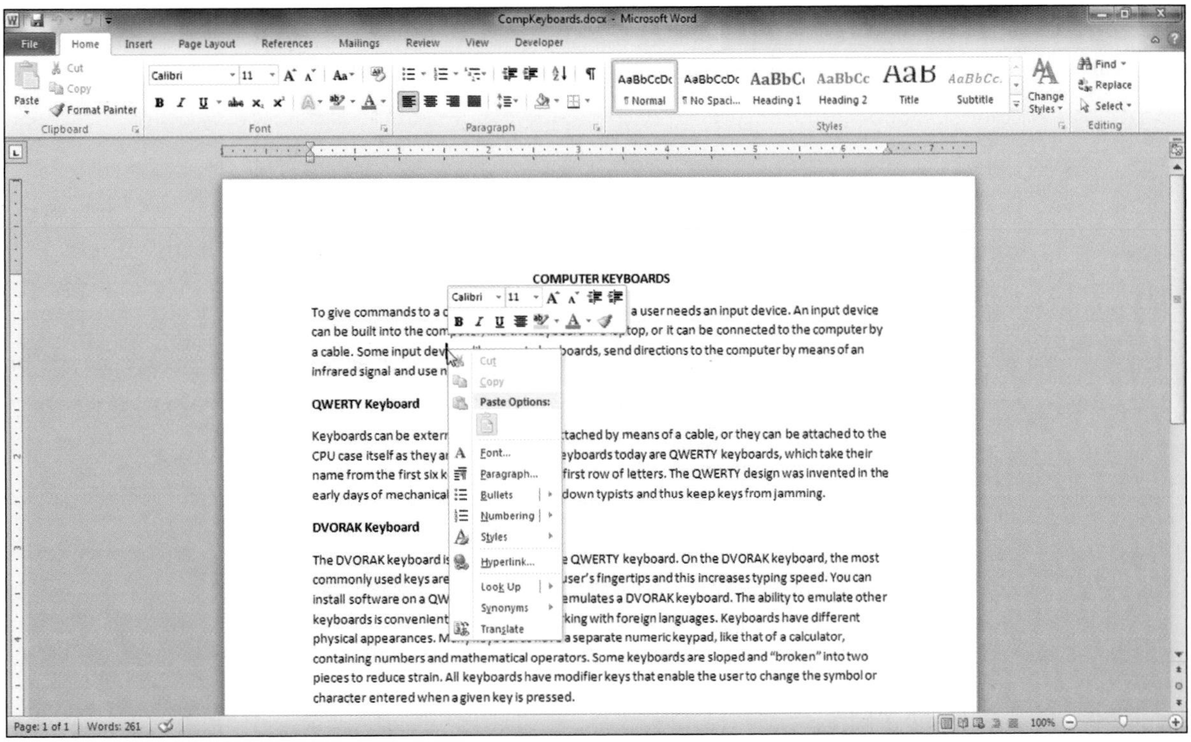

Figure G.9 Taskbar with Word, Excel, and PowerPoint Open

When you open a program, a button displays on the Taskbar containing an icon representing the program. If you open another program, a button containing an icon representing the program displays to the right of the first program button. Figure G.9 shows the Taskbar with Word, Excel, and PowerPoint open. To move from one program to another, click the button on the Taskbar representing the desired program file.

Customizing Settings

Before beginning computer projects in this textbook, you may need to customize the monitor settings and turn on the display of file extensions. Projects in the chapters in this textbook assume that the monitor display is set at 1280 by 800 pixels and that the display of file extensions is turned on.

Changing Monitor Resolutions

Before you begin learning the applications in the Microsoft Office 2010 suite, take a moment to check the display settings on the computer you are using. The ribbon in the Microsoft Office suite adjusts to the screen resolution setting of your computer monitor. Computer monitors set at a high resolution will have the ability to show more buttons in the ribbon than will a monitor set to a low resolution. The illustrations in this textbook were created with a screen resolution display set at 1280 × 800 pixels. In Figure G.10 the Word ribbon is shown three ways: at a lower screen resolution (1024 × 768 pixels), at the screen resolution featured

Figure G.10 Monitor Resolution

1024 × 768 screen resolution

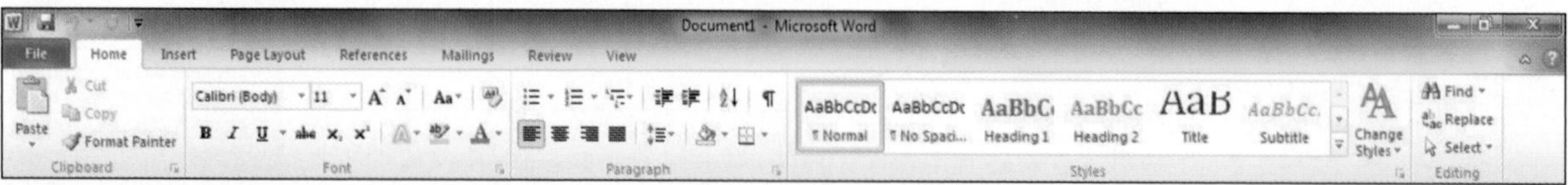

1280 × 800 screen resolution

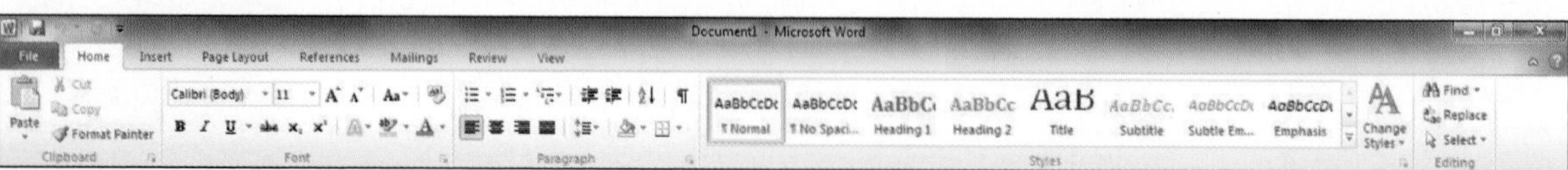

1440 × 900 screen resolution

throughout this textbook, and at a higher screen resolution (1440 × 900 pixels). Note the variances in the ribbon in all three examples. If possible, set your display to 1280 × 800 pixels to match the illustrations you will see in this textbook.

Project 1 Setting Monitor Display to 1280 by 800

1. At the Windows 7 desktop, click the Start button and then click *Control Panel.*
2. At the Control Panel dialog box, click the *Adjust screen resolution* option in the Appearance and Personalization category.
3. At the Control Panel Screen Resolution window, click the Resolution option button. (This displays a drop-down slider bar. Your drop-down slider bar may display differently than what you see in the image at the right.)
4. Drag the slider bar button on the slider bar until *1280 × 800* displays to the right of the slider button.
5. Click in the Control Panel Screen Resolution window to remove the slider bar.
6. Click the Apply button.
7. Click the Keep Changes button.
8. Click the OK button.
9. Close the Control Panel window.

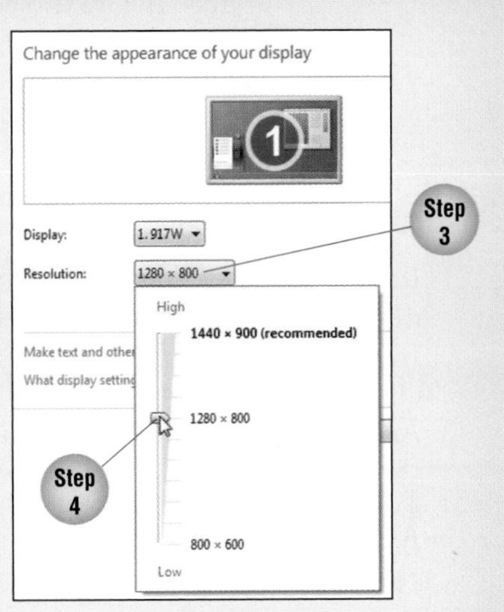

Project 2 Displaying File Extensions

1. At the Windows 7 desktop, click the Start button and then click *Computer.*
2. At the Computer window, click the Organize button on the toolbar and then click *Folder and search options* at the drop-down list.
3. At the Folder Options dialog box, click the View tab.
4. Click the *Hide extensions for known file types* check box to remove the check mark.
5. Click the Apply button.
6. Click the OK button.
7. Close the Computer window.

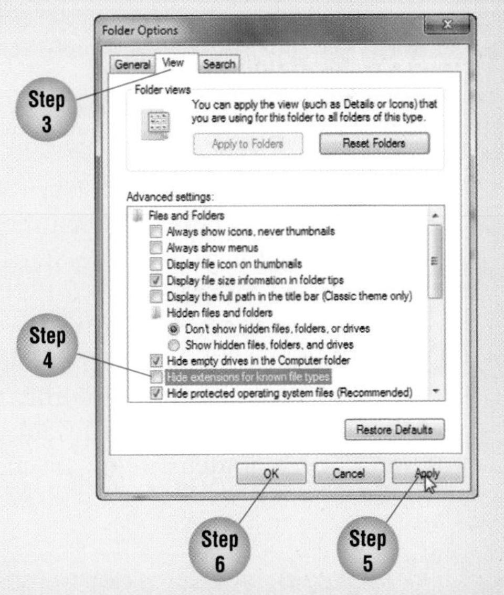

Completing Computer Projects

Some computer projects in this textbook require that you open an existing file. Project files are saved on the Student Resources CD that accompanies this textbook. The files you need for each chapter are saved in individual folders. Before beginning a chapter, copy the necessary folder from the CD to your storage medium (such as a USB flash drive) using the Computer window. If storage capacity is an issue with your storage medium, delete any previous chapter folders before copying a chapter folder onto your storage medium.

Project 3 Copying a Folder from the Student Resources CD

1. Insert the CD that accompanies this textbook in the CD drive. At the AutoPlay window that displays, click the Close button located in the upper right corner of the window.
2. Insert your USB flash drive in an available USB port. If an AutoPlay window displays, click the Close button.
3. At the Windows desktop, open the Computer window by clicking the Start button and then clicking *Computer* at the Start menu.
4. Double-click the CD drive in the Content pane (displays with the name *BM10StudentResources* preceded by the drive letter).
5. Double-click the desired program folder name in the Content pane.
6. Click once on the desired chapter subfolder name to select it.
7. Click the Organize button on the toolbar and then click *Copy* at the drop-down list.
8. In the Computer window Content pane, click the drive containing your storage medium.
9. Click the Organize button on the toolbar and then click *Paste* at the drop-down list.
10. Close the Computer window by clicking the Close button located in the upper right corner of the window.

Project 4 Deleting a Folder

Note: Check with your instructor before deleting a folder.

1. Insert your storage medium (such as a USB flash drive) in the USB port.
2. At the Windows desktop, open the Computer window by clicking the Start button and then clicking *Computer* at the Start menu.
3. Double-click the drive letter for your storage medium (drive containing your USB flash drive such as *Removable Disk (F:)*).
4. Click the chapter folder in the Content pane.
5. Click the Organize button on the toolbar and then click *Delete* at the drop-down list.
6. At the message asking if you want to delete the folder, click the Yes button.
7. Close the Computer window by clicking the Close button located in the upper right corner of the window.

Using Windows 7

A computer requires an operating system to provide necessary instructions on a multitude of processes including loading programs, managing data, directing the flow of information to peripheral equipment, and displaying information. Windows 7 is an operating system that provides functions of this type (along with much more) in a graphical environment. Windows is referred to as a ***graphical user interface*** (GUI—pronounced *gooey*) that provides a visual display of information with features such as icons (pictures) and buttons. In this introduction, you will learn these basic features of Windows 7:

- Use desktop icons and the Taskbar to launch programs and open files or folders
- Add and remove gadgets
- Organize and manage data, including copying, moving, creating, and deleting files and folders; and create a shortcut
- Explore the Control Panel and personalize the desktop
- Use the Windows Help and Support features
- Use search tools
- Customize monitor settings

Before using one of the software programs in the Microsoft Office suite, you will need to start the Windows 7 operating system. To do this, turn on the computer. Depending on your computer equipment configuration, you may also need to turn on the monitor and printer. If you are using a computer that is part of a network system or if your computer is set up for multiple users, a screen will display showing the user accounts defined for your computer system. At this screen, click your user account name and, if necessary, type your password and then press the Enter key. The Windows 7 operating system will start and, after a few moments, the desktop will display as shown in Figure W.1. (Your desktop may vary from what you see in Figure W.1.)

Exploring the Desktop

When Windows is loaded, the main portion of the screen is called the ***desktop***. Think of the desktop in Windows as the top of a desk in an office. A business person places necessary tools—such as pencils, pens, paper, files, calculator—on the desktop to perform functions. Like the tools that are located on a desk, the desktop contains tools for operating the computer. These tools are logically grouped and placed in dialog boxes or panels that you can display using icons on the desktop. The desktop contains a variety of features for using your computer and software programs installed on the computer. The features available on the desktop are represented by icons and buttons.

Figure W.1 Windows 7 Desktop

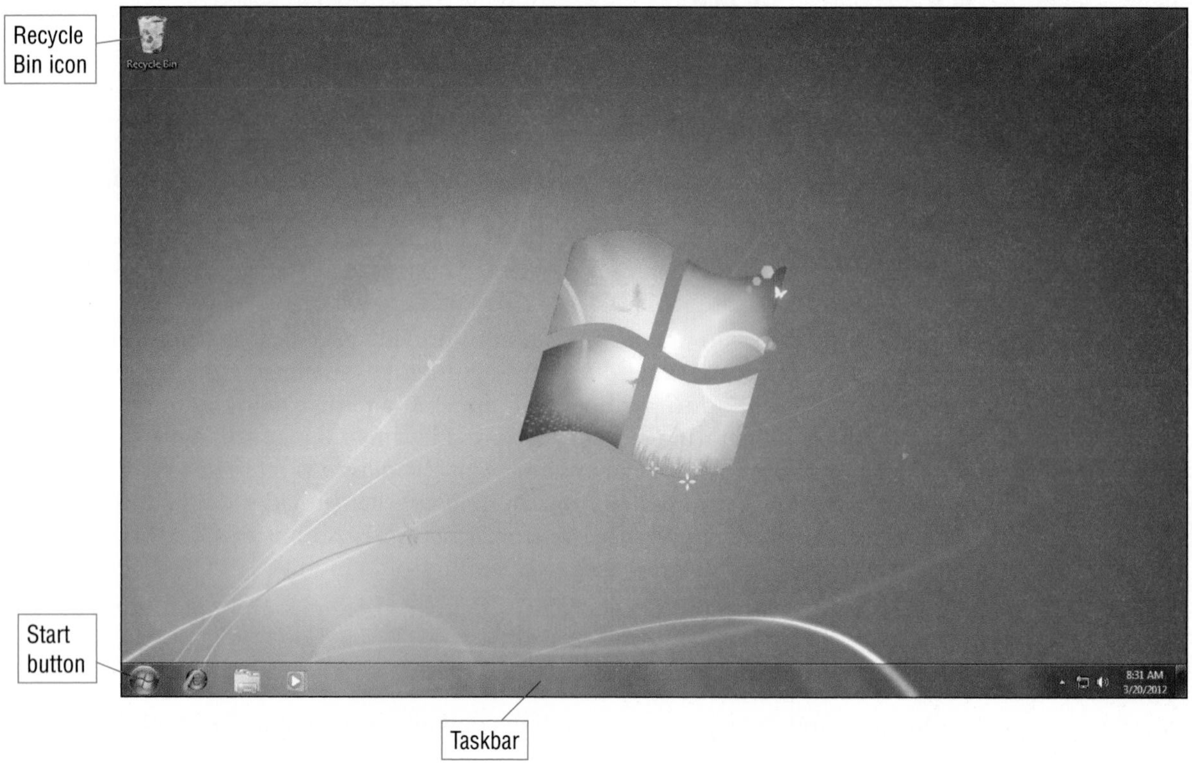

Using Icons

Icons are visual symbols that represent programs, files, or folders. Figure W.1 identifies the Recycle Bin icon located on the Windows desktop. The Windows desktop on your computer may contain additional icons. Programs that have been installed on your computer may be represented by an icon on the desktop. Also, icons may display on your desktop representing files or folders. Double-click an icon and the program, file, or folder it represents opens on the desktop.

Using the Taskbar

The bar that displays at the bottom of the desktop (see Figure W.1) is called the Taskbar. The Taskbar, shown in Figure W.2, contains the Start button, pinned items, a section that displays task buttons representing active tasks, the notification area, and the Show Desktop button.

Figure W.2 Windows 7 Taskbar

Click the Start button, located at the left side of the Taskbar, and the Start menu displays as shown in Figure W.3 (your Start menu may vary). You can also display the Start menu by pressing the Windows key on your keyboard or by pressing Ctrl + Esc. The left side of the Start menu contains links to the most recently and frequently used programs. The name of the currently logged on user displays at the top of the darker right portion of the menu followed by the user's libraries. The two sections below the personal libraries provide links to other Windows features, such as games, the Control Panel, and Windows Help and Support. Use the Shut down button to put the system in a power-conserving state or into a locked, shut down, or sleep mode.

To choose an option from the Start menu, drag the arrow pointer to the desired option (referred to as ***pointing***) and then click the left mouse button. Pointing to options at the Start menu that are followed by a right-pointing arrow will cause a side menu to display with additional options. When a program is open, a task button representing the program appears on the Taskbar. If multiple programs are open, each program will appear as a task button on the Taskbar (a few specialized tools may not).

Manipulating Windows

When you open a program, a defined work area displays on the screen, which is referred to as a ***window***. A Title bar displays at the top of a window and contains buttons at the right side for closing the window and minimizing, maximizing, and restoring the size of the window. You can open more than one window at a time and the open windows can be cascaded or stacked. Windows 7 contains a Snap feature that causes a window to "stick" to the edge of the screen when the window

Figure W.3 Start Menu

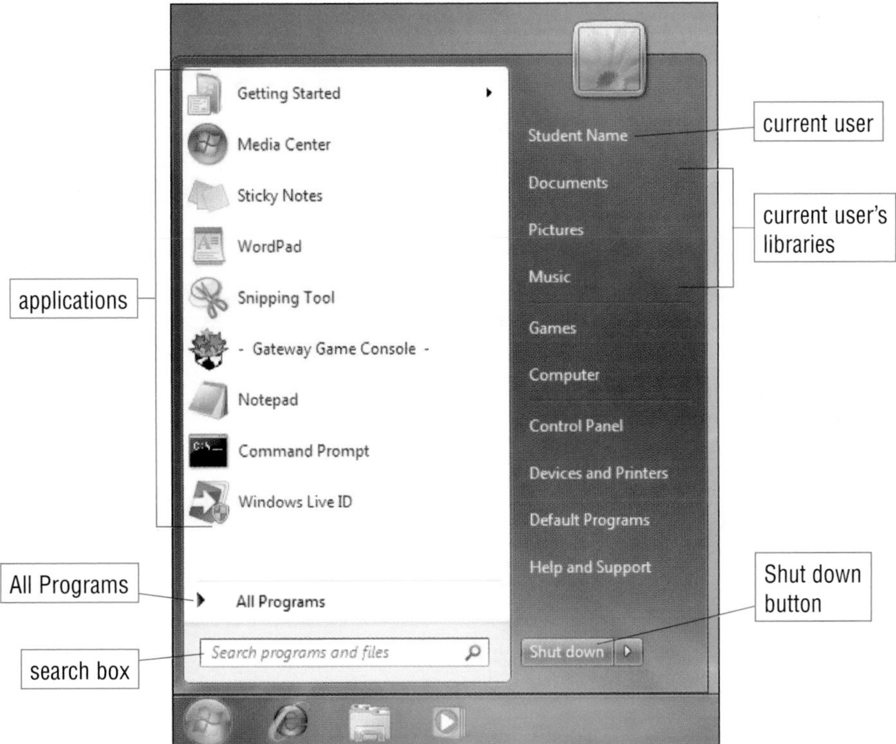

is moved to the left or right side of the screen. Move a window to the top of the screen and the window is automatically maximized. If you drag down a maximized window, the window is automatically restored down.

In addition to moving and sizing a window, you can change the display of all open windows. To do this, position the mouse pointer on the Taskbar and then click the right mouse button and a pop-up list displays with options for displaying multiple open windows. You can cascade the windows, stack the windows, and display the windows side by side.

Project 1 Opening Programs, Switching between Programs, and Manipulating Windows

1. Open Windows 7. (To do this, turn on the computer and, if necessary, turn on the monitor and/or printer. If you are using a computer that is part of a network system or if your computer is set up for multiple users, you may need to click your user account name and, if necessary, type your password and then press the Enter key. Check with your instructor to determine if you need to complete any additional steps.)
2. When the Windows 7 desktop displays, open Microsoft Word by completing the following steps:
   a. Position the arrow pointer on the Start button on the Taskbar and then click the left mouse button.
   b. At the Start menu, click *All Programs* and then click *Microsoft Office* (this displays programs in the Office suite below Microsoft Office).
   c. Drag the arrow pointer down to *Microsoft Word 2010* and then click the left mouse button.
   d. When the Microsoft Word program is open, notice that a task button representing Word displays on the Taskbar.

Step 2d

3. Open Microsoft Excel by completing the following steps:
   a. Position the arrow pointer on the Start button on the Taskbar and then click the left mouse button.
   b. At the Start menu, click *All Programs* and then click *Microsoft Office*.
   c. Drag the arrow pointer down to *Microsoft Excel 2010* and then click the left mouse button.
   d. When the Microsoft Excel program is open, notice that a task button representing Excel displays on the Taskbar to the right of the task button representing Word.
4. Switch to the Word program by clicking the task button on the Taskbar representing Word.
5. Switch to the Excel program by clicking the task button on the Taskbar representing Excel.

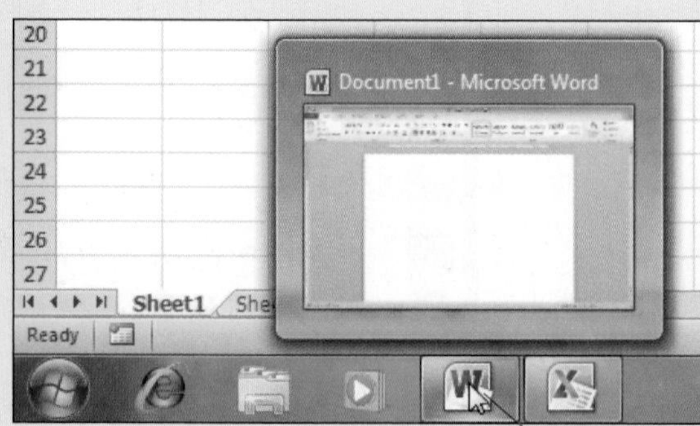

6. Restore down the Excel window by clicking the Restore Down button that displays immediately left of the Close button in the upper right corner of the screen. (This reduces the Excel window so it displays along the bottom half of the screen.)

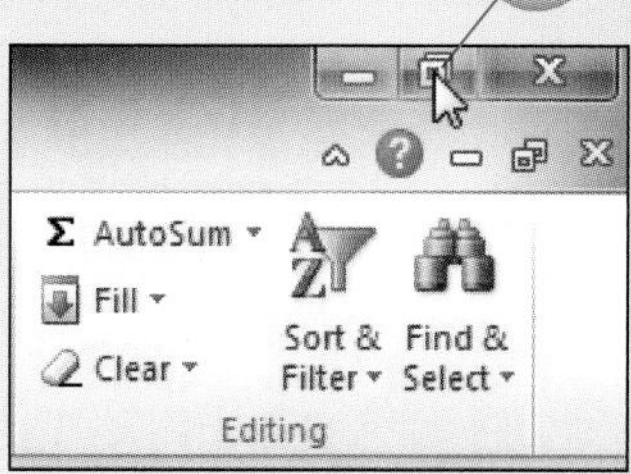

7. Restore down the Word window by clicking the Restore Down button located immediately left of the Close button in the upper right corner of the screen.
8. Position the mouse pointer on the Word window Title bar, hold down the left mouse button, drag to the left side of the screen until an outline of the window displays in the left half of the screen, and then release the mouse button. (This "sticks" the window to the left side of the screen.)
9. Position the mouse pointer on the Excel window Title bar, hold down the left mouse button, drag to the right until an outline of the window displays in the right half of the screen, and then release the mouse button.

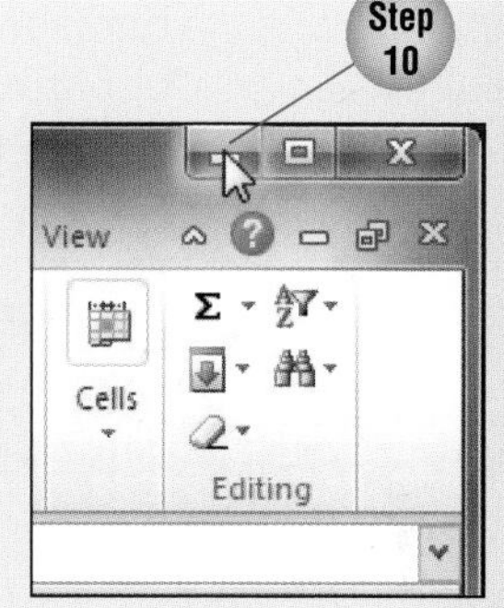

10. Minimize the Excel window by clicking the Minimize button that displays in the upper right corner of the Excel window Title bar.
11. Hover your mouse over the Excel button on the Taskbar and notice the Excel window thumbnail that displays above the button and then click the thumbnail. (This displays the Excel window at the right side of the screen.)

12. Cascade the Word and Excel windows by positioning the arrow pointer on an empty area on the Taskbar, clicking the right mouse button, and then clicking *Cascade windows* at the pop-up list.
13. After viewing the windows cascaded, display them stacked by right-clicking an empty area on the Taskbar and then clicking *Show windows stacked* at the pop-up list.

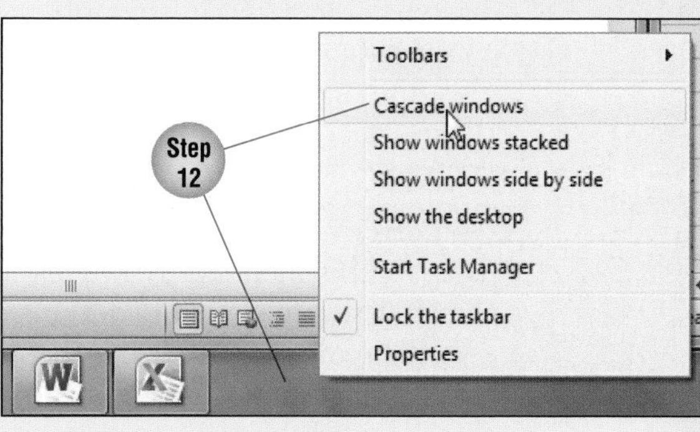

14. Display the desktop by right-clicking an empty area on the Taskbar and then clicking *Show the desktop* at the pop-up list.
15. Display the windows stacked by right-clicking an empty area on the Taskbar and then clicking *Show open windows* at the pop-up list.
16. Position the mouse pointer on the Word window Title bar, hold down the left mouse button, drag the window to the top of the screen, and then release the mouse button. This maximizes the Word window so it fills the screen.
17. Close the Word window by clicking the Close button located in the upper right corner of the window.
18. At the Excel window, click the Maximize button located immediately left of the Close button in the upper right corner of the Excel window.
19. Close the Excel window by clicking the Close button located in the upper right corner of the window.

Using the Pinned Area

The icons that display immediately right of the Start button are pinned programs. Clicking an icon opens the program associated with the icon. Click the first icon to open the Internet Explorer web browser, click the second icon to open a window containing Libraries, and click the third icon to open the Windows media player window.

Exploring the Notification Area

The notification area is located at the right side of the Taskbar and contains icons that show the status of certain system functions such as a network connection or battery power. It also contains icons you can use to manage certain programs and Windows 7 features. The notification area also contains the system clock and date. Click the time or date in the notification area and a window displays with a clock and a calendar of the current month. Click the Change date and time settings hyperlink that displays at the bottom of the window and the Date and Time dialog box displays. To change the date and/or time, click the Change date and time button and the Date and Time Settings dialog box displays similar to the dialog box shown in Figure W.4. (If a dialog box displays telling you that Windows needs your permission to continue, click the Continue button.)

Change the month and year by clicking the left-pointing or right-pointing arrow at the top of the calendar in the *Date* section. Click the left-pointing arrow to display the previous month(s) and click the right-pointing arrow to display the next month(s).

To change the day, click the desired day in the monthly calendar that displays in the dialog box. To change the time, double-click either the hour, minute, or seconds and then type the appropriate time or use the up- and down-pointing arrows in the spin boxes to adjust the time.

Some programs, when installed, will add an icon to the notification area of the Taskbar. Display the name of the icon by positioning the mouse pointer on the icon and, after approximately one second, the icon label displays. If more icons have been inserted in the notification area than can be viewed at one time, an up-pointing arrow button displays at the left side of the notification area. Click this up-pointing arrow button and the remaining icons display.

Setting Taskbar Properties

You can customize the Taskbar with options from the Taskbar shortcut menu. Display this menu by right-clicking on an empty portion of the Taskbar. The Taskbar shortcut menu contains options for turning on or off the display of specific toolbars, specifying the display of multiple windows, displaying the Start Task Manager dialog box, locking or unlocking the Taskbar, and displaying the Taskbar and Start Menu Properties dialog box.

With options in the Taskbar and Start Menu Properties dialog box shown in Figure W.5, you can change settings for the Taskbar as well as the Start menu. Display this dialog box by right-clicking on an empty area on the Taskbar and then clicking *Properties* at the shortcut menu.

Each property is controlled by a check box. Property options containing a check mark are active. Click the option to remove the check mark and make the option inactive. If an option is inactive, clicking the option will insert a check mark in the check box and turn on the option (make it active).

Figure W.4 Date and Time Settings Dialog Box

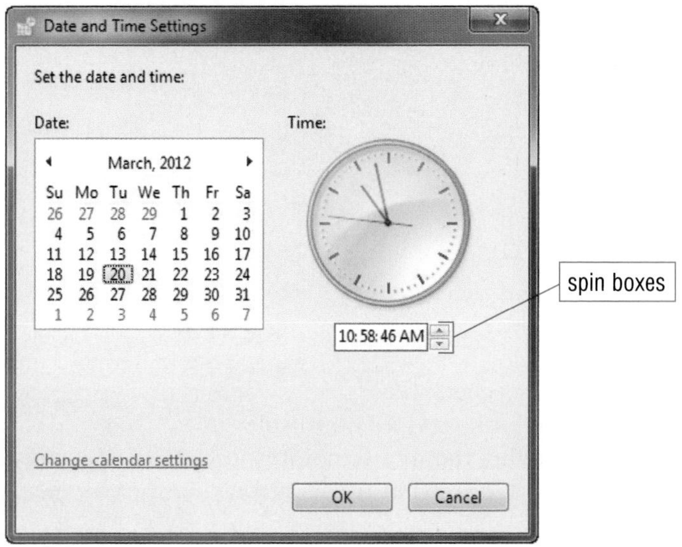

Figure W.5 Taskbar and Start Menu Properties Dialog Box

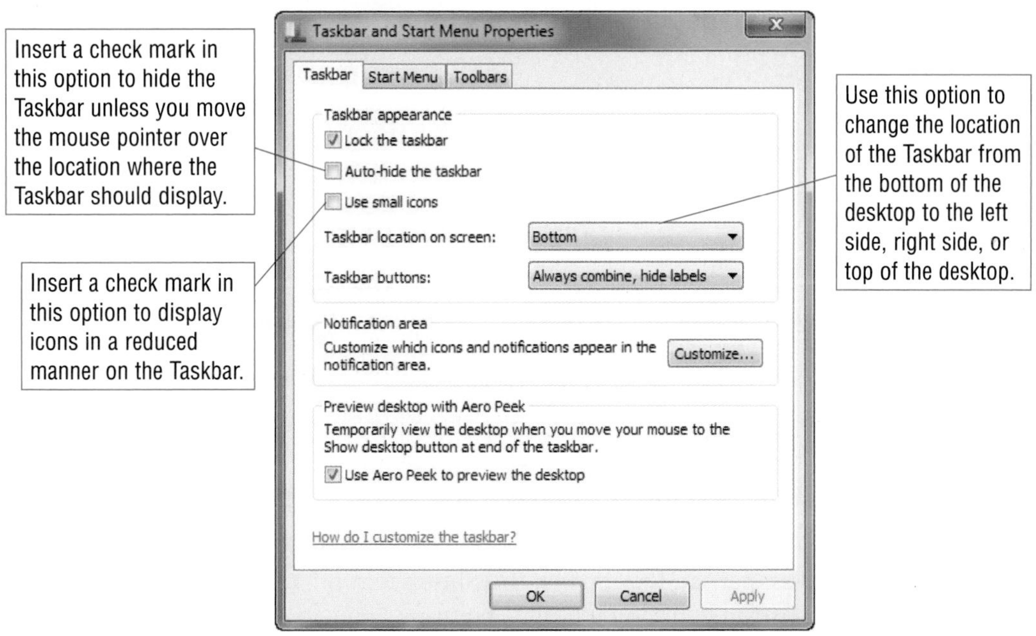

Project 2 Changing Taskbar Properties

1. Make sure the Windows 7 desktop displays.
2. Change Taskbar properties by completing the following steps:
   a. Position the arrow pointer on any empty area on the Taskbar and then click the right mouse button.
   b. At the shortcut menu that displays, click *Properties*.

c. At the Taskbar and Start Menu Properties dialog box, click the *Auto-hide the taskbar* check box to insert a check mark.
d. Click the *Use small icons* check box to insert a check mark.
e. Click the button (displays with the word *Bottom*) that displays at the right side of the *Taskbar location on screen* option and then click *Right* at the drop-down list.
f. Click OK to close the dialog box.

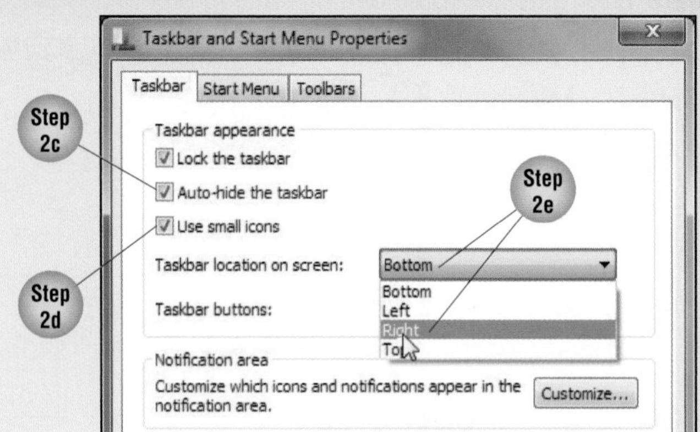

3. Since the *Auto-hide the taskbar* check box contains a check mark, the Taskbar does not display. Display the Taskbar by moving the mouse pointer to the right side of the screen. Notice that the icons on the Taskbar are smaller.
4. Return to the default settings for the Taskbar by completing the following steps:
   a. Move the mouse pointer to the right side of the screen to display the Taskbar.
   b. Right-click any empty area on the Taskbar and then click *Properties* at the shortcut menu.
   c. Click the *Auto-hide the taskbar* check box to remove the check mark.
   d. Click the *Use small icons* check box to remove the check mark.
   e. Click the button (displays with the word *Right*) that displays at the right side of the *Taskbar location on screen* option and then click *Bottom* at the drop-down list.
   f. Click OK to close the dialog box.

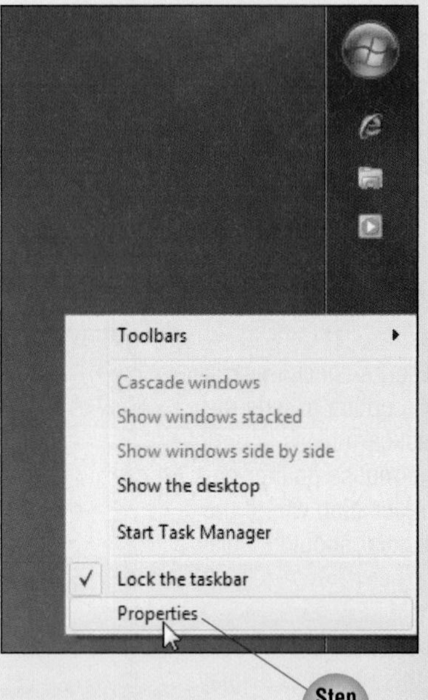

Powering Down the Computer

If you want to shut down Windows, close any open programs, click the Start button on the Taskbar, and then click the Shut down button as shown in Figure W.6. Click the button containing a right-pointing triangle that displays at the right side of the Shut down button and a drop-down list displays with options for powering down the computer.

In a multi-user environment, click the *Switch user* option to change users or click the *Log off* option to log off your computer, which shuts down your applications and files and makes system resources available to other users logged on to the system. If you need to walk away from your computer and you want to protect your work, consider locking the computer by clicking the *Lock* option. When you lock the computer, the desktop is hidden but the system is not shut down and the power is not conserved. To unlock the computer, click the icon on the desktop representing your account, type your password, and then press Enter. Click the *Restart* option to shut down and then restart the computer and click

Figure W.6 Shut Down Button and Power Options Button

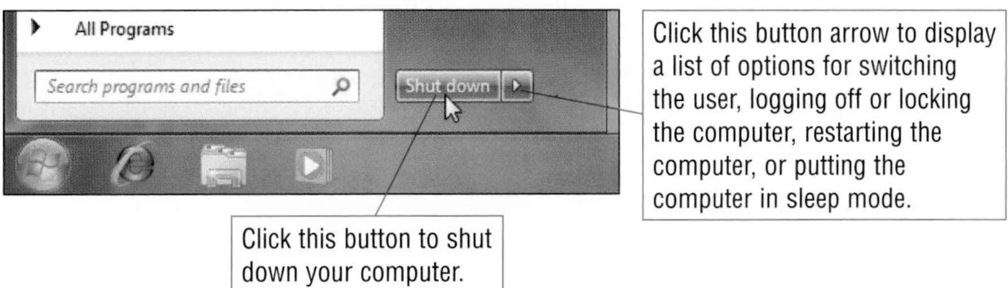

the *Sleep* option to save power without having to close all files and applications. In sleep mode, Windows saves files and information about programs and then powers down the computer to a low-power state. To "wake" the computer back up, quickly press the computer's power button.

Using Gadgets

You can add gadgets to your desktop. A gadget is a mini program providing information at a glance and easy access to frequently used tools. For example, you can add a Clock gadget to your desktop that shows the current time, a Weather gadget that displays the current temperature where you live, or a Calendar gadget that displays the current date. Gadgets are added to the Sidebar, which is a location at the right side of the Windows 7 desktop.

To view available gadgets, right-click in a blank area on the desktop and then click *Gadgets* at the shortcut menu. This displays the gadget gallery similar to what you see in Figure W.7. To add a gadget to the Sidebar, double-click the desired gadget. To remove a gadget from the Sidebar, hover the mouse pointer over the gadget and then click the Close button that displays at the upper right side of the gadget. ***Note: The Gadget option on the shortcut menu may be missing if the computer you are using is located in a school setting where customization options have been disabled. If you do not see*** **Gadget** ***on the shortcut menu, please skip Project 3.***

Figure W.7 Gadget Gallery

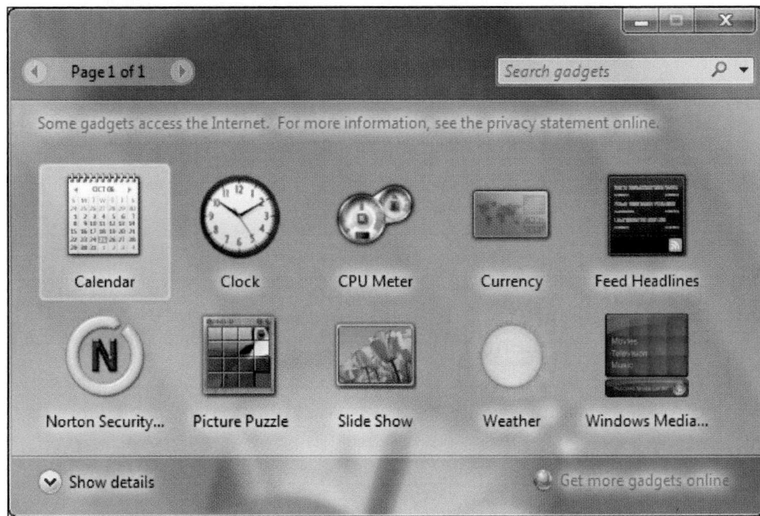

Project 3 Adding and Removing Gadgets

1. At the Windows 7 desktop, right-click in a blank area on the desktop and then click *Gadgets* at the shortcut menu.
2. At the Gadgets Gallery, double-click the *Clock* gadget.
3. Double-click the *Weather* gadget.
4. Double-click the *Calendar* gadget.
5. Close the Gadget Gallery by clicking the Close button located in the upper right corner of the gallery.
6. Hover your mouse over the Calendar gadget until buttons display at the right side of the gadget and then click the Larger size button. (This expands the calendar to display the days of the month.)
7. Hover your mouse over the Weather gadget and then click the Options button.
8. At the Weather dialog box that displays, type in the *Select current location* text box the name of your city followed by your state (or province) and then press Enter.
9. If a drop-down list displays with city names, scroll down the list to display your city and then click your city and state (or province).
10. Click OK to close the Weather dialog box.
11. After viewing the gadgets, remove the Clock gadget by hovering the mouse over the clock and then clicking the Close button that displays at the upper right side of the clock.
12. Close the Weather gadget by hovering the mouse over the gadget and then clicking the Close button that displays.
13. Close the Calendar gadget by hovering the mouse over the gadget and then clicking the Close button that displays.

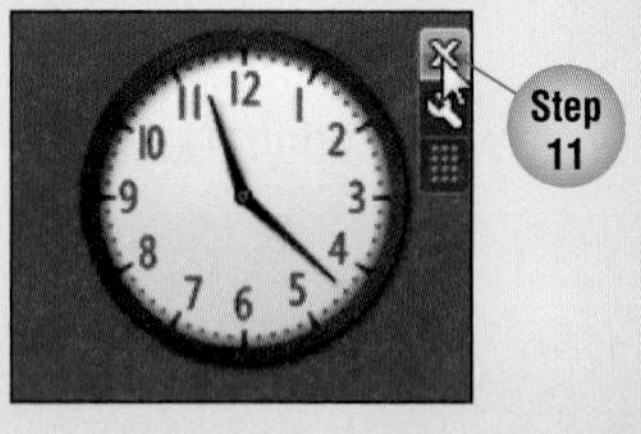

Managing Files and Folders

As you begin working with programs in Windows 7, you will create files in which data (information) is saved. A file might contain a Word document, an Excel workbook, or a PowerPoint presentation. As you begin creating files, consider creating folders into which those files will be stored. You can complete file management tasks such as creating a folder and copying and moving files and folders at the Computer window. To display the Computer window shown in Figure W.8, click the Start button on the Taskbar and then click *Computer*. The various components of the Computer window are identified in Figure W.8.

Figure W.8 Computer Window

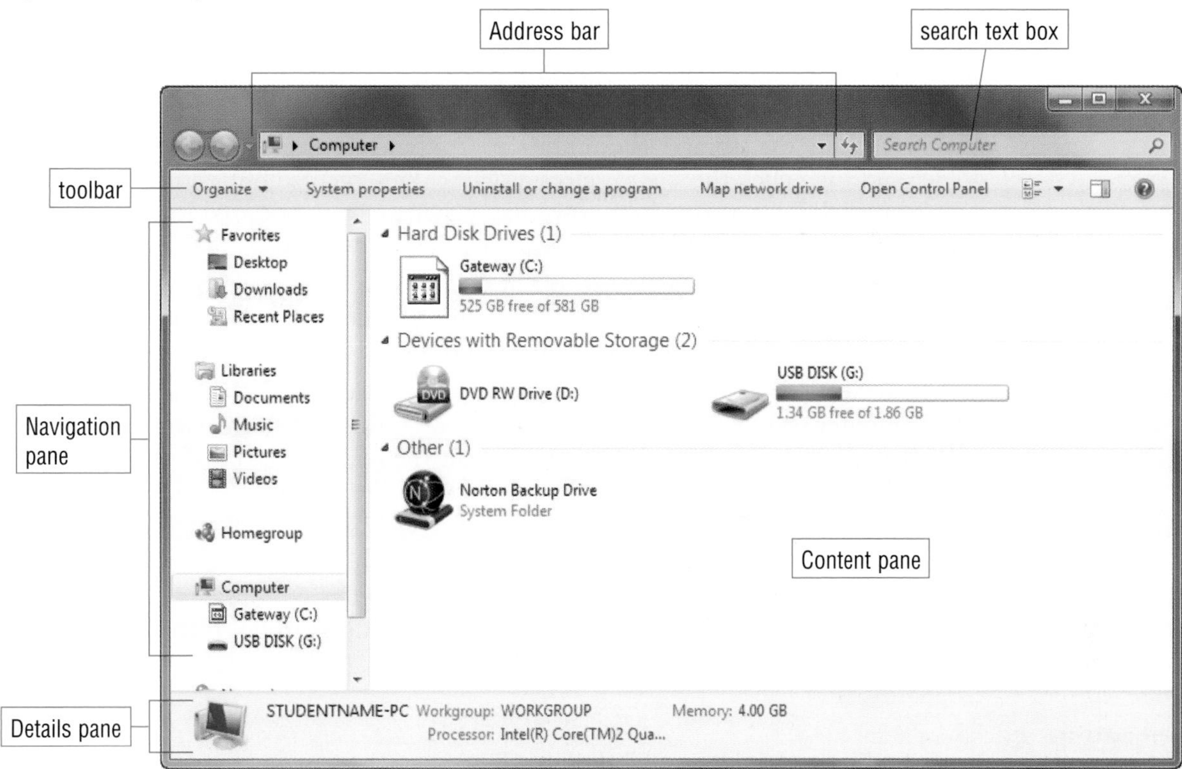

In the Content pane of the Computer window, icons display representing each hard disk drive and removable storage medium such as a CD, DVD, or USB device connected to your computer. Next to each storage device icon, Windows provides the amount of storage space available as well as a bar with the amount of used space shaded with color. This visual cue allows you to see at a glance the proportion of space available relative to the capacity of the device. Double-click a device icon in the Content pane to change the display to show the contents stored on the device. You can display contents from another device or folder using the Navigation pane or the Address bar on the Computer window.

Copying, Moving, and Deleting Files and Folders

File and folder management activities might include copying and moving files or folders from one folder or drive to another, or deleting files or folders. The Computer window offers a variety of methods for copying, moving, and deleting files and folders. This section will provide you with steps for copying, moving, and deleting files and folders using options from the Organize button on the toolbar and the shortcut menu.

To copy a file to another folder or drive, first display the file in the Content pane by identifying the location of the file. If the file is located in the Documents folder, click the *Documents* folder in the *Libraries* section in the Navigation pane and then click the file name in the Content pane that you want to copy. Click the Organize button on the toolbar and then click *Copy* at the drop-down list. In the Navigation pane, click the location where you want to copy the file. Click the Organize button and then click *Paste* at the drop-down list. You would complete similar steps to copy and paste a folder to another location.

If the desired file is located on a storage medium such as a CD, DVD, or USB device, double-click the device in the section of the Content pane labeled *Devices with Removable Storage*. (Each removable device is assigned an alphabetic drive letter by Windows, usually starting at F or G and continuing through the alphabet depending on the number of removable devices that are currently in use.) After double-clicking the storage medium in the Content pane, navigate to the desired folder and then click the file to select it. Click the Organize button on the toolbar and then click *Copy* at the drop-down list. Navigate to the desired folder, click the Organize button, and then click *Paste* at the drop-down list.

To move a file, click the desired file in the Content pane, click the Organize button on the toolbar, and then click *Cut* at the drop-down list. Navigate to the desired location, click the Organize button, and then click *Paste* at the drop-down list.

To delete a file(s) or folder(s), click the file or folder in the Content pane in the Computer window or select multiple files or folders. Click the Organize button and then click *Delete* at the drop-down list. At the message asking if you want to move the file or folder to the Recycle Bin, click the Yes button.

In Project 4, you will insert the CD that accompanies this book into the DVD or CD drive. When the CD is inserted, the drive may automatically activate and a dialog box may display telling you that the disc or device contains more than one type of content and asking what you want Windows to do. If this dialog box displays, click the Cancel button.

Project 4 Copying a File and Folder and Deleting a File

1. Insert the CD that accompanies this textbook into the appropriate drive. If a dialog box displays telling you that the disc or device contains more than one type of content and asking what you want Windows to do, click the Cancel button.
2. Insert your storage medium (such as a USB flash drive) in the USB port (or other drive). If an AutoPlay window displays, click the Close button.
3. At the Windows 7 desktop, click the Start button and then click *Computer* located at the right side of the Start menu.
4. Copy a file from the CD that accompanies this textbook to the drive containing your storage medium by completing the following steps:
   a. Double-click the CD drive in the Content pane containing the CD from the book.
   b. Double-click the *StudentDataFiles* folder in the Content pane.
   c. Double-click the *Windows7* folder in the Content pane.
   d. Click ***WordDocument01.docx*** in the Content pane.
   e. Click the Organize button on the toolbar and then click *Copy* at the drop-down list.

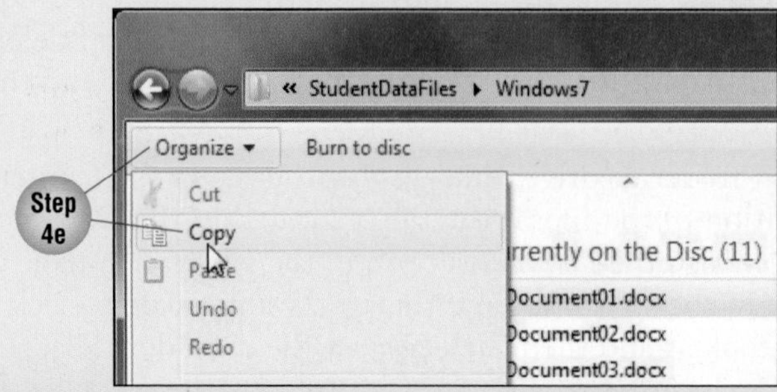

f. In the Computer section in the Navigation pane, click the drive containing your storage medium. (You may need to scroll down the Navigation pane.)
g. Click the Organize button and then click *Paste* at the drop-down list.

5. Delete ***WordDocument01.docx*** from your storage medium by completing the following steps:
   a. Make sure the contents of your storage medium display in the Content pane in the Computer window.
   b. Click ***WordDocument01.docx*** in the Content pane to select it.
   c. Click the Organize button and then click *Delete* at the drop-down list.
   d. At the message asking if you want to permanently delete the file, click the Yes button.
6. Copy the Windows7 folder from the CD to your storage medium by completing the following steps:
   a. With the Computer window open, click the drive in the *Computer* section in the Navigation pane that contains the CD that accompanies this book.
   b. Double-click *StudentDataFiles* in the Content pane.
   c. Click the *Windows7* folder in the Content pane.
   d. Click the Organize button and then click *Copy* at the drop-down list.
   e. In the *Computer* section in the Navigation pane, click the drive containing your storage medium.
   f. Click the Organize button and then click *Paste* at the drop-down list.
7. Close the Computer window by clicking the Close button located in the upper right corner of the window.

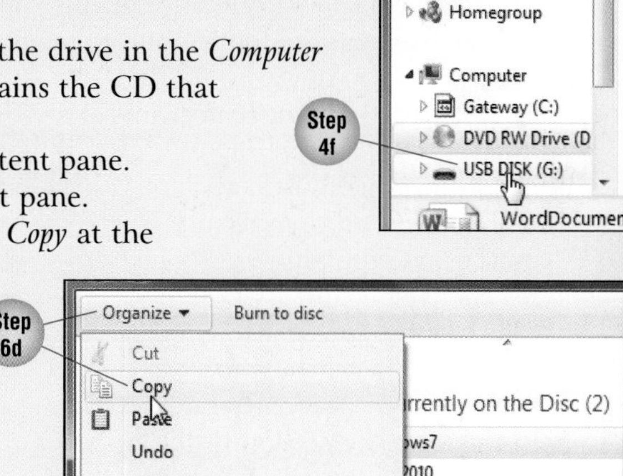

In addition to options in the Organize button drop-down list, you can use options in a shortcut menu to copy, move, and delete files or folders. To use a shortcut menu, select the desired file(s) or folder(s), position the mouse pointer on the selected item, and then click the right mouse button. At the shortcut menu that displays, click the desired option such as Copy, Cut, or Delete.

Selecting Files and Folders

You can move, copy, or delete more than one file or folder at the same time. Before moving, copying, or deleting files or folders, select the desired files or folders. To make selecting easier, consider changing the display in the Content pane to List or Details. To change the display, click the Views button arrow on the toolbar in the Computer window and then click *List* or *Details* at the drop-down list. You can also cycle through the various views by clicking the Views button. Hover your mouse over the Views button and the ScreenTip *Change your view* displays.

To select adjacent files or folders, click the first file or folder, hold down the Shift key, and then click the last file or folder. To select nonadjacent files or folders, click the first file or folder, hold down the Ctrl key, and then click any other files or folders.

Project 5 Copying and Deleting Files

1. At the Windows 7 desktop, click the Start button and then click *Computer*.
2. Copy files from the CD that accompanies this textbook to the drive containing your storage medium by completing the following steps:
   a. Make sure the CD that accompanies this textbook and your storage medium are inserted in the appropriate drives.
   b. Double-click the CD drive in the Content pane in the Computer window.
   c. Double-click the *StudentDataFiles* folder in the Content pane.
   d. Double-click the *Windows7* folder in the Content pane.
   e. Change the display to List by clicking the Views button arrow on the toolbar and then clicking *List* at the drop-down list.

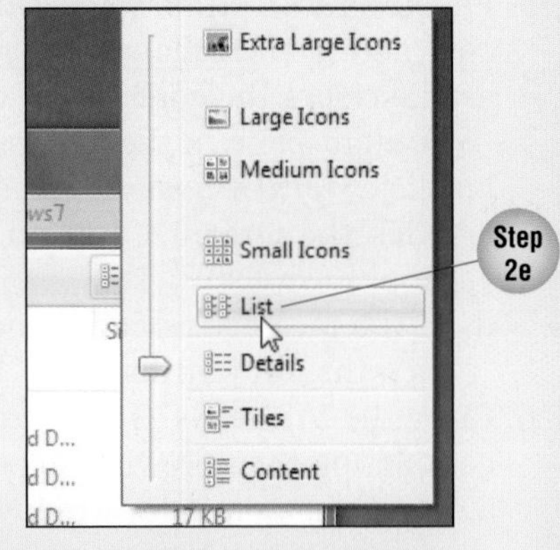

   f. Click ***WordDocument01.docx*** in the Content pane.
   g. Hold down the Shift key, click ***WordDocument05.docx***, and then release the Shift key. (This selects five documents.)
   h. Click the Organize button and then click *Copy* at the drop-down list.
   i. In the *Computer* section in the Navigation pane, click the drive containing your storage medium.
   j. Click the Organize button and then click *Paste* at the drop-down list.
3. Delete the files from your storage medium that you just copied by completing the following steps:
   a. Change the view by clicking the Views button arrow bar and then clicking *List* at the drop-down list.
   b. Click ***WordDocument01.docx*** in the Content pane.
   c. Hold down the Shift key, click ***WordDocument05.docx***, and then release the Shift key.
   d. Position the mouse pointer on any selected file, click the right mouse button, and then click *Delete* at the shortcut menu.
   e. At the message asking if you are sure you want to permanently delete the files, click Yes.
4. Close the Computer window by clicking the Close button located in the upper right corner of the window.

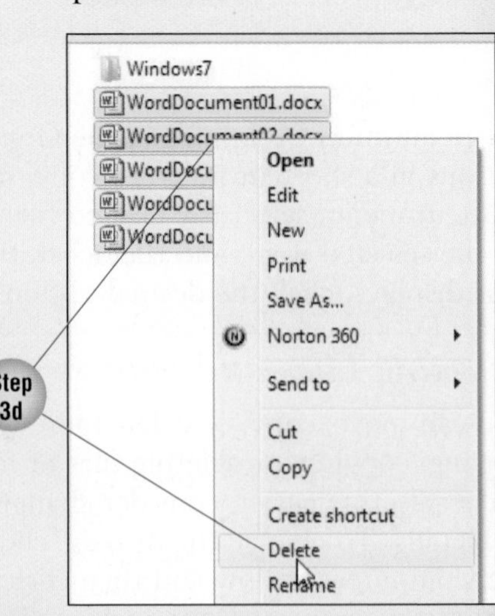

Manipulating and Creating Folders

As you begin working with and creating a number of files, consider creating folders in which you can logically group the files. To create a folder, display the Computer window and then display in the Content pane the drive or folder where you want to create the folder. Position the mouse pointer in a blank area in the Content pane, click the right mouse button, point to *New* in the shortcut menu, and then click *Folder* at the side menu. This inserts a folder icon in the Content pane and names the folder *New folder*. Type the desired name for the new folder and then press Enter.

Project 6 Creating a New Folder

1. At the Windows 7 desktop, open the Computer window.
2. Create a new folder by completing the following steps:
   a. Double-click in the Content pane the drive that contains your storage medium.
   b. Double-click the *Windows7* folder in the Content pane. (This opens the folder.)
   c. Click the Views button arrow and then click *List* at the drop-down list.
   d. Position the mouse pointer in a blank area in the Content pane and then click the right mouse button.
   e. Point to *New* in the shortcut menu and then click *Folder* at the side menu.
   f. Type SpellCheckFiles and then press Enter. (This changes the name from *New folder* to *SpellCheckFiles*.)

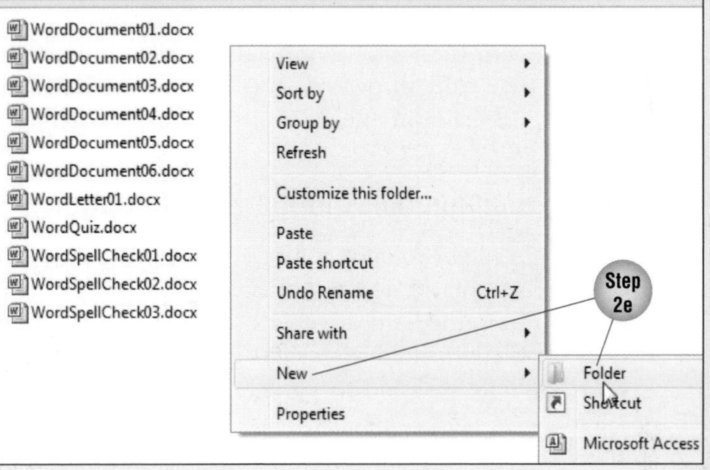

3. Copy **WordSpellCheck01.docx**, **WordSpellCheck02.docx**, and **WordSpellCheck03.docx** into the SpellCheckFiles folder you just created by completing the following steps:
   a. Click the Views button arrow and then click *List* at the drop-down list. (Skip this step if *List* is already selected.)
   b. Click once on the file named **WordSpellCheck01.docx** located in the Content pane.
   c. Hold down the Shift key, click once on the file named **WordSpellCheck03.docx**, and then release the Shift key. (This selects three documents.)
   d. Click the Organize button and then click *Copy* at the drop-down list.
   e. Double-click the *SpellCheckFiles* folder in the Content pane.
   f. Click the Organize button and then click *Paste* at the drop-down list.

4. Delete the SpellCheckFiles folder and its contents by completing the following steps:
   a. Click the Back button (contains a left-pointing arrow) located at the left side of the Address bar.
   b. With the SpellCheckFiles folder selected in the Content pane, click the Organize button and then click *Delete* at the drop-down list.
   c. At the message asking you to confirm the deletion, click Yes.

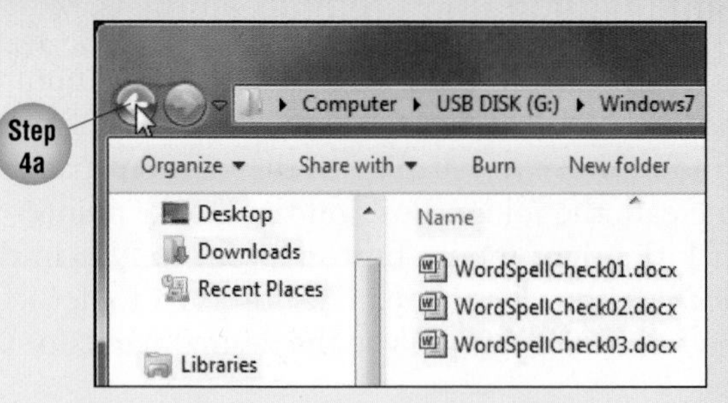

5. Close the window by clicking the Close button located in the upper right corner of the window.

Using the Recycle Bin

Deleting the wrong file can be a disaster but Windows 7 helps protect your work with the Recycle Bin. The Recycle Bin acts just like an office wastepaper basket; you can "throw away" (delete) unwanted files, but you can "reach in" to the Recycle Bin and take out (restore) a file if you threw it away by accident.

Deleting Files to the Recycle Bin

A file or folder or selected files or folders you delete from the hard drive are sent automatically to the Recycle Bin. If you want to permanently delete files or folders from the hard drive without first sending them to the Recycle Bin, select the desired file(s) or folder(s), right click on one of the selected files or folders, hold down the Shift key, and then click *Delete* at the shortcut menu.

Files and folders deleted from a USB flash drive or disc are deleted permanently. (Recovery programs are available, however, that will help you recover deleted files or folders. If you accidentally delete a file or folder from a USB flash drive or disc, do not do anything more with the USB flash drive or disc until you can run a recovery program.)

You can delete files in the manner described earlier in this section and you can also delete a file by dragging the file icon to the Recycle Bin. To do this, click the desired file in the Content pane in the Computer window, drag the file icon on top of the Recycle Bin icon on the desktop until the text *Move to Recycle Bin* displays, and then release the mouse button.

Restoring Files from the Recycle Bin

To restore a file from the Recycle Bin, double-click the Recycle Bin icon on the desktop. This opens the Recycle Bin window shown in Figure W.9. (The contents of the Recycle Bin will vary.) To restore a file, click the file you want restored and then click the Restore this item button on the toolbar. This removes the file from the Recycle Bin and returns it to its original location. You can also restore a file by positioning the mouse pointer on the file, clicking the right mouse button, and then clicking *Restore* at the shortcut menu.

Figure W.9 Recycle Bin Window

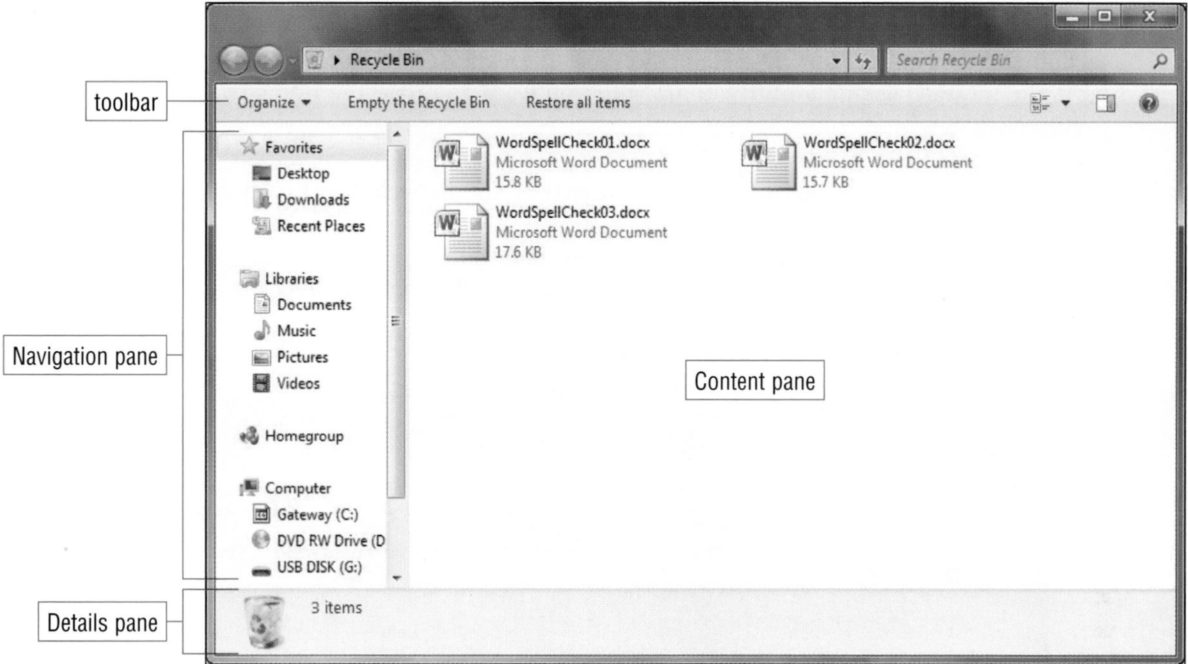

Project 7 Deleting Files to and Restoring Files from the Recycle Bin

Before beginning this project, check with your instructor to determine if you can copy files to the hard drive.

1. At the Windows 7 desktop, open the Computer window.
2. Copy files from your storage medium to the Documents folder on your hard drive by completing the following steps:
   a. Double-click in the Content pane the drive containing your storage medium.
   b. Double-click the *Windows7* folder in the Content pane.
   c. Click the Views button arrow and then click *List* at the drop-down list. (Skip this step if *List* is already selected.)
   d. Click ***WordSpellCheck01.docx*** in the Content pane.
   e. Hold down the Shift key, click ***WordSpellCheck03.docx***, and then release the Shift key.
   f. Click the Organize button and then click *Copy* at the drop-down list.
   g. Click the *Documents* folder in the *Libraries* section in the Navigation pane.
   h. Click the Organize button and then click *Paste* at the drop-down list.

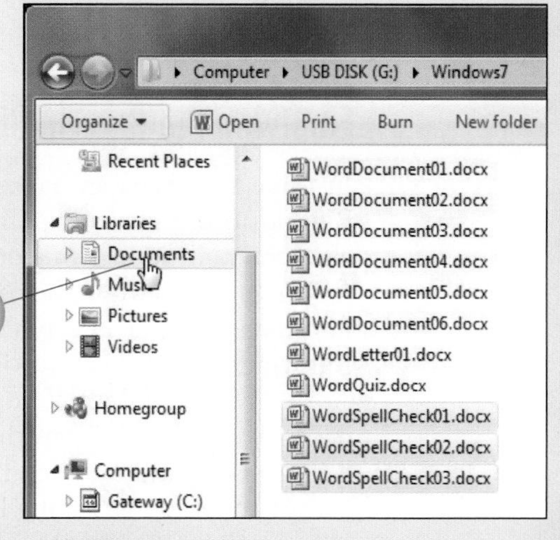

3. Delete to the Recycle Bin the files you just copied by completing the following steps:
   a. With **WordSpellCheck01.docx** through **WordSpellCheck03.docx** selected in the Content pane, click the Organize button and then click *Delete* at the drop-down list.
   b. At the message asking you if you are sure you want to move the items to the Recycle Bin, click Yes.
4. Close the Computer window.
5. At the Windows 7 desktop, display the contents of the Recycle Bin by double-clicking the Recycle Bin icon.
6. Restore the files you just deleted by completing the following steps:
   a. Select **WordSpellCheck01.docx** through **WordSpellCheck03.docx** in the Recycle Bin Content pane. (If these files are not visible, you will need to scroll down the list of files in the Content pane.)
   b. Click the Restore the selected items button on the toolbar.

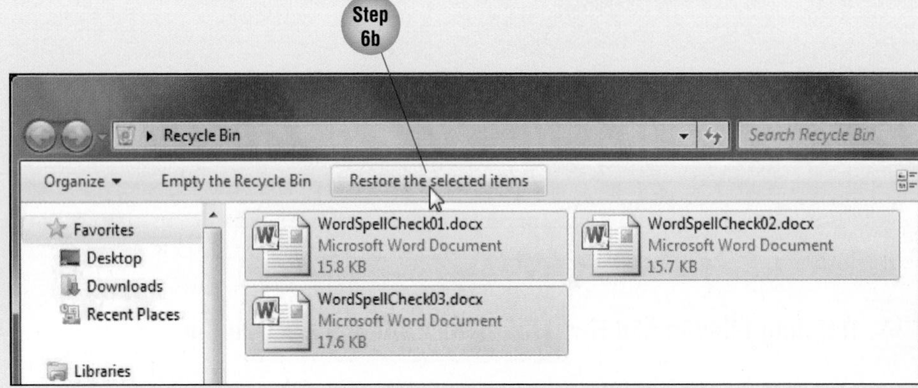

7. Close the Recycle Bin by clicking the Close button located in the upper right corner of the window.
8. Display the Computer window.
9. Click the *Documents* folder in the *Libraries* section in the Navigation pane.
10. Delete the files you restored.
11. Close the Computer window.

Emptying the Recycle Bin

Just like a wastepaper basket, the Recycle Bin can get full. To empty the Recycle Bin, position the arrow pointer on the Recycle Bin icon on the desktop and then click the right mouse button. At the shortcut menu that displays, click the *Empty Recycle Bin* option. At the message asking if you want to permanently delete the items, click Yes. You can also empty the Recycle Bin by displaying the Recycle Bin window and then clicking the Empty the Recycle Bin button on the toolbar. At the message asking if you want to permanently delete the items, click Yes. To delete a specific file from the Recycle Bin window, click the desired file in the Recycle Bin window, click the Organize button, and then *Delete* at the drop-down list. At the message asking if you want to permanently delete the file, click Yes. When you empty the Recycle Bin, the files cannot be recovered by the Recycle Bin or by Windows 7. If you have to recover a file, you will need to use a file recovery program.

Project 8 Emptying the Recycle Bin

Before beginning this project, check with your instructor to determine if you can delete files/folders from the Recycle Bin.

1. At the Windows 7 desktop, double-click the Recycle Bin icon.
2. At the Recycle Bin window, empty the contents by clicking the Empty the Recycle Bin button on the toolbar.
3. At the message asking you if you want to permanently delete the items, click Yes.
4. Close the Recycle Bin by clicking the Close button located in the upper right corner of the window.

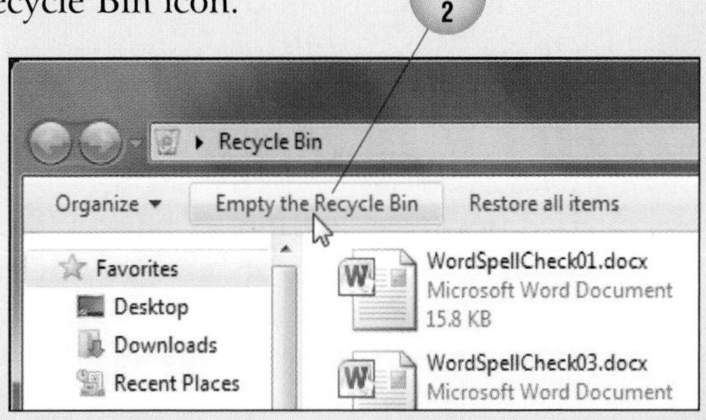

Creating a Shortcut

If you use a file or program on a consistent basis, consider creating a shortcut to the file or program. A shortcut is a specialized icon that represents very small files that point the operating system to the actual item, whether it is a file, a folder, or an application. If you create a shortcut to a Word document, the shortcut icon is not the actual document but a path to the document. Double-click the shortcut icon and Windows 7 opens the document in Word.

One method for creating a shortcut is to display the Computer window and then make active the drive or folder where the file is located. Right-click the desired file, point to *Send To*, and then click *Desktop (create shortcut)*. You can easily delete a shortcut icon from the desktop by dragging the shortcut icon to the Recycle Bin icon. This deletes the shortcut icon but does not delete the file to which the shortcut pointed.

Project 9 Creating a Shortcut

1. At the Windows 7 desktop, display the Computer window.
2. Double-click the drive containing your storage medium.
3. Double-click the *Windows7* folder in the Content pane.
4. Change the display of files to a list by clicking the Views button arrow and then clicking *List* at the drop-down list. (Skip this step if *List* is already selected.)
5. Create a shortcut to the file named **WordLetter01.docx** by right-clicking ***WordLetter01.docx***, pointing to *Send to*, and then clicking *Desktop (create shortcut)*.

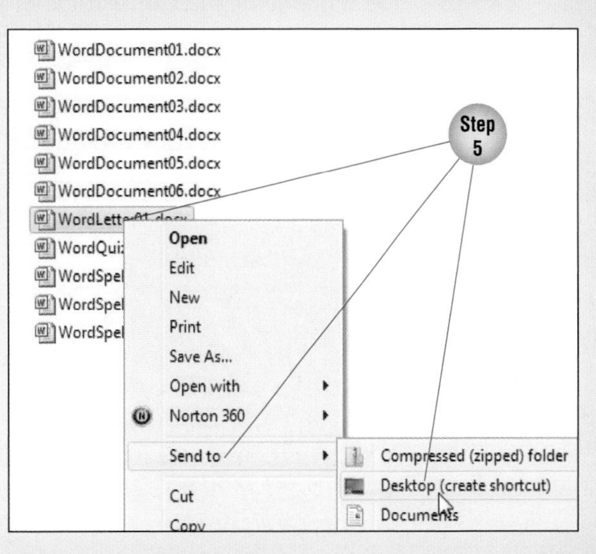

6. Close the Computer window.
7. Open Word and the file named **WordLetter01.docx** by double-clicking the *WordLetter01.docx* shortcut icon on the desktop.
8. After viewing the file in Word, exit Word by clicking the Close button that displays in the upper right corner of the window.
9. Delete the *WordLetter01.docx* shortcut icon by completing the following steps:
   a. At the desktop, position the mouse pointer on the *WordLetter01.docx* shortcut icon.
   b. Hold down the left mouse button, drag the icon on top of the Recycle Bin icon, and then release the mouse button.

Exploring the Control Panel

The Control Panel, shown in Figure W.10, contains a variety of icons you can use to customize the appearance and functionality of your computer as well as access and change system settings. Display the Control Panel by clicking the Start button on the Taskbar and then clicking *Control Panel* at the Start menu. The Control Panel organizes settings into categories to make them easier to find. Click a category icon and the Control Panel displays lower-level categories and tasks within each of them.

Hover your mouse over a category icon in the Control Panel and a ScreenTip displays with an explanation of what options are available. For example, if you hover the mouse over the Appearance and Personalization icon, a ScreenTip displays with information about the tasks available in the category such as changing the appearance of desktop items, applying a theme or screen saver to your computer, or customizing the Start menu and Taskbar.

If you click a category icon in the Control Panel, the Control Panel displays all of the available subcategories and tasks in the category. Also, the categories display in text form at the left side of the Control Panel. For example, if you click the Appearance and Personalization category icon, the Control Panel displays as shown in Figure W.11. Notice how the Control Panel categories display at the left side of the Control Panel and options for changing the appearance and personalizing your computer display in the middle of the Control Panel.

By default, the Control Panel displays categories of tasks in what is called Category view. You can change this view to *Large icons* or *Small icons*. To change the view, click the down-pointing arrow that displays at the right side of the text *View by* that displays in the upper right corner of the Control Panel, and then click the desired view at the drop-down list (see Figure W.10).

Figure W.10 The Control Panel

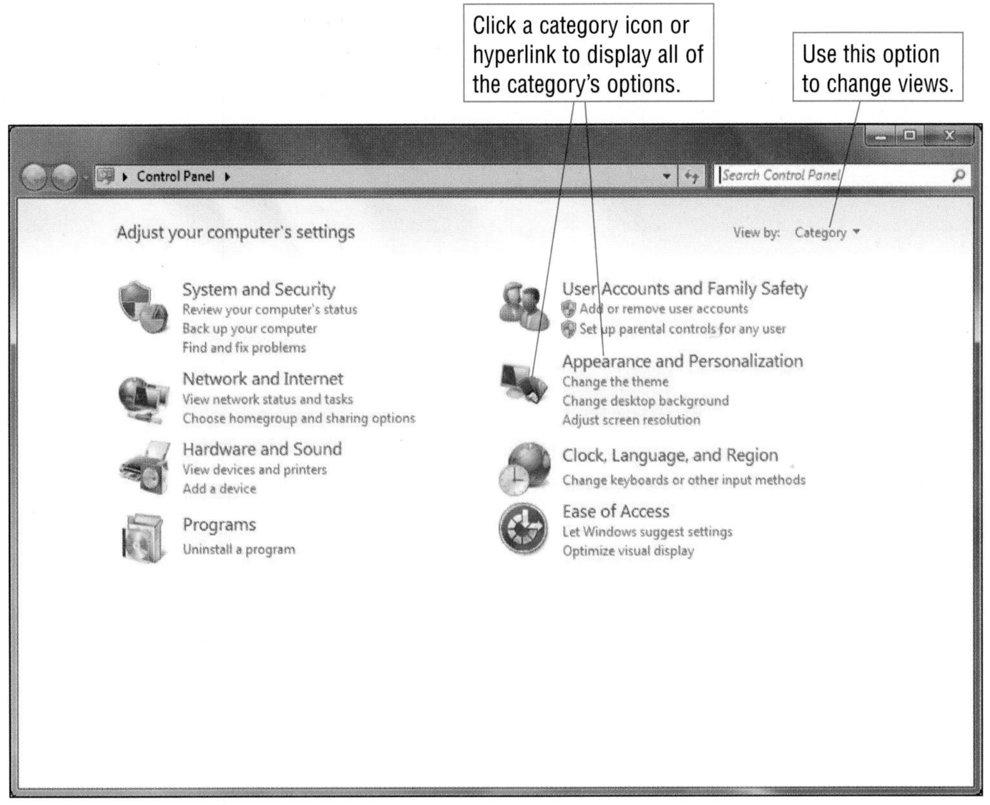

Figure W.11 Appearance and Personalization Window

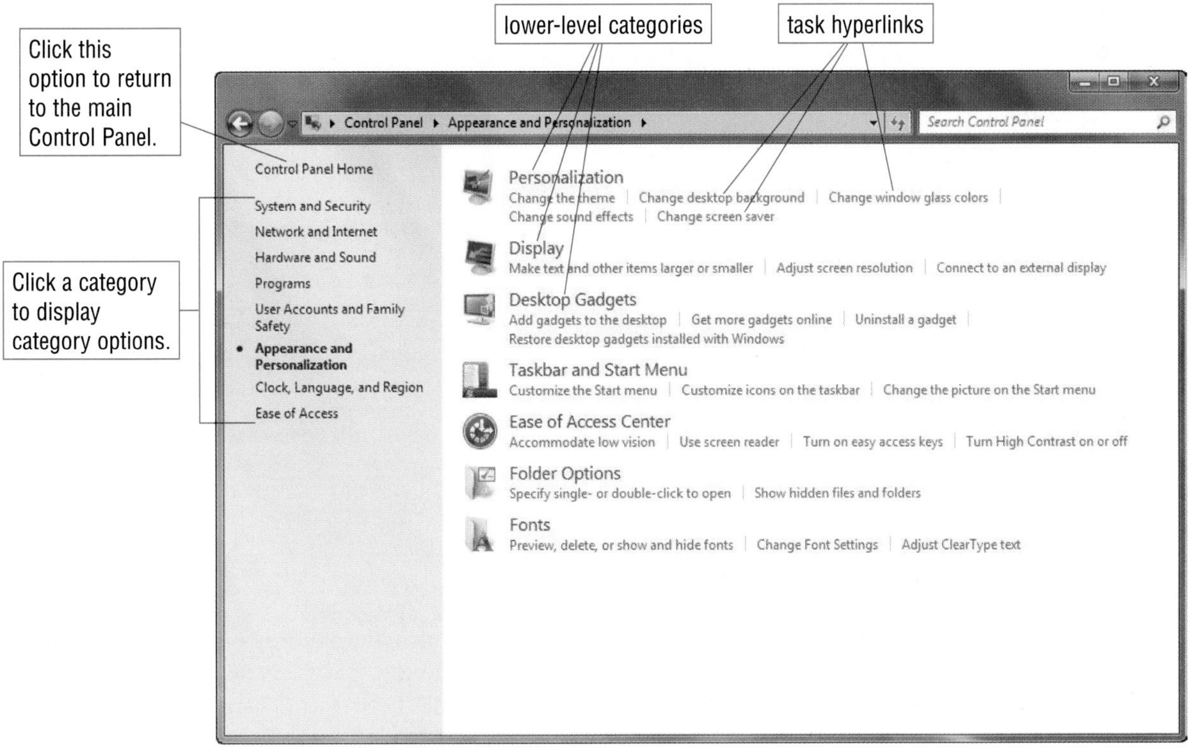

Project 10 Changing the Desktop Theme

1. At the Windows 7 desktop, click the Start button and then click *Control Panel* at the Start menu.
2. At the Control Panel, click the Appearance and Personalization category icon.

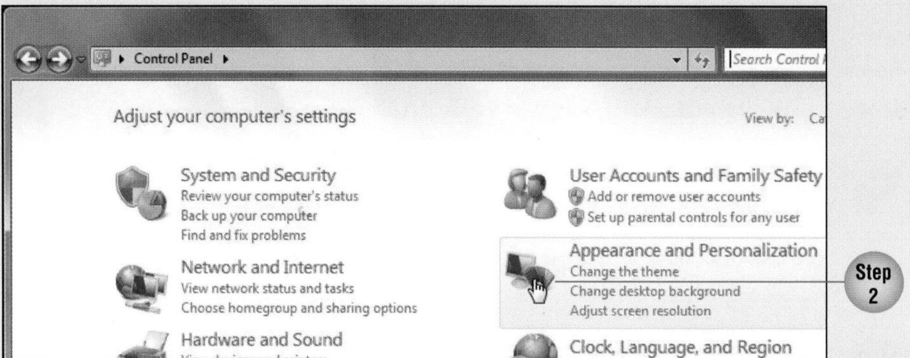

3. Click the Change the theme hyperlink that displays below the Personalization category in the panel at the right in the Control Panel.
4. At the window that displays with options for changing visuals and sounds on your computer, click the *Landscapes* theme.

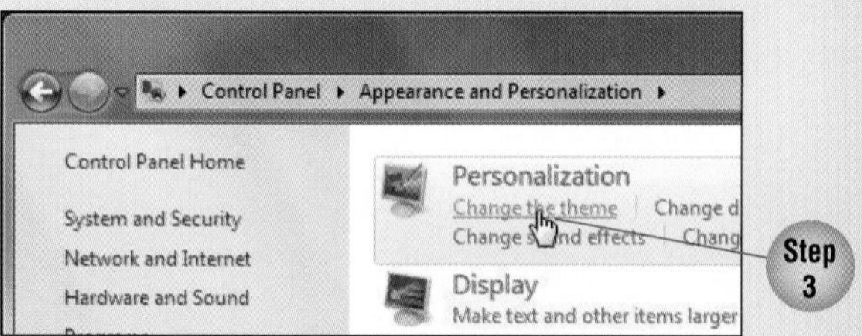

5. Click the Desktop Background hyperlink that displays in the lower left corner of the panel at the right.
6. Click the button that displays below the text *Change picture every* and then click *10 Seconds* at the drop-down list. (This tells Windows to change the picture on your desktop every 10 seconds.)
7. Click the Save changes button that displays in the lower right corner of the Control Panel.
8. Click the Close button located in the upper right corner to close the Control Panel.
9. Look at the picture that displays as the background at the desktop. Wait for 10 seconds and then look at the second picture that displays.
10. Click the Start button and then click *Control Panel* at the Start menu.
11. At the Control Panel, click the Appearance and Personalization category icon.
12. Click the Change the theme hyperlink that displays below the Personalization category in the panel at the right.
13. At the window that displays with options for changing visuals and sounds on your computer, click the *Windows 7* theme in the *Aero Themes* section. (This is the default theme.)
14. Click the Close button located in the upper right corner of the Control Panel.

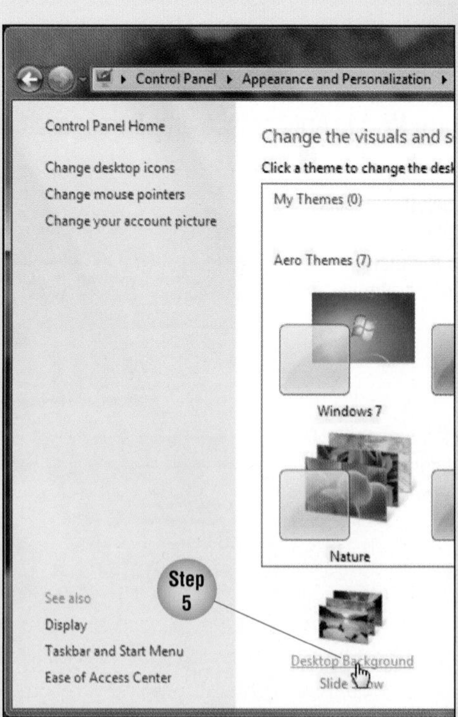

Searching in the Control Panel

The Control Panel contains a large number of options for customizing the appearance and functionality of your computer. If you want to customize a feature and are not sure where the options for the feature are located, search for the feature. To do this, display the Control Panel and then type the name of the desired feature. By default, the insertion point is positioned in the *Search Control Panel* text box. When you type the feature name in the Search Control Panel, options related to the feature display in the Control Panel.

Project 11 **Customizing the Mouse**

1. Click the Start button and then click *Control Panel.*
2. At the Control Panel, type mouse. (The insertion point is automatically located in the *Search Control Panel* text box when you open the Control Panel. When you type *mouse,* features for customizing the mouse display in the Control Panel.)
3. Click the Mouse icon that displays in the Control Panel.
4. At the Mouse Properties dialog box, notice the options that display. (The *Switch primary and secondary buttons* option might be useful, for example, if you are left-handed and want to switch the buttons on the mouse.)
5. Click the Cancel button to remove the dialog box.
6. At the Control Panel, click the Change the mouse pointer display or speed hyperlink.

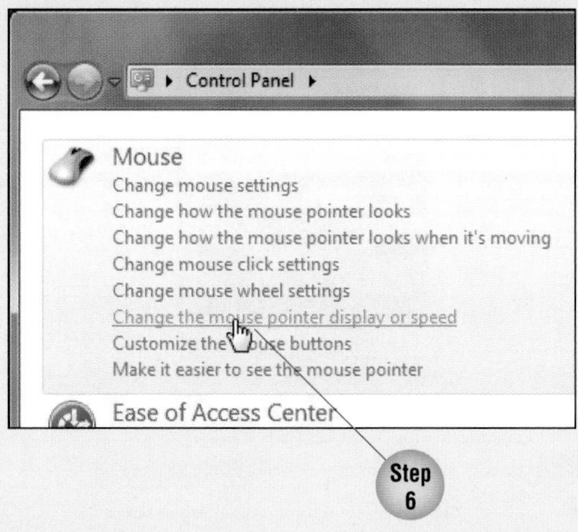

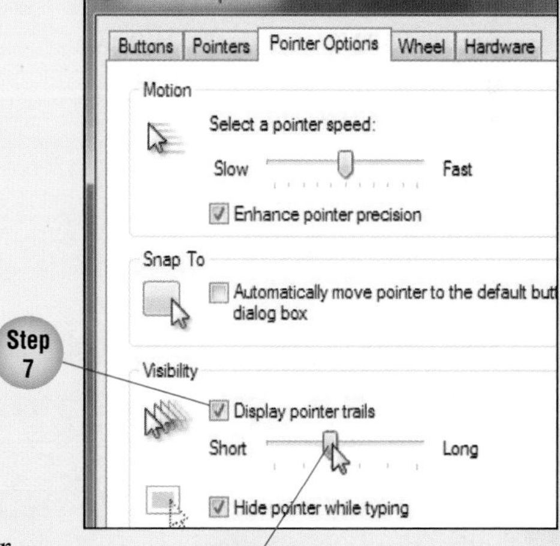

7. At the Mouse Properties dialog box with the Pointer Options tab selected, click the *Display pointer trails* check box in the *Visibility* section to insert a check mark.
8. Drag the button on the slider bar (located below the *Display pointer trails* check box) approximately to the middle of the bar.
9. Click OK to close the dialog box.
10. Close the Control Panel.
11. Move the mouse pointer around the screen to see the pointer trails as well as the speed at which the mouse moves.

Displaying Personalize Options with a Shortcut Command

In addition to the Control Panel, you can display customization options with a command from a shortcut menu. Display a shortcut menu by positioning the mouse pointer in the desired position and then clicking the right mouse button. For example, display a shortcut menu with options for customizing the desktop by positioning the mouse pointer in an empty area on the desktop and then clicking the right mouse button. At the shortcut menu that displays, click the desired shortcut command.

Project 12 Customizing with a Shortcut Command

1. At the Windows 7 desktop, position the mouse pointer in an empty area on the desktop, click the right mouse button, and then click *Personalize* at the shortcut menu.
2. At the Control Panel Appearance and Personalization window that displays, click the Change mouse pointers hyperlink that displays at the left side of the window.
3. At the Mouse Properties dialog box, click the Pointer Options tab.
4. Click in the *Display pointer trails* check box to remove the check mark.
5. Click OK to close the dialog box.
6. At the Control Panel Appearance and Personalization window, click the Screen Saver hyperlink that displays in the lower right corner of the window.
7. At the Screen Saver Settings dialog box, click the option button below the *Screen saver* option and then click *Ribbons* at the drop-down list.
8. Check the number in the *Wait* text box. If a number other than *1* displays, click the down-pointing arrow in the spin box at the right side of the text box until *1* displays. (This tells Windows to display the screen saver after one minute of inactivity.)
9. Click OK to close the dialog box.
10. Close the Control Panel by clicking the Close button located in the upper right corner of the window.

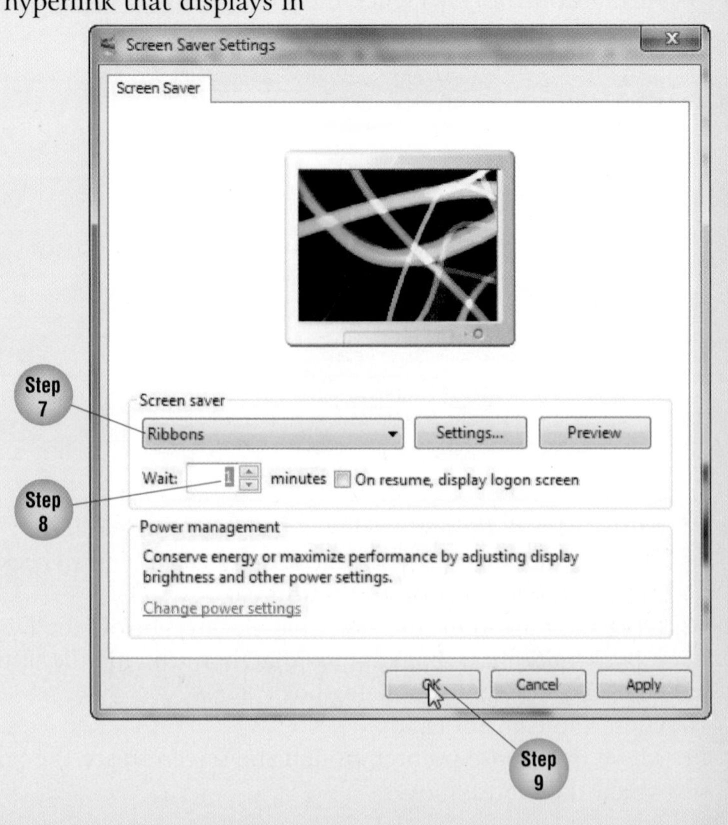

11. Do not touch the mouse or keyboard and wait over one minute for the screen saver to display. After watching the screen saver, move the mouse. (This redisplays the desktop.)
12. Right-click in an empty area on the desktop and then click *Personalize* at the shortcut menu.
13. At the Control Panel Appearance and Personalization window, click the Screen Saver hyperlink.
14. At the Screen Saver Settings dialog box, click the option button below the *Screen saver* option and then click *(None)* at the drop-down list.
15. Click OK to close the dialog box.
16. Close the Control Panel Appearance and Personalization window.

Exploring Windows Help and Support

Windows 7 includes an on-screen reference guide providing information, explanations, and interactive help on learning Windows features. Get help at the Windows Help and Support window shown in Figure W.12. Display this window by clicking the Start button and then clicking *Help and Support* at the Start menu. Use buttons in the window toolbar to display the opening Windows Help and Support window, print the current information, display a list of contents, get customer support or other types of services, and display a list of Help options.

Figure W.12 Windows Help and Support Window

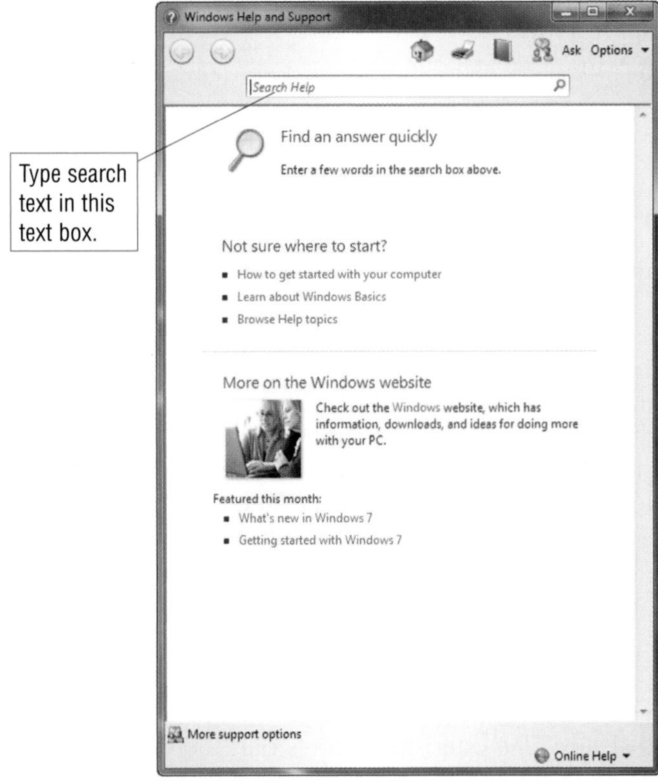

Project 13 Getting Help

1. At the Windows 7 desktop, click the Start button and then click *Help and Support* at the Start menu.
2. At the Windows Help and Support window, click the Learn about Windows Basics hyperlink.
3. Click a hyperlink that interests you, read the information, and then click the Back button on the Windows Help and Support window toolbar. (The Back button is located in the upper left corner of the window.)
4. Click another hyperlink that interests you and then read the information.
5. Click the Help and Support home button that displays on the window toolbar. (This returns you to the opening Windows Help and Support window.)
6. Click in the *Search Help* text box, type **delete files**, and then press Enter.
7. Click the Delete a file or folder hyperlink that displays in the window.
8. Read the information that displays about deleting files or folders and then click the
Print button on the window toolbar.
9. At the Print dialog box, click the Print button.
10. Click the Close button to close the Windows Help and Support window.

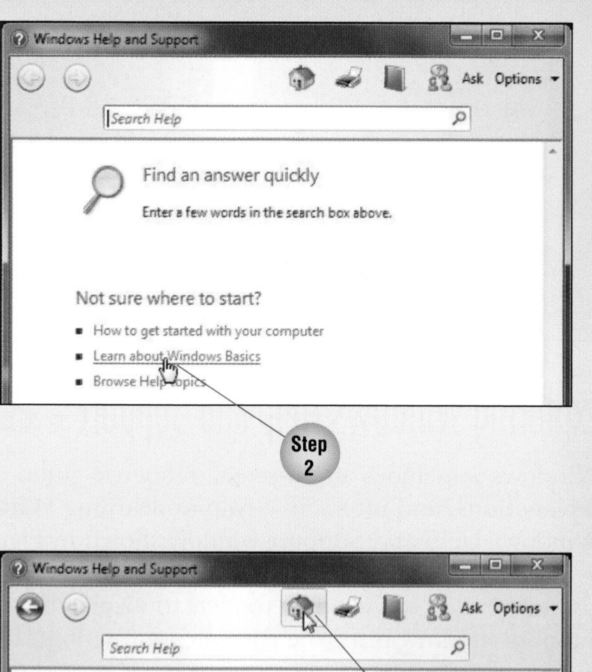

Using Search Tools

The Start menu contains a search tool you can use to quickly find a program or file on your computer. To use the search tool, click the Start button and then type the first few characters of the program or file for which you are searching in the *Search programs and files* text box. As you type characters in the text box, a pop-up list displays with program names or file names that begin with the characters. As you continue typing characters, the search tool refines the list.

You can also search for programs or files with the search text box in the Computer window. The search text box displays in the upper right corner of the Computer window at the right side of the Address bar. If you want to search a specific folder, make that folder active in the Content pane and then type the search text in the text box.

When conducting a search, you can use the asterisk (*) as a wildcard character in place of any letters, numbers, or symbols within a file name. For example, in the following project you will search for file names containing *check* by typing ***check** in the search text box. The asterisk indicates that the file name can start with any letter but it must contain the letters *check* somewhere in the file name.

Project 14 Searching for Programs and Files

1. At the Windows 7 desktop, click the Start button.
2. With the insertion point positioned in the *Search programs and files* text box, type paint. (Notice as you type the letters that Windows displays programs and/or files that begin with the same letters you are typing or that are associated with the same letters in a keyword. Notice that the Paint program displays below the heading *Programs* at the top of the list. Depending on the contents stored in the computer you are using, additional items may display below Paint.)

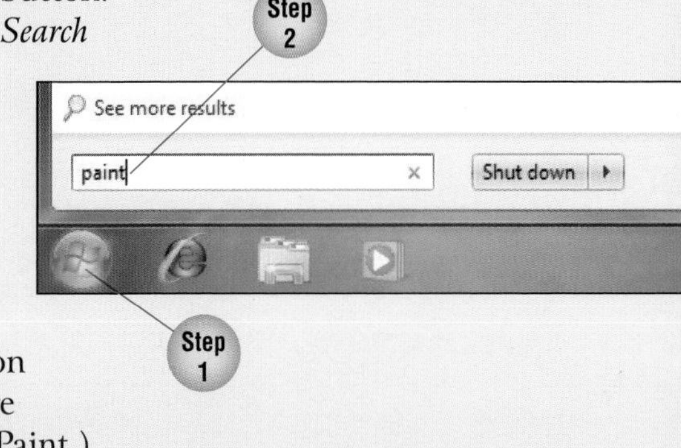

3. Click *Paint* that displays below the *Programs* heading.
4. Close the Paint window.
5. Click the Start button and then click *Computer*.
6. At the Computer window, double-click the icon representing your storage medium.
7. Double-click the *Windows7* folder.
8. Click in the search text box located at the right of the Address bar and then type document. (As you begin typing the letters, Windows filters the list of files in the Content pane to those that contain the letters you type. Notice that the Address bar displays *Search Results in Windows7* to indicate that the files that display matching your criteria were limited to the current folder.)

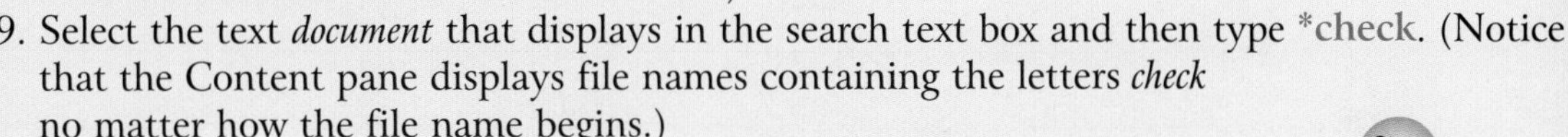

9. Select the text *document* that displays in the search text box and then type *check. (Notice that the Content pane displays file names containing the letters *check* no matter how the file name begins.)
10. Double-click ***WordSpellCheck02.docx*** to open the document in Word.
11. Close the document and exit Word by clicking the Close button located in the upper right corner of the window.
12. Close the Computer window.

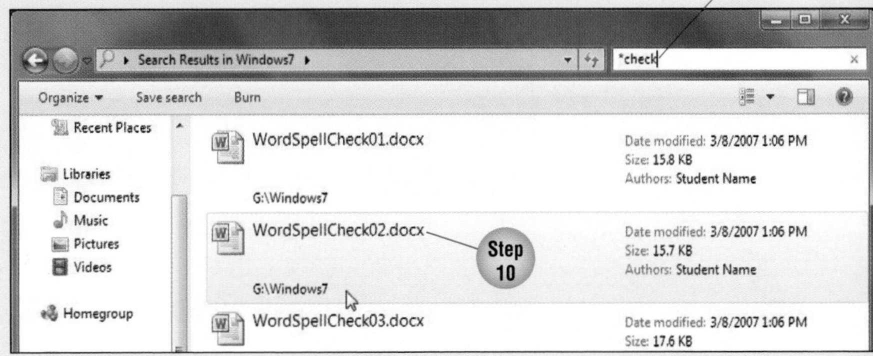

Browsing the Internet Using Internet Explorer 8.0

Microsoft Internet Explorer 8.0 is a web browser program with options and features for displaying sites as well as navigating and searching for information on the Internet. The ***Internet*** is a network of computers connected around the world. Users access the Internet for several purposes: to communicate using instant messaging and/or email, to subscribe to newsgroups, to transfer files, to socialize with other users around the globe in chat rooms, and also to access virtually any kind of information imaginable.

Using the Internet, people can find a phenomenal amount of information for private or public use. To use the Internet, three things are generally required: an Internet Service Provider (ISP), a program to browse the Web (called a ***web browser***), and a ***search engine***. In this section, you will learn how to:

- Navigate the Internet using URLs and hyperlinks
- Use search engines to locate information
- Download web pages and images

You will use the Microsoft Internet Explorer web browser to locate information on the Internet. Uniform Resource Locators, referred to as URLs, are the method used to identify locations on the Internet. The steps for browsing the Internet vary but generally include: opening Internet Explorer, typing the URL for the desired site, navigating the various pages of the site, navigating to other sites using links, and then closing Internet Explorer.

To launch Internet Explorer 8.0, click the Internet Explorer icon on the Taskbar at the Windows desktop. Figure IE.1 identifies the elements of the Internet Explorer, version 8.0, window. The web page that displays in your Internet Explorer window may vary from what you see in Figure IE.1.

If you know the URL for the desired website, click in the Address bar, type the URL, and then press Enter. The website's home page displays in a tab within the Internet Explorer window. URLs (Uniform Resource Locators) are the method used to identify locations on the Internet. The format of a URL is *http://server-name.path*. The first part of the URL, *http*, stands for HyperText Transfer Protocol, which is the protocol or language used to transfer data within the World Wide Web. The colon and slashes separate the protocol from the server name. The server name is the second component of the URL. For example, in the URL http://www.microsoft.com, the server name is *microsoft*. The last part of the URL specifies the domain to which the server belongs. For example, *.com* refers to "commercial" and establishes that the URL is a commercial company. Examples of other domains include *.edu* for "educational," *.gov* for "government," and *.mil* for "military."

Figure IE.1 Internet Explorer Window

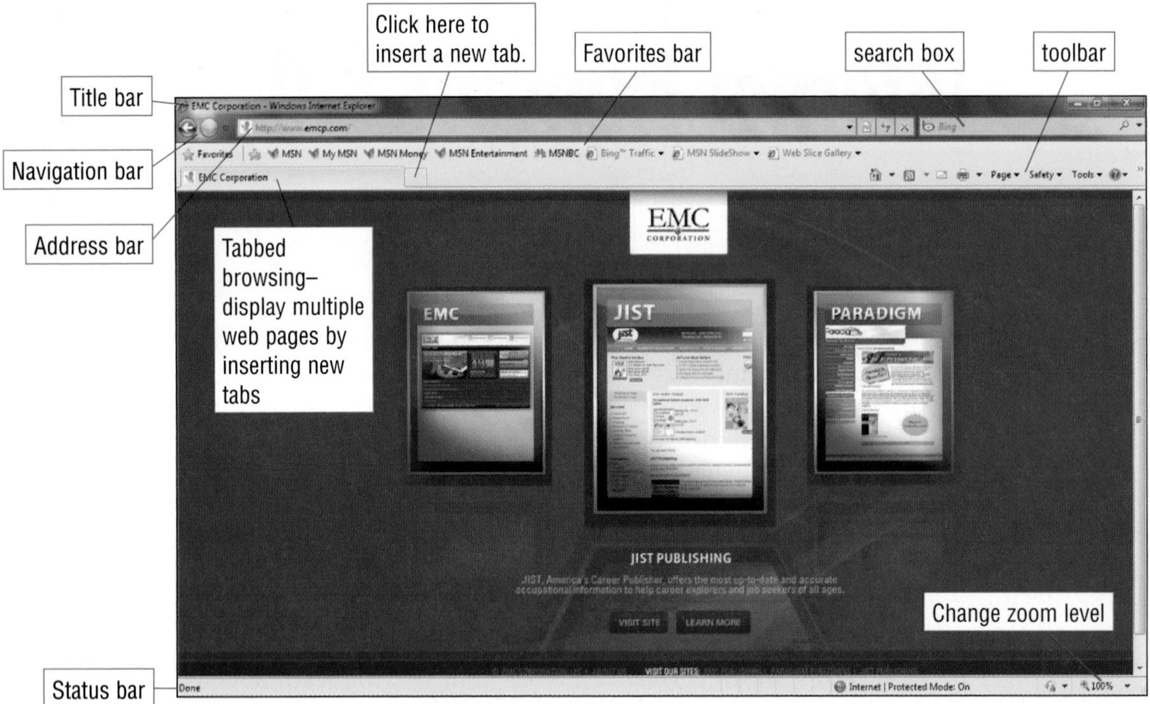

Project 1 Browsing the Internet Using URLs

1. Make sure you are connected to the Internet through an Internet Service Provider and that the Windows desktop displays. (Check with your instructor to determine if you need to complete steps for accessing the Internet such as typing a user name and password to log on.)
2. Launch Microsoft Internet Explorer by clicking the Internet Explorer icon located on the Taskbar located at the bottom of the Windows desktop.
3. At the Internet Explorer window, explore the website for Yosemite National Park by completing the following steps:
   a. Click in the Address bar, type www.nps.gov/yose, and then press Enter.
   b. Scroll down the home page for Yosemite National Park by clicking the down-pointing arrow on the vertical scroll bar located at the right side of the Internet Explorer window.
   c. Print the home page by clicking the Print button located on the Internet Explorer toolbar. (Some websites have a printer friendly button you can click to print the page.)

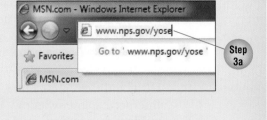

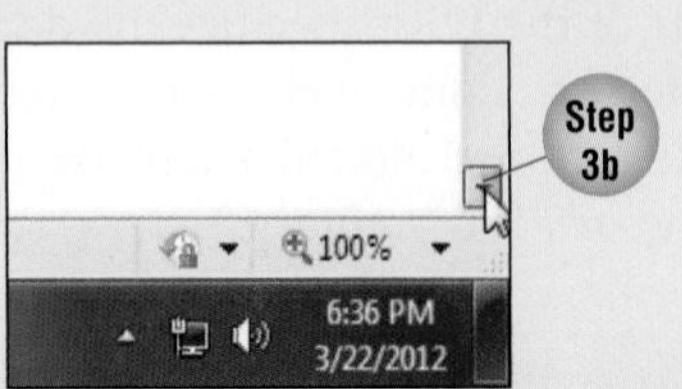

4. Explore the website for Glacier National Park by completing the following steps:
   a. Click in the Address bar, type www.nps.gov/glac, and then press Enter.
   b. Print the home page by clicking the Print button located on the Internet Explorer toolbar.
5. Close Internet Explorer by clicking the Close button (contains an X) located in the upper right corner of the Internet Explorer window.

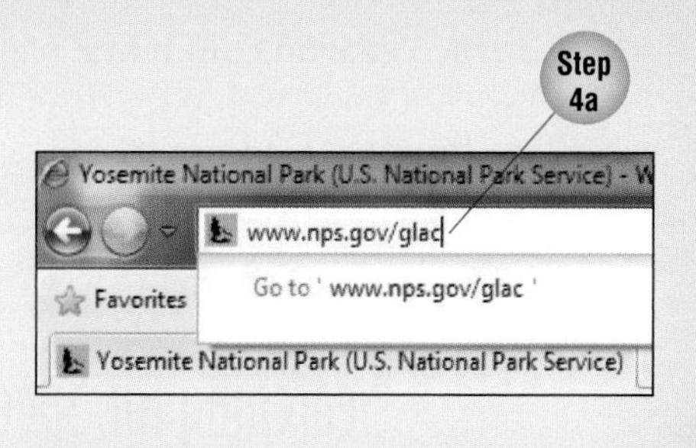

Navigating Using Hyperlinks

Most web pages contain "hyperlinks" that you click to connect to another page within the website or to another site on the Internet. Hyperlinks may display in a web page as underlined text in a specific color or as images or icons. To use a hyperlink, position the mouse pointer on the desired hyperlink until the mouse pointer turns into a hand, and then click the left mouse button. Use hyperlinks to navigate within and between sites on the Internet. The navigation bar in the Internet Explorer window contains a Back button that, when clicked, takes you to the previous web page viewed. If you click the Back button and then want to return to the previous page, click the Forward button. You can continue clicking the Back button to back your way out of several linked pages in reverse order since Internet Explorer maintains a history of the websites you visit.

Project 2 Navigating Using Hyperlinks

1. Make sure you are connected to the Internet and then click the Internet Explorer icon on the Taskbar.
2. At the Internet Explorer window, display the White House web page and navigate in the page by completing the following steps:
   a. Click in the Address bar, type whitehouse.gov, and then press Enter.
   b. At the White House home page, position the mouse pointer on a hyperlink that interests you until the pointer turns into a hand, and then click the left mouse button.
   c. At the linked web page, click the Back button. (This returns you to the White House home page.)
   d. At the White House home page, click the Forward button to return to the previous web page viewed.
   e. Print the web page by clicking the Print button on the Internet Explorer toolbar.
3. Display the website for Amazon.com and navigate in the site by completing the following steps:
   a. Click in the Address bar, type www.amazon.com, and then press Enter.

b. At the Amazon.com home page, click a hyperlink related to books.
c. When a book web page displays, click the Print button on the Internet Explorer toolbar.
4. Close Internet Explorer by clicking the Close button (contains an X) located in the upper right corner of the Internet Explorer window.

Searching for Specific Sites

If you do not know the URL for a specific site or you want to find information on the Internet but do not know what site to visit, complete a search with a search engine. A search engine is a software program created to search quickly and easily for desired information. A variety of search engines are available on the Internet, each offering the opportunity to search for specific information. One method for searching for information is to click in the search box located to the right of the Address bar, type a keyword or phrase related to your search, and then click the Search button or press Enter. Another method for completing a search is to visit the website for a search engine and use options at the site.

Bing is Microsoft's online search portal and is the default search engine used by Internet Explorer. Bing organizes search results by topic category and provides related search suggestions.

Project 3 Searching for Information by Topic

1. Start Internet Explorer.
2. At the Internet Explorer window, search for sites on bluegrass music by completing the following steps:
   a. Click in the search box (may display *Bing*) located at the right side of the Address bar.
   b. Type bluegrass music and then press Enter.
   c. When a list of sites displays in the Bing results window, click a site that interests you.
   d. When the page displays, click the Print button.

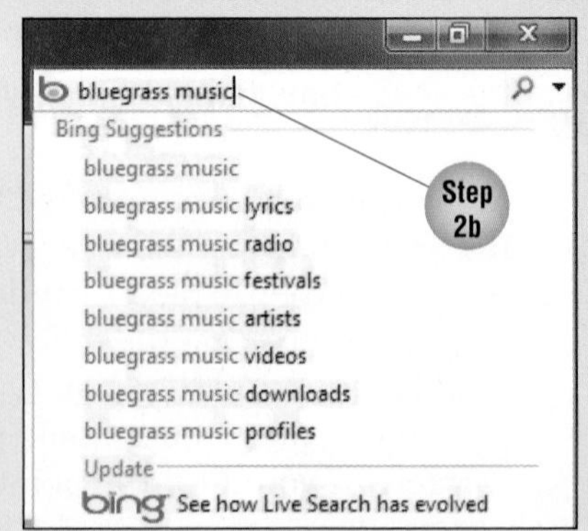

3. Use the Yahoo! search engine to find sites on bluegrass music by completing the following steps:
   a. Click in the Address bar, type www.yahoo.com, and then press Enter.
   b. At the Yahoo! website, with the insertion point positioned in the search text box, type bluegrass music and then press Enter. (Notice that the sites displayed vary from sites displayed in the earlier search.)
   c. Click hyperlinks until a website displays that interests you.
   d. Print the page.

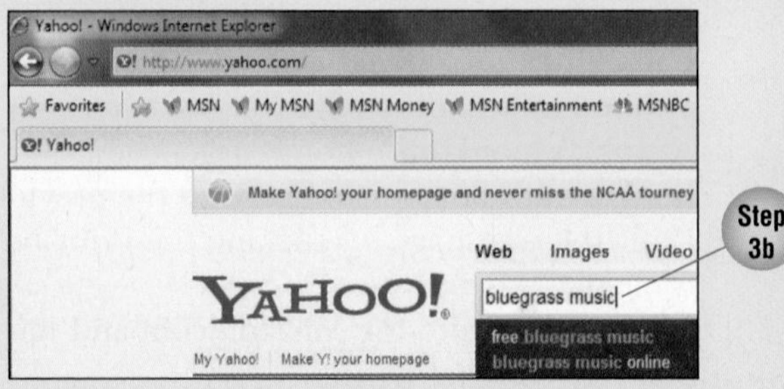

4. Use the Google search engine to find sites on jazz music by completing the following steps:
   a. Click in the Address bar, type www.google.com, and then press Enter.
   b. At the Google website, with the insertion point positioned in the search text box, type jazz music and then press Enter.
   c. Click a site that interests you.
   d. Print the page.
5. Close Internet Explorer.

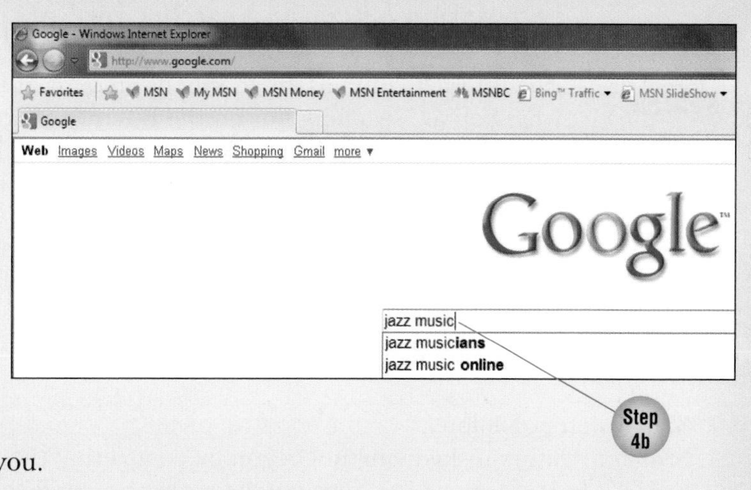

Using a Metasearch Engine

Bing, Yahoo!, and Google are search engines that search the Web for content and display search results. In addition to individual search engines, you can use a metasearch engine, such as Dogpile, that sends your search text to other search engines and then compiles the results in one list. With a metasearch engine, you type the search text once and then access results from a wider group of search engines. The Dogpile metasearch engine provides search results from Google, Yahoo!, Bing, and Ask.

Project 4 Searching with a Metasearch Search Engine

1. At the Windows desktop, click the Internet Explorer icon on the Taskbar.
2. Click in the Address bar.
3. Type www.dogpile.com and then press Enter.
4. At the Dogpile website, type jazz music in the search text box and then press Enter.
5. Click a hyperlink that interests you.
6. Close the Internet Explorer window.

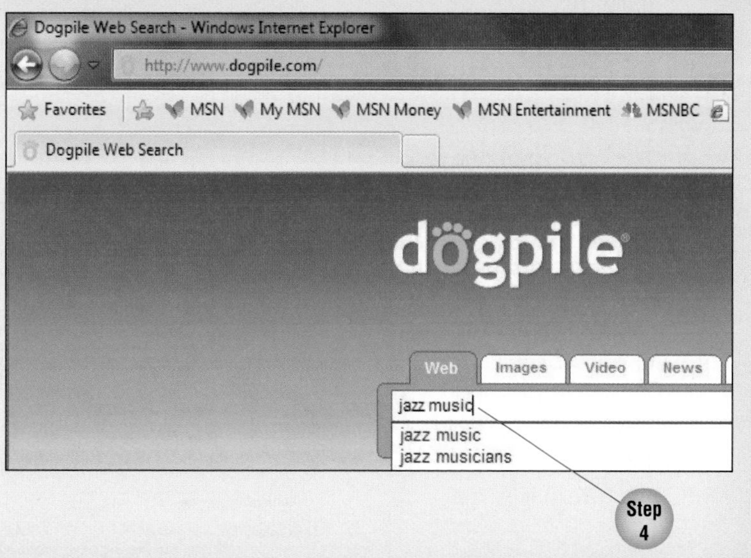

Completing Advanced Searches for Specific Sites

Web Search

The Internet contains an enormous amount of information. Depending on what you are searching for on the Internet and the search engine you use, some searches can result in several thousand "hits" (sites). Wading through a large number of sites can be very time-consuming and counterproductive. Narrowing a search to very specific criteria can greatly reduce the number of hits for a search. To narrow a search, use the advanced search options offered by the search engine.

Project 5 Narrowing a Search

1. Start Internet Explorer.
2. Search for sites on skydiving in Oregon by completing the following steps:
   a. Click in the Address bar, type www.yahoo.com, and then press Enter.
   b. At the Yahoo! home page, click the Web Search button next to the search text box.
   c. Click the <u>more</u> hyperlink located above the search text box and then click Advanced Search at the drop-down list.
   d. At the Advanced Web Search page, click in the search text box next to *all of these words*.
   e. Type skydiving Oregon tandem static line. (This limits the search to web pages containing all of the words typed in the search text box.)
   f. Click the Yahoo! Search button.
   g. When the list of websites displays, click a hyperlink that interests you.
   h. Click the Back button until the Yahoo! Advanced Web Search page displays.
   i. Click in the *the exact phrase* text box and then type skydiving in Oregon.
   j. Click the *Only .com domains* in the *Site/Domain* section.
   k. Click the Yahoo! Search button.
   l. When the list of websites displays, click a hyperlink that interests you.
   m. Print the page.
3. Close Internet Explorer.

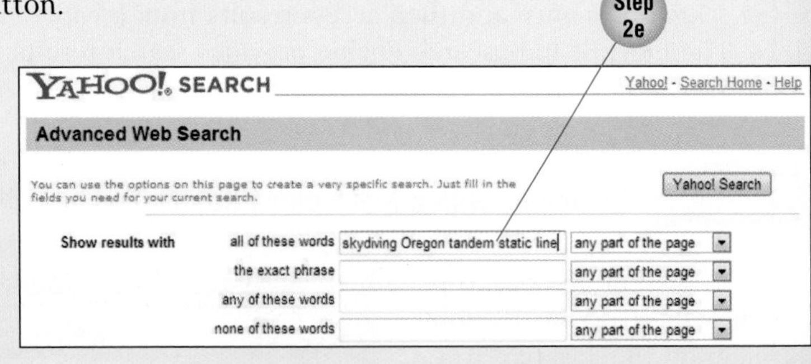

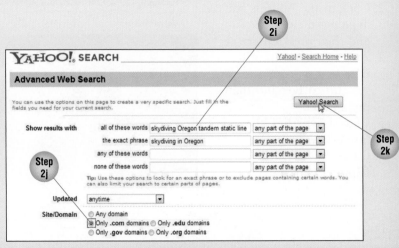

Downloading Images, Text, and Web Pages from the Internet

The image(s) and/or text that display when you open a web page as well as the web page itself can be saved as a separate file. This separate file can be viewed, printed, or inserted in another file. The information you want to save in a separate file is downloaded from the Internet by Internet Explorer and saved in a folder of your choosing with the name you specify. Copyright laws protect much of the information on the Internet. Before using information downloaded from the Internet, check the site for restrictions. If you do use information, make sure you properly cite the source.

Project 6 Downloading Images and Web Pages

1. Start Internet Explorer.
2. Download a web page and image from Banff National Park by completing the following steps:
   a. Search for sites on the Internet for Banff National Park.
   b. From the list of sites that displays, choose a site that contains information about Banff National Park and at least one image of the park.
   c. Save the web page as a separate file by clicking the Page button on the Internet Explorer toolbar and then clicking *Save As* at the drop-down list.
   d. At the Save Webpage dialog box, type BanffWebPage.

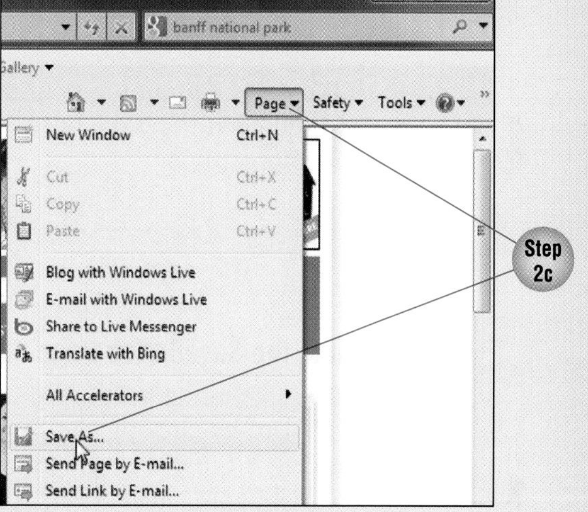

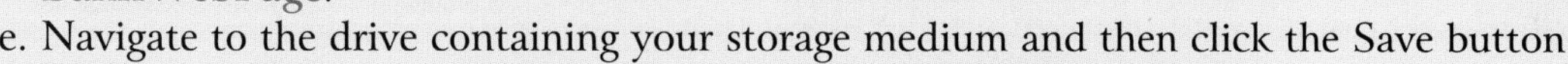

   e. Navigate to the drive containing your storage medium and then click the Save button.

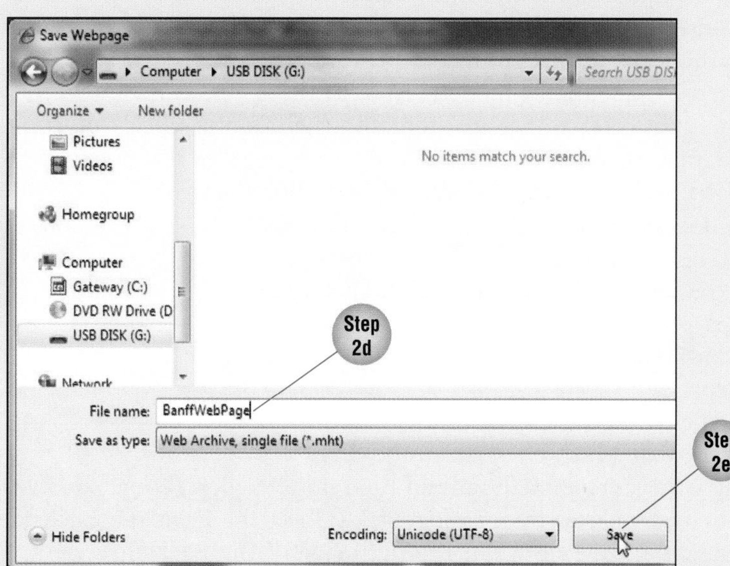

3. Save an image file by completing the following steps:
   a. Right-click an image that displays at the website. (The image that displays may vary from what you see below.)
   b. At the shortcut menu that displays, click *Save Picture As*.
   c. At the Save Picture dialog box, type BanffImage in the *File name* text box.

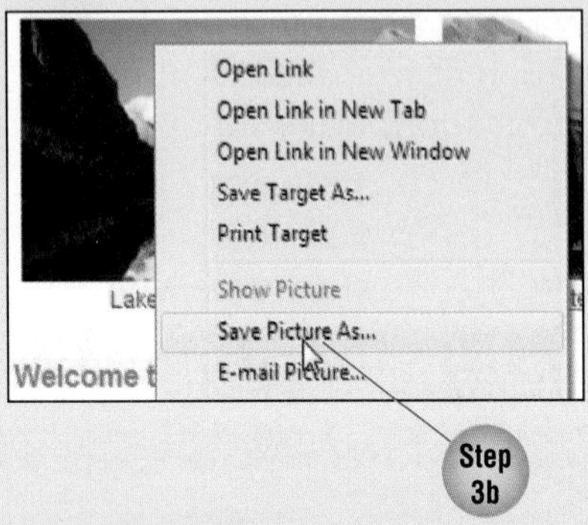

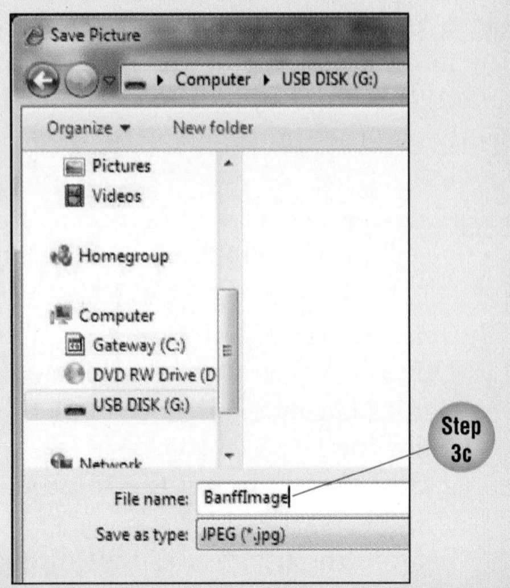

   d. Navigate to the drive containing your storage medium and then click the Save button.
4. Close Internet Explorer.

Project 7 Opening the Saved Web Page and Image in a Word Document

1. Open Microsoft Word by clicking the Start button on the Taskbar, clicking *All Programs*, clicking *Microsoft Office*, and then clicking *Microsoft Word 2010*.
2. With Microsoft Word open, insert the image in a document by completing the following steps:
   a. Click the Insert tab and then click the Picture button in the Illustrations group.

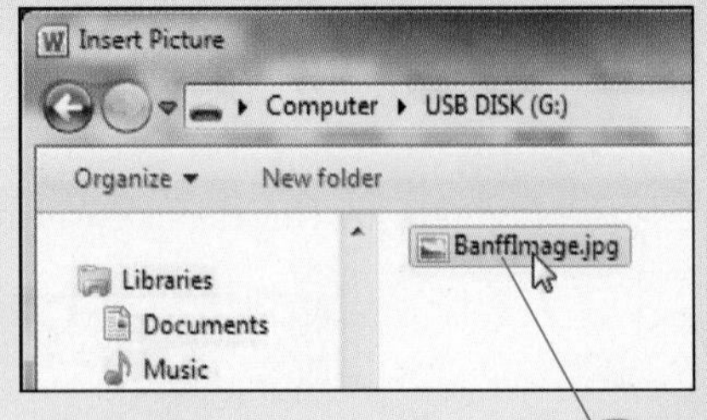

   b. At the Insert Picture dialog box, navigate to the drive containing your storage medium and then double-click ***BanffImage.jpg***.
   c. When the image displays in the Word document, print the document by pressing Ctrl + P and then clicking the Print button.
   d. Close the document by clicking the File tab and then clicking the Close button. At the message asking if you want to save the changes, click *Don't Save*.
3. Open the **BanffWebPage.mht** file by completing the following steps:
   a. Click the File tab and then click the Open button.

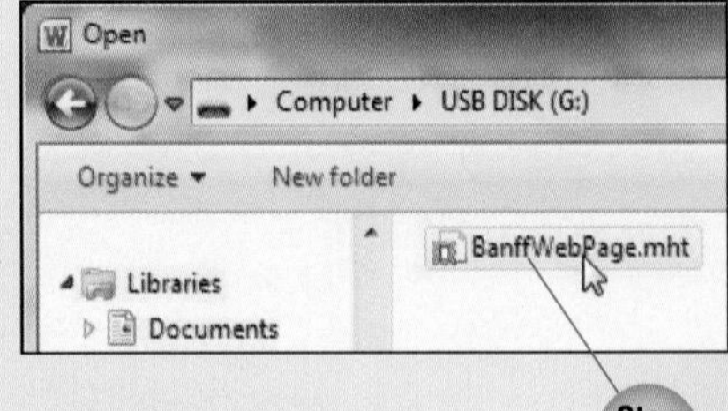

   b. At the Open dialog box, navigate to the drive containing your storage medium and then double-click ***BanffWebPage.mht***.
   c. Preview the web page(s) by pressing Ctrl + P. At the Print tab Backstage view, preview the page shown at the right side of the Backstage view.
4. Close Word by clicking the Close button (contains an X) that displays in the upper right corner of the screen.

Microsoft® Excel® Level 1

Unit 1 ■ Editing and Formatting Documents

Microsoft® Excel®

CHAPTER 1

Preparing an Excel Workbook

PERFORMANCE OBJECTIVES

Upon successful completion of Chapter 1, you will be able to:

- **Identify the various elements of an Excel workbook**
- **Create, save, and print a workbook**
- **Enter data in a workbook**
- **Edit data in a workbook**
- **Insert a formula using the AutoSum button**
- **Apply basic formatting to cells in a workbook**
- **Use the Help feature**

Tutorials

1.1 Creating and Saving a Workbook

1.2 Editing Cells and Using Proofing Tools

1.3 Displaying Formulas and Navigating a Worksheet

1.4 Applying Basic Formatting

1.5 Applying Formatting; Using Undo and Redo; Changing Alignment

Many companies use a spreadsheet for numerical and financial data and to analyze and evaluate information. An Excel spreadsheet can be used for such activities as creating financial statements, preparing budgets, managing inventory, and analyzing cash flow. In addition, numbers and values can be easily manipulated to create "what if" situations. For example, using a spreadsheet, a person in a company can ask questions such as "What if the value in this category is decreased? How would that change affect the department budget?" Questions like these can be easily answered in an Excel spreadsheet. Change the value in a category and Excel will recalculate formulas for the other values. In this way, a spreadsheet can be used not only for creating financial statements or budgets, but also as a planning tool. Model answers for this chapter's projects appear on the following page.

Excel2010L1C1

Note: Before beginning the projects, copy to your storage medium the Excel2010L1C1 subfolder from the Excel2010L1 folder on the CD that accompanies this textbook. Steps on how to copy a folder are presented on the inside of the back cover of this textbook. Do this every time you start a chapter's projects.

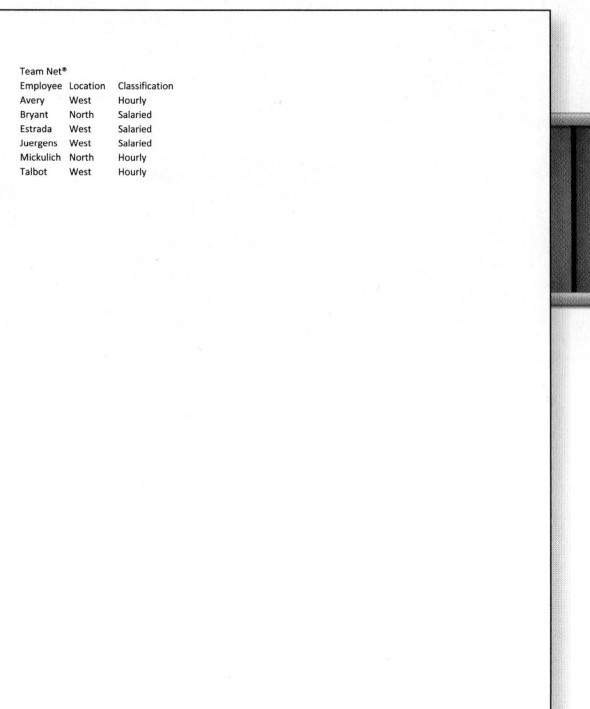

Team Net®

Employee	Location	Classification
Avery	West	Hourly
Bryant	North	Salaried
Estrada	West	Salaried
Juergens	West	Salaried
Mickulich	North	Hourly
Talbot	West	Hourly

Project 1 Prepare a Worksheet with Employee Information

EL1-C1-P1-EmpBene.xlsx

	January	February	March	April	May	June
Year 1	**100**	100	100	100	125	125
Year 3	**150**	150	150	150	175	175
Year 5	**200**	200	200	150	150	150
Year 7	**250**	250	250	250	250	250
Total	700	700	700	650	700	700

Qtr 1	$5,500	$6,250	$7,000	$8,500	$5,500	$4,500
Qtr 2	$6,000	$7,250	$6,500	$9,000	$4,000	$5,000
Qtr 3	$4,500	$8,000	$6,000	$7,500	$6,000	$5,000
Qtr 4	$6,500	$8,500	$7,000	$8,000	$5,500	$6,000
Average	$5,625	$7,500	$6,625	$8,250	$5,250	$5,125

Project 2 Open and Format a Workbook and Insert Formulas

EL1-C1-P2-FillCells.xlsx

Monthly Expenses
January, 2013

Expense	Budget	Actual
Accounting Services	$ 500	$ 423
Advertising	3,200	3,475
Utilities	2,700	3,045
Estimated Taxes	25,000	25,000
Health Insurance	9,420	9,595
Inventory Purchases	4,200	2,155
Equipment Repair	500	214
Loan Payment	5,586	5,586
Office Supplies	225	415
Total	$ 51,331	$ 49,908

Budget Percentages

Department	Percentage
Personnel	26%
Development	22%
Sales	18%
Production	13%
Maintenance	8%
Accounting	7%
Administration	6%

Project 3 Format a Worksheet

EL1-C1-P3-MoExps.xlsx

Prepare a Worksheet with Employee Information 3 Parts

You will create a worksheet containing employee information, edit the contents, and then save and close the workbook.

Creating a Worksheet

Open Excel by clicking the Start button at the left side of the Taskbar, pointing to *All Programs*, clicking *Microsoft Office*, and then clicking *Microsoft Excel 2010*. (Depending on your operating system, these steps may vary.) When Excel is open, you are presented with a blank worksheet like the one shown in Figure 1.1. The elements of a blank Excel worksheet are described in Table 1.1.

Start

A file created in Excel is referred to as a ***workbook***. An Excel workbook consists of individual worksheets (or *sheets*) like the sheets of paper in a notebook. Notice the tabs located toward the bottom of the Excel window that are named *Sheet1*, *Sheet2*, and so on. The area containing the gridlines in the Excel window is called the ***worksheet area***. Figure 1.2 identifies the elements of the worksheet area. Create a worksheet in the worksheet area that will be saved as part of a workbook. Columns in a worksheet are labeled with letters of the alphabet and rows are numbered.

Figure 1.1 Blank Excel Worksheet

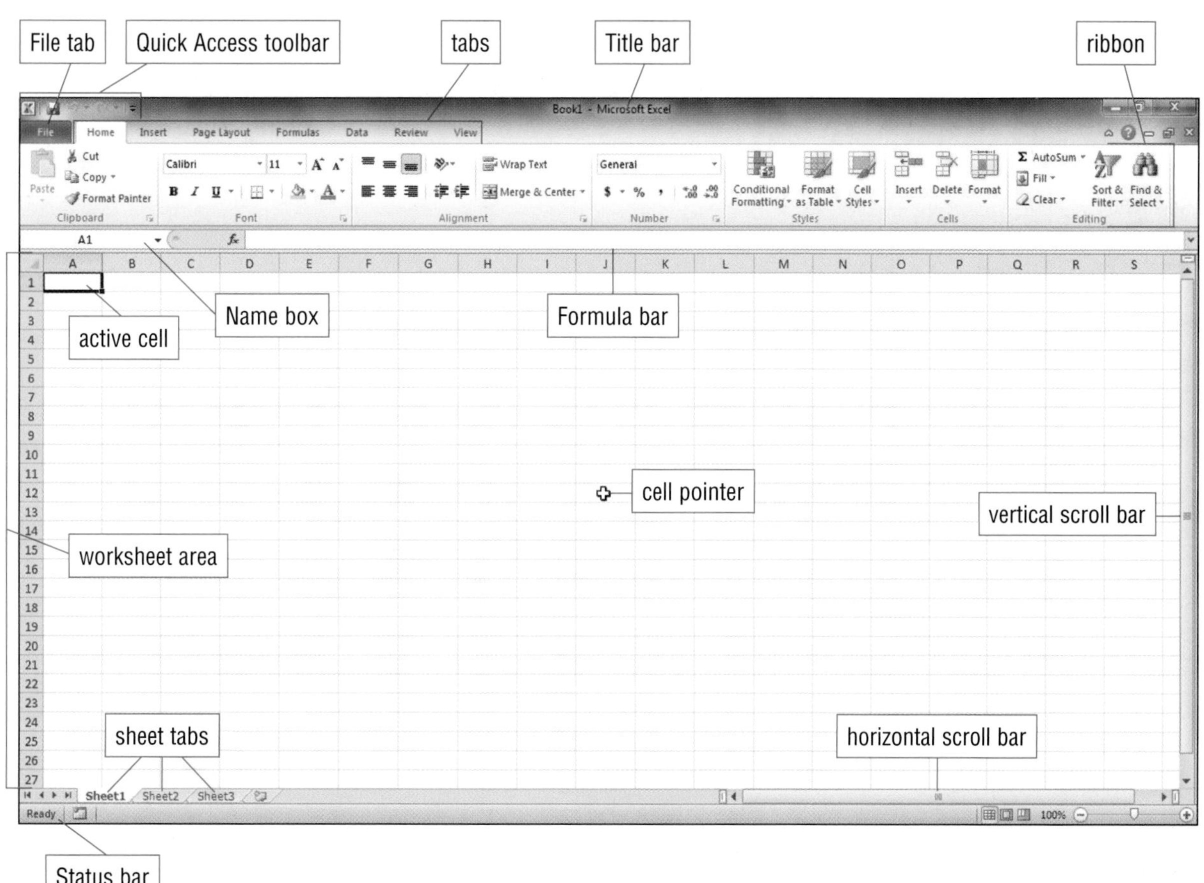

Table 1.1 Elements of an Excel Worksheet

Feature	*Description*
Quick Access toolbar	Contains buttons for commonly used commands.
File tab	Click the File tab and the Backstage view displays containing buttons and tabs for working with and managing files.
Title bar	Displays workbook name followed by program name.
Tabs	Contain commands and features organized into groups.
Ribbon	Area containing the tabs and commands divided into groups.
Name box	Displays cell address (also called the cell reference) and includes the column letter and row number.
Formula bar	Provides information about active cell; enter and edit formulas in this bar.
Scroll bars	Use vertical and horizontal scroll bars to navigate within a worksheet.
Sheet tab	Displays toward bottom of screen and identifies current worksheet.
Status bar	Displays information about worksheet and active cell, view buttons, and Zoom slider bar.

Figure 1.2 Elements of a Worksheet Area

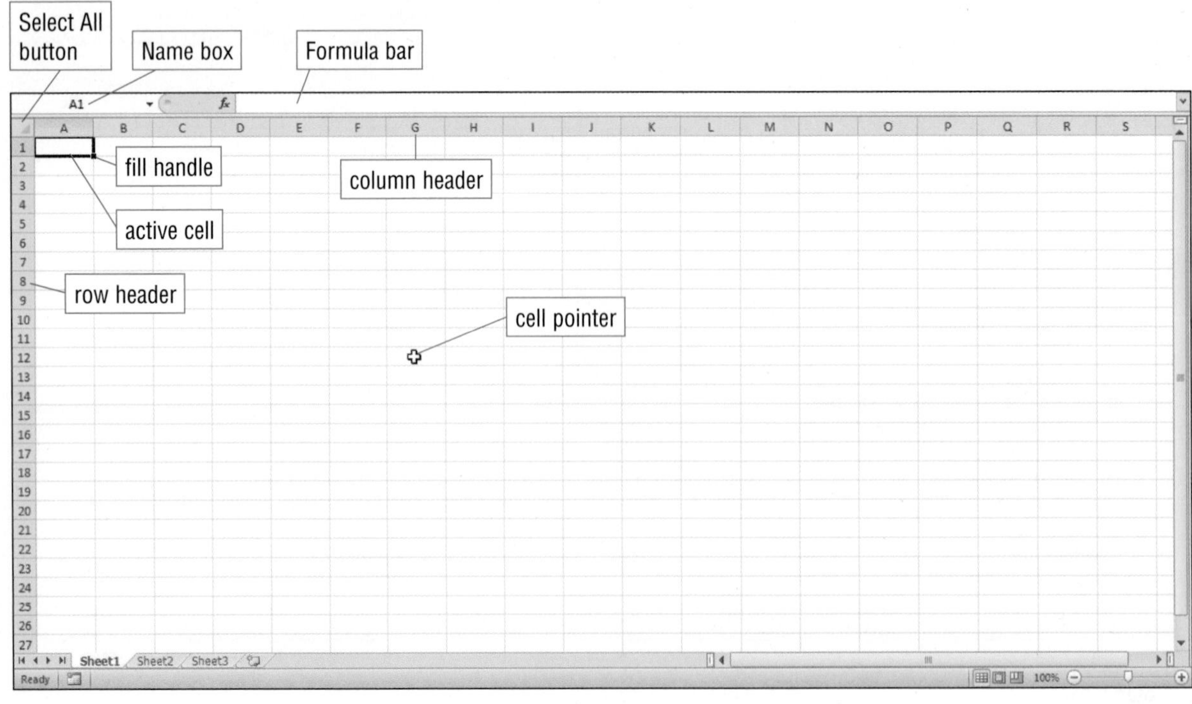

The horizontal and vertical lines that define the cells in the worksheet area are called ***gridlines***. When a cell is active (displays with a black border), the ***cell address***, also called the ***cell reference***, displays in the ***Name box***. The cell reference includes the column letter and row number. For example, if the first cell of the worksheet is active, the cell reference *A1* displays in the Name box. A thick black border surrounds the active cell.

To make a cell active, position the cell pointer in the cell and then click the left mouse button.

Enter data such as text, a number, or a value in a cell. To enter data in a cell, make the desired cell active and then type the data. To make the next cell active, press the Tab key. Table 1.2 displays additional commands for making a specific cell active.

Ctrl + G is the keyboard command to display the Go To dialog box.

Another method for making a specific cell active is to use the Go To feature. To use this feature, click the Find & Select button in the Editing group in the Home tab and then click Go To. At the Go To dialog box, type the cell reference in the *Reference* text box, and then click OK.

Find & Select

When you are ready to type data into the active cell, check the Status bar. The word *Ready* should display at the left side. As you type data, the word *Ready* changes to *Enter*. Data you type in a cell displays in the cell as well as in the Formula bar. If the data you type is longer than the cell can accommodate, the data overlaps the next cell to the right. (It does not become a part of the next cell—it simply overlaps it.) You will learn how to change column widths to accommodate data later in this chapter.

Table 1.2 Commands for Making a Specific Cell Active

To make this cell active	*Press*
Cell below current cell	Enter
Cell above current cell	Shift + Enter
Next cell	Tab
Previous cell	Shift + Tab
Cell at beginning of row	Home
Next cell in the direction of the arrow	Up, Down, Left, or Right Arrow keys
Last cell in worksheet	Ctrl + End
First cell in worksheet	Ctrl + Home
Cell in next window	Page Down
Cell in previous window	Page Up
Cell in window to right	Alt + Page Down
Cell in window to left	Alt + Page Up

If the data you enter in a cell consists of text and the text does not fit into the cell, it overlaps the next cell. If, however, you enter a number in a cell, specify it as a number (rather than text) and the number is too long to fit in the cell, Excel changes the display of the number to number symbols *(###)*. This is because Excel does not want you to be misled by a number when you see only a portion of it in the cell.

Along with the keyboard, you can use the mouse to make a specific cell active. To make a specific cell active with the mouse, position the mouse pointer, which displays as a white plus sign (called the ***cell pointer***), on the desired cell, and then click the left mouse button. The cell pointer displays as a white plus sign when positioned in a cell in the worksheet and displays as an arrow pointer when positioned on other elements of the Excel window such as options in tabs or scroll bars.

Scroll through a worksheet using the horizontal and/or vertical scroll bars. Scrolling shifts the display of cells in the worksheet area, but does not change the active cell. Scroll through a worksheet until the desired cell is visible and then click the desired cell.

Saving a Workbook

Quick Steps
Save a Workbook
1. Click Save button.
2. Type workbook name.
3. Press Enter.

Ctrl + S is the keyboard command to save a workbook.

Save

Save an Excel workbook, which may consist of a worksheet or several worksheets, by clicking the Save button on the Quick Access toolbar or by clicking the File tab and then clicking the Save button in the Quick commands area of the Backstage view. At the Save As dialog box, type a name for the workbook in the *File name* text box and then press Enter or click the Save button. A workbook file name can contain up to 255 characters, including drive letter and any folder names, and can include spaces. Note that you cannot give a workbook the same name in first uppercase and then lowercase letters. Also, some symbols cannot be used in a file name such as:

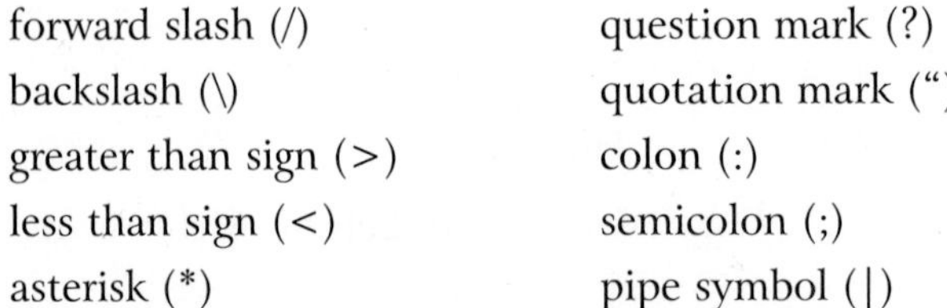

forward slash (/)	question mark (?)
backslash (\)	quotation mark (“)
greater than sign (>)	colon (:)
less than sign (<)	semicolon (;)
asterisk (*)	pipe symbol (|)

To save an Excel workbook in the Excel2010L1C1 folder on your storage medium, display the Save As dialog box, click the drive representing your storage medium in the Navigation pane, and then double-click *Excel2010L1C1* in the Content pane.

Project 1a Creating and Saving a Document

Part 1 of 3

1. Open Excel by clicking the Start button on the Taskbar, pointing to *All Programs*, clicking *Microsoft Office*, and then clicking *Microsoft Excel 2010*. (Depending on your operating system, these steps may vary.)
2. At the Excel worksheet that displays, create the worksheet shown in Figure 1.3 by completing the following steps:
   a. Press the Enter key once to make cell A2 the active cell.
   b. With cell A2 active (displays with a thick black border), type **Employee**.
   c. Press the Tab key. (This makes cell B2 active.)
   d. Type **Location** and then press the Tab key. (This makes cell C2 active.)
   e. Type **Benefits** and then press the Enter key to move the insertion point to cell A3.
   f. With cell A3 active, type the name **Avery**.
   g. Continue typing the data shown in Figure 1.3. (For commands for making specific cells active, refer to Table 1.2.)

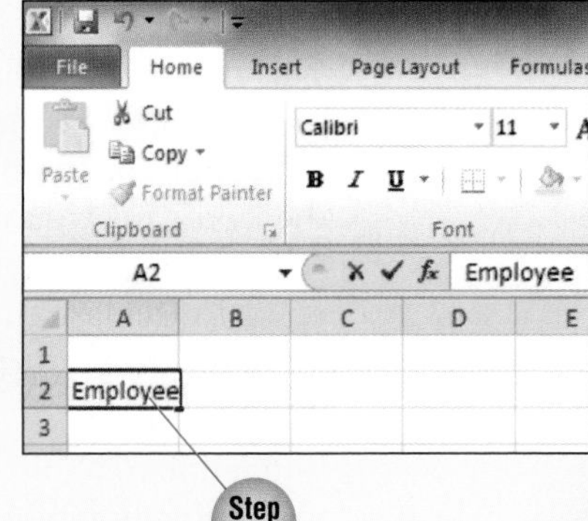

3. After typing the data shown in the cells in Figure 1.3, save the workbook by completing the following steps:
   a. Click the Save button on the Quick Access toolbar.
   b. At the Save As dialog box, click the drive representing your storage medium in the Navigation pane.
   c. Double-click the *Excel2010L1C1* folder that displays in the Content pane.
   d. Select the text in the *File name* text box and then type **EL1-C1-P1-EmpBene** (for Excel Level 1, Chapter 1, Project 1, and the workbook that contains information about employee benefits).
   e. Press the Enter key or click the Save button.

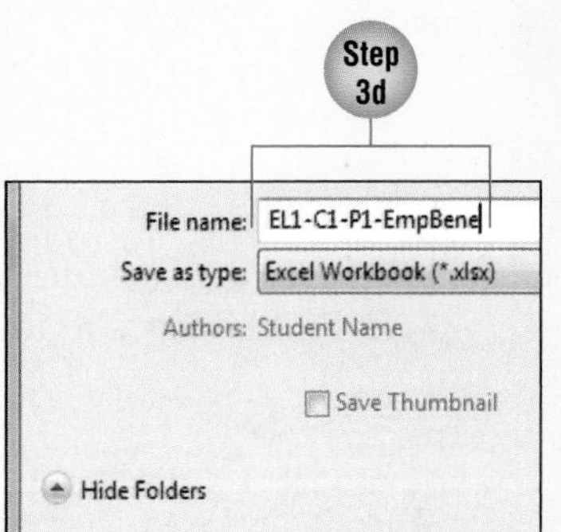

Figure 1.3 Project 1a

	A	B	C	D
1				
2	Employee	Location	Benefits	
3	Avery			
4	Connors			
5	Estrada			
6	Juergens			
7	Mikulich			
8	Talbot			
9				

Editing Data in a Cell

Edit data being typed in a cell by pressing the Backspace key to delete the character to the left of the insertion point or pressing the Delete key to delete the character to the right of the insertion point. To change the data in a cell, click the cell once to make it active and then type the new data. When a cell containing data is active, anything typed will take the place of the existing data.

If you want to edit only a portion of the data in a cell, double-click the cell. This makes the cell active, moves the insertion point inside the cell, and displays the word *Edit* at the left side of the Status bar. Move the insertion point using the arrow keys or the mouse and then make the needed corrections. If you are using the keyboard, you can press the Home key to move the insertion point to the first character in the cell or Formula bar, or press the End key to move the insertion point to the last character.

When you are finished editing the data in the cell, be sure to change out of the Edit mode. To do this, make another cell active. You can do this by pressing Enter, Tab, or Shift + Tab. You can also change out of the Edit mode and return to the Ready mode by clicking another cell or clicking the Enter button on the Formula bar.

Cancel

Enter

If the active cell does not contain data, the Formula bar displays only the cell reference (by column letter and row number). As you type data, the two buttons shown in Figure 1.4 display on the Formula bar to the right of the Name box. Click the Cancel button to delete the current cell entry. You can also delete the cell entry by pressing the Delete key. Click the Enter button to indicate that you are finished typing or editing the cell entry. When you click the Enter button on the Formula bar, the word *Enter* (or *Edit*) located at the left side of the Status bar changes to *Ready*.

Project 1b **Editing Data in a Cell** Part 2 of 3

1. With **EL1-C1-P1-EmpBene.xlsx** open, double-click cell A7 (contains *Mikulich*).
2. Move the insertion point immediately left of the *k* and then type a c. (This changes the spelling to *Mickulich*.)
3. Click once in cell A4 (contains *Connors*), type Bryant, and then press the Tab key. (Clicking only once allows you to type over the existing data.)
4. Edit cell C2 by completing the following steps:
   a. Click the Find & Select button in the Editing group in the Home tab and then click *Go To* at the drop-down list.
   b. At the Go To dialog box, type C2 in the *Reference* text box and then click OK.
   c. Type Classification (over *Benefits*).
5. Click once in any other cell.
6. Click the Save button on the Quick Access toolbar to save the workbook again.

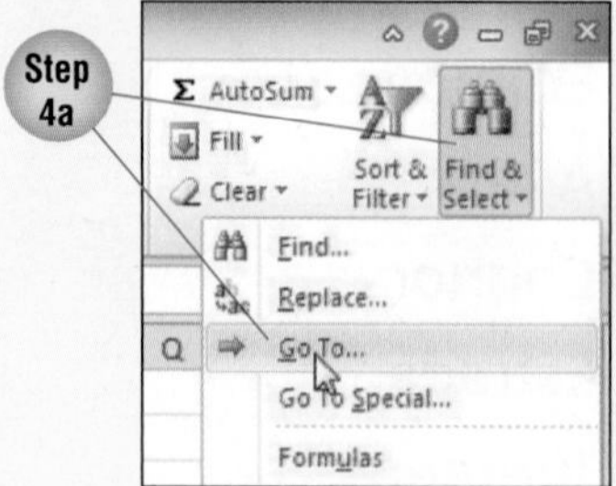

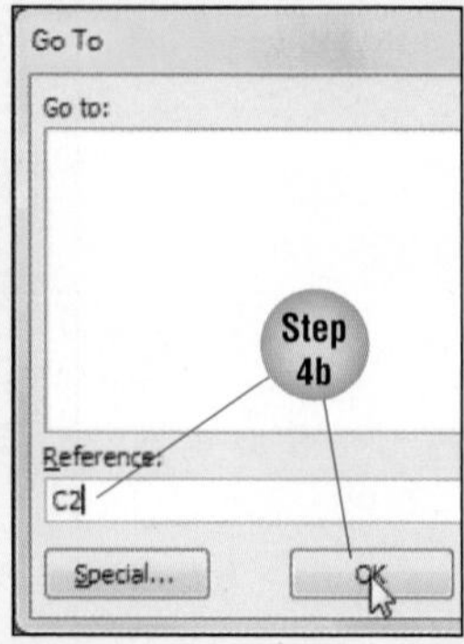

Figure 1.4 Buttons on the Formula Bar

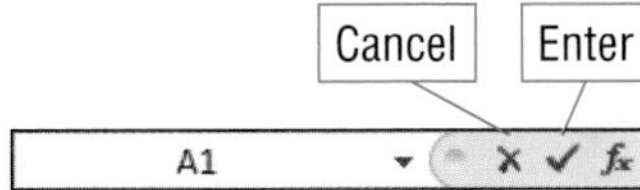

Printing a Workbook

Click the File tab and the Backstage view displays as shown in Figure 1.5. Use buttons and tabs at this view to work with and manage workbooks such as opening, closing, saving, and printing a workbook. If you want to remove the Backstage view without completing an action, click the File tab, click any other tab in the ribbon, or press the Esc key on your keyboard.

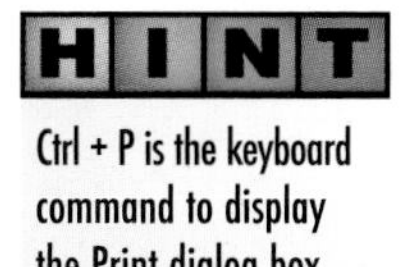

Ctrl + P is the keyboard command to display the Print dialog box.

Many of the computer projects you will be creating will need to be printed. Print a workbook from the Print tab of the Backstage view shown in Figure 1.6. To display this view, click the File tab and then click the Print tab. You can also display the Print tab Backstage view with the keyboard command Ctrl + P.

Figure 1.5 Backstage View

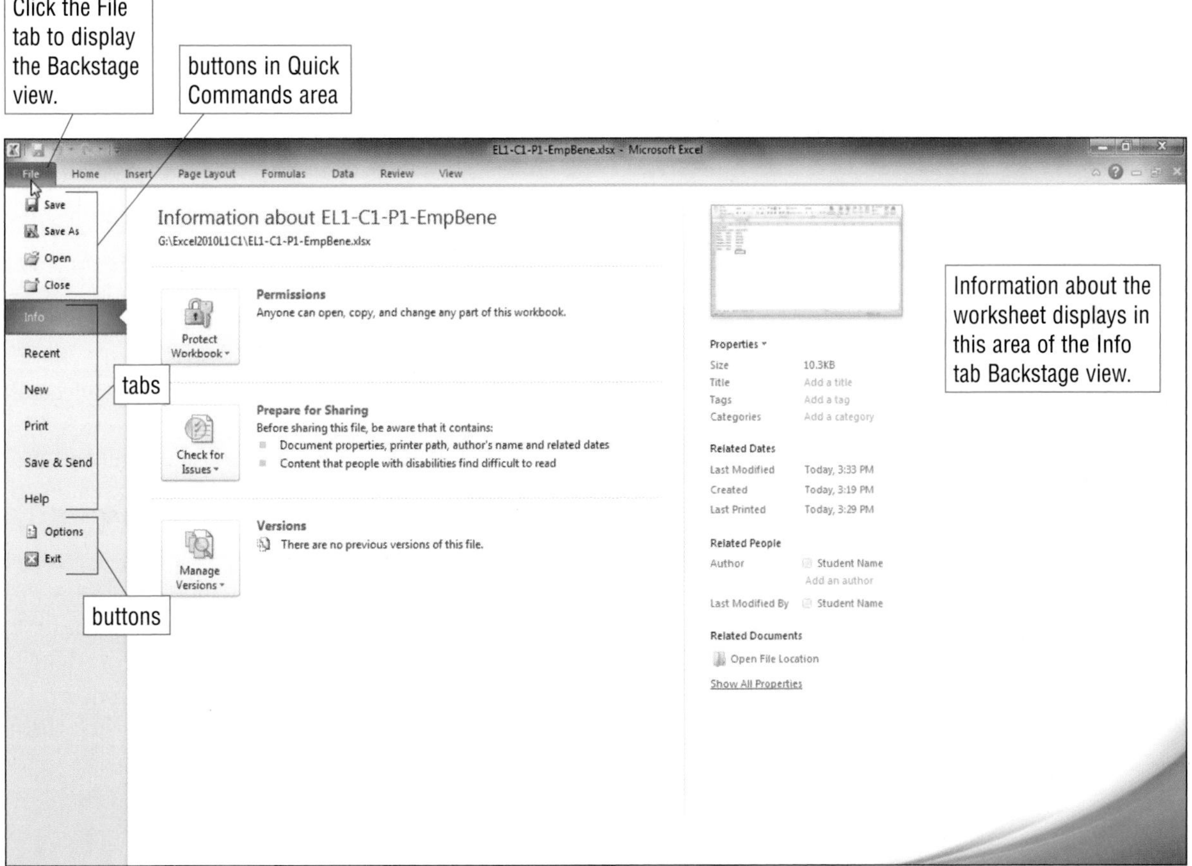

Figure 1.6 Print Tab Backstage View

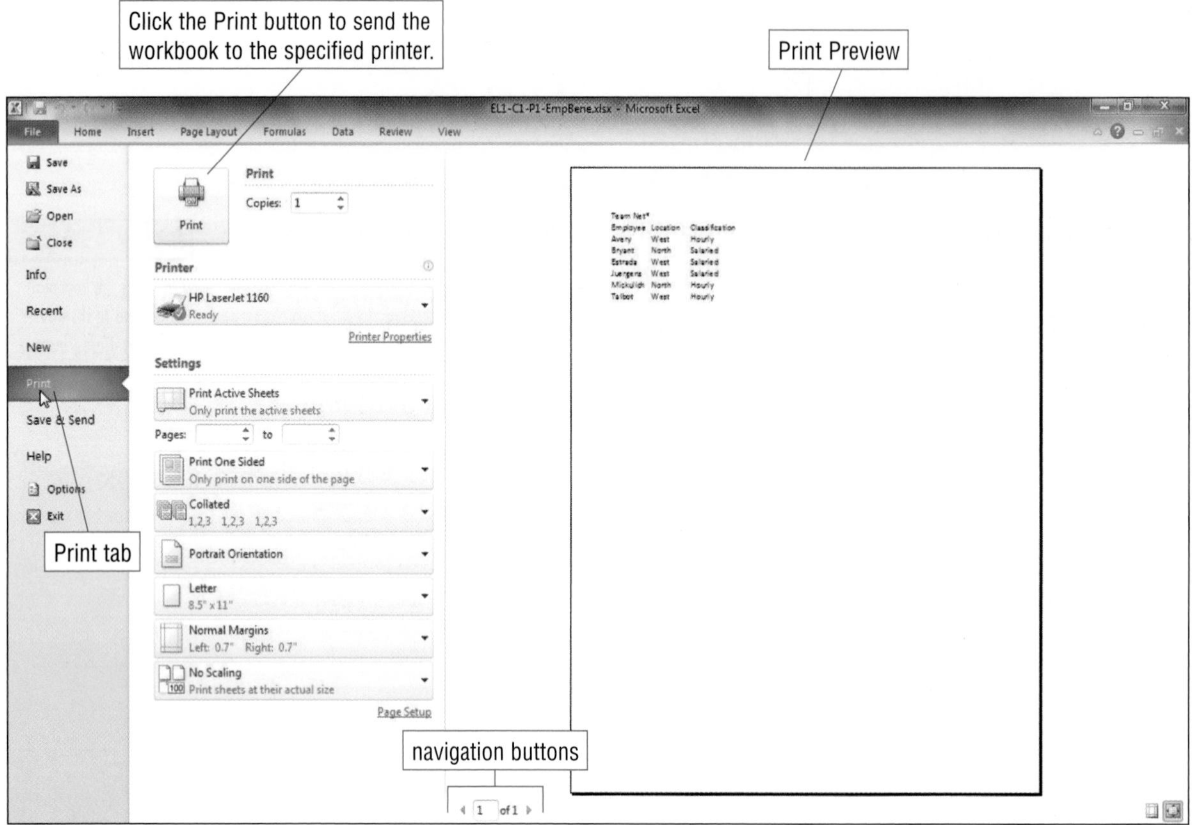

Quick Steps

Print a Workbook
1. Click File tab.
2. Click Print tab.
3. Click Print button.
OR
Click Quick Print button.

Close a Workbook
Click Close Window button.
OR
Click File tab, Close button.

Exit Excel
Click Close button.
OR
Click File tab, Exit button.

The left side of the Print tab Backstage view displays three categories—*Print, Printer*, and *Settings*. Click the Print button in the Print category to send the workbook to the printer and specify the number of copies you want printed in the *Copies* option text box. Use the gallery in the Printer category to specify the desired printer. The Settings category contains a number of galleries, each with options for specifying how you want your workbook printed. Use the galleries to specify whether or not you want the pages collated when printed; the orientation, page size, and margins of your workbook; and if you want the worksheet scaled to print all rows and columns of data on one page.

Another method for printing a workbook is to insert the Quick Print button on the Quick Access toolbar and then click the button. This sends the workbook directly to the printer without displaying the Print tab Backstage view. To insert the button on the Quick Access toolbar, click the Customize Quick Access Toolbar button that displays at the right side of the toolbar and then click *Quick Print* at the drop-down list. To remove the Quick Print button from the Quick Access toolbar, right-click the button and then click *Remove from Quick Access Toolbar* at the drop-down list.

Closing a Workbook

Close Window

To close an Excel workbook, click the File tab and then click the Close button. You can also close a workbook by clicking the Close Window button located toward the upper right corner of the screen. Position the mouse pointer on the button and a ScreenTip displays with the name *Close Window*.

Exiting Excel

To exit Excel, click the Close button that displays in the upper right corner of the screen. The Close button contains an X and if you position the mouse pointer on the button a ScreenTip displays with the name *Close*. You can also exit Excel by clicking the File tab and then clicking the Exit button.

Close

Using Automatic Entering Features

Excel contains several features that help you enter data into cells quickly and efficiently. These features include ***AutoComplete***, which automatically inserts data in a cell that begins the same as a previous entry; ***AutoCorrect***, which automatically corrects many common typographical errors; and ***AutoFill***, which will automatically insert words, numbers, or formulas in a series.

Using AutoComplete and AutoCorrect

The AutoComplete feature will automatically insert data in a cell that begins the same as a previous entry. If the data inserted by AutoComplete is the data you want in the cell, press Enter. If it is not the desired data, simply continue typing the correct data. This feature can be very useful in a worksheet that contains repetitive data entries. For example, consider a worksheet that repeats the word *Payroll*. The second and subsequent times this word is to be inserted in a cell, simply typing the letter *P* will cause AutoComplete to insert the entire word.

The AutoCorrect feature automatically corrects many common typing errors. To see what symbols and words are in the AutoCorrect feature, click the File tab and then click the Options button located below the Help tab. At the Excel Options dialog box, click *Proofing* in the left panel and then click the AutoCorrect Options button located in the right panel. This displays the AutoCorrect dialog box with the AutoCorrect tab selected as shown in Figure 1.7 with a list box containing the replacement data.

Figure 1.7 AutoCorrect Dialog Box with AutoCorrect Tab Selected

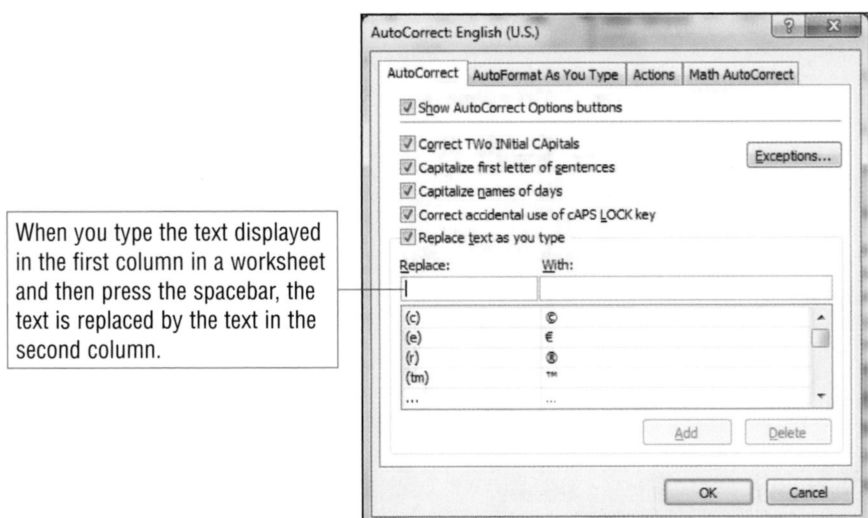

At the AutoCorrect dialog box, type the text shown in the first column in the list box and the text in the second column is inserted in the cell. Along with symbols, the AutoCorrect dialog box contains commonly misspelled words and common typographical errors.

Project 1c Inserting Data in Cells with AutoComplete

Part 3 of 3

1. With **EL1-C1-P1-EmpBene.xlsx** open make cell A1 active.
2. Type the text in cell A1 as shown in Figure 1.8. Insert the ® symbol by typing (r). [AutoCorrect will change (r) to ®.]
3. Type the remaining text in the cells. When you type the W in *West* in cell B5, the AutoComplete feature will insert *West*. Accept this by pressing the Enter key. (Pressing the Enter key accepts *West* and also makes the cell below active.) Use the AutoComplete feature to enter *West* in B6 and B8 and *North* in cell B7. Use AutoComplete to enter the second and subsequent occurrences of *Salaried* and *Hourly*.
4. Click the Save button on the Quick Access toolbar.
5. Print **EL1-C1-P1-EmpBene.xlsx** by clicking the File tab, clicking the Print tab, and then clicking the Print button at the Print tab Backstage view. (The gridlines will not print.)
6. Close the workbook by clicking the Close Window button (contains an X) that displays in the upper right corner of the screen. (Make sure you click the Close Window button and not the Close button.)

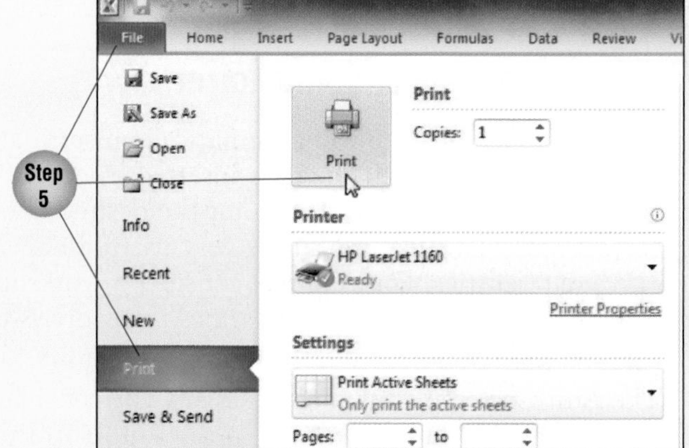

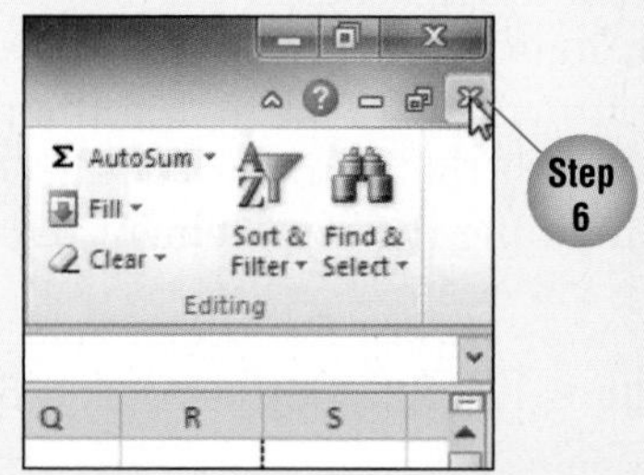

Figure 1.8 Project 1c

	A	B	C	D
1	Team Net®			
2	Employee	Location	Classification	
3	Avery	West	Hourly	
4	Bryant	North	Salaried	
5	Estrada	West	Salaried	
6	Juergens	West	Salaried	
7	Mickulich	North	Hourly	
8	Talbot	West	Hourly	
9				

Project 2 Open and Format a Workbook and Insert Formulas — 3 Parts

You will open an existing workbook and insert formulas to find the sum and averages of numbers.

Using AutoFill

When a cell is active, a thick black border surrounds it and a small black square displays in the bottom right corner of the border. This black square is called the AutoFill ***fill handle*** (see Figure 1.2). With the fill handle, you can quickly fill a range of cells with the same data or with consecutive data. For example, suppose you need to insert the year 2012 in a row or column of cells. To do this quickly, type 2012 in the first cell, position the mouse pointer on the fill handle, hold down the left mouse button, drag across the cells in which you want the year inserted, and then release the mouse button.

You can also use the fill handle to insert a series in a row or column of cells. For example, suppose you are creating a worksheet with data for all of the months in the year. Type January in the first cell, position the mouse pointer on the fill handle, hold down the left mouse button, drag down or across to 11 more cells, and then release the mouse button. Excel automatically inserts the other 11 months in the year in the proper order. When using the fill handle, the cells must be adjacent. Table 1.3 identifies the sequence inserted in cells by Excel when specific data is entered.

If you do not want a series to increment, hold down the Ctrl key while dragging the fill handle.

Certain sequences, such as *2, 4* and *Jan 12, Jan 13,* require that both cells be selected before using the fill handle. If only the cell containing *2* is active, the fill handle will insert *2*s in the selected cells. The list in Table 1.3 is only a sampling of what the fill handle can do. You may find a variety of other sequences that can be inserted in a worksheet using the fill handle.

An Auto Fill Options button displays when you fill cells with the fill handle. Click this button and a list of options displays for filling the cells. By default, data and formatting are filled in each cell. You can choose to fill only the formatting in the cells or fill only the data without the formatting.

Auto Fill Options

Table 1.3 AutoFill Fill Handle Series

Enter this data *(Commas represent data in separate cells.)*	***And the fill handle will insert this sequence in adjacent cells***
January	February, March, April, and so on . . .
Jan	Feb, Mar, Apr, and so on . . .
Jan 12, Jan 13	14-Jan, 15-Jan, 16-Jan, and so on . . .
Monday	Tuesday, Wednesday, Thursday, and so on . . .
Product 1	Product 2, Product 3, Product 4, and so on . . .
Qtr 1	Qtr 2, Qtr 3, Qtr 4
2, 4	6, 8, 10, and so on . . .

Quick Steps

Open a Workbook
1. Click File tab.
2. Click Open button.
3. Display desired folder.
4. Double-click workbook name.

Opening a Workbook

Open an Excel workbook by displaying the Open dialog box and then double-clicking the desired workbook name. Display the Open dialog box by clicking the File tab and then clicking the Open button. You can also use the keyboard command Ctrl + O to display the Open dialog box.

Project 2a Inserting Data in Cells with the Fill Handle

Part 1 of 3

1. Open **FillCells.xlsx**. (This workbook is located in the Excel2010L1C1 folder on your storage medium.)
2. Save the workbook with Save As and name it **EL1-C1-P2-FillCells**.
3. Add data to cells as shown in Figure 1.9. Begin by making cell B1 active and then typing January.
4. Position the mouse pointer on the fill handle for cell B1, hold down the left mouse button, drag across to cell G1, and then release the mouse button.

	A	B	C	D	E	F	G
1		January	February	March	April	May	June
2		100				125	125
3		150	150	150	150	175	175

5. Type a sequence and then use the fill handle to fill the remaining cells by completing the following steps:
   a. Make cell A2 active and then type Year 1.
   b. Make cell A3 active and then type Year 3.
   c. Select cells A2 and A3 by positioning the mouse pointer in cell A2, holding down the left mouse button, dragging down to cell A3, and then releasing the mouse button.
   d. Drag the fill handle for cell A3 to cell A5. (This inserts *Year 5* in cell A4 and *Year 7* in cell A5.)
6. Use the fill handle to fill adjacent cells with a number but not the formatting by completing the following steps:
   a. Make cell B2 active. (This cell contains *100* with bold formatting.)
   b. Drag the fill handle for cell B2 to cell E2. (This inserts ***100*** in cells C2, D2, and E2.)
   c. Click the Auto Fill Options button that displays at the bottom right of the selected cells.
   d. Click the *Fill Without Formatting* option at the drop-down list.

Step 6c

	A	B	C	D	E	F	G	H
1		January	February	March	April	May	June	
2	Year 1	100	100	100	100	125	125	
3	Year 3	150	150	150	150	175	175	
4	Year 5	200	200	200	150			
5	Year 7	250	250	250	250			

Copy Cells
Fill Series
Fill Formatting Only
Fill Without Formatting

Step 6d

7. Use the fill handle to apply formatting only by completing the following steps:
   a. Make cell B2 active.
   b. Drag the fill handle to cell B5.
   c. Click the Auto Fill Options button and then click *Fill Formatting Only* at the drop-down list.
8. Make cell A10 active and then type Qtr 1.
9. Drag the fill handle for cell A10 to cell A13.
10. Save **EL1-C1-P2-FillCells.xlsx**.

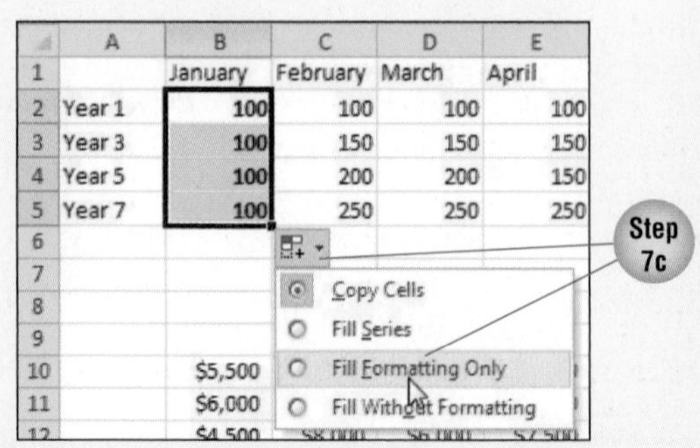

Figure 1.9 Project 2a

	A	B	C	D	E	F	G	H
1		January	February	March	April	May	June	
2	Year 1	**100**	100	100	100	125	125	
3	Year 3	**150**	150	150	150	175	175	
4	Year 5	**200**	200	200	150	150	150	
5	Year 7	**250**	250	250	250	250	250	
6								
7								
8								
9								
10	Qtr 1	$5,500	$6,250	$7,000	$8,500	$5,500	$4,500	
11	Qtr 2	$6,000	$7,250	$6,500	$9,000	$4,000	$5,000	
12	Qtr 3	$4,500	$8,000	$6,000	$7,500	$6,000	$5,000	
13	Qtr 4	$6,500	$8,500	$7,000	$8,000	$5,500	$6,000	
14								

Inserting Formulas

Excel is a powerful decision-making tool you can use to manipulate data to answer "what if" situations. Insert a formula in a worksheet and then manipulate the data to make projections, answer specific questions, and use as a planning tool. For example, the manager of a department might use an Excel worksheet to prepare a department budget and then determine the impact on the budget of hiring a new employee or increasing the volume of production.

Insert a ***formula*** in a worksheet to perform calculations on values. A formula contains a mathematical operator, value, cell reference, cell range, and a function. Formulas can be written that add, subtract, multiply, and/or divide values. Formulas can also be written that calculate averages, percentages, minimum and maximum values, and much more. Excel includes an AutoSum button in the Editing group in the Home tab that inserts a formula to calculate the total of a range of cells.

Quick Steps

Insert Formula Using Sum Button

1. Click in desired cell.
2. Click AutoSum button.
3. Check range identified and make changes if necessary.
4. Press Enter.

HINT

You can use the keyboard command Alt + = to insert the SUM function in the cell.

Using the AutoSum Button to Add Numbers

You can use the AutoSum button in the Editing group in the Home tab to insert a formula. The AutoSum button adds numbers automatically with the SUM function. Make active the cell in which you want to insert the formula (this cell should be empty) and then click the AutoSum button. Excel looks for a range of cells containing numbers above the active cell. If no cell above contains numbers, then Excel looks to the left of the active cell. Excel suggests the range of cells to be added. If the suggested range is not correct, drag through the desired range of cells with the mouse, and then press Enter. You can also just double-click the AutoSum button and this will insert the SUM function with the range Excel chooses.

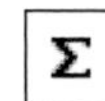

AutoSum

Project 2b Adding Values with the AutoSum Button

Part 2 of 3

1. With **EL1-C1-P2-FillCells.xlsx** open, make cell A6 active and then type Total.
2. Make cell B6 active and then calculate the sum of cells by clicking the AutoSum button in the Editing group in the Home tab.
3. Excel inserts the formula *=SUM(B2:B5)* in cell B6. This is the correct range of cells, so press Enter.

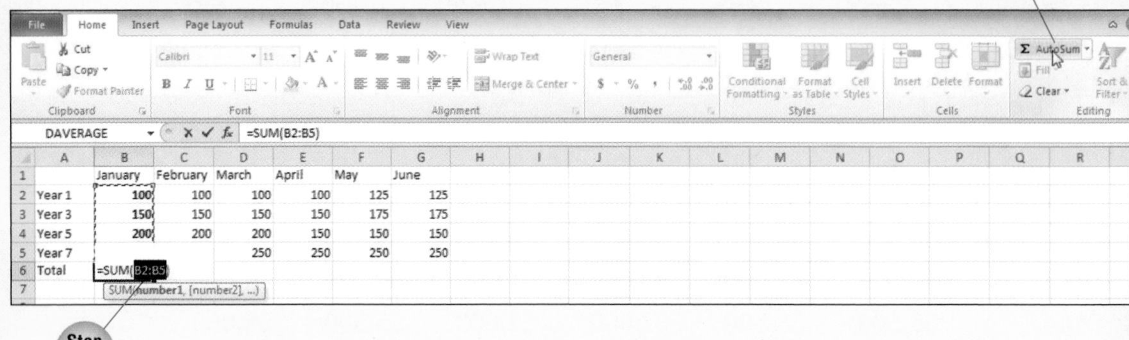

4. Make cell C6 active and then click the AutoSum button in the Editing group.
5. Excel inserts the formula *=SUM(C2:C5)* in cell C6. This is the correct range of cells, so press Enter.
6. Make cell D6 active.
7. Double-click the AutoSum button. [This inserts the formula *=SUM(D2:D5)* in cell D6 and inserts the sum *700*.]
8. Insert the sum in cells E6, F6, and G6.
9. Save **EL1-C1-P2-FillCells**.

Quick Steps

Insert Average Formula Using Sum Button
1. Click in desired cell.
2. Click AutoSum button arrow.
3. Click *Average*.
4. Specify range.
5. Press Enter.

Copy Formula Using Fill Handle
1. Insert formula in cell.
2. Make active the cell containing formula.
3. Using fill handle, drag through cells you want to contain formula.

Using the AutoSum Button to Average Numbers

A common function in a formula is the AVERAGE function. With this function, a range of cells is added together and then divided by the number of cell entries. The AVERAGE function is available on the AutoSum button. Click the AutoSum button arrow and a drop-down list displays with a number of common functions.

Using the Fill Handle to Copy a Formula

In a worksheet, you may want to insert the same basic formula in other cells. In a situation where a formula is copied to other locations in a worksheet, use a ***relative cell reference***. Copy a formula containing relative cell references and the cell references change. For example, if you enter the formula *=SUM(A2:C2)* in cell D2 and then copy it relatively to cell D3, the formula in cell D3 displays as *=SUM(A3:C3)*. You can use the fill handle to copy a formula relatively in a worksheet. To do this, position the mouse pointer on the fill handle until the mouse pointer turns into a thin black cross, hold down the left mouse button, drag and select the desired cells, and then release the mouse button.

Project 2c Inserting the AVERAGE Function and Copying a Formula Relatively

Part 3 of 3

1. With **EL1-C1-P2-FillCells.xlsx** open, make cell A14 active, and then type Average.
2. Insert the average of cells B10 through B13 by completing the following steps:
   a. Make cell B14 active.
   b. Click the AutoSum button arrow in the Editing group and then click *Average* at the drop-down list.
   c. Excel inserts the formula =*AVERAGE(B10:B13)* in cell B14. This is the correct range of cells, so press Enter.
3. Copy the formula relatively to cells C14 through G14 by completing the following steps:
   a. Make cell B14 active.
   b. Position the mouse pointer on the fill handle, hold down the left mouse button, drag across to cell G14, and then release the mouse button.

9							
10	Qtr 1	$5,500	$6,250	$7,000	$8,500	$5,500	$4,500
11	Qtr 2	$6,000	$7,250	$6,500	$9,000	$4,000	$5,000
12	Qtr 3	$4,500	$8,000	$6,000	$7,500	$6,000	$5,000
13	Qtr 4	$6,500	$8,500	$7,000	$8,000	$5,500	$6,000
14	Average	$5,625	$7,500	$6,625	$8,250	$5,250	$5,125
15							
16							

4. Save, print, and then close **EL1-C1-P2-FillCells.xlsx**.

Format a Worksheet

2 Parts

You will open a monthly expenses workbook and then change column width, merge and center cells, and apply number formatting to numbers in cells.

Selecting Cells

You can use a variety of methods for formatting cells in a worksheet. For example, you can change the alignment of data in cells or rows or add character formatting. To identify the cells that are to be affected by the formatting, select the specific cells.

Selecting Cells Using the Mouse

Select specific cells in a worksheet using the mouse or select columns or rows. Table 1.4 displays the methods for selecting cells using the mouse.

The first cell in a range displays with a white background and is the active cell.

Selected cells, except the active cell, display with a light blue background (this may vary) rather than a white background. The active cell is the first cell in the selection block and displays in the normal manner (white background with black data). Selected cells remain selected until you click a cell with the mouse or press an arrow key on the keyboard.

Table 1.4 Selecting with the Mouse

To select this	*Do this*
Column	Position the cell pointer on the column header (a letter) and then click the left mouse button.
Row	Position the cell pointer on the row header (a number) and then click the left mouse button.
Adjacent cells	Drag with mouse to select specific cells.
Nonadjacent cells	Hold down the Ctrl key while clicking column header, row header, or specific cells.
All cells in worksheet	Click Select All button (refer to Figure 1.2).

Selecting Cells Using the Keyboard

You can use the keyboard to select specific cells within a worksheet. Table 1.5 displays the commands for selecting specific cells. If a worksheet contains data, the last entry in Table 1.5 will select the cells containing data. If the worksheet contains groups of data separated by empty cells, Ctrl + A or Ctrl + Shift + spacebar will select a group of cells rather than all of the cells.

Selecting Data within Cells

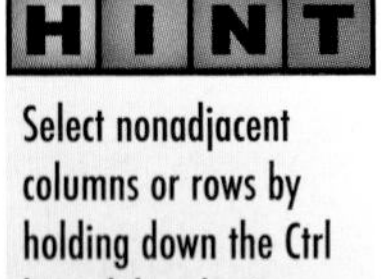

Select nonadjacent columns or rows by holding down the Ctrl key while selecting cells.

The selection commands presented select the entire cell. You can also select specific characters within a cell. To do this with the mouse, position the cell pointer in the desired cell, and then double-click the left mouse button. Drag with the I-beam pointer through the data you want selected. Data selected within a cell displays in white with a black background. If you are using the keyboard to select data in a cell, hold down the Shift key, and then press the arrow key that moves the insertion point in the desired direction. Data the insertion point passes through will be selected. You can also press F8 to turn on the Extend Selection mode, move the insertion point in the desired direction to select the data, and then press F8 to turn off the Extend Selection mode. When the Extend Selection mode is on, the words *Extend Selection* display toward the left side of the Status bar.

Table 1.5 Selecting Cells Using the Keyboard

To select	*Press*
Cells in direction of arrow key	Shift + arrow key
From active cell to beginning of row	Shift + Home
From active cell to beginning of worksheet	Shift + Ctrl + Home
From active cell to last cell in worksheet containing data	Shift + Ctrl + End
An entire column	Ctrl + spacebar
An entire row	Shift + spacebar
An entire worksheet	Ctrl + A

Applying Basic Formatting

Excel provides a wide range of formatting options you can apply to cells in a worksheet. Some basic formatting options that are helpful when creating a worksheet include changing column width, merging and centering cells, and formatting numbers.

Changing Column Width

If data such as text or numbers overlaps in a cell, you can increase the width of the column to accommodate the data. To do this, position the mouse pointer on the blue boundary line between columns in the column header (Figure 1.2 identifies the column header) until the pointer turns into a double-headed arrow pointing left and right and then drag the boundary to the desired location. If the column contains data, you can double-click the column boundary at the right side of the column and the column will increase in size to accommodate the longest entry.

Quick Steps

Change Column Width
Drag column boundary line.
OR
Double-click column boundary.

Merge and Center Cells
1. Select cells.
2. Click Merge & Center button.

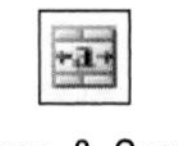

Merge & Center

Merging and Centering Cells

As you learned earlier in this chapter, if text you type is longer than the cell can accommodate, the text overlaps the next cell to the right. You can merge cells to accommodate the text and also center the text within the merged cells. To merge cells and center text, select the desired cells and then click the Merge & Center button located in the Alignment group in the Home tab.

Project 3a **Changing Column Width and Merging and Centering Cells** Part 1 of 2

1. Open **MoExps.xlsx** from the Excel2010L1C1 folder on your storage medium.
2. Save the workbook with Save As and name it **EL1-C1-P3-MoExps**.
3. Change column width by completing the following steps:
   a. Position the mouse pointer in the column header on the boundary line between columns A and B until the pointer turns into a double-headed arrow pointing left and right.

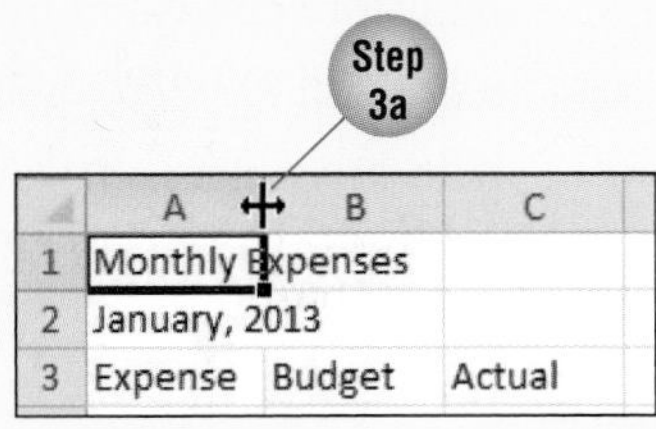

   b. Double-click the left mouse button.
   c. Position the mouse pointer in the column header on the boundary line between columns E and F and then double-click the left mouse button.
   d. Position the mouse pointer in the column header on the boundary line between columns F and G and then double-click the left mouse button.

4. Merge and center cells by completing the following steps:
   a. Select cells A1 through C1.
   b. Click the Merge & Center button in the Alignment group in the Home tab.
   c. Select cells A2 through C2.
   d. Click the Merge & Center button.
   e. Select cells E1 and F1 and then click the Merge & Center button.
5. Save **EL1-C1-P3-MoExps.xlsx**.

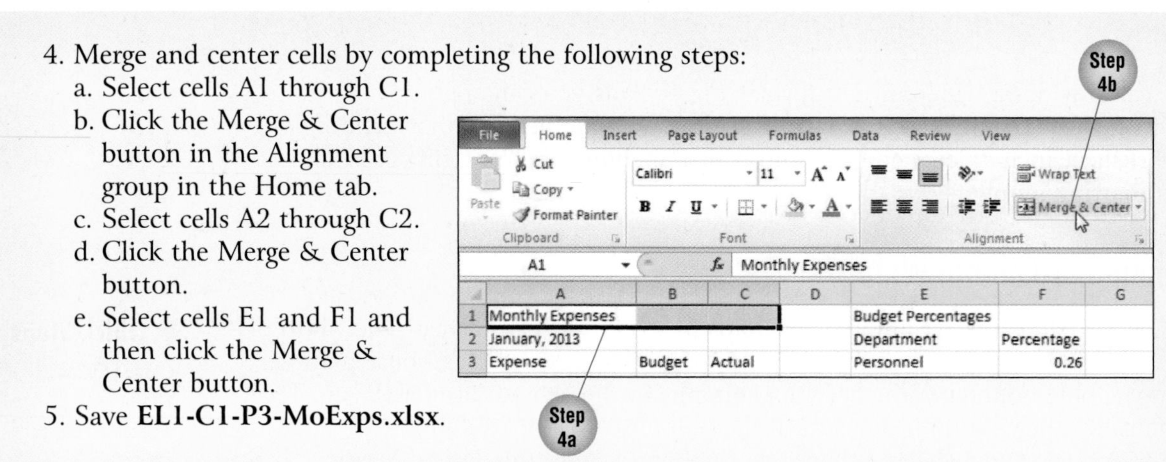

Formatting Numbers

Numbers in a cell, by default, are aligned at the right and decimals and commas do not display unless they are typed in the cell. You can change the format of numbers with buttons in the Number group in the Home tab. Symbols you can use to format numbers include a percent sign (%), a comma (,), and a dollar sign ($). For example, if you type the number *$45.50* in a cell, Excel automatically applies Currency formatting to the number. If you type *45%*, Excel automatically applies the Percent formatting to the number. The Number group in the Home tab contains five buttons you can use to format numbers in cells. The five buttons are shown and described in Table 1.6.

Table 1.6 Number Formatting Buttons

	Click this button	*To do this*
$ ▾	Accounting Number Format	Add a dollar sign, any necessary commas, and a decimal point followed by two decimal digits, if none are typed; right-align number in cell.
%	Percent Style	Multiply cell value by 100 and display result with a percent symbol; right-align number in cell.
,	Comma Style	Add any necessary commas and a decimal point followed by two decimal digits, if none are typed; right-align number in cell.
←.0 .00	Increase Decimal	Increase number of decimal places displayed after decimal point in selected cell.
.00 →.0	Decrease Decimal	Decrease number of decimal places displayed after decimal point in selected cell.

Specify the formatting for numbers in cells in a worksheet before typing the numbers, or format existing numbers in a worksheet. The Increase Decimal and Decrease Decimal buttons in the Number group in the Home tab will change decimal places for existing numbers only. The Number group in the Home tab also contains the Number Format button. Click the Number Format button arrow and a drop-down list displays of common number formats. Click the desired format at the drop-down list to apply the number formatting to the cell or selected cells.

A general guideline in accounting is to insert a dollar sign before the first number amount in a column and before the total number amount but not before the number amounts in between. You can format a worksheet following this guideline by applying the Accounting Number Format to the first amount and total amount and apply the Comma Style formatting to the number amounts in between.

Project 3b Formatting Numbers

Part 2 of 2

1. With **EL1-C1-P3-MoExps.xlsx** open, make cell B13 active and then double-click the AutoSum button. (This inserts the total of the numbers in cells B4 through B12.)
2. Make cell C13 active and then double-click the AutoSum button.
3. Apply Accounting Number Format to cells by completing the following steps:
   a. Select cells B4 and C4.
   b. Click the Accounting Number Format button in the Number group in the Home tab.
   c. Decrease the decimals by clicking twice on the Decrease Decimal button in the Number group.

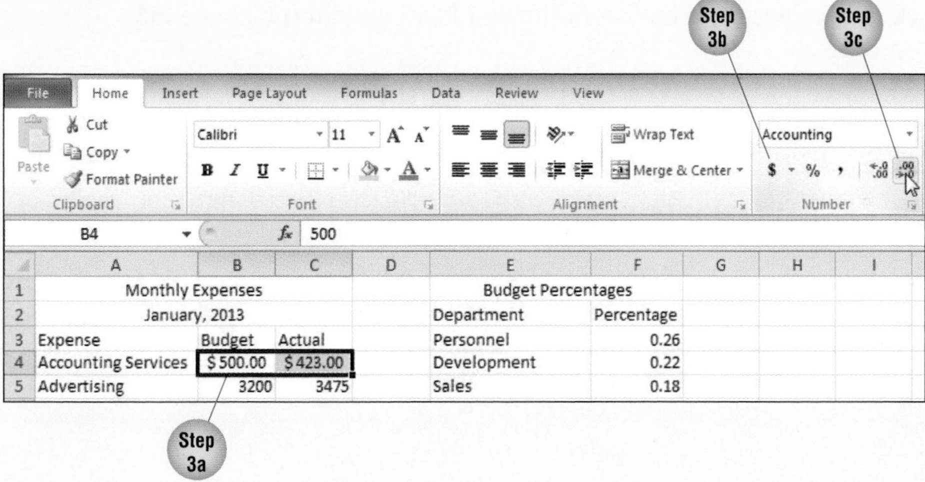

   d. Select cells B13 and C13.
   e. Click the Accounting Number Format button.
   f. Click twice on the Decrease Decimal button.

4. Apply Comma Style formatting to numbers by completing the following steps:
   a. Select cells B5 through C12.
   b. Click the Comma Style button in the Number group.
   c. Click twice on the Decrease Decimal button.

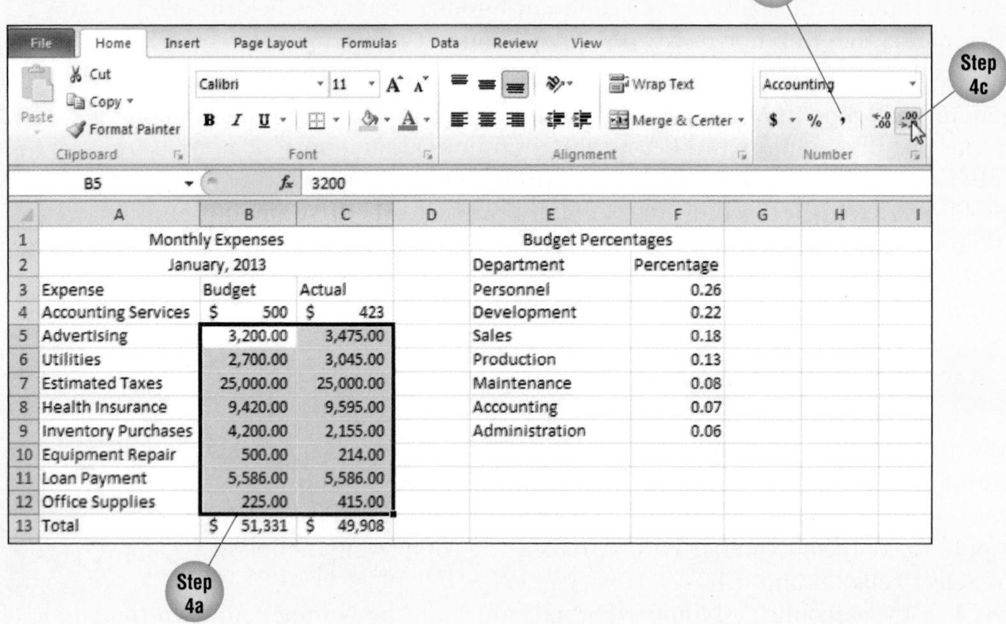

5. Apply Percent Style formatting to numbers by completing the following steps:
   a. Select cells F3 through F9.
   b. Click the Percent Style button in the Number group in the Home tab.
6. Click in cell A1.
7. Save, print, and then close **EL1-C1-P3-MoExps.xlsx**.

Project 4 Use the Help Feature — 3 Parts

You will use the Help feature to learn more about entering data in cells and saving a workbook and use the ScreenTip to display information about a specific button. You will also learn about options available at the Help tab Backstage view and how to customize Help to search for information offline.

Using Help

Quick Steps

Use the Help Feature
1. Click Microsoft Excel Help button.
2. Type topic or feature.
3. Press Enter.
4. Click desired topic.

Microsoft Excel includes a Help feature that contains information about Excel features and commands. This on-screen reference manual is similar to Windows Help and the Help features in Word, PowerPoint, and Access. Click the Microsoft Excel Help button (the circle with the question mark) located in the upper right corner of the screen or press the keyboard shortcut F1 to display the Excel Help window. In this window, type a topic, feature, or question in the search text box and then press the Enter key. Topics related to the search text display in the Excel Help window. Click a topic that interests you. If the topic window contains a

Show All hyperlink in the upper right corner, click this hyperlink and the topic options expand to show additional help information related to the topic. When you click the Show All hyperlink, it becomes the Hide All hyperlink.

Help

Getting Help at the Help Tab Backstage View

The Help tab Backstage view, shown in Figure 1.10, contains an option for displaying the Excel Help window as well as other options. Click the Microsoft Office Help button in the Support category to display the Excel Help window and click the Getting Started button to access the Microsoft website that displays information about getting started with Excel 2010. Click the Contact Us button in the Support category and the Microsoft Support website displays. Click the Options button in the Tools for Working With Office category and the Excel Options dialog box displays. You will learn about this dialog box in a later chapter. Click the Check for Updates button and the Microsoft Update website displays with information on available updates. The right side of the Help tab Backstage view displays information about Office and Excel.

Quick Steps

Display Help Tab Backstage View
1. Click File tab.
2. Click Help button.

Getting Help on a Button

When you position the mouse pointer on a button, a ScreenTip displays with information about the button. Some button ScreenTips display with the message "Press F1 for more help" that is preceded by an image of the Help button. With the ScreenTip visible, press the F1 function key on your keyboard and the Excel Help window opens and displays information about the specific button.

Figure 1.10 Help Tab Backstage View

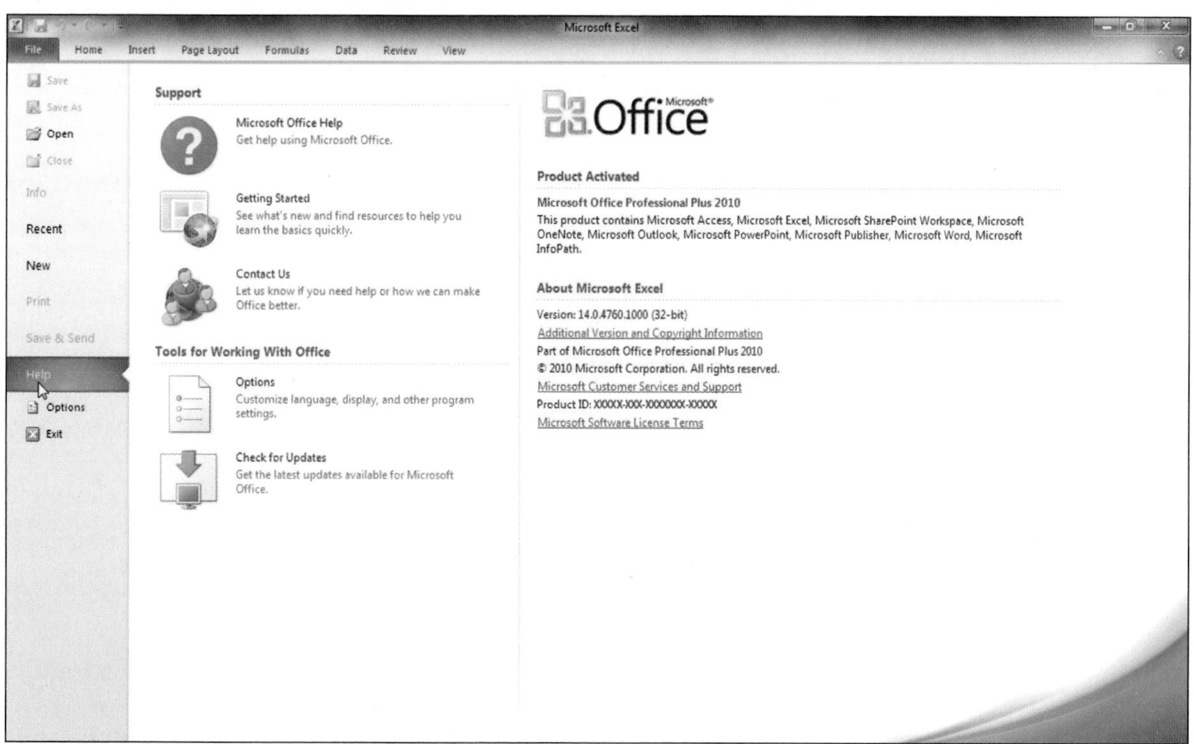

Project 4a Using the Help Feature

Part 1 of 3

1. At the blank screen, press Ctrl + N to display a blank workbook. (Ctrl + N is the keyboard command to open a blank workbook.)
2. Click the Microsoft Excel Help button located in the upper right corner of the screen.

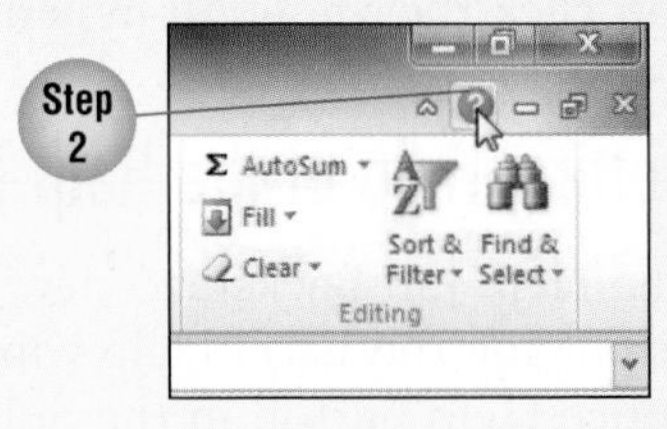

3. At the Excel Help window, type **enter data** in the search text box and then press the Enter key. (Make sure that *Connected to Office.com* displays in the lower right corner of the window. If not, click the Search button arrow and then click *Content from Office.com* at the drop-down list.)
4. When the list of topics displays, click the Enter data manually in worksheet cells hyperlink.
5. Read the information about entering data in cells. (If you want a printing of the information, you can click the Print button located toward the top of the Excel Help window and then click the Print button at the Print dialog box.)

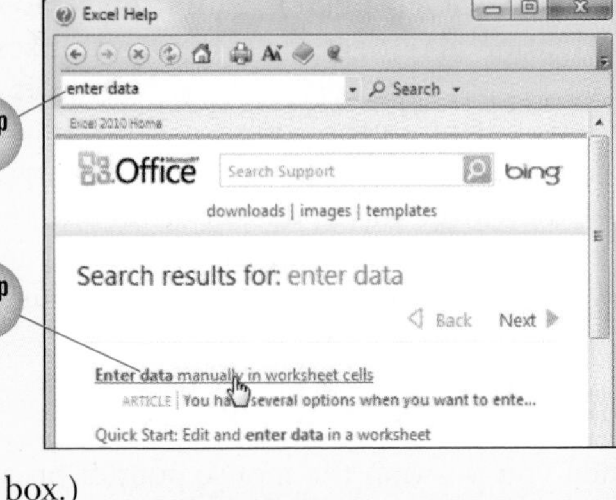

6. Close the Excel Help window by clicking the Close button located in the upper right corner of the window.
7. Click the File tab and then click the Help tab.
8. At the Help tab Backstage view, click the Getting Started button in the Support category. (You must be connected to the Internet to display the web page.)
9. Look at the information that displays at the website and then click the Close button located in the upper right corner of the web page.
10. Click the File tab and then click the Help tab.
11. Click the Contact Us button, look at the information that displays at the website, and then close the web page.

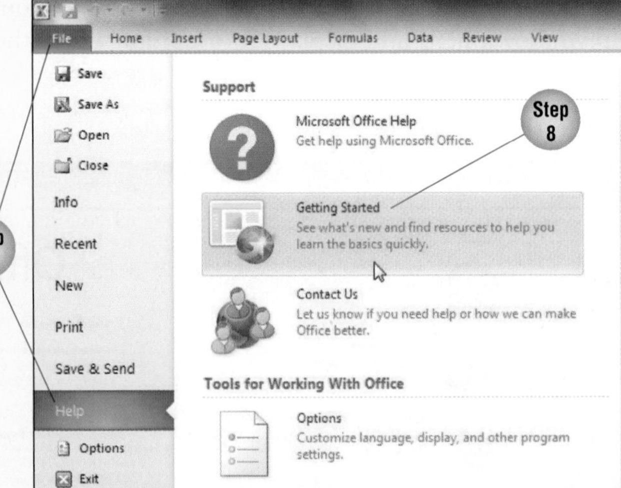

12. Hover the mouse pointer over the Wrap Text button in the Alignment group in the Home tab until the ScreenTip displays and then press F1.
13. At the Excel Help window, read the information that displays and then close the window.

Getting Help in a Dialog Box or Backstage View

Some dialog boxes, as well as the Backstage view, contain a Help button you can click to display a help window with specific information about the dialog box or Backstage view. After reading and/or printing the information, close a dialog box by clicking the Close button located in the upper right corner of the dialog box or close the Backstage view by clicking the File tab or clicking any other tab in the ribbon.

Project 4b Getting Help in a Dialog Box and Backstage View

Part 2 of 3

1. At the blank workbook, click the File tab and then click the Save As button.
2. At the Save As dialog box, click the Help button located near the upper right corner of the dialog box.
3. Read the information about saving files that displays in the Windows Help and Support window.
4. Close the window by clicking the Close button located in the upper right corner of the window.
5. Close the Save As dialog box.
6. Click the File tab.
7. At the Backstage view, click the Help button located near the upper right corner of the window.
8. At the Excel Help window, click a hyperlink that interests you.
9. Read the information and then close the Excel Help window by clicking the Close button located in the upper right corner of the window.
10. Click the File tab to return to the blank workbook.

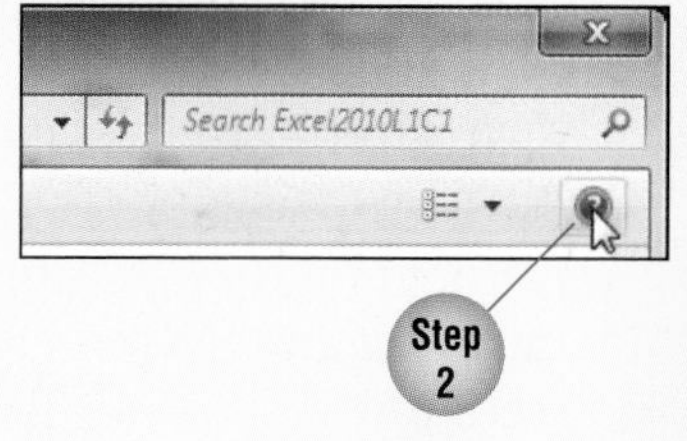

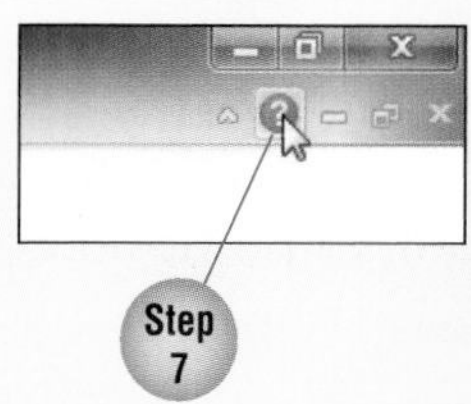

Customizing Help

By default, the Excel Help feature will search for an Internet connection and, if one is found, display help resources from Office Online. If you are connected online to help resources, the message "Connected to Office.com" displays in the lower right corner of the Excel Help window. If you are not connected to the Internet, the message displays as "Offline."

Office Online provides additional help resources such as training and templates. To view the resources, display the Excel Help window and then click the down-pointing arrow at the right side of the Search button. This displays a drop-down list similar to the one shown in Figure 1.11. Generally, the *All Excel* option in the *Content from Office.com* section is selected. If you want to search only the Help resources available with your computer (offline), click the *Excel Help* option in the *Content from this computer* section. To access Office.com training, click the *Excel Training* option in the *Content from Office.com* section, type a training topic in the search text box, and then click OK.

Figure 1.11 Excel Help Search Drop-down List

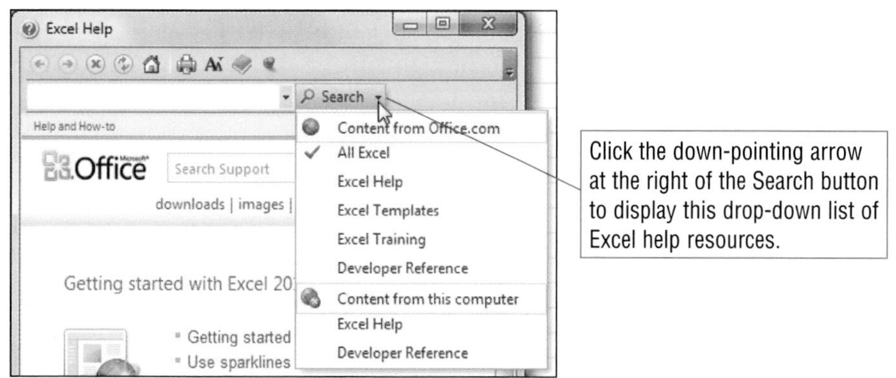

Project 4c Customizing Help

Part 3 of 3

1. At a blank worksheet, click the Microsoft Excel Help button located toward the upper right corner of the screen.
2. Click the down-pointing arrow at the right side of the Search button in the Excel Help window.
3. At the drop-down list that displays, click *Excel Help* in the *Content from this computer* section.
4. Click in the search text box, type formulas, and then press Enter.
5. Click a hyperlink that interests you and then read the information that displays.
6. Click the down-pointing arrow at the right side of the Search button and then click *Excel Training* in the *Content from Office.com* section.

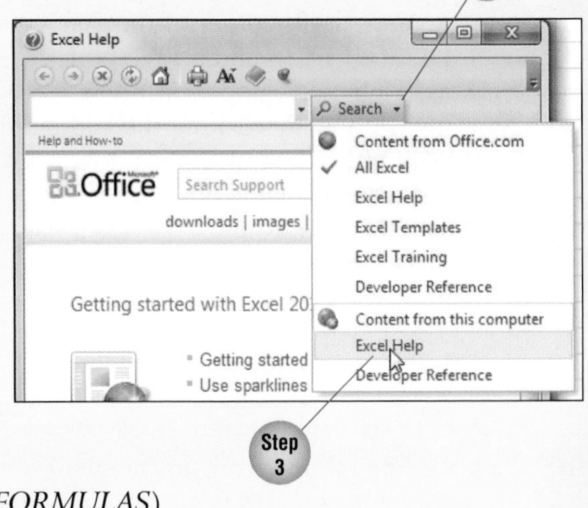

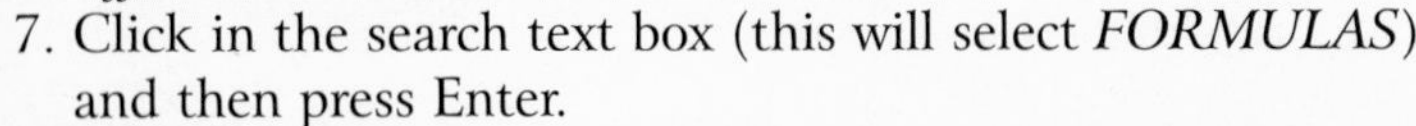

7. Click in the search text box (this will select *FORMULAS*) and then press Enter.
8. Click the hyperlink of a training about formulas that interests you.
9. After completing the training, close Internet Explorer and then close the Excel Help window.

Chapter Summary

- A file created in Excel is called a workbook, which consists of individual worksheets. The intersection of columns and rows is referred to as a cell. Gridlines are the horizontal and vertical lines that define cells.
- An Excel window contains the following elements: Quick Access toolbar, File tab, Title bar, tabs, ribbon, Name box, Formula bar, scroll bars, sheet tabs, and Status bar.
- When the insertion point is positioned in a cell, the cell name (also called the cell reference) displays in the Name box located at the left side of the Formula bar. The cell name includes the column letter and row number.
- If data entered in a cell consists of text (letters) and it does not fit into the cell, it overlaps the cell to the right. If the data consists of numbers and it does not fit into the cell, the numbers are changed to number symbols (###).
- Save a workbook by clicking the Save button on the Quick Access toolbar or by clicking the File tab and then clicking the Save button.
- To replace data in a cell, click the cell once and then type the new data. To edit data within a cell, double-click the cell and then make necessary changes.
- Print a workbook by clicking the File tab, clicking the Print tab, and then clicking the Print button.

- Close a workbook by clicking the Close Window button located in the upper right corner of the screen or by clicking the File tab and then clicking the Close button.
- Exit Excel by clicking the Close button located in the upper right corner of the screen or by clicking the File tab and then clicking the Exit button.
- The AutoComplete feature will automatically insert a previous entry if the character or characters being typed in a cell match a previous entry. The AutoCorrect feature corrects many common typographical errors. Use the AutoFill fill handle to fill a range of cells with the same or consecutive data.
- Open a workbook by clicking the File tab and then clicking the Open button. At the Open dialog box, double-click the desired workbook.
- Use the AutoSum button in the Editing group in the Home tab to find the total or average of data in columns or rows.
- Select all cells in a column by clicking the column header. Select all cells in a row by clicking the row header. Select all cells in a worksheet by clicking the Select All button located immediately to the left of the column headers.
- Change column width by dragging the column boundary or double-clicking the column boundary.
- Merge and center cells by selecting the desired cells and then clicking the Merge & Center button in the Alignment group in the Home tab.
- Format numbers in cells with buttons in the Number group in the Home tab.
- Click the Microsoft Excel Help button or press F1 to display the Excel Help window. At this window, type a topic in the search text box and then press Enter.
- Some dialog boxes as well as the Backstage view contain a Help button you can click to display information specific to the dialog box or Backstage view.
- The ScreenTip for some buttons displays with a message telling you to press F1. Press F1 and the Excel Help window opens with information about the button.

Commands Review

FEATURE	RIBBON TAB, GROUP	BUTTON	FILE TAB	KEYBOARD SHORTCUT
Close workbook			Close	Ctrl + F4
Exit Excel			Exit	
Go To dialog box	Home, Editing			Ctrl + G
Excel Help window				F1
Open workbook			Open	Ctrl + O
Print tab Backstage view			Print	
Save workbook			Save	Ctrl + S

FEATURE	RIBBON TAB, GROUP	BUTTON	FILE TAB	KEYBOARD SHORTCUT
AutoSum button	Home, Editing	Σ		Alt + =
Merge & Center	Home, Alignment			
Accounting Number Format	Home, Number	$		
Comma Style	Home, Number	,		
Percent Style	Home, Number	%		Ctrl + Shift + %
Increase Decimal	Home, Number			
Decrease Decimal	Home, Number			

Concepts Check Test Your Knowledge

Completion: In the space provided at the right, indicate the correct term, symbol, or command.

1. The horizontal and vertical lines that define the cells in a worksheet area are referred to as this. ____________________
2. Columns in a worksheet are labeled with these. ____________________
3. Rows in a worksheet are labeled with these. ____________________
4. Press this key on the keyboard to move the insertion point to the next cell. ____________________
5. Press these keys on the keyboard to move the insertion point to the previous cell. ____________________
6. Data being typed in a cell displays in the cell as well as here. ____________________
7. If a number entered in a cell is too long to fit inside the cell, the number is changed to this. ____________________
8. This feature will automatically insert words, numbers, or formulas in a series. ____________________
9. This is the name of the small black square that displays in the bottom right corner of the active cell. ____________________
10. Use this button in the Editing group in the Home tab to insert a formula in a cell. ____________________

11. With this function, a range of cells is added together and then divided by the number of cell entries. ________________

12. To select nonadjacent columns using the mouse, hold down this key on the keyboard while clicking the column headers. ________________

13. Click this button in the worksheet area to select all of the cells in the table. ________________

14. Click this button to merge selected cells and center data within the merged cells. ________________

15. The Accounting Number Format button is located in this group in the Home tab. ________________

16. Press this function key to display the Excel Help window. ________________

Skills Check Assess Your Performance

Assessment

1 CREATE A WORKSHEET USING AUTOCOMPLETE

1. Create the worksheet shown in Figure 1.12 with the following specifications:
   a. To create the © symbols in cell A1, type (c).
   b. Type the misspelled words as shown and let the AutoCorrect feature correct the spelling. Use the AutoComplete feature to insert the second occurrence of *Category, Available,* and *Balance*.
   c. Merge and center cells A1 and B1.
2. Save the workbook and name it **EL1-C1-A1-Plan**.
3. Print and then close **EL1-C1-A1-Plan.xlsx**.

Figure 1.12 Assessment 1

	A	B	C
1	Premiere Plan©		
2	Plan A	Catagory	
3		Availalbe	
4		Balence	
5	Plan B	Category	
6		Available	
7		Balance	
8			

Assessment 2

CREATE AND FORMAT A WORKSHEET

1. Create the worksheet shown in Figure 1.13 with the following specifications:
   a. Merge and center cells A1 through C1.
   b. After typing the data, automatically adjust the width of column A.
   c. Insert in cell B8 the sum of cells B3 through B7 and insert in cell C8 the sum of cells C3 through C7.
   d. Apply the Accounting Number Format style and decrease the decimal point by two positions to cells B3, C3, B8, and C8.
   e. Apply the Comma Style and decrease the decimal point two times to cells B4 through C7.
   f. If any of the number amounts displays as number symbols (###), automatically adjust the width of the appropriate columns.
2. Save the workbook and name it **EL1-C1-A2-Exp**.
3. Print and then close **EL1-C1-A2-Exp.xlsx**.

Figure 1.13 Assessment 2

	A	B	C	D
1	Construction Project			
2	Expense	Original	Current	
3	Material	$129,000	$153,000	
4	Labor	97,000	98,500	
5	Equipmental rental	14,500	11,750	
6	Permits	1,200	1,350	
7	Tax	1,950	2,145	
8	Total	$243,650	$266,745	
9				

Assessment 3

CREATE A WORKSHEET USING THE FILL HANDLE

1. Type the worksheet data shown in Figure 1.14 with the following specifications:
   a. Type Monday in cell B2 and then use the fill handle to fill in the remaining days of the week.
   b. Type 350 in cell B3 and then use the fill handle to fill in the remaining numbers in the row.
   c. Merge and center cells A1 through G1.
2. Insert in cell G3 the sum of cells B3 through F3 and insert in cell G4 the sum of cells B4 through F4.
3. After typing the data, select cells B3 through G4 and then change to the accounting number format with two decimal points.
4. If necessary, adjust column widths.
5. Save the workbook and name it **EL1-C1-A3-Invest**.
6. Print and then close **EL1-C1-A3-Invest.xlsx**.

Figure 1.14 Assessment 3

	A	B	C	D	E	F	G	H
1	CAPITAL INVESTMENTS							
2		Monday	Tuesday	Wednesday	Thursday	Friday	Total	
3	Budget	350	350	350	350	350		
4	Actual	310	425	290	375	400		
5								

Assessment

INSERT FORMULAS IN A WORKSHEET

1. Open **DIAnalysis.xlsx** and then save the workbook with Save As and name it **EL1-C1-A4-DIAnalysis**.
2. Insert a formula in cell B15 that totals the amounts in cells B4 through B14.
3. Use the fill handle to copy relatively the formula in cell B15 to cell C15.
4. Insert a formula in cell D4 that finds the average of cells B4 and C4.
5. Use the fill handle to copy relatively the formula in cell D4 down to cells D5 through D14.
6. Select cells D5 through D14 and then apply the Comma Style with zero decimals.
7. Save, print, and then close **EL1-C1-A4-DIAnalysis.xlsx**.

Visual Benchmark Demonstrate Your Proficiency

CREATE, FORMAT, AND INSERT FORMULAS IN A WORKSHEET

1. At a blank workbook, create the worksheet shown in Figure 1.15 with the following specifications:
   a. Type the data in cells as shown in the figure. Use the fill handle when appropriate, merge and center the text *Personal Expenses – July through December*, and automatically adjust column widths.
   b. Insert formulas to determine averages and totals.
   c. Apply the Accounting Number Format style with zero decimal places to the amounts in cells B4 through H4 and cells B12 through H12.
   d. Apply the Comma Style with zero decimals to the amounts in cells B5 through G11.
2. Save the workbook and name it **EL1-C1-VB-PersExps**.
3. Print and then close **EL1-C1-VB-PersExps.xlsx**.

Figure 1.15 Visual Benchmark

	A	B	C	D	E	F	G	H	I
1									
2	Personal Expenses - July through December								
3	Expense	July	August	September	October	November	December	Average	
4	Rent	$ 850	$ 850	$ 850	$ 850	$ 850	$ 850		
5	Rental Insurance	55	55	55	55	55	55		
6	Health Insurance	120	120	120	120	120	120		
7	Electricity	129	135	110	151	168	173		
8	Utilities	53	62	49	32	55	61		
9	Telephone	73	81	67	80	82	75		
10	Groceries	143	137	126	150	147	173		
11	Gasoline	89	101	86	99	76	116		
12	Total								
13									

Case Study Apply Your Skills

Part 1

You are the office manager for Deering Industries. One of your responsibilities is creating a monthly calendar containing information on staff meetings, training, and due dates for time cards. Open **DICalendar.xlsx** and then insert the following information:

- Insert the text *October, 2012* in cell A2.
- Insert the days of the week (*Sunday*, *Monday*, *Tuesday*, *Wednesday*, *Thursday*, *Friday*, and *Saturday*) in cells A3 through G3. (Use the fill handle to fill in the days of the week and fill without formatting.)
- Insert the number *1* in cell B4, number *2* in cell C4, number *3* in cell D4, number *4* in cell E4, number *5* in cell F4, and number *6* in cell G4.
- Insert in the calendar the remaining numbers of the days (numbers *7* through *13* in cells A6 through G6, numbers *14* through *20* in cells A8 through G8, numbers *21* through *27* in cells A10 through G10, and numbers *28* through *31* in cells A12 through D12). If you use the fill handle, fill without formatting.
- Excel training will be held Thursday, October 4, from 9-11 a.m. Insert this information in cell E5. (Insert the text on two lines by typing Excel Training, pressing Alt + Enter to move the insertion point to the next line, and then typing 9-11 a.m.)
- A staff meeting is held the second and fourth Monday of each month from 9-10 a.m. Insert this information in cell B7 and cell B11.
- Time cards are due the first and third Fridays of the month. Insert in cells F5 and F9 information indicating that time cards are due.
- A production team meeting is scheduled for Tuesday, October 23, from 1-3 p.m. Insert this information in cell C11.

Save the workbook and name it **EL1-C1-CS-DICalendar**. Print and then close the workbook.

Part 2

The manager of the Purchasing Department has asked you to prepare a worksheet containing information on quarterly purchases. Open **DIExpenditures.xlsx** and then insert the data as shown in Figure 1.16. After typing the data, insert in the appropriate cells formulas to calculate averages and totals. Save the workbook and name it **EL1-C1-CS-DIExpenditures**. Print and then close the workbook.

Figure 1.16 Case Study, Part 2

	A	B	C	D	E	F	G
1			DEERING INDUSTRIES				
2			PURCHASING DEPARTMENT - EXPENDITURES				
3	*Category*					*Average*	
4	Supplies	$ 645.75	$ 756.25	$ 534.78	$ 78,950.00		
5	Equipment	4,520.55	10,789.35	3,825.00	12,890.72		
6	Furniture	458.94	2,490.72	851.75	743.20		
7	Training	1,000.00	250.00	1,200.00	800.00		
8	Software	249.00	1,574.30	155.45	3,458.70		
9	Total						
10							

Part 3

The manager of the Purchasing Department has asked you to prepare a note to the finances coordinator, Jennifer Strauss. In Word, type a note to Jennifer Strauss explaining that you have prepared an Excel worksheet with the Purchasing Department expenditures. You are including the cells from the worksheet containing the expenditure information. In Excel, open **EL1-C1-CS-DIExpenditures.xlsx**, copy cells A3 through F9, and then paste them in the Word document. Make any corrections to the table so the information is readable. Save the document and name it **EL1-C1-CS-DINotetoJS**. Print and then close the document. Close **EL1-C1-CS-DIExpenditures.xlsx**.

Part 4

You will be ordering copy machines for several departments in the company and decide to research prices. Using the Internet, find three companies that sell copiers and write down information on different copier models. Open **DICopiers.xlsx** and then type the company, model number, and price in the designated cells. Save the completed workbook and name it **EL1-C1-CS-DICopiers**. Print and then close **EL1-C1-CS-DICopiers.xlsx**.

Microsoft® Excel®

CHAPTER 2

Inserting Formulas in a Worksheet

PERFORMANCE OBJECTIVES

Upon successful completion of Chapter 2, you will be able to:

- **Write formulas with mathematical operators**
- **Type a formula in the Formula bar**
- **Copy a formula**
- **Use the Insert Function feature to insert a formula in a cell**
- **Write formulas with the AVERAGE, MAX, MIN, COUNT, PMT, FV, DATE, NOW, and IF functions**
- **Create an absolute and mixed cell reference**

Tutorials

2.1 Performing Calculations Using Formulas

2.2 Writing Formulas in Excel

2.3 Copying and Testing Formulas

2.4 Creating Formulas with Absolute Addressing

2.5 Using Financial Functions

2.6 Writing Formulas with the FV Function

2.7 Using the Logical IF Function

Excel is a powerful decision-making tool containing data that can be manipulated to answer "what if" situations. Insert a formula in a worksheet and then manipulate the data to make projections, answer specific questions, and use as a planning tool. For example, the owner of a company might prepare a worksheet on production costs and then determine the impact on company revenues if production is increased or decreased.

Insert a formula in a worksheet to perform calculations on values. A formula contains a mathematical operator, value, cell reference, cell range, and a function. Formulas can be written that add, subtract, multiply, and/or divide values. Formulas can also be written that calculate averages, percentages, minimum and maximum values, and much more. As you learned in Chapter 1, Excel includes an AutoSum button in the Editing group in the Home tab that inserts a formula to calculate the total of a range of cells and also includes some commonly used formulas. Along with the AutoSum button, Excel includes a Formulas tab that offers a variety of functions to create formulas. Model answers for this chapter's projects appear on the following pages.

Excel2010L1C2

Note: Before beginning the projects, copy to your storage medium the Excel2010L1C2 subfolder from the Excel2010L1 folder on the CD that accompanies this textbook and make Excel2010L1C2 the active folder.

Model Answers

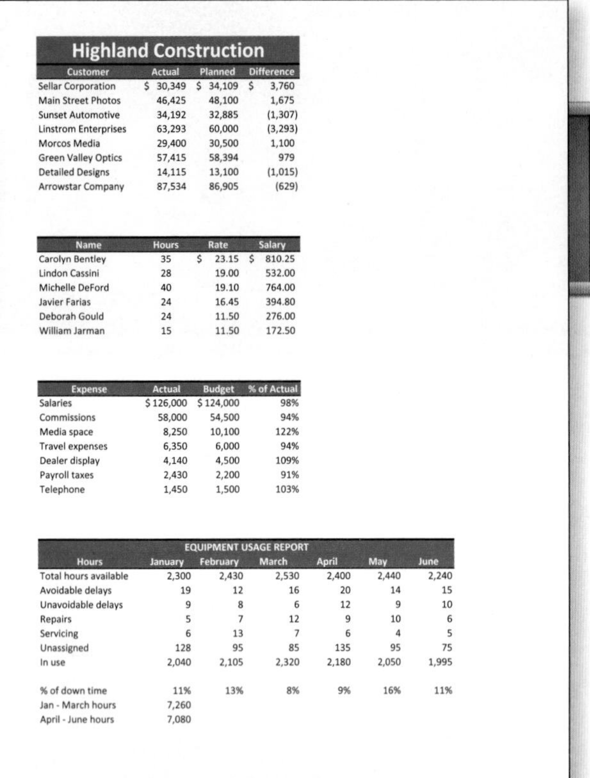

Highland Construction

Customer	Actual	Planned	Difference
Sellar Corporation	$ 30,349	$ 34,109	$ 3,760
Main Street Photos	46,425	48,100	1,675
Sunset Automotive	34,192	32,885	(1,307)
Linstrom Enterprises	63,293	60,000	(3,293)
Morcos Media	29,400	30,500	1,100
Green Valley Optics	57,415	58,394	979
Detailed Designs	14,115	13,100	(1,015)
Arrowstar Company	87,534	86,905	(629)

Name	Hours	Rate	Salary
Carolyn Bentley	35	$ 23.15	$ 810.25
Lindon Cassini	28	19.00	532.00
Michelle DeFord	40	19.10	764.00
Javier Farias	24	16.45	394.80
Deborah Gould	24	11.50	276.00
William Jarman	15	11.50	172.50

Expense	Actual	Budget	% of Actual
Salaries	$ 126,000	$ 124,000	98%
Commissions	58,000	54,500	94%
Media space	8,250	10,100	122%
Travel expenses	6,350	6,000	94%
Dealer display	4,140	4,500	109%
Payroll taxes	2,430	2,200	91%
Telephone	1,450	1,500	103%

EQUIPMENT USAGE REPORT						
Hours	January	February	March	April	May	June
Total hours available	2,300	2,430	2,530	2,400	2,440	2,240
Avoidable delays	19	12	16	20	14	15
Unavoidable delays	9	8	6	12	9	10
Repairs	5	7	12	9	10	6
Servicing	6	13	7	6	4	5
Unassigned	128	95	85	135	95	75
In use	2,040	2,105	2,320	2,180	2,050	1,995
% of down time	11%	13%	8%	9%	16%	11%
Jan - March hours	7,260					
April - June hours	7,080					

Project 1 Insert Formulas in a Worksheet

EL1-C2-P1-HCReports.xlsx

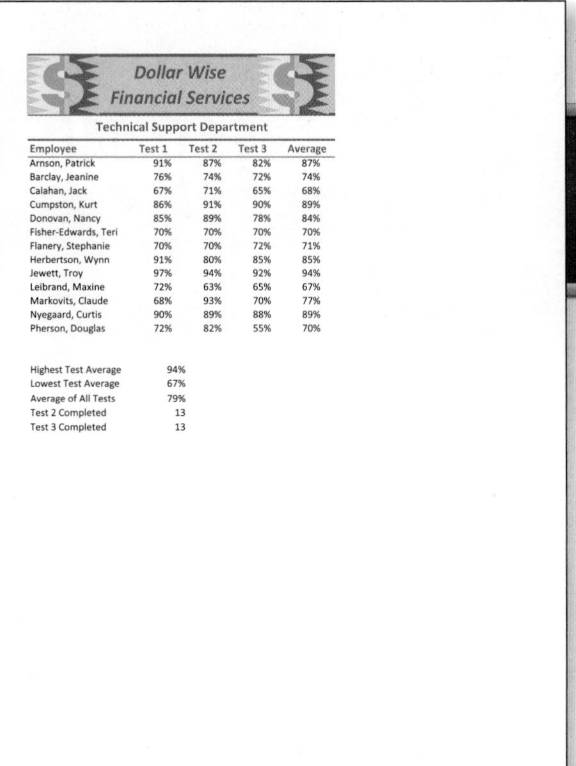

Dollar Wise
Financial Services

Technical Support Department

Employee	Test 1	Test 2	Test 3	Average
Arnson, Patrick	91%	87%	82%	87%
Barclay, Jeanine	76%	74%	72%	74%
Calahan, Jack	67%	71%	65%	68%
Cumpston, Kurt	86%	91%	90%	89%
Donovan, Nancy	85%	89%	78%	84%
Fisher-Edwards, Teri	70%	70%	70%	70%
Flanery, Stephanie	70%	70%	72%	71%
Herbertson, Wynn	91%	80%	85%	85%
Jewett, Troy	97%	94%	92%	94%
Leibrand, Maxine	72%	63%	65%	67%
Markovits, Claude	68%	93%	70%	77%
Nyegaard, Curtis	90%	89%	88%	89%
Pherson, Douglas	72%	82%	55%	70%

Highest Test Average	94%
Lowest Test Average	67%
Average of All Tests	79%
Test 2 Completed	13
Test 3 Completed	13

Project 2 Insert Formulas with Statistical Functions

EL1-C2-P2-DWTests.xlsx

Dollar Wise
Financial Services

Technical Support Department

Employee	Test 1	Test 2
Arnson, Patrick	0.91	0.87
Barclay, Jeanine	0.76	0.74
Calahan, Jack	0.67	0.71
Cumpston, Kurt	0.86	0.91
Donovan, Nancy	0.85	0.89
Fisher-Edwards, Teri	0.7	0.7
Flanery, Stephanie	0.7	0.7
Herbertson, Wynn	0.91	0.8
Jewett, Troy	0.97	0.94
Leibrand, Maxine	0.72	0.63
Markovits, Claude	0.68	0.93
Nyegaard, Curtis	0.9	0.89
Pherson, Douglas	0.72	0.82

Highest Test Average	=MAX(E4:E16)
Lowest Test Average	=MIN(E4:E16)
Average of All Tests	=AVERAGE(E4:E16)
Test 2 Completed	=COUNT(C4:C16)
Test 3 Completed	=COUNT(D4:D16)

Page 1

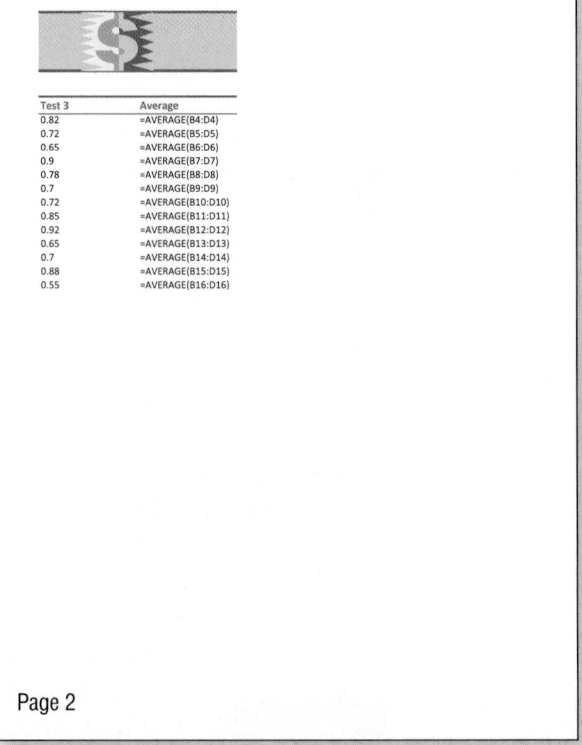

Test 3	Average
0.82	=AVERAGE(B4:D4)
0.72	=AVERAGE(B5:D5)
0.65	=AVERAGE(B6:D6)
0.9	=AVERAGE(B7:D7)
0.78	=AVERAGE(B8:D8)
0.7	=AVERAGE(B9:D9)
0.72	=AVERAGE(B10:D10)
0.85	=AVERAGE(B11:D11)
0.92	=AVERAGE(B12:D12)
0.65	=AVERAGE(B13:D13)
0.7	=AVERAGE(B14:D14)
0.88	=AVERAGE(B15:D15)
0.55	=AVERAGE(B16:D16)

Page 2

EL1-C2-P2-DWTests.xlsx, Formulas

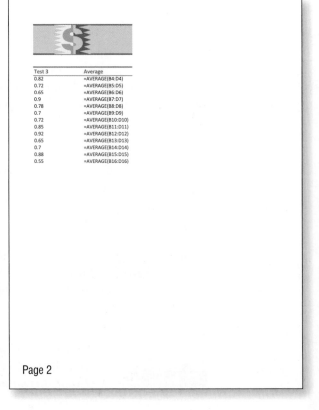

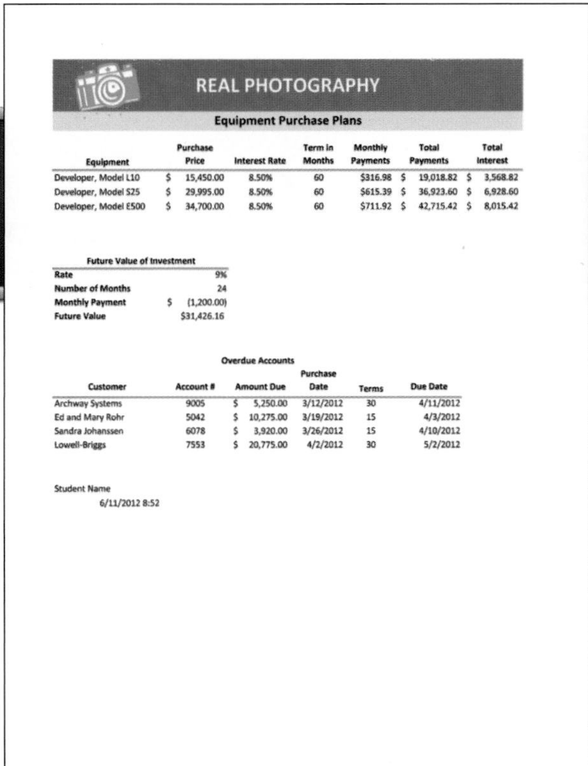

REAL PHOTOGRAPHY

Equipment Purchase Plans

Equipment	Purchase Price	Interest Rate	Term in Months	Monthly Payments	Total Payments	Total Interest
Developer, Model L10	$ 15,450.00	8.50%	60	$316.98	$ 19,018.82	$ 3,568.82
Developer, Model S25	$ 29,995.00	8.50%	60	$615.39	$ 36,923.60	$ 6,928.60
Developer, Model E500	$ 34,700.00	8.50%	60	$711.92	$ 42,715.42	$ 8,015.42

Future Value of Investment	
Rate	9%
Number of Months	24
Monthly Payment	$ (1,200.00)
Future Value	$31,426.16

Overdue Accounts

Customer	Account #	Amount Due	Purchase Date	Terms	Due Date
Archway Systems	9005	$ 5,250.00	3/12/2012	30	4/11/2012
Ed and Mary Rohr	5042	$ 10,275.00	3/19/2012	15	4/3/2012
Sandra Johanssen	6078	$ 3,920.00	3/26/2012	15	4/10/2012
Lowell-Briggs	7553	$ 20,775.00	4/2/2012	30	5/2/2012

Student Name
6/11/2012 8:52

Project 3 Insert Formulas with Financial and Date and Time Functions EL1-C2-P3-RPReports.xlsx

Capstan Marine Products

Sales Department			
Salesperson	**Quota**	**Actual Sales**	**Bonus**
Allejandro	$ 95,500.00	$ 103,295.00	$ 25,823.75
Crispin	137,000.00	129,890.00	-
Frankel	124,000.00	133,255.00	33,313.75
Hiesmann	85,500.00	94,350.00	23,587.50
Jarvis	159,000.00	167,410.00	41,852.50
Littleman	110,500.00	109,980.00	-

New Employee Orientation					
Name	**Quiz 1**	**Quiz 2**	**Quiz 3**	**Average**	**Grade**
Angelo	78	69	88	78	FAIL
Cunningham	90	95	86	90	PASS
Elliot	82	88	94	88	PASS
Kennedy	100	98	96	98	PASS
Lipscomb	64	76	62	67	FAIL

Sales Department			
Product #	**Price**	**Discount**	**Discount %**
C-2340	$ 1,250.00	YES	5%
C-3215	$ 695.00	YES	5%
C-4390	$ 475.00	NO	0%
E-2306	$ 225.00	NO	0%
E-3420	$ 520.00	NO	0%
G-2312	$ 2,150.00	YES	5%
G-4393	$ 2,450.00	YES	5%
J-1203	$ 755.00	YES	5%
J-3288	$ 455.00	NO	0%
J-4594	$ 1,050.00	YES	5%
M-2355	$ 890.00	YES	5%
M-3129	$ 645.00	YES	5%
M-4392	$ 475.00	NO	0%

Project 4 Insert Formulas with the IF Logical Function EL1-C2-P4-CMPReports.xlsx

Capstan Marin

Sales Department		
Salesperson	**Quota**	**Actual Sales**
Allejandro	95500	103295
Crispin	137000	129890
Frankel	124000	133255
Hiesmann	85500	94350
Jarvis	159000	167410
Littleman	110500	109980

New Employee Ori		
Name	**Quiz 1**	**Quiz 2**
Angelo	78	69
Cunningham	90	95
Elliot	82	88
Kennedy	100	98
Lipscomb	64	76

Sales Department		
Product #	**Price**	**Discount**
C-2340	1250	=IF(B26>599,"YES","NO")
C-3215	695	=IF(B27>599,"YES","NO")
C-4390	475	=IF(B28>599,"YES","NO")
E-2306	225	=IF(B29>599,"YES","NO")
E-3420	520	=IF(B30>599,"YES","NO")
G-2312	2150	=IF(B31>599,"YES","NO")
G-4393	2450	=IF(B32>599,"YES","NO")
J-1203	755	=IF(B33>599,"YES","NO")
J-3288	455	=IF(B34>599,"YES","NO")
J-4594	1050	=IF(B35>599,"YES","NO")
M-2355	890	=IF(B36>599,"YES","NO")
M-3129	645	=IF(B37>599,"YES","NO")
M-4392	475	=IF(B38>599,"YES","NO")

Page 1

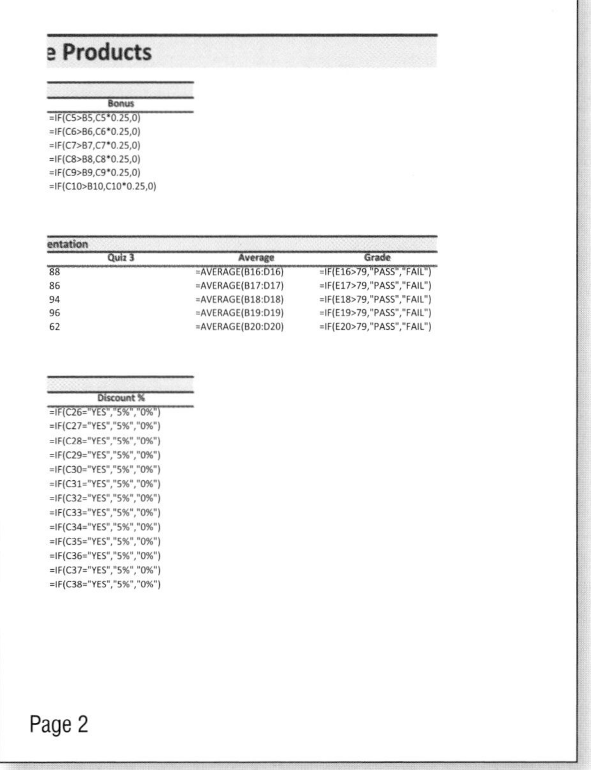

e Products

Bonus
=IF(C5>B5,C5*0.25,0)
=IF(C6>B6,C6*0.25,0)
=IF(C7>B7,C7*0.25,0)
=IF(C8>B8,C8*0.25,0)
=IF(C9>B9,C9*0.25,0)
=IF(C10>B10,C10*0.25,0)

entation		
Quiz 3	**Average**	**Grade**
88	=AVERAGE(B16:D16)	=IF(E16>79,"PASS","FAIL")
86	=AVERAGE(B17:D17)	=IF(E17>79,"PASS","FAIL")
94	=AVERAGE(B18:D18)	=IF(E18>79,"PASS","FAIL")
96	=AVERAGE(B19:D19)	=IF(E19>79,"PASS","FAIL")
62	=AVERAGE(B20:D20)	=IF(E20>79,"PASS","FAIL")

Discount %
=IF(C26="YES","5%","0%")
=IF(C27="YES","5%","0%")
=IF(C28="YES","5%","0%")
=IF(C29="YES","5%","0%")
=IF(C30="YES","5%","0%")
=IF(C31="YES","5%","0%")
=IF(C32="YES","5%","0%")
=IF(C33="YES","5%","0%")
=IF(C34="YES","5%","0%")
=IF(C35="YES","5%","0%")
=IF(C36="YES","5%","0%")
=IF(C37="YES","5%","0%")
=IF(C38="YES","5%","0%")

Page 2

EL1-C2-P4-CMPReports.xlsx, Formulas

Model Answers

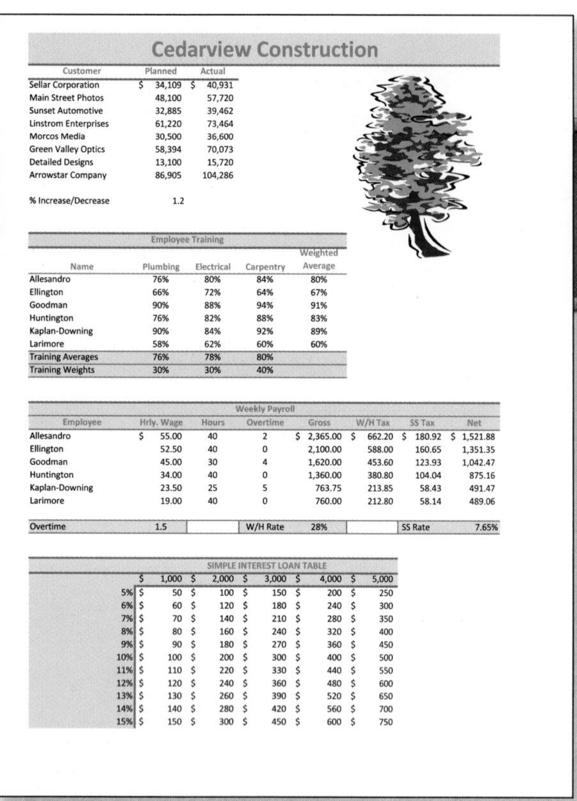

Cedarview Construction

Customer	Planned	Actual
Sellar Corporation	$ 34,109	$ 40,931
Main Street Photos	48,100	57,720
Sunset Automotive	32,885	39,462
Linstrom Enterprises	61,220	73,464
Morcos Media	30,500	36,600
Green Valley Optics	58,394	70,073
Detailed Designs	13,100	15,720
Arrowstar Company	86,905	104,286
% Increase/Decrease	1.2	

Employee Training				
Name	Plumbing	Electrical	Carpentry	Weighted Average
Allesandro	76%	80%	84%	80%
Ellington	66%	72%	64%	67%
Goodman	90%	88%	94%	91%
Huntington	76%	82%	88%	83%
Kaplan-Downing	90%	84%	92%	89%
Larimore	58%	62%	60%	60%
Training Averages	76%	78%	80%	
Training Weights	30%	30%	40%	

Weekly Payroll							
Employee	Hrly. Wage	Hours	Overtime	Gross	W/H Tax	SS Tax	Net
Allesandro	$ 55.00	40	2	$ 2,365.00	$ 662.20	$ 180.92	$ 1,521.88
Ellington	52.50	40	0	2,100.00	588.00	160.65	1,351.35
Goodman	45.00	30	4	1,620.00	453.60	123.93	1,042.47
Huntington	34.00	40	0	1,360.00	380.80	104.04	875.16
Kaplan-Downing	23.50	25	5	763.75	213.85	58.43	491.47
Larimore	19.00	40	0	760.00	212.80	58.14	489.06
Overtime	1.5		W/H Rate	28%		SS Rate	7.65%

SIMPLE INTEREST LOAN TABLE					
	$ 1,000	$ 2,000	$ 3,000	$ 4,000	$ 5,000
5%	$ 50	$ 100	$ 150	$ 200	$ 250
6%	$ 60	$ 120	$ 180	$ 240	$ 300
7%	$ 70	$ 140	$ 210	$ 280	$ 350
8%	$ 80	$ 160	$ 240	$ 320	$ 400
9%	$ 90	$ 180	$ 270	$ 360	$ 450
10%	$ 100	$ 200	$ 300	$ 400	$ 500
11%	$ 110	$ 220	$ 330	$ 440	$ 550
12%	$ 120	$ 240	$ 360	$ 480	$ 600
13%	$ 130	$ 260	$ 390	$ 520	$ 650
14%	$ 140	$ 280	$ 420	$ 560	$ 700
15%	$ 150	$ 300	$ 450	$ 600	$ 750

Project 5 Insert Formulas Using Absolute and Mixed Cell References EL1-C2-P5-CCReports.xlsx

Project 1 Insert Formulas in a Worksheet — 4 Parts

You will open a worksheet containing data and then insert formulas to calculate differences, salaries, and percentages of budgets.

Writing Formulas with Mathematical Operators

HINT

After typing a formula in a cell, press the Enter key, the Tab key, Shift + Tab, or click the Enter button on the Formula bar.

As you learned in Chapter 1, the AutoSum button in the Editing group in the Home tab creates the formula for you. You can also write your own formulas using ***mathematical operators***. Commonly used mathematical operators and their functions are displayed in Table 2.1. When writing your own formula, begin the formula with the equals sign (=). For example, to create a formula that divides the contents of cell B2 by the contents of cell C2 and inserts the result in cell D2, you would make D2 the active cell and then type =B2/C2.

If a formula contains two or more operators, Excel uses the same order of operations used in algebra. From left to right in a formula, this order, called the ***order of operations***, is: negations (negative number — a number preceded by -) first, then percents (%), then exponentiations (^), followed by multiplications (*), divisions (/), additions (+), and finally subtractions (-). If you want to change the order of operations, use parentheses around the part of the formula you want calculated first.

Table 2.1 Mathematical Operators

Operator	*Function*
+	Addition
-	Subtraction
*	Multiplication
/	Division
%	Percent
^	Exponentiation

Copying a Formula with Relative Cell References

In many worksheets, the same basic formula is used repetitively. In a situation where a formula is copied to other locations in a worksheet, use a ***relative cell reference***. Copy a formula containing relative cell references and the cell references change. For example, if you enter the formula *=SUM(A2:C2)* in cell D2 and then copy it relatively to cell D3, the formula in cell D3 displays as *=SUM(A3:C3)*. (Additional information on cell references is discussed later in this chapter in the "Using an Absolute Cell Reference in a Formula" section.)

To copy a formula relatively in a worksheet, use the Fill button or the fill handle. (You used the fill handle to copy a formula in Chapter 1.) To use the Fill button, select the cell containing the formula as well as the cells to which you want the formula copied and then click the Fill button in the Editing group in the Home tab. At the Fill button drop-down list, click the desired direction. For example, if you are copying the formula down cells, click the *Down* option.

Quick Steps

Copy Relative Formula

1. Insert formula in cell.
2. Select cell containing formula and all cells you want to contain formula.
3. Click Fill button.
4. Click desired direction.

Fill

Project 1a **Finding Differences by Inserting and Copying a Formula** Part 1 of 4

1. Open **HCReports.xlsx**.
2. Save the workbook with Save As and name it **EL1-C2-P1-HCReports**.
3. Insert a formula by completing the following steps:
   a. Make cell D3 active.
   b. Type the formula =C3-B3.
   c. Press Enter.
4. Copy the formula to cells D4 through D10 by completing the following steps:
   a. Select cells D3 through D10.
   b. Click the Fill button in the Editing group in the Home tab and then click *Down* at the drop-down list.
5. Save **EL1-C2-P1-HCReports.xlsx**.
6. With the worksheet open, make the following changes to cell contents:

   B4: Change *48,290* to *46425*
   C6: Change *61,220* to *60000*
   B8: Change *55,309* to *57415*
   B9: Change *12,398* to *14115*

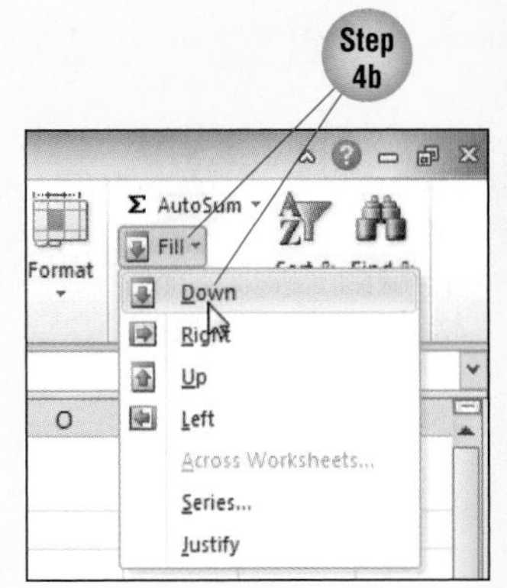

7. Make cell D3 active, apply the Accounting Number Format, and decrease the decimal point by two positions.
8. Save **EL1-C2-P1-HCReports.xlsx**.

Copying Formulas with the Fill Handle

Use the fill handle to copy a relative version of a formula.

Use the fill handle to copy a formula up, down, left, or right within a worksheet. To use the fill handle, insert the desired data in the cell (text, value, formula, etc.). With the cell active, position the mouse pointer on the fill handle until the mouse pointer turns into a thin, black cross. Hold down the left mouse button, drag and select the desired cells, and then release the mouse button. If you are dragging a cell containing a formula, a relative version of the formula is copied to the selected cells.

Project 1b Calculating Salary by Inserting and Copying a Formula with the Fill Handle

Part 2 of 4

1. With **EL1-C2-P1-HCReports.xlsx** open, insert a formula by completing the following steps:
   a. Make cell D15 active.
   b. Click in the Formula bar text box and then type =C15*B15.
   c. Click the Enter button on the Formula bar.
2. Copy the formula to cells D16 through D20 by completing the following steps:
   a. Make sure cell D15 is the active cell.
   b. Position the mouse pointer on the fill handle that displays at the lower right corner of cell D15 until the pointer turns into a thin, black cross.
   c. Hold down the left mouse button, drag down to cell D20, and then release the mouse button.
3. Save **EL1-C2-P1-HCReports.xlsx**.
4. With the worksheet still open, make the following changes to cell contents:
   B16: Change *20* to *28*
   C17: Change *18.75* to *19.10*
   B19: Change *15* to *24*
5. Select cells D16 through D20 and then apply the Comma Style.
6. Save **EL1-C2-P1-HCReports.xlsx**.

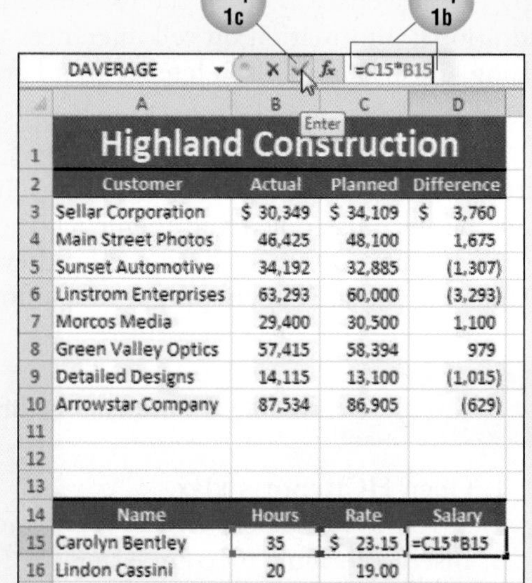

	Name	Hours	Rate	Salary
13				
14	Name	Hours	Rate	Salary
15	Carolyn Bentley	35	$ 23.15	$ 810.25
16	Lindon Cassini	20	19.00	$ 380.00
17	Michelle DeFord	40	18.75	$ 750.00
18	Javier Farias	24	16.45	$ 394.80
19	Deborah Gould	15	11.50	$ 172.50
20	William Jarman	15	11.50	$ 172.50
21				

Step 2c

Writing a Formula by Pointing

In Project 1a and Project 1b, you wrote formulas using cell references such as *=C3-B3*. Another method for writing a formula is to "point" to the specific cells that are to be part of the formula. Creating a formula by pointing is more accurate than typing the cell reference since a mistake can happen when typing the cell reference.

To write a formula by pointing, click the cell that will contain the formula, type the equals sign to begin the formula, and then click the cell you want to reference in the formula. This inserts a moving border around the cell and also changes the mode from Enter to Point. (The word *Point* displays at the left side of the Status bar.) Type the desired mathematical operator and then click the next cell reference. Continue in this manner until all cell references are specified and then press the Enter key. This ends the formula and inserts the result of the calculation of the formula in the active cell. When writing a formula by pointing, you can also select a range of cells you want included in a formula.

Quick Steps

Write Formula by Pointing

1. Click cell that will contain formula.
2. Type equals sign.
3. Click cell you want to reference in formula.
4. Type desired mathematical operator.
5. Click next cell reference.

Project 1c **Writing a Formula by Pointing that Calculates Percentage of Actual Budget**

Part 3 of 4

1. With **EL1-C2-P1-HCReports.xlsx** open, enter a formula by pointing that calculates the percentage of actual budget by completing the following steps:
   a. Make cell D25 active.
   b. Type the equals sign.
   c. Click cell C25. (This inserts a moving border around the cell and the mode changes from Enter to Point.)
   d. Type the forward slash symbol (/).
   e. Click cell B25.
   f. Make sure the formula in D25 is *=C25/B25* and then press Enter.
2. Make cell D25 active, position the mouse pointer on the fill handle, drag down to cell D31, and then release the mouse button.
3. Save **EL1-C2-P1-HCReports.xlsx**.

	A	B	C	D	E
22					
23					
24	Expense	Actual	Budget	% of Actual	
25	Salaries	$126,000	$124,000	=C25/B25	
26	Commissions	58,000	54,500		
27	Media space	8,250	10,100		
28	Travel expenses	6,350	6,000		
29	Dealer display	4,140	4,500		
30	Payroll taxes	2,430	2,200		
31	Telephone	1,450	1,500		

Steps 1a-1e

C	D	E
Budget	% of Actual	
$124,000	98%	
54,500	94%	
10,100	122%	
6,000	94%	
4,500	109%	
2,200	91%	
1,500	103%	

Step 2

Using the Trace Error Button

Trace Error

As you are working in a worksheet, you may occasionally notice a button pop up near the active cell. The general term for this button is ***smart tag***. The display of the smart tag button varies depending on the action performed. In Project 1d, you will insert a formula that will cause a smart tag button, named the Trace Error button, to appear. When the Trace Error button appears, a small dark green triangle also displays in the upper left corner of the cell. Click the Trace Error button and a drop-down list displays with options for updating the formula to include specific cells, getting help on the error, ignoring the error, editing the error in the Formula bar, and completing an error check. In Project 1d, two of the formulas you insert return the desired results. You will click the Trace Error button, read information on what Excel perceives as the error, and then tell Excel to ignore the error.

Project 1d Writing a Formula by Pointing that Calculates Percentage of Down Time

Part 4 of 4

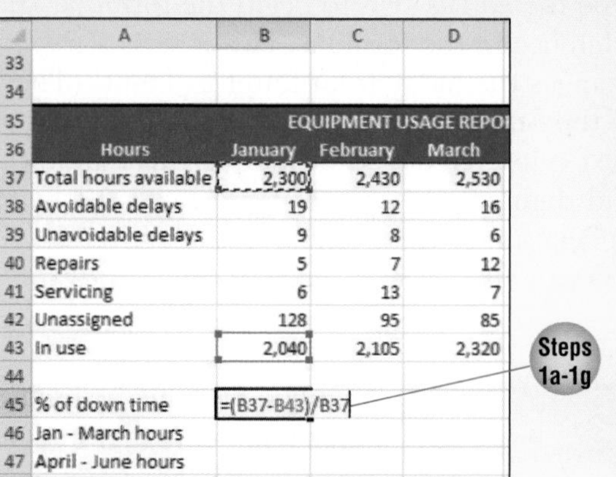

	A	B	C	D
33				
34				
35		EQUIPMENT USAGE REPOI		
36	Hours	January	February	March
37	Total hours available	2,300	2,430	2,530
38	Avoidable delays	19	12	16
39	Unavoidable delays	9	8	6
40	Repairs	5	7	12
41	Servicing	6	13	7
42	Unassigned	128	95	85
43	In use	2,040	2,105	2,320
44				
45	% of down time	=(B37-B43)/B37		
46	Jan - March hours			
47	April - June hours			

1. With **EL1-C2-P1-HCReports.xlsx** open, enter a formula by pointing that computes the percentage of equipment down time by completing the following steps:
   a. Make cell B45 active.
   b. Type the equals sign followed by the left parenthesis (=().
   c. Click cell B37. (This inserts a moving border around the cell and the mode changes from Enter to Point.)
   d. Type the minus symbol (-).
   e. Click cell B43.
   f. Type the right parenthesis followed by the forward slash ()/).
   g. Click cell B37.
   h. Make sure the formula in B45 is *=(B37-B43)/B37* and then press Enter.
2. Make cell B45 active, position the mouse pointer on the fill handle, drag across to cell G45, and then release the mouse button.
3. Enter a formula by dragging through a range of cells by completing the following steps:
   a. Click in cell B46 and then click the AutoSum button in the Editing group in the Home tab.
   b. Select cells B37 through D37.
   c. Click the Enter button on the Formula bar. (This inserts *7,260* in cell B46.)

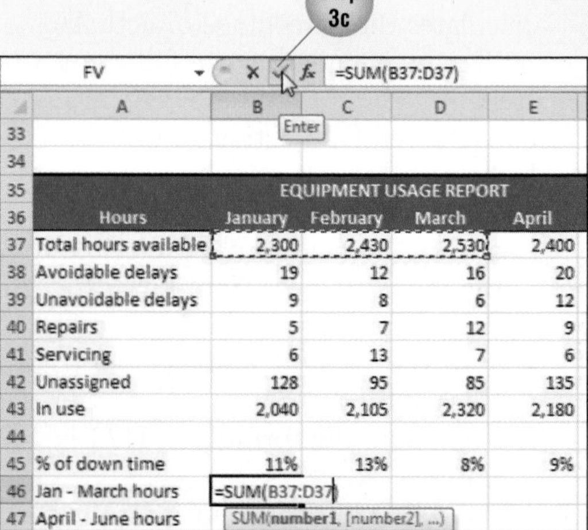

	A	B	C	D	E
33					
34					
35		EQUIPMENT USAGE REPORT			
36	Hours	January	February	March	April
37	Total hours available	2,300	2,430	2,530	2,400
38	Avoidable delays	19	12	16	20
39	Unavoidable delays	9	8	6	12
40	Repairs	5	7	12	9
41	Servicing	6	13	7	6
42	Unassigned	128	95	85	135
43	In use	2,040	2,105	2,320	2,180
44					
45	% of down time	11%	13%	8%	9%
46	Jan - March hours	=SUM(B37:D37)			
47	April - June hours	SUM(number1, [number2], ...)			

4. Click in cell B47 and then complete steps similar to those in Step 3 to create a formula that totals hours available from April through June (cells E37 through G37). (This inserts *7,080* in cell B47.)
5. Click in cell B46 and notice the Trace Error button that displays. Complete the following steps to read about the error and then tell Excel to ignore the error:
   a. Click the Trace Error button.
   b. At the drop-down list that displays, click the *Help on this error* option.
   c. Read the information that displays in the Excel Help window and then close the window.
   d. Click the Trace Error button again and then click *Ignore Error* at the drop-down list.

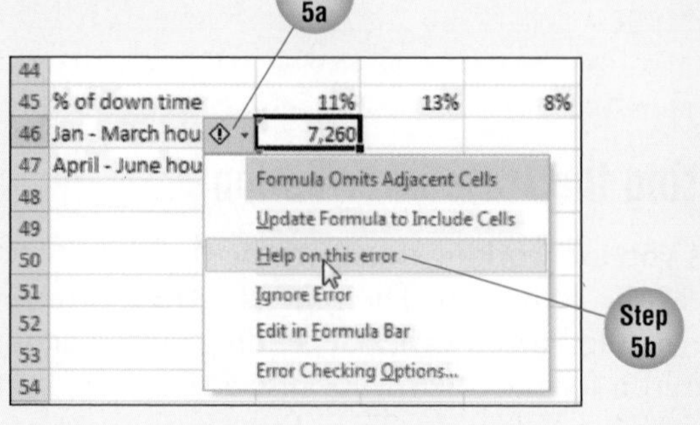

6. Remove the dark green triangle from cell B47 by completing the following steps:
   a. Click in cell B47.
   b. Click the Trace Error button and then click *Ignore Error* at the drop-down list.
7. Save, print, and then close **EL1-C2-P1-HCReports.xlsx**.

Project 2 Insert Formulas with Statistical Functions — 4 Parts

You will use the AVERAGE function to determine average test scores, use the MINIMUM and MAXIMUM functions to determine lowest and highest averages, use the COUNT function to count number of students taking a test, and display formulas in a cell rather than the result of the formula.

Inserting Formulas with Functions

In Project 2a in Chapter 1, you used the AutoSum button to insert the formula *=SUM(B2:B5)* in a cell. The beginning section of the formula, *=SUM*, is called a ***function***, which is a built-in formula. Using a function takes fewer keystrokes when creating a formula. For example, the *=SUM* function saved you from having to type each cell to be included in the formula with the plus (+) symbol between cell entries.

Excel provides other functions for writing formulas. A function operates on what is referred to as an ***argument***. An argument may consist of a constant, a cell reference, or another function. In the formula *=SUM(B2:B5)*, the cell range *(B2:B5)* is an example of a cell reference argument. An argument may also contain a ***constant***. A constant is a value entered directly into the formula. For example, if you enter the formula *=SUM(B3:B9,100)*, the cell range *B3:B9* is a cell reference argument and *100* is a constant. In this formula, 100 is always added to the sum of the cells.

When a value calculated by the formula is inserted in a cell, this process is referred to as ***returning the result***. The term *returning* refers to the process of calculating the formula and the term *result* refers to inserting the value in the cell.

Insert Function

You can type a function in a cell in a worksheet or you can use the Insert Function button on the Formula bar or in the Formulas tab to help you write the formula. Figure 2.1 displays the Formulas tab. The Formulas tab provides the Insert Function button as well as other buttons for inserting functions in a worksheet. The Function Library group in the Formulas tab contains a number of buttons for inserting functions from a variety of categories such as Financial, Logical, Text, and Date & Time.

Click the Insert Function button on the Formula bar or in the Formulas tab and the Insert Function dialog box displays as shown in Figure 2.2. At the

Figure 2.1 Formulas Tab

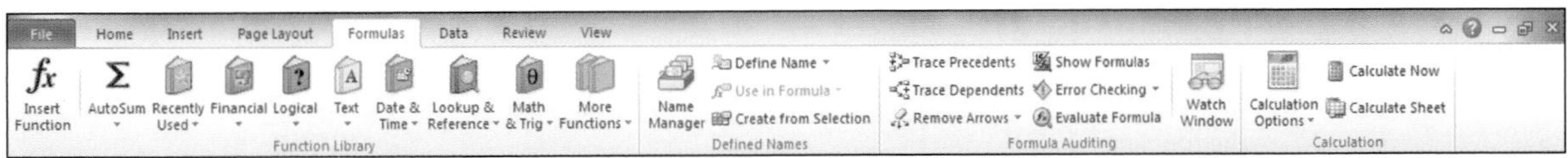

Figure 2.2 Insert Function Dialog Box

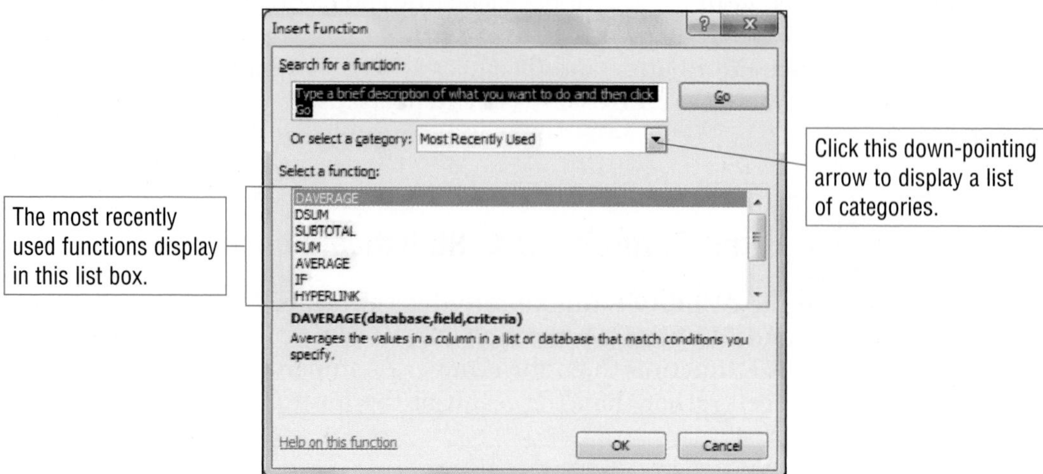

You can also display the Insert Function dialog box by clicking the down-pointing arrow at the right side of the AutoSum button and then clicking *More Functions.*

Click the AutoSum button arrow in the Formulas tab and common functions display in a drop-down list.

Insert Function dialog box, the most recently used functions display in the *Select a function* list box. You can choose a function category by clicking the down-pointing arrow at the right side of the *Or select a category* list box and then clicking the desired category at the drop-down list. Use the *Search for a function* option to locate a specific function.

With the desired function category selected, choose a function in the *Select a function* list box and then click OK. This displays a Function Arguments palette like the one shown in Figure 2.3. At this palette, enter in the *Number1* text box the range of cells you want included in the formula, enter any constants that are to be included as part of the formula, or enter another function. After entering a range of cells, a constant, or another function, click the OK button. You can include more than one argument in a function. If the function you are creating contains more than one argument, press the Tab key to move the insertion point to the *Number2* text box, and then enter the second argument. If you need to display a specific cell or cells behind the function palette, move the palette by clicking and dragging it.

Figure 2.3 Example Function Arguments Palette

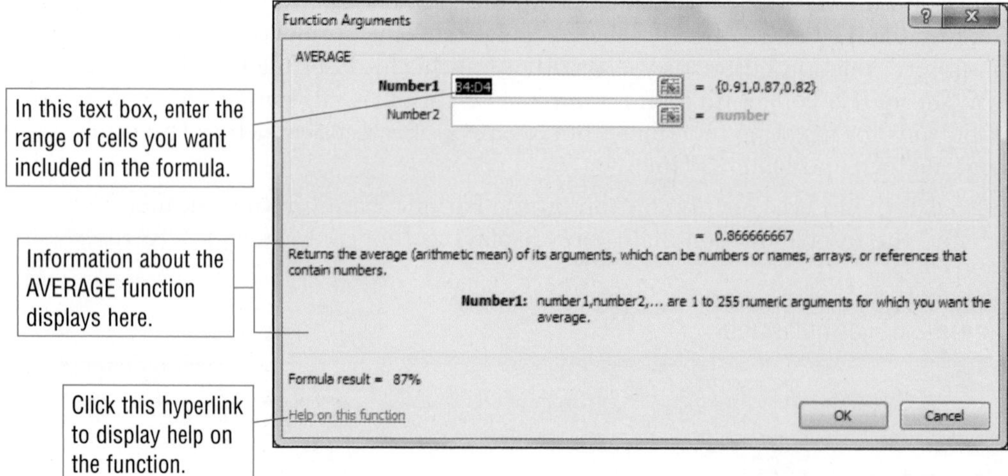

Excel includes over 200 functions that are divided into twelve different categories including *Financial*, *Date & Time*, *Math & Trig*, *Statistical*, *Lookup & Reference*, *Database*, *Text*, *Logical*, *Information*, *Engineering*, *Cube*, and *Compatibility*. Clicking the AutoSum button in the Function Library group in the Formulas tab or the Editing group in the Home tab automatically adds numbers with the SUM function. The SUM function is included in the *Math & Trig* category. In some projects in this chapter, you will write formulas with functions in other categories including *Statistical*, *Financial*, *Date & Time*, and *Logical*.

Excel includes the Formula AutoComplete feature that displays a drop-down list of functions. To use this feature, click in the desired cell or click in the Formula bar text box, type the equals sign (=), and then type the first letter of the desired function. This displays a drop-down list with functions that begin with the letter. Double-click the desired function, enter the cell references, and then press Enter.

Writing Formulas with Statistical Functions

In this section, you will learn to write formulas with the statistical functions AVERAGE, MAX, MIN, and COUNT. The AVERAGE function returns the average (arithmetic mean) of the arguments. The MAX function returns the largest value in a set of values and the MIN function returns the smallest value in a set of values. Use the COUNT function to count the number of cells that contain numbers within the list of arguments.

Finding Averages

A common function in a formula is the AVERAGE function. With this function, a range of cells is added together and then divided by the number of cell entries. In Project 2a you will use the AVERAGE function, which will add all of the test scores for a student and then divide that number by the total number of tests. You will use the Insert Function button to simplify the creation of the formula containing an AVERAGE function.

One of the advantages to using formulas in a worksheet is the ability to easily manipulate data to answer certain questions. In Project 2a you will learn the impact of retaking certain tests on the final average score.

Project 2a **Averaging Test Scores in a Worksheet** Part 1 of 4

1. Open **DWTests.xlsx**.
2. Save the workbook with Save As and name it **EL1-C2-P2-DWTests**.
3. Use the Insert Function button to find the average of test scores by completing the following steps:
   a. Make cell E4 active.
   b. Click the Insert Function button on the Formula bar.

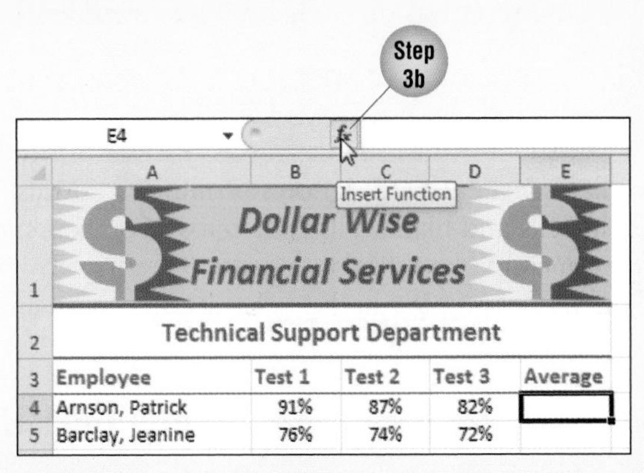

c. At the Insert Function dialog box, click the down-pointing arrow at the right side of the *Or select a category* list box and then click *Statistical* at the drop-down list.
d. Click *AVERAGE* in the *Select a function* list box.
e. Click OK.
f. At the Function Arguments palette, make sure *B4:D4* displays in the *Number1* text box. (If not, type B4:D4 in the *Number1* text box.)
g. Click OK.

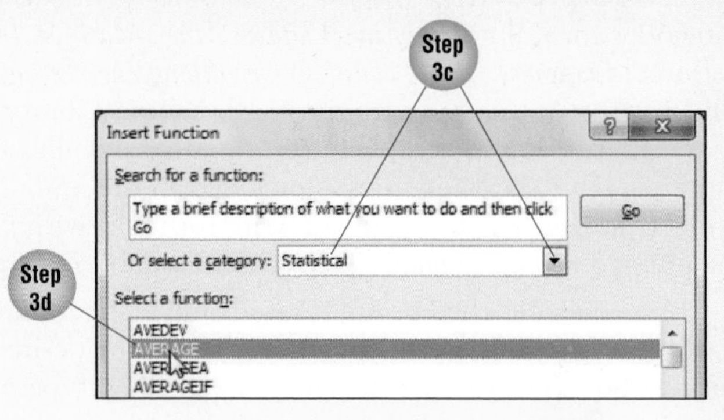

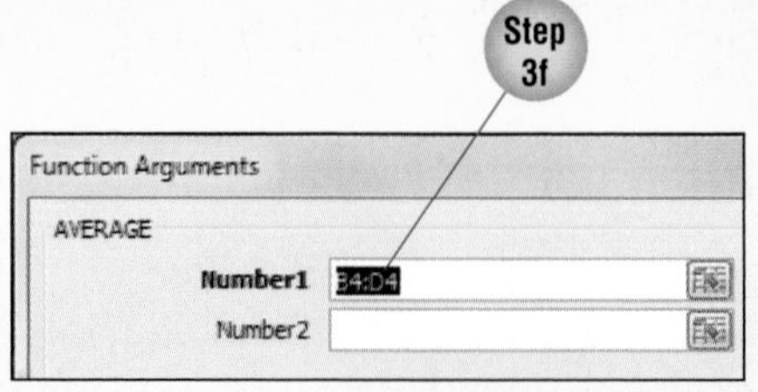

4. Copy the formula by completing the following steps:
   a. Make sure cell E4 is active.
   b. Position the mouse pointer on the fill handle until the pointer turns into a thin black cross.
   c. Hold down the left mouse button, drag down to cell E16, and then release the mouse button.
5. Save and then print **EL1-C2-P2-DWTests.xlsx**.
6. After viewing the averages of test scores, you notice that a couple of people have a low average. You decide to see what happens to the average score if students make up tests where they scored the lowest. You decide that a student can score a maximum of 70% on a retake of the test. Make the following changes to test scores to see how the changes will affect the test average.
   B9: Change *50* to *70*
   C9: Change *52* to *70*
   D9: Change *60* to *70*
   B10: Change *62* to *70*
   B14: Change *0* to *70*
   D14: Change *0* to *70*
   D16: Change *0* to *70*
7. Save and then print **EL1-C2-P2-DWTests.xlsx**. (Compare the test averages for Teri Fisher-Edwards, Stephanie Flanery, Claude Markovits, and Douglas Pherson to see what the effect of retaking the tests has on their final test averages.)

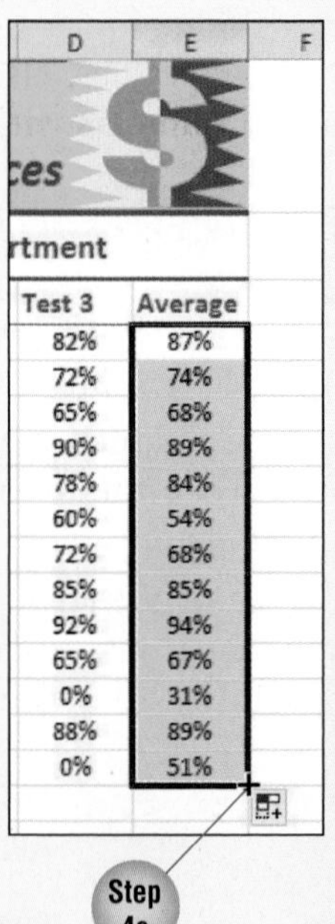

When a formula such as the AVERAGE formula you inserted in a cell in Project 2a calculates cell entries, it ignores certain cell entries. The AVERAGE function will ignore text in cells and blank cells (not zeros). For example, in the worksheet containing test scores, a couple of cells contained a *0%* entry. This entry was included in the averaging of the test scores. If you did not want that particular test to be included in the average, enter text in the cell such as *N/A* (for *not applicable*) or leave the cell blank.

Finding Maximum and Minimum Values

The MAX function in a formula returns the maximum value in a cell range and the MIN function returns the minimum value in a cell range. As an example, you could use the MAX and MIN functions in a worksheet containing employee hours to determine which employee worked the most number of hours and which worked the least. In a worksheet containing sales commissions, you could use the MAX and MIN functions to determine the salesperson who earned the most commission dollars and the one who earned the least.

Insert a MAX and MIN function into a formula in the same manner as an AVERAGE function. In Project 2b, you will use the Formula AutoComplete feature to insert the MAX function in cells to determine the highest test score average and the Insert Function button to insert the MIN function to determine the lowest test score average.

Project 2b Finding Maximum and Minimum Values in a Worksheet

Part 2 of 4

1. With **EL1-C2-P2-DWTests.xlsx** open, type the following in the specified cells:
   A19: Highest Test Average
   A20: Lowest Test Average
   A21: Average of All Tests

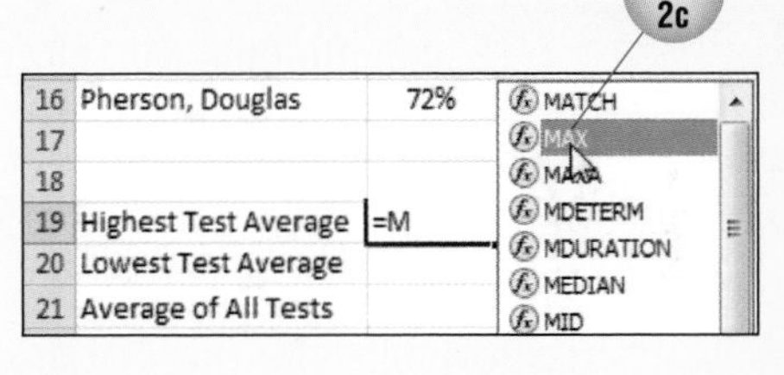

2. Insert a formula to identify the highest test score average by completing the following steps:
   a. Make cell B19 active.
   b. Type =M. (This displays the Formula AutoComplete list.)
   c. Double-click *MAX* in the Formula AutoComplete list.
   d. Type E4:E16) and then press Enter.

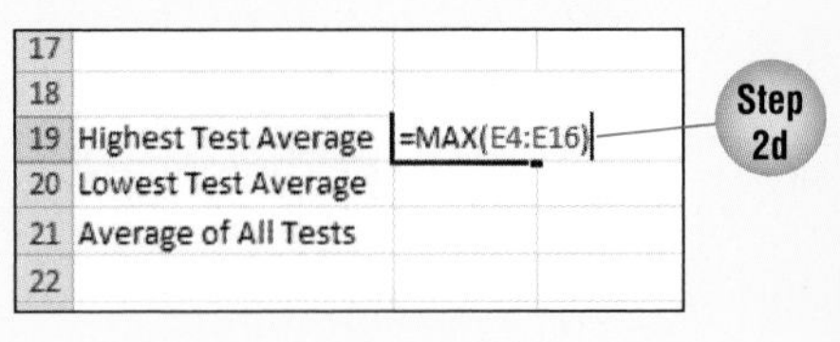

3. Insert a formula to identify the lowest test score average by completing the following steps:
   a. Make cell B20 active.
   b. Click the Insert Function button on the Formula bar.
   c. At the Insert Function dialog box, make sure *Statistical* is selected in the *Or select a category* list box, and then click *MIN* in the *Select a function* list box. (You will need to scroll down the list to display *MIN*.)
   d. Click OK.
   e. At the Function Arguments palette, type E4:E16 in the *Number1* text box.
   f. Click OK.

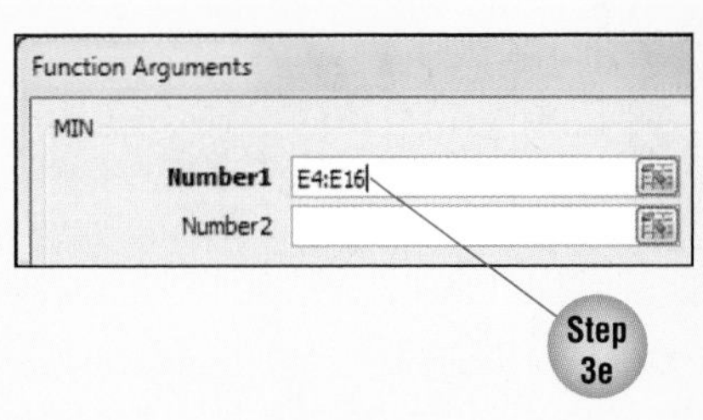

4. Insert a formula to determine the average of all test scores by completing the following steps:
   a. Make cell B21 active.
   b. Click the Formulas tab.
   c. Click the Insert Function button in the Function Library group.
   d. At the Insert Function dialog box, make sure *Statistical* is selected in the *Or select a category* list box and then click *AVERAGE* in the *Select a function* list box.
   e. Click OK.
   f. At the Function Arguments palette, type E4:E16 in the *Number1* text box, and then click OK.

5. Save and then print **EL1-C2-P2-DWTests.xlsx**.
6. Change the *70%* values (which were previously *0%*) in cells B14, D14, and D16 to *N/A*. (This will cause the average of test scores for Claude Markovits and Douglas Pherson to increase and will change the minimum number and average of all test scores.)
7. Save and then print **EL1-C2-P2-DWTests.xlsx**.

Counting Numbers in a Range

Use the COUNT function to count the numeric values in a range. For example, in a range of cells containing cells with text and cells with numbers, you can count how many cells in the range contain numbers. In Project 2c, you will use the COUNT function to specify the number of students taking Test 2 and Test 3. In the worksheet, the cells containing the text N/A are not counted by the COUNT function.

Project 2c **Counting the Number of Students Taking Tests** Part 3 of 4

1. With **EL1-C2-P2-DWTests.xlsx** open, make cell A22 active.
2. Type Test 2 Completed.
3. Make cell B22 active.
4. Insert a formula counting the number of students who have taken Test 2 by completing the following steps:
   a. With cell B22 active, click in the Formula bar text box.
   b. Type =C.
   c. At the Formula AutoComplete list that displays, scroll down the list until *COUNT* displays and then double-click *COUNT*.
   d. Type C4:C16) and then press Enter.

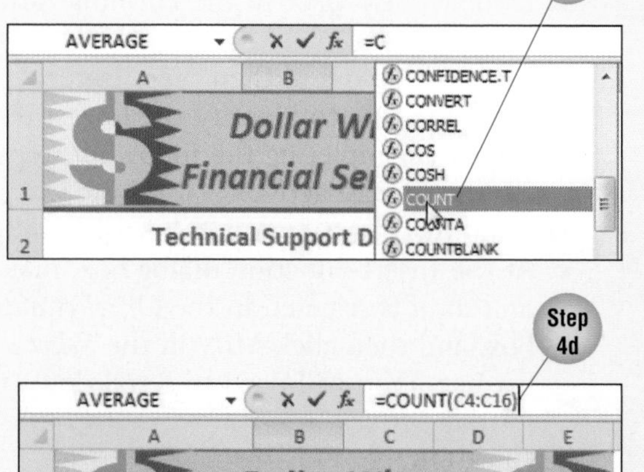

5. Count the number of students who have taken Test 3 by completing the following steps:
   a. Make cell A23 active.
   b. Type Test 3 Completed.
   c. Make cell B23 active.
   d. Click the Insert Function button on the Formula bar.
   e. At the Insert Function dialog box, make sure *Statistical* is selected in the *Or select a category* list box.
   f. Scroll down the list of functions in the *Select a function* list box until *COUNT* is visible and then double-click *COUNT*.
   g. At the formula palette, type D4:D16 in the *Value1* text box and then click OK.
6. Save and then print **EL1-C2-P2-DWTests.xlsx**.
7. Add test scores by completing the following steps:
   a. Make cell B14 active and then type 68.
   b. Make cell D14 active and then type 70.
   c. Make cell D16 active and then type 55.
   d. Press Enter.
8. Save and then print **EL1-C2-P2-DWTests.xlsx**.

Displaying Formulas

In some situations, you may need to display the formulas in a worksheet rather than the results of the formula. You may want to turn on formulas for auditing purposes or check formulas for accuracy. Display all formulas in a worksheet rather than the results by pressing Ctrl + ` (this is the grave accent, generally located to the left of the 1 key on the keyboard). Press Ctrl + ` to turn off the display of formulas.

Press Ctrl + ` to display formulas in a worksheet rather than the results.

Displaying Formulas Part 4 of 4

1. With **EL1-C2-P2-DWTests.xlsx** open, make cell A3 active.
2. Press Ctrl + ` to turn on the display of formulas.
3. Print the worksheet with the formulas. (The worksheet will print on two pages.)
4. Press Ctrl + ` to turn off the display of formulas.
5. Save and then close **EL1-C2-P2-DWTests.xlsx**.

Project 3 **Insert Formulas with Financial and Date and Time Functions** **3 Parts**

You will use the PMT financial function to calculate payments and the FV function to find the future value of an investment. You will also use the DATE function to return the serial number for a date and the NOW function to insert the current date and time as a serial number.

Writing Formulas with Financial Functions

In this section, you will learn to write formulas with the financial functions PMT and FV. The PMT function calculates the payment for a loan based on constant payments and a constant interest rate. Use the FV function to return the future value of an investment.

Finding the Periodic Payments for a Loan

The PMT function finds the payment for a loan based on constant payments and a constant interest rate. The PMT function contains the arguments Rate, Nper, Pv, Fv, and Type. The Rate argument is the interest rate per period for a loan, the Nper is the number of payments that will be made to an investment or loan, Pv is the current value of amounts to be received or paid in the future, Fv is the value of a loan or investment at the end of all periods, and Type determines whether calculations will be based on payments made in arrears (at the end of each period) or in advance (at the beginning of each period).

Project 3a Calculating Payments

1. Open **RPReports.xlsx**.
2. Save the workbook with Save As and name it **EL1-C2-P3-RPReports**.
3. The owner of Real Photography is interested in purchasing a new developer and needs to determine monthly payments on three different models. Insert a formula that calculates monthly payments and then copy that formula by completing the following steps:
   a. Make cell E5 active.
   b. Click the Formulas tab.
   c. Click the Financial button in the Function Library group, scroll down the drop-down list until *PMT* displays, and then click *PMT*.
   d. At the Function Arguments palette, type C5/12 in the *Rate* text box. (This tells Excel to divide the interest rate by 12 months.)
   e. Press the Tab key. (This moves the insertion point to the *Nper* text box).
   f. Type D5. (This is the total number of months in the payment period.)
   g. Press the Tab key. (This moves the insertion point to the *Pv* text box.)
   h. Type -B5. (Excel displays the result of the PMT function as a negative number since the loan represents a negative cash flow to the borrower. Insert a minus sign before *B5* to show the monthly payment as a positive number rather than a negative number.)
   i. Click OK. (This closes the palette and inserts the monthly payment of *$316.98* in cell E5.)
   j. Copy the formula in cell E5 down to cells E6 and E7.

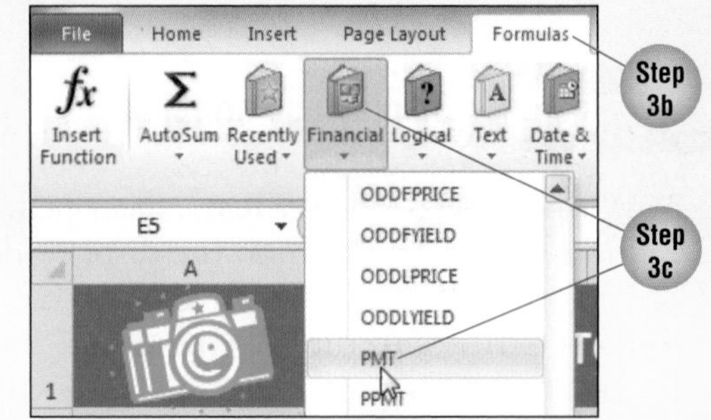

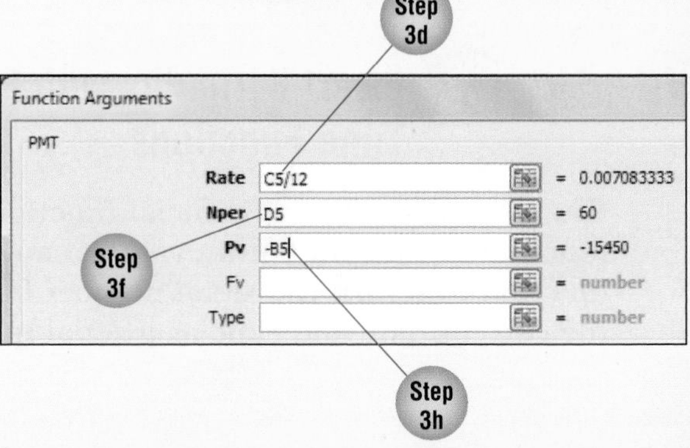

4. Insert a formula in cell F5 that calculates the total amount of the payments by completing the following steps:
   a. Make cell F5 active.
   b. Type =E5*D5 and then press Enter.
   c. Make cell F5 active and then copy the formula down to cells F6 and F7.
5. Insert a formula in cell G5 that calculates the total amount of interest paid by completing the following steps:
   a. Make cell G5 active.
   b. Type =F5-B5 and then press Enter.
   c. Make cell G5 active and then copy the formula down to cells G6 and G7.
6. Save **EL1-C2-P3-RPReports.xlsx**.

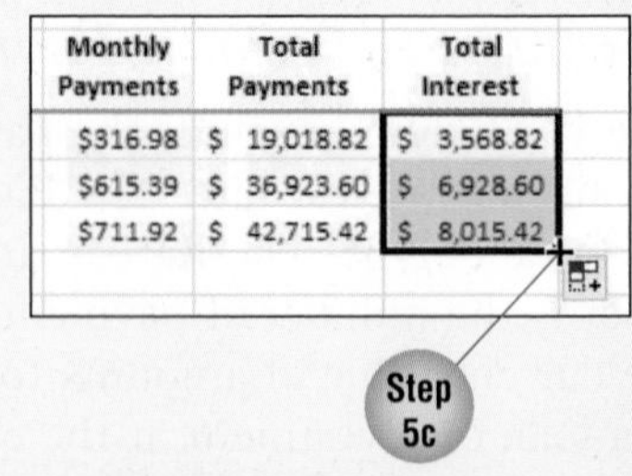

Monthly Payments	Total Payments	Total Interest
$316.98	$ 19,018.82	$ 3,568.82
$615.39	$ 36,923.60	$ 6,928.60
$711.92	$ 42,715.42	$ 8,015.42

Finding the Future Value of a Series of Payments

The FV function calculates the future value of a series of equal payments or an annuity. Use this function to determine information such as how much money can be earned in an investment account with a specific interest rate and over a specific period of time.

Project 3b Finding the Future Value of an Investment

Part 2 of 3

1. Make sure **EL1-C2-P3-RPReports.xlsx** is open.
2. The owner of Real Photography has decided to save money to purchase a new developer and wants to compute how much money can be earned by investing the money in an investment account that returns 9% annual interest. The owner determines that $1,200 per month can be invested in the account for three years. Complete the following steps to determine the future value of the investment account by completing the following steps:
   a. Make cell B15 active.
   b. Click the Financial button in the Function Library group in the Formulas tab.
   c. At the drop-down list that displays, scroll down the list until *FV* is visible and then click *FV*.
   d. At the Function Arguments palette, type B12/12 in the *Rate* text box.
   e. Press the Tab key.
   f. Type B13 in the *Nper* text box.
   g. Press the Tab key.
   h. Type B14 in the *Pmt* text box.
   i. Click OK. (This closes the palette and also inserts the future value of *$49,383.26* in cell B15.)

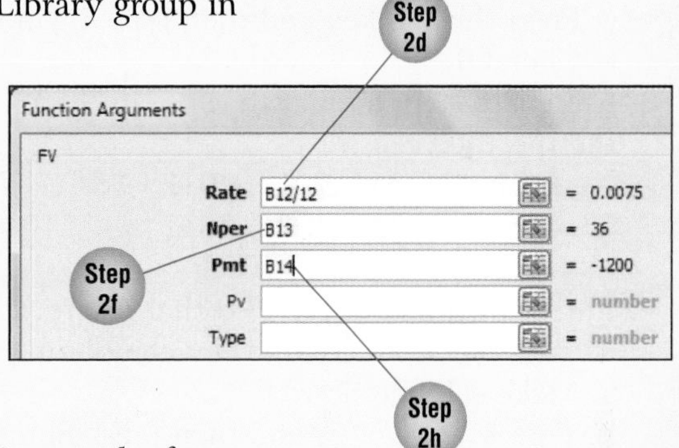

3. Save and then print **EL1-C2-P3-RPReports.xlsx**.
4. The owner decides to determine the future return after two years. To do this, change the amount in cell B13 from *36* to *24* and then press Enter. (This recalculates the future investment amount in cell B15.)
5. Save and then print **EL1-C2-P3-RPReports.xlsx**.

10		
11	Future Value of Investment	
12	Rate	9%
13	Number of Months	24
14	Monthly Payment	$ (1,200.00)
15	Future Value	$31,426.16
16		

Step 4

Writing Formulas with Date and Time Functions

In this section, you will learn to write formulas with the date and time functions NOW and DATE. The NOW function returns the serial number of the current date and time. The DATE function returns the serial number that represents a particular date. Excel can make calculations using dates because the dates are represented as serial numbers. To calculate a date's serial number, Excel counts the days since the beginning of the twentieth century. The date serial number for January 1, 1900, is 1. The date serial number for January 1, 2000, is 36,526. To access the DATE and NOW functions, click the Date & Time button in the Function Library group in the Formulas tab.

Ctrl + ; is the keyboard shortcut to insert the current date in the active cell.

Date & Time

Project 3c Using the DATE and NOW Functions

Part 3 of 3

1. Make sure **EL1-C2-P3-RPReports.xlsx** is open.
2. Certain cells in this worksheet establish overdue dates for Real Photography accounts. Enter a formula in cell D20 that returns the serial number for the date March 12, 2012, by completing the following steps:

a. Make cell D20 active.
b. Click the Formulas tab.
c. Click the Date & Time button in the Function Library group.
d. At the drop-down list that displays, click *DATE*.
e. At the Function Arguments palette, type 2012 in the *Year* text box.
f. Press the Tab key and then type 03 in the *Month* text box.
g. Press the Tab key and then type 12 in the *Day* text box.
h. Click OK.

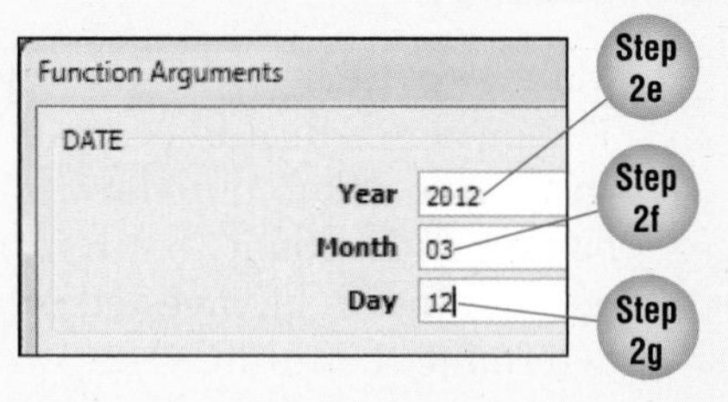

3. Complete steps similar to those in Step 2 to enter the following dates as serial numbers in the specified cells:
   D21 = March 19, 2012
   D22 = March 26, 2012
   D23 = April 2, 2012
4. Enter a formula in cell F20 that inserts the due date (the purchase date plus the number of days in the *Terms* column) by completing the following steps:
   a. Make cell F20 active.
   b. Type =D20+E20 and then press Enter.
   c. Make cell F20 active and then copy the formula down to cells F21, F22, and F23.

Purchase Date	Terms	Due Date
3/12/2012	30	4/11/2012
3/19/2012	15	4/3/2012
3/26/2012	15	4/10/2012
4/2/2012	30	5/2/2012

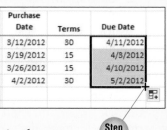

5. Make cell A26 active and then type your name.
6. Insert the current date and time as a serial number by completing the following steps:
   a. Make cell A27 active.
   b. Click the Date & Time button in the Function Library group in the Formulas tab and then click *NOW* at the drop-down list.
   c. At the Function Arguments palette telling you that the function takes no argument, click OK.
7. Save, print, and then close **EL1-C2-P3-RPReports.xlsx**.

Project 4 Insert Formulas with the IF Logical Function — 2 Parts

You will use the IF logical function to calculate sales bonuses, determine letter grades based on test averages, and identify discounts and discount amounts.

Writing a Formula with the IF Logical Function

The IF function is considered a ***conditional function***. With the IF function you can perform conditional tests on values and formulas. A question that can be answered with true or false is considered a ***logical test***. The IF function makes a logical test and then performs a particular action if the answer is true and another action if the answer is false.

For example, an IF function can be used to write a formula that calculates a salesperson's bonus as 10% if the quota of $100,000 is met or exceeded, and zero if the quota is less than $100,000. That formula would look like this: *=IF(quota=>100000,quota*0.1,0)*. The formula contains three parts—the condition or logical test, *IF(quota=>100000*, action taken if the condition or logical test is true, *quota*0.1*, and the action taken if the condition or logical test is false, *0*. Commas separate the condition and the actions. In the bonus formula, if the quota is equal to or greater than $100,000, then the quota is multiplied by 10%. If the quota is less than $100,000, then the bonus is zero.

In Project 4a, you will write a formula with cell references rather than cell data. The formula in Project 4a is *=IF(C5>B5,C5*0.15,0)*. In this formula the condition or logical test is whether or not the number in cell C5 is greater than the number in cell B5. If the condition is true and the number is greater, then the number in cell C5 is multiplied by 0.15 (providing a 15% bonus). If the condition is false and the number in cell C5 is less than the number in cell B5, then nothing happens (no bonus). Notice how commas are used to separate the logical test from the actions.

Editing a Formula

Edit a formula by making active the cell containing the formula and then editing the formula in the cell or in the Formula bar text box. After editing the formula, press Enter or click the Enter button on the Formula bar and Excel will recalculate the result of the formula.

Enter

Project 4a Writing a Formula with an IF Function and Editing the Formula

Part 1 of 2

1. Open **CMPReports.xlsx**.
2. Save the workbook with Save As and name it **EL1-C2-P4-CMPReports**.
3. Write a formula with the IF function by completing the following steps. (The formula will determine if the quota has been met and, if it has, will insert the bonus [15% of the actual sales]. If the quota has not been met, the formula will insert a zero.)
   a. Make cell D5 active.
   b. Type =IF(C5>B5,C5*0.15,0) and then press Enter.
   c. Make cell D5 active and then use the fill handle to copy the formula to cells D6 through D10.
4. Print the worksheet.
5. Revise the formula so it will insert a 25% bonus if the quota has been met by completing the following steps:
   a. Make cell D5 active.
   b. Click in the Formula bar, edit the formula so it displays as *=IF(C5>B5,C5*0.25,0)*, and then click the Enter button on the Formula bar.
   c. Copy the formula down to cells D6 through D10.
   d. Apply the Accounting Number Format to cell D5.

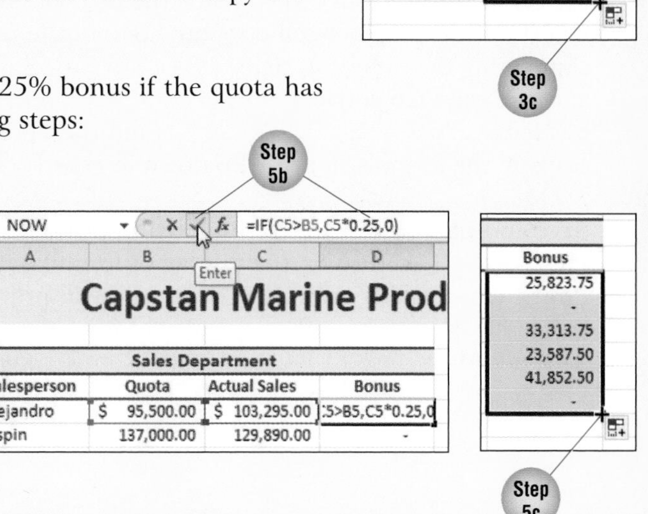

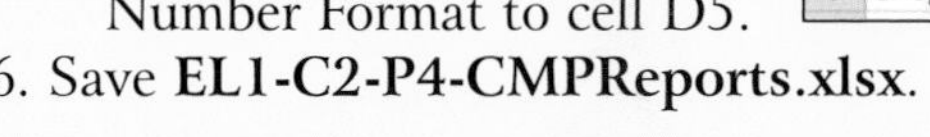
6. Save **EL1-C2-P4-CMPReports.xlsx**.

Writing IF Formulas Containing Text

If you write a formula with an IF function and you want text inserted in a cell rather than a value, you must insert quotation marks around the text. For example, in Project 4b, you will write a formula with an IF function that inserts the word *PASS* in a cell if the average of the new employee quizzes is greater than 79 and inserts the word *FAIL* if the condition is not met. To write this formula in Project 4b, you will type *=IF(E16>79,"PASS","FAIL")*. The quotation marks before and after PASS and FAIL identify the data as text rather than a value.

Project 4b Writing IF Statements with Text — Part 2 of 2

1. With **EL1-C2-P4-CMPReports.xlsx** open, insert quiz averages by completing the following steps:
   a. Make E16 active and then insert a formula that calculates the average of the test scores in cells B16 through D16.
   b. Copy the formula in cell E16 down to cells E17 through E20.

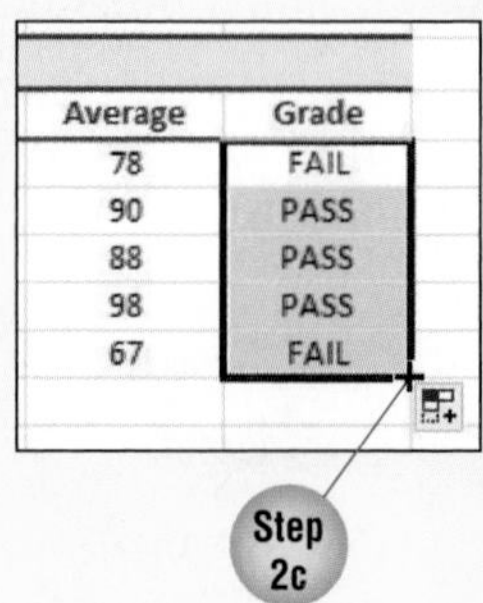

Average
Grade
78
FAIL
90
PASS
88
PASS
98
PASS
67
FAIL
Step 2c

2. Write a formula with an IF function that inserts the word *PASS* if the quiz average is greater than 79 and inserts the word *FAIL* if the quiz average is not greater than 79 by completing the following steps:
   a. Make cell F16 active.
   b. Type **=IF(E16>79,"PASS","FAIL")** and then press Enter.
   c. Copy the formula in cell F16 down to cells F17 through F20.
3. Write a formula with an IF function that inserts the word *YES* in the cell if the product price is greater than $599 and inserts the word *NO* if the price is not greater than $599 by completing the following steps:
   a. Make cell C26 active.
   b. Type **=IF(B26>599,"YES","NO")** and then press Enter.
   c. Copy the formula in cell C26 down to cells C27 through C38.

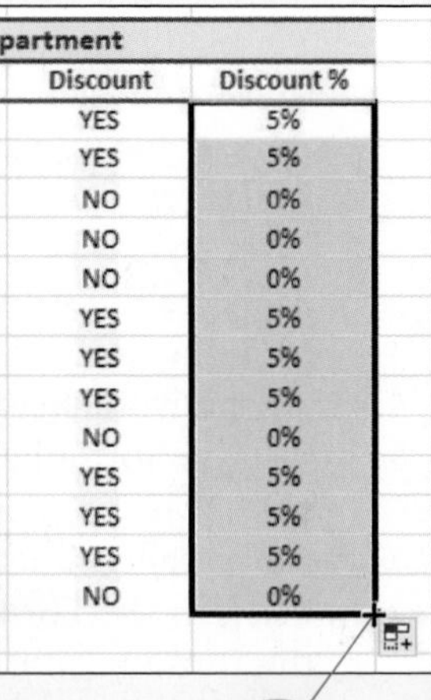

partment
Discount
Discount %
YES
5%
YES
5%
NO
0%
NO
0%
NO
0%
YES
5%
YES
5%
YES
5%
NO
0%
YES
5%
YES
5%
YES
5%
NO
0%
Step 4c

4. Write a formula with an IF function that inserts the text *5%* in the cell if the previous cell contains the text *YES* and inserts the text *0%* if the previous cell does not contain the text *YES* by completing the following steps:
   a. Make cell D26 active.
   b. Type **=IF(C26="YES","5%","0%")** and then press Enter.
   c. Copy the formula in cell D26 down to cells D27 through D38.
5. Save and then print **EL1-C2-P4-CMPReports.xlsx**.
6. Press Ctrl + ` to turn on the display of formulas.
7. Print the worksheet again (the worksheet will print on two pages).
8. Press Ctrl + ` to turn off the display of formulas.
9. Save and then close **EL1-C2-P4-CMPReports.xlsx**.

Project 5 Insert Formulas Using Absolute and Mixed Cell References

4 Parts

You will insert a formula containing an absolute cell reference that determines the effect on earnings with specific increases, insert a formula with multiple absolute cell references that determine the weighted average of scores, and use mixed cell references to determine simple interest.

Using Absolute and Mixed Cell References in Formulas

A reference identifies a cell or a range of cells in a worksheet and can be relative, absolute, or mixed. ***Relative cell references*** refer to cells relative to a position in a formula. ***Absolute cell references*** refer to cells in a specific location. When a formula is copied, a relative cell reference adjusts while an absolute cell reference remains constant. A ***mixed cell reference*** does both—either the column remains absolute and the row is relative or the column is relative and the row is absolute. Distinguish between relative, absolute, and mixed cell references using the dollar sign ($). Type a dollar sign before the column and/or row cell reference in a formula to specify that the column or row is an absolute cell reference.

Using an Absolute Cell Reference in a Formula

In this chapter you have learned to copy a relative formula. For example, if the formula *=SUM(A2:C2)* in cell D2 is copied relatively to cell D3, the formula changes to *=SUM(A3:C3)*. In some situations, you may want a formula to contain an absolute cell reference, which always refers to a cell in a specific location. In Project 5a, you will add a column for projected job earnings and then perform "what if" situations using a formula with an absolute cell reference. To identify an absolute cell reference, insert a $ sign before the row and the column. For example, the absolute cell reference C12 would be typed as *$C$12* in a formula.

Project 5a Inserting and Copying a Formula with an Absolute Cell Reference

Part 1 of 4

1. Open **CCReports.xlsx**.
2. Save the workbook with Save As and name it **EL1-C2-P5-CCReports**.
3. Determine the effect on actual job earnings with a 10% increase by completing the following steps:
   a. Make cell C3 active, type the formula =B3*$B$12, and then press Enter.
   b. Make cell C3 active and then use the fill handle to copy the formula to cells C4 through C10.

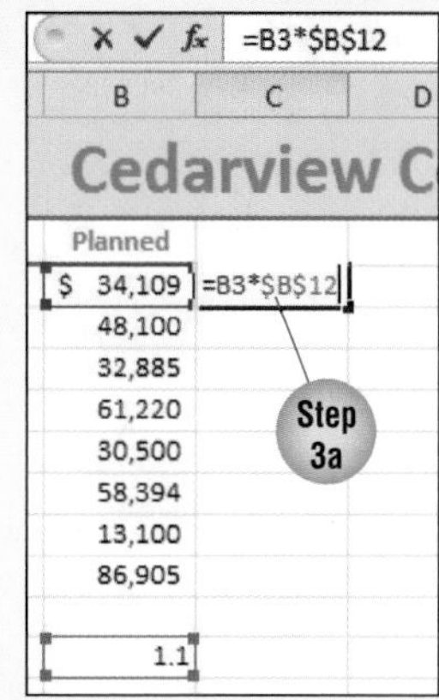

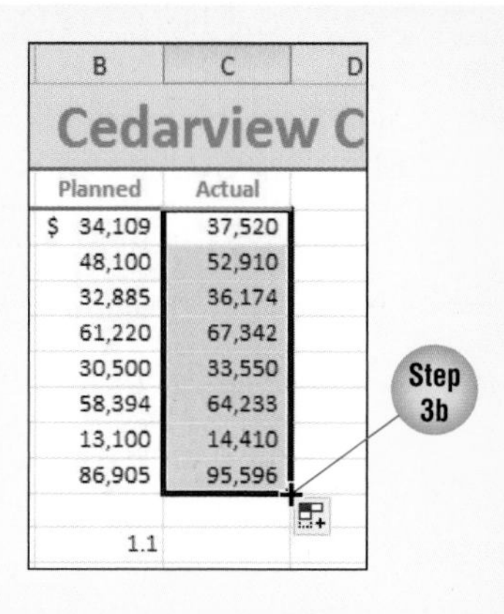

c. Make C3 active, click the Accounting Number Format button, and then click twice on the Decrease Decimal button.
4. Save and then print **EL1-C2-P5-CCReports.xlsx**.
5. With the worksheet still open, determine the effect on actual job earnings with a 10% decrease by completing the following steps:
   a. Make cell B12 active.
   b. Type 0.9 and then press Enter.
6. Save and then print the **EL1-C2-P5-CCReports.xlsx**.
7. Determine the effects on actual job earnings with a 20% increase. (To do this, type 1.2 in cell B12.)
8. Save and then print **EL1-C2-P5-CCReports.xlsx**.

B	C
Cedarview	
Planned	Actual
$ 34,109	$ 30,698
48,100	43,290
32,885	29,597
61,220	55,098
30,500	27,450
58,394	52,555
13,100	11,790
86,905	78,215
0.9	

Step 5b

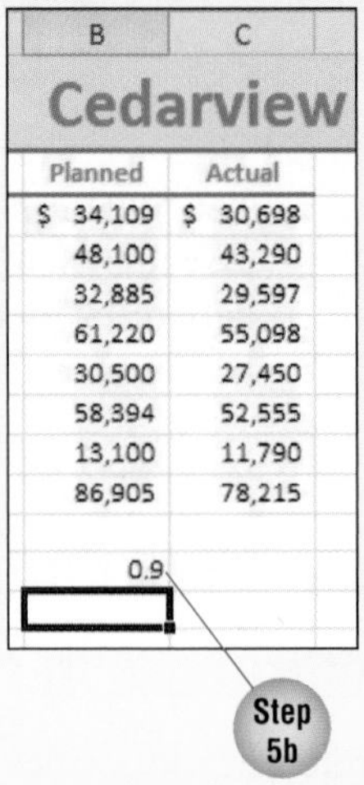

In Project 5a, you created a formula with one absolute cell reference. You can also create a formula with multiple absolute cell references. For example, in Project 5b you will create a formula that contains both relative and absolute cell references to determine the average of training scores based on specific weight percentages.

Project 5b Inserting and Copying a Formula with Multiple Absolute Cell References

Part 2 of 4

1. With **EL1-C2-P5-CCReports.xlsx** open, insert the following formulas:
   a. Insert a formula in cell B23 that averages the percentages in cells B17 through B22.
   b. Copy the formula in cell B23 to the right to cells C23 and D23.
2. Insert a formula that determines the weighted average of training scores by completing the following steps:
   a. Make cell E17 active.
   b. Type the following formula:
      =$B$24*B17+$C$24*C17+$D$24*D17
   c. Press the Enter key.
   d. Copy the formula in cell E17 down to cells E18 through E22.
   e. With cells E17 through E22 selected, click the Decrease Decimal button three times.
3. Save and then print the **EL1-C2-P5-CCReports.xlsx**.
4. With the worksheet still open, determine the effect on weighted training scores if the weighted values change by completing the following steps:
   a. Make cell B24 active, type 30, and then press Enter.
   b. Make cell D24 active, type 40, and then press Enter.
5. Save and then print **EL1-C2-P5-CCReports.xlsx**.

	Name	Plumbing	Electrical	Carpentry	Weighted Average
15	Employee Training				
16	Name	Plumbing	Electrical	Carpentry	Weighted Average
17	Allesandro	76%	80%	84%	80%
18	Ellington	66%	72%	64%	67%
19	Goodman	90%	88%	94%	91%
20	Huntington	76%	82%	88%	83%
21	Kaplan-Downing	90%	84%	92%	89%
22	Larimore	58%	62%	60%	60%
23	Training Averages	76%	78%	80%	
24	Training Weights	30%	30%	40%	
25					
26					

Step 4a

Step 4b

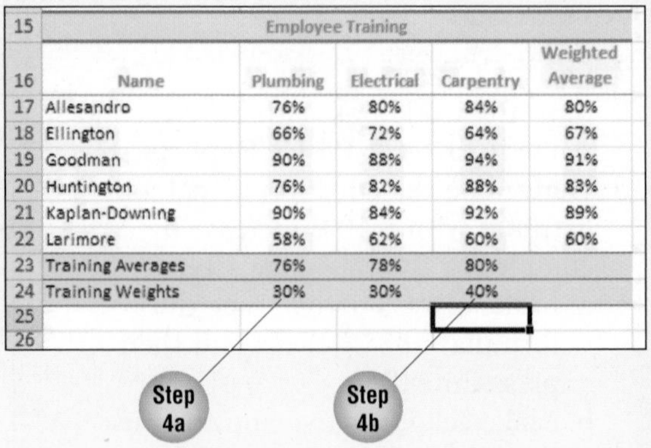

Using a Mixed Cell Reference in a Formula

The formula you created in Step 3a in Project 5a contained a relative cell reference (B3) and an absolute cell reference ($B$12). A formula can also contain a mixed cell reference. In a mixed cell reference either the column remains absolute and the row is relative or the column is relative and the row is absolute. In Project 5c you will insert a number of formulas, two of which will contain mixed cell references. You will insert the formula *=E29*E$26* to calculate withholding tax and *=E29*H$36* to calculate Social Security tax. The dollar sign before the rows indicates that the row is an absolute cell reference.

Project 5c **Determining Payroll Using Formulas with Absolute and Mixed Cell References** Part 3 of 4

1. With **EL1-C2-P5-CCReports.xlsx** open, make cell E29 active and then type the following formula containing mixed cell references:
   =(B29*C29+(B29*$B$36*D29))
2. Copy the formula in cell E29 down to cells E30 through E34.
3. Make cell F29 active and then type the following formula that calculates the amount of withholding tax:
   =E29*E$36
4. Copy the formula in cell F29 down to cells F30 through F34.
5. Make cell G29 active and then type the following formula that calculates the amount of Social Security tax:
   =E29*H$36
6. Copy the formula in cell G29 down to cells G30 through G34.
7. Make cell H29 active and then type the following formula that calculates net pay:
   =E29-(F29+G29)
8. Copy the formula in cell H29 down to cells H30 through H34.
9. Select cells E29 through H29 and then click the Accounting Number Format button.
10. Save **EL1-C2-P5-CCReports.xlsx**.

As you learned in Project 5c, a formula can contain a mixed cell reference. In a mixed cell reference either the column remains absolute and the row is relative or the column is relative and the row is absolute. In Project 5d, you will create the formula *=$A41*B$40*. In the first cell reference in the formula, *$A41*, the column is absolute and the row is relative. In the second cell reference, *B$40*, the column is relative and the row is absolute. The formula containing the mixed cell references allows you to fill in the column and row data using only one formula.

Identify an absolute or mixed cell reference by typing a dollar sign before the column and/or row reference or press the F4 function key to cycle through the various cell references. For example, type *=A41* in a cell, press F4, and the cell reference changes to *=$A$41*. Press F4 again and the cell reference changes to *=A$41*. The next time you press F4, the cell reference changes to *=$A41* and press it again to change the cell reference back to *=A41*.

Project 5d Determining Simple Interest Using a Formula with Mixed Cell References

Part 4 of 4

1. With **EL1-C2-P5-CCReports.xlsx** open, make cell B41 the active cell and then insert a formula containing mixed cell references by completing the following steps:
   a. Type =A41 and then press the F4 function key three times. (This changes the cell reference to *$A41*.)
   b. Type *B40 and then press the F4 function key twice. (This changes the cell reference to *B$40*.)
   c. Make sure the formula displays as *=$A41*B$40* and then press Enter.
2. Copy the formula to the right by completing the following steps:
   a. Make cell B41 active and then use the fill handle to copy the formula right to cell F41.
   b. With cells B41 through F41 selected, use the fill handle to copy the formula down to cell F51.
3. Save, print, and then close **EL1-C2-P5-CCReports.xlsx**.

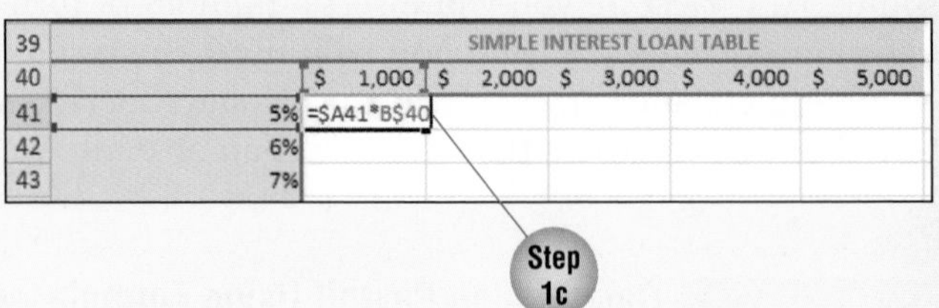

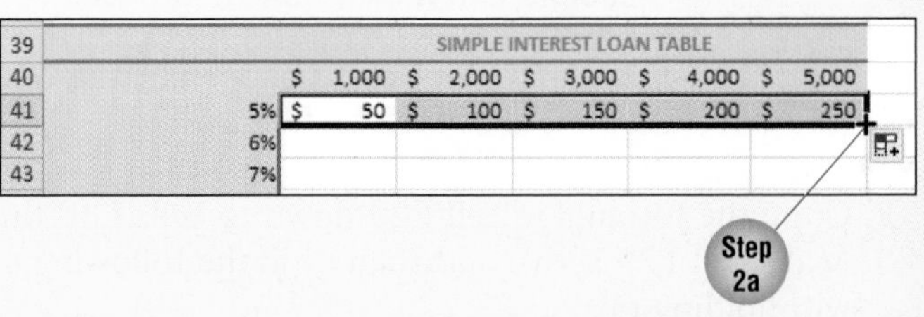

	A	B	C	D	E	F
39	SIMPLE INTEREST LOAN TABLE					
40		$ 1,000	$ 2,000	$ 3,000	$ 4,000	$ 5,000
41	5%	$ 50	$ 100	$ 150	$ 200	$ 250
42	6%	$ 60	$ 120	$ 180	$ 240	$ 300
43	7%	$ 70	$ 140	$ 210	$ 280	$ 350
44	8%	$ 80	$ 160	$ 240	$ 320	$ 400
45	9%	$ 90	$ 180	$ 270	$ 360	$ 450
46	10%	$ 100	$ 200	$ 300	$ 400	$ 500
47	11%	$ 110	$ 220	$ 330	$ 440	$ 550
48	12%	$ 120	$ 240	$ 360	$ 480	$ 600
49	13%	$ 130	$ 260	$ 390	$ 520	$ 650
50	14%	$ 140	$ 280	$ 420	$ 560	$ 700
51	15%	$ 150	$ 300	$ 450	$ 600	$ 750
52						
53						

Step 2b

Chapter Summary

- Type a formula in a cell and the formula displays in the cell as well as in the Formula bar. If cell entries are changed, a formula will automatically recalculate the values and insert the result in the cell.
- Create your own formula with commonly used operators such as addition (+), subtraction (-), multiplication (*), division (/), percent (%), and exponentiation (^). When writing a formula, begin with the equals sign (=).
- Copy a formula to other cells in a row or column with the Fill button in the Editing group in the Home tab or with the fill handle that displays in the bottom right corner of the active cell.

- Another method for writing a formula is to point to specific cells that are part of the formula as the formula is being built.
- If Excel detects an error in a formula, a Trace Error button appears and a dark green triangle displays in the upper left corner of the cell containing the formula.
- Excel includes over 200 functions that are divided into twelve categories. Use the Insert Function feature to create formulas using built-in functions.
- A function operates on an argument, which may consist of a cell reference, a constant, or another function. When a value calculated by a formula is inserted in a cell, this is referred to as returning the result.
- The AVERAGE function returns the average (arithmetic mean) of the arguments. The MAX function returns the largest value in a set of values, and the MIN function returns the smallest value in a set of values. The COUNT function counts the number of cells containing numbers within the list of arguments.
- Use the keyboard shortcut Ctrl + ` (grave accent) to turn on the display of formulas in a worksheet.
- The PMT function calculates the payment for a loan based on constant payments and a constant interest rate. The FV function returns the future value of an investment based on periodic, constant payments and a constant interest rate.
- The NOW function returns the serial number of the current date and time and the DATE function returns the serial number that represents a particular date.
- Use the IF function, considered a conditional function, to perform conditional tests on values and formulas. Use quotation marks around data in an IF statement to identify the data as text rather than a value.
- A reference identifies a cell or a range of cells in a worksheet and can be relative, absolute, or mixed. Identify an absolute cell reference by inserting a $ sign before the column and row. Cycle through the various cell reference options by typing the cell reference and then pressing F4.

Commands Review

FEATURE	RIBBON TAB, GROUP	BUTTON	KEYBOARD SHORTCUT
SUM function	Home, Editing OR Formulas, Function Library	Σ	Alt + =
Insert Function dialog box	Formulas, Function Library	fx	Shift + F3
Display formulas			Ctrl + `

Concepts Check Test Your Knowledge

Completion: In the space provided at the right, indicate the correct term, symbol, or command.

1. When typing a formula, begin the formula with this sign. __________
2. This is the operator for division that is used when writing a formula. __________
3. This is the operator for multiplication that is used when writing a formula. __________
4. As an alternative to the fill handle, use this button to copy a formula relatively in a worksheet. __________
5. A function operates on this, which may consist of a constant, a cell reference, or other function. __________
6. This function returns the largest value in a set of values. __________
7. This is the keyboard shortcut to display formulas in a worksheet. __________
8. This function finds the periodic payment for a loan based on constant payments and a constant interest rate. __________
9. This function returns the serial number of the current date and time. __________
10. This function is considered a conditional function. __________
11. Suppose cell B2 contains the total sales amount. Write a formula that would insert the word *BONUS* in cell C2 if the sales amount was greater than $99,999 and inserts the words *NO BONUS* if the sales amount is not greater than $99,999. __________
12. To identify an absolute cell reference, type this symbol before the column and row. __________

Skills Check Assess Your Performance

Assessment 1

INSERT AVERAGE, MAX, AND MIN FUNCTIONS

1. Open **DISalesAnalysis.xlsx**.
2. Save the workbook with Save As and name it **EL1-C2-A1-DISalesAnalysis**.
3. Use the AVERAGE function to determine the monthly sales (cells H4 through H9).
4. Format cell H4 with the Accounting Number Format with no decimal places.
5. Total each monthly column including the Average column (cells B10 through H10).
6. Use the MAX function to determine the highest monthly total (for cells B10 through G10) and insert the amount in cell B11.
7. Use the MIN function to determine the lowest monthly total (for cells B10 through G10) and insert the amount in cell B12.
8. Save, print, and then close **EL1-C2-A1-DISalesAnalysis.xlsx**.

Assessment 2

INSERT PMT FUNCTION

1. Open **CMRefiPlan.xlsx**.
2. Save the workbook with Save As and name it **EL1-C2-A2-CMRefiPlan**.
3. The manager of Clearline Manufacturing is interested in refinancing a loan for either $125,000 or $300,000 and wants to determine the monthly payments, total payments, and total interest paid. Insert a formula with the following specifications:
   a. Make cell E5 active.
   b. Use the Insert Function button on the Formula bar to insert a formula using the PMT function. At the formula palette, enter the following:
      Rate = C5/12
      Nper = D5
      Pv = -B5
   c. Copy the formula in cell E5 down to cells E6 through E8.
4. Insert a formula in cell F5 that multiplies the amount in E5 by the amount in D5.
5. Copy the formula in cell F5 down to cells F6 through F8.
6. Insert a formula in cell G5 that subtracts the amount in B5 from the amount in F5. (The formula is *=F5-B5*.)
7. Copy the formula in cell G5 down to cells G6 through G8.
8. Save, print, and then close **EL1-C2-A2-CMRefiPlan.xlsx**.

Assessment 3

INSERT FV FUNCTION

1. Open **RPInvest.xlsx**.
2. Save the workbook with Save As and name it **EL1-C2-A3-RPInvest**.
3. Make the following changes to the worksheet:
   a. Change the percentage in cell B3 from *9%* to *10%*.

b. Change the number in cell B4 from *36* to *60*.
c. Change the amount in cell B5 from *($1,200) to -500*.
d. Use the FV function to insert a formula that calculates the future value of the investment. ***Hint: For help with the formula, refer to Project 3b.***

4. Save, print, and then close **EL1-C2-A3-RPInvest.xlsx**.

Assessment 4

WRITE IF STATEMENT FORMULAS

1. Open **DISalesBonuses.xlsx**.
2. Save the workbook with Save As and name it **EL1-C2-A4-DISalesBonuses**.
3. Insert a formula in cell C4 that inserts the word *YES* if the amount in B4 is greater than 99999 and inserts *NO* if the amount is not greater than 99999. Copy the formula in cell C4 down to cells C5 through C14.
4. Make cell D4 active and then insert the formula =IF(C4="YES",B4*0.05,0). If sales are over $99,000, this formula will multiply the amount of sales by 5 percent and then insert the product (result) of the formula in the cell. Copy the formula in cell D4 down to cells D5 through D14.
5. Format cell D4 with the accounting number format with no decimal places.
6. Save and then print **EL1-C2-A4-DISalesBonuses.xlsx**.
7. Display the formulas in the worksheet and then print the worksheet.
8. Turn off the display of formulas.
9. Save and then close **EL1-C2-A4-DISalesBonuses.xlsx**.

Assessment 5

WRITE FORMULAS WITH ABSOLUTE CELL REFERENCES

1. Open **CCQuotas.xlsx**.
2. Save the workbook with Save As and name it **EL1-C2-A5-CCQuotas**.
3. Make the following changes to the worksheet:
   a. Insert a formula using an absolute reference to determine the projected quotas with a 10% increase from the current quotas.
   b. Save and then print **EL1-C2-A5-CCQuotas.xlsx**.
   c. Determine the projected quotas with a 15% increase from the current quota by changing cell A15 to *15% Increase* and cell B15 to *1.15*.
   d. Save and then print **EL1-C2-A5-CCQuotas.xlsx**.
   e. Determine the projected quotas with a 20% increase from the current quota.
4. Format cell C4 with the Accounting Number Format with no decimal places.
5. Save, print, and then close **EL1-C2-A5-CCQuotas.xlsx**.

Assessment 6

USE HELP TO LEARN ABOUT EXCEL OPTIONS

1. Learn about specific options in the Excel Options dialog box by completing the following steps:
   a. At a blank workbook, display the Excel Options dialog box by clicking the File tab and then clicking the Options button.
   b. At the Excel Options dialog box, click the *Advanced* option located in the left panel.

c. Scroll down and look for the section *Display options for this workbook* and then read the information in the section. Read the information that displays in the *Display options for this worksheet* section.
d. Write down the check box options available in the *Display options for this workbook* section and the *Display options for this worksheet* section and identify whether or not the check box contains a check mark. (Record only check box options and ignore buttons and options preceded by circles.)

2. With the information you wrote down about the options, create an Excel spreadsheet with the following information:
   a. In column C, type each option you wrote down. (Include an appropriate heading.)
   b. In column B, insert an X in the cell that precedes any option that contains a check mark in the check box. (Include an appropriate heading.)
   c. In column A, write a formula with the IF function that inserts the word ON in the cell if the cell in column B contains an X and inserts the word OFF if it does not (the cell is blank). (Include an appropriate heading.)
   d. Apply formatting to improve the visual appeal of the worksheet.
3. Save the workbook and name it **EL1-C2-A6-DisplayOptions**.
4. Turn on the display of formulas.
5. Print the worksheet.
6. Turn off the display of formulas.
7. Save, print, and then close **EL1-C2-A6-DisplayOptions.xlsx**.

Visual Benchmark Demonstrate Your Proficiency

CREATE A WORKSHEET AND INSERT FORMULAS

1. At a blank workbook, type the data in the cells indicated in Figure 2.4 but <u>**do not**</u> type the data in the following cells—instead insert the formulas as indicated (the results of your formulas should match the results you see in the figure):
   - Cells D3 through D9: Insert a formula that calculates the salary.
   - Cells D14 through D19: Insert a formula that calculates the differences.
   - Cells D24 through D27: Insert the dates as serial numbers.
   - Cells F24 through F27: Insert a formula that calculates the due date.
   - Cells B37 through D37: Insert a formula that calculates the averages.
   - Cells E32 through E36: Insert a formula that calculates the weighted average of test scores.
2. Apply any other formatting so your worksheet looks similar to the worksheet shown in Figure 2.4.
3. Save the workbook and name it **EL1-C2-VB-Formulas**.
4. Print **EL1-C2-VB-Formulas.xlsx**.
5. Press Ctrl + ` to turn on the display of formulas and then print the worksheet again.
6. Turn off the display of formulas and then close the workbook.

Figure 2.4 Visual Benchmark

	A	B	C	D	E	F	G
1	Weekly Payroll						
2	Employee	Hours	Rate	Salary			
3	Alvarez, Rita	40	$ 22.50	$ 900.00			
4	Campbell, Owen	15	22.50	337.50			
5	Heitmann, Luanne	25	19.00	475.00			
6	Malina, Susan	40	18.75	750.00			
7	Parker, Kenneth	40	18.75	750.00			
8	Reitz, Collette	20	15.00	300.00			
9	Shepard, Gregory	15	12.00	180.00			
10							
11							
12	Construction Projects						
13	Project	Projected	Actual	Difference			
14	South Cascade	$145,000	$ 141,597	$ (3,403)			
15	Rogue River Park	120,000	124,670	4,670			
16	Meridian	120,500	99,450	(21,050)			
17	Lowell Ridge	95,250	98,455	3,205			
18	Walker Canyon	70,000	68,420	(1,580)			
19	Nettleson Creek	52,000	49,517	(2,483)			
20							
21							
22	Overdue Accounts						
23	Client	Account #	Amount Due	Pur. Date	Terms	Due Date	
24	Sunrise Marketing	120	$ 9,875	12/4/2012	15	12/19/2012	
25	National Systems	398	8,525	12/7/2012	30	1/6/2013	
26	First Street Signs	188	5,000	12/12/2012	15	12/27/2012	
27	Valley Services	286	3,250	12/19/2012	30	1/18/2013	
28							
29							
30	Test Scores						
31	Employee	Test No. 1	Test No. 2	Test No. 3	Wgt. Avg.		
32	Coffey, Annette	62%	64%	76%	70%		
33	Halverson, Ted	88%	96%	90%	91%		
34	Kohler, Jeremy	80%	76%	82%	80%		
35	McKnight, Carol	68%	72%	78%	74%		
36	Parkhurst, Jody	98%	96%	98%	98%		
37	Test Averages	79%	81%	85%			
38	Test Weights	25%	25%	50%			

Case Study Apply Your Skills

Part 1

You are a loan officer for Dollar Wise Financial Services and work in the department that specializes in home loans. You have decided to prepare a sample home mortgage worksheet to show prospective clients. This sample home mortgage worksheet will show the monthly payments on variously priced homes with varying interest rates. Open the **DWMortgages.xlsx** worksheet and then complete the home mortgage worksheet by inserting the following formulas:

- Since many homes in your area sell for at least $400,000, you decide to add that amount to the worksheet with a 5%, 10%, 15%, and 20% down payment.
- In column C, insert a formula that determines the down payment amount.
- In column D, insert a formula that determines the loan amount.
- In column G, insert a formula using the PMT function. (The monthly payment will display as a negative number.)

Save the worksheet and name it **EL1-C2-CS-DWMortgages**.

Part 2

If home buyers put down less than 20 percent of the home's purchase price, mortgage insurance is required. With **EL1-C2-CS-DWMortgages.xlsx** open, insert an IF statement in the cells in column H that inserts the word "No" if the percentage in column B is equal to or greater than 20% or inserts the word "Yes" if the percentage in column B is less than 20%. Save and then print **EL1-C2-CS-DWMortgages.xlsx**.

Part 3

Interest rates fluctuate on a regular basis. Using the resources available to you, determine a current interest rate in your area. Delete the interest rate of 7% in the Dollar Wise worksheet and insert the interest rate for your area. Save and then print **EL1-C2-CS-DWMortgages.xlsx**.

Part 4

When a client is required to purchase mortgage insurance, you would like to provide information to the client concerning this insurance. Use the Help feature to learn about creating hyperlinks in Excel. Locate a helpful website that specializes in private mortgage insurance. Create a hyperlink in the worksheet that will display the website. Save, print, and then close **EL1-C2-CS-DWMortage.xlsx**.

Part 5

Once a loan has been approved and finalized, a letter is sent to the client explaining the details of the loan. Use a letter template in Word to create a letter that is sent to the client. Copy and link the information in the **EL1-C2-CS-DWMortage.xlsx** worksheet to the client letter. Save the letter document and name it **DWLetter**. Print and then close **DWLetter.docx**.

Microsoft Excel

CHAPTER 3

Formatting an Excel Worksheet

PERFORMANCE OBJECTIVES

Upon successful completion of Chapter 3, you will be able to:

- **Change column widths**
- **Change row heights**
- **Insert rows and columns in a worksheet**
- **Delete cells, rows, and columns in a worksheet**
- **Clear data in cells**
- **Apply formatting to data in cells**
- **Apply formatting to selected data using the Mini toolbar**
- **Preview a worksheet**
- **Apply a theme and customize the theme font and color**
- **Format numbers**
- **Repeat the last action**
- **Automate formatting with Format Painter**
- **Hide and unhide rows and columns**

Tutorials

3.1 Inserting, Adjusting, and Deleting Rows and Columns

3.2 Using Cell Styles and Themes

3.3 Formatting Numbers

3.4 Adding Borders and Shading; Copying Formats with Format Painter

3.5 Hiding and Unhiding Rows and Columns

The appearance of a worksheet on the screen and how it looks when printed is called the ***format***. In Chapter 1, you learned how to apply basic formatting to cells in a worksheet. Additional types of formatting you may want to apply to a worksheet include changing column width and row height; applying character formatting such as bold, italics, and underlining; specifying number formatting; inserting and deleting rows and columns; and applying borders, shading, and patterns to cells. You can also apply formatting to a worksheet with a theme. A theme is a set of formatting choices that include colors and fonts. Model answers for this chapter's projects appear on the following page.

Excel2010L1C3

Note: Before beginning the projects, copy to your storage medium the Excel2010L1C3 subfolder from the Excel2010L1 folder on the CD that accompanies this textbook and then make Excel2010L1C3 the active folder.

Model Answers

Capstan Marine Products

Purchasing Department

Company	Product #	Price	Number	Total
RD Manufacturing	240-490-B	$ 85.75	7	$ 600.25
	443-22-0	148.50	8	1,188.00
	855-495	42.75	5	213.75
Ray Enterprises	S894-T	4.99	30	149.70
	B-3448	25.50	12	306.00
	43-GB-39	45.00	20	900.00
Sunrise Corporation	341-453	19.99	8	159.92
	CT-342	304.75	5	1,523.75
	83-492	9.75	35	341.25
	L-756-M	95.40	4	381.60
Geneva Systems	340-19	15.99	20	319.80
	T-3491-S	450.50	5	2,252.50
	900-599	35.95	15	539.25
	43-49CE	120.00	5	600.00
	Total			$ 9,475.77

Project 1 Format a Product Pricing Worksheet

EL1-C3-P1-CMProducts.xlsx

Stanton & Barnett Associates

Weekly Payroll

Employee	Hrly. Rate	Hours	Overtime	Gross	W/H Tax	SS Tax	Net
Lowell	$ 40.00	40	1	$1,660.00	$ 464.80	$126.99	$1,068.21
McIntyre	$ 40.00	40	3	$1,780.00	$ 498.40	$136.17	$1,145.43
Rawlings	$ 37.50	30	0	$1,125.00	$ 315.00	$ 86.06	$ 723.94
Fratzke	$ 32.00	40	2	$1,376.00	$ 385.28	$105.26	$ 885.46
Singleton	$ 25.00	25	0	$ 625.00	$ 175.00	$ 47.81	$ 402.19
Gleason	$ 22.00	40	1	$ 913.00	$ 255.64	$ 69.84	$ 587.52

Overtime	1.5		W/H Rate	28%		SS Rate	7.65%

Project 2 Apply a Theme to a Payroll Worksheet

EL1-C3-P2-SBAPayroll.xlsx

REAL PHOTOGRAPHY

Invoices

Invoice #	Client #	Service	Amount	Tax	Amount Due
2930	03-392	Family Portraits	$ 450.00	8.5%	$ 488.25
2942	02-498	Wedding Portraits	$ 1,075.00	8.8%	$ 1,169.60
2002	11-279	Development	$ 225.00	0.0%	$ 225.00
2007	04-325	Sports Portraits	$ 750.00	8.5%	$ 813.75
2376	03-392	Senior Portraits	$ 850.00	8.5%	$ 922.25
2129	11-279	Development	$ 350.00	0.0%	$ 350.00
2048	11-325	Wedding Portraits	$ 875.00	8.5%	$ 949.38
2054	04-325	Sports Portraits	$ 750.00	8.5%	$ 813.75
2064	05-665	Family Portraits	$ 560.00	8.8%	$ 609.28
2077	11-279	Development	$ 400.00	0.0%	$ 400.00
2079	04-325	Sports Portraits	$ 600.00	8.5%	$ 651.00
2908	55-340	Senior Portraits	$ 725.00	8.8%	$ 788.80
3001	11-279	Development	$ 310.00	8.8%	$ 337.28

Project 3 Format an Invoices Worksheet

EL1-C3-P3-RPInvoices.xlsx

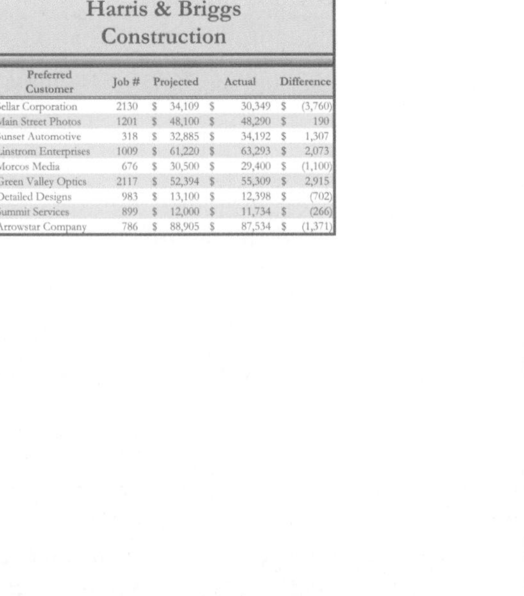

Harris & Briggs Construction

Preferred Customer	Job #	Projected	Actual	Difference
Sellar Corporation	2130	$ 34,109	$ 30,349	$ (3,760)
Main Street Photos	1201	$ 48,100	$ 48,290	$ 190
Sunset Automotive	318	$ 32,885	$ 34,192	$ 1,307
Linstrom Enterprises	1009	$ 61,220	$ 63,293	$ 2,073
Morcos Media	676	$ 30,500	$ 29,400	$ (1,100)
Green Valley Optics	2117	$ 52,394	$ 55,309	$ 2,915
Detailed Designs	983	$ 13,100	$ 12,398	$ (702)
Summit Services	899	$ 12,000	$ 11,734	$ (266)
Arrowstar Company	786	$ 88,905	$ 87,534	$ (1,371)

Project 4 Format a Company Budget Worksheet

EL1-C3-P4-HBCJobs.xlsx

Format a Product Pricing Worksheet — 7 Parts

You will open a workbook containing a worksheet with product pricing data, and then format the worksheet by changing column widths and row heights, inserting and deleting rows and columns, deleting rows and columns, and clearing data in cells. You will also apply font and alignment formatting to data in cells and then preview the worksheet.

Changing Column Width

Columns in a worksheet are the same width by default. In some worksheets you may want to change column widths to accommodate more or less data. You can change column width using the mouse on column boundaries or at a dialog box.

Changing Column Width Using Column Boundaries

As you learned in Chapter 1, you can adjust the width of a column by dragging the column boundary line or adjust a column width to the longest entry by double-clicking the boundary line. When you drag a column boundary, the column width displays in a box above the mouse pointer. The column width number that displays represents the average number of characters in the standard font that can fit in a cell.

To change the width of all columns in a worksheet, click the Select All button and then drag a column boundary to the desired position.

You can change the width of selected adjacent columns at the same time. To do this, select the columns and then drag one of the column boundaries within the selected columns. As you drag the boundary the column width changes for all selected columns. To select adjacent columns, position the cell pointer on the first desired column header (the mouse pointer turns into a black, down-pointing arrow), hold down the left mouse button, drag the cell pointer to the last desired column header, and then release the mouse button.

Project 1a — Changing Column Width Using a Column Boundary — Part 1 of 7

1. Open **CMProducts.xlsx**.
2. Save the workbook with Save As and name it **EL1-C3-P1-CMProducts**.
3. Insert a formula in cell D2 that multiplies the price in cell B2 with the number in cell C2. Copy the formula in cell D2 down to cells D3 through D14.
4. Change the width of column D by completing the following steps:
   a. Position the mouse pointer on the column boundary in the column header between columns D and E until it turns into a double-headed arrow pointing left and right.
   b. Hold down the left mouse button, drag the column boundary to the right until *Width: 11.00 (82 pixels)* displays in the box, and then release the mouse button.

D2 | fx =B2* | Width: 11.00 (82 pixels)

	A	B	C	D	E	F
1	Product #	Price	Number	Total		
2	240-490-B	$ 85.75	7	$ 600.25		
3	1203-3422	$ 20.99	15	$ 314.85		

Step 4b

5. Make cell D15 active and then insert the sum of cells D2 through D14.
6. Change the width of columns A and B by completing the following steps:
   a. Select columns A and B. To do this, position the cell pointer on the column A header, hold down the left mouse button, drag the cell pointer to the column B header, and then release the mouse button.

b. Position the cell pointer on the column boundary between columns A and B until it turns into a double-headed arrow pointing left and right.
c. Hold down the left mouse button, drag the column boundary to the right until *Width: 10.14 (76 pixels)* displays in the box, and then release the mouse button.

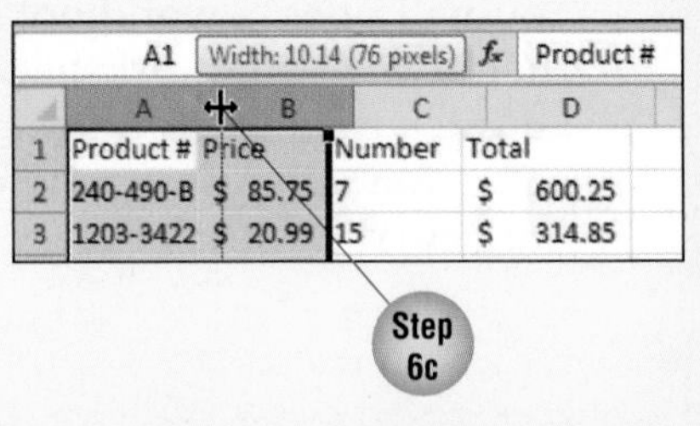

A1
Width: 10.14 (76 pixels)
Product #
Product # Price Number Total
240-490-B $ 85.75 7 $ 600.25
1203-3422 $ 20.99 15 $ 314.85
Step 6c

7. Adjust the width of column C to accommodate the longest entry by double-clicking on the column boundary between columns C and D.
8. Save **EL1-C3-P1-CMProducts.xlsx**.

Quick Steps

Change Column Width
Drag column boundary line.
OR
Double-click column boundary.
OR
1. Click Format button.
2. Click *Column Width* at drop-down list.
3. Type desired width.
4. Click OK.

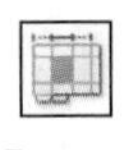

Format

Changing Column Width at the Column Width Dialog Box

At the Column Width dialog box shown in Figure 3.1, you can specify a column width number. Increase the column width number to make the column wider or decrease the column width number to make the column narrower.

To display the Column Width dialog box, click the Format button in the Cells group in the Home tab and then click *Column Width* at the drop-down list. At the Column Width dialog box, type the number representing the average number of characters in the standard font that you want to fit in the column and then press Enter or click OK.

Figure 3.1 Column Width Dialog Box

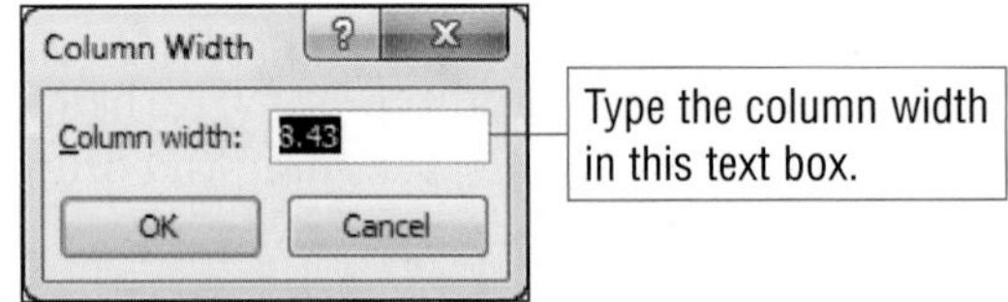

Project 1b **Changing Column Width at the Column Width Dialog Box** Part 2 of 7

1. With **EL1-C3-P1-CMProducts.xlsx** open, change the width of column A by completing the following steps:
   a. Make any cell in column A active.
   b. Click the Format button in the Cells group in the Home tab and then click *Column Width* at the drop-down list.
   c. At the Column Width dialog box, type 12.75 in the *Column width* text box.
   d. Click OK to close the dialog box.

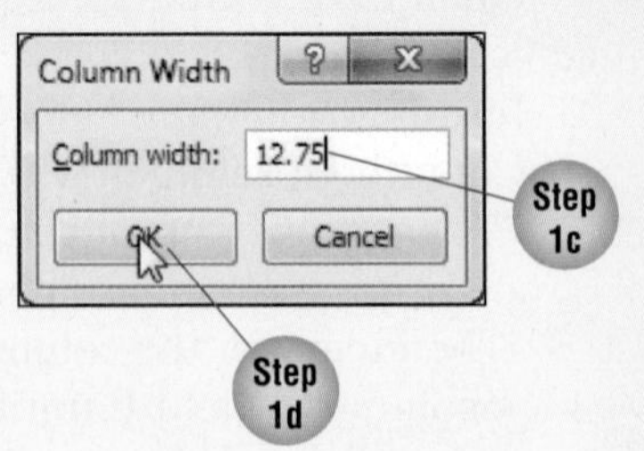

2. Make any cell in column B active and then change the width of column B to *12.75* by completing steps similar to those in Step 1.
3. Make any cell in column C active and then change the width of column C to *8* by completing steps similar to those in Step 1.
4. Save **EL1-C3-P1-CMProducts.xlsx**.

Changing Row Height

Row height can be changed in much the same manner as column width. For example, you can change the row height using the mouse on a row boundary, or at the Row Height dialog box. Change row height using a row boundary in the same manner as you learned to change column width. To do this, position the cell pointer on the boundary between rows in the row header until it turns into a double-headed arrow pointing up and down, hold down the left mouse button, drag up or down until the row is the desired height, and then release the mouse button.

Quick Steps

Change Row Height
Drag row boundary line.
OR
1. Click Format button.
2. Click *Row Height* at drop-down list.
3. Type desired height.
4. Click OK.

The height of selected rows that are adjacent can be changed at the same time. (The height of nonadjacent rows will not all change at the same time.) To do this, select the rows and then drag one of the row boundaries within the selected rows. As the boundary is being dragged the row height changes for all selected rows.

To change the height of all rows in a worksheet, click the Select All button and then drag a row boundary to the desired position.

As a row boundary is being dragged, the row height displays in a box above the mouse pointer. The row height number that displays represents a point measurement. A vertical inch contains approximately 72 points. Increase the point size to increase the row height; decrease the point size to decrease the row height.

At the Row Height dialog box shown in Figure 3.2, you can specify a row height number. To display the Row Height dialog box, click the Format button in the Cells group in the Home tab and then click *Row Height* at the drop-down list.

Figure 3.2 Row Height Dialog Box

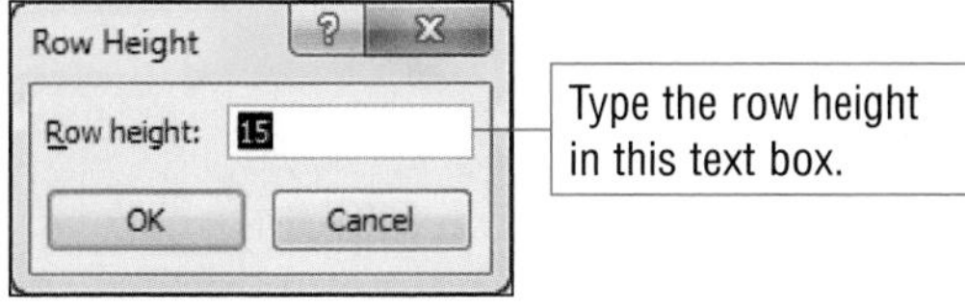

Project 1c **Changing Row Height** Part 3 of 7

1. With **EL1-C3-P1-CMProducts.xlsx** open, change the height of row 1 by completing the following steps:
   a. Position the cell pointer in the row header on the row boundary between rows 1 and 2 until it turns into a double-headed arrow pointing up and down.
   b. Hold down the left mouse button, drag the row boundary down until *Height: 19.50 (26 pixels)* displays in the box, and then release the mouse button.
2. Change the height of rows 2 through 14 by completing the following steps:
   a. Select rows 2 through 14. To do this, position the cell pointer on the number 2 in the row header, hold down the left mouse button, drag the cell pointer to the number 14 in the row header, and then release the mouse button.
   b. Position the cell pointer on the row boundary between rows 2 and 3 until it turns into a double-headed arrow pointing up and down.

c. Hold down the left mouse button, drag the row boundary down until *Height: 16.50 (22 pixels)* displays in the box, and then release the mouse button.

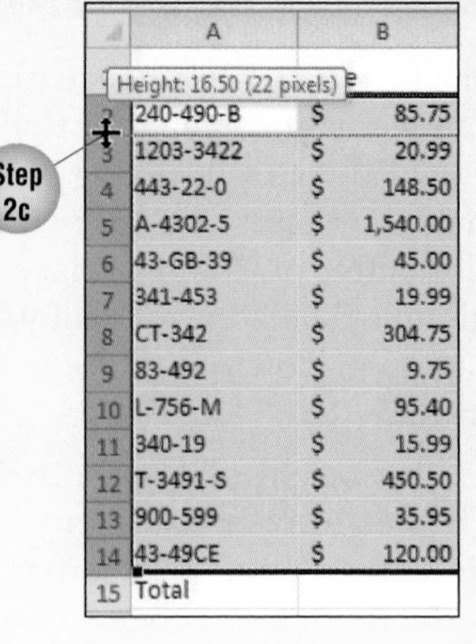

3. Change the height of row 15 by completing the following steps:
   a. Make cell A15 active.
   b. Click the Format button in the Cells group in the Home tab and then click *Row Height* at the drop-down list.
   c. At the Row Height dialog box, type 20 in the *Row height* text box and then click OK.

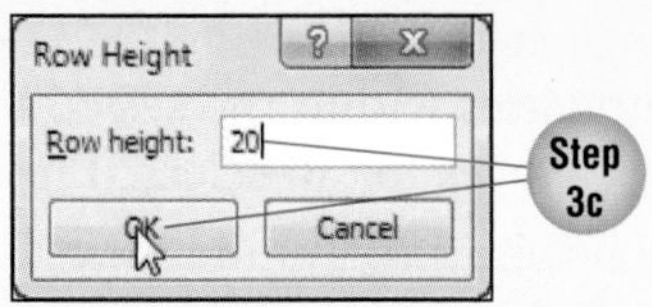

4. Save **EL1-C3-P1-CMProducts.xlsx**.

Inserting and Deleting Cells, Rows, and Columns

Quick Steps

Insert Row
Click Insert button.
OR
1. Click Insert button arrow.
2. Click *Insert Sheet Rows* at drop-down list.

OR
1. Click Insert button arrow.
2. Click *Insert Cells.*
3. Click *Entire row* in dialog box.
4. Click OK.

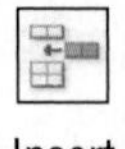

Insert

HINT

When you insert rows in a worksheet, all references affected by the insertion are automatically adjusted.

New data may need to be included in an existing worksheet. For example, a row or several rows of new data may need to be inserted into a worksheet or data may need to be removed from a worksheet.

Inserting Rows

After you create a worksheet, you can add (insert) rows to the worksheet. Insert a row with the Insert button in the Cells group in the Home tab or with options at the Insert dialog box. By default, a row is inserted above the row containing the active cell. To insert a row in a worksheet, select the row below where the row is to be inserted and then click the Insert button. If you want to insert more than one row, select the number of rows in the worksheet that you want inserted and then click the Insert button.

You can also insert a row by making a cell active in the row below where the row is to be inserted, clicking the Insert button arrow, and then clicking *Insert Sheet Rows*. Another method for inserting a row is to click the Insert button arrow and then click *Insert Cells*. This displays the Insert dialog box as shown in Figure 3.3. At the Insert dialog box, click *Entire row*. This inserts a row above the active cell.

Figure 3.3 Insert Dialog Box

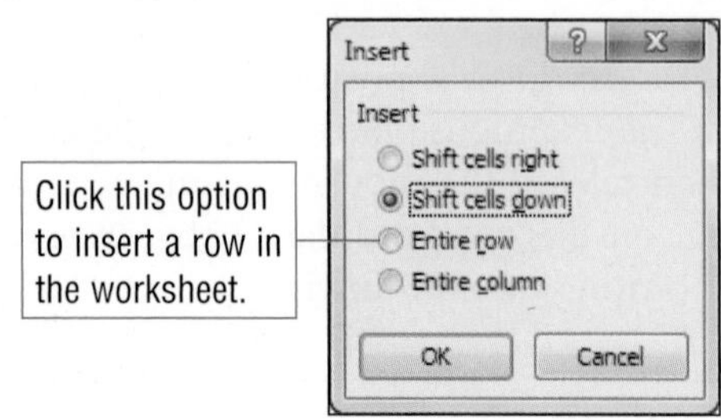

Project 1d Inserting Rows

Part 4 of 7

1. With **EL1-C3-P1-CMProducts.xlsx** open, insert two rows at the beginning of the worksheet by completing the following steps:
   a. Make cell A1 active.
   b. Click the Insert button arrow in the Cells group in the Home tab.
   c. At the drop-down list that displays, click *Insert Sheet Rows*.
   d. With cell A1 active, click the Insert button arrow and then click *Insert Sheet Rows* at the drop-down list.

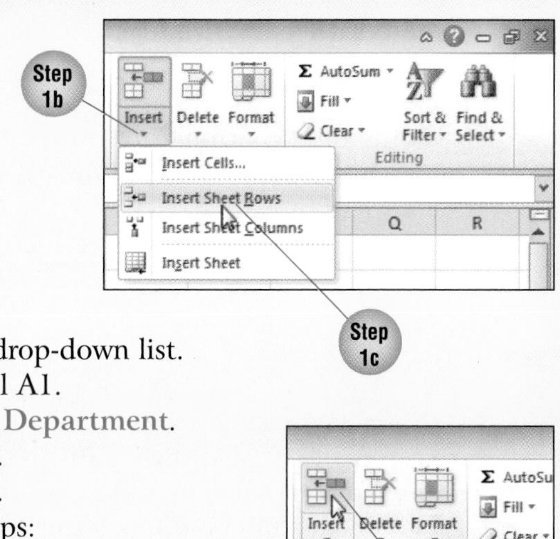

2. Type the text Capstan Marine Products in cell A1.
3. Make cell A2 active and then type Purchasing Department.
4. Change the height of row 1 to *42.00 (56 pixels)*.
5. Change the height of row 2 to *21.00 (28 pixels)*.
6. Insert two rows by completing the following steps:
   a. Select rows 7 and 8 in the worksheet.
   b. Click the Insert button in the Cells group in the Home tab.

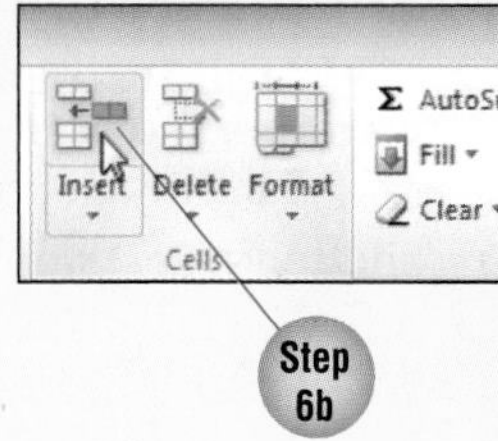

7. Type the following data in the specified cells: (You do not need to type the dollar sign in cells containing money amounts.)
   A7 = 855-495
   B7 = 42.75
   C7 = 5
   A8 = ST039
   B8 = 12.99
   C8 = 25
8. Make D6 the active cell and then use the fill handle to copy the formula down to cells D7 and D8.
9. Save **EL1-C3-P1-CMProducts.xlsx**.

Inserting Columns

Insert columns in a worksheet in much the same way as rows. Insert a column with options from the Insert button drop-down list or with options at the Insert dialog box. By default, a column is inserted immediately to the left of the column containing the active cell. To insert a column in a worksheet, make a cell active in the column immediately to the right of where the new column is to be inserted, click the Insert button arrow, and then click *Insert Sheet Columns* at the drop-down list. If you want to insert more than one column, select the number of columns in the worksheet that you want inserted, click the Insert button arrow, and then click *Insert Sheet Columns*.

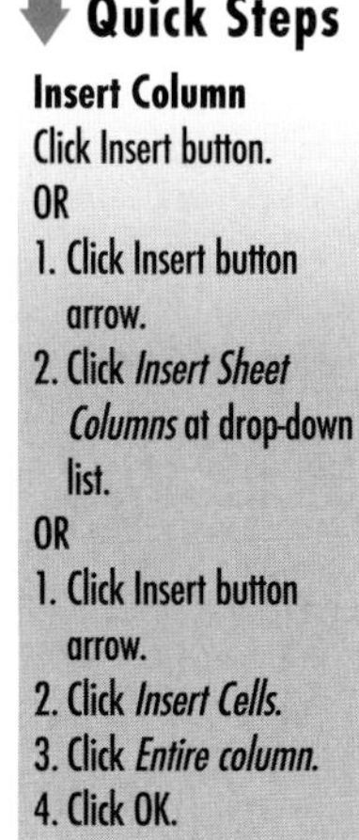

Quick Steps

Insert Column
Click Insert button.
OR
1. Click Insert button arrow.
2. Click *Insert Sheet Columns* at drop-down list.
OR
1. Click Insert button arrow.
2. Click *Insert Cells*.
3. Click *Entire column*.
4. Click OK.

You also can insert a column by making a cell active in the column immediately to the right of where the new column is to be inserted, clicking the Insert button arrow, and then clicking *Insert Cells* at the drop-down list. This causes the Insert dialog box to display. At the Insert dialog box, click *Entire column*. This inserts an entire column immediately to the left of the active cell.

Excel includes an especially helpful and time-saving feature related to inserting columns. When you insert columns in a worksheet, all references affected by the insertion are automatically adjusted.

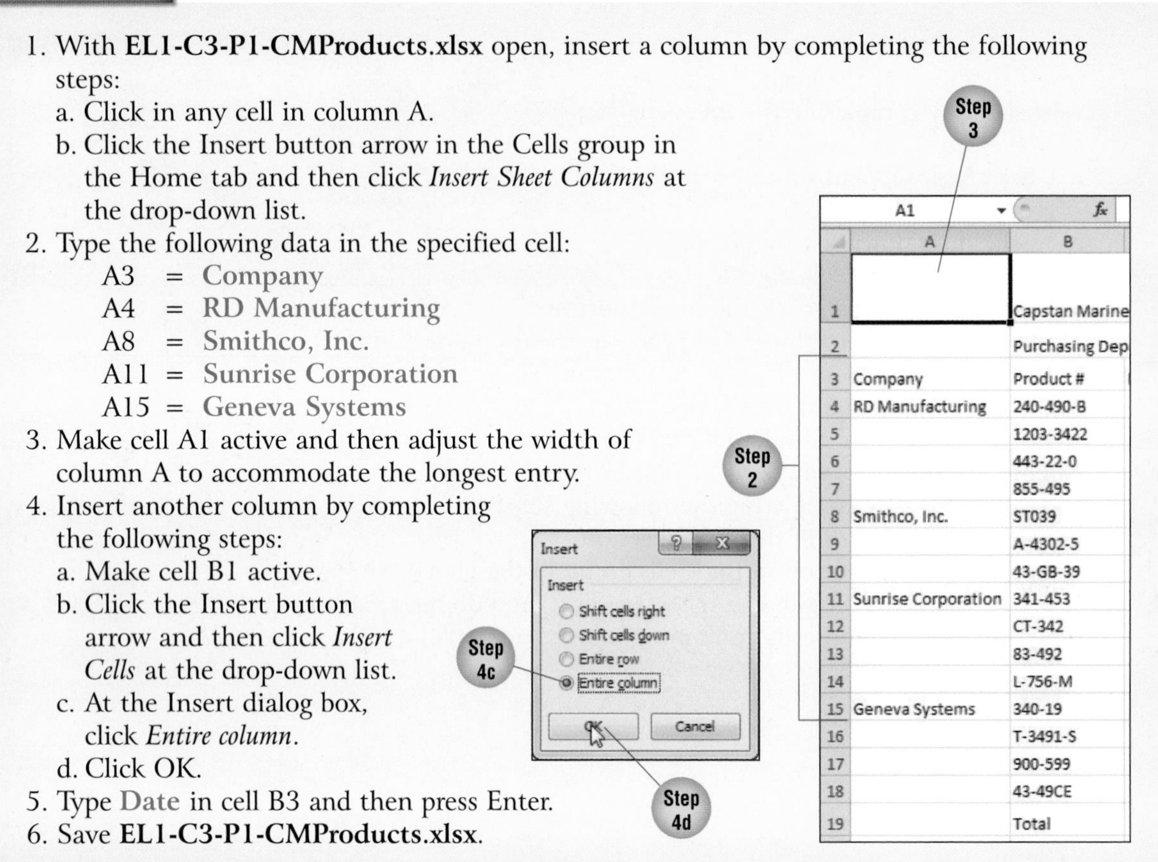

Project 1e Inserting a Column

Part 5 of 7

1. With **EL1-C3-P1-CMProducts.xlsx** open, insert a column by completing the following steps:
   a. Click in any cell in column A.
   b. Click the Insert button arrow in the Cells group in the Home tab and then click *Insert Sheet Columns* at the drop-down list.
2. Type the following data in the specified cell:
   A3 = Company
   A4 = RD Manufacturing
   A8 = Smithco, Inc.
   A11 = Sunrise Corporation
   A15 = Geneva Systems
3. Make cell A1 active and then adjust the width of column A to accommodate the longest entry.
4. Insert another column by completing the following steps:
   a. Make cell B1 active.
   b. Click the Insert button arrow and then click *Insert Cells* at the drop-down list.
   c. At the Insert dialog box, click *Entire column*.
   d. Click OK.
5. Type Date in cell B3 and then press Enter.
6. Save **EL1-C3-P1-CMProducts.xlsx**.

Deleting Cells, Rows, or Columns

HINT

Display the Delete dialog box by positioning the cell pointer in the worksheet, clicking the right mouse button, and then clicking *Delete* at the shortcut menu.

You can delete specific cells in a worksheet or rows or columns in a worksheet. To delete a row, select the row and then click the Delete button in the Cells group in the Home tab. To delete a column, select the column and then click the Delete button. Delete a specific cell by making the cell active, clicking the Delete button arrow, and then clicking *Delete Cells* at the drop-down list. This displays the Delete dialog box shown in Figure 3.4. At the Delete dialog box, specify what you want deleted and then click OK. You can also delete adjacent cells by selecting the cells and then displaying the Delete dialog box.

Delete

Figure 3.4 Delete Dialog Box

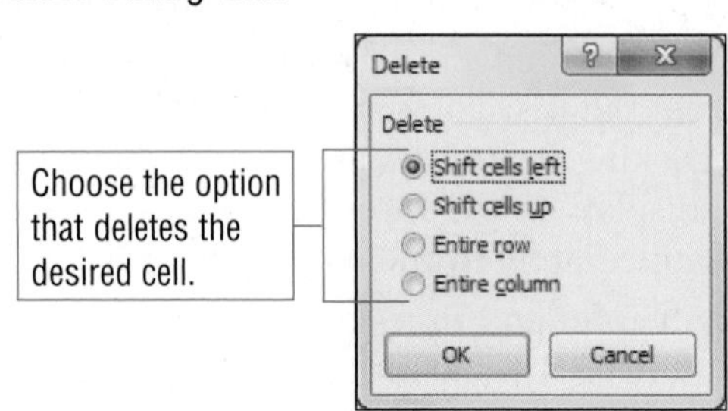

Clearing Data in Cells

If you want to delete cell contents but not the cell, make the cell active or select desired cells and then press the Delete key. A quick method for clearing the contents of a cell is to right-click the cell and then click *Clear Contents* at the shortcut menu. Another method for deleting cell contents is to make the cell active or select desired cells, click the Clear button in the Editing group in the Home tab, and then click *Clear Contents* at the drop-down list.

With the options at the Clear button drop-down list you can clear the contents of the cell or selected cells as well as formatting and comments. Click the *Clear Formats* option to remove formatting from cells or selected cells while leaving the data. You can also click the *Clear All* option to clear the contents of the cell or selected cells as well as the formatting.

Quick Steps

Clear Data in Cells
1. Select desired cells.
2. Press Delete key.

OR
1. Select desired cells.
2. Click Clear button.
3. Click *Clear Contents* at drop-down list.

Clear

Project 1f **Deleting and Clearing Rows in a Worksheet** Part 6 of 7

1. With **EL1-C3-P1-CMProducts.xlsx** open, delete column B in the worksheet by completing the following steps:
   a. Click in any cell in column B.
   b. Click the Delete button arrow in the Cells group in the Home tab and then click *Delete Sheet Columns* at the drop-down list.
2. Delete row 5 by completing the following steps:
   a. Select row 5.
   b. Click the Delete button in the Cells group.
3. Clear row contents by completing the following steps:
   a. Select rows 7 and 8.
   b. Click the Clear button in the Editing group in the Home tab and then click *Clear Contents* at the drop-down list.
4. Type the following data in the specified cell:
   A7 = Ray Enterprises
   B7 = S894-T
   C7 = 4.99
   D7 = 30
   B8 = B-3448
   C8 = 25.50
   D8 = 12
5. Make cell E6 active and then copy the formula down to cells E7 and E8.
6. Save **EL1-C3-P1-CMProducts.xlsx**.

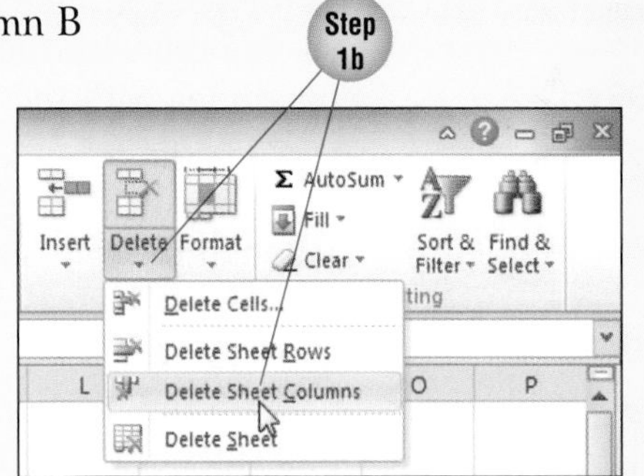

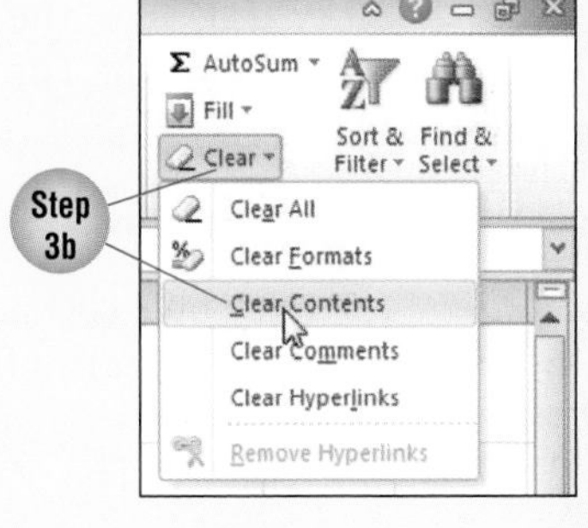

Step 4

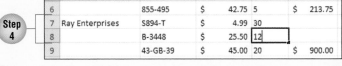

6		855-495	$	42.75	5	$	213.75
7	Ray Enterprises	S894-T	$	4.99	30		
8		B-3448	$	25.50	12		
9		43-GB-39	$	45.00	20	$	900.00

Applying Formatting

With many of the groups in the Home tab you can apply formatting to text in the active cells or selected cells. Use buttons in the Font group to apply font formatting to text and use buttons in the Alignment group to apply alignment formatting to text.

Figure 3.5 Font Group

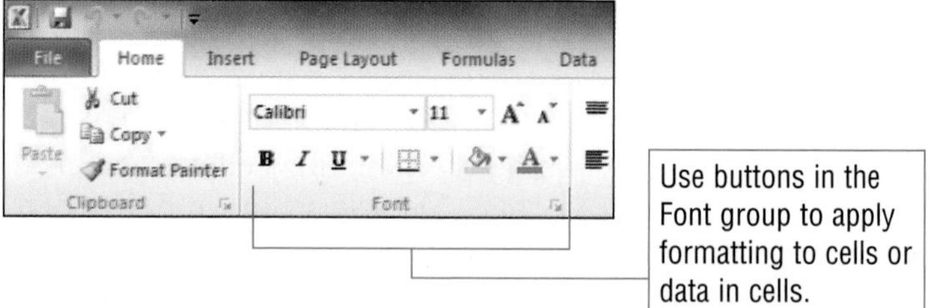

Use buttons in the Font group to apply formatting to cells or data in cells.

Applying Font Formatting

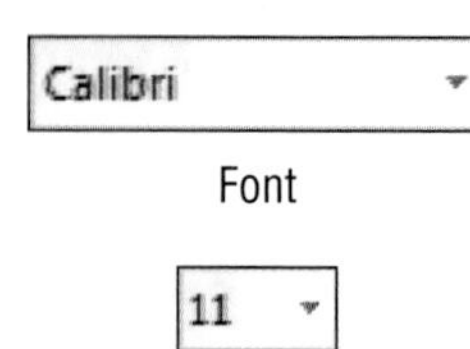

Font

Font Size

Bold

Italic

Underline

You can apply a variety of formatting to cells in a worksheet with buttons in the Font group in the Home tab. With buttons in the Font group shown in Figure 3.5, you can change the font, font size, and font color; bold, italicize, and underline data in cells; change the text color; and apply a border or add fill to cells.

Use the Font button in the Font group to change the font of text in a cell and use the Font Size button to specify size for the text. Apply bold formatting to text in a cell with the Bold button, italic formatting with the Italic button, and underlining with the Underline button.

Click the Increase Font Size button and the text in the active cell or selected cells increases from 11 points to 12 points. Click the Increase Font Size button again and the font size increases to 14. Each additional time you click the button, the font size increases by two points. Click the Decrease Font Size button and text in the active cell or selected cells decreases in point size.

With the Borders button in the Font group, you can insert a border on any or all sides of the active cell or any or all sides of selected cells. The name of the button changes depending on the most recent border applied to a cell or selected cells. Use the Fill Color button to insert color in the active cell or in selected cells. With the Font Color button, you can change the color of text within a cell.

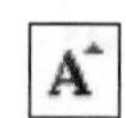

Increase Font Size

Formatting with the Mini Toolbar

Decrease Font Size

Double-click in a cell and then select data within the cell and the Mini toolbar displays in a dimmed fashion above the selected data. The Mini toolbar also displays when you right-click in any cell. Hover the mouse pointer over the Mini toolbar and it becomes active. The Mini toolbar contains buttons for applying font formatting such as font, font size, and font color as well as bold and italic formatting. Click a button on the Mini toolbar to apply formatting to selected text.

Borders

Applying Alignment Formatting

Fill Color

Font Color

Merge & Center

The alignment of data in cells depends on the type of data entered. Enter words or text combined with numbers in a cell and the text is aligned at the left edge of the cell. Enter numbers in a cell and the numbers are aligned at the right side of the cell. Use options in the Alignment group to align text at the left, center, or right side of the cell; align text at the top, center, or bottom of the cell; increase and/or decrease the indent of text; and change the orientation of text in a cell. As you learned in Chapter 1, you can merge selected cells by clicking the Merge & Center button. If you merged cells, you can split the merged cell into the original cells by selecting the cell and then clicking the Merge & Center button. If you click the Merge & Center button arrow, a drop-down list of options displays. Click the *Merge & Center* option to merge all of the selected cells and change to center cell alignment. Click the *Merge Across* to merge each row of the selected cells. For example, if you select three cells and two rows, clicking the *Merge Across* option will merge the three cells in the first row and merge the three cells in the second row so you end up with two cells. Click the *Merge Cells* option to merge all selected cells but not change to center cell alignment. Use the last option, *Unmerge Cells* to split cells that were previously merged. If you select and merge cells containing data, only the data in the upper-left cell will remain. Data in any other cells in the merged cells is deleted.

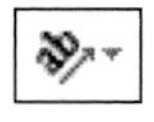

Orientation

Click the Orientation button to rotate data in a cell. Click the Orientation button and a drop-down list displays with options for rotating text in a cell. If data typed in a cell is longer than the cell, it overlaps the next cell to the right. If you want data to remain in a cell and wrap to the next line within the same cell, click the Wrap Text button in the Alignment group.

Wrap Text

Project 1g Applying Font and Alignment Formatting

Part 7 of 7

1. With **EL1-C3-P1-CMProducts.xlsx** open, make cell B1 active and then click the Wrap Text button in the Alignment group in the Home tab. (This wraps the company name within the cell.)
2. Select cells B1 through C2, click the Merge & Center button arrow in the Alignment group in the Home tab, and then click *Merge Across* at the drop-down list.
3. After looking at the merged cells, you decide to merge additional cells and horizontally and vertically center text in the cells by completing the following steps:
   a. With cells B1 through C2 selected, click the Merge & Center button and then click *Unmerge Cells* at the drop-down list.
   b. Select cells A1 through E2.
   c. Click the Merge & Center button arrow in the Alignment group in the Home tab and then click the *Merge Across* option at the drop-down list.
   d. Click the Middle Align button in the Alignment group and then click the Center button.

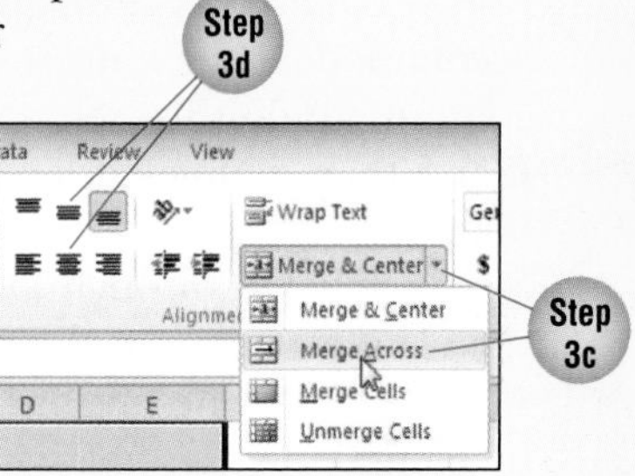

4. Rotate text in the third row by completing the following steps:
   a. Select cells A3 through E3.
   b. Click the Orientation button in the Alignment group in the Home tab and then click *Angle Counterclockwise* at the drop-down list.
   c. After looking at the rotated text, you decide to return the orientation back to the horizontal by clicking the Undo button on the Quick Access toolbar.

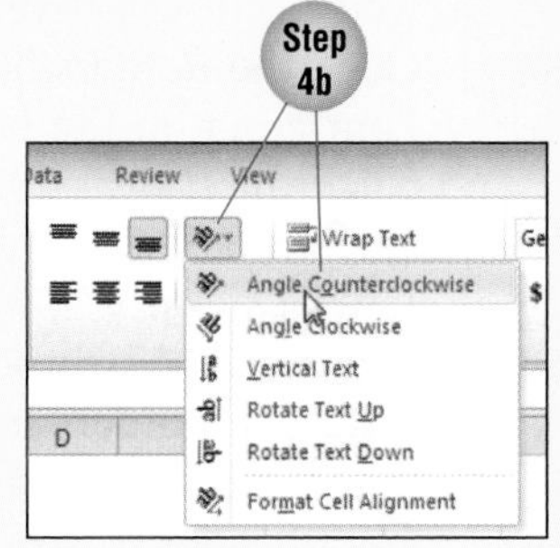

5. Change the font, font size, and font color for text in specific cells by completing the following steps:
   a. Make cell A1 active.
   b. Click the Font button arrow in the Font group in the Home tab, scroll down the drop-down gallery, and then click *Bookman Old Style*.
   c. Click the Font Size button arrow in the Font group and then click *22* at the drop-down gallery.

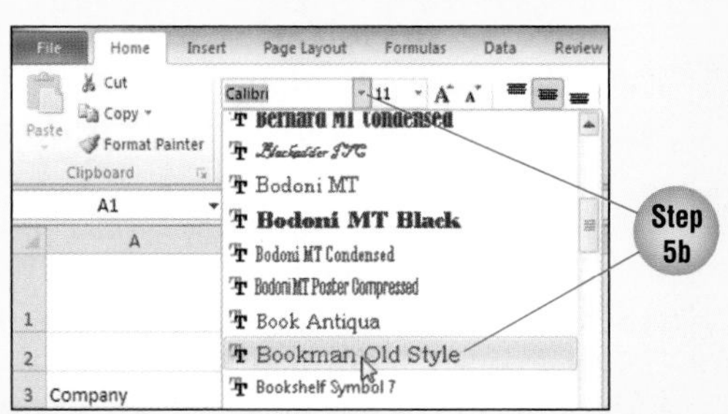

d. Click the Font Color button arrow and then click *Dark Blue* in the *Standard Colors* section of the drop-down color palette.

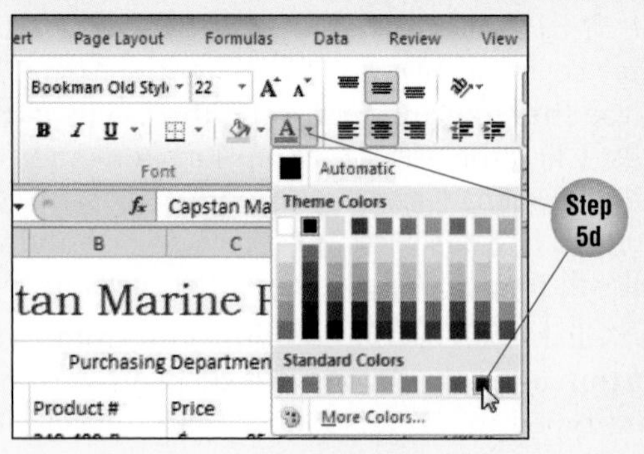

6. Make cell A2 active and then complete steps similar to those in Step 5 to change the font to Bookman Old Style, the font size to 16, and the font color to Dark Blue.
7. Select cells A3 through E3 and then click the Center button in the Alignment group.
8. With cells A3 through E3 still selected, click the Bold button in the Font group and then click the Italic button.
9. Select cells A3 through E18 and then change the font to Bookman Old Style.

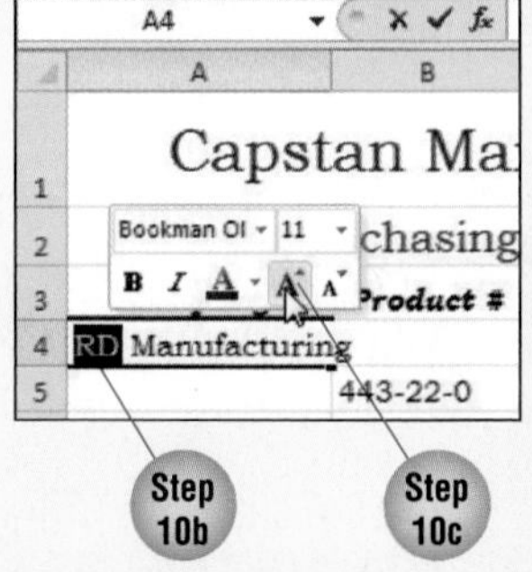

10. Apply formatting to selected data using the Mini toolbar by completing the following steps:
    a. Double-click cell A4.
    b. Select the letters *RD*. (This displays the dimmed Mini toolbar above the selected word.)
    c. Click the Increase Font Size button on the Mini toolbar.
    d. Double-click cell A14.
    e. Select the word *Geneva* and then click the Italic button on the Mini toolbar.

11. Adjust columns A through E to accommodate the longest entry in each column. To do this, select columns A through E and then double-click any selected column boundary.
12. Select cells D4 through D17 and then click the Center button in the Alignment group.
13. Add a double-line bottom border to cell A2 by completing the following steps:
    a. Make cell A2 active.
    b. Click the Borders button arrow in the Font group in the Home tab.
    c. Click the *Bottom Double Border* option at the drop-down list.
14. Add a single-line bottom border to cells A3 through E3 by completing the following steps:
    a. Select cells A3 through E3.
    b. Click the Borders button arrow and then click the *Bottom Border* option.

15. Apply fill color to specific cells by completing the following steps:
    a. Select cells A1 through E3.
    b. Click the Fill Color button arrow in the Font group.
    c. Click the *Aqua, Accent 5, Lighter 80%* color option.
16. Select cells C5 through C17 and then click the Comma Style button.
17. Select cells E5 through E17 and then click the Comma Style button.
18. Save, print, and then close **EL1-C3-P1-CMProducts.xlsx**.

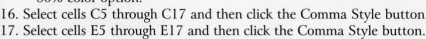

Apply a Theme to a Payroll Worksheet — 1 Part

You will open a workbook containing a worksheet with payroll information and then insert text, apply formatting to cells and cell contents, apply a theme, and then change the theme font and colors.

Applying a Theme

Excel provides a number of themes you can use to format text and cells in a worksheet. A theme is a set of formatting choices that include a color theme (a set of colors), a font theme (a set of heading and body text fonts), and an effects theme (a set of lines and fill effects). To apply a theme, click the Page Layout tab and then click the Themes button in the Themes group. At the drop-down gallery that displays, click the desired theme. Position the mouse pointer over a theme and the ***live preview*** feature will display the worksheet with the theme formatting applied. With the live preview feature you can see how the theme formatting affects your worksheet before you make your final choice.

Apply a theme to give your worksheet a professional look.

Themes

Project 2 Applying a Theme — Part 1 of 1

1. Open **SBAPayroll.xlsx** and then save it with Save As and name it **EL1-C3-P2-SBAPayroll**.
2. Make G4 the active cell and then insert a formula that calculates the amount of Social Security tax. (Multiply the gross pay amount in E4 with the Social Security rate in cell H11; you will need to use the mixed cell reference H$11 when writing the formula.)
3. Copy the formula in cell G4 down to cells G5 through G9.
4. Make H4 the active cell and then insert a formula that calculates the net pay (gross pay minus withholding and Social Security tax).
5. Copy the formula in H4 down to cells H5 through H9.
6. Increase the height of row 1 to 36.00.
7. Make A1 the active cell, click the Middle Align button in the Alignment group, click the Font Size button arrow, click *18* at the drop-down list, and then click the Bold button.
8. Type Stanton & Barnett Associates in cell A1.
9. Select cells A2 through H3 and then click the Bold button in the Font group.
10. Apply a theme and customize the font and colors by completing the following steps:
    a. Click the Page Layout tab.
    b. Click the Themes button in the Themes group and then click *Apothecary* at the drop-down gallery. (You might want to point the mouse to various themes to see how each theme's formatting affects the worksheet.)

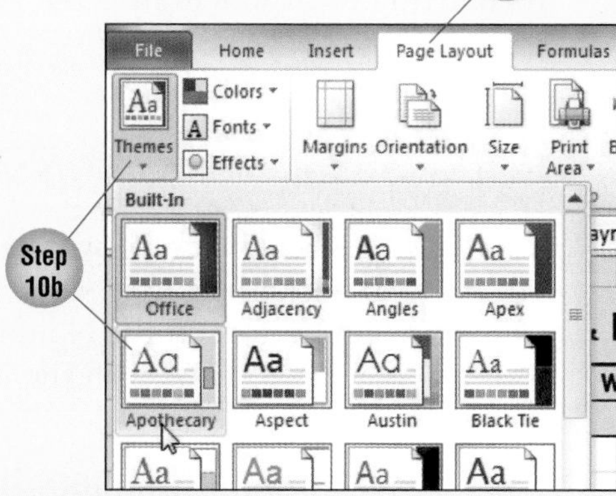

c. Click the Colors button in the Themes group and then click *Flow* at the drop-down gallery.
d. Click the Fonts button in the Themes group, scroll down the drop-down gallery, and then click *Black Tie*.

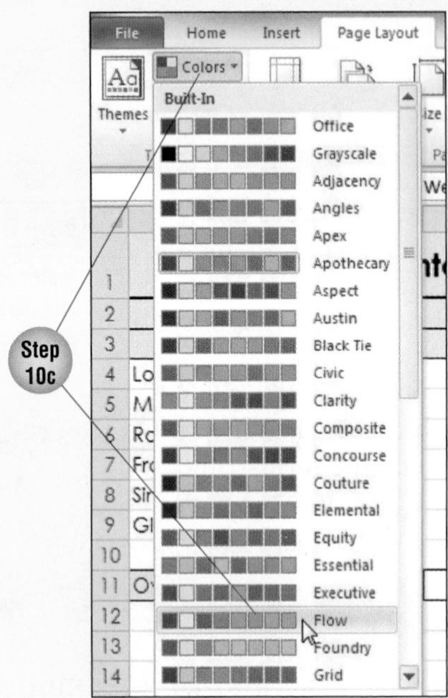

11. Select columns A through H and then adjust the width of the columns to accommodate the longest entries.
12. Save, print, and then close **EL1-C3-P2-SBAPayroll.xlsx**.

Project 3 Format an Invoices Worksheet — 2 Parts

You will open a workbook containing an invoice worksheet and apply number formatting to numbers in cells.

Formatting Numbers

Numbers in a cell, by default, are aligned at the right and decimals and commas do not display unless they are typed in the cell. Change the format of numbers with buttons in the Number group in the Home tab or with options at the Format Cells dialog box with the Number tab selected.

Formatting Numbers Using Number Group Buttons

Format symbols you can use to format numbers include a percent sign (%), a comma (,), and a dollar sign ($). For example, if you type the number *$45.50* in a cell, Excel automatically applies Currency formatting to the number. If you type *45%*, Excel automatically applies the Percent formatting to the number.

The Number group in the Home tab contains five buttons you can use to format numbers in cells. You learned about these buttons in Chapter 1.

Specify the formatting for numbers in cells in a worksheet before typing the numbers, or format existing numbers in a worksheet. The Increase Decimal and Decrease Decimal buttons in the Number group in the Home tab will change decimal places for existing numbers only.

The Number group in the Home tab also contains the Number Format button. Click the Number Format button arrow and a drop-down list displays of common number formats. Click the desired format at the drop-down list to apply the number formatting to the cell or selected cells.

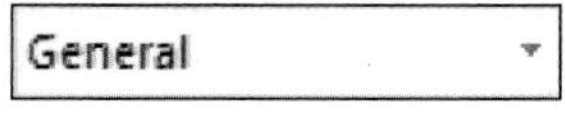

Number Format

Project 3a Formatting Numbers with Buttons in the Number Group

Part 1 of 2

1. Open **RPInvoices.xlsx**.
2. Save the workbook with Save As and name it **EL1-C3-P3-RPInvoices**.
3. Make the following changes to column widths:
   a. Change the width of column C to 17.00.
   b. Change the width of column D to 10.00.
   c. Change the width of column E to 7.00.
   d. Change the width of column F to 12.00.
4. Select row 1 and then click the Insert button in the Cells group.
5. Change the height of row 1 to 42.00.
6. Select cells A1 through F1 and then make the following changes:
   a. Click the Merge & Center button in the Alignment group in the Home tab.
   b. With cell A1 active, change the font size to 24 points.
   c. Click the Fill Color button arrow in the Font group and then click *Olive Green, Accent 3, Lighter 80%*.
   d. Click the Borders button arrow in the Font group and then click the *Top and Thick Bottom Border* option.
   e. With cell A1 active, type **REAL PHOTOGRAPHY** and then press Enter.
7. Change the height of row 2 to 24.00.
8. Select cells A2 through F2 and then make the following changes:
   a. Click the Merge & Center button in the Alignment group.
   b. With cell A2 active, change the font size to 18.
   c. Click the Fill Color button in the Font group. (This will fill the cell with light green color.)
   d. Click the Borders button arrow in the Font group and then click the *Bottom Border* option.
9. Make the following changes to row 3:
   a. Change the height of row 3 to 18.00.
   b. Select cells A3 through F3, click the Bold button in the Font group, and then click the Center button in the Alignment group.

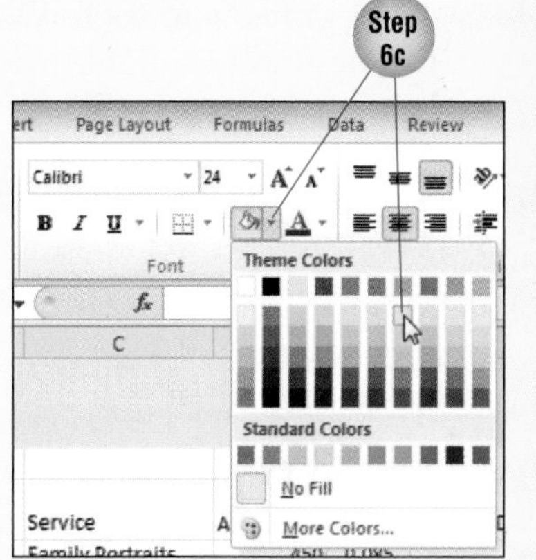

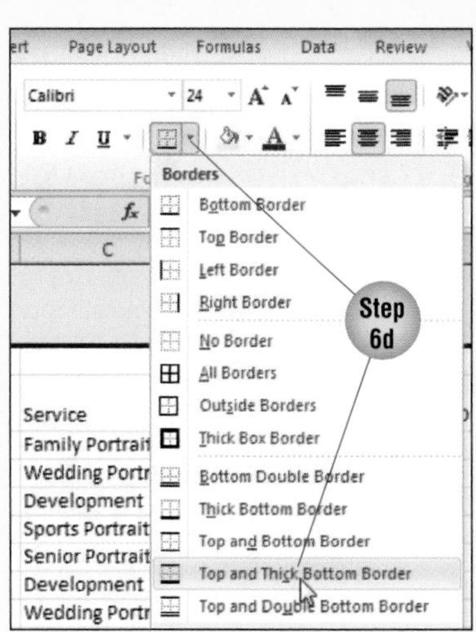

c. With the cells still selected, click the Borders button arrow and then click the *Bottom Border* option.

10. Make the following number formatting changes:
    a. Select cells E4 through E16 and then click the *Percent Style* button in the Number group in the Home tab.
    b. With the cells still selected, click once on the Increase Decimal button in the Number group. (The percent numbers should contain one decimal place.)

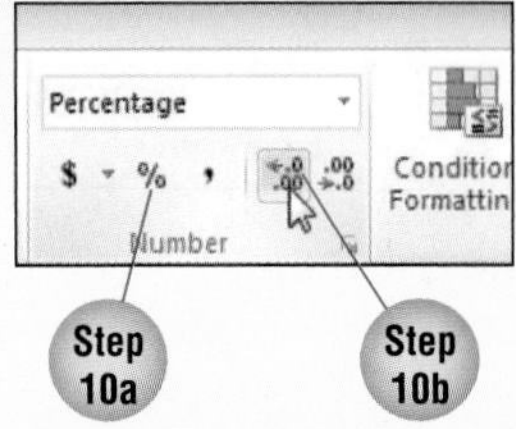

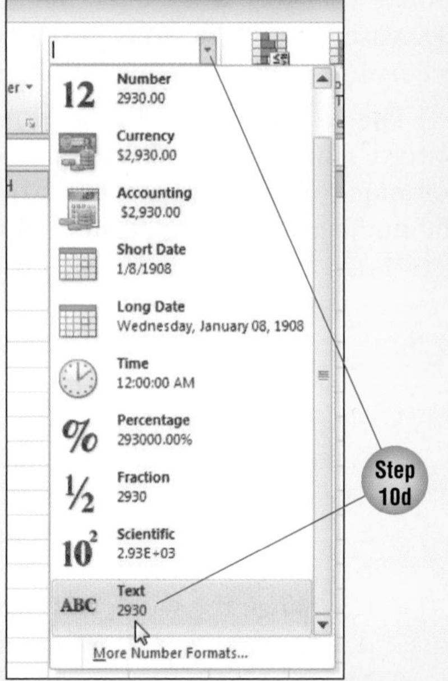

    c. Select cells A4 through B16.
    d. Click the Number Format button arrow, scroll down the drop-down list, and then click *Text*.
    e. With A4 through B16 still selected, click the Center button in the Alignment group.

11. Save **EL1-C3-P3-RPInvoices.xlsx**.

Formatting Numbers Using the Format Cells Dialog Box

Along with buttons in the Number group, you can format numbers with options at the Format Cells dialog box with the Number tab selected as shown in Figure 3.6. Display this dialog box by clicking the Number group dialog box

Figure 3.6 Format Cells Dialog Box with Number Tab Selected

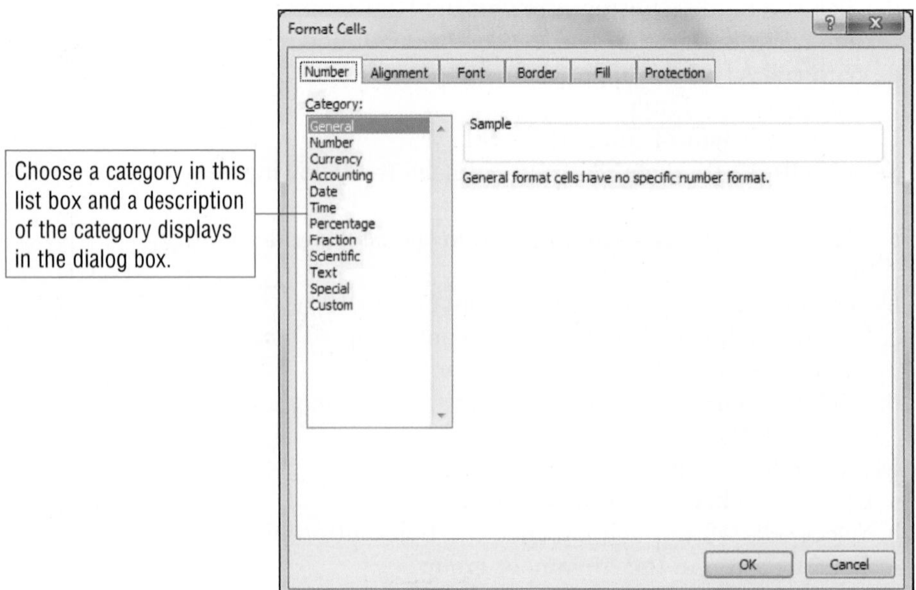

launcher or by clicking the Number Format button arrow and then clicking *More Number Formats* at the drop-down list. The left side of the dialog box displays number categories with a default category of *General*. At this setting no specific formatting is applied to numbers except right-aligning numbers in cells. The other number categories are described in Table 3.1.

Table 3.1 Number Categories at the Format Cells Dialog Box

Click this category	*To apply this number formatting*
Number	Specify number of decimal places and whether or not a thousand separator should be used; choose the display of negative numbers; right-align numbers in cell.
Currency	Apply general monetary values; dollar sign is added as well as commas and decimal points, if needed; right-align numbers in cell.
Accounting	Line up the currency symbol and decimal points in a column; add dollar sign and two digits after a decimal point; right-align numbers in cell.
Date	Display date as date value; specify the type of formatting desired by clicking an option in the *Type* list box; right-align date in cell.
Time	Display time as time value; specify the type of formatting desired by clicking an option in the *Type* list box; right-align time in cell.
Percentage	Multiply cell value by 100 and display result with a percent symbol; add decimal point followed by two digits by default; number of digits can be changed with the *Decimal places* option; right-align number in cell.
Fraction	Specify how fraction displays in cell by clicking an option in the *Type* list box; right-align fraction in cell.
Scientific	Use for very large or very small numbers. Use the letter *E* to tell Excel to move a decimal point a specified number of positions.
Text	Treat number in cell as text; number is displayed in cell exactly as typed.
Special	Choose a number type, such as *Zip Code*, *Phone Number*, or *Social Security Number* in the *Type* option list box; useful for tracking list and database values.
Custom	Specify a numbering type by choosing an option in the *Type* list box.

Project 3b Formatting Numbers at the Format Cells Dialog Box

Part 2 of 2

1. With **EL1-C3-P3-PRInvoices.xlsx** open, make cell F4 active, insert the following formula: =(D4*E4)+D4, and then press Enter.
2. Make cell F4 active and then copy the formula down to cells F5 through F16.
3. Change number formatting by completing the following steps:
   a. Select cells D4 through D16.
   b. Click the Number group dialog box launcher.

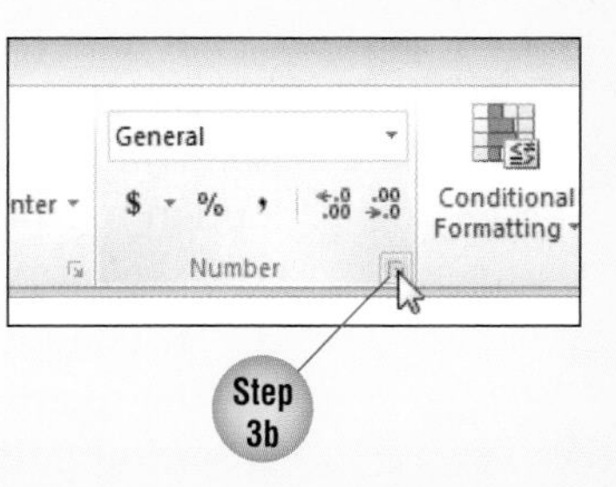

c. At the Format Cells dialog box with the Number tab selected, click *Accounting* in the *Category* section.
d. Make sure a *2* displays in the *Decimal places* option box and a dollar sign *$* displays in the *Symbol* option box.
e. Click OK.

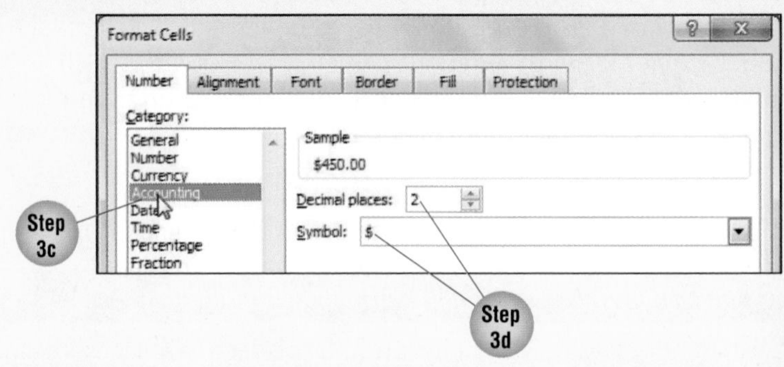

4. Apply Accounting formatting to cells F4 through F16 by completing steps similar to those in Step 3.
5. Save, print, and then close **EL1-C3-P3-RPInvoices.xlsx**.

Format a Company Budget Worksheet **6 Parts**

You will open a workbook containing a company budget worksheet and then apply formatting to cells with options at the Format Cells dialog box, use the Format Painter to apply formatting, and hide and unhide rows and columns in the worksheet.

Formatting Cells Using the Format Cells Dialog Box

In the previous section, you learned how to format numbers with options at the Format Cells dialog box with the Number tab selected. This dialog box contains a number of other tabs you can select to format cells.

Aligning and Indenting Data

You can align and indent data in cells using buttons in the Alignment group in the Home tab or with options at the Format Cells dialog box with the Alignment tab selected as shown in Figure 3.7. Display this dialog box by clicking the Alignment group dialog box launcher.

In the *Orientation* section, you can choose to rotate data. A portion of the *Orientation* section shows points on an arc. Click a point on the arc to rotate the text along that point. You can also type a rotation degree in the *Degrees* text box. Type a positive number to rotate selected text from the lower left to the upper right of the cell. Type a negative number to rotate selected text from the upper left to the lower right of the cell.

If data typed in a cell is longer than the cell, it overlaps the next cell to the right. If you want data to remain in a cell and wrap to the next line within the same cell, click the *Wrap text* option in the *Text control* section of the dialog box. Click the *Shrink to fit* option to reduce the size of the text font so all selected data fits within the column. Use the *Merge cells* option to combine two or more selected cells into a single cell.

If you want to enter data on more than one line within a cell, enter the data on the first line and then press Alt + Enter. Pressing Alt + Enter moves the insertion point to the next line within the same cell.

Figure 3.7 Format Cells Dialog Box with Alignment Tab Selected

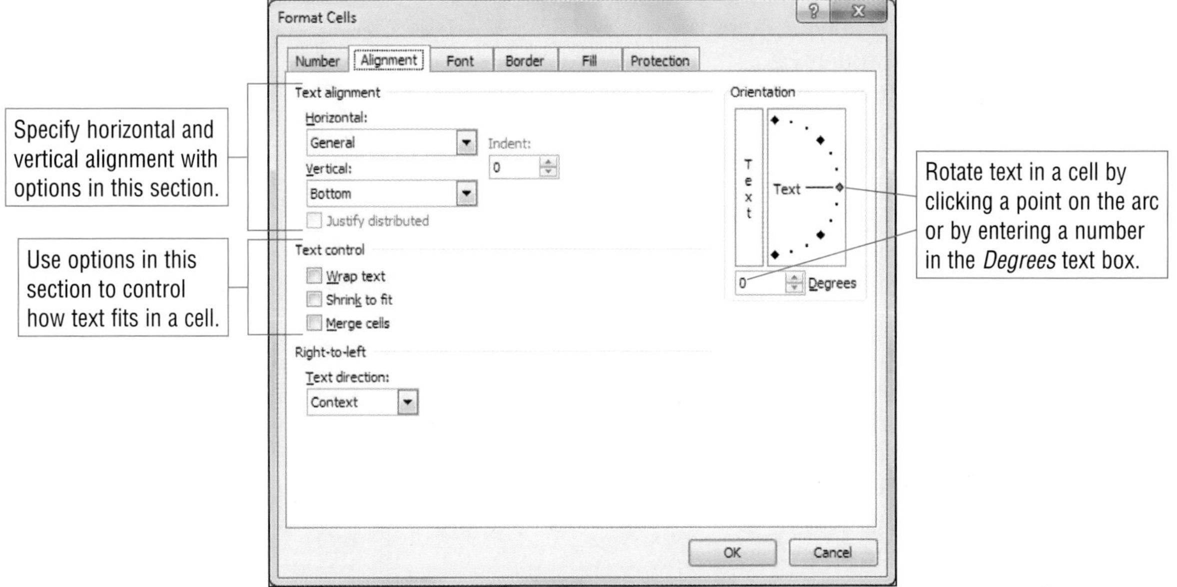

Project 4a Aligning and Rotating Data in Cells

Part 1 of 6

1. Open **HBCJobs.xlsx**.
2. Save the workbook with Save As and name it **EL1-C3-P4-HBCJobs**.
3. Make the following changes to the worksheet:
   a. Insert a new row at the beginning of the worksheet.
   b. Change the height of row 1 to 66.00.
   c. Merge and center cells A1 through E1.
   d. Type Harris & Briggs in cell A1 and then press Alt + Enter. (This moves the insertion point down to the next line in the same cell.)
   e. Type Construction and then press Enter.
   f. With cell A2 active, type Preferred, press Alt + Enter, type Customer, and then press Enter.
   g. Change the width of column A to 20.00.
   h. Change the width of column B to 7.00.
   i. Change the width of columns C, D, and E to 10.00.
4. Change number formatting for specific cells by completing the following steps:
   a. Select cells C3 through E11.
   b. Click the Number group dialog box launcher.
   c. At the Format Cells dialog box with the Number tab selected, click *Accounting* in the *Category* section.
   d. Click the down-pointing arrow at the right side of the *Decimal places* option until *0* displays.
   e. Make sure a dollar sign *$* displays in the *Symbol* option box.
   f. Click OK.

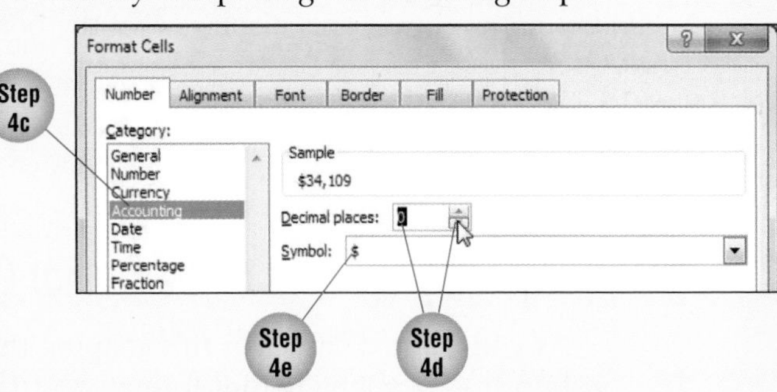

5. Make cell E3 active and then insert the formula =D3-C3. Copy this formula down to cells E4 through E11.

6. Change the orientation of data in cells by completing the following steps:
   a. Select cells B2 through E2.
   b. Click the Alignment group dialog box launcher.
   c. At the Format Cells dialog box with the Alignment tab selected, select *0* in the *Degrees* text box and then type 45.
   d. Click OK.

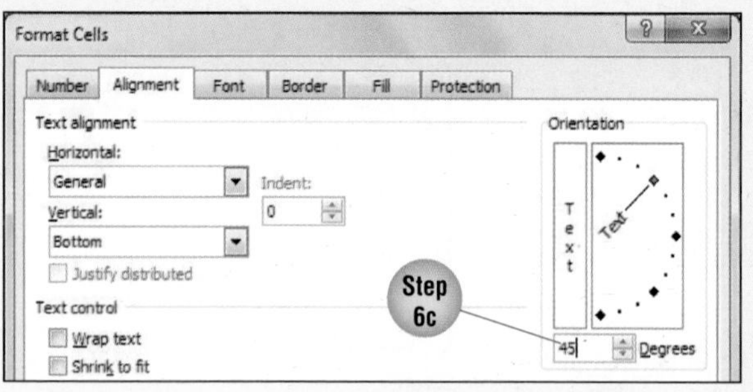

7. Change the vertical alignment of text in cells by completing the following steps:
   a. Select cells A1 through E2.
   b. Click the Alignment group dialog box launcher.
   c. At the Format Cells dialog box with the Alignment tab selected, click the down-pointing arrow at the right side of the *Vertical* alignment option.
   d. Click *Center* at the drop-down list.
   e. Click OK.

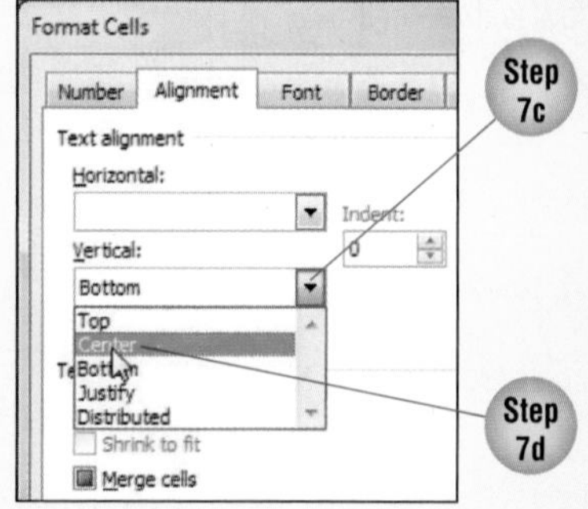

8. Change the horizontal alignment of text in cells by completing the following steps:
   a. Select cells A2 through E2.
   b. Click the Alignment group dialog box launcher.
   c. At the Format Cells dialog box with the Alignment tab selected, click the down-pointing arrow at the right side of the *Horizontal* alignment option.
   d. Click *Center* at the drop-down list.
   e. Click OK.

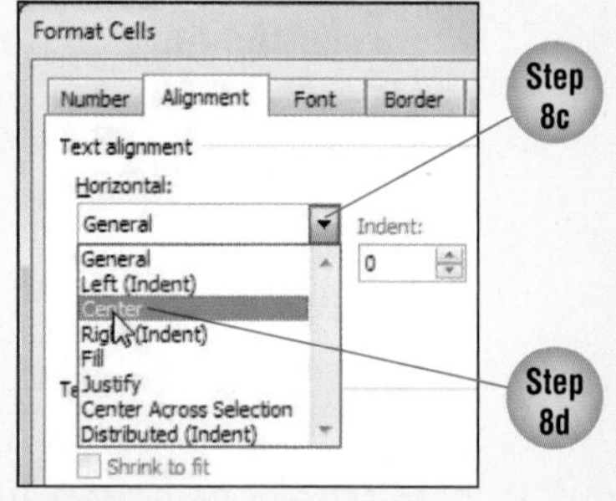

9. Change the horizontal alignment and indent of text in cells by completing the following steps:
   a. Select cells B3 through B11.
   b. Click the Alignment group dialog box launcher.
   c. At the Format Cells dialog box with the Alignment tab selected, click the down-pointing arrow at the right side of the *Horizontal* alignment option and then click *Right (Indent)* at the drop-down list.
   d. Click once on the up-pointing arrow at the right side of the *Indent* option box. (This displays *1* in the box.)
   e. Click OK.
10. Save **EL1-C3-P4-HBCJobs.xlsx**.

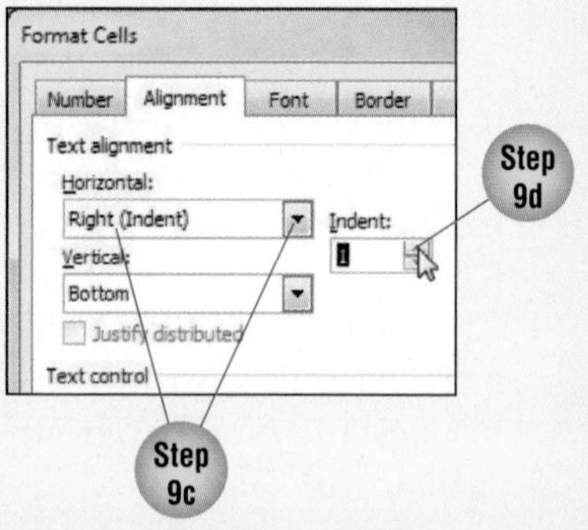

Changing the Font at the Format Cells Dialog Box

As you learned earlier in this chapter, the Font group in the Home tab contains buttons for applying font formatting to data in cells. You can also change the font for data in cells with options at the Format Cells dialog box with the Font tab selected as shown in Figure 3.8. At the Format Cells dialog box with the Font tab selected, you can change the font, font style, font size, and font color. You can also change the underlining method and add effects such as superscript and subscript. Click the Font group dialog box launcher to display this dialog box.

Figure 3.8 Format Cells Dialog Box with Font Tab Selected

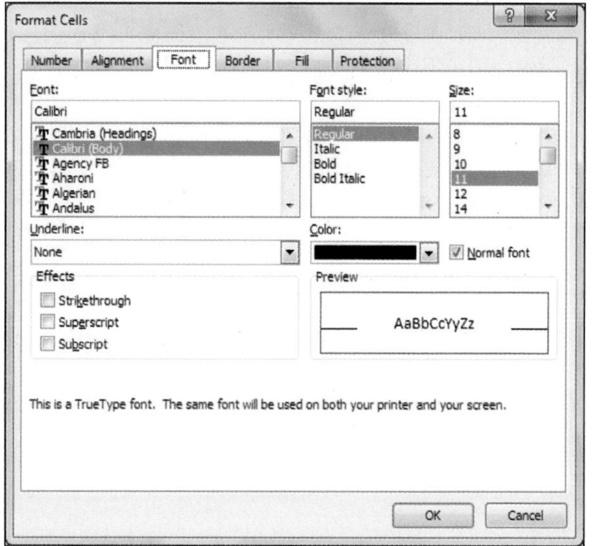

Project 4b Applying Font Formatting at the Format Cells Dialog Box

Part 2 of 6

1. With **EL1-C3-P4-HBCJobs.xlsx** open, change the font and font color by completing the following steps:
   a. Select cells A1 through E11.
   b. Click the Font group dialog box launcher.
   c. At the Format Cells dialog box with the Font tab selected, click *Garamond* in the *Font* list box. (You will need to scroll down the list to make this font visible.)
   d. Click *12* in the *Size* list box.
   e. Click the down-pointing arrow at the right of the *Color* option box.
   f. At the palette of color choices that displays, click the *Dark Red* color (first color option from the left in the *Standard Colors* section).
   g. Click OK to close the dialog box.
2. Make cell A1 active and then change the font to 24-point Garamond bold.
3. Select cells A2 through E2 and then apply bold formatting.
4. Save and then print **EL1-C3-P4-HBCJobs.xlsx**.

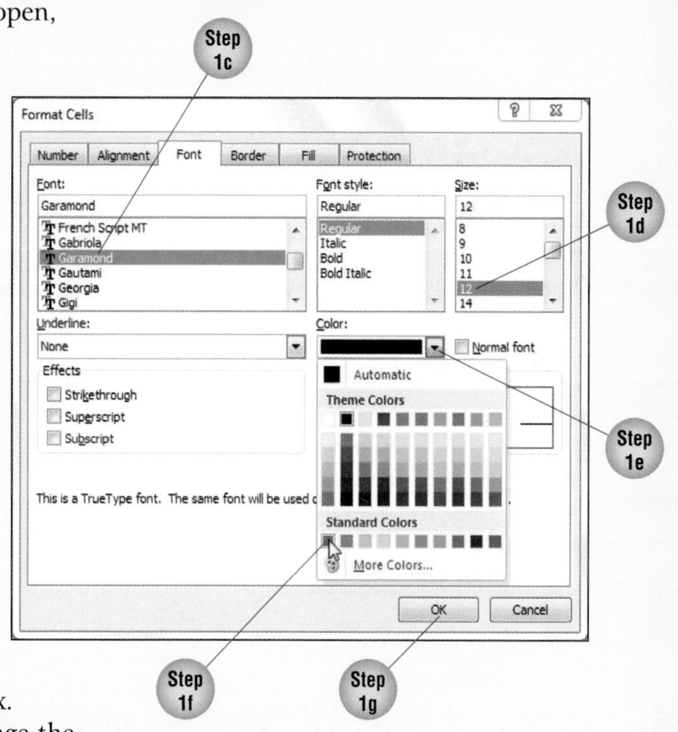

Adding Borders to Cells

Quick Steps

Add Borders to Cells
1. Select cells.
2. Click Borders button arrow.
3. Click desired border.

OR
1. Select cells.
2. Click Borders button arrow.
3. Click *More Borders.*
4. Use options in dialog box to apply desired border.
5. Click OK.

The gridlines that display in a worksheet do not print. As you learned earlier in this chapter, you can use the Borders button in the Font group to add borders to cells that will print. You can also add borders to cells with options at the Format Cells dialog box with the Border tab selected as shown in Figure 3.9. Display this dialog box by clicking the Borders button arrow in the Font group and then clicking *More Borders* at the drop-down list.

With options in the *Presets* section, you can remove borders with the *None* option, add only outside borders with the *Outline* option, or click the *Inside* option to add borders to the inside of selected cells. In the *Border* section of the dialog box, specify the side of the cell or selected cells to which you want to apply a border. Choose the style of line desired for the border with the options that display in the *Style* list box. Add color to border lines with choices from the color palette that displays when you click the down-pointing arrow located at the right side of the *Color* option box.

Figure 3.9 Format Cells Dialog Box with Border Tab Selected

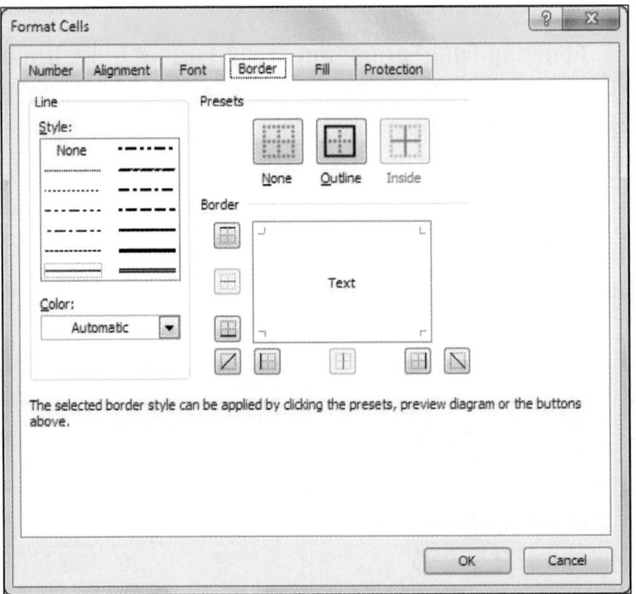

Project 4c **Adding Borders to Cells** Part 3 of 6

1. With **EL1-C3-P4-HBCJobs.xlsx** open, remove the 45 degrees orientation you applied in Project 4a by completing the following steps:
   a. Select cells B2 through E2.
   b. Click the Alignment group dialog box launcher.
   c. At the Format Cells dialog box with the Alignment tab selected, select *45* in the *Degrees* text box and then type 0.
   d. Click OK.

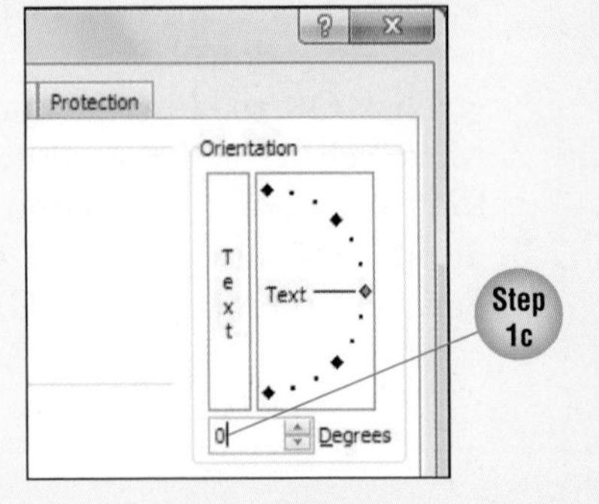

2. Change the height of row 2 to 33.00.
3. Add a thick, dark red border line to cells by completing the following steps:
   a. Select cells A1 through E11 (cells containing data).
   b. Click the Border button arrow in the Font group and then click the *More Borders* option at the drop-down list.
   c. At the Format Cells dialog box with the Border tab selected, click the down-pointing arrow at the right side of the *Color* option and then click *Dark Red* at the color palette (first color option from the left in the *Standard Colors* section).
   d. Click the thick single line option located in the second column (sixth option from the top) in the *Style* option box in the *Line* section.
   e. Click the *Outline* option in the *Presets* section.
   f. Click OK.
4. Add a border above and below cells by completing the following steps:
   a. Select cells A2 through E2.
   b. Click the Border button arrow in the Font group and then click *More Borders* at the drop-down list.
   c. At the Format Cells dialog box with the Border tab selected, make sure the color is Dark Red.
   d. Make sure the thick single line option (sixth option from the top in the second column) is selected in the *Style* option box in the *Line* section.
   e. Click the top border of the sample cell in the *Border* section of the dialog box.

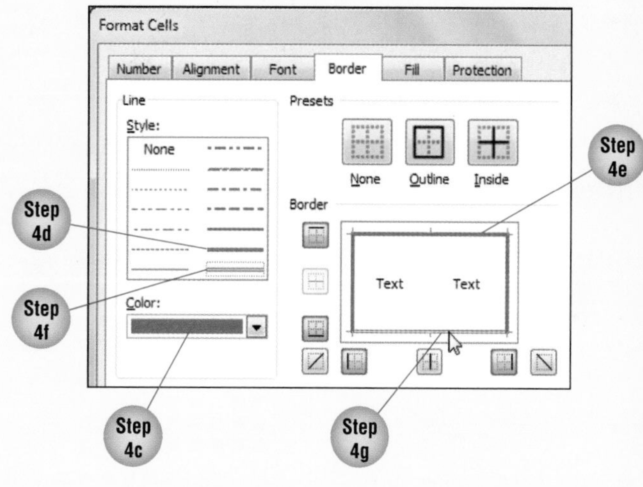

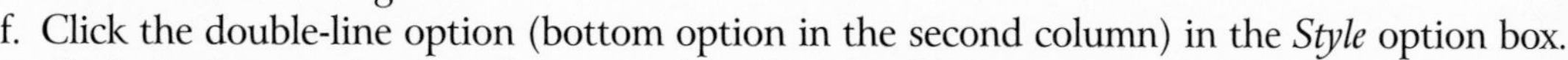

   f. Click the double-line option (bottom option in the second column) in the *Style* option box.
   g. Click the bottom border of the sample cell in the *Border* section of the dialog box.
   h. Click OK.
5. Save **EL1-C3-P4-HBCJobs.xlsx**.

Adding Fill and Shading to Cells

Quick Steps

Add Shading to Cells
1. Select cells.
2. Click Fill Color button arrow.
3. Click desired color.

OR

1. Select cells.
2. Click Format button.
3. Click *Format Cells* at drop-down list.
4. Click Fill tab.
5. Use options in dialog box to apply desired shading.
6. Click OK.

Repeat Last Action
1. Apply formatting.
2. Move to desired location.
3. Press F4 or Ctrl + Y.

To enhance the visual display of cells and data within cells, consider adding fill and/or shading to cells. As you learned earlier in this chapter, you can add fill color to cells with the Fill Color button in the Font group. You can also add fill color and/or shading to cells in a worksheet with options at the Format Cells dialog box with the Fill tab selected as shown in Figure 3.10. Display the Format Cells dialog box by clicking the Format button in the Cells group and then clicking *Format Cells* at the drop-down list. You can also display the dialog box by clicking the Font group, Alignment group, or Number group dialog box launcher. At the Format Cells dialog box, click the Fill tab or right-click in a cell and then click Format Cells at the shortcut menu.

Choose a fill color for a cell or selected cells by clicking a color choice in the Color palette. To add shading to a cell or selected cells, click the Fill Effects button and then click the desired shading style at the Fill Effects dialog box.

Repeating the Last Action

If you want to apply other types of formatting, such as number, border, or shading formatting to other cells in a worksheet, use the Repeat command by pressing F4 or Ctrl + Y. The Repeat command repeats the last action performed.

Figure 3.10 Format Cells Dialog Box with Fill Tab Selected

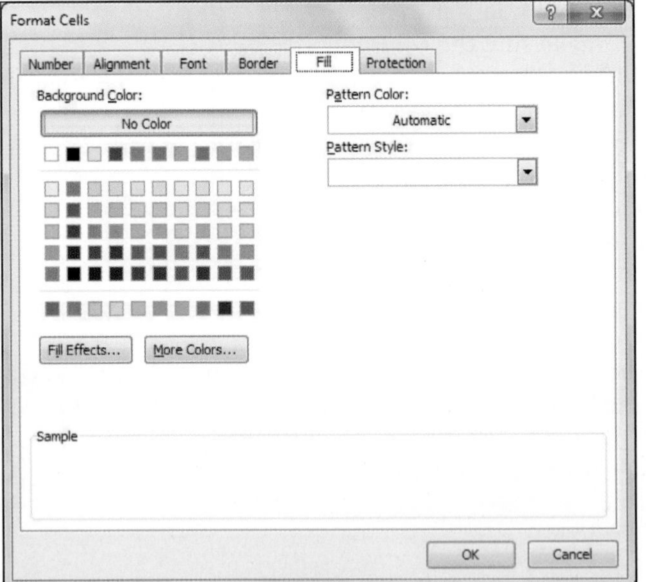

Adding Fill Color and Shading to Cells

1. With **EL1-C3-P4-HBCJobs.xlsx** open, add fill color to cell A1 and repeat the formatting by completing the following steps:
   a. Make cell A1 active.
   b. Click the Format button in the Cells group and then click *Format Cells* at the drop-down list.
   c. At the Format Cells dialog box, click the Fill tab.
   d. Click a light purple color in the *Background Color* section. (Click the eighth color from the left in the second row.)

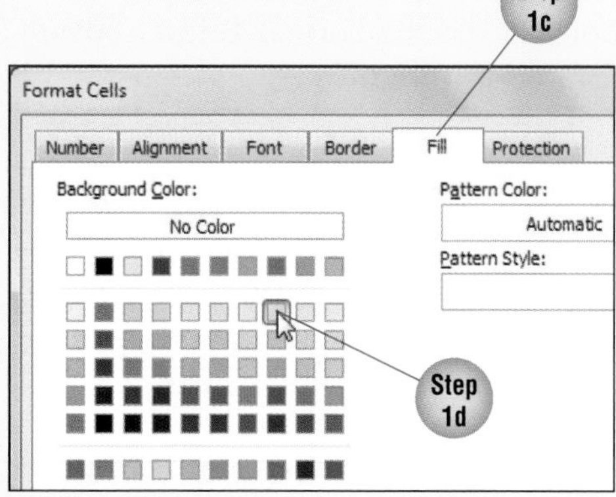

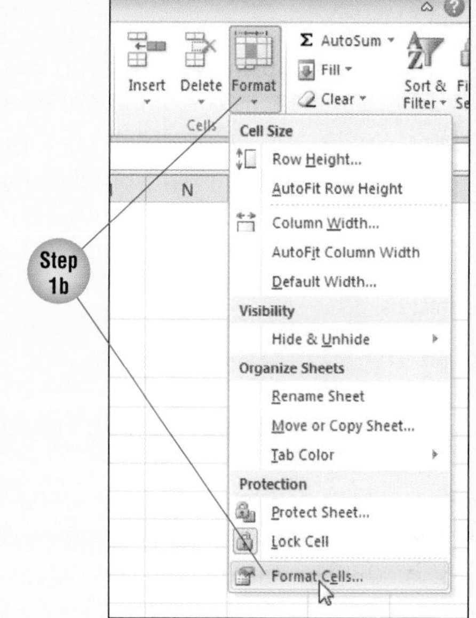

   e. Click OK.
   f. Select cells A2 through E2 and then press the F4 function key. (This repeats the light purple fill.)
2. Select row 2, insert a new row, and then change the height of the new row to 12.00.
3. Add shading to cells by completing the following steps:
   a. Select cells A2 through E2.
   b. Click the Format button in the Cells group and then click *Format Cells* at the drop-down list.
   c. At the Format Cells dialog box, if necessary, click the Fill tab.
   d. Click the Fill Effects button.
   e. At the Fill Effects dialog box, click the down-pointing arrow at the right side of the *Color 2* option box and then click *Purple, Accent 4* (eighth color from the left in the top row).
   f. Click OK to close the Fill Effects dialog box.
   g. Click OK to close the Format Cells dialog box.

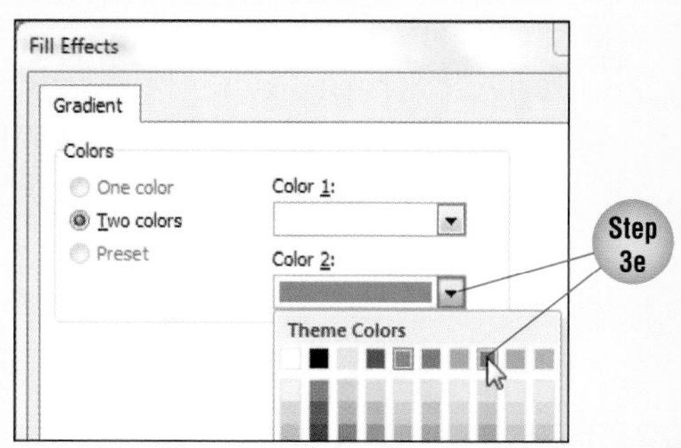

4. Save **EL1-C3-P4-HBCJobs.xlsx**.

Quick Steps

Format with Format Painter

1. Select cells with desired formatting.
2. Double-click Format Painter button.
3. Select cells.
4. Click Format Painter button.

Format Painter

Formatting with Format Painter

The Clipboard group in the Home tab contains a button you can use to copy formatting to different locations in the worksheet. This button is the Format Painter button and displays in the Clipboard group as a paintbrush. To use the Format Painter button, make a cell or selected cells active that contain the desired formatting, click the Format Painter button, and then click the cell or selected cells to which you want the formatting applied.

When you click the Format Painter button, the mouse pointer displays with a paintbrush attached. If you want to apply formatting a single time, click the Format Painter button once. If, however, you want to apply the character formatting in more than one location in the worksheet, double-click the Format Painter button. If you have double-clicked the Format Painter button, turn off the feature by clicking the Format Painter button once.

Project 4e Formatting with Format Painter

Part 5 of 6

1. With **EL1-C3-P4-HBCJobs.xlsx** open, select cells A5 through E5.
2. Click the Font group dialog box launcher.
3. At the Format Cells dialog box, click the Fill tab.
4. Click the light green color (seventh color from the left in the second row).
5. Click OK to close the dialog box.
6. Use Format Painter to "paint" formatting to rows by completing the following steps:
   a. With A5 through E5 selected, double-click the Format Painter button in the Clipboard group.
   b. Select cells A7 through E7.
   c. Select cells A9 through E9.
   d. Select cells A11 through E11.
   e. Turn off Format Painter by clicking the Format Painter button in the Clipboard group.
7. Save and then print **EL1-C3-P4-HBCJobs.xlsx**.

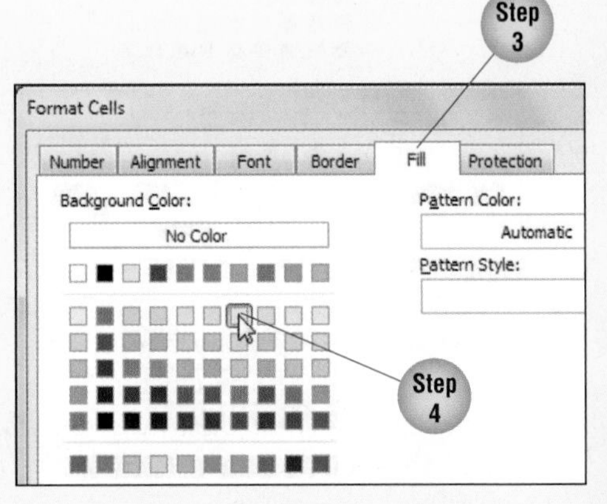

Hiding and Unhiding Columns and/or Rows

Set the column width to zero and the column is hidden. Set the row height to zero and the row is hidden.

If a worksheet contains columns and/or rows of sensitive data or data that you are not using or do not want to view, consider hiding the columns and/or rows. To hide columns in a worksheet, select the columns to be hidden, click the Format button in the Cells group in the Home tab, point to *Hide & Unhide*, and then click *Hide Columns*. To hide selected rows, click the Format button in the Cells group, point to *Hide & Unhide*, and then click *Hide Rows*. To make a hidden column visible, select the column to the left and the column to the right of the hidden column, click the Format button in the Cells group, point to *Hide & Unhide*, and then click *Unhide Columns*. To make a hidden row visible, select the row above and the row below the hidden row, click the Format button in the Cells group, point to *Hide & Unhide*, and then click *Unhide Rows*.

If the first row or column is hidden, use the Go To feature to make the row or column visible. To do this, click the Find & Select button in the Editing group in the Home tab and then click *Go To* at the drop-down list. At the Go To dialog box, type *A1* in the *Reference* text box and then click OK. At the worksheet, click the Format button in the Cells group, point to *Hide & Unhide*, and then click *Unhide Columns* or click *Unhide Rows*.

You can also unhide columns or rows using the mouse. If a column or row is hidden, the light blue boundary line in the column or row header displays as a slightly thicker blue line. To unhide a column, position the mouse pointer on the slightly thicker blue line that displays in the column header until the mouse pointer changes to left- and right-pointing arrows with a double line between. (Make sure the mouse pointer displays with two lines between the arrows. If a single line displays, you will simply change the size of the visible column.) Hold down the left mouse button, drag to the right until the column displays at the desired width, and then release the mouse button. Unhide a row in a similar manner. Position the mouse pointer on the slightly thicker blue line in the row header until the mouse pointer changes to up- and down-pointing arrows with a double line between. Drag down to display the row and then release the mouse button. If two or more adjacent columns or rows are hidden, you will need to unhide each column or row separately.

Quick Steps

Hide Columns
1. Select columns.
2. Click Format button.
3. Point to *Hide & Unhide.*
4. Click *Hide Columns.*

Hide Rows
1. Select rows.
2. Click Format button.
3. Point to *Hide & Unhide.*
4. Click *Hide Rows.*

Project 4f **Hiding and Unhiding Columns and Rows** Part 6 of 6

1. With **EL1-C3-P4-HBCJobs.xlsx** open, hide the row for Linstrom Enterprises and the row for Summit Services by completing the following steps:
   a. Click the row 7 header to select the entire row.
   b. Hold down the Ctrl key and then click the row 11 header to select the entire row.
   c. Click the Format button in the Cells group in the Home tab, point to *Hide & Unhide*, and then click *Hide Rows*.
2. Hide the column containing the actual amounts by completing the following steps:
   a. Click cell D3 to make it the active cell.
   b. Click the Format button in the Cells group, point to *Hide & Unhide*, and then click *Hide Columns*.
3. Save and then print **EL1-C3-P4-HBCJobs.xlsx**.
4. Unhide the rows by completing the following steps:
   a. Select rows 6 through 12.
   b. Click the Format button in the Cells group, point to *Hide & Unhide*, and then click *Unhide Rows*.
   c. Click in cell A4.
5. Unhide column D by completing the following steps:
   a. Position the mouse pointer on the thicker gray line that displays between columns C and E in the column header until the pointer turns into arrows pointing left and right with a double line between.

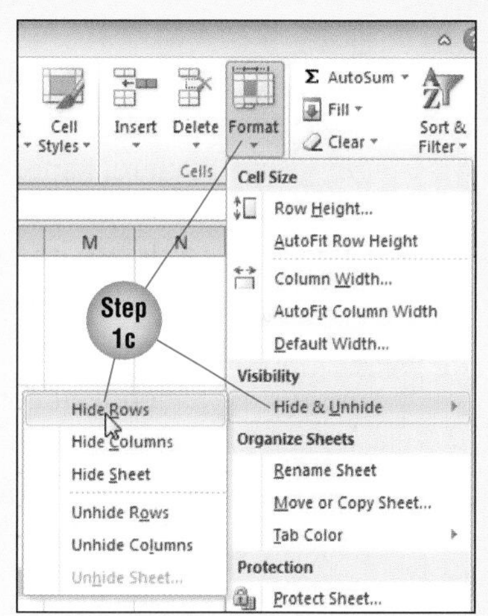

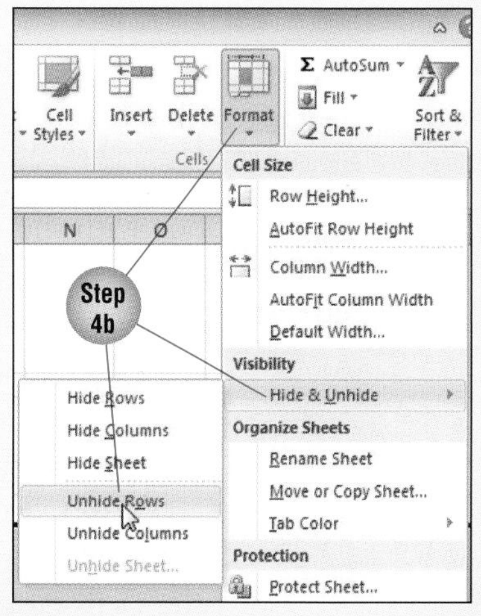

b. Hold down the left mouse button, drag to the right until *Width: 12.57 (93 pixels)* displays in a box above the mouse pointer, and then release the mouse button.

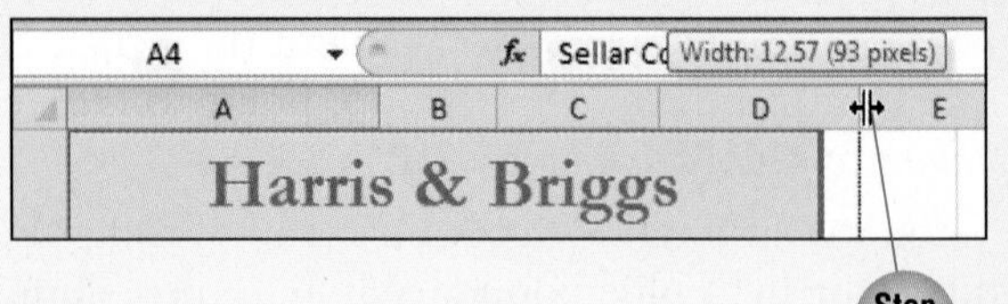

6. Save, print, and then close **EL1-C3-P4-HBCJobs.xlsx**.

Chapter Summary

- Change column width using the mouse on column boundaries or with options at the Column Width dialog box.
- Change row height using the mouse on row boundaries or with options at the Row Height dialog box.
- Insert a row in a worksheet with the Insert button in the Cells group in the Home tab or with options at the Insert dialog box.
- Insert a column in a worksheet with the Insert button in the Cells group or with options at the Insert dialog box.
- Delete a specific cell by clicking the Delete button arrow and then clicking *Delete Cells* at the drop-down list. At the Delete dialog box, specify if you want to delete just the cell or an entire row or column.
- Delete a selected row(s) or column(s) by clicking the Delete button in the Cells group.
- Delete cell contents by pressing the Delete key or clicking the Clear button in the Editing group and then clicking *Clear Contents* at the drop-down list.
- Apply font formatting with buttons in the Font group in the Home tab.
- Use the Mini toolbar to apply font formatting to selected data in a cell.
- Apply alignment formatting with buttons in the Alignment group in the Home tab.
- Use the Themes button in the Themes group in the Page Layout tab to apply a theme to cells in a worksheet that applies formatting such as color, font, and effects. Use the other buttons in the Themes group to customize the theme.
- Format numbers in cells with buttons in the Number group in the Home tab. You can also apply number formatting with options at the Format Cells dialog box with the Number tab selected.
- Apply formatting to cells in a worksheet with options at the Format Cells dialog box. This dialog box includes the following tabs for formatting cells: Number, Alignment, Font, Border, and Fill.
- Press F4 or Ctrl + Y to repeat the last action performed.
- Use the Format Painter button in the Clipboard group in the Home tab to apply formatting to different locations in a worksheet.
- Hide selected columns or rows in a worksheet by clicking the Format button in the Cells group in the Home tab, pointing to *Hide & Unhide*, and then clicking *Hide Columns* or *Hide Rows*.

- To make a hidden column visible, select the column to the left and right, click the Format button in the Cells group, point to *Hide & Unhide*, and then click *Unhide Columns*.
- To make a hidden row visible, select the row above and below, click the Format button in the Cells group, point to *Hide & Unhide*, and then click *Unhide Rows*.

Commands Review

FEATURE	RIBBON TAB, GROUP	BUTTON	KEYBOARD SHORTCUT
Format	Home, Cells		
Insert cells, rows, columns	Home, Cells		
Delete cells, rows, columns	Home, Cells		
Clear cell or cell contents	Home, Editing	Clear	
Font	Home, Font	Calibri	
Font size	Home, Font	11	
Increase font size	Home, Font	A	
Decrease font size	Home, Font	A	
Bold	Home, Font	B	Ctrl + B
Italic	Home, Font	I	Ctrl + I
Underline	Home, Font	U	Ctrl + U
Borders	Home, Font		
Fill color	Home, Font		
Font color	Home, Font	A	
Top align	Home, Alignment		
Middle align	Home, Alignment		
Bottom align	Home, Alignment		
Orientation	Home, Alignment		

FEATURE	RIBBON TAB, GROUP	BUTTON	KEYBOARD SHORTCUT
Align text left	Home, Alignment		
Center	Home, Alignment		
Align text right	Home, Alignment		
Decrease indent	Home, Alignment		Ctrl + Alt + Shift + Tab
Increase indent	Home, Alignment		Ctrl + Alt + Tab
Wrap text	Home, Alignment		
Merge & Center	Home, Alignment		
Themes	Page Layout, Themes		
Number Format	Home, Number	General	
Format Painter	Home, Clipboard		
Repeat			F4 or Ctrl + Y

Concepts Check Test Your Knowledge

Completion: In the space provided at the right, indicate the correct term, symbol, or command.

1. By default, a column is inserted in this direction from the column containing the active cell. __________
2. To delete a row, select the row and then click the Delete button in this group in the Home tab. __________
3. With the options at this button's drop-down list, you can clear the contents of the cell or selected cells. __________
4. Use this button to insert color in the active cell or selected cells. __________
5. Select data in a cell and this displays in a dimmed fashion above the selected text. __________
6. By default, numbers are aligned at this side of a cell. __________
7. Click this button in the Alignment group in the Home tab to rotate data in a cell. __________

8. The Themes button is located in this tab. ____________

9. If you type a number with a dollar sign, such as $50.25, Excel automatically applies this formatting to the number. ____________

10. If you type a number with a percent sign, such as 25%, Excel automatically applies this formatting to the number. ____________

11. Align and indent data in cells using buttons in the Alignment group in the Home tab or with options at this dialog box with the Alignment tab selected. ____________

12. You can repeat the last action performed with the command Ctrl + Y or by pressing this function key. ____________

13. The Format Painter button is located in this group in the Home tab. ____________

14. To hide a column, select the column, click this button in the Cells group in the Home tab, point to *Hide & Unhide*, and then click *Hide Columns*. ____________

Skills Check Assess Your Performance

Assessment 1

FORMAT A SALES AND BONUSES WORKSHEET

1. Open **NSPSales.xlsx**.
2. Save the workbook with Save As and name it **EL1-C3-A1-NSPSales**.
3. Change the width of columns as follows:
   Column A = 14.00
   Columns B – E = 10.00
   Column F = 6.00
4. Select row 2 and then insert a new row.
5. Merge and center cells A2 through F2.
6. Type Sales Department in cell A2 and then press Enter.
7. Increase the height of row 1 to 33.00.
8. Increase the height of row 2 to 21.00.
9. Increase the height of row 3 to 18.00.
10. Make the following formatting changes to the worksheet:
    a. Make cell A1 active, change the font size to 18 points, and turn on bold.
    b. Make cell A2 active, change the font size to 14 points, and turn on bold.
    c. Select cells A3 through F3, click the Bold button in the Font group, and then click the Center button in the Alignment group.
    d. Select cells A1 through F3, change the vertical alignment to Middle Align.
11. Insert the following formulas in the worksheet:
    a. Insert a formula in D4 that adds the amounts in B4 and C4. Copy the formula down to cells D5 through D11.

b. Insert a formula in E4 that averages the amounts in B4 and C4. Copy the formula down to cells E5 through E11.
c. Insert an IF statement in cell F4 that says that if the amount in cell E4 is greater than 74999, then insert the word "Yes" and if the amount is not greater than 74999, then insert the word "No." Copy this formula down to cells F5 through F11.

12. Make the following changes to the worksheet:
    a. Select cells F4 through F11 and then click the Center button in the Alignment group.
    b. Select cells B4 through E4 and then change the number formatting to Accounting with 0 decimal places and a dollar sign.
    c. Select cells B5 through E11, click the Comma Style button, and then click twice on the Decrease Decimal button.
    d. Add a double-line border around cells A1 through F11.
    e. Select cells A1 and A2 and then apply a light orange fill color.
    f. Select cells A3 through F3 and then apply an orange fill color.
13. Save and then print the worksheet.
14. Apply the Verve theme to the worksheet.
15. Save, print, and then close **EL1-C3-A1-NSPSales.xlsx**.

Assessment 2

FORMAT AN OVERDUE ACCOUNTS WORKSHEET

1. Open **CCorpAccts.xlsx**.
2. Save the workbook with Save As and name it **EL1-C3-A2-CCorpAccts**.
3. Change the width of columns as follows:

   Column A = 21.00
   Column B = 10.00
   Column C = 10.00
   Column D = 12.00
   Column E = 7.00
   Column F = 12.00
4. Make cell A1 active and then insert a new row.
5. Merge and center cells A1 through F1.
6. Type **Compass Corporation** in cell A1 and then press Enter.
7. Increase the height of row 1 to 42.00.
8. Increase the height of row 2 to 24.00.
9. Make the following formatting changes to the worksheet:
    a. Select cells A1 through F11 and then change the font to 10-point Cambria.
    b. Make cell A1 active, change the font size to 24 points, and turn on bold.
    c. Make cell A2 active, change the font size to 18 points, and turn on bold.
    d. Select cells A3 through F3, click the Bold button in the Font group and then click the Center button in the Alignment group.
    e. Select cells A1 through F3, click the Middle Align button in the Alignment group.
    f. Select cells B4 through B11 and then click the Center button in the Alignment group.
    g. Select cells E4 through E11 and then click the Center button in the Alignment group.

10. Use the DATE function in the following cells to enter a formula that returns the serial number for the following dates:
    D4 = October 1, 2012
    D5 = October 3, 2012
    D6 = October 8, 2012
    D7 = October 10, 2012
    D8 = October 15, 2012
    D9 = October 30, 2012
    D10 = November 6, 2012
    D11 = November 13, 2012
11. Enter a formula in cell F4 that inserts the due date (the purchase date plus the number of days in the Terms column). Copy the formula down to cells F5 through F11.
12. Apply the following borders and fill color:
    a. Add a thick line border around cells A1 through F11.
    b. Make cell A2 active and then add a double-line border at the top and bottom of the cell.
    c. Select cells A3 through F3 and then add a single line border to the bottom of the cells.
    d. Select cells A1 and A2 and then apply a light blue fill color.
13. Save, print, and then close **EL1-C3-A2-CCorpAccts.xlsx**.

Assessment 3

FORMAT A SUPPLIES AND EQUIPMENT WORKSHEET

1. Open **OEBudget.xlsx**.
2. Save the workbook with Save As and name it **EL1-C3-A3-OEBudget**.
3. Select and then merge across cells A1 through D2. ***Hint: Use the* Merge Across *option at the Merge & Center button drop-down list.***
4. With cells A1 and A2 selected, click the Middle Align button in the Alignment group and then click the Center button.
5. Make cell A1 active and then change the font size to 22 points and turn on bold.
6. Make cell A2 active and then change the font size to 12 points and turn on bold.
7. Change the height of row 1 to 36.00.
8. Change the height of row 2 to 21.00.
9. Change the width of column A to 15.00.
10. Select cells A3 through A17, turn on bold, and then click the Wrap Text button in the Alignment group.
11. Make cell B3 active and then change the number formatting to Currency with no decimal places.
12. Select cells C6 through C19 and then change the number formatting to Percentage with one decimal place.
13. Automatically adjust the width of column B.
14. Make cell D6 active and then type a formula that multiplies the absolute cell reference $B$3 with the percentage in cell C6. Copy the formula down to cells D7 through D19.
15. With cells D6 through D19 selected, change the number formatting to Currency with no decimal places.
16. Make cell D8 active and then clear the cell contents. Use the Repeat command, F4, to clear the contents from cells D11, D14, and D17.
17. Select cells A1 through D19, change the font to Constantia, and then change the font color to dark blue.

18. Add light green fill color to the following cells: A1, A2, A5–D5, A8–D8, A11–D11, A14–D14, and A17–D17.
19. Add borders and/or additional shading of your choosing to enhance the visual appeal of the worksheet.
20. Save, print, and then close **EL1-C3-A3-OEBudget.xlsx**.

Assessment

4 FORMAT A FINANCIAL ANALYSIS WORKSHEET

1. At a blank workbook, display the Format Cells dialog box with the Alignment tab selected and then experiment with the options in the *Text control* section.
2. Open **FinAnalysis.xlsx**.
3. Save the workbook with Save As and name it **EL1-C3-A4-FinAnalysis**.
4. Make cell B9 active and then insert a formula that averages the percentages in cells B3 through B8. Copy the formula to the right to cells C9 and D9.
5. Select cells B3 through D9, display the Format Cells dialog box with the Alignment tab selected, change the horizontal alignment to *Right (Indent)* and the indent to *2*, and then close the dialog box.
6. Select cells A1 through D9 and then change the font size to 14.
7. Select cells B2 through D2 and then change the orientation to 45 degrees.
8. With cells B2 through D2 still selected, shrink the font size to show all data in the cells.
9. Save, print, and then close **EL1-C3-A4-FinAnalysis.xlsx**.

Visual Benchmark Demonstrate Your Proficiency

CREATE A WORKSHEET AND INSERT FORMULAS

1. At a blank workbook, type the data in the cells indicated in Figure 3.11 but **do not** type the data in the following cells—instead insert the formulas as indicated (the results of your formulas should match the results you see in the figure):
   - Cells C4 through C14: Insert a formula with an IF statement that inserts the word *Yes* if the sales amount is greater than $114,999 and inserts the word *No* if the sales amount is not greater than $114,999.
   - Cells D4 through D14: Insert a formula with an IF statement that if the content of the previous cell is *Yes*, then multiply the amount in the cell in column B by 0.05 and if the previous cell does not contain the word *Yes*, then insert a zero.
2. Apply formatting so your worksheet looks similar to the worksheet shown in Figure 3.11.
3. Save the workbook and name it **EL1-C3-VB-BonusAmounts**.
4. Print **EL1-C3-VB-BonusAmounts.xlsx**.
5. Press Ctrl + ` to turn on the display of formulas and then print the worksheet again.
6. Turn off the display of formulas and then close the workbook.

Figure 3.11 Visual Benchmark

	A	B	C	D	E
1	Capstan Marine Products				
2	Sales Department Bonuses				
3	Salesperson	Sales	Bonus	Amount	
4	Abrams, Warner	$ 130,490.00	Yes	$ 6,524.50	
5	Allejandro, Elaine	95,500.00	No	-	
6	Crispin, Nicolaus	137,000.00	Yes	6,850.00	
7	Frankel, Maria	124,000.00	Yes	6,200.00	
8	Hiesmann, Thomas	85,500.00	No	-	
9	Jarvis, Lawrence	159,000.00	Yes	7,950.00	
10	Littleman, Shirley	110,500.00	No	-	
11	McBride, Leah	78,420.00	No	-	
12	Ostlund, Sonya	101,435.00	No	-	
13	Ryckman, Graham	83,255.00	No	-	
14	Sharma, Anja	121,488.00	Yes	6,074.40	
15					

Case Study Apply Your Skills

Part 1

You are the office manager for HealthWise Fitness Center and you decide to prepare an Excel worksheet that displays the various plans offered by the health club. In this worksheet, you want to include yearly dues for each plan as well as quarterly and monthly payments. Open the **HFCDues.xlsx** workbook and then save it with Save As and name it **EL1-C3-CS-HFCDues-1**. Make the following changes to the worksheet:

- Select cells B3 through D8 and then change the number formatting to Accounting with two decimal places and a dollar sign.
- Make cell B3 active and then insert *500.00*.
- Make cell B4 active and then insert a formula that adds the amount in B3 with the product (multiplication) of B3 multiplied by 10%. (The formula should look like this: **=B3+(B3*10%)**. The Economy plan is the base plan and each additional plan costs 10% more than the previous plan.)
- Copy the formula in cell B4 down to cells B5 through B8.
- Insert a formula in cell C3 that divides the amount in cell B3 by 4 and then copy the formula down to cells C4 through C8.
- Insert a formula in cell D3 that divides the amount in cell B3 by 12 and then copy the formula down to cells D4 through D8.
- Apply formatting to enhance the visual display of the worksheet.

Save and print the completed worksheet.

With **EL1-C3-CS-HFCDues-1.xlsx** open, save the workbook with Save As and name it **EL1-C3-CS-HFCDues-2**, and then make the following changes:

- You have been informed that the base rate for yearly dues has increased from $500.00 to $600.00. Change this amount in cell B3 of the worksheet.
- If clients are late with their quarterly or monthly dues payments, a late fee is charged. You decide to add the late fee information to the worksheet. Insert a new column to the right of Column C. Type Late Fees in cell D2 and also in cell F2.
- Insert a formula in cell D3 that multiplies the amount in C3 by 5%. Copy this formula down to cells D4 through D8.
- Insert a formula in cell F3 that multiplies the amount in E3 by 7%. Copy this formula down to cells F4 through F8. If necessary, change the number formatting for cells F3 through F8 to Accounting with two decimal places and a dollar sign.
- Apply any additional formatting to enhance the visual display of the worksheet.

Save, print, and then close **EL1-C3-CS-HFCDues-2.xlsx**.

Part 2

Prepare a payroll sheet for the employees of the fitness center and include the following information:

HealthWise Fitness Center

Weekly Payroll

Employee	Hourly Wage	Hours	Weekly Salary	Benefits
Heaton, Kelly	$26.50	40		
Severson, Joel	$25.00	40		
Turney, Amanda	$20.00	15		
Walters, Leslie	$19.65	30		
Overmeyer, Jean	$18.00	20		
Haddon, Bonnie	$16.00	20		
Baker, Grant	$15.00	40		
Calveri, Shannon	$12.00	15		
Dugan, Emily	$10.50	10		
Joyner, Daniel	$10.50	10		
Lee, Alexander	$10.50	10		

Insert a formula in the *Weekly Salary* column that multiplies the hourly wage by the number of hours. Insert an IF statement in the *Benefits* column that states that if the number in the *Hours* column is greater than 19, then insert "Yes" and if not, then insert "No." Apply formatting to enhance the visual display of the worksheet. Save the workbook and name it **EL1-C3-CS-HFCPayroll**. Print **EL1-C3-CS-HFCPayroll.xlsx**. Press Ctrl + ` to turn on the display of formulas, print the worksheet, and then press Ctrl + ` to turn off the display of formulas.

Make the following changes to the worksheet:

- Change the hourly wage for Amanda Turney to *$22.00*.
- Increase the hours for Emily Dugan to *20*.
- Remove the row for Grant Baker.
- Insert a row between Jean Overmeyer and Bonnie Haddon and then type the following information in the cells in the new row: Employee: Tonya McGuire; Hourly Wage: $17.50; Hours: 15.

Save and then print **EL1-C3-CS-HFCPayroll.xlsx**. Press Ctrl + ` to turn on the display of formulas and then print the worksheet. Press Ctrl + ` to turn off the display of formulas and then save and close **EL1-C3-CS-HFCPayroll.xlsx**.

Part 3

Your boss is interested in ordering new equipment for the health club. She is interested in ordering three elliptical machines, three recumbent bikes, and three upright bikes. She has asked you to use the Internet to research models and prices for this new equipment. She then wants you to prepare a worksheet with the information. Using the Internet, search for the following equipment:

- Search for elliptical machines for sale. Locate two different models and, if possible, find at least two companies that sell each model. Make a note of the company names, model numbers, and prices.
- Search for recumbent bikes for sale. Locate two different models and, if possible, find at least two companies that sell each model. Make a note of the company names, model numbers, and prices.
- Search for upright bikes for sale. Locate two different models and, if possible, find at least two companies that sell each model. Make a note of the company names, model numbers, and prices.

Using the information you found on the Internet, prepare an Excel worksheet with the following information:

- Equipment name
- Equipment model
- Price
- A column that multiplies the price by the number required (which is 3).

Include the fitness center name, HealthWise Fitness Center, and any other information you determine is necessary to the worksheet. Apply formatting to enhance the visual display of the worksheet. Save the workbook and name it **EL1-C3-CS-HFCEquip**. Print and then close **EL1-C3-CS-HFCEquip.xlsx**.

Part 4

When a prospective client contacts HealthWise about joining, you send a letter containing information about the fitness center, the plans offered, and the dues amounts. Use a letter template in Word to create a letter to send to a prospective client (you determine the client's name and address). Copy the cells in **EL1-C3-CS-HFCDues-02.xlsx** containing data and paste them into the body of the letter. Make any formatting changes to make the data readable. Save the document and name it **HFCLetter**. Print and then close **HFCLetter.docx**.

Enhancing a Worksheet

PERFORMANCE OBJECTIVES

Upon successful completion of Chapter 4, you will be able to:

- **Change worksheet margins**
- **Center a worksheet horizontally and vertically on the page**
- **Insert a page break in a worksheet**
- **Print gridlines and row and column headings**
- **Set and clear a print area**
- **Insert headers and footers**
- **Customize print jobs**
- **Complete a spelling check on a worksheet**
- **Find and replace data and cell formatting in a worksheet**
- **Sort data in cells in ascending and descending order**
- **Filter a list using AutoFilter**

Tutorials

4.1 Changing Page Margins and Layout Options
4.2 Formatting and Printing Options
4.3 Inserting a Page Break
4.4 Formatting a Worksheet Page
4.5 Adding Headers and Footers
4.6 Using Undo and Redo
4.7 Using Find and Replace
4.8 Sorting Data and Using Help

Excel contains features you can use to enhance and control the formatting of a worksheet. In this chapter, you will learn how to change worksheet margins, orientation, size, and scale; print column and row titles; print gridlines; and center a worksheet horizontally and vertically on the page. You will also learn how to complete a spell check on text in a worksheet, find and replace specific data and formatting in a worksheet, sort and filter data, and plan and create a worksheet. Model answers for this chapter's projects appear on the following pages.

Excel2010L1C4

Note: Before beginning the projects, copy to your storage medium the Excel2010L1C4 subfolder from the Excel2010L1 folder on the CD that accompanies this textbook and make Excel2010L1C4 the active folder.

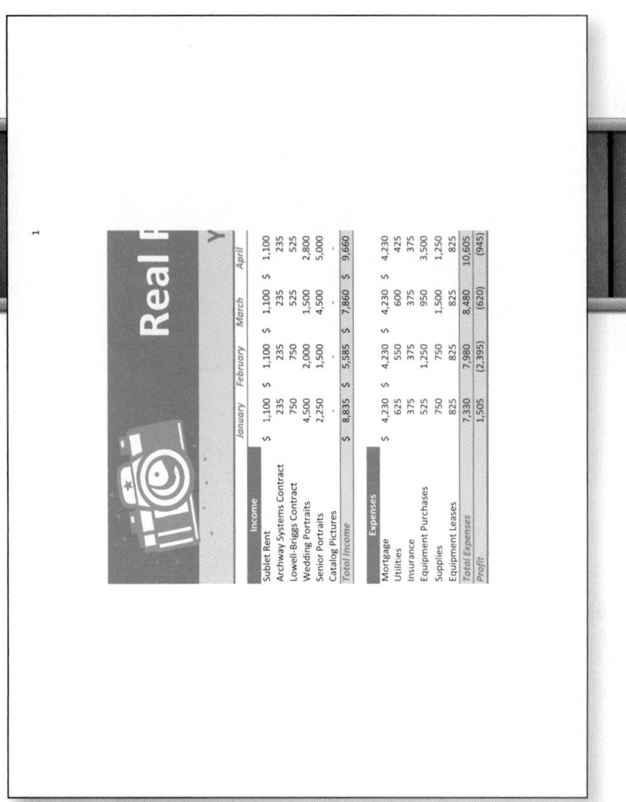

1

Real P

Y

Income	January	February	March	April
Sublet Rent	$ 1,100	$ 1,100	$ 1,100	$ 1,100
Archway Systems Contract	235	235	235	235
Lowell-Briggs Contract	750	750	525	525
Wedding Portraits	4,500	2,000	1,500	2,800
Senior Portraits	2,250	1,500	4,500	5,000
Catalog Pictures	-	-	-	-
Total Income	$ 8,835	$ 5,585	$ 7,860	$ 9,660
Expenses				
Mortgage	$ 4,230	$ 4,230	$ 4,230	$ 4,230
Utilities	625	550	600	425
Insurance	375	375	375	375
Equipment Purchases	525	1,250	950	3,500
Supplies	750	750	1,500	1,250
Equipment Leases	825	825	825	825
Total Expenses	7,330	7,980	8,480	10,605
Profit	1,505	(2,395)	(620)	(945)

2

Yearly Budget

hotography

early Budget

May	June	July	August	September	October
$ 1,100	$ 1,100	$ 1,100	$ 1,100	$ 1,100	$ 1,100
235	235	235	235	235	235
-	-	450	450	450	575
4,000	8,250	7,500	6,850	4,500	3,500
3,250	1,000	300	500	650	650
500	500	500	500	500	-
$ 9,085	$ 11,085	$ 10,085	$ 9,635	$ 7,435	$ 6,060
$ 4,230	$ 4,230	$ 4,230	$ 4,230	$ 4,230	$ 4,230
400	500	650	700	700	500
375	375	375	375	375	375
-	-	-	-	-	-
1,500	2,500	2,250	1,750	950	850
825	825	825	825	825	825
7,330	8,430	8,330	7,880	7,080	6,780
1,755	2,655	1,755	1,755	355	(720)

Student Name

Project 1 Format a Yearly Budget Worksheet

EL1-C4-P1-RPBudget.xlsx

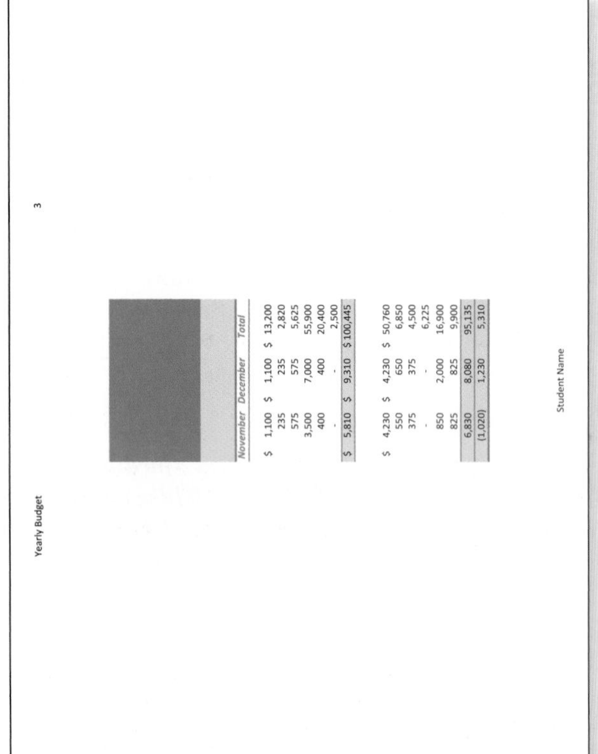

3

Yearly Budget

November	December	Total
$ 1,100	$ 1,100	$ 13,200
235	235	2,820
575	575	5,625
3,500	7,000	55,900
400	400	20,400
-	-	2,500
$ 5,810	$ 9,310	$ 100,445
$ 4,230	$ 4,230	$ 50,760
550	650	6,850
375	375	4,500
-	-	6,225
850	2,000	16,900
825	825	9,900
6,830	8,080	95,135
(1,020)	1,230	5,310

Student Name

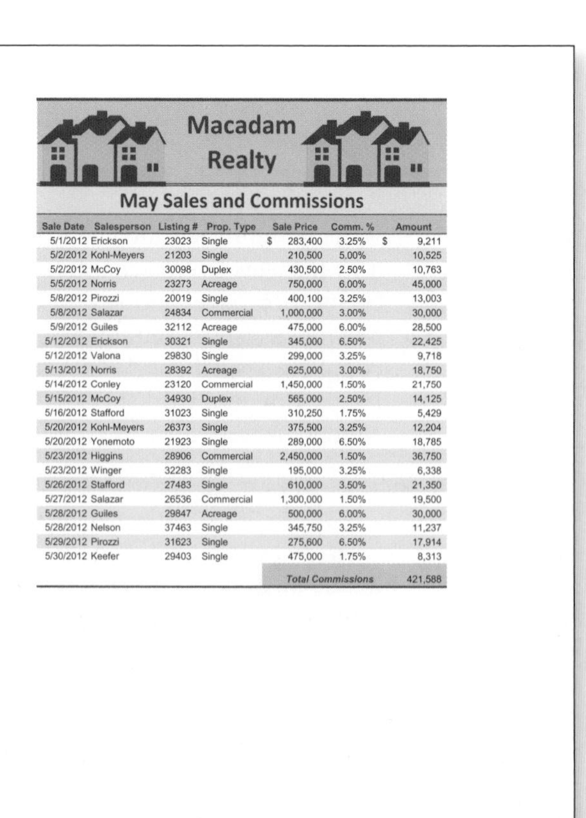

Macadam Realty

May Sales and Commissions

Sale Date	Salesperson	Listing #	Prop. Type	Sale Price	Comm. %	Amount
5/1/2012	Erickson	23023	Single	$ 283,400	3.25%	$ 9,211
5/2/2012	Kohl-Meyers	21203	Single	210,500	5.00%	10,525
5/2/2012	McCoy	30098	Duplex	430,500	2.50%	10,763
5/5/2012	Norris	23273	Acreage	750,000	6.00%	45,000
5/8/2012	Pirozzi	20019	Single	400,100	3.25%	13,003
5/8/2012	Salazar	24834	Commercial	1,000,000	3.00%	30,000
5/9/2012	Guiles	32112	Acreage	475,000	6.00%	28,500
5/12/2012	Erickson	30321	Single	345,000	6.50%	22,425
5/12/2012	Valona	29830	Single	299,000	3.25%	9,718
5/13/2012	Norris	28392	Acreage	625,000	3.00%	18,750
5/14/2012	Conley	23120	Commercial	1,450,000	1.50%	21,750
5/15/2012	McCoy	34930	Duplex	565,000	2.50%	14,125
5/16/2012	Stafford	31023	Single	310,250	1.75%	5,429
5/20/2012	Kohl-Meyers	26373	Single	375,500	3.25%	12,204
5/20/2012	Yonemoto	21923	Single	289,000	6.50%	18,785
5/23/2012	Higgins	28906	Commercial	2,450,000	1.50%	36,750
5/23/2012	Winger	32283	Single	195,000	3.25%	6,338
5/26/2012	Stafford	27483	Single	610,000	3.50%	21,350
5/27/2012	Salazar	26536	Commercial	1,300,000	1.50%	19,500
5/28/2012	Guiles	29847	Acreage	500,000	6.00%	30,000
5/28/2012	Nelson	37463	Single	345,750	3.25%	11,237
5/29/2012	Pirozzi	31623	Single	275,600	6.50%	17,914
5/30/2012	Keefer	29403	Single	475,000	1.75%	8,313
				Total Commissions		421,588

Project 2 Format a May Sales and Commissions Worksheet

EL1-C4-P2-MRSales.xlsx

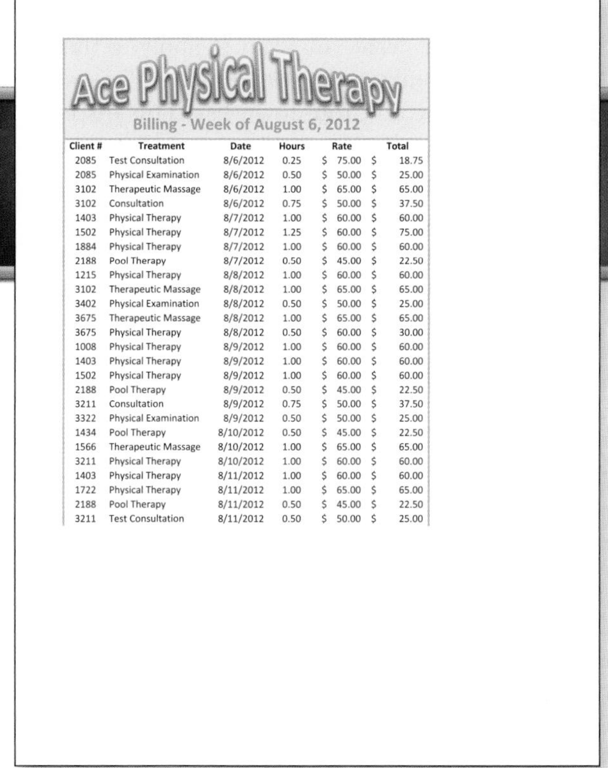

Ace Physical Therapy

Billing - Week of August 6, 2012

Client #	Treatment	Date	Hours	Rate	Total
2085	Test Consultation	8/6/2012	0.25	$ 75.00	$ 18.75
2085	Physical Examination	8/6/2012	0.50	$ 50.00	$ 25.00
3102	Therapeutic Massage	8/6/2012	1.00	$ 65.00	$ 65.00
3102	Consultation	8/6/2012	0.75	$ 50.00	$ 37.50
1403	Physical Therapy	8/7/2012	1.00	$ 60.00	$ 60.00
1502	Physical Therapy	8/7/2012	1.25	$ 60.00	$ 75.00
1884	Physical Therapy	8/7/2012	1.00	$ 60.00	$ 60.00
2188	Pool Therapy	8/7/2012	0.50	$ 45.00	$ 22.50
1215	Physical Therapy	8/8/2012	1.00	$ 60.00	$ 60.00
3102	Therapeutic Massage	8/8/2012	1.00	$ 65.00	$ 65.00
3402	Physical Examination	8/8/2012	0.50	$ 50.00	$ 25.00
3675	Therapeutic Massage	8/8/2012	1.00	$ 65.00	$ 65.00
3675	Physical Therapy	8/8/2012	0.50	$ 60.00	$ 30.00
1008	Physical Therapy	8/9/2012	1.00	$ 60.00	$ 60.00
1403	Physical Therapy	8/9/2012	1.00	$ 60.00	$ 60.00
1502	Physical Therapy	8/9/2012	1.00	$ 60.00	$ 60.00
2188	Pool Therapy	8/9/2012	0.50	$ 45.00	$ 22.50
3211	Consultation	8/9/2012	0.75	$ 50.00	$ 37.50
3322	Physical Examination	8/9/2012	0.50	$ 50.00	$ 25.00
1434	Pool Therapy	8/10/2012	0.50	$ 45.00	$ 22.50
1566	Therapeutic Massage	8/10/2012	1.00	$ 65.00	$ 65.00
3211	Physical Therapy	8/10/2012	1.00	$ 60.00	$ 60.00
1403	Physical Therapy	8/11/2012	1.00	$ 60.00	$ 60.00
1722	Physical Therapy	8/11/2012	1.00	$ 65.00	$ 65.00
2188	Pool Therapy	8/11/2012	0.50	$ 45.00	$ 22.50
3211	Test Consultation	8/11/2012	0.50	$ 50.00	$ 25.00

Project 3 Format a Billing Worksheet

EL1-C4-P3-APTBilling.xlsx

Project 1 Format a Yearly Budget Worksheet — 12 Parts

You will format a yearly budget worksheet by inserting formulas; changing margins, page orientation, and page size; inserting a page break; printing column headings on multiple pages; scaling data to print on one page; inserting a background picture; inserting headers and footers; and identifying a print area and customizing print jobs.

Formatting a Worksheet Page

An Excel worksheet contains default page formatting. For example, a worksheet contains left and right margins of 0.7 inch and top and bottom margins of 0.75 inch, a worksheet prints in portrait orientation, and the worksheet page size is 8.5 inches by 11 inches. These default settings as well as additional options can be changed and/or controlled with options in the Page Layout tab.

Changing Margins

The Page Setup group in the Page Layout tab contains buttons for changing margins, the page orientation and size, as well as buttons for establishing a print area, inserting a page break, applying a picture background, and printing titles.

Change the worksheet margins by clicking the Margins button in the Page Setup group in the Page Layout tab. This displays a drop-down list of predesigned

Quick Steps

Change Worksheet Margins

1. Click Page Layout tab.
2. Click Margins button.
3. Click desired predesigned margin.

OR

1. Click Page Layout tab.
2. Click Margins button.
3. Click *Custom Margins* at drop-down list.
4. Change the top, left, right, and/or bottom measurements.
5. Click OK.

Margins

margin choices. If one of the predesigned choices is what you want to apply to the worksheet, click the option. If you want to customize margins, click the *Custom Margins* option at the bottom of the Margins button drop-down list. This displays the Page Setup dialog box with the Margins tab selected as shown in Figure 4.1.

A worksheet page showing the cells and margins displays in the dialog box. As you increase or decrease the top, bottom, left, or right margin measurements, the sample worksheet page reflects the change. You can also increase or decrease the measurement from the top of the page to the header with the *Header* option or the measurement from the footer to the bottom of the page with the *Footer* option. (You will learn about headers and footers later in this chapter.)

Figure 4.1 Page Setup Dialog Box with Margins Tab Selected

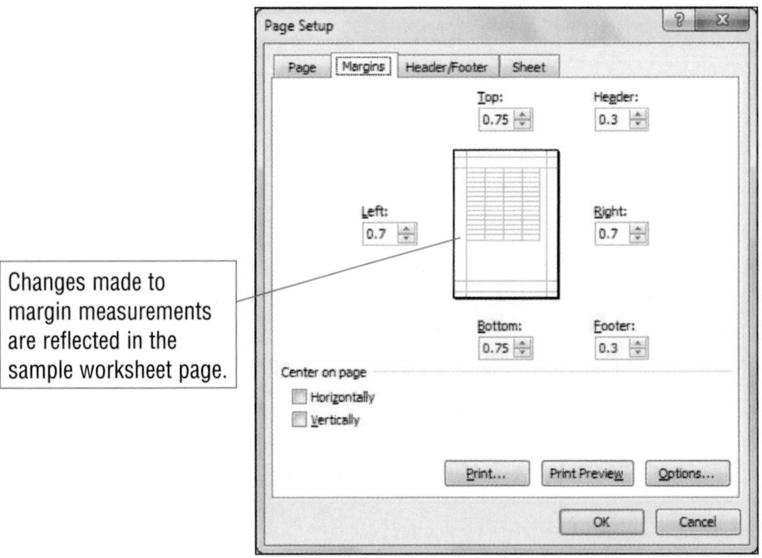

Quick Steps

Center Worksheet Horizontally/ Vertically
1. Click Page Layout tab.
2. Click Margins button.
3. Click *Custom Margins* at drop-down list.
4. Click *Horizontally* option and/or click *Vertically* option.
5. Click OK.

Centering a Worksheet Horizontally and/or Vertically

By default, worksheets print in the upper left corner of the page. You can center a worksheet on the page by changing the margins; however, an easier method for centering a worksheet is to use the *Horizontally* and/or *Vertically* options that display in the Page Setup dialog box with the Margins tab selected. If you choose one or both of these options, the worksheet page in the preview section displays how the worksheet will print on the page.

Changing Margins and Horizontally and Vertically Centering a Worksheet Part 1 of 12

1. Open **RPBudget.xlsx**.
2. Save the workbook with Save As and name it **EL1-C4-P1-RPBudget**.
3. Insert the following formulas in the worksheet:
   a. Insert formulas in column N, rows 5 through 10 that sum the totals for each income item.
   b. Insert formulas in row 11, columns B through N that sum the income as well as the total for all income items.

c. Insert formulas in column N, rows 14 through 19 that sum the totals for each expense item.
d. Insert formulas in row 20, columns B through N that sum the expenses as well as the total of expenses.
e. Insert formulas in row 21, columns B through N that subtract the total expenses from the income. (To begin the formula, make cell B21 active and then type the formula *=B11-B20*. Copy this formula to columns C through N.)
f. Apply the Accounting Number Format style with no decimal places to cells N5 and N14.

4. Click the Page Layout tab.
5. Click the Margins button in the Page Setup group and then click *Custom Margins* at the drop-down list.
6. At the Page Setup dialog box with the Margins tab selected, click the up-pointing arrow at the right side of the *Top* text box until *3.5* displays.
7. Click the up-pointing arrow at the right side of the *Bottom* text box until *1.5* displays.
8. Preview the worksheet by clicking the Print Preview button located toward the bottom of the Page Setup dialog box. The worksheet appears to be a little low on the page so you decide to horizontally and vertically center it by completing the following steps:
   a. Click the Page Setup hyperlink that displays below the categories in the Print tab Backstage view.
   b. Click the Margins tab at the Page Setup dialog box.
   c. Change the *Top* and *Bottom* measurements to *1*.
   d. Click the *Horizontally* option. (This inserts a check mark.)
   e. Click the *Vertically* option. (This inserts a check mark.)
   f. Click OK to close the dialog box.
   g. Look at the preview of the worksheet and then click the File tab to return to the worksheet.
9. Save **EL1-C4-P1-RPBudget.xlsx**.

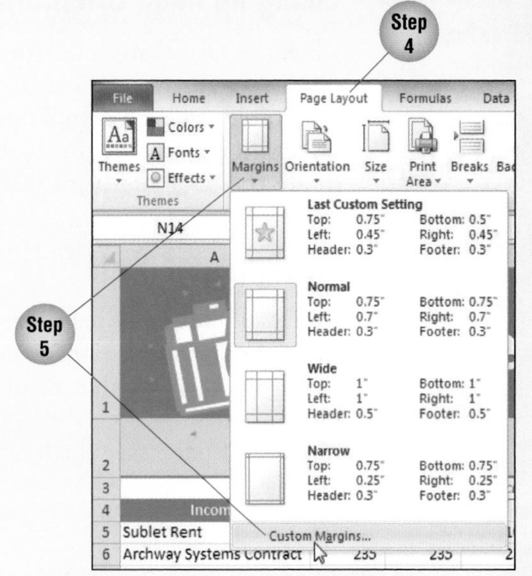

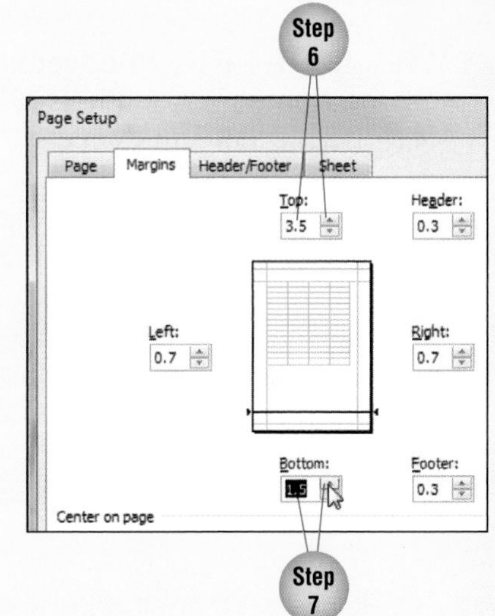

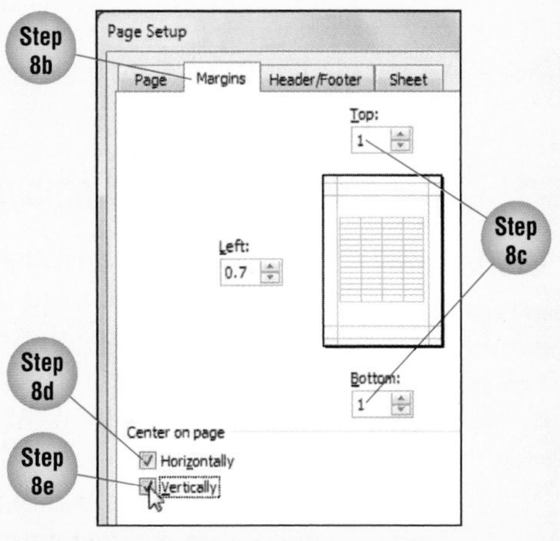

Quick Steps

Change Page Orientation
1. Click Page Layout tab.
2. Click Orientation button.
3. Click desired orientation at drop-down list.

Change Page Size
1. Click Page Layout tab.
2. Click Size button.
3. Click desired size at drop-down list.

Orientation

Size

Changing Page Orientation

Click the Orientation button in the Page Setup group and a drop-down list displays with two choices, *Portrait* and *Landscape*. The two choices are represented by sample pages. A sample page that is taller than it is wide shows how the default orientation (*Portrait*) prints data on the page. The other choice, *Landscape*, will rotate the data and print it on a page that is wider than it is tall.

Changing the Page Size

An Excel worksheet page size, by default, is set at 8.5 × 11 inches. You can change this default page size by clicking the Size button in the Page Setup group. At the drop-down list that displays, notice that the default setting is *Letter* and the measurement *8.5″ × 11″* displays below *Letter*. This drop-down list also contains a number of page sizes such as *Executive*, *Legal*, and a number of envelope sizes.

Project 1b **Changing Page Orientation and Size** Part 2 of 12

1. With **EL1-C4-P1-RPBudget.xlsx** open, click the Orientation button in the Page Setup group in the Page Layout tab and then click *Landscape* at the drop-down list.
2. Click the Size button in the Page Setup group and then click *Legal* at the drop-down list.
3. Preview the worksheet by clicking the File tab and then clicking the Print tab. After viewing the worksheet in the Print tab Backstage view, click the File tab to return to the worksheet.
4. Save **EL1-C4-P1-RPBudget.xlsx**.

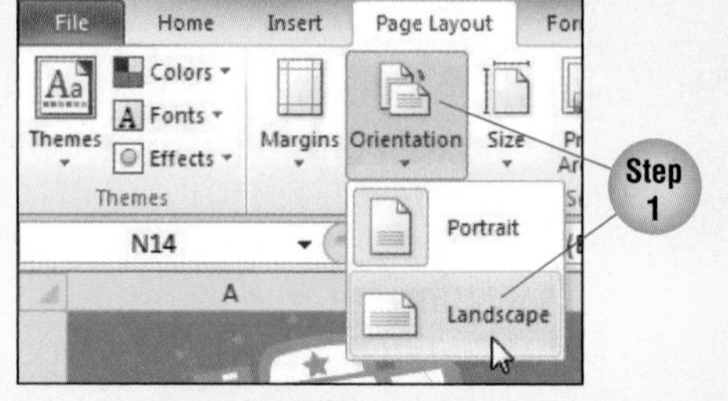

Inserting and Removing Page Breaks

Quick Steps

Insert Page Break
1. Select column or row.
2. Click Page Layout tab.
3. Click Breaks button.
4. Click *Insert Page Break* at drop-down list.

The default left and right margins of 0.7 inch allow approximately 7 inches of cells across the page (8.5 inches minus 1.4 inches equals 7.1 inches). If a worksheet contains more than 7 inches of cells across the page, a page break is inserted in the worksheet and the remaining columns are moved to the next page. A page break displays as a broken line along cell borders. Figure 4.2 shows the page break in **EL1-C4-P1-RPBudget.xlsx**.

A page break also displays horizontally in a worksheet. By default, a worksheet can contain approximately 9.5 inches of cells vertically down the page. This is because the paper size is set by default at 11 inches. With the default top and bottom margins of 0.75 inch, this allows 9.5 inches of cells to print on one page.

Figure 4.2 Page Break

Real Photography

Yearly Budget

page break

	January	February	March	April	May	June	July	August	September	October	November	December	Total
Income													
Sublet Rent	$ 1,100	$ 1,100	$ 1,100	$ 1,100	$ 1,100	$ 1,100	$ 1,100	$ 1,100	$ 1,100	$ 1,100	$ 1,100	$ 1,100	$ 13,200
Archway Systems Contract	235	235	235	235	235	235	235	235	235	235	235	235	2,820
Lowell-Briggs Contract	750	750	525	525	-	-	450	450	450	575	575	575	5,625
Wedding Portraits	4,500	2,000	1,500	2,800	4,000	8,250	7,500	6,850	4,500	3,500	3,500	7,000	55,900
Senior Portraits	2,250	1,500	4,500	5,000	3,250	1,000	300	500	650	650	400	400	20,400
Catalog Pictures	-	-	-	-	500	500	500	500	500	-	-	-	2,500
Total Income	$ 8,835	$ 5,585	$ 7,860	$ 9,660	$ 9,085	$ 11,085	$ 10,085	$ 9,635	$ 7,435	$ 6,060	$ 5,810	$ 9,310	$100,445
Expenses													
Mortgage	$ 4,230	$ 4,230	$ 4,230	$ 4,230	$ 4,230	$ 4,230	$ 4,230	$ 4,230	$ 4,230	$ 4,230	$ 4,230	$ 4,230	$ 50,760
Utilities	625	550	600	425	400	500	650	700	700	500	550	650	6,850
Insurance	375	375	375	375	375	375	375	375	375	375	375	375	4,500
Equipment Purchases	525	1,250	950	3,500	-	-	-	-	-	-	-	-	6,225
Supplies	750	750	1,500	1,250	1,500	2,500	2,250	1,750	950	850	850	2,000	16,900
Equipment Leases	825	825	825	825	825	825	825	825	825	825	825	825	9,900
Total Expenses	7,330	7,980	8,480	10,605	7,330	8,430	8,330	7,880	7,080	6,780	6,830	8,080	95,135
Profit	1,505	(2,395)	(620)	(945)	1,755	2,655	1,755	1,755	355	(720)	(1,020)	1,230	5,310

Sheet1 Sheet2 Sheet3

Excel automatically inserts a page break in a worksheet. You can insert your own if you would like more control over what cells print on a page. To insert your own page break, select the column or row, click the Breaks button in the Page Setup group in the Page Layout tab, and then click *Insert Page Break* at the drop-down list. A page break is inserted immediately left of the selected column or immediately above the selected row.

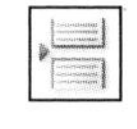

Breaks

If you want to insert both a horizontal and vertical page break at the same time, make a cell active, click the Breaks button in the Page Setup group and then click *Insert Page Break*. This causes a horizontal page break to be inserted immediately above the active cell, and a vertical page break to be inserted at the left side of the active cell. To remove a page break, select the column or row or make the desired cell active, click the Breaks button in the Page Setup group, and then click *Remove Page Break* at the drop-down list.

The page break automatically inserted by Excel may not be visible initially in a worksheet. One way to display the page break is to display the worksheet in the Print tab Backstage view. When you return to the worksheet, the page break will display in the worksheet.

Excel provides a page break view that displays worksheet pages and page breaks. To display this view, click the Page Break Preview button located in the view area at the right side of the Status bar or click the View tab and then click the Page Break Preview button in the Workbook Views group. This causes the worksheet to display similar to the worksheet shown in Figure 4.3. The word *Page* along with the page number is displayed in gray behind the cells in the worksheet. A solid blue line indicates a page break inserted by Excel and a dashed blue line indicates a page break inserted manually.

You can edit a worksheet in Page Break Preview.

Page Break Preview

You can move the page break by positioning the arrow pointer on the blue line, holding down the left mouse button, dragging the line to the desired location, and then releasing the mouse button. To return to the Normal view, click the Normal button in the view area on the Status bar or click the View tab and then click the Normal button in the Workbook Views group.

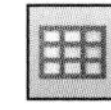

Normal

Figure 4.3 Worksheet in Page Break Preview

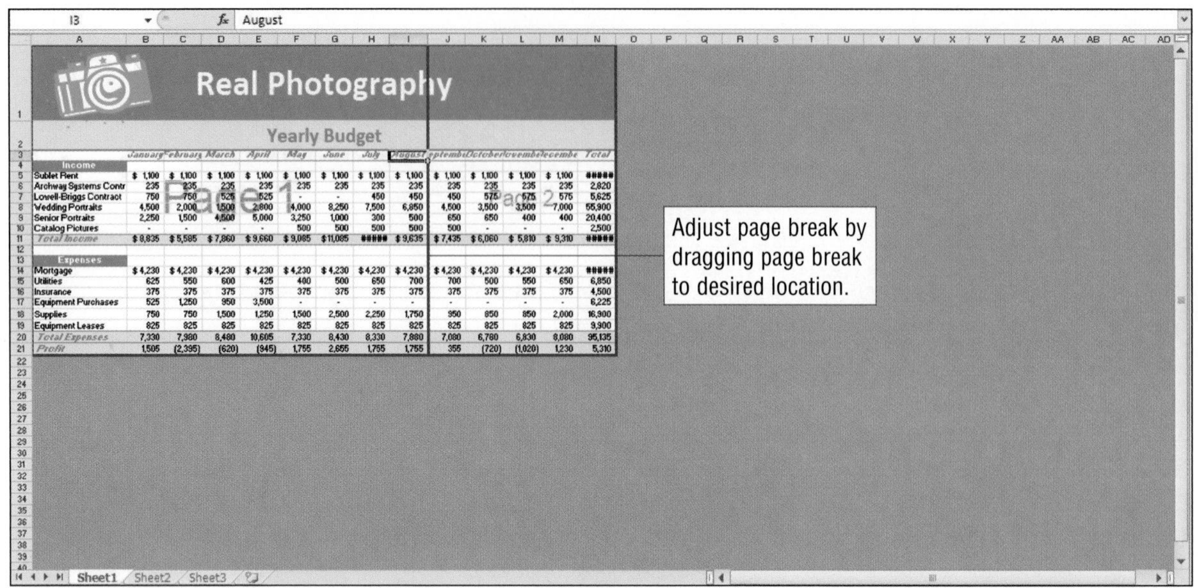

Project 1c Inserting a Page Break in a Worksheet

Part 3 of 12

1. With **EL1-C4-P1-RPBudget.xlsx** open, click the Size button in the Page Setup group in the Page Layout tab and then click *Letter* at the drop-down list.
2. Click the Margins button and then click *Custom Margins* at the drop-down list.
3. At the Page Setup dialog box with the Margins tab selected, click *Horizontally* to remove the check mark, click *Vertically* to remove the check mark, and then click OK to close the dialog box.
4. Insert a page break between columns I and J by completing the following steps:
   a. Select column J.
   b. Click the Breaks button in the Page Setup group and then click *Insert Page Break* at the drop-down list. Click in any cell in column I.

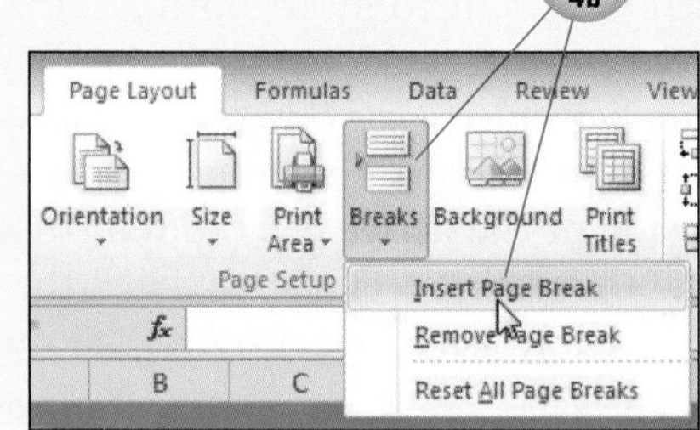

5. View the worksheet in Page Break Preview by completing the following steps:
   a. Click the Page Break Preview button located in the view area on the Status bar. (If a welcome message displays, click OK.)
   b. View the pages and page breaks in the worksheet.
   c. You decide to include the first six months of the year on one page. To do this, position the arrow pointer on the vertical blue line, hold down the left mouse button, drag the line to the left so it is positioned between columns G and H, and then release the mouse button.

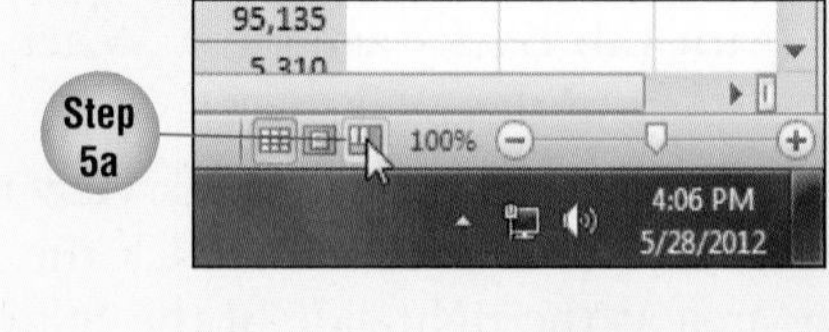

d. Click the Normal button located in the view area on the Status bar.

6. Save **EL1-C4-P1-RPBudget.xlsx**.

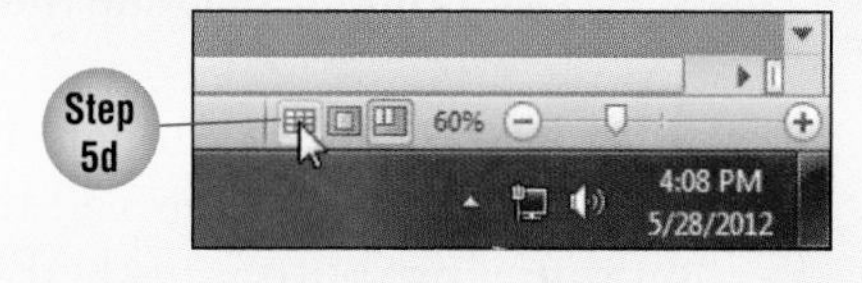

Printing Column and Row Titles on Multiple Pages

Columns and rows in a worksheet are usually titled. For example, in **EL1-C4-P1-RPBudget.xlsx**, column titles include *Income*, *Expenses*, *January*, *February*, *March*, and so on. Row titles include the income and expenses categories. If a worksheet prints on more than one page, having column and/or row titles printing on each page can be useful. To do this, click the Print Titles button in the Page Setup group in the Page Layout tab. This displays the Page Setup dialog box with the Sheet tab selected as shown in Figure 4.4.

At the Page Setup dialog box with the Sheet tab selected, specify the range of row cells you want to print on every page in the *Rows to repeat at top* text box. Type a cell range using a colon. For example, if you want cells A1 through J1 to print on every page, you would type *A1:J1* in the *Rows to repeat at top* text box. Type the range of column cells you want to print on every page in the *Columns to repeat at left* text box. To make rows and columns easier to identify on the printed page, specify that row and/or column headings print on each page.

Quick Steps

Print Column and Row Titles

1. Click Page Layout tab.
2. Click Print Titles button.
3. Type row range in *Rows to repeat at top* option.
4. Type column range in *Columns to repeat at left* option.
5. Click OK.

Print Titles

Figure 4.4 Page Setup Dialog Box with Sheet Tab Selected

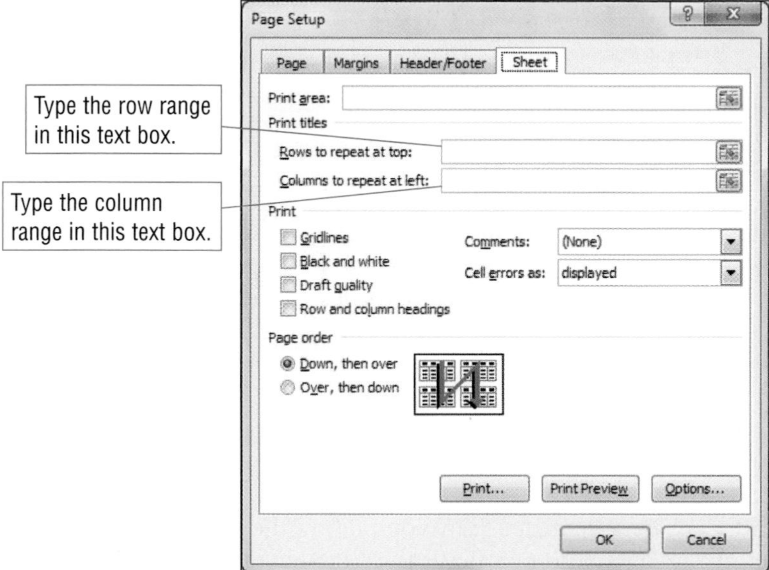

Project 1d Printing Column Titles on Each Page of a Worksheet Part 4 of 12

1. With **EL1-C4-P1-RPBudget.xlsx** open, click the Page Layout tab and then click the Print Titles button in the Page Setup group.
2. At the Page Setup dialog box with the Sheet tab selected, click in the *Columns to repeat at left* text box.
3. Type A1:A21.
4. Click OK to close the dialog box.
5. Save and then print **EL1-C4-P1-RPBudget.xlsx**.

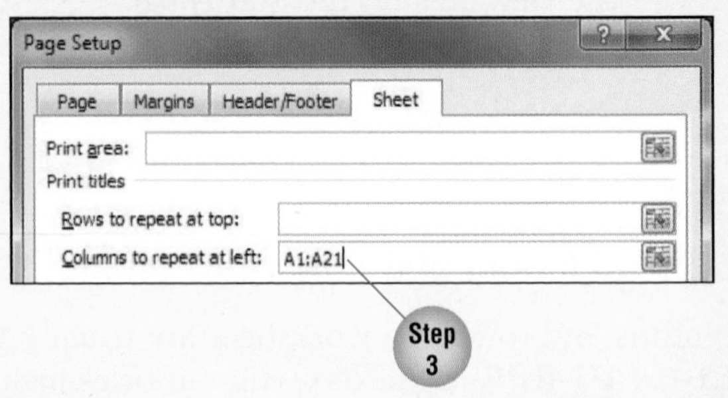

Scaling Data

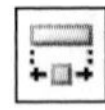
Width

With buttons in the Scale to Fit group in the Page Layout tab, you can adjust the printed output by a percentage to fit the number of pages specified. For example, if a worksheet contains too many columns to print on one page, click the down-pointing arrow at the right side of the *Width* box in the Scale to Fit group in the Page Layout tab and then click *1 page*. This causes the data to shrink so all columns display and print on one page.

Project 1e Scaling Data to Fit on One Page and Printing Row Titles on Each Page Part 5 of 12

1. With **EL1-C4-P1-RPBudget.xlsx** open, click the down-pointing arrow at the right side of the *Width* box in the Scale to Fit group in the Page Layout tab.
2. At the drop-down list that displays, click the *1 page* option.
3. Display the Print tab Backstage view, notice that all cells containing data display on one page in the worksheet, and then return to the worksheet.
4. Change margins by completing the following steps:
   a. Click the Page Layout tab.
   b. Click the Margins button in the Page Setup group and then click *Custom Margins* at the drop-down list.
   c. At the Page Setup dialog box with the Margins tab selected, select the current number in the *Top* text box and then type 3.5.
   d. Select the current number in the *Left* text box and then type 0.3.
   e. Select the current number in the *Right* text box and then type 0.3.
   f. Click OK to close the Page Setup dialog box.
5. Specify that you want row titles to print on each page by completing the following steps:
   a. Click the Print Titles button in the Page Setup group in the Page Layout tab.
   b. At the Page Setup dialog box with the Sheet tab selected, select and then delete the text that displays in the *Columns to repeat at left* text box.

c. Click in the *Rows to repeat at top* text box and then type A3:N3.

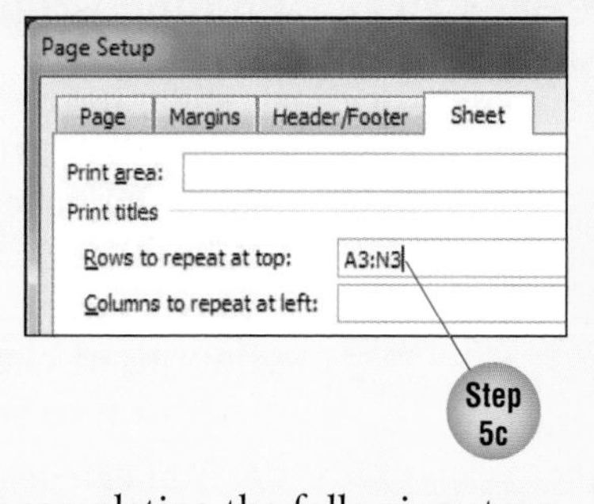

d. Click OK to close the dialog box.

6. Save and then print **EL1-C4-P1-RPBudget.xlsx**. (The worksheet will print on two pages with the row titles repeated on the second page.)
7. At the worksheet, return to the default margins by clicking the Page Layout tab, clicking the Margins button, and then clicking the *Normal* option at the drop-down list.
8. Remove titles from printing on second and subsequent pages by completing the following steps:
   a. Click the Print Titles button in the Page Setup group.
   b. At the Page Setup dialog box with the Sheet tab selected, select and then delete the text that displays in the *Rows to repeat at top* text box.
   c. Click OK to close the dialog box.
9. Change the scaling back to the default by completing the following steps:
   a. Click the down-pointing arrow at the right side of the *Width* box in the Scale to Fit group and then click *Automatic* at the drop-down list.

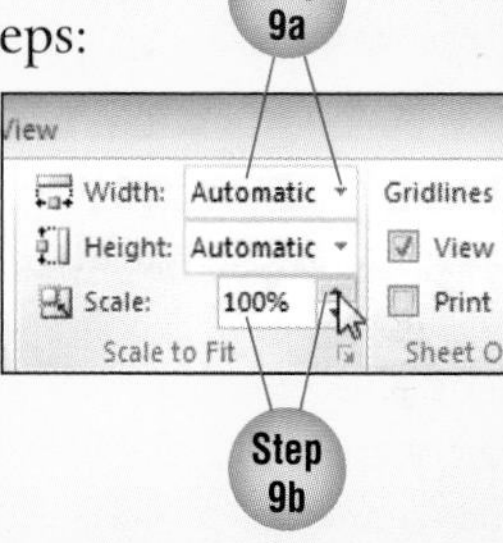

   b. Click the up-pointing arrow at the right side of the *Scale* measurement box until *100%* displays in the box.
10. Save **EL1-C4-P1-RPBudget.xlsx**.

Inserting a Background Picture

With the Background button in the Page Setup group in the Page Layout tab you can insert a picture as a background to the worksheet. The picture displays only on the screen and does not print. To insert a picture, click the Background button in the Page Setup group. At the Sheet Background dialog box navigate to the folder containing the desired picture and then double-click the picture. To remove the picture from the worksheet, click the Delete Background button.

Quick Steps

Insert Background Picture

1. Click Page Layout tab.
2. Click Background button.
3. Navigate to desired picture and double-click picture.

Background

Project 1f **Inserting a Background Picture** Part 6 of 12

1. With **EL1-C4-P1-RPBudget.xlsx** open, insert a background picture by completing the following steps:
   a. Click the Background button in the Page Setup group in the Page Layout tab.
   b. At the Sheet Background dialog box, navigate to the Excel2010L1C4 folder, and then double-click ***Ship.jpg***.
   c. Scroll down the worksheet to display the ship.

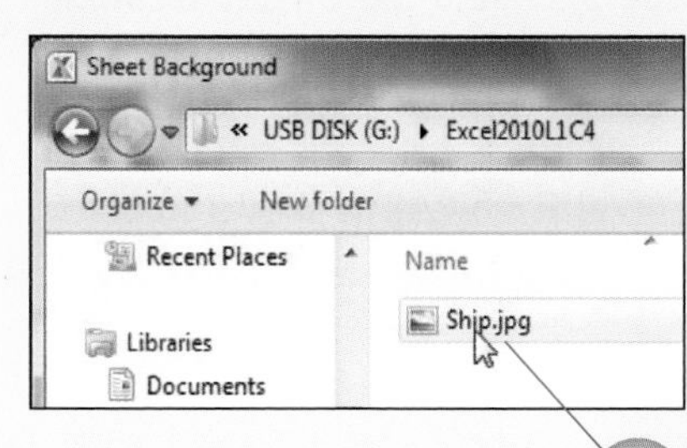

2. Display the Print tab Backstage view, notice that the picture does not display in the preview worksheet, and then return to the worksheet.
3. Remove the picture by clicking the Delete Background button in the Page Setup group in the Page Layout tab.
4. Save **EL1-C4-P1-RPBudget.xlsx**.

Quick Steps

Print Gridlines
1. Click Page Layout tab.
2. Click *Print* check box in *Gridlines* section in Sheet Options group.

OR

1. Click Page Layout tab.
2. Click Sheet Options dialog box launcher.
3. Click *Gridlines* option.
4. Click OK.

Print Row and Column Headings
1. Click Page Layout tab.
2. Click *Print* check box in *Headings* section in Sheet Options group.

OR

1. Click Page Layout tab.
2. Click Sheet Options dialog box launcher.
3. Click *Row and column headings* option.
4. Click OK.

Printing Gridlines and Row and Column Headings

By default, the gridlines that create the cells in a worksheet and the row numbers and column letters do not print. The Sheet Options group in the Page Layout tab contain check boxes for gridlines and headings. The *View* check boxes for Gridlines and Headings contain check marks. At these settings, gridlines and row and column headings display on the screen but do not print. If you want them to print, insert check marks in the *Print* check boxes. Complex worksheets may be easier to read with the gridlines printed.

You can also control the display and printing of gridlines and headings with options at the Page Setup dialog box with the Sheet tab selected. Display this dialog box by clicking the Sheet Options dialog box launcher. To print gridlines and headings, insert check marks in the check boxes located in the *Print* section of the dialog box. The *Print* section contains two additional options — *Black and white* and *Draft quality*. If you are printing with a color printer, you can print the worksheet in black and white by inserting a check mark in the *Black and white* check box. Insert a check mark in the *Draft* option if you want to print a draft of the worksheet. With this option checked, some formatting such as shading and fill do not print.

Project 1g **Printing Gridlines and Row and Column Headings** Part 7 of 12

1. With **EL1-C4-P1-RPBudget.xlsx** open, click in the *Print* check box below Gridlines in the Sheet Options group in the Page Layout tab to insert a check mark.
2. Click in the *Print* check box below Headings in the Sheet Options group to insert a check mark.
3. Click the Margins button in the Page Setup group and then click *Custom Margins* at the drop-down list.
4. At the Page Setup dialog box with the Margins tab selected, click in the *Horizontally* check box to insert a check mark.
5. Click in the *Vertically* check box to insert a check mark.
6. Click OK to close the dialog box.
7. Save and then print **EL1-C4-P1-RPBudget.xlsx**.
8. Click in the *Print* check box below Headings in the Sheet Options group to remove the check mark.
9. Click in the *Print* check box below Gridlines in the Sheet Options group to remove the check mark.
10. Save **EL1-C4-P1-RPBudget.xlsx**.

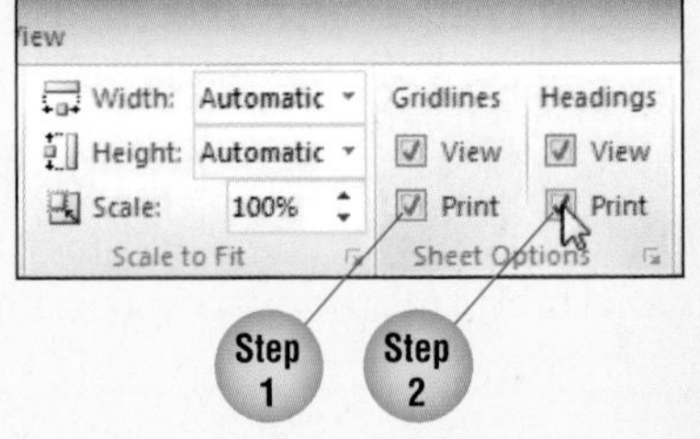

Printing a Specific Area of a Worksheet

Print Area

With the Print Area button in the Page Setup group in the Page Layout tab you can select and print specific areas in a worksheet. To do this, select the cells you want to print, click the Print Area button in the Page Setup group in the Page Layout tab, and then click *Set Print Area* at the drop-down list. This inserts a border around the selected cells. Display the Print tab Backstage view, click the Print button, and the cells within the border are printed.

You can specify more than one print area in a worksheet. To do this, select the first group of cells, click the Print Area button in the Page Setup group, and then click *Set Print Area*. Select the next group of cells, click the Print Area button, and then click *Add to Print Area*. Clear a print area by clicking the Print Area button in the Page Setup group and then clicking *Clear Print Area* at the drop-down list.

Each area specified as a print area will print on a separate page. If you want nonadjacent print areas to print on the same page, consider hiding columns and/or rows in the worksheet to bring the areas together.

Project 1h Printing Specific Areas

Part 8 of 12

1. With **EL1-C4-P1-RPBudget.xlsx** open, print the first half of the year's income and expenses by completing the following steps:
   a. Select cells A3 through G21.
   b. Click the Print Area button in the Page Setup group in the Page Layout tab and then click *Set Print Area* at the drop-down list.
   c. With the border surrounding the cells A3 through G21, click the File tab, click the Print tab, and then click the Print button at the Print tab Backstage view.
   d. Clear the print area by clicking the Print Area button in the Page Setup group and then clicking *Clear Print Area* at the drop-down list.

Step 1b

Page Layout Formulas Data Review
Orientation Size Print Area Breaks Background
Set Print Area
Clear Print Area

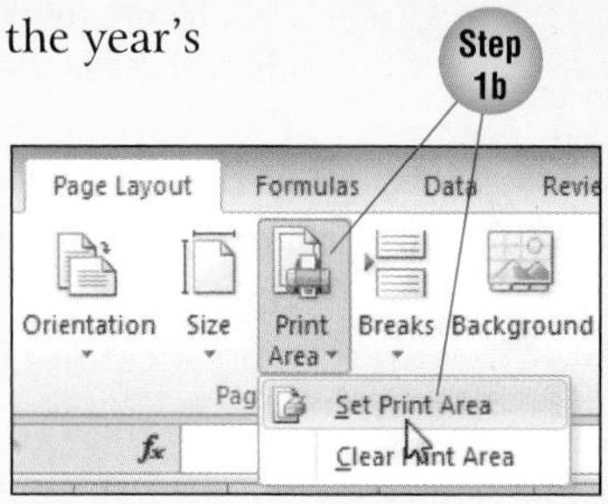

2. Suppose you want to print the income and expenses information as well as the totals for the month of April. To do this, hide columns and select a print area by completing the following steps:
   a. Select columns B through D.
   b. Click the Home tab.
   c. Click the Format button in the Cells group, point to *Hide & Unhide*, and then click *Hide Columns*.
   d. Click the Page Layout tab.
   e. Select cells A3 through E21. (Columns A and E are now adjacent.)
   f. Click the Print Area button in the Page Setup group and then click *Set Print Area* at the drop-down list.
3. Click the File tab, click the Print tab, and then click the Print button.
4. Clear the print area by making sure cells A3 through E21 are selected, clicking the Print Area button in the Page Setup group, and then clicking *Clear Print Area* at the drop-down list.
5. Unhide the columns by completing the following steps:
   a. Click the Home tab.
   b. Select columns A and E. (These columns are adjacent.)
   c. Click the Format button in the Cells group, point to *Hide & Unhide*, and then click *Unhide Columns*.
   d. Deselect the text by clicking in any cell containing data in the worksheet.
6. Save **EL1-C4-P1-RPBudget.xlsx**.

Figure 4.5 Header & Footer Tools Design Tab

Inserting Headers and Footers

Text that prints at the top of each worksheet page is called a ***header*** and text that prints at the bottom of each worksheet page is called a ***footer***. You can create a header and/or footer with the Header & Footer button in the Text group in the Insert tab, in Page Layout View, or with options at the Page Setup dialog box with the Header/Footer tab selected.

To create a header with the Header & Footer button, click the Insert tab and then click the Header & Footer button in the Text group. This displays the worksheet in Page Layout view and displays the Header & Footer Tools Design tab. Use buttons in this tab, shown in Figure 4.5, to insert predesigned headers and/or footers or insert header and footer elements such as the page number, date, time, path name, and file name. You can also create a different header or footer on the first page of the worksheet or create a header or footer for even pages and another for odd pages.

At the Print tab Backstage view, you can preview your headers and footers before printing. Click the File tab and then the Print tab to display the Print tab Backstage view. A preview of the worksheet displays at the right side of the Backstage view. If your worksheet will print on more than one page, you can view different pages by clicking the Next Page button or the Previous Page button. These buttons are located below and to the left of the preview worksheet at the Print tab Backstage view. Two buttons display in the bottom right corner of the Print tab Backstage view. Click the Show Margins button and margin guidelines display in the preview of the worksheet. Click the Zoom to Page button to zoom in or out of the preview of the worksheet.

Quick Steps

Insert a Header or Footer

1. Click Insert tab.
2. Click Header & Footer button.
3. Click Header button and then click predesigned header or click Footer button and then click predesigned footer.

OR

1. Click Insert tab.
2. Click Header & Footer button.
3. Click desired header or footer elements.

Close the header or footer pane by clicking in the worksheet or pressing Esc.

Header & Footer

Project 1i Inserting a Header in a Worksheet

Part 9 of 12

1. With **EL1-C4-P1-RPBudget.xlsx** open, create a header by completing the following steps:
   a. Click the Insert tab.
   b. Click the Header & Footer button in the Text group.

Step 1a

Step 1b

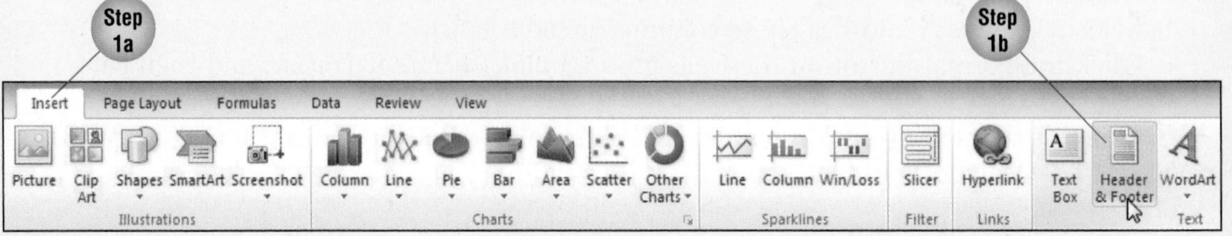

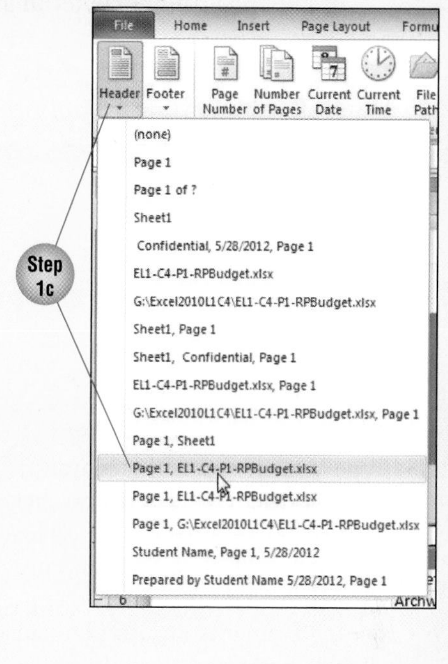

c. Click the Header button located at the left side of the Header & Footer Tools Design tab and then click *Page 1, EL1-C4-P1-RPBudget.xlsx* at the drop-down list. (This inserts the page number in the middle header box and the workbook name in the right header box.)

2. Preview the worksheet by completing the following steps:
   a. Click the File tab and then click the Print tab.
   b. At the Print tab Backstage view look at the preview worksheet that displays at the right.
   c. View the next page of the worksheet by clicking the Next Page button that displays below and to the left of the preview worksheet.

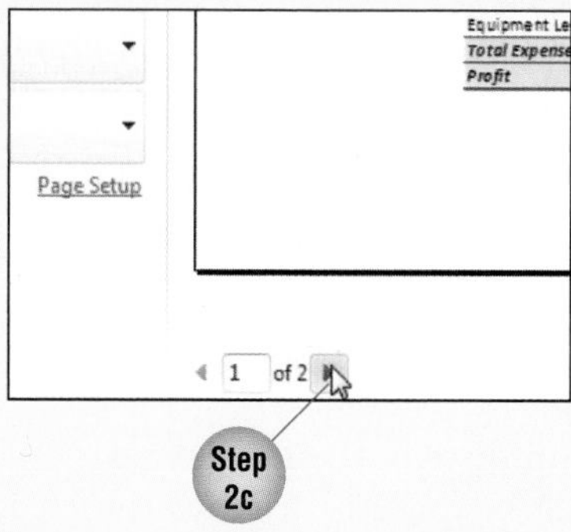

   d. View the first page by clicking the Previous Page button that displays left of the Next Page button.
   e. Click the File tab to return to the workbook.
3. Save **EL1-C4-P1-RPBudget.xlsx**.

You also can insert a header and/or footer by switching to Page Layout view. In Page Layout view, the top of the worksheet page displays with the text *Click to add header*. Click this text and the insertion point is positioned in the middle header box. Type the desired header in this box or click in the left box or the right box and then type the header. Create a footer in a similar manner. Scroll down the worksheet until the bottom of the page displays and then click the text *Click to add footer*. Type the footer in the center footer box or click the left or right box and then type the footer.

Project 1j Inserting a Footer and Modifying a Header in a Worksheet

Part 10 of 12

1. With **EL1-C4-P1-RPBudget.xlsx** open, make sure the workbook displays in Page Layout view.
2. Scroll down the worksheet until the text *Click to add footer* displays and then click the text.

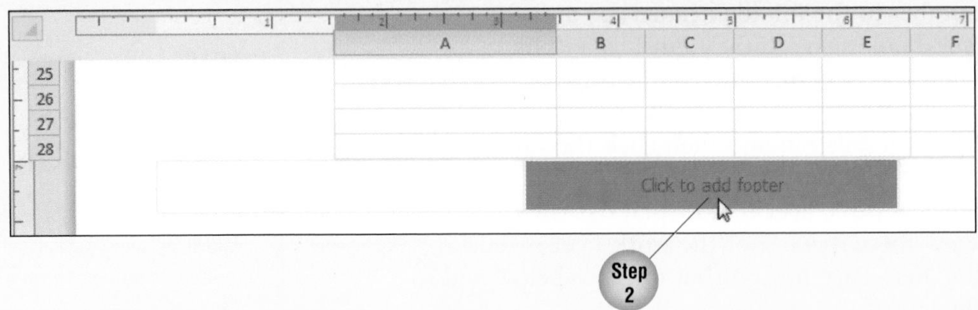

3. Type your first and last names.
4. Click in the left footer box, click the Header & Footer Tools Design tab, and then click the Current Date button in the Header & Footer Elements group. (This inserts a date code. The date will display when you click outside the footer box.)
5. Click in the right footer box and then click the Current Time button in the Header & Footer Elements group. (This inserts the time as a code. The time will display when you click outside the footer box.)
6. View the headers and footers at the Print tab Backstage view and then return to the worksheet.
7. Modify the header by completing the following steps:
   a. Scroll to the beginning of the worksheet and display the header text.
   b. Click the page number in the middle header box. (This displays the Header & Footer Tools Design tab, changes the header to a field, and selects the field.)
   c. Press the Delete key to delete the header.
   d. Click the header text that displays in the right header box and then press the Delete key.
   e. With the insertion point positioned in the right header box, insert the page number by clicking the Header & Footer Tools Design tab and then clicking the Page Number button in the Header & Footer Elements group.
   f. Click in the left header box and then click the File Name button in the Header & Footer Elements group.

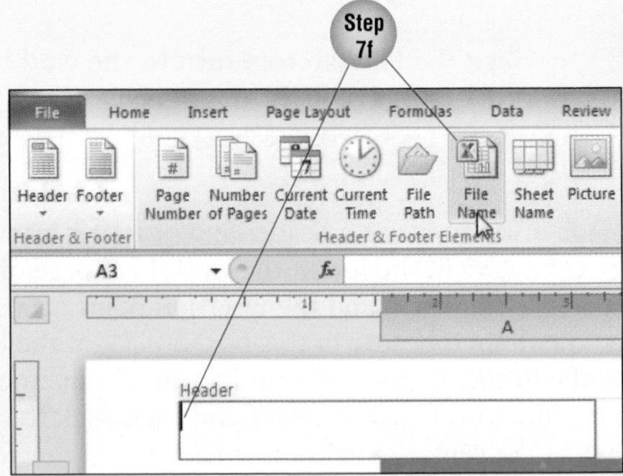

8. Click in any cell in the worksheet containing data.
9. View the headers and footers at the Print tab Backstage view and then return to the worksheet.
10. Save **EL1-C4-P1-RPBudget.xlsx**.

In addition to options in the Header & Footer Tools Design tab, you can insert and customize headers and footers with options at the Page Setup dialog box with the Header/Footer tab selected that displays in Figure 4.6. Display this dialog box by clicking the Page Layout tab and then clicking the Page Setup group dialog box launcher. At the Page Setup dialog box, click the Header/Footer tab. If your worksheet contains headers or footers, they will display in the dialog box.

Figure 4.6 Page Setup Dialog Box with Header/Footer Tab Selected

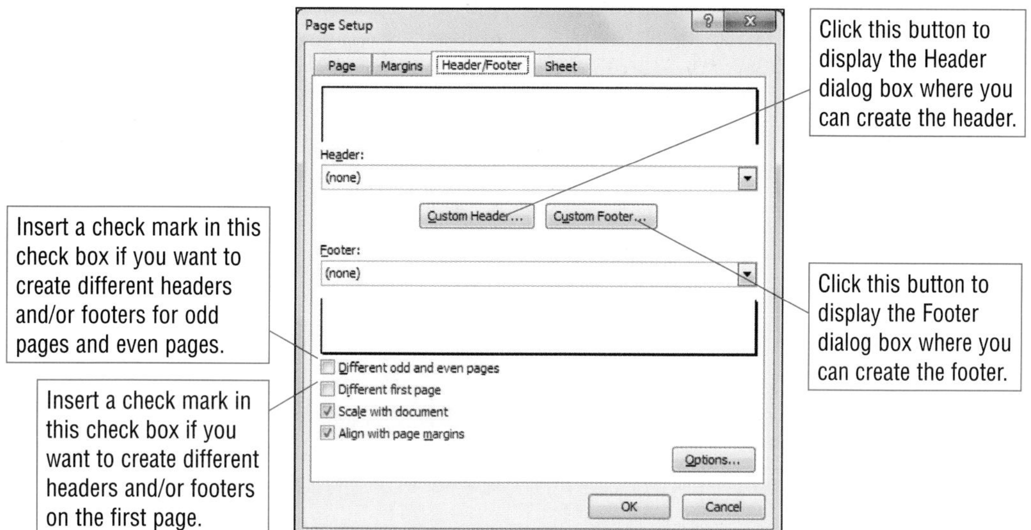
Page Setup
Page
Margins
Header/Footer
Sheet
Header:
(none)
Custom Header...
Custom Footer...
Footer:
(none)
Different odd and even pages
Different first page
Scale with document
Align with page margins
Options...
OK
Cancel
Click this button to display the Header dialog box where you can create the header.
Click this button to display the Footer dialog box where you can create the footer.
Insert a check mark in this check box if you want to create different headers and/or footers for odd pages and even pages.
Insert a check mark in this check box if you want to create different headers and/or footers on the first page.

With the check box options that display in the lower left corner of the dialog box, you can specify that you want to insert a different odd and even page header or footer or insert a different first page header or footer. The bottom two check box options are active by default. These defaults scale the header and footer text with the worksheet text and align the header and footer with the page margins.

To create different odd and even page headers, click the *Different odd and even pages* check box to insert a check mark and then click the Custom Header button. This displays the Header dialog box with the Odd Page Header tab selected. Type or insert the desired odd page header data in the left, center, or right section boxes and then click the Even Page Header tab. Type or insert the desired even page header data in the section boxes and then click OK. Use the buttons that display above the section boxes to format the header text and insert information such as the page number, current date, current time, file name, worksheet name, and so on. Complete similar steps to create different odd and even page footers and different first page headers or footers.

Project 1k

Creating Different Odd and Even Page Headers and Footers and a Different First Page Header and Footer

Part 11 of 12

1. With **EL1-C4-P1-RPBudget.xlsx** open, remove the page break by clicking the Page Layout tab, clicking the Breaks button in the Page Setup group, and then clicking *Reset All Page Breaks* at the drop-down list.
2. Change the margins by completing the following steps:
   a. Click the Margins button in the Page Setup group in the Page Layout tab and then click *Custom Margins* at the drop-down list.
   b. At the Page Setup dialog box with the Margins tab selected, select the current number in the *Left* text box and then type 3.
   c. Select the current number in the *Right* text box and then type 3.
   d. Click OK to close the dialog box.
3. Click the Page Layout tab and then click the Page Setup group dialog box launcher.

4. At the Page Setup dialog box, click the Header/Footer tab.
5. At the Page Setup dialog box with the Header/Footer tab selected, click the *Different odd and even pages* check box to insert a check mark and then click the Custom Header button.
6. At the Header dialog box with the Odd Page Header tab selected, click the Format Text button (located above the left section box). At the Font dialog box, click *12* in the *Size* text box and then click OK.
7. At the Header dialog box, type Yearly Budget.

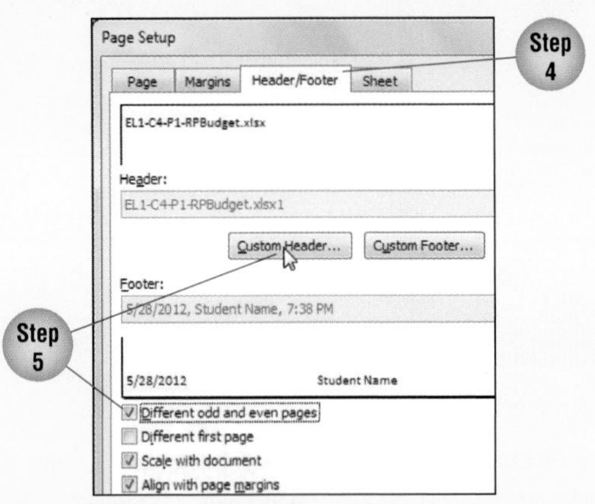

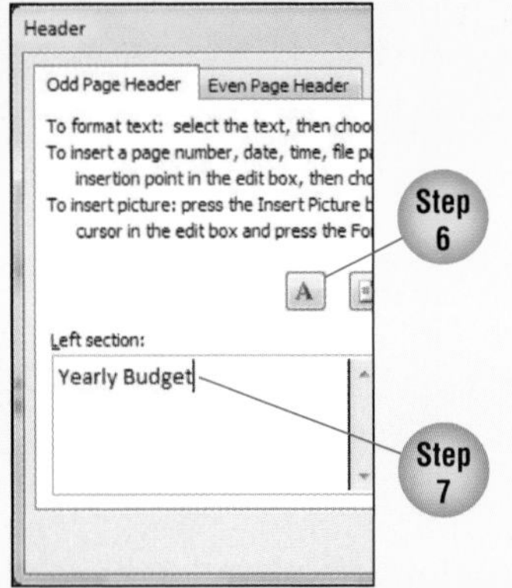

8. Click the Even Page Header tab, click in the left section box, and then click the Insert Page Number button.
9. Click in the right section box and then type Yearly Budget.
10. Select *Yearly Budget*, click the Format Text button, click *12* in the *Size* text box, and then click OK.
11. Click OK to close the Header dialog box.
12. Click the Custom Footer button and, at the Footer dialog box with the Odd Page Footer tab selected, delete the data in the left section box and select and delete the data in the right section box. (The footer should only contain your name.)
13. Select your name, click the Format Text button, click *12* in the *Size* text box, and then click OK.
14. Click the Even Page Footer tab, type your name in the center section box, select your name, and then change the font size to *12*.
15. Click OK to close the Footer dialog box and then click OK to close the Page Setup dialog box. (View the headers and footers in Print tab Backstage view and then return to the worksheet.)
16. Click the Page Setup group dialog box launcher in the Page Layout tab.
17. At the Page Setup dialog box, click the Header/Footer tab.
18. At the Page Setup dialog box with the Header/Footer tab selected, click the *Different odd and even pages* check box to remove the check mark.
19. Click the *Different first page* check box to insert a check mark and then click the Custom Header button.
20. At the Header dialog box with the Header tab selected, click the First Page Header tab.
21. Click in the right section box and then click the Insert Page Number button located above the section boxes.

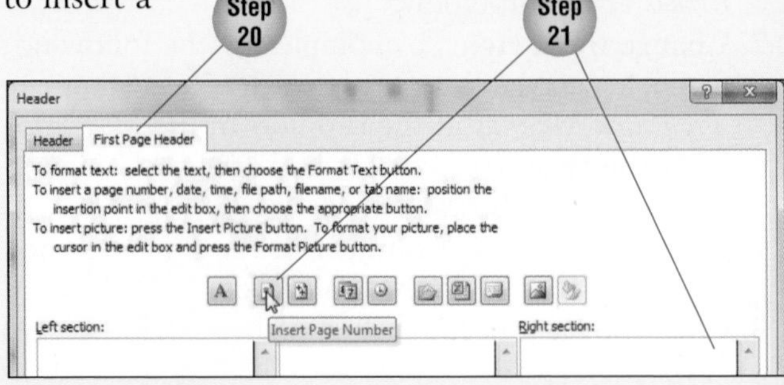

22. Click OK to close the Header dialog box and then click OK to close the Page Setup dialog box.
23. View the headers and footers in the Print tab Backstage view and then return to the worksheet.
24. Save **EL1-C4-P1-RPBudget.xlsx**.

Customizing Print Jobs

As you learned in this chapter, you can preview worksheets in the Print tab Backstage view. With options in the Settings category at the Print tab Backstage view, you can also specify what you want printed. By default, the active worksheet prints. You can change this by clicking the first gallery that displays in the Settings category. At the drop-down list that displays, you can specify that you want the entire workbook to print (this is useful when a workbook contains more than one worksheet) or print the selected cells. With the other galleries in the Settings category, you can specify if you want pages printed on one side or both sides (this is dependent on your printer) and collated. You can also specify the worksheet orientation, size, and margins as well as specify if you want the worksheet scaled to fit all columns or rows on one page.

With the *Pages* text boxes in the Settings category, you can specify the pages you want printed of your worksheet. For example, if you wanted to print pages 2 and 3 of your active worksheet, you would type 2 in the text box immediately right of the word *Pages* in the Settings category and then type 3 in the text box immediately right of the word *to*. You can also use the up- and down-pointing arrows to insert page numbers.

Project 1l Printing Specific Pages of a Worksheet

Part 12 of 12

1. With **EL1-C4-P1-RPBudget.xlsx** open, print the first two pages of the worksheet by completing the following steps:
   a. Click the File tab and then click the Print tab.
   b. At the Print tab Backstage view, click in the text box immediately right of *Pages* located below the first gallery in the Settings category and then type 1.
   c. Click in the text box immediately right of *to* in the Settings category and then type 2.
   d. Click the Print button.

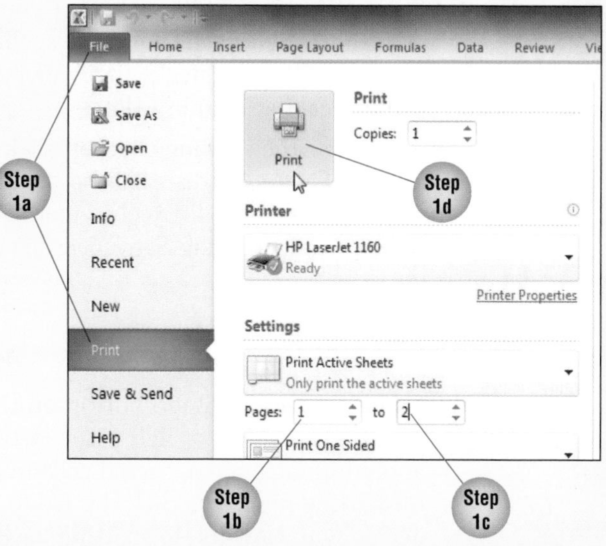

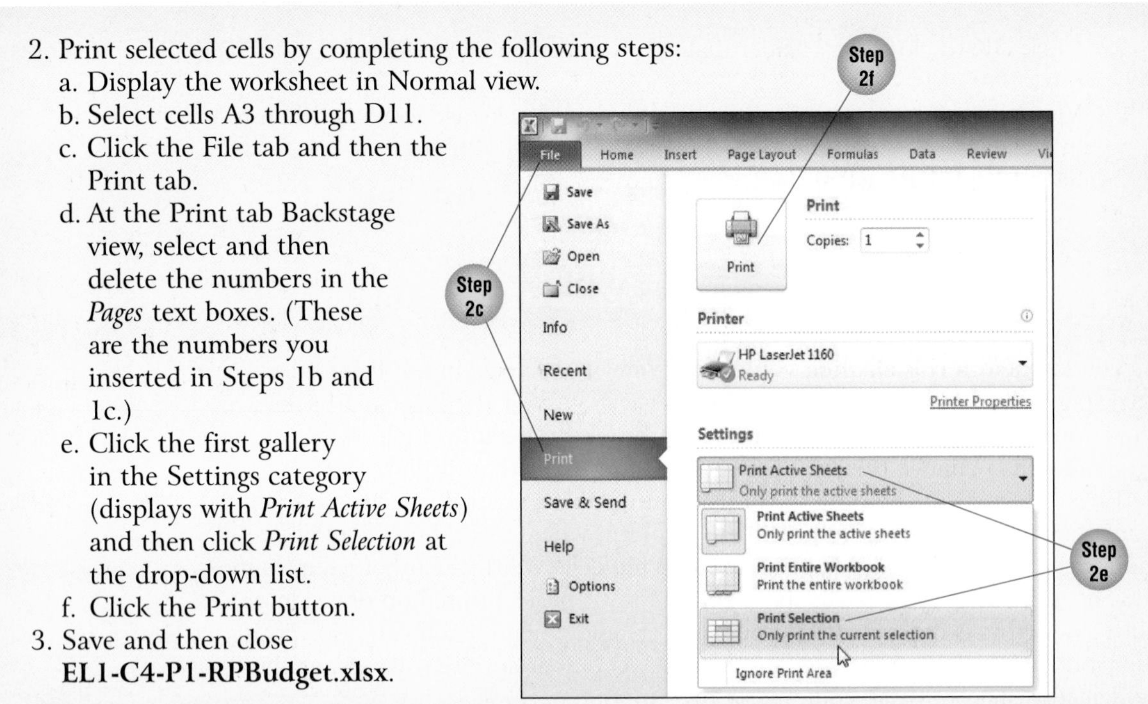

2. Print selected cells by completing the following steps:
   a. Display the worksheet in Normal view.
   b. Select cells A3 through D11.
   c. Click the File tab and then the Print tab.
   d. At the Print tab Backstage view, select and then delete the numbers in the *Pages* text boxes. (These are the numbers you inserted in Steps 1b and 1c.)
   e. Click the first gallery in the Settings category (displays with *Print Active Sheets*) and then click *Print Selection* at the drop-down list.
   f. Click the Print button.
3. Save and then close **EL1-C4-P1-RPBudget.xlsx**.

Project 2 Format a May Sales and Commissions Worksheet 3 Parts

You will format a sales commission worksheet by inserting a formula, completing a spelling check, and finding and replacing data and cell formatting.

Completing a Spelling Check

Quick Steps

Complete a Spelling Check
1. Click Review tab.
2. Click Spelling button.
3. Replace or ignore selected words.

Customize spell checking options at the Excel Options dialog box with *Proofing* selected.

Spelling

Excel includes a spelling checker you can use to check the spelling of text in a worksheet. Before checking the spelling in a worksheet, make the first cell active. The spell checker checks the worksheet from the active cell to the last cell in the worksheet that contains data.

To use the spelling checker, click the Review tab and then click the Spelling button. Figure 4.7 displays the Spelling dialog box. At this dialog box, you can click a button to tell Excel to ignore a word or you can replace a misspelled word with a word from the *Suggestions* list box.

Using Undo and Redo

Excel includes an Undo button on the Quick Access toolbar that will reverse certain commands or delete the last data typed in a cell. For example, if you apply formatting to selected cells in a worksheet and then decide you want the formatting removed, click the Undo button on the Quick Access toolbar. If you decide you want the formatting back again, click the Redo button on the Quick Access toolbar.

Figure 4.7 Excel Spelling Dialog Box

HINT

Ctrl + Z is the keyboard shortcut to undo a command.

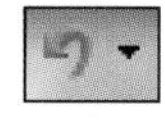

Undo

Redo

Excel maintains actions in temporary memory. If you want to undo an action performed earlier, click the down-pointing arrow at the right side of the Undo button and a drop-down list displays containing the actions performed on the worksheet. Click the desired action at the drop-down list. Any actions preceding a chosen action are also undone. You can do the same with the Redo drop-down list. Multiple actions must be undone or redone in sequence.

Project 2a Spell Checking and Formatting a Worksheet

Part 1 of 3

1. Open **MRSales.xlsx**.
2. Save the workbook with Save As and name it **EL1-C4-P2-MRSales**.
3. Complete a spelling check on the worksheet by completing the following steps:
   a. Make cell A1 active.
   b. Click the Review tab.
   c. Click the Spelling button in the Proofing group.
   d. Click the Change button as needed to correct misspelled words in the worksheet. (When the spell checker stops at proper names *Pirozzi* and *Yonemoto*, click the Ignore All button.)
   e. At the message telling you the spelling check is completed, click OK.

4. Insert a formula and then copy the formula without the formatting by completing the following steps:
   a. Make cell G4 active and then insert a formula that multiplies the sale price by the commission percentage.
   b. Copy the formula down to cells G5 through G26.
   c. Some of the cells contain shading that you do not want removed, so click the Auto Fill Options button that displays at the bottom right of the selected cells and then click the *Fill Without Formatting* option at the drop-down list.

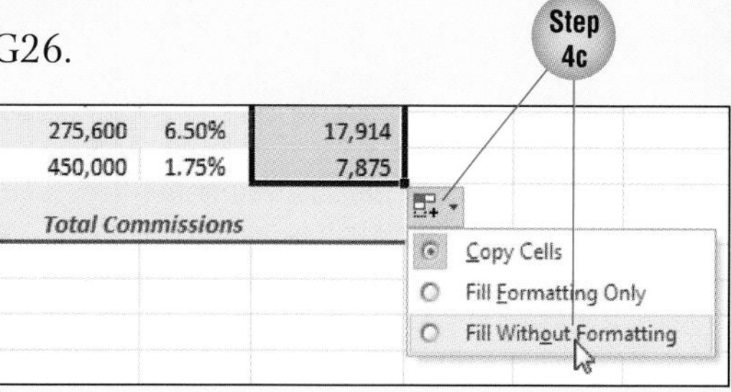

5. Apply the Accounting Number Format style with no decimal places to cell G4.

6. Make cell G27 active and then insert the sum of cells G4 through G26.
7. Apply a theme by clicking the Page Layout button, clicking the Themes button, and then clicking *Elemental* at the drop-down gallery.
8. After looking at the worksheet with the Elemental theme applied, you decide you want to return to the original formatting. To do this, click the Undo button on the Quick Access toolbar.

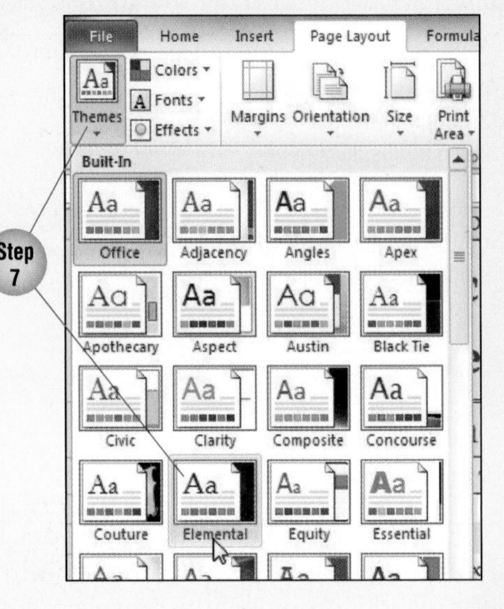

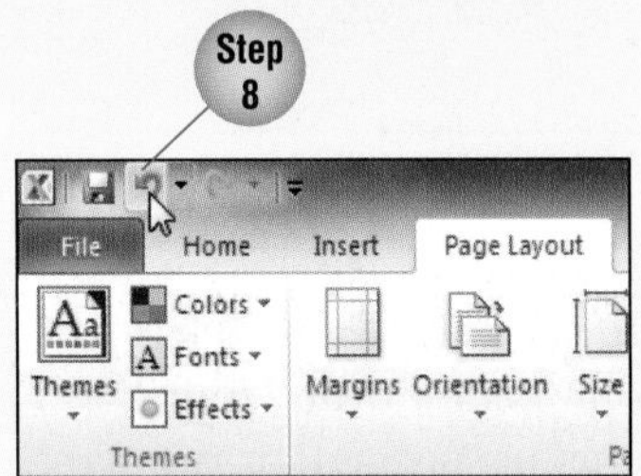

9. Save **EL1-C4-P2-MRSales.xlsx**.

Finding and Replacing Data and Cell Formatting in a Worksheet

Quick Steps

Find Data
1. Click Find & Select button.
2. Click *Find* at drop-down list.
3. Type data in *Find what* text box.
4. Click Find Next button.

Find & Select

Excel provides a Find feature you can use to look for specific data and either replace it with nothing or replace it with other data. This feature is particularly helpful in a large worksheet with data you want to find quickly. Excel also includes a find and replace feature. Use this to look for specific data in a worksheet and replace it with other data.

To find specific data in a worksheet, click the Find & Select button located in the Editing group in the Home tab and then click *Find* at the drop-down list. This displays the Find and Replace dialog box with the Find tab selected as shown in Figure 4.8. Type the data you want to find in the *Find what* text box and then click the Find Next button. Continue clicking the Find Next button to move to the next occurrence of the data. If the Find and Replace dialog box obstructs your view of the worksheet, use the mouse pointer on the title bar to drag the box to a different location.

Figure 4.8 Find and Replace Dialog Box with Find Tab Selected

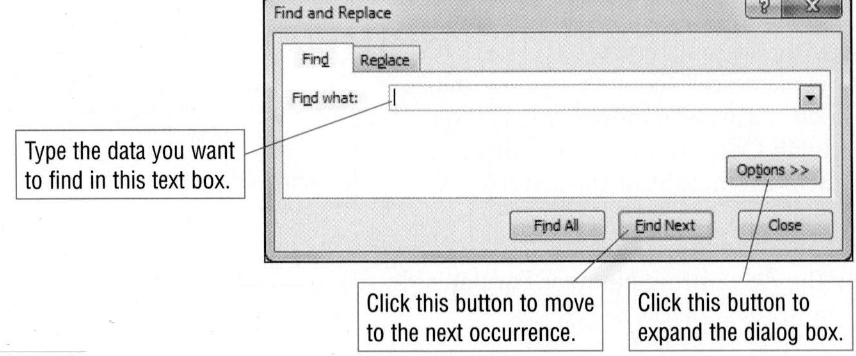

To find specific data in a worksheet and replace it with other data, click the Find & Select button in the Editing group in the Home tab and then click *Replace* at the drop-down list. This displays the Find and Replace dialog box with the Replace tab selected as shown in Figure 4.9. Enter the data for which you are looking in the *Find what* text box. Press the Tab key or click in the *Replace with* text box and then enter the data that is to replace the data in the *Find what* text box.

Click the Find Next button to tell Excel to find the next occurrence of the data. Click the Replace button to replace the data and find the next occurrence. If you know that you want all occurrences of the data in the *Find what* text box replaced with the data in the *Replace with* text box, click the Replace All button. Click the Close button to close the Replace dialog box.

Display additional find and replace options by clicking the Options button. This expands the dialog box as shown in Figure 4.10. By default, Excel will look for any data that contains the same characters as the data in the *Find what* text box, without concern for the characters before or after the entered data. For example, in Project 2b, you will be looking for sale prices of $450,000 and replacing with $475,000. If you do not specify to Excel that you want to find cells that contain only *450000,* Excel will stop at any cell containing *450000.* In this example, Excel would stop at a cell containing *$1,450,000* or a cell containing *$2,450,000.* To specify that the only data that should be contained in the cell is what is entered in the *Find what* text box, click the Options button to expand the dialog box and then insert a check mark in the *Match entire cell contents* check box.

Quick Steps

Find and Replace Data
1. Click Find & Select button.
2. Click *Replace* at drop-down list.
3. Type data in *Find what* text box.
4. Type data in *Replace with* text box.
5. Click Replace button or Replace All button.

Figure 4.9 Find and Replace Dialog Box with Replace Tab Selected

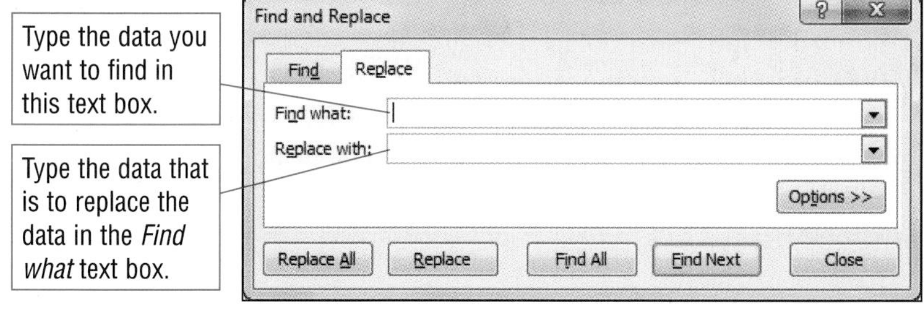

Figure 4.10 Expanded Find and Replace Dialog Box

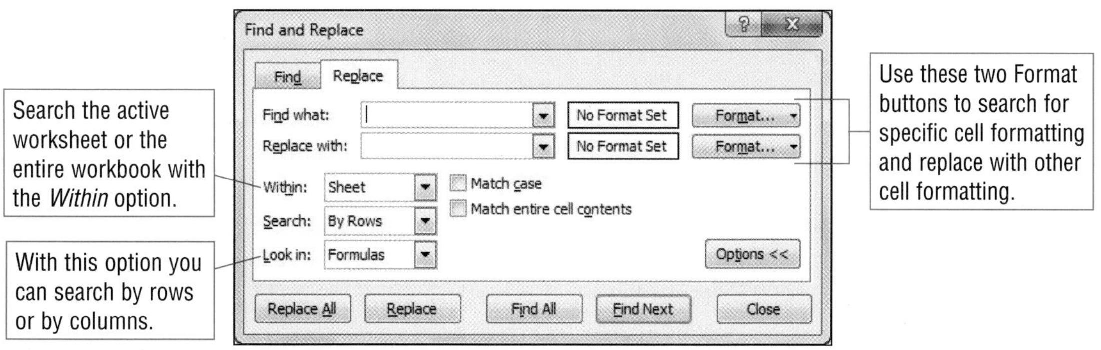

If the *Match case* option is active (contains a check mark), Excel will look for only that data that exactly matches the case of the data entered in the *Find what* text box. Remove the check mark from this check box if you do not want Excel to find exact case matches. Excel will search in the current worksheet. If you want Excel to search an entire workbook, change the *Within* option to *Workbook*. Excel, by default, searches by rows in a worksheet. You can change this to *By Columns* with the *Search* option.

Project 2b Finding and Replacing Data — Part 2 of 3

1. With **EL1-C4-P2-MRSales.xlsx** open, find all occurrences of *Land* in the worksheet and replace with *Acreage* by completing the following steps:
   a. Click the Find & Select button in the Editing group in the Home tab and then click *Replace* at the drop-down list.
   b. At the Find and Replace dialog box with the Replace tab selected, type Land in the *Find what* text box.
   c. Press the Tab key. (This moves the insertion point to the *Replace with* text box.)
   d. Type Acreage.
   e. Click the Replace All button.
   f. At the message telling you that four replacements were made, click OK.
   g. Click the Close button to close the Find and Replace dialog box.
2. Find all occurrences of *$450,000* and replace with *$475,000* by completing the following steps:
   a. Click the Find & Select button in the Editing group and then click *Replace* at the drop-down list.
   b. At the Find and Replace dialog box with the Replace tab selected, type 450000 in the *Find what* text box.
   c. Press the Tab key.
   d. Type 475000.
   e. Click the Options button to display additional options. (If additional options already display, skip this step.)
   f. Click the *Match entire cell contents* option to insert a check mark in the check box.
   g. Click Replace All.
   h. At the message telling you that two replacements were made, click OK.
   i. At the Find and Replace dialog box, click the *Match entire cell contents* option to remove the check mark.
   j. Click the Close button to close the Find and Replace dialog box.
3. Save **EL1-C4-P2-MRSales.xlsx**.

Use the Format buttons at the expanded Find and Replace dialog box (see Figure 4.10) to search for specific cell formatting and replace with other formatting. Click the down-pointing arrow at the right side of the Format button and a drop-down list displays. Click the *Format* option and the Find Format dialog box displays with the Number, Alignment, Font, Border, Fill, and Protection tabs. Specify formatting at this dialog box. Click the *Choose Format From Cell* option and the mouse pointer displays with a pointer tool attached. Click in the cell containing the desired formatting and the formatting displays in the *Preview* box to the left of the Format button. Click the *Clear Find Format* option and any formatting in the *Preview* box is removed.

Project 2c Finding and Replacing Cell Formatting

Part 3 of 3

1. With **EL1-C4-P2-MRSales.xlsx** open, search for light turquoise fill color and replace with a purple fill color by completing the following steps:
   a. Click the Find & Select button in the Editing group in the Home tab and then click *Replace* at the drop-down list.
   b. At the Find and Replace dialog box with the Replace tab selected, make sure the dialog box is expanded. (If not, click the Options button.)
   c. Select and then delete any text that displays in the *Find what* text box.
   d. Select and then delete any text that displays in the *Replace with* text box.
   e. Make sure the boxes immediately preceding the two Format buttons display with the text *No Format Set*. (If not, click the down-pointing arrow at the right of the Format button, and then click the *Clear Find Format* option at the drop-down list. Do this for each Format button.)
   f. Click the top Format button.
   g. At the Find Format dialog box, click the Fill tab.
   h. Click the More Colors button.
   i. At the Colors dialog box with the Standard tab selected, click the light turquoise color shown at the right.
   j. Click OK to close the Colors dialog box.
   k. Click OK to close the Find Format dialog box.
   l. Click the bottom Format button.
   m. At the Replace Format dialog box with the Fill tab selected, click the purple color shown at the right.
   n. Click OK to close the dialog box.
   o. At the Find and Replace dialog box, click the Replace All button.
   p. At the message telling you that 10 replacements were made, click OK.

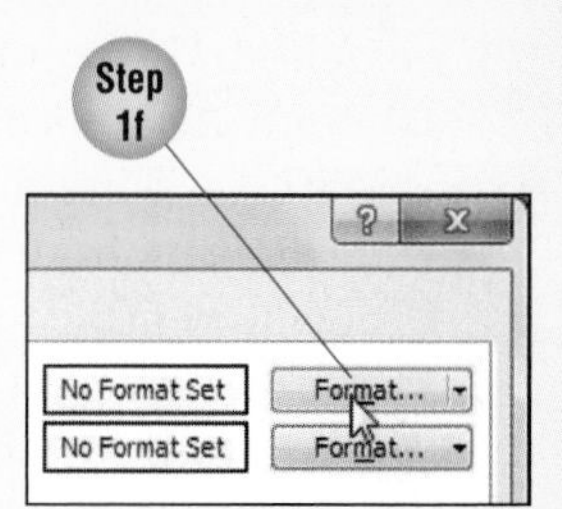

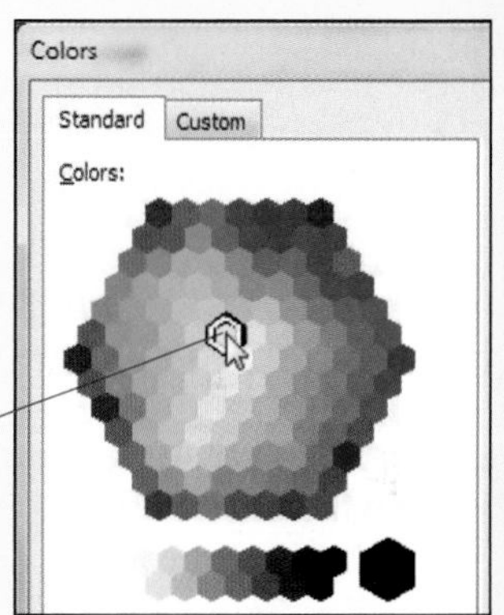

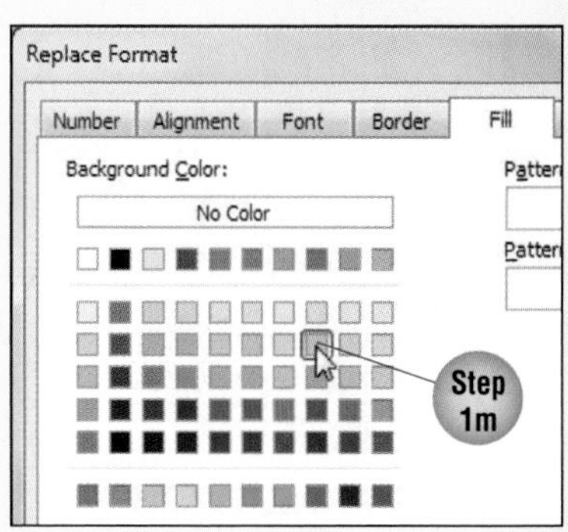

2. Search for yellow fill color and replace with a green fill color by completing the following steps:
   a. At the Find and Replace dialog box, click the top Format button.
   b. At the Find Format dialog box with the Fill tab selected, click the More Colors button.

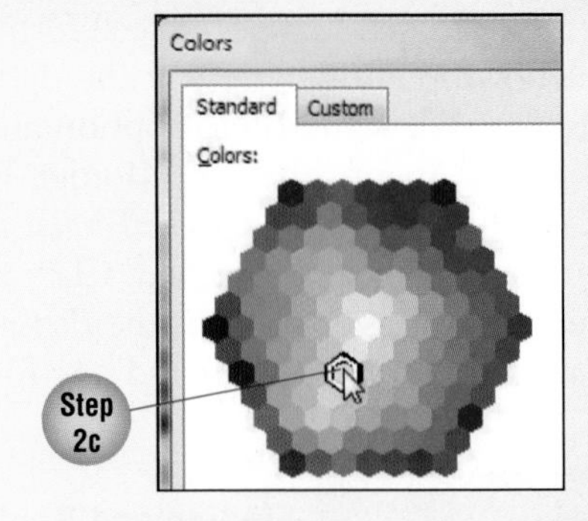

c. At the Colors dialog box with the Standard tab selected, click the yellow color as shown at the right.
d. Click OK to close the Colors dialog box.
e. Click OK to close the Find Format dialog box.
f. Click the bottom Format button.
g. At the Replace Format dialog box with the Fill tab selected, click the green color shown below and to the right.
h. Click OK to close the dialog box.
i. At the Find and Replace dialog box, click the Replace All button.
j. At the message telling you that 78 replacements were made, click OK.

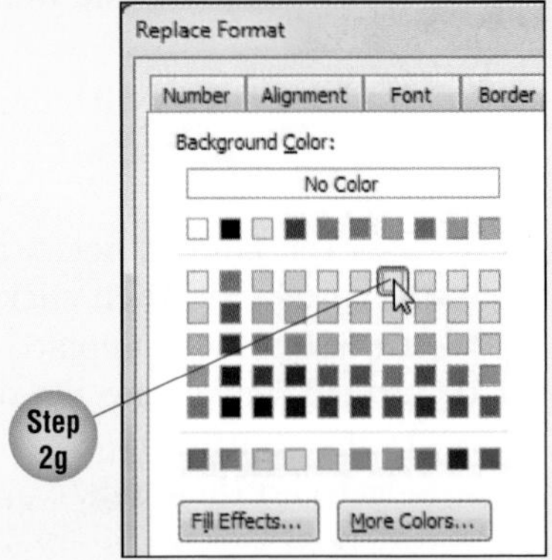

3. Search for 11-point Calibri formatting and replace with 10-point Arial formatting by completing the following steps:
   a. With the Find and Replace dialog box open, clear formatting from the top Format button by clicking the down-pointing arrow at the right side of the top Format button and then clicking the *Clear Find Format* option at the drop-down list.
   b. Clear formatting from the bottom Format button by clicking the down-pointing arrow at the right side of the bottom Format button and then clicking *Clear Replace Format.*

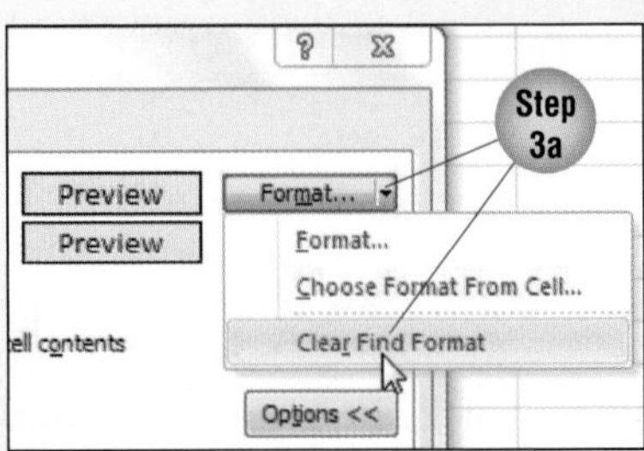

   c. Click the top Format button.
   d. At the Find Format dialog box, click the Font tab.
   e. Click *Calibri* in the *Font* list box. (You may need to scroll down the list to display this typeface.)
   f. Click *11* in the *Size* text box.
   g. Click OK to close the dialog box.
   h. Click the bottom Format button.
   i. At the Replace Format dialog box with the Font tab selected, click *Arial* in the *Font* list box (you may need to scroll down the list to display this typeface).
   j. Click *10* in the *Size* list box.
   k. Click OK to close the dialog box.
   l. At the Find and Replace dialog box, click the Replace All button.
   m. At the message telling you that 174 replacements were made, click OK.
   n. At the Find and Replace dialog box, remove formatting from both Format buttons.
   o. Click the Close button to close the Find and Replace dialog box.
4. Save, print, and then close **EL1-C4-P2-MRSales.xlsx**.

Project 3 Format a Billing Worksheet — 4 Parts

You will insert a formula in a weekly billing worksheet and then sort and filter specific data in the worksheet.

Sorting Data

Excel is primarily a spreadsheet program, but it also includes some basic database functions. With a database program, you can alphabetize information or arrange numbers numerically. Data can be sorted by columns in a worksheet. Sort data in a worksheet with the Sort & Filter button in the Editing group in the Home tab.

To sort data in a worksheet, select the cells containing data you want to sort, click the Sort & Filter button in the Editing group and then click the option representing the desired sort. The sort option names vary depending on the data in selected cells. For example, if the first column of selected cells contains text, the sort options in the drop-down list display as *Sort A to Z* and *Sort Z to A*. If the selected cells contain dates, the sort options in the drop-down list display as *Sort Oldest to Newest* and *Sort Newest to Oldest* and if the cells contain numbers or values, the sort options display as *Sort Smallest to Largest* and *Sort Largest to Smallest*. If you select more than one column in a worksheet, Excel will sort the data in the first selected column.

Quick Steps

Sort Data

1. Select cells.
2. Click Sort & Filter button.
3. Click desired sort option at drop-down list.

If you are not satisfied with the results of the sort, immediately click the Undo button.

Sort & Filter

Project 3a **Sorting Data** Part 1 of 4

1. Open **APTBilling.xlsx** and save it with Save As and name it **EL1-C4-P3-APTBilling**.
2. Insert a formula in cell F4 that multiplies the rate by the hours. Copy the formula down to cells F5 through F29.
3. Sort the data in the first column in descending order by completing the following steps:
   a. Make cell A4 active.
   b. Click the Sort & Filter button in the Editing group in the Home tab.
   c. Click the *Sort Largest to Smallest* option at the drop-down list.
4. Sort in ascending order by clicking the Sort & Filter button and then clicking *Sort Smallest to Largest* at the drop-down list.
5. Save **EL1-C4-P3-APTBilling.xlsx**.

Step 3b

Step 3c

Completing a Custom Sort

If you want to sort data in a column other than the first column, use the Sort dialog box. If you select just one column in a worksheet, click the Sort & Filter button, and then click the desired sort option, only the data in that column is sorted. If this data is related to data to the left or right of the data in the sorted column, that relationship is broken. For example, if you sort cells C4 through C29 in EL1-C4-P3-APTBilling.xlsx, the client number, treatment, hours, and total would no longer match the date.

Use the Sort dialog box to sort data and maintain the relationship of all cells. To sort using the Sort dialog box, select the cells you want sorted, click the Sort & Filter button, and then click *Custom Sort*. This displays the Sort dialog box shown in Figure 4.11.

The data displayed in the *Sort by* option box will vary depending on what you have selected. Generally, the data that displays is the title of the first column

Quick Steps

Complete Custom Sort

1. Select cells.
2. Click Sort & Filter button.
3. Click *Custom Sort* at drop-down list.
4. Specify options at Sort dialog box.
5. Click OK.

Figure 4.11 Sort Dialog Box

Click this down-pointing arrow to specify if you are sorting on values, cell color, font color, or cell icon.

Click this button to specify a second column for sorting.

Click this down-pointing arrow and then specify the sort order.

Click this down-pointing arrow and then click the desired column in the drop-down list.

of selected cells. If the selected cells do not have a title, the data may display as *Column A*. Use this option to specify what column you want sorted. Using the Sort dialog box to sort data in a column maintains the relationship of the data.

Project 3b **Sorting Data Using the Sort Dialog Box** Part 2 of 4

1. With **EL1-C4-P3-APTBilling.xlsx** open, sort the rates in cells E4 through E29 in descending order and maintain the relationship to the other data by completing the following steps:
   a. Select cells A3 through F29.
   b. Click the Sort & Filter button and then click *Custom Sort*.
   c. At the Sort dialog box, click the down-pointing arrow at the right of the *Sort by* option box, and then click *Rate* at the drop-down list.
   d. Click the down-pointing arrow at the right of the *Order* option box and then click *Largest to Smallest* at the drop-down list.
   e. Click OK to close the Sort dialog box.
   f. Deselect the cells.

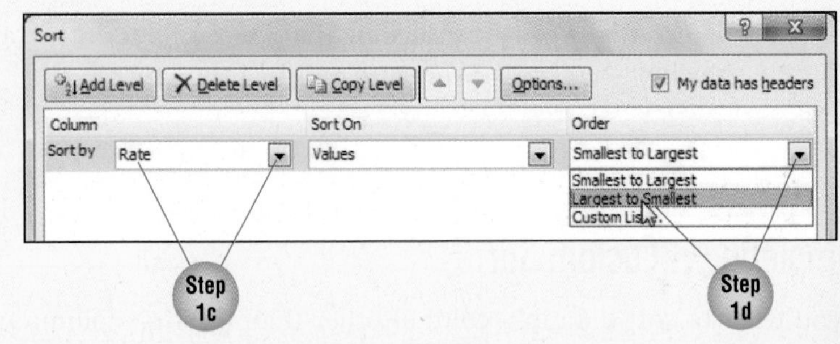

2. Sort the dates in ascending order (oldest to newest) by completing steps similar to those in Step 1.
3. Save and then print **EL1-C4-P3-APTBilling.xlsx**.

Sorting More Than One Column

When sorting data in cells, you can sort in more than one column. For example, in Project 3c you will be sorting the date from oldest to newest and then sorting client numbers from lowest to highest. In this sort, the dates are sorted first and then client numbers are sorted in ascending order within the same date.

To sort in more than one column, select all columns in the worksheet that need to remain relative and then display the Sort dialog box. At the Sort dialog box, specify the first column you want sorted in the *Sort by* option box, click the *Add Level* button, and then specify the second column in the first *Then by* option box. In Excel, you can sort on multiple columns. Add additional *Then by* option boxes by clicking the *Add Level* button.

Project 3c Sorting Data in Two Columns

Part 3 of 4

1. With **EL1-C4-P3-APTBilling.xlsx** open, select cells A3 through F29.
2. Click the Sort & Filter button and then click *Custom Sort*.
3. At the Sort dialog box, click the down-pointing arrow at the right side of the *Sort by* option box, and then click *Date* in the drop-down list. (Skip this step if Date already displays in the Sort by option box.)
4. Make sure *Oldest to Newest* displays in the *Order* option box.
5. Click the *Add Level* button.
6. Click the down-pointing arrow at the right of the *Then by* option box and then click *Client #* in the drop-down list.
7. Click OK to close the dialog box.
8. Deselect the cells.
9. Save and then print **EL1-C4-P3-APTBilling.xlsx**.

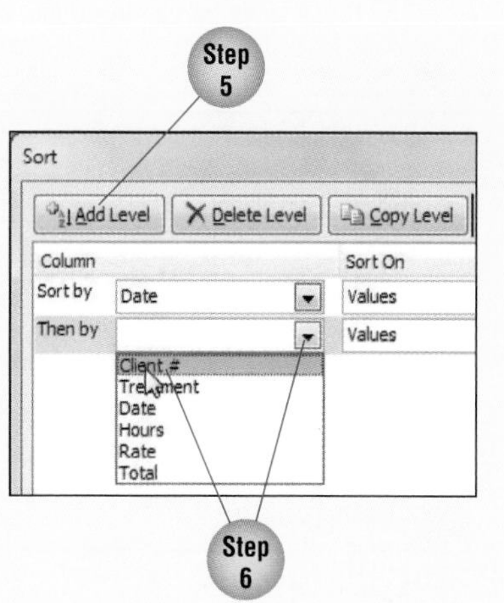

Filtering Data

You can place a restriction, called a *filter*, on data in a worksheet to temporarily isolate specific data. To turn on filtering, make a cell containing data active, click the Sort & Filter button in the Editing group in the Home tab, and then click *Filter* at the drop-down list. This turns on filtering and causes a filter arrow to appear in each column label in the worksheet as shown in Figure 4.12. You do not need to select before turning on filtering because Excel automatically searches for column labels in a worksheet.

To filter data in a worksheet, click the filter arrow in the heading you want to filter. This causes a drop-down list to display with options to filter all records, create a custom filter, or select an entry that appears in one or more of the cells in the column. When you filter data, the filter arrow changes to a funnel icon. The funnel icon indicates that rows in the worksheet have been filtered. To turn off filtering, click the Sort & Filter button and then click *Filter*.

If a column contains numbers, click the filter arrow, point to *Number Filters*, and a side menu displays with options for filtering numbers. For example, you can filter numbers that are equal to, greater than, or less than a number you specify; filter the top ten numbers; and filter numbers that are above or below a specified number.

Quick Steps

Filter a List

1. Select cells.
2. Click Sort & Filter button.
3. Click *Filter* at drop-down list.
4. Click down-pointing arrow of heading to filter.
5. Click desired option at drop-down list.

Figure 4.12 Filtering Data

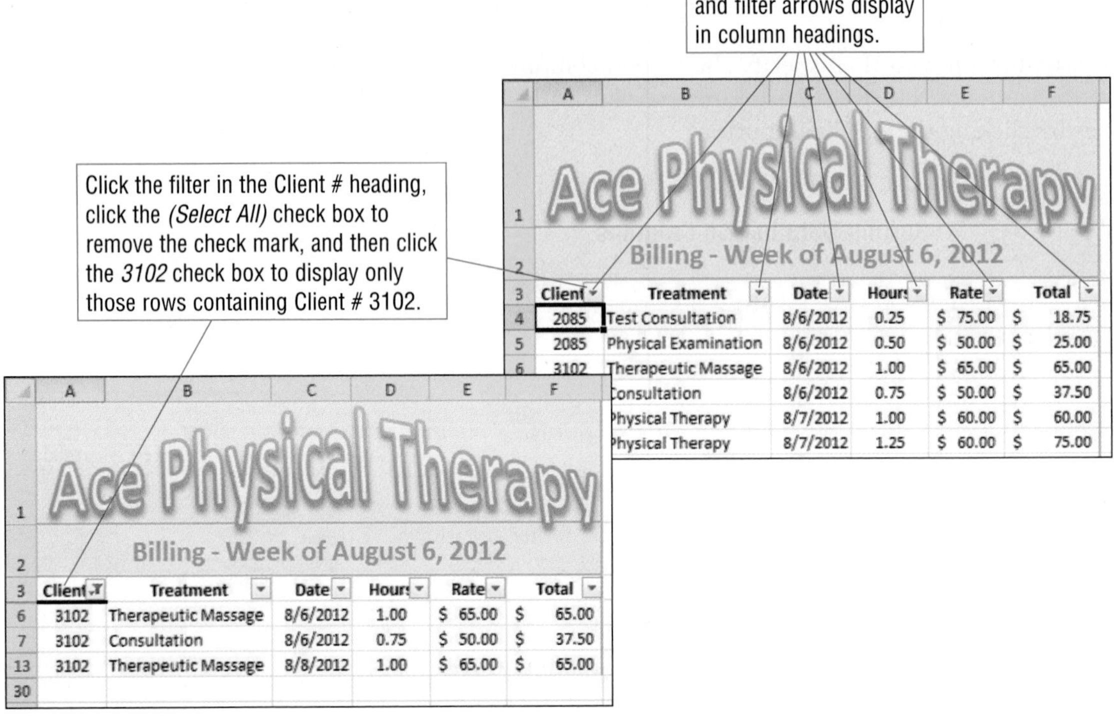

Project 3d Filtering Data

Part 4 of 4

1. With **EL1-C4-P3-APTBilling.xlsx** open, click in cell A4.
2. Turn on filtering by clicking the Sort & Filter button in the Editing group in the Home tab and then clicking *Filter* at the drop-down list.
3. Filter rows for client number 3102 by completing the following steps:
   a. Click the filter arrow in the *Client #* heading.
   b. Click the *(Select All)* check box to remove the check mark.
   c. Scroll down the list box and then click *3102* to insert a check mark in the check box.
   d. Click OK.

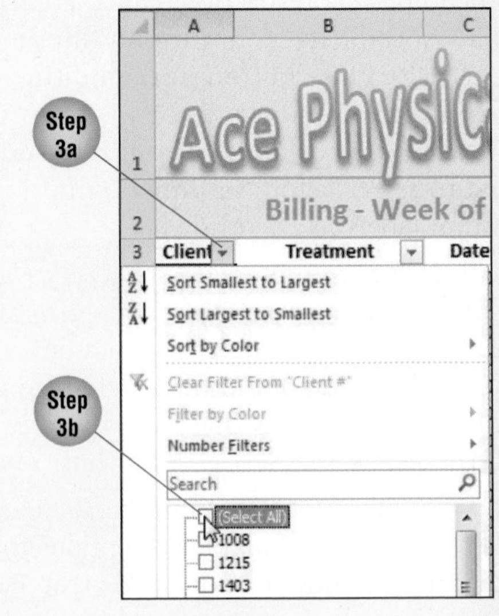

4. Redisplay all rows containing data by completing the following steps:
   a. Click the funnel icon in the *Client #* heading.
   b. Click the *(Select All)* check box to insert a check mark. (This also inserts a check mark for all items in the list.)
   c. Click OK.
5. Filter a list of clients receiving physical therapy by completing the following steps:
   a. Click the filter arrow in the *Treatment* heading.
   b. Click the *(Select All)* check box.
   c. Click the *Physical Therapy* check box.
   d. Click OK.

6. Redisplay all rows containing data by completing the following steps:
   a. Click the funnel icon in the *Treatment* heading.
   b. Click the *(Select All)* check box to insert a check mark. (This also inserts a check mark for all items in the list.)
   c. Click OK.
7. Display the top two highest rates by completing the following steps:
   a. Click the filter arrow in the *Rate* heading.
   b. Point to *Number Filters* and then click *Top 10* at the side menu.
   c. At the Top 10 AutoFilter dialog box, select the *10* that displays in the middle text box and then type 2.
   d. Click OK to close the dialog box.

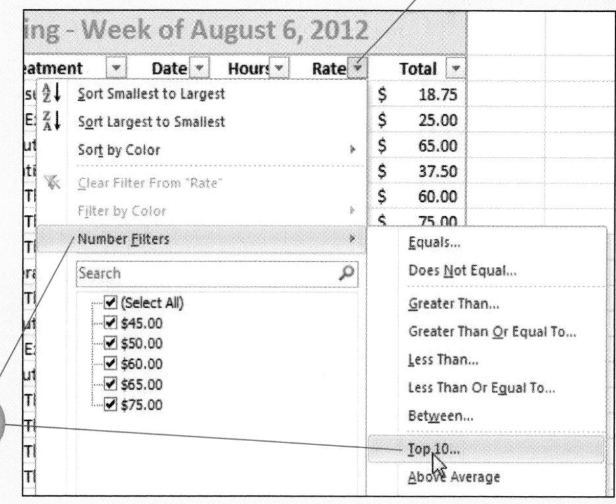

8. Redisplay all rows containing data by completing the following steps:
   a. Click the funnel icon in the *Rate* heading.
   b. Click the *(Select All)* check box to insert a check mark. (This also inserts a check mark for all items in the list.)
   c. Click OK.

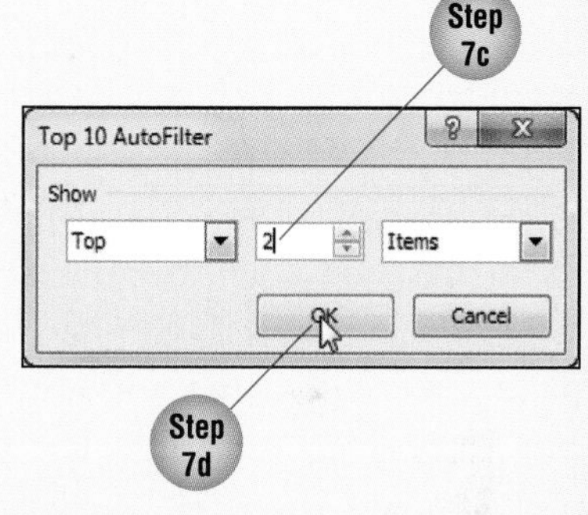

9. Display totals greater than $60 by completing the following steps:
   a. Click the filter arrow in the *Total* heading.
   b. Point to *Number Filters* and then click *Greater Than*.
   c. At the Custom AutoFilter dialog box, type 60 and then click OK.
   d. Print the worksheet by clicking the File tab, clicking the Print tab, and then clicking the Print button.
10. Turn off the filtering feature by clicking the Sort & Filter button and then clicking *Filter* at the drop-down list.
11. Save, print, and then close **EL1-C4-P3-APTBilling.xlsx**.

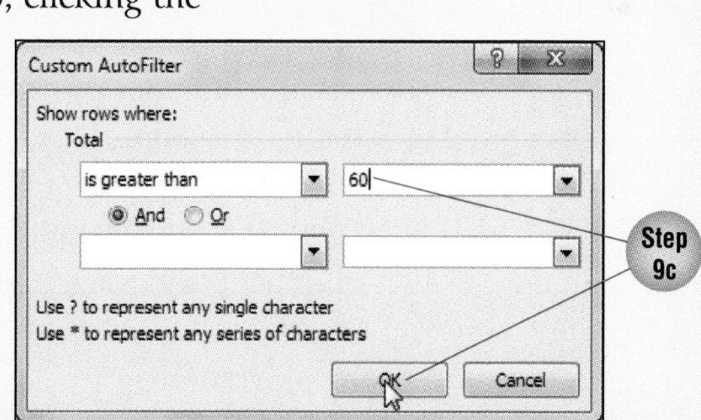

Chapter Summary

- The Page Setup group in the Page Layout tab contains buttons for changing margins, page orientation and size, and buttons for establishing a print area, inserting a page break, applying a picture background, and printing titles.
- The default left and right margins are 0.7 inch and the default top and bottom margins are 0.75 inch. Change these default margins with the Margins button in the Page Setup group in the Page Layout tab.
- Display the Page Setup dialog box with the Margins tab selected by clicking the Margins button and then clicking *Custom Margins* at the drop-down list.
- Center a worksheet on the page with the *Horizontally* and *Vertically* options at the Page Setup dialog box with the Margins tab selected.
- Click the Orientation button in the Page Setup group in the Page Layout tab to display the two orientation choices — *Portrait* and *Landscape*.
- Insert a page break by selecting the column or row, clicking the Breaks button in the Page Setup group in the Page Layout tab, and then clicking *Insert Page Break* at the drop-down list.
- To insert both a horizontal and vertical page break at the same time, make a cell active, click the Breaks button, and then click *Insert Page Break* at the drop-down list.
- Display a worksheet in page break preview by clicking the Page Break Preview button in the view area on the Status bar or clicking the View tab and then clicking the Page Break Preview button.
- Use options at the Page Setup dialog box with the Sheet tab selected to specify that you want column or row titles to print on each page. Display this dialog box by clicking the Print Titles button in the Page Setup group in the Page Layout tab.
- Use options in the Scale to Fit group in the Page Layout tab to scale data to fit on a specific number of pages.
- Use the Background button in the Page Setup group in the Page Layout tab to insert a worksheet background picture. A background picture displays on the screen but does not print.
- Use options in the Sheet Options group in the Page Layout tab to specify if you want gridlines and headings to view and/or print.
- Specify a print area by selecting the desired cells, clicking the Print Area button in the Page Setup group in the Page Layout tab, and then clicking *Set Print Area* at the drop-down list. Add another print area by selecting the desired cells, clicking the Print Area button, and then clicking *Add to Print Area* at the drop-down list.
- Create a header and/or footer with the Header & Footer button in the Text group in the Insert tab, in Page Layout view, or with options at the Page Setup dialog box with the Header/Footer tab selected.
- Customize print jobs with options at the Print tab Backstage view.
- To check spelling in a worksheet, click the Review tab and then click the Spelling button.

- Click the Undo button on the Quick Access toolbar to reverse the most recent action and click the Redo button to redo a previously reversed action.
- Use options at the Find and Replace dialog box with the Find tab selected to find specific data and/or formatting in a worksheet.
- Use options at the Find and Replace dialog box with the Replace tab selected to find specific data and/or formatting and replace with other data and/or formatting.
- Sort data in a worksheet with options from the Sort & Filter button in the Editing group in the Home tab.
- Create a custom sort with options at the Sort dialog box. Display this dialog box by clicking the Sort & Filter button and then clicking *Custom Sort* at the drop-down list.
- Use the filter feature to temporarily isolate specific data. Turn on the filter feature by clicking the Sort & Filter button in the Editing group in the Home tab and then clicking *Filter* at the drop-down list. This inserts filter arrows in each column label. Click a filter arrow and then use options at the drop-down list that displays to specify the filter data.

Commands Review

FEATURE	RIBBON TAB, GROUP	BUTTON, OPTION	KEYBOARD SHORTCUT
Margins	Page Layout, Page Setup		
Page Setup dialog box with Margins tab selected	Page Layout, Page Setup	, Custom Margins	
Orientation	Page Layout, Page Setup		
Size	Page Layout, Page Setup		
Insert page break	Page Layout, Page Setup	, Insert Page Break	
Remove page break	Page Layout, Page Setup	, Remove Page Break	
Page Break Preview	View, Workbook Views		
Page Setup dialog box with Sheet tab selected	Page Layout, Page Setup		
Scale width	Page Layout, Scale to Fit		
Scale height	Page Layout, Scale to Fit		
Scale	Page Layout, Scale to Fit		
Background picture	Page Layout, Page Setup		

FEATURE	RIBBON TAB, GROUP	BUTTON, OPTION	KEYBOARD SHORTCUT
Print Area	Page Layout, Page Setup		
Header and footer	Insert, Text		
Page Layout view	View, Workbook Views		
Spelling	Review, Proofing		F7
Find and Replace dialog box with Find tab selected	Home, Editing	, Find	Ctrl + F
Find and Replace dialog box with Replace tab selected	Home, Editing	, Replace	Ctrl + H
Sort data	Home, Editing		
Filter data	Home, Editing		

Concepts Check Test Your Knowledge

Completion: In the space provided at the right, indicate the correct term, symbol, or command.

1. This is the default left and right margin measurement. ____________
2. This is the default top and bottom margin measurement. ____________
3. The Margins button is located in this tab. ____________
4. By default, a worksheet prints in this orientation on a page. ____________
5. Click the Print Titles button in the Page Setup group in the Page Layout tab and the Page Setup dialog box displays with this tab selected. ____________
6. Use options in this group in the Page Layout tab to adjust the printed output by a percentage to fit the number of pages specified. ____________
7. Use this button in the Page Setup group in the Page Layout tab to select and print specific areas in a worksheet. ____________
8. Click the Header & Footer button in the Text group in the Insert tab and the worksheet displays in this view. ____________

9. This tab contains options for formatting and customizing a header and/or footer. __________

10. Click this tab to display the Spelling button. __________

11. The Undo and Redo buttons are located on this toolbar. __________

12. Click this button in the Find and Replace dialog box to expand the dialog box. __________

13. Use these two buttons at the expanded Find and Replace dialog box to search for specific cell formatting and replace with other formatting. __________

14. Use this button in the Editing group in the Home tab to sort data in a worksheet. __________

15. Use this feature to temporarily isolate specific data in a worksheet. __________

Skills Check Assess Your Performance

Assessment

1 FORMAT A DATA ANALYSIS WORKSHEET

1. Open **DISemiSales.xlsx**.
2. Save the workbook with Save As and name it **EL1-C4-A1-DISemiSales**.
3. Make the following changes to the worksheet:
   a. Insert a formula in cell H4 that averages the amounts in cells B4 through G4.
   b. Copy the formula in cell H4 down to cells H5 through H9.
   c. Insert a formula in cell B10 that adds the amounts in cells B4 through B9.
   d. Copy the formula in cell B10 over to cells C10 through H10. (Click the Auto Fill Options button and then click *Fill Without Formatting* at the drop-down list.)
   e. Apply the Accounting Number Format style to cell H4.
   f. Change the orientation of the worksheet to landscape.
   g. Change the top margin to 3 inches and the left margin to 1.5 inches.
4. Save and then print **EL1-C4-A1-DISemiSales.xlsx**.
5. Make the following changes to the worksheet:
   a. Change the orientation back to portrait.
   b. Change the top margin to 1 inch and the left margin to 0.7 inch.
   c. Horizontally and vertically center the worksheet on the page.
   d. Scale the worksheet so it fits on one page.
6. Save, print, and then close **EL1-C4-A1-DISemiSales.xlsx**.

Assessment 2

FORMAT A TEST RESULTS WORKSHEET

1. Open **CMTests.xlsx**.
2. Save the workbook with Save As and name it **EL1-C4-A2-CMTests**.
3. Make the following changes to the worksheet.
   a. Insert a formula in cell N4 that averages the test scores in cells B4 through M4.
   b. Copy the formula in cell N4 down to cells N5 through N21.
   c. Type Average in cell A22.
   d. Insert a formula in cell B22 that averages the test scores in cells B4 through B21.
   e. Copy the formula in cell B22 across to cells C22 through N22.
   f. Insert a page break between columns G and H.
4. View the worksheet in Page Break Preview.
5. Change back to the Normal view.
6. Specify that the column titles (A3 through A22) are to print on each page.
7. Create a header that prints the page number at the right side of the page.
8. Create a footer that prints your name at the left side of the page and the workbook file name at the right side of the page.
9. Save and then print the worksheet.
10. Set a print area for cells N3 through N22 and then print the cells.
11. Clear the print area.
12. Save and then close **EL1-C4-A2-CMTests.xlsx**.

Assessment 3

FORMAT AN EQUIPMENT RENTAL WORKSHEET

1. Open **HERInvoices.xlsx**.
2. Save the workbook with Save As and name it **EL1-C4-A3-HERInvoices**.
3. Insert a formula in cell H3 that multiplies the rate in cell G3 by the hours in cell F3. Copy the formula in cell H3 down to cells H4 through H16.
4. Insert a formula in cell H17 that sums the amounts in cells H3 through H16.
5. Complete the following find and replaces:
   a. Find all occurrences of cells containing *75* and replace with *90*.
   b. Find all occurrences of cells containing *55* and replace with *60*.
   c. Find all occurrences of *Barrier Concrete* and replace with *Lee Sand and Gravel*.
   d. Find all occurrences of 11-point Calibri and replace with 10-point Cambria.
   e. After completing the find and replace, clear all formatting from the Format buttons.
6. Insert a header that prints the date at the left side of the page and the time at the right side of the page.
7. Insert a footer that prints your name at the left side of the page and the workbook file name at the right side of the page.
8. Print the worksheet horizontally and vertically centered on the page.
9. Save and then close **EL1-C4-A3-HERInvoices.xlsx**.

Assessment 4

FORMAT AN INVOICES WORKSHEET

1. Open **RPInvoices.xlsx**.
2. Save the workbook with Save As and name it **EL1-C4-A4-RPInvoices**.
3. Insert a formula in G4 that multiplies the amount in E4 with the percentage in F4 and then adds the product to cell E4. (If you write the formula correctly, the result in G4 will display as *$488.25*.)
4. Copy the formula in cell G4 down to cells G5 through G17, click the Auto Fill Options button, and then click the *Fill Without Formatting* option.
5. Complete a spelling check on the worksheet.
6. Find all occurrences of *Picture* and replace with *Portrait*. (Do not type a space after *Picture* or *Portrait* because you want to find occurrences that end with an "s." Make sure the *Match entire cell contents* check box does not contain a check mark.)
7. Sort the records by invoice number in ascending order (smallest to largest).
8. Complete a new sort that sorts the records by client number in ascending order (A to Z).
9. Complete a new sort that sorts the date in ascending order (oldest to newest).
10. Insert a footer in the worksheet that prints your name at the left side of the page and the current date at the right side of the page.
11. Center the worksheet horizontally and vertically on the page.
12. Save and then print **EL1-C4-A4-RPInvoices.xlsx**.
13. Select cells A3 through G3 and then turn on the filter feature and complete the following filters:
    a. Filter and then print a list of rows containing client number 11-279 and then clear the filter.
    b. Filter and then print a list of rows containing the top three highest amounts due and then clear the filter.
    c. Filter and then print a list of rows containing amounts due that are less than $500 and then clear the filter.
14. Save and then close **EL1-C4-A4-RPInvoices.xlsx**.

Assessment 5

CREATE A WORKSHEET CONTAINING KEYBOARD SHORTCUTS

1. Use Excel's Help feature and learn about keyboard shortcuts in Excel. After reading the information presented, create a worksheet with the following feature:
    - Create a title for the worksheet.
    - Include at least 10 keyboard shortcuts along with an explanation of the keyboard shortcut.
    - Set the data in cells in a typeface other than Calibri and change the data color.
    - Add borders to the cells. (You determine the border style.)
    - Add a color shading to cells. (You determine the color—make it complementary to the data color.)
    - Create a header that prints the date at the right margin and create a footer that prints your name at the left margin and the file name at the right margin.
2. Save the workbook and name it **EL1-C4-A5-KeyboardShortcuts**.
3. Print and then close **EL1-C4-A5-KeyboardShortcuts.xlsx**.

Visual Benchmark Demonstrate Your Proficiency

CREATE AND FORMAT AN EXPENSE WORKSHEET

1. At a blank workbook, type the data in the cells indicated in Figure 4.13 but **do not** type the data in the following cells—instead insert the formulas as indicated (the results of your formulas should match the results you see in the figure):
   - Cells N3 through N8: Insert a formula that sums the monthly expenses for the year.
   - Cells B9 through N9: Insert a formula that sums the monthly expenses for each month and the entire year.
2. Change the left and right margins to *0.45* and change the top margin to *1.5*.
3. Apply formatting so your worksheet looks similar to the worksheet shown in Figure 4.13. (Set the heading in 26-point Cambria and set the remaining data in 10-point Cambria. Apply bold formatting as shown in the figure.)
4. Save the workbook and name it **EL1-C4-VB-HERExpenses**.
5. Look at the printing of the worksheet shown in Figure 4.14 and then make the following changes:
   - Insert a page break between columns G and H.
   - Insert the headers and footer as shown.
   - Specify that the column titles print on the second page as shown in Figure 4.14.
6. Save and then print **EL1-C4-VB-HERExpenses.xlsx**. (Your worksheet should print on two pages and appear as shown in Figure 4.14.)
7. Close **EL1-C4-VB-HERExpenses.xlsx**.

Figure 4.13 Visual Benchmark Data

	A	B	C	D	E	F	G	H	I	J	K	L	M	N
1	**Hilltop Equipment Rental**													
2	**Expenses**	**January**	**February**	**March**	**April**	**May**	**June**	**July**	**August**	**September**	**October**	**November**	**December**	***Total***
3	Lease	$ 3,250	$ 3,250	$ 3,250	$ 3,250	$ 3,250	$ 3,250	$ 3,250	$ 3,250	$ 3,250	$ 3,250	$ 3,250	$ 3,250	$ 39,000
4	Utilities	3,209	2,994	2,987	2,500	2,057	1,988	1,845	1,555	1,890	2,451	2,899	3,005	29,380
5	Payroll	10,545	9,533	11,542	10,548	11,499	12,675	13,503	13,258	12,475	10,548	10,122	9,359	135,607
6	Insurance	895	895	895	895	895	895	895	895	895	895	895	895	10,740
7	Maintenance	2,439	1,856	2,455	5,410	3,498	3,110	2,479	3,100	1,870	6,105	4,220	3,544	40,086
8	Supplies	341	580	457	330	675	319	451	550	211	580	433	601	5,528
9	***Total Expenses***	$ 20,679	$ 19,108	$ 21,586	$ 22,933	$ 21,874	$ 22,237	$ 22,423	$ 22,608	$ 20,591	$ 23,829	$ 21,819	$ 20,654	$ 260,341
10														

Figure 4.14 Visual Benchmark Printed Pages

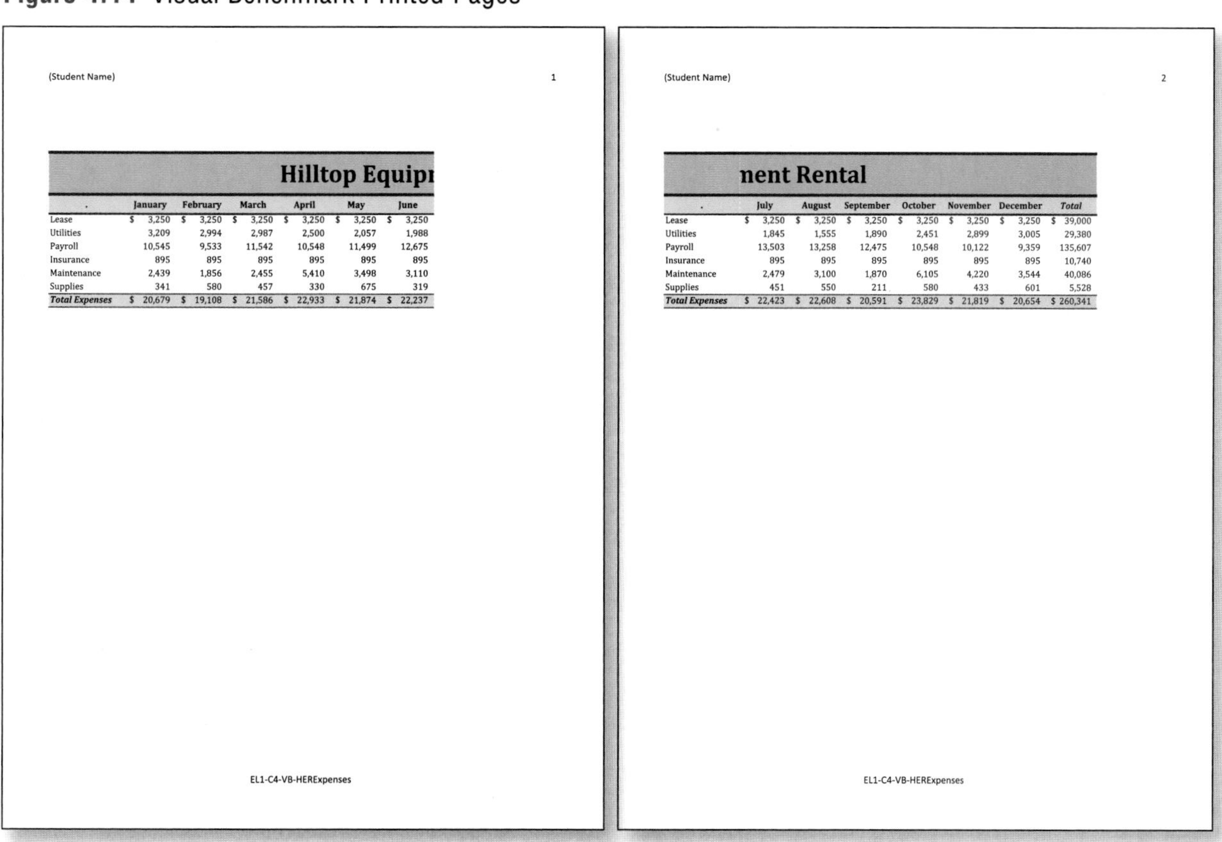

(Student Name) 1

Hilltop Equipı

.	January	February	March	April	May	June
Lease	$ 3,250	$ 3,250	$ 3,250	$ 3,250	$ 3,250	$ 3,250
Utilities	3,209	2,994	2,987	2,500	2,057	1,988
Payroll	10,545	9,533	11,542	10,548	11,499	12,675
Insurance	895	895	895	895	895	895
Maintenance	2,439	1,856	2,455	5,410	3,498	3,110
Supplies	341	580	457	330	675	319
Total Expenses	$ 20,679	$ 19,108	$ 21,586	$ 22,933	$ 21,874	$ 22,237

EL1-C4-VB-HERExpenses

(Student Name) 2

nent Rental

.	July	August	September	October	November	December	*Total*
Lease	$ 3,250	$ 3,250	$ 3,250	$ 3,250	$ 3,250	$ 3,250	$ 39,000
Utilities	1,845	1,555	1,890	2,451	2,899	3,005	29,380
Payroll	13,503	13,258	12,475	10,548	10,122	9,359	135,607
Insurance	895	895	895	895	895	895	10,740
Maintenance	2,479	3,100	1,870	6,105	4,220	3,544	40,086
Supplies	451	550	211	580	433	601	5,528
Total Expenses	$ 22,423	$ 22,608	$ 20,591	$ 23,829	$ 21,819	$ 20,654	$ 260,341

EL1-C4-VB-HERExpenses

Case Study Apply Your Skills

Part 1

You are the sales manager for Macadam Realty. You decide that you want to display sample mortgage worksheets in the reception area display rack. Open the **MRMortgages.xlsx** workbook, save it with Save As and name it **EL1-C4-CS-MRMortgages-01**, and then add the following information and make the following changes:

- In column C, insert a formula that determines the down payment amount.
- In column D, insert a formula that determines the loan amount.
- In column G, insert a formula using the PMT function. (Enter the *Pv* as a negative.)
- Insert the date and time as a header and your name and the workbook name (**EL1-C4-CS-MRMortgages-01.xlsx**) as a footer.
- Find 11-point Calibri formatting and replace with 11-point Candara formatting.
- Scale the worksheet so it prints on one page.

Save and then print **EL1-C4-CS-MRMortgages-01.xlsx**. After looking at the printed worksheet, you decide that you need to make the following changes:

- Sort the *Price of Home* column from smallest to largest.
- Change the percentage amount in column E from 6% to 7%.
- Shade the cells in row 4 in the light yellow color that matches the fill in cell A2. Copy this shading to every other row of cells in the worksheet (stopping at row 46).

Save the edited worksheet with Save As and name it **EL1-C4-CS-MRMortgages-02**. Edit the footer to reflect the workbook name change. Save, print, and then close **EL1-C4-CS-MRMortgages-02.xlsx**. (Make sure the worksheet prints on one page.)

Part 2

You are preparing for a quarterly sales meeting during which you will discuss retirement issues with the sales officers. You want to encourage them to consider opening an Individual Retirement Account (IRA) to supplement the retirement contributions made by Macadam Realty. You have begun an IRA worksheet but need to complete it. Open **MRIRA.xlsx** and then save it with Save As and name it **EL1-C4-CS-MRIRA-01**. Make the following changes to the worksheet:

- Insert in cell C6 a formula that calculates the future value of an investment. Use the FV function to write the formula. You must use absolute and mixed cell references for the formula. When entering the *Rate* (percentage), the column letter is variable but the row number is fixed; when entering the *Nper* (years), the column letter is fixed but the row number is variable; and when entering the *Pmt* (the contribution amount), both the column letter and row number are absolute.
- Copy the formula in cell C6 down to cells C7 through C19. Copy the formula in cell C6 across to cells D6 through K6. Continue in this manner until the amounts are entered in all the appropriate cells.

- Select and then merge and center cells A6 through A19. Type the text Number of Years and then rotate the text up. Make sure the text is centered in the merged cell. Apply 12-point Calibri bold formatting to the text.
- Adjust the column widths so all text is visible in the cells.
- Change the page orientation to landscape.
- Vertically and horizontally center the worksheet.
- Include a header that prints the page number and insert a footer that prints your name.

Save the worksheet and then print it so that the row titles print on both pages. After looking at the worksheet, you decide to make the following changes:

- Remove the header containing the page number.
- Edit the footer so the date prints at the left margin and your name prints at the right margin.
- Scale the worksheet so it prints on one page.

Save the workbook with Save As and name it **EL1-C4-CS-MRIRA-02** and then print the worksheet. Change the amount in cell D3 to *$3,000* and then print the worksheet again. Save and then close **EL1-C4-CS-MRIRA-02.xlsx**.

Part 3

You have clients living in Canada that are interested in purchasing real estate in the United States. For those clients, you like to keep a conversion worksheet available. Using the Internet, search for the MS MoneyCentral Investor Currency Rates site. Determine the current currency exchange rate for Canada and then create a worksheet with the following specifications:

- Apply formatting that is similar to the formatting in the worksheets you worked with in the first two parts of the case study.
- Create the following columns:
  - Column for home price in American dollars.
  - Column for home price in Canadian dollars.
  - Column for amount of down payment.
  - Column for loan total.
  - Column for monthly payment.
- In the column for home prices, insert home amounts beginning with $100,000, incrementing every $50,000, and ending with $1,000,000.
- Insert a formula in the home price in the Canadian dollars column that displays the home price in Canadian dollars.
- Insert a formula in the down payment column that multiplies the Canadian home price by 20%.
- Insert a formula in the loan total column that subtracts the down payment from the Canadian home price.
- Insert a formula in the monthly payment column that determines the monthly payment using the PMT function. Use 6% as the rate (be sure to divide by 12 months), 360 as the number of payments, and the loan amount as a negative as the present value.
- Apply any other formatting you feel necessary to improve the worksheet.

Save the completed workbook and name it **EL1-C4-CS-CanadaPrices**. Display formulas and then print the worksheet. Turn off the display of formulas and then save and close the workbook.

UNIT 1

Performance Assessment

Excel2010L1U1

Note: Before beginning unit assessments, copy to your storage medium the Excel2010L1U1 subfolder from the Excel2010L1 folder on the CD that accompanies this textbook and then make Excel2010L1U1 the active folder.

Assessing Proficiency

In this unit, you have learned to create, save, print, edit, and format Excel worksheets; create and insert formulas; and enhance worksheets with features such as headers and footers, page numbering, sorting, and filtering.

Assessment 1 Create Sales Bonuses Workbook

1. Create the Excel worksheet shown in Figure U1.1. Format the cells as you see them in the figure.
2. Insert an IF statement in cell C4 that inserts *7%* if B4 is greater than 99999 and inserts *3%* if B4 is not greater than 99999.
3. Format the number in cell C4 so it displays as a percentage with no decimal places. Copy the formula in cell C4 down to cells C5 through C11. Center the percents in cells C4 through C11.
4. Insert a formula in cell D4 that multiplies the amount in B4 with the percentage in cell C4. Copy the formula in D4 down to cells D5 through D11.
5. Insert the sum of cells B4 through B11 in B12 and insert the sum of cells D4 through D11 in cell D12.
6. Apply the Accounting Number Format style with two decimal places to cells B4, B12, D4, and D12. Apply the Comma style with two decimal places to cells B5 through B11 and cells D5 through D11.
7. Insert a footer that contains your first and last names and the current date.
8. Print the worksheet horizontally and vertically centered on the page.
9. Save the workbook and name it **EL1-U1-A1-SBASales**.
10. Close **EL1-U1-A1-SBASales.xlsx**.

Figure U1.1 Assessment 1

	A	B	C	D	E
1	Stanton & Barnet Associates				
2	Sales Department				
3	Associate	Sales	Bonus	Bonus Amount	
4	Conway, Edward	$ 101,450.00			
5	Eckhart, Geneva	94,375.00			
6	Farris, Amanda	73,270.00			
7	Greenwood, Wayne	110,459.00			
8	Hagen, Chandra	120,485.00			
9	Logan, Courtney	97,520.00			
10	Pena, Geraldo	115,850.00			
11	Rubin, Alice	76,422.00			
12	Total				
13					

Assessment 2 Format Equipment Purchase Plan Workbook

1. Open **HERPurPlans.xlsx** and then save the workbook with Save As and name it **EL1-U1-A2-HERPurPlans**.
2. The owner of Hilltop Equipment Rental is interested in purchasing a new tractor and needs to determine monthly payments on three different models. Insert a formula in cell E4 that uses the PMT function to calculate monthly payments. Copy the formula down to cells E5 and E6.
3. Insert a formula in cell F4 that multiplies the amount in E4 by the amount in D4.
4. Copy the formula in cell F4 down to cells F5 and F6.
5. Insert a formula in cell G4 that subtracts the amount in B4 from the amount in F4. ***Hint: The formula should return a positive number, not a negative number (a number surrounded by parentheses).***
6. Copy the formula in cell G4 down to cells G5 and G6.
7. Change the vertical alignment of cell A2 to Middle Align.
8. Change the vertical alignment of cells A3 through G3 to Bottom Align.
9. Save, print, and then close **EL1-U1-A2-HERPurPlans.xlsx**.

Assessment 3 Format Accounts Due Workbook

1. Open **RPAccts.xlsx** and then save the workbook with Save As and name it **EL1-U1-A3-RPAccts**.
2. Using the DATE function, enter a formula in each of the specified cells that returns the serial number for the specified date:

   C4 = October 29, 2012
   C5 = October 30, 2012
   C6 = October 30, 2012
   C7 = November 1, 2012
   C8 = November 5, 2012
   C9 = November 7, 2012
   C10 = November 7, 2012
   C11 = November 14, 2012
   C12 = November 14, 2012
3. Enter a formula in cell E4 that inserts the due date (date of service plus the number of days in the *Terms* column).
4. Copy the formula in cell E4 down to cells E5 through E12.
5. Make cell A14 active and then type your name.
6. Make cell A15 active and then use the NOW function to insert the current date and time as a serial number.
7. Save, print, and then close **EL1-U1-A3-RPAccts.xlsx**.

Assessment 4 Format First Quarter Sales Workbook

1. Open **PSQtrlySales.xlsx** and then save the workbook with Save As and name it **EL1-U1-A4-PSQtrlySales**.
2. Insert a formula in cell E4 that totals the amounts in B4, C4, and D4. Copy the formula in cell E4 down to cells E5 through E18. Apply the Accounting Number Format style with no decimal places to cell E4.
3. Insert an IF statement in cell F4 that inserts *5%* if E4 is greater than 74999 and inserts *0%* if E4 is not greater than 74999.
4. Make sure the result of the IF formula displays in cell F4 as a percentage with no decimal points and then copy the formula down to cells F5 through F18. Center the percent amounts in cells F4 through F18.
5. Select cells A5 through F5 and then insert the same yellow fill as cell A2. Apply the same yellow fill to cells A7 through F7, A9 through F9, A11 through F11, A13 through F13, A15 through F15, and cells A17 through F17.
6. Insert a footer that prints your name at the left, the current date at the middle, and the current time at the right.
7. Print the worksheet horizontally and vertically centered on the page.
8. Save, print, and then close **EL1-U1-A4-PSQtrlySales.xlsx**.

Assessment 5 Format Weekly Payroll Workbook

1. Open **CCPayroll.xlsx** and then save the workbook with Save As and name it **EL1-U1-A5-CCPayroll**.
2. Insert a formula in cell E3 that multiplies the hourly rate by the hours and then adds that to the multiplication of the hourly rate by the overtime pay rate (1.5) and then overtime hours. (Use parentheses in the formula and use an absolute cell reference for the overtime pay rate (1.5). Refer to Chapter 2, Project 5c.) Copy the formula down to cells E4 through E16.

3. Insert a formula in cell F3 that multiplies the gross pay by the withholding tax rate (W/H Rate). (Use an absolute cell reference for the cell containing the withholding rate. Refer to Chapter 2, Project 5c.) Copy the formula down to cells F4 through F16.
4. Insert a formula in cell G3 that multiplies the gross pay by the Social Security rate (SS Rate). Use an absolute cell reference for the cell containing the Social Security rate. (Refer to Chapter 2, Project 5c.) Copy the formula down to cells G4 through G16.
5. Insert a formula in cell H4 that adds together the Social Security tax and the withholding tax and subtracts that from the gross pay. (Refer to Chapter 2, Project 5c.) Copy the formula down to cells H4 through H16.
6. Sort the employee last names alphabetically in ascending order (A to Z).
7. Center the worksheet horizontally and vertically on the page.
8. Insert a footer that prints your name at the left side of the page and the file name at the right side of the page.
9. Save, print, and then close **EL1-U1-A5-CCPayroll.xlsx**.

Assessment 6 Format Customer Sales Analysis Workbook

1. Open **DIAnnualSales.xlsx** and then save the workbook with Save As and name it **EL1-U1-A6-DIAnnualSales**.
2. Insert formulas and drag formulas to complete the worksheet. After dragging the total formula in row 10, specify that you want to fill without formatting. (This retains the right border in cell N10.) Do this with the AutoFill Options button.
3. Insert in cell B11 the highest total from cells B10 through M10. Insert in cell B12 the lowest total from cells B10 through M10.
4. Change the orientation to landscape.
5. Insert a header that prints the page number at the right side of the page.
6. Insert a footer that prints your name at the right side of the page.
7. Horizontally and vertically center the worksheet on the page.
8. Specify that the column headings in cells A3 through A12 print on both pages.
9. Save, print, and then close **EL1-U1-A6-DIAnnualSales.xlsx**.

Assessment 7 Format Invoices Workbook

1. Open **RPInvoices.xlsx** and then save the workbook with Save As and name it **EL1-U1-A7-RPInvoices**.
2. Insert a formula in cell G4 that multiplies the amount in E4 by the percentage in F4 and then adds that total to the amount in E4. (Use parentheses in this formula.)
3. Copy the formula in cell G4 down to cells G5 through G18.
4. Find all occurrences of cells containing *11-279* and replace with *10-005*.
5. Find all occurrences of cells containing *8.5* and replace with *9.0*.
6. Search for the Calibri font and replace with the Candara font. (Do not specify a type size so that Excel replaces all sizes of Calibri with Candara.)
7. Print **EL1-U1-A7-RPInvoices.xlsx**.
8. Filter and then print a list of rows containing only the client number *04-325*. (After printing, return the list to *(Select All)*.)
9. Filter and then print a list of rows containing only the service *Development*. (After printing, return the list to *(Select All)*.)
10. Filter and then print a list of rows containing the top three highest totals in the *Amount Due* column. (After printing, turn off the filter feature.)
11. Save and then close **EL1-U1-A7-RPInvoices.xlsx**.

Writing Activities

The following activities give you the opportunity to practice your writing skills along with demonstrating an understanding of some of the important Excel features you have mastered in this unit. Use correct grammar, appropriate word choices, and clear sentence construction.

Activity 1 Plan and Prepare Orders Summary Workbook

Plan and prepare a worksheet with the information shown in Figure U1.2. Apply formatting of your choosing to the worksheet. Save the completed worksheet and name it **EL1-U1-Act1-OrdersSumm**. Print and then close **EL1-U1-Act1-OrdersSumm.xlsx**.

Figure U1.2 Activity 1

Prepare a weekly summary of orders taken that itemizes the products coming into the company and the average order size.
The products and average order size include:

Black and gold wall clock: $2,450 worth of orders, average order size of $125
Traveling alarm clock: $l,358 worth of orders, average order size of $195
Waterproof watch: $890 worth of orders, average order size of $90
Dashboard clock: $2,135 worth of orders, average order size of $230
Pyramid clock: $3,050 worth of orders, average order size of $375
Gold chain watch: $755 worth of orders, average order size of $80

In the worksheet, total the amount ordered and also calculate the average weekly order size. Sort the data in the worksheet by the order amount in descending order.

Activity 2 Prepare Depreciation Workbook

Assets within a company, such as equipment, can be depreciated over time. Several methods are available for determining the amount of depreciation such as the straight-line depreciation method, fixed-declining balance method, and the double-declining method. Use Excel's Help feature to learn about two depreciation methods — straight-line and double-declining depreciation. (The straight-line depreciation function, SNL, and the double-declining depreciation function, DDB, are located in the Financial category.) After reading about the two methods, create an Excel worksheet with the following information:

- An appropriate title
- A heading for straight-line depreciation
- The straight-line depreciation function
- The name and a description for each straight-line depreciation function argument category
- A heading for double-declining depreciation

- The double-declining depreciation function
- The name and a description for each double-declining depreciation function argument category

Apply formatting of your choosing to the worksheet. Save the completed workbook and name it **EL1-U1-Act2-DepMethods**. Print the worksheet horizontally and vertically centered on the page. Close **EL1-U1-Act2-DepMethods.xlsx**.

Activity 3 Insert Straight-Line Depreciation Formula

Open **RPDepreciation.xlsx** and then save the workbook and name it **EL1-U1-Act3-RPDepreciation**. Insert the function to determine straight-line depreciation in cell E3. Copy the formula down to cells E4 through E10. Apply formatting of your choosing to the worksheet. Print the worksheet horizontally and vertically centered on the page. Save and then close **EL1-U1-Act3-RPDepreciation.xlsx**.

Optional: Briefly research the topic of straight-line and double-declining depreciation to find out why businesses depreciate their assets. What purpose does it serve? Locate information about the topic on the Internet or in your school library. Then use Word 2010 to write a half-page, single-spaced report explaining the financial reasons for using depreciation methods. Save the document and name it **EL1-U1-Act3-DepReport**. Print and then close the document.

Internet Research

Activity 4 Create a Travel Planning Worksheet

Make sure you are connected to the Internet. Use a search engine of your choosing to look for information on traveling to a specific country that interests you. Find sites that provide cost information for airlines, hotels, meals, entertainment, and car rentals. Create a travel planning worksheet for the country that includes the following:

- appropriate title
- appropriate headings
- airline costs
- hotel costs (off-season and in-season rates if available)
- estimated meal costs
- entertainment costs
- car rental costs

Save the completed workbook and name it **EL1-U1-Act4-TrvlWksht**. Print and then close the workbook.

Microsoft® Excel®

Level 1

Unit 2 ■ Enhancing the Display of Workbooks

Chapter 5 ■ Moving Data within and between Workbooks

Chapter 6 ■ Maintaining Workbooks

Chapter 7 ■ Creating a Chart in Excel

Chapter 8 ■ Adding Visual Interest to Workbooks

Microsoft® Excel

CHAPTER 5

Moving Data within and between Workbooks

PERFORMANCE OBJECTIVES

Upon successful completion of Chapter 5, you will be able to:

- **Create a workbook with multiple worksheets**
- **Move, copy, and paste cells within a worksheet**
- **Split a worksheet into windows and freeze panes**
- **Name a range of cells and use a range in a formula**
- **Open multiple workbooks**
- **Arrange, size, and move workbooks**
- **Copy and paste data between workbooks**
- **Link data between worksheets**

Tutorials

5.1 Moving and Copying Cells
5.2 Inserting, Moving, Renaming, and Hiding a Worksheet
5.3 Formatting Multiple Worksheets
5.4 Setting a Print Area and Printing Multiple Worksheets
5.5 Splitting a Worksheet into Windows
5.6 Freezing Panes and Changing the Zoom
5.7 Naming and Using a Range
5.8 Working with Windows
5.9 Linking Data and Using 3-D References
5.10 Copying and Pasting Data between Programs

Up to this point, the workbooks in which you have been working have consisted of only one worksheet. In this chapter, you will learn to create a workbook with several worksheets and complete tasks such as copying and pasting data within and between worksheets. Moving and pasting or copying and pasting selected cells in and between worksheets is useful for rearranging data or for saving time. You will also work with multiple workbooks and complete tasks such as arranging, sizing, and moving workbooks, and opening and closing multiple workbooks. Model answers for this chapter's projects appear on the following pages.

Excel2010L1C5

Note: Before beginning the projects, copy to your storage medium the Excel2010L1C5 subfolder from the Excel2010L1 folder on the CD that accompanies this textbook and then make Excel2010L1C5 the active folder.

Model Answers

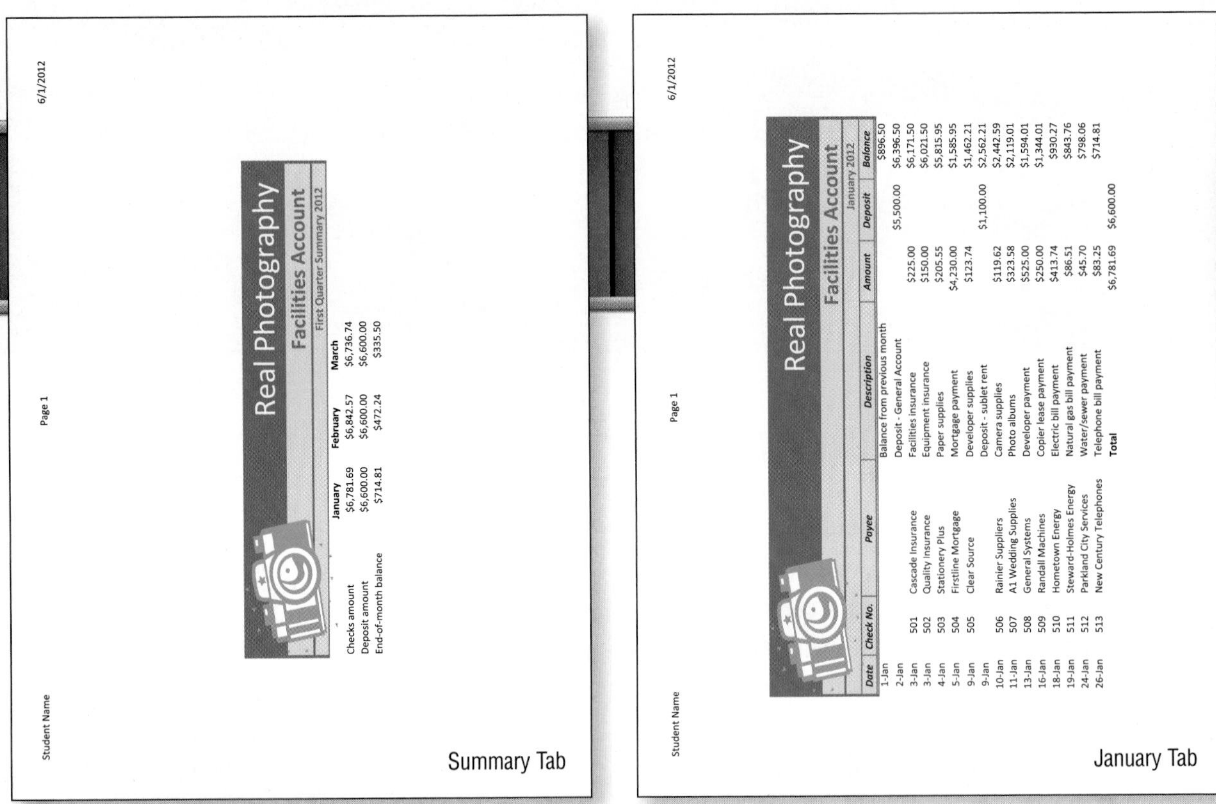
Student Name | Page 1 | 6/1/2012

Real Photography
Facilities Account
First Quarter Summary 2012

	January	February	March
Checks amount	$6,781.69	$6,842.57	$6,736.74
Deposit amount	$6,600.00	$6,600.00	$6,600.00
End-of-month balance	$714.81	$472.24	$335.50

Summary Tab

Student Name | Page 1 | 6/1/2012

Real Photography
Facilities Account
January 2012

Date	Check No.	Payee	Description	Amount	Deposit	Balance
1-Jan			Balance from previous month			$896.50
2-Jan			Deposit - General Account		$5,500.00	$6,396.50
3-Jan	501	Cascade Insurance	Facilities insurance	$225.00		$6,171.50
3-Jan	502	Quality Insurance	Equipment insurance	$150.00		$6,021.50
4-Jan	503	Stationery Plus	Paper supplies	$205.55		$5,815.95
5-Jan	504	Firstline Mortgage	Mortgage payment	$4,230.00		$1,585.95
9-Jan	505	Clear Source	Developer supplies	$123.74		$1,462.21
9-Jan			Deposit - sublet rent		$1,100.00	$2,562.21
10-Jan	506	Rainier Suppliers	Camera supplies	$119.62		$2,442.59
11-Jan	507	A1 Wedding Supplies	Photo albums	$323.58		$2,119.01
13-Jan	508	General Systems	Developer payment	$525.00		$1,594.01
16-Jan	509	Randall Machines	Copier lease payment	$250.00		$1,344.01
18-Jan	510	Hometown Energy	Electric bill payment	$413.74		$930.27
19-Jan	511	Steward-Holmes Energy	Natural gas bill payment	$86.51		$843.76
24-Jan	512	Parkland City Services	Water/sewer payment	$45.70		$798.06
26-Jan	513	New Century Telephones	Telephone bill payment	$83.25		$714.81
			Total	$6,781.69	$6,600.00	

January Tab

Project 1 Manage Data in a Multiple-Worksheet Account Workbook EL1-C5-P1-RPFacAccts.xlsx

Student Name | Page 1 | 6/1/2012

Real Photography
Facilities Account
February 2012

Date	Check No.	Payee	Description	Amount	Deposit	Balance
1-Feb			Balance from previous month			$714.81
1-Feb			Deposit - General Account		$5,500.00	$6,214.81
6-Feb	514	Firstline Mortgage	Mortgage payment	$4,230.00		$1,984.81
6-Feb	515	Cascade Insurance	Facilities insurance	$225.00		$1,759.81
10-Feb	516	Quality Insurance	Equipment insurance	$150.00		$1,609.81
11-Feb	517	Stationery Plus	Paper supplies	$266.43		$1,343.38
12-Feb	518	Clear Source	Developer supplies	$123.74		$1,219.64
12-Feb			Deposit - sublet rent		$1,100.00	$2,319.64
16-Feb	519	Rainier Suppliers	Camera supplies	$119.62		$2,200.02
17-Feb	520	A1 Wedding Supplies	Photo albums	$323.58		$1,876.44
17-Feb	521	General Systems	Developer payment	$525.00		$1,351.44
20-Feb	522	Randall Machines	Copier lease payment	$250.00		$1,101.44
20-Feb	523	Hometown Energy	Electric bill payment	$413.74		$687.70
21-Feb	524	Steward-Holmes Energy	Natural gas bill payment	$86.51		$601.19
23-Feb	525	Parkland City Services	Water/sewer payment	$45.70		$555.49
26-Feb	526	New Century Telephones	Telephone bill payment	$83.25		$472.24
			Total	$6,842.57	$6,600.00	

February Tab

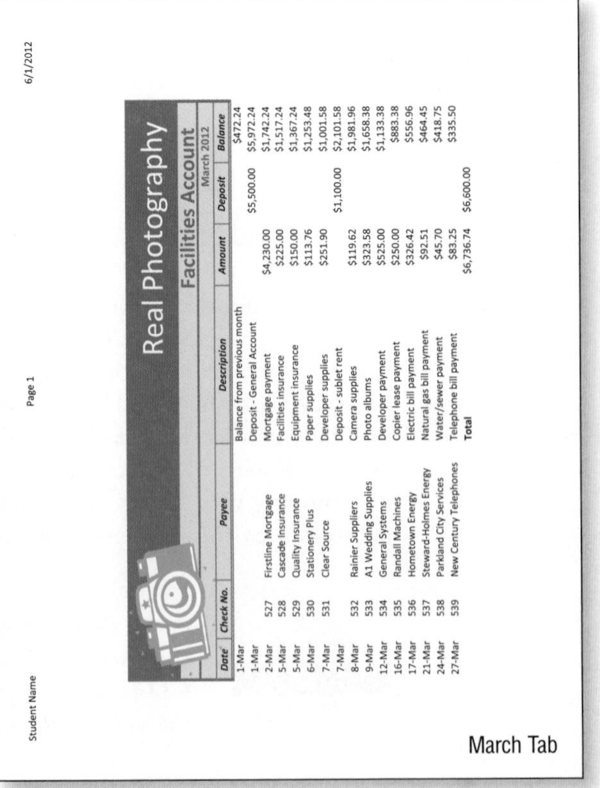
Student Name | Page 1 | 6/1/2012

Real Photography
Facilities Account
March 2012

Date	Check No.	Payee	Description	Amount	Deposit	Balance
1-Mar			Balance from previous month			$472.24
1-Mar			Deposit - General Account		$5,500.00	$5,972.24
2-Mar	527	Firstline Mortgage	Mortgage payment	$4,230.00		$1,742.24
5-Mar	528	Cascade Insurance	Facilities insurance	$225.00		$1,517.24
5-Mar	529	Quality Insurance	Equipment insurance	$150.00		$1,367.24
6-Mar	530	Stationery Plus	Paper supplies	$113.76		$1,253.48
7-Mar	531	Clear Source	Developer supplies	$251.90		$1,001.58
7-Mar			Deposit - sublet rent		$1,100.00	$2,101.58
8-Mar	532	Rainier Suppliers	Camera supplies	$119.62		$1,981.96
9-Mar	533	A1 Wedding Supplies	Photo albums	$323.58		$1,658.38
12-Mar	534	General Systems	Developer payment	$525.00		$1,133.38
16-Mar	535	Randall Machines	Copier lease payment	$250.00		$883.38
17-Mar	536	Hometown Energy	Electric bill payment	$326.42		$556.96
21-Mar	537	Steward-Holmes Energy	Natural gas bill payment	$92.51		$464.45
24-Mar	538	Parkland City Services	Water/sewer payment	$45.70		$418.75
27-Mar	539	New Century Telephones	Telephone bill payment	$83.25		$335.50
			Total	$6,736.74	$6,600.00	

March Tab

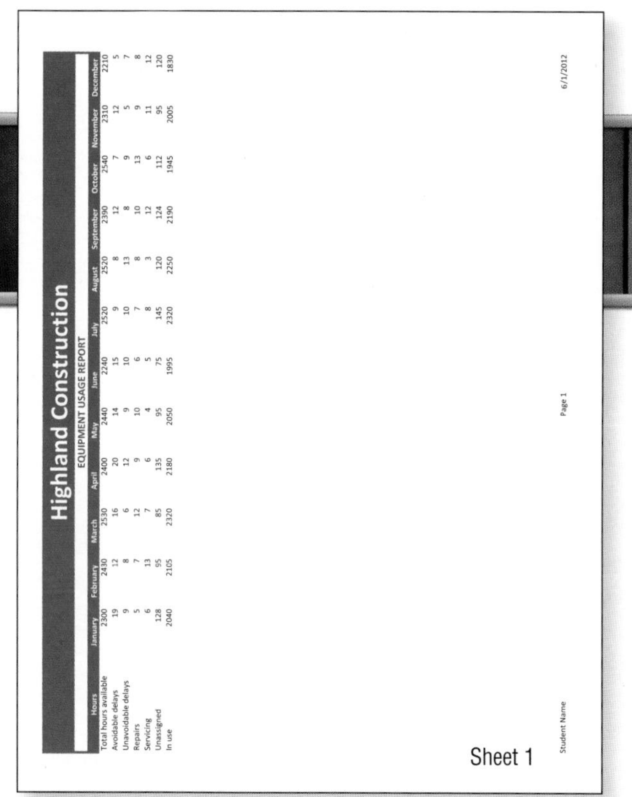

Highland Construction

EQUIPMENT USAGE REPORT

Hours	January	February	March	April	May	June	July	August	September	October	November	December
Total hours available	2300	2430	2530	2400	2440	2240	2520	2520	2390	2540	2310	2210
Avoidable delays	19	12	16	20	14	15	9	8	12	7	12	5
Unavoidable delays	9	8	6	12	9	10	10	13	8	9	5	7
Repairs	5	7	12	9	10	6	7	8	10	13	9	8
Servicing	6	13	7	6	4	5	8	3	12	6	11	12
Unassigned	128	95	85	135	95	75	145	120	124	112	95	120
In use	2040	2105	2320	2180	2050	1995	2320	2250	2190	1945	2005	1830

Student Name Page 1 6/1/2012

Sheet 1

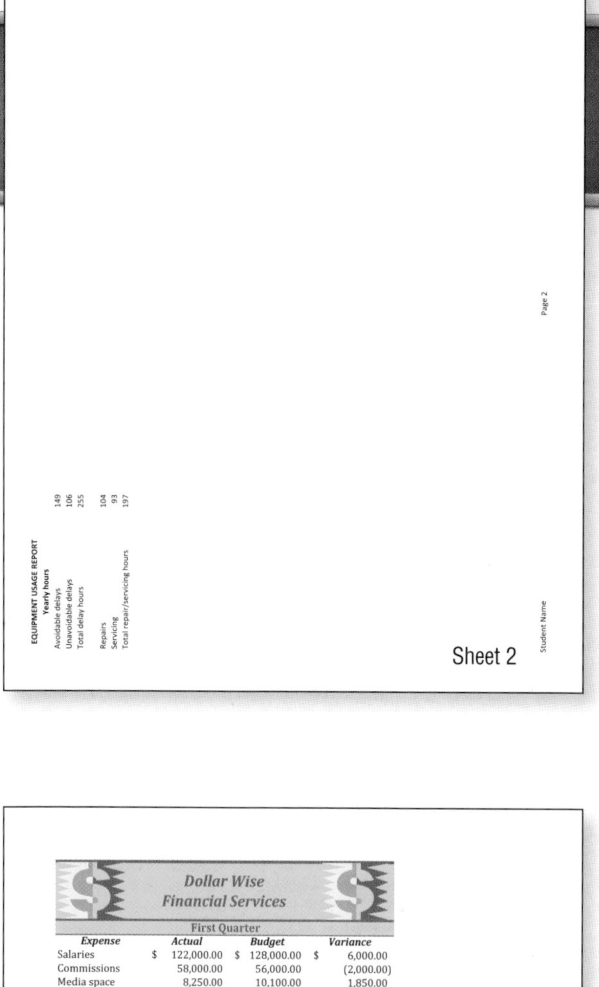

EQUIPMENT USAGE REPORT	
Yearly hours	
Avoidable delays	149
Unavoidable delays	106
Total delay hours	255
Repairs	104
Servicing	93
Total repair/servicing hours	197

Student Name Page 2 6/1/2012

Sheet 2

Project 2 Write Formulas Using Ranges in an Equipment Usage Workbook EL1-C5-P2-HCEqpRpt.xlsx

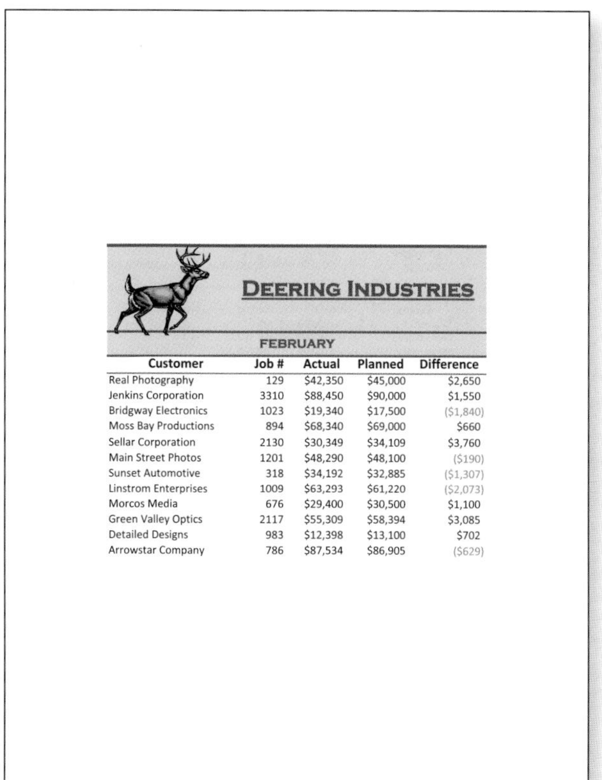

DEERING INDUSTRIES

FEBRUARY

Customer	Job #	Actual	Planned	Difference
Real Photography	129	$42,350	$45,000	$2,650
Jenkins Corporation	3310	$88,450	$90,000	$1,550
Bridgway Electronics	1023	$19,340	$17,500	($1,840)
Moss Bay Productions	894	$68,340	$69,000	$660
Sellar Corporation	2130	$30,349	$34,109	$3,760
Main Street Photos	1201	$48,290	$48,100	($190)
Sunset Automotive	318	$34,192	$32,885	($1,307)
Linstrom Enterprises	1009	$63,293	$61,220	($2,073)
Morcos Media	676	$29,400	$30,500	$1,100
Green Valley Optics	2117	$55,309	$58,394	$3,085
Detailed Designs	983	$12,398	$13,100	$702
Arrowstar Company	786	$87,534	$86,905	($629)

Project 3 Arrange, Size, and Copy Data between Workbooks EL1-C5-P3-DIFebJobs.xlsx

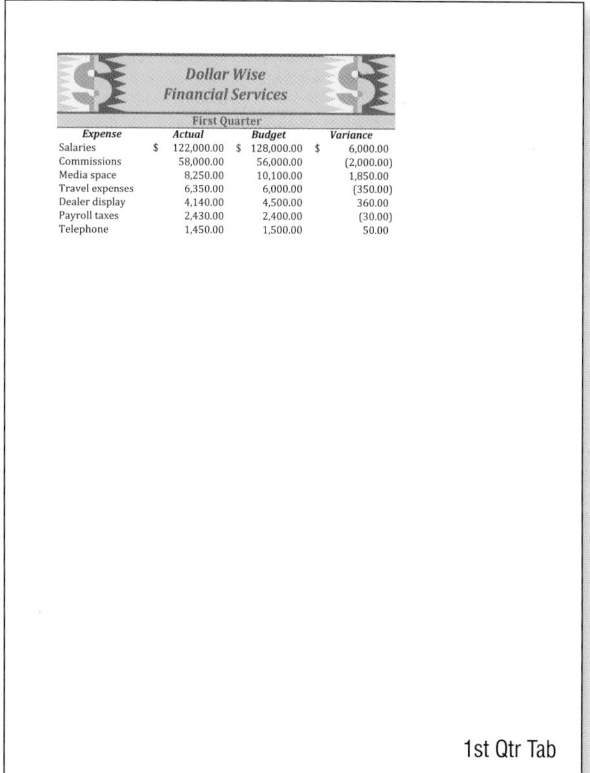

Dollar Wise Financial Services

First Quarter

Expense	*Actual*	*Budget*	*Variance*
Salaries	$ 122,000.00	$ 128,000.00	$ 6,000.00
Commissions	58,000.00	56,000.00	(2,000.00)
Media space	8,250.00	10,100.00	1,850.00
Travel expenses	6,350.00	6,000.00	(350.00)
Dealer display	4,140.00	4,500.00	360.00
Payroll taxes	2,430.00	2,400.00	(30.00)
Telephone	1,450.00	1,500.00	50.00

1st Qtr Tab

Project 4 Linking and Copying Data within and between Worksheets and Word EL1-C5-P4-DWQtrlyExp.xlsx

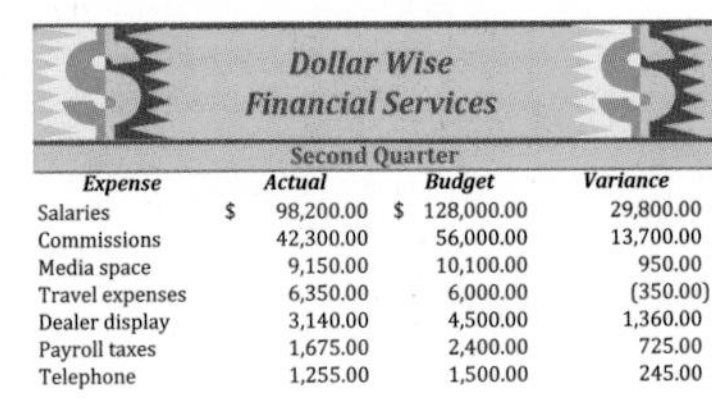

Second Quarter			
Expense	*Actual*	*Budget*	*Variance*
Salaries	$ 98,200.00	$ 128,000.00	29,800.00
Commissions	42,300.00	56,000.00	13,700.00
Media space	9,150.00	10,100.00	950.00
Travel expenses	6,350.00	6,000.00	(350.00)
Dealer display	3,140.00	4,500.00	1,360.00
Payroll taxes	1,675.00	2,400.00	725.00
Telephone	1,255.00	1,500.00	245.00

2nd Qtr Tab

Dollar Wise Financial Services

Third Quarter			
Expense	*Actual*	*Budget*	*Variance*
Salaries	$ 129,000.00	$ 128,000.00	(1,000.00)
Commissions	48,000.00	56,000.00	8,000.00
Media space	9,000.00	10,100.00	1,100.00
Travel expenses	5,250.00	6,000.00	750.00
Dealer display	5,140.00	4,500.00	(640.00)
Payroll taxes	2,150.00	2,400.00	250.00
Telephone	1,250.00	1,500.00	250.00

3rd Qtr Tab

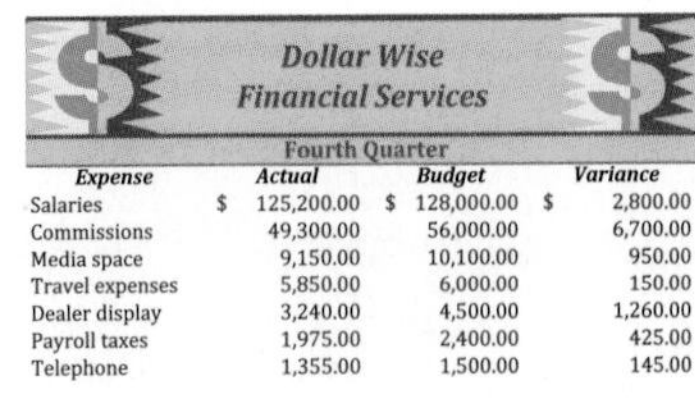

Fourth Quarter			
Expense	*Actual*	*Budget*	*Variance*
Salaries	$ 125,200.00	$ 128,000.00	$ 2,800.00
Commissions	49,300.00	56,000.00	6,700.00
Media space	9,150.00	10,100.00	950.00
Travel expenses	5,850.00	6,000.00	150.00
Dealer display	3,240.00	4,500.00	1,260.00
Payroll taxes	1,975.00	2,400.00	425.00
Telephone	1,355.00	1,500.00	145.00

4th Qtr Tab

Dollar Wise Financial Services

Quarterly Expenses

First Quarter			
Expense	*Actual*	*Budget*	*Variance*
Salaries	$ 122,000.00	$ 128,000.00	6,000.00
Commissions	58,000.00	56,000.00	(2,000.00)
Media space	8,250.00	10,100.00	1,850.00
Travel expenses	6,350.00	6,000.00	(350.00)
Dealer display	4,140.00	4,500.00	360.00
Payroll taxes	2,430.00	2,400.00	(30.00)
Telephone	1,450.00	1,500.00	50.00

Second Quarter			
Expense	*Actual*	*Budget*	*Variance*
Salaries	$ 98,200.00	$ 128,000.00	29,800.00
Commissions	42,300.00	56,000.00	13,700.00
Media space	9,150.00	10,100.00	950.00
Travel expenses	6,350.00	6,000.00	(350.00)
Dealer display	3,140.00	4,500.00	1,360.00
Payroll taxes	1,675.00	2,400.00	725.00
Telephone	1,255.00	1,500.00	245.00

Third Quarter			
Expense	*Actual*	*Budget*	*Variance*
Salaries	$ 129,000.00	$ 128,000.00	(1,000.00)
Commissions	48,000.00	56,000.00	8,000.00
Media space	9,000.00	10,100.00	1,100.00
Travel expenses	5,250.00	6,000.00	750.00
Dealer display	5,140.00	4,500.00	(640.00)
Payroll taxes	2,150.00	2,400.00	250.00
Telephone	1,250.00	1,500.00	250.00

Fourth Quarter			
Expense	*Actual*	*Budget*	*Variance*
Salaries	$ 125,200.00	$ 128,000.00	2,800.00
Commissions	49,300.00	56,000.00	6,700.00
Media space	9,150.00	10,100.00	950.00
Travel expenses	5,850.00	6,000.00	150.00
Dealer display	3,240.00	4,500.00	1,260.00
Payroll taxes	1,975.00	2,400.00	425.00
Telephone	1,355.00	1,500.00	145.00

5005 Tenth Avenue ◆ Omaha, NE 68121 ◆ 1-800-555-5005

EL1-C5-P4-DWQtrlyRpt.docx

Project 1 Manage Data in a Multiple-Worksheet Account Workbook — 9 Parts

You will open an account workbook containing three worksheets and then move, copy, and paste data between the worksheets. You will also hide and unhide worksheets, and format and print multiple worksheets in the workbook.

Creating a Workbook with Multiple Worksheets

An Excel workbook can contain multiple worksheets. You can create a variety of worksheets within a workbook for related data. For example, a workbook may contain a worksheet for the expenses for each salesperson in a company and another worksheet for the monthly payroll for each department within the company. Another example is recording sales statistics for each quarter in individual worksheets within a workbook.

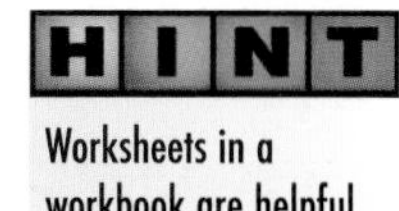

Worksheets in a workbook are helpful for saving related data.

By default, a workbook contains three worksheets named *Sheet1*, *Sheet2*, and *Sheet3*. (Later in this chapter, you will learn how to change these default names.) Display various worksheets in the workbook by clicking the desired tab.

Project 1a Displaying Worksheets in a Workbook — Part 1 of 9

1. Open **RPFacAccts.xlsx** and then save the workbook with Save As and name it **EL1-C5-P1-RPFacAccts**.
2. This workbook contains three worksheets. Display the various worksheets by completing the following steps:
   a. Display the second worksheet by clicking the Sheet2 tab that displays immediately above the Status bar.
   b. Display the third worksheet by clicking the Sheet3 tab that displays immediately above the Status bar.
   c. Return to the first worksheet by clicking the Sheet1 tab.
3. Make the following changes to worksheets in the workbook:
   a. Click the Sheet2 tab and then change the column width for columns E, F, and G to 10.00.
   b. Click the Sheet3 tab and then change the column width for columns E, F, and G to 10.00.
   c. Click the Sheet1 tab to display the first worksheet.
4. Save **EL1-C5-P1-RPFacAccts.xlsx**.

Cutting, Copying, and Pasting Selected Cells

Situations may arise where you need to move cells to a different location within a worksheet, or you may need to copy repetitive data in a worksheet. You can perform these actions by selecting cells and then using the Cut, Copy, and/or Paste buttons in the Clipboard group in the Home tab. You can also perform these actions with the mouse.

Quick Steps

Move and Paste Cells
1. Select cells.
2. Click Cut button.
3. Click desired cell.
4. Click Paste button.

HINT

Ctrl + X is the keyboard shortcut to cut selected data. Ctrl + V is the keyboard shortcut to paste data.

Cut

Paste

Moving Selected Cells

You can move selected cells and cell contents in a worksheet and between worksheets. Move selected cells with the Cut and Paste buttons in the Clipboard group in the Home tab or by dragging with the mouse.

To move selected cells with buttons in the Home tab, select the cells and then click the Cut button in the Clipboard group. This causes a moving dashed line border (called a ***marquee***) to display around the selected cells. Click the cell where you want the first selected cell inserted and then click the Paste button in the Clipboard group. If you change your mind and do not want to move the selected cells, press the Esc key to remove the moving dashed line border or double-click in any cell.

To move selected cells with the mouse, select the cells and then position the mouse pointer on any border of the selected cells until the pointer turns into an arrow pointer with a four-headed arrow attached. Hold down the left mouse button, drag the outline of the selected cells to the desired location, and then release the mouse button.

Project 1b **Moving Selected Cells** Part 2 of 9

1. With **EL1-C5-P1-RPFacAccts.xlsx** open, you realize that the sublet rent deposit was recorded on the wrong day. The correct day is January 9. To move the cells containing information on the deposit, complete the following steps:
   a. Make cell A13 active and then insert a row. (The new row should display above the row containing information on *Rainer Suppliers*.)
   b. Select cells A7 through F7.
   c. Click the Cut button in the Clipboard group in the Home tab.

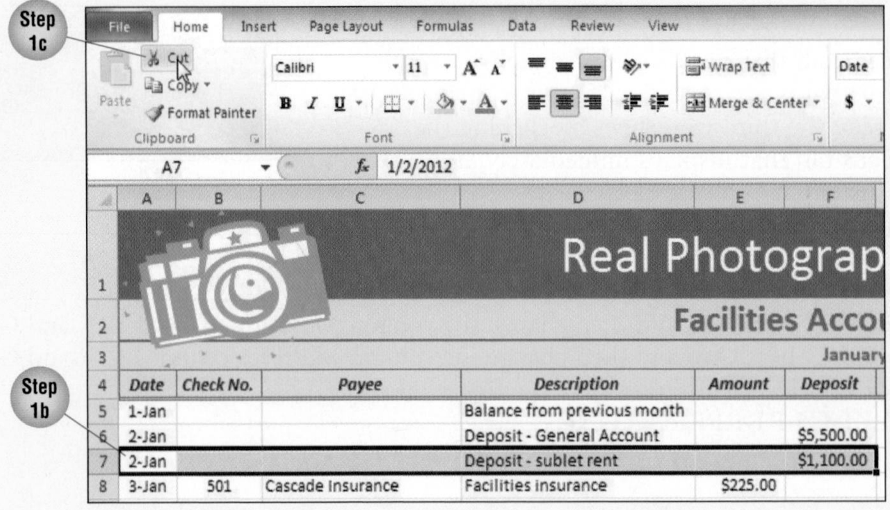

   d. Click cell A13 to make it active.
   e. Click the Paste button in the Clipboard group.
   f. Change the date of the deposit from January 2 to January 9.
   g. Select row 7 and then delete it.

2. Click the Sheet2 tab and then complete steps similar to those in Step 1 to move the sublet deposit row so it is positioned above the *Rainier Suppliers* row and below the *Clear Source* row. Change the date of the deposit to February 12 and make sure you delete row 7.
3. Move cells using the mouse by completing the following steps:
   a. Click the Sheet3 tab.
   b. Make cell A13 active and then insert a new row.
   c. Using the mouse, select cells A7 through F7.
   d. Position the mouse pointer on any boundary of the selected cells until it turns into an arrow pointer with a four-headed arrow attached.
   e. Hold down the left mouse button, drag the outline of the selected cells to row 13, and then release the mouse button.

Step 3c

4	Date	Check No.	Payee	Description	Amount	Deposit
5	1-Mar			Balance from previous month		
6	1-Mar			Deposit - General Account		$5,500.00
7	1-Mar			Deposit - sublet rent		$1,100.00
8	2-Mar	527				
9	5-Mar	528				
10	5-Mar	529				
11	6-Mar	530	Stationery Plus	Paper supplies	$113.76	
12	7-Mar	531	Clear Source	Developer supplies	$251.90	
13						
14	8-Mar	53 A13:F13	inier Suppliers	Camera supplies	$119.62	
15	9-Mar	533	A1 Wedding Supplies	Photo albums	$323.58	

Step 3e

   f. Change the date of the deposit to March 7.
   g. Delete row 7.
4. Save **EL1-C5-P1-RPFacAccts.xlsx**.

Copying Selected Cells

Quick Steps

Copy and Paste Cells
1. Select cells.
2. Click Copy button.
3. Click desired cell.
4. Click Paste button.

Copying selected cells can be useful in worksheets that contain repetitive data. To copy cells, select the cells and then click the Copy button in the Clipboard group in the Home tab. Click the cell where you want the first selected cell copied and then click the Paste button in the Clipboard group.

You can also copy selected cells using the mouse and the Ctrl key. To do this, select the cells you want to copy and then position the mouse pointer on any border around the selected cells until it turns into an arrow pointer. Hold down the Ctrl key and the left mouse button, drag the outline of the selected cells to the desired location, release the left mouse button, and then release the Ctrl key.

Ctrl + C is the keyboard shortcut to copy selected data.

Using the Paste Options Button

Copy

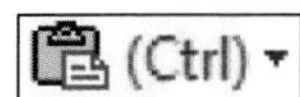

Paste Options

The Paste Options button displays in the lower right corner of the pasted cell(s) when you paste a cell or cells. Display a list of paste options by hovering the mouse pointer over the button and then clicking the button or by pressing the Ctrl key. This causes a drop-down list to display as shown in Figure 5.1. Hover your mouse over a button in the drop-down list and the descriptive name of the button displays along with the keyboard shortcut. With buttons in this drop-down list, you can specify what you want pasted.

Figure 5.1 Paste Options Button Drop-down List

C8 Firstline Mortgage

	A	B	C	D	E	F	G
1				Real Photography			
2				Facilities Account			
3				March 2012			
4	Date	Check No.	Payee	Description	Amount	Deposit	Balance
5	1-Mar			Balance from previous month			
6	1-Mar			Deposit - General Account		$5,500.00	
7	2-Mar	527					
8	5-Mar	528	Firstline Mortgage	Mortgage payment	$4,230.00		
9	5-Mar	529	Cascade Insurance	Facilities insurance	$225.00		
10	6-Mar	530	Quality Insurance	Equipment insurance	$150.00		
11	7-Mar	531	Clear Source	Developer supplies	$251.90		
12	7-Mar			Deposit - sublet rent			
13	8-Mar	532	Rainier Suppliers	Camera supplies	$119.62		
14	9-Mar	533	A1 Wedding Supplies	Photo albums	$323.58		
15	12-Mar	534					
16	16-Mar	535					
17	17-Mar	536	Hometown Energy	Electric bill payment	$326.42		
18	21-Mar	537	Steward-Holmes Energ	Natural gas bill payment	$92.51		
19	24-Mar	538					
20	27-Mar	539	New Century Telephor	Telephone bill payment	$83.25		
21							

(Ctrl)
Paste
Paste Values
Other Paste Options

Click the button that specifies the formatting you desire for the pasted data.

Project 1c Copying Selected Cells in a Worksheet

Part 3 of 9

1. With **EL1-C5-P1-RPFacAccts.xlsx** open, make Sheet2 active.
2. Select cells C7 through E9.
3. Click the Copy button in the Clipboard group in the Home tab.

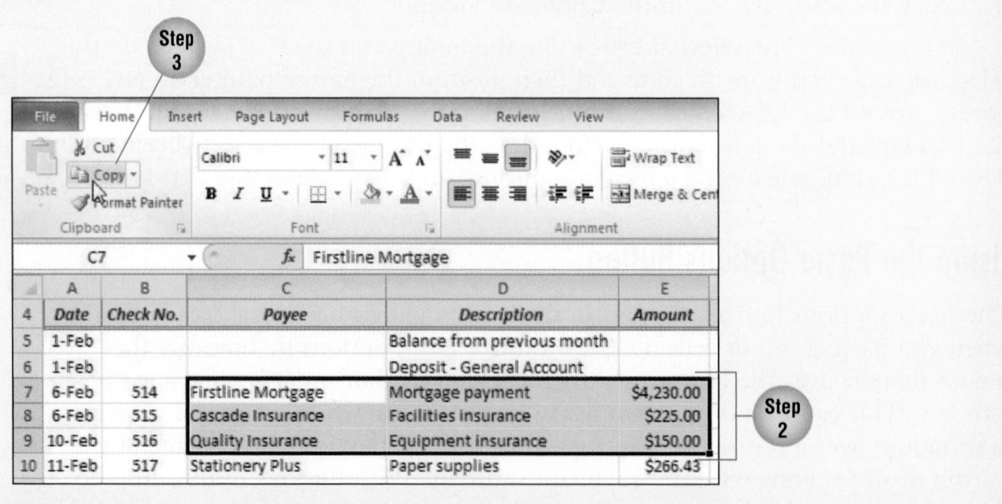

4. Make Sheet3 active.
5. Make cell C7 active.
6. Click the Paste button in the Clipboard group.
7. Click the Paste Options button that displays in the lower right corner of the pasted cells and then click the Keep Source Column Widths button at the drop-down list.
8. Make Sheet2 active and then press the Esc key to remove the moving marquee.
9. Save **EL1-C5-P1-RPFacAccts.xlsx**.

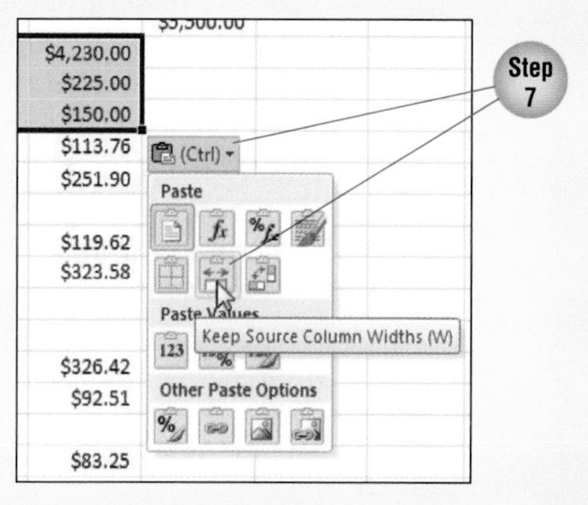

Using the Office Clipboard

Use the Office Clipboard feature to collect and paste multiple items. To use the Office Clipboard, display the Clipboard task pane by clicking the Clipboard group dialog box launcher. This button is located in the lower right corner of the Clipboard group in the Home tab. The Clipboard task pane displays at the left side of the screen in a manner similar to what you see in Figure 5.2.

Quick Steps

Copy and Paste Multiple Items

1. Click Clipboard group dialog box launcher.
2. Select desired cells.
3. Click Copy button.
4. Continue selecting desired cells and then clicking the Copy button.
5. Make desired cell active.
6. Click item in Clipboard task pane that you want inserted in the worksheet.
7. Continue pasting desired items from the Clipboard task pane.

Figure 5.2 Clipboard Task Pane

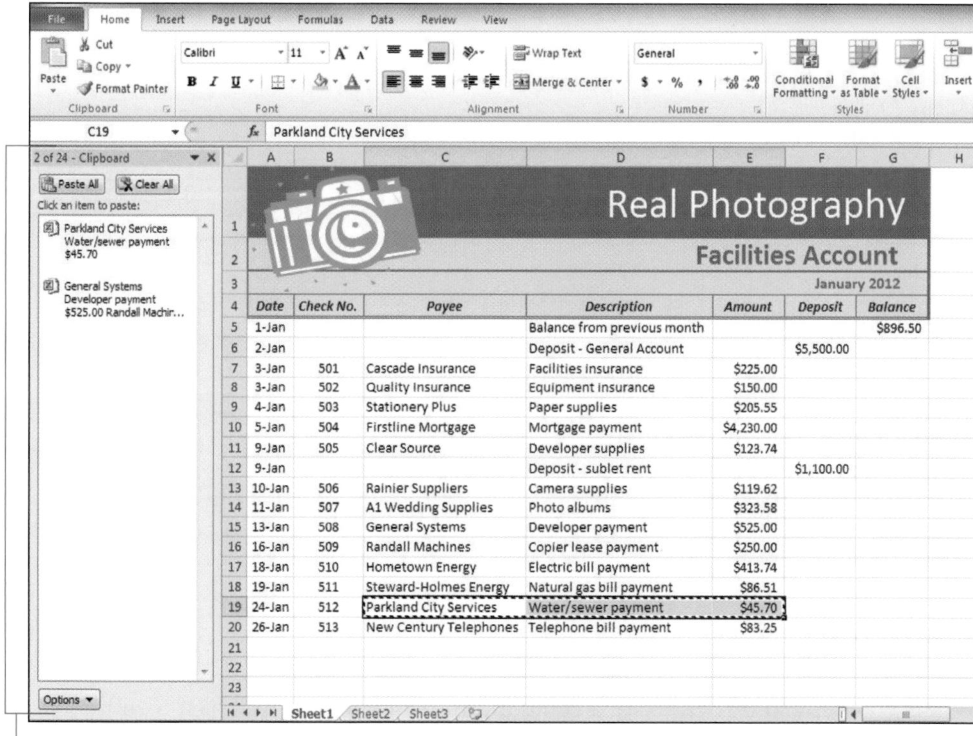

Date	Check No.	Payee	Description	Amount	Deposit	Balance
1-Jan			Balance from previous month			$896.50
2-Jan			Deposit - General Account		$5,500.00	
3-Jan	501	Cascade Insurance	Facilities insurance	$225.00		
3-Jan	502	Quality Insurance	Equipment insurance	$150.00		
4-Jan	503	Stationery Plus	Paper supplies	$205.55		
5-Jan	504	Firstline Mortgage	Mortgage payment	$4,230.00		
9-Jan	505	Clear Source	Developer supplies	$123.74		
9-Jan			Deposit - sublet rent		$1,100.00	
10-Jan	506	Rainier Suppliers	Camera supplies	$119.62		
11-Jan	507	A1 Wedding Supplies	Photo albums	$323.58		
13-Jan	508	General Systems	Developer payment	$525.00		
16-Jan	509	Randall Machines	Copier lease payment	$250.00		
18-Jan	510	Hometown Energy	Electric bill payment	$413.74		
19-Jan	511	Steward-Holmes Energy	Natural gas bill payment	$86.51		
24-Jan	512	Parkland City Services	Water/sewer payment	$45.70		
26-Jan	513	New Century Telephones	Telephone bill payment	$83.25		

Select data or an object you want to copy and then click the Copy button in the Clipboard group. Continue selecting text or items and clicking the Copy button. To insert an item, position the insertion point in the desired location and then click the item in the Clipboard task pane. If the copied item is text, the first 50 characters display. When all desired items are inserted, click the Clear All button to remove any remaining items. Sometimes, you may have a situation in which you want to copy all of the selected items to a single location. If so, position the insertion point in the desired location and then click the Paste All button in the Clipboard task pane.

Project 1d Copying and Pasting Cells Using the Office Clipboard

Part 4 of 9

1. With **EL1-C5-P1-RPFacAccts.xlsx** open, select cells for copying by completing the following steps:
   a. Display the Clipboard task pane by clicking the Clipboard group dialog box launcher. (If the Clipboard contains any copied data, click the Clear All button.)
   b. Click the Sheet1 tab.
   c. Select cells C15 through E16.
   d. Click the Copy button in the Clipboard group.
   e. Select cells C19 through E19.
   f. Click the Copy button in the Clipboard group.
2. Paste the copied cells by completing the following steps:
   a. Click the Sheet2 tab.
   b. Make cell C15 active.
   c. Click the item in the Clipboard task pane representing *General Systems Developer*.
   d. Click the Sheet3 tab.
   e. Make C15 active.
   f. Click the item in the Clipboard task pane representing *General Systems Developer*.
   g. Make cell C19 active.
   h. Click the item in the Clipboard task pane representing *Parkland City Services*.
3. Click the Clear All button located toward the top of the Clipboard task pane.
4. Close the Clipboard task pane by clicking the Close button (contains an X) located in the upper right corner of the task pane.
5. Save **EL1-C5-P1-RPFacAccts.xlsx**.

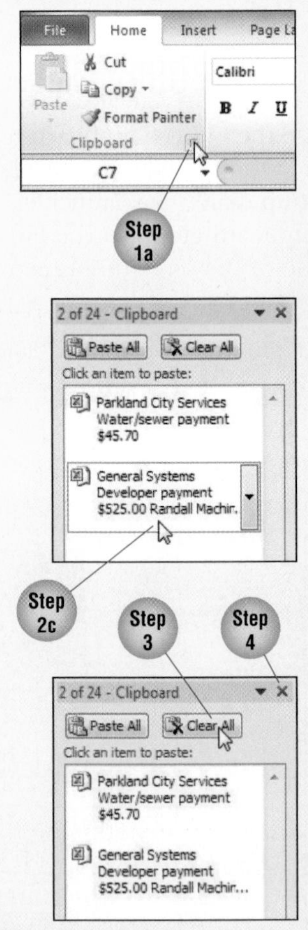

Pasting Values Only and Formulas

When you copy and then paste a cell containing a value as well as a formula, you can use buttons in the Paste Options button drop-down list to specify what you want pasted. For example, you can paste all data and formatting, only the formula, or only the value. Click the Paste Options button and a drop-down list of buttons displays in three sections—*Paste*, *Paste Values*, and *Other Paste Options*. To paste only the formula, click the Formulas button in the *Paste* section and to paste only the value, click the Values button in the *Paste Values* section.

Project 1e Copying and Pasting Values

Part 5 of 9

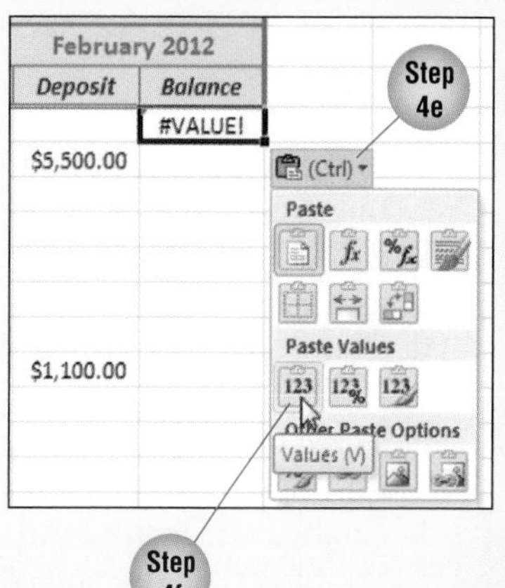

1. With **EL1-C5-P1-RPFacAccts.xlsx** open, make Sheet1 active.
2. Make cell G6 active, insert the formula =(F6-E6)+G5, and then press Enter.
3. Copy the formula in cell G6 down to cells G7 through G20.
4. Copy the final balance amount from Sheet1 to Sheet2 by completing the following steps:
   a. Make cell G20 active.
   b. Click the Copy button in the Clipboard group.
   c. Click the Sheet2 tab.
   d. Make cell G5 active and then click the Paste button in the Clipboard group.
   e. Click the Paste Options button.
   f. At the drop-down list, click the Values button in the *Paste Values* section of the drop-down list. (This inserts the value and not the formula.)
5. Make Sheet1 active, make cell G6 active, click the Bold button, and then click the Copy button.
6. Make Sheet2 active, make cell G6 active, and then click the Paste button.
7. Click the Paste Options button and then click the Formulas button in the *Paste* section.
8. Copy the formula in G6 down to cells G7 through G20.
9. Copy the amount in cell G20 and then paste the value only into cell G5 in Sheet3.
10. Make Sheet2 active, make cell G6 active, and then click the Copy button.
11. Make Sheet3 active, make cell G6 active, and then click the Paste button. Copy the formula in cell G6 down to cells G7 through G20.
12. Make Sheet1 active, make cell G6 active, and then click the Bold button to remove bold formatting.
13. Save **EL1-C5-P1-RPFacAccts.xlsx**.

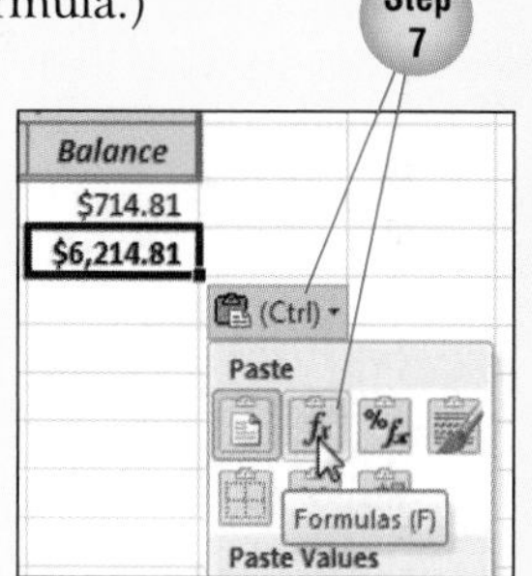

Inserting and Deleting Worksheets

A workbook, by default, contains three worksheets. You can insert additional worksheets in a workbook by clicking the Insert Worksheet tab located to the right of the Sheet3 tab. You can also press Shift + F11 to insert a worksheet or click the Insert button arrow in the Cells group in the Home tab and then click *Insert Sheet*. Insert multiple worksheets by selecting the desired number of worksheet tabs in the current workbook, clicking the Insert button in the Home tab, and then clicking *Insert Sheet* at the drop-down list.

Delete an individual worksheet from a workbook by clicking the desired worksheet tab, clicking the Delete button arrow in the Cells group in the Home tab, and then clicking *Delete Sheet* at the drop-down list. You can also delete a worksheet by right-clicking the desired tab and then clicking *Delete* at the shortcut menu. Delete multiple worksheets by selecting the desired worksheet tabs, clicking the Delete button arrow, and then clicking *Delete Sheet*. You can delete multiple worksheets by selecting the worksheet tabs, right-clicking one of the tabs, and then clicking *Delete* at the shortcut menu.

Quick Steps

Insert Worksheet
Click Insert Worksheet tab.
OR
Press Shift + F11.

Delete a Worksheet
1. Click worksheet tab.
2. Click Delete button arrow.
3. Click *Delete Sheet*.

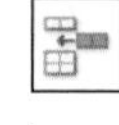
Insert

Project 1f Inserting a Worksheet

1. With **EL1-C5-P1-RPFacAccts.xlsx** open, make the following changes:
   a. Make Sheet1 active.
   b. Make cell D21 active, turn on bold, and then type Total.
   c. Make cell E21 active and then click once on the AutoSum button located in the Editing group in the Home tab. (This inserts the formula *=SUM(E13:E20)*.)
   d. Change the formula to *=SUM(E7:E20)* and then press Enter.
   e. Make cell F21 active and then click once on the AutoSum button in the Editing group. (This inserts the formula *=SUM(F12:F20)*.)

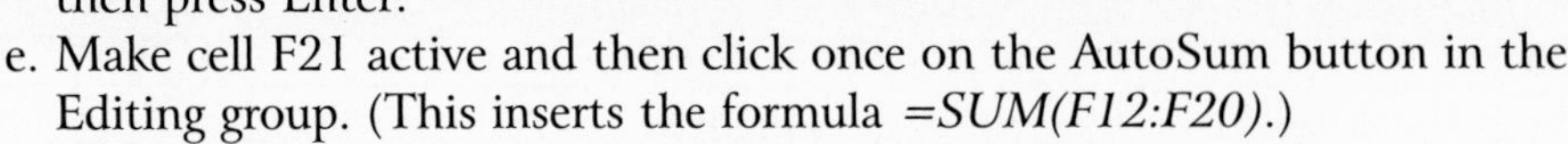

   f. Change the formula to *=SUM(F6:F20)* and then press Enter.
2. Make Sheet2 active and then complete the steps in Step 1 to insert the totals of the *Amount* and *Deposit* columns.
3. Make Sheet3 active and then complete the steps in Step 1 to insert the totals of the *Amount* and *Deposit* columns.
4. Insert a new worksheet by clicking the Insert Worksheet tab located to the right of the Sheet3 tab.
5. Make Sheet1 active, copy cells A1 through G3, make Sheet4 active (with cell A1 active), and then paste the cells. (When copying the cells, position the cell pointer to the right of the image, make sure the pointer displays as a white plus symbol, and then drag to select the cells.)
6. Make the following changes to the worksheet:
   a. Make cell A3 active and then type First Quarter Summary 2012.
   b. Change the width of column A to 20.00.
   c. Change the width of columns B, C, and D to 12.00.
   d. Select cells B4 through D4, click the Bold button in the Font group in the Home tab, and then click the Center button in the Alignment group.
   e. Select cells B5 through D7 and then change the number formatting to Currency with two decimal places and include the dollar sign symbol.
   f. Type the following text in the specified cells:
      B4 = January
      C4 = February
      D4 = March
      A5 = Checks amount
      A6 = Deposit amount
      A7 = End-of-month balance

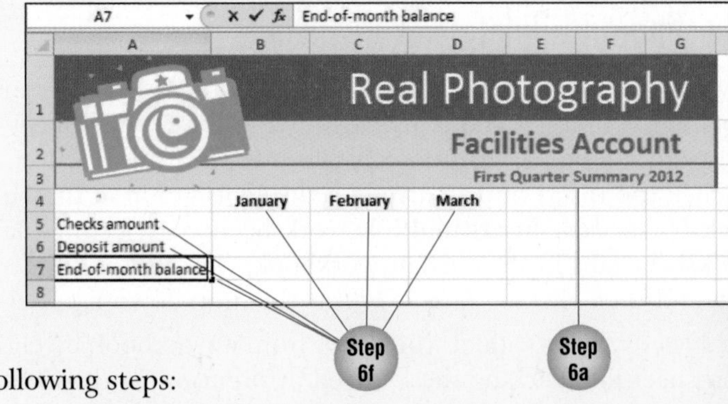

7. Copy a value by completing the following steps:
   a. Make Sheet1 active.
   b. Make cell E21 active and then click the Copy button in the Clipboard group in the Home tab.
   c. Make Sheet4 active.
   d. Make cell B5 active and then click the Paste button in the Clipboard group.

e. Click the Paste Options button and then click the Values button in the *Paste Values* section of the drop-down list.
f. Make Sheet1 active.
g. Press the Esc key to remove the moving marquee.
h. Make cell F21 active and then click the Copy button.
i. Make Sheet4 active.
j. Make cell B6 active and then click the Paste button.
k. Click the Paste Options button and then click the Values button at the drop-down list.
l. Make Sheet1 active.
m. Press the Esc key to remove the moving marquee.
n. Make cell G20 active and then click the Copy button.
o. Make Sheet4 active.
p. Make cell B7 active and then click the Paste button.
q. Click the Paste Options button and then click the Values button at the drop-down list.

8. Complete steps like those in Step 7 to insert amounts and balances for February and March.
9. Insert two new worksheets by completing the following steps:
   a. Click the Sheet1 tab, hold down the Shift key, and then click the Sheet2 tab. (This selects both tabs.)
   b. Make sure the Home tab is active, click the Insert button arrow in the Cells group, and then click *Insert Sheet* at the drop-down list. (This inserts a new Sheet5 and Sheet6.)
10. Click each of the sheet tabs in the workbook.
11. Remove the two worksheets you inserted by completing the following steps:
   a. Click the Sheet5 tab, hold down the Shift key, and then click the Sheet6 tab.
   b. Click the Delete button arrow in the Cells group in the Home tab and then click *Delete Sheet* at the drop-down list.
12. Save **EL1-C5-P1-RPFacAccts.xlsx**.

Managing Worksheets

Right-click a sheet tab and a shortcut menu displays as shown in Figure 5.3 with the options for managing worksheets. For example, remove a worksheet by clicking the *Delete* option. Move or copy a worksheet by clicking the *Move or Copy* option. Clicking this option causes a Move or Copy dialog box to display where

Quick Steps

Move or Copy a Worksheet
1. Right-click sheet tab.
2. Click *Move or Copy*.
3. At Move or Copy dialog box, click desired worksheet name in *Before sheet* list box.
4. Click OK.

OR

Drag worksheet tab to the desired position. (To copy, hold down Ctrl key while dragging.)

Figure 5.3 Sheet Tab Shortcut Menu

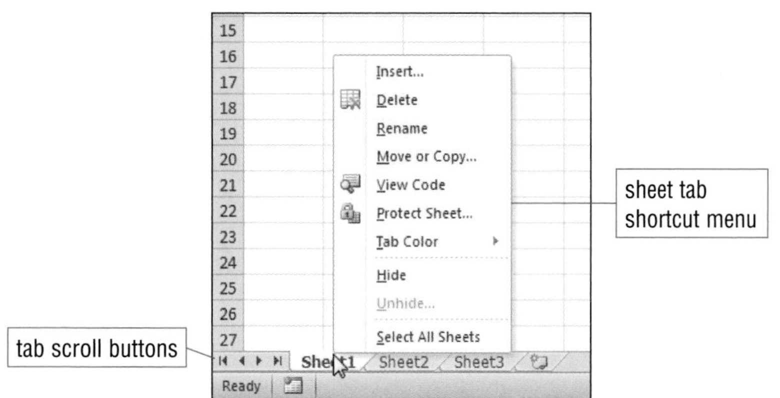

Use the tab scroll button to bring into view any worksheet tabs not currently visible.

Quick Steps

Recolor Sheet Tab
1. Right-click sheet tab.
2. Point to *Tab Color.*
3. Click desired color at color palette.

you specify before what sheet you want to move or copy the selected sheet. By default, Excel names worksheets in a workbook *Sheet1, Sheet2, Sheet3,* and so on. To rename a worksheet, click the *Rename* option (this selects the default sheet name) and then type the desired name.

In addition to the shortcut menu options, you can use the mouse to move or copy worksheets. To move a worksheet, position the mouse pointer on the worksheet tab, hold down the left mouse button (a page icon displays next to the mouse pointer), drag the page icon to the desired position, and then release the mouse button. For example, to move the Sheet2 tab after the Sheet3 tab you would position the mouse pointer on the Sheet2 tab, hold down the left mouse button, drag the page icon so it is positioned after the Sheet3 tab, and then release the mouse button. To copy a worksheet, hold down the Ctrl key while dragging the sheet tab.

Use the *Tab Color* option at the shortcut menu to apply a color to a worksheet tab. Right-click a worksheet tab, point to *Tab Color* at the shortcut menu, and then click the desired color at the color palette.

Project 1g Selecting, Moving, Renaming, and Changing the Color of Worksheet Tabs Part 7 of 9

1. With **EL1-C5-P1-RPFacAccts.xlsx** open, move Sheet4 by completing the following steps:
   a. Right-click Sheet4 and then click *Move or Copy* at the shortcut menu.
   b. At the Move or Copy dialog box, make sure *Sheet1* is selected in the *Before sheet* section, and then click OK.

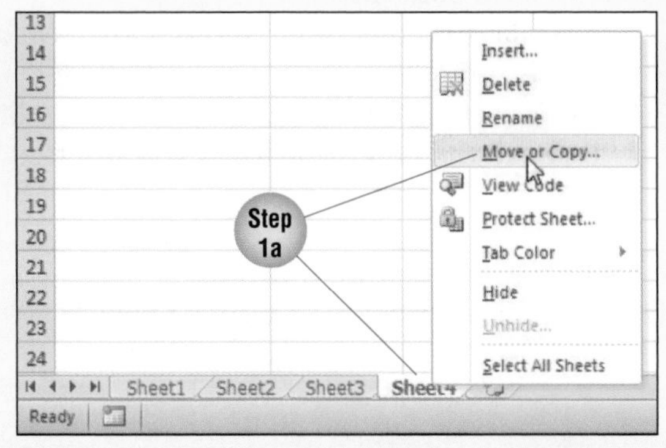

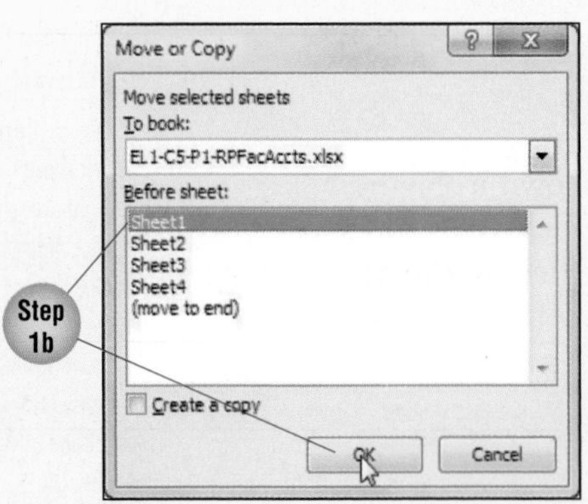

2. Rename Sheet4 by completing the following steps:
   a. Right-click the Sheet4 tab and then click *Rename.*
   b. Type Summary and then press Enter.

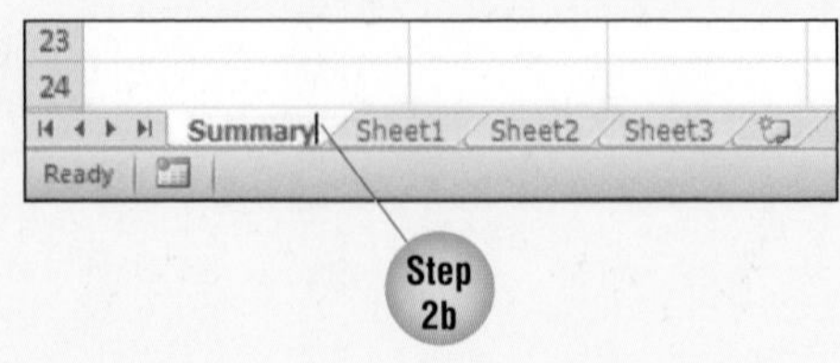

3. Complete steps similar to those in Step 2 to rename Sheet1 to January, Sheet2 to February, and Sheet3 to March.
4. Change the color of the Summary sheet tab by completing the following steps:
   a. Right-click the Summary sheet tab.
   b. Point to *Tab Color* at the shortcut menu.
   c. Click a red color of your choosing at the color palette.
5. Follow steps similar to those in Step 4 to change the January sheet tab to a blue color, the February sheet tab to a purple color, and the March sheet tab to a green color.
6. Save **EL1-C5-P1-RPFacAccts.xlsx**.

Hiding a Worksheet in a Workbook

In a workbook containing multiple worksheets, you can hide a worksheet that may contain sensitive data or data you do not want to display or print with the workbook. To hide a worksheet in a workbook, click the Format button in the Cells group in the Home tab, point to *Hide & Unhide*, and then click *Hide Sheet*. You can also hide a worksheet by right-clicking a worksheet tab and then clicking the *Hide* option at the shortcut menu. To make a hidden worksheet visible, click the Format button in the Cells group, point to *Hide & Unhide*, and then click *Unhide Sheet*, or right-click a worksheet tab and then click *Unhide* at the shortcut menu. At the Unhide dialog box shown in Figure 5.4, double-click the name of the hidden worksheet you want to display.

Quick Steps

Hide a Worksheet
1. Click Format button.
2. Point to *Hide & Unhide*.
3. Click *Hide Sheet*.

OR
1. Right-click worksheet tab.
2. Click *Hide* at shortcut menu.

Unhide a Worksheet
1. Click Format button.
2. Point to *Hide & Unhide*.
3. Click *Unhide Sheet*.
4. Double-click desired hidden worksheet in Unhide dialog box.

OR
1. Right-click worksheet tab.
2. Click *Unhide* at shortcut menu.
3. Double-click desired hidden worksheet in Unhide dialog box.

If the *Hide* option is unavailable, the workbook is protected from change.

Format

Formatting Multiple Worksheets

When you apply formatting to a worksheet, such as changing margins, orientation, or inserting a header or footer, and so on, the formatting is applied only to the active worksheet. If you want formatting to apply to multiple worksheets in a workbook, select the tabs of the desired worksheets and then apply the formatting. For example, if a workbook contains three worksheets and you want to apply formatting to the first and second worksheets only, select the tabs for the first and second worksheets and then apply the formatting.

To select adjacent worksheet tabs, click the first tab, hold down the Shift key, and then click the last tab. To select nonadjacent worksheet tabs, click the first tab, hold down the Ctrl key, and then click any other tabs you want selected.

Figure 5.4 Unhide Dialog Box

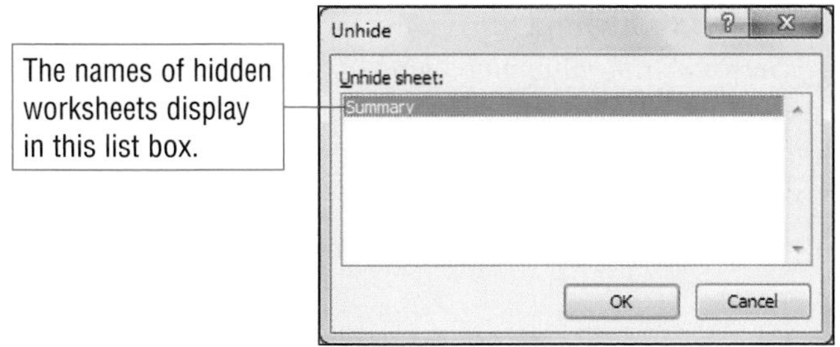

Project 1h Hiding a Worksheet and Formatting Multiple Worksheets

Part 8 of 9

1. With **EL1-C5-P1-RPFacAccts.xlsx** open, hide the Summary worksheet by completing the following steps:
   a. Click the Summary tab.
   b. Click the Format button in the Cells group in the Home tab, point to *Hide & Unhide*, and then click *Hide Sheet*.

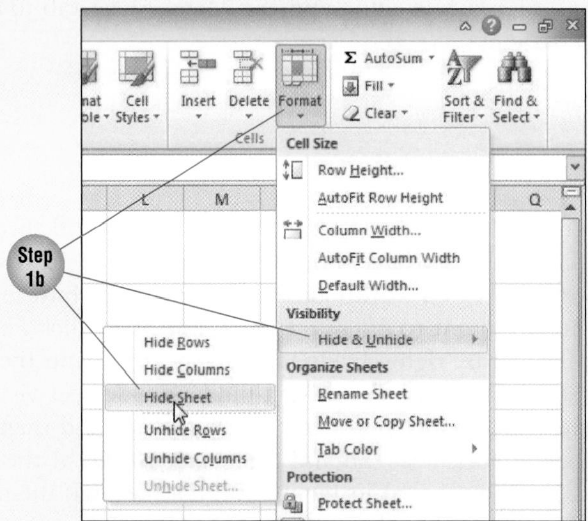

2. Unhide the worksheet by completing the following steps:
   a. Click the Format button in the Cells group, point to *Hide & Unhide*, and then click *Unhide Sheet*.
   b. At the Unhide dialog box, make sure *Summary* is selected and then click OK.

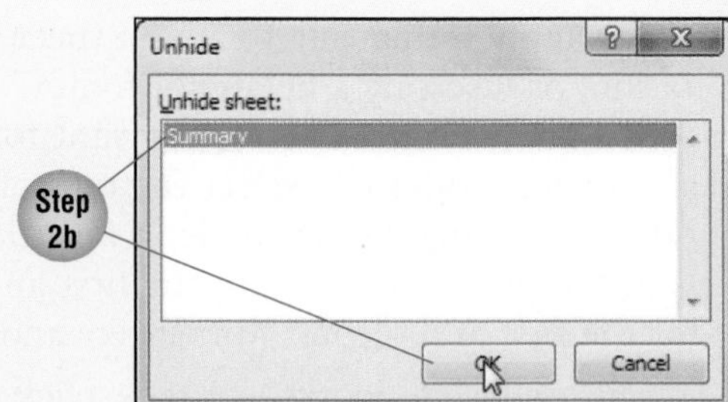

3. Insert a header for each worksheet by completing the following steps:
   a. Click the Summary tab.
   b. Hold down the Shift key and then click the March tab. (This selects all four tabs.)
   c. Click the Insert tab.
   d. Click the Header & Footer button in the Text group.
   e. Click the Header button in the Header & Footer group in the Header & Footer Tools Design tab and then click the option at the drop-down list that prints your name at the left side of the page, the page number in the middle, and the date at the right side of the page.
4. With all the sheet tabs selected, horizontally and vertically center each worksheet on the page. ***Hint: Do this at the Page Setup dialog box with the Margins tab selected.***
5. With all of the sheet tabs still selected, change the page orientation to landscape. ***Hint: Do this with the Orientation button in the Page Layout tab.***
6. Save **EL1-C5-P1-RPFacAccts.xlsx**.

Printing a Workbook Containing Multiple Worksheets

By default, Excel prints the currently displayed worksheet. If you want to print all worksheets in a workbook, display the Print tab Backstage view, click the first gallery in the Settings category, click *Print Entire Workbook* at the drop-down list, and then click the Print button. You can also print specific worksheets in a workbook by selecting the tabs of the worksheets you want printed. With the desired worksheet tabs selected, display the Print tab Backstage view and then click the Print button.

Quick Steps

Print All Worksheets in Workbook
1. Click File tab.
2. Click Print tab.
3. Click first gallery in Settings category.
4. Click *Print Entire Workbook.*
5. Click Print button.

Project 1i **Printing All Worksheets in a Workbook** Part 9 of 9

1. With **EL1-C5-P1-RPFacAccts.xlsx** open, click the File tab and then click the Print tab.
2. At the Print tab Backstage view, click the first gallery in the Settings category and then click *Print Entire Workbook* at the drop-down list.
3. Click the Print button.

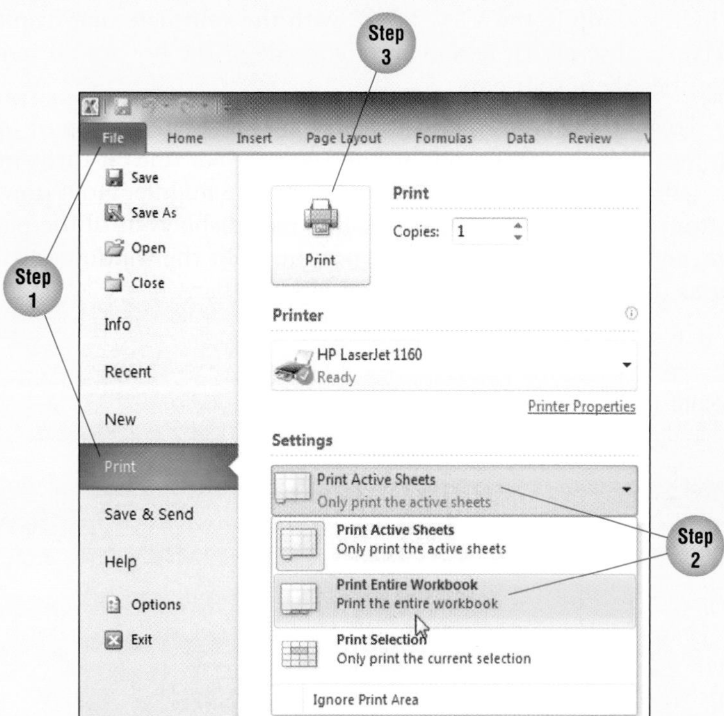

4. Save and then close **EL1-C5-P1-RPFacAccts.xlsx**.

Project 2 Write Formulas Using Ranges in an Equipment Usage Workbook — 2 Parts

You will open an equipment usage workbook and then split the window and edit cells. You will also name ranges and then use the range names to write formulas in the workbook.

Quick Steps

Split a Worksheet
1. Click View tab.
2. Click Split button.

OR

Drag horizontal and/or vertical split bars.

Restore a split window by double-clicking anywhere on the split bar that divides the panes.

Split

Splitting a Worksheet into Windows and Freezing and Unfreezing Panes

In some worksheets, not all cells display at one time in the worksheet area (such as EL1-C5-P2-HCEqpRpt.xlsx). When working in worksheets with more cells than can display at one time, you may find splitting the worksheet window into panes helpful. Split the worksheet window into panes with the Split button in the Window group in the View tab or with the split bars that display at the top of the vertical scroll bar and at the right side of the horizontal scroll bar. Figure 5.5 identifies these split bars.

To split a window with the split bar located at the top of the vertical scroll bar, position the mouse pointer on the split bar until it turns into a double-headed arrow with a short double line in the middle. Hold down the left mouse button, drag down the thick gray line that displays until the pane is the desired size, and then release the mouse button. Split the window vertically with the split bar at the right side of the horizontal scroll bar.

Figure 5.5 Split Bars

horizontal split bar

Highland Construction

EQUIPMENT USAGE REPORT

Hours	January	February	March	April	May	June	July	August	September	October	November	December
Total hours available	2300	2430	2530	2400	2440	2240	2520	2520	2390	2540		
Avoidable delays	19	12	16	20	14	15	9	8	12	7		
Unavoidable delays	9	8	6	12	9	10	10	13	8	9		
Repairs	5	7	12	9	10	6	7	8	10	13		
Servicing	6	13	7	6	4	5	8	3	12	6		
Unassigned	128	95	85	135	95	75	145	120	124	112		
In use	2040	2105	2320	2180	2050	1995	2320	2250	2190	1945		

vertical split bar

Figure 5.6 Split Window

Highland Construction

EQUIPMENT USAGE REPORT

Hours	January	February	March	April	May	June	July	August	September	October	November	December
Total hours available	2300	2430	2530	2400	2440	2240	2520	2520	2390	2540		
Avoidable delays	19	12	16	20	14	15	9	8	12	7		
Unavoidable delays	9	8	6	12	9	10	10	13	8	9		
Repairs	5	7	12	9	10	6	7	8	10	13		
Servicing	6	13	7	6	4	5	8	3	12	6		
Unassigned	128	95	85	135	95	75	145	120	124	112		
In use	2040	2105	2320	2180	2050	1995	2320	2250	2190	1945		

To split a worksheet window with the Split button, click the View tab and then click the Split button. This causes the worksheet to split into four window panes as shown in Figure 5.6. The windows are split by thick, light blue lines (with a three-dimensional look). To remove a split from a worksheet click the Split button to deactivate it or drag the split bars to the upper left corner of the worksheet.

A window pane will display the active cell. As the insertion point is moved through the pane, another active cell with a blue background may display. This additional active cell displays when the insertion point passes over one of the light blue lines that creates the pane. As you move through a worksheet, you may see both active cells — one with a normal background and one with a blue background. If you make a change to the active cell, the change is made in both. If you want only one active cell to display, freeze the window panes by clicking the Freeze Panes button in the Window group in the View tab and then clicking *Freeze Panes* at the drop-down list. You can maintain the display of column headings while editing or typing text in cells by clicking the Freeze Panes button and then clicking *Freeze Top Row*. Maintain the display of row headings by clicking the Freeze Panes button and then clicking *Freeze First Column*. Unfreeze window panes by clicking the Freeze Panes button and then clicking *Unfreeze Panes* at the drop-down list.

Freeze Panes

Using the mouse, you can move the thick, light blue lines that divide the window into panes. To do this, position the mouse pointer on the line until the pointer turns into a double-headed arrow with a double line in the middle. Hold down the left mouse button, drag the outline of the light blue line to the desired location, and then release the mouse button. If you want to move both the horizontal and vertical lines at the same time, position the mouse pointer on the intersection of the thick, light blue lines until it turns into a four-headed arrow. Hold down the left mouse button, drag the thick, light blue lines in the desired direction, and then release the mouse button.

Project 2a Splitting Windows and Editing Cells

1. Open **HCEqpRpt.xlsx** and then save the workbook with Save As and name it **EL1-C5-P2-HCEqpRpt**.
2. Make sure cell A1 is active and then split the window by clicking the View tab and then clicking the Split button in the Window group. (This splits the window into four panes.)
3. Drag the vertical light gray line by completing the following steps:
   a. Position the mouse pointer on the vertical split line until the pointer turns into a double-headed arrow pointing left and right with a double-line between.
   b. Hold down the left mouse button, drag to the left until the vertical light gray line is immediately to the right of the first column, and then release the mouse button.

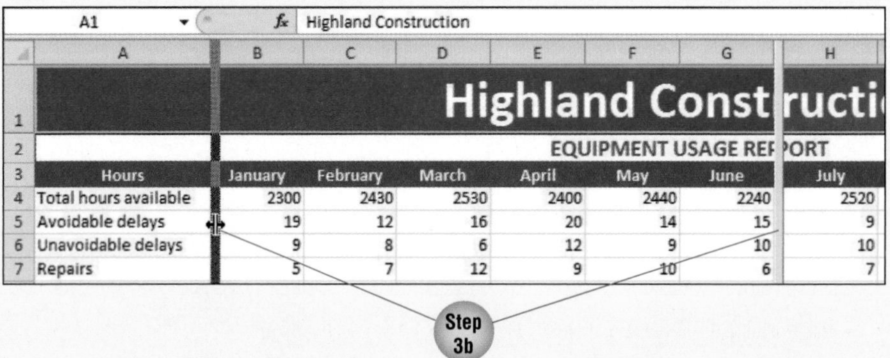

4. Freeze the window panes by clicking the Freeze Panes button in the Window group in the View tab and then clicking *Freeze Panes* at the drop-down list.

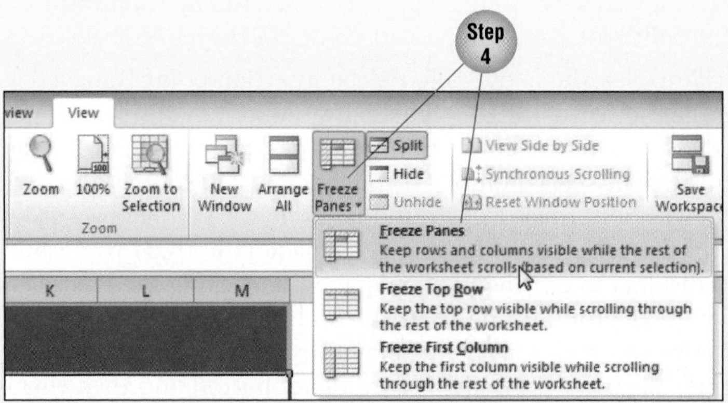

5. Make cell L4 active and then type the following data in the specified cells:

L4	=	2310	M4	=	2210
L5	=	12	M5	=	5
L6	=	5	M6	=	7
L7	=	9	M7	=	8
L8	=	11	M8	=	12
L9	=	95	M9	=	120
L10	=	2005	M10	=	1830

6. Unfreeze the window panes by clicking the Freeze Panes button and then clicking *Unfreeze Panes* at the drop-down list.
7. Remove the panes by clicking the Split button in the Window group to deactivate it.
8. Save **EL1-C5-P2-HCEqpRpt.xlsx**.

Working with Ranges

A selected group of cells is referred to as a ***range***. A range of cells can be formatted, moved, copied, or deleted. You can also name a range of cells and then move the insertion point to the range or use a named range as part of a formula.

To name a range, select the cells and then click in the Name Box located at the left of the Formula bar. Type a name for the range (do not use a space) and then press Enter. To move the insertion point to a specific range and select the range, click the down-pointing arrow at the right side of the Name Box and then click the range name.

You can also name a range using the Define Name button in the Formulas tab. To do this, click the Formulas tab and then click the Define Name button in the Defined Names group. At the New Name dialog box, type a name for the range and then click OK.

You can use a range name in a formula. For example, if a range is named *Profit* and you want to insert the average of all cells in the *Profit* range, you would make the desired cell active and then type *=AVERAGE(Profit)*. You can use a named range in the current worksheet or in another worksheet within the workbook.

Name a Range
1. Select cells.
2. Click in Name Box.
3. Type range name.
4. Press Enter.

HINT

Another method for moving to a range is to click the Find & Select button in the Editing group in the Home tab and then click *Go To*. At the Go To dialog box, double-click the range name.

Define Name

Project 2b Naming a Range and Using a Range in a Formula

Part 2 of 2

1. With **EL1-C5-P2-HCEqpRpt.xlsx** open, click the Sheet2 tab and then type the following text in the specified cells:
   - A1 = EQUIPMENT USAGE REPORT
   - A2 = Yearly hours
   - A3 = Avoidable delays
   - A4 = Unavoidable delays
   - A5 = Total delay hours
   - A6 = (leave blank)
   - A7 = Repairs
   - A8 = Servicing
   - A9 = Total repair/servicing hours
2. Make the following formatting changes to the worksheet:
   a. Automatically adjust the width of column A.
   b. Center and bold the text in cells A1 and A2.
3. Select a range of cells in worksheet 1, name the range, and use it in a formula in worksheet 2 by completing the following steps:
   a. Click the Sheet1 tab.
   b. Select cells B5 through M5.
   c. Click in the Name Box located to the left of the Formula bar.
   d. Type adhours (for Avoidable Delays Hours) and then press Enter.
   e. Click the Sheet2 tab.
   f. Make cell B3 active.
   g. Type the equation =SUM(adhours) and then press Enter.

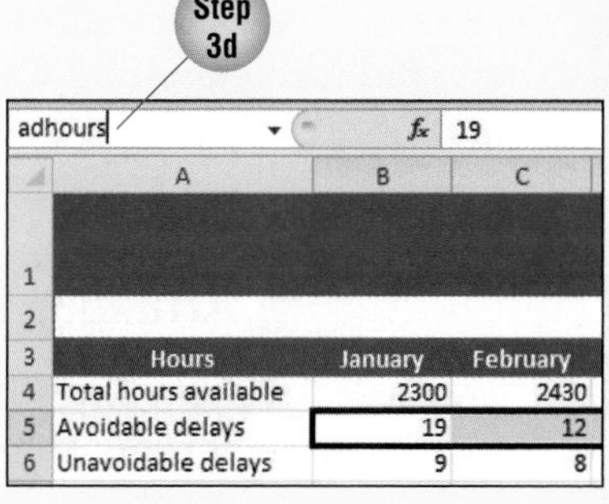

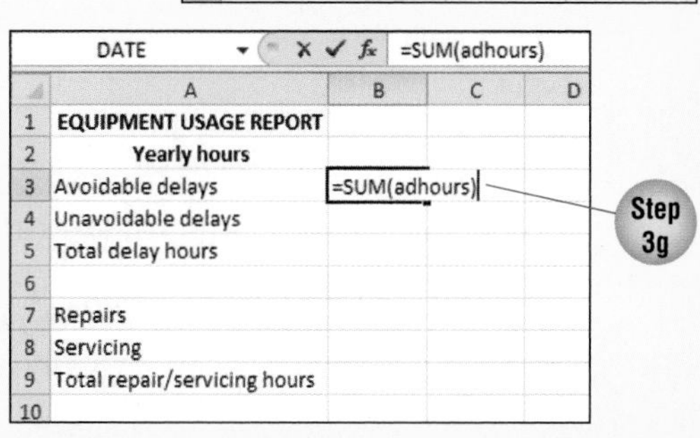

4. Click the Sheet1 tab and then complete the following steps:
   a. Select cells B6 through M6.
   b. Click the Formulas tab.
   c. Click the Define Name button in the Defined Names group.
   d. At the New Name dialog box, type **udhours** and then click OK.
   e. Make worksheet 2 active, make cell B4 active, and then type the equation **=SUM(udhours)**.

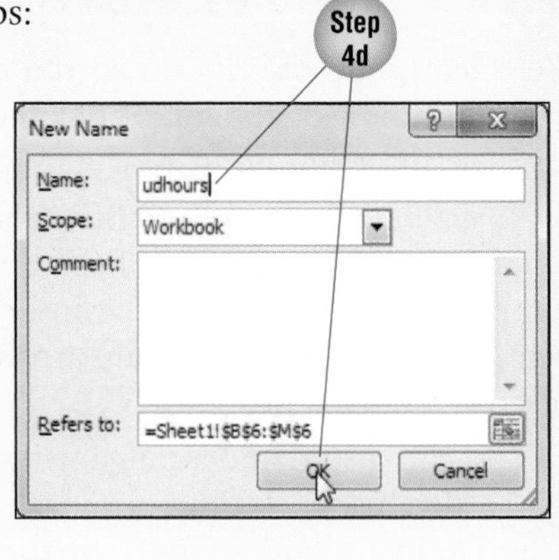

5. Make worksheet 1 active and then complete the following steps:
   a. Select cells B7 through M7 and then name the range *rhours*.
   b. Make worksheet 2 active, make cell B7 active, and then type the equation **=SUM(rhours)**.
   c. Make worksheet 1 active.
   d. Select cells B8 through M8 and then name the range *shours*.
   e. Make worksheet 2 active, make cell B8 active, and then type the equation **=SUM(shours)**.
6. With worksheet 2 still active, make the following changes:
   a. Make cell B5 active.
   b. Double-click the AutoSum button in the Editing group in the Home tab.
   c. Make cell B9 active.
   d. Double-click the AutoSum button in the Editing group in the Home tab.
7. Make worksheet 1 active and then move to the range *adhours* by clicking the down-pointing arrow at the right side of the Name Box and then clicking *adhours* at the drop-down list.

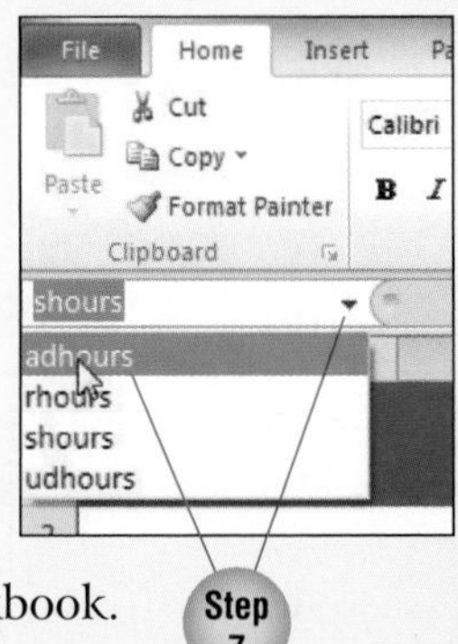

8. Select both sheet tabs, change the orientation to landscape, scale the contents to fit on one page (in Page Layout tab, change width to *1 page*), and insert a custom footer with your name, page number, and date.
9. With both worksheet tabs selected, print both worksheets in the workbook.
10. Save and then close **EL1-C5-P2-HCEqpRpt.xlsx**.

Project 3 Arrange, Size, and Copy Data between Workbooks — 3 Parts

You will open, arrange, hide, unhide, size, and move multiple workbooks. You will also copy cells from one workbook and paste in another workbook.

Working with Windows

You can open multiple workbooks in Excel, open a new window with the current workbook, and arrange the open workbooks in the Excel window. With multiple workbooks open, you can cut and paste or copy and paste cell entries from one workbook to another using the same techniques discussed earlier in this chapter with the exception that you activate the destination workbook before executing the Paste command.

Opening Multiple Workbooks

New Window

With multiple workbooks open, or more than one version of the current workbook open, you can move or copy information between workbooks and compare the contents of several workbooks. When you open a new workbook or a new window of the current workbook, it is placed on top of the original workbook. Open a new window of the current workbook by clicking the View tab and then clicking the New Window button in the Window group. Excel adds a colon followed by the number *2* to the end of the workbook title and adds a colon followed by the number *1* to the end of the originating workbook name. Open multiple workbooks at one time at the Open dialog box. Select adjacent workbooks by clicking the name of the first workbook to be opened, holding down the Shift key, clicking the name of the last workbook to be opened, and then clicking the Open button. If workbooks are nonadjacent, click the name of the first workbook to be opened, hold down the Ctrl key, and then click the names of any other workbooks you want to open.

Switch Windows

To see what workbooks are currently open, click the View tab and then click the Switch Windows button in the Window group. The names of the open workbooks display in a drop-down list and the workbook name preceded by a check mark is the active workbook. To make one of the other workbooks active, click the desired workbook name at the drop-down list.

Another method for determining which workbooks are open is to hover your mouse over the Excel icon button that displays on the Taskbar. This causes a thumbnail to display of each open workbook. If you have more than one workbook open, the Excel button on the Taskbar displays another layer in a cascaded manner. The layer behind the Excel button displays only a portion of the edge at the right side of the button. If you have multiple workbooks open, hovering the mouse over the Excel button on the Taskbar will cause thumbnails of all of the workbooks to display above the button. (This is dependent on your monitor size.) To change to the desired workbook, click the thumbnail that represents the workbook.

Arranging Workbooks

If you have more than one workbook open, you can arrange the workbooks at the Arrange Windows dialog box shown in Figure 5.7. To display this dialog box, open several workbooks and then click the Arrange All button in the Window group in the View tab. At the Arrange Windows dialog box, click *Tiled* to display a portion of each open workbook. Figure 5.8 displays four tiled workbooks.

Quick Steps

Arrange Workbooks

1. Click View tab.
2. Click Arrange All button.
3. At Arrange Windows dialog box, click desired arrangement.
4. Click OK.

Arrange All

Figure 5.7 Arrange Windows Dialog Box

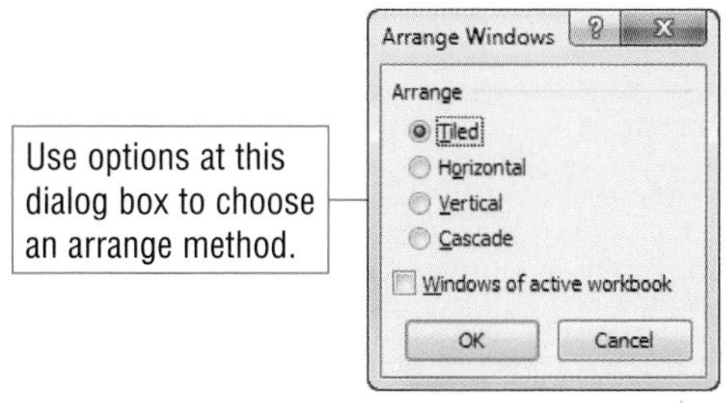

Figure 5.8 Tiled Workbooks

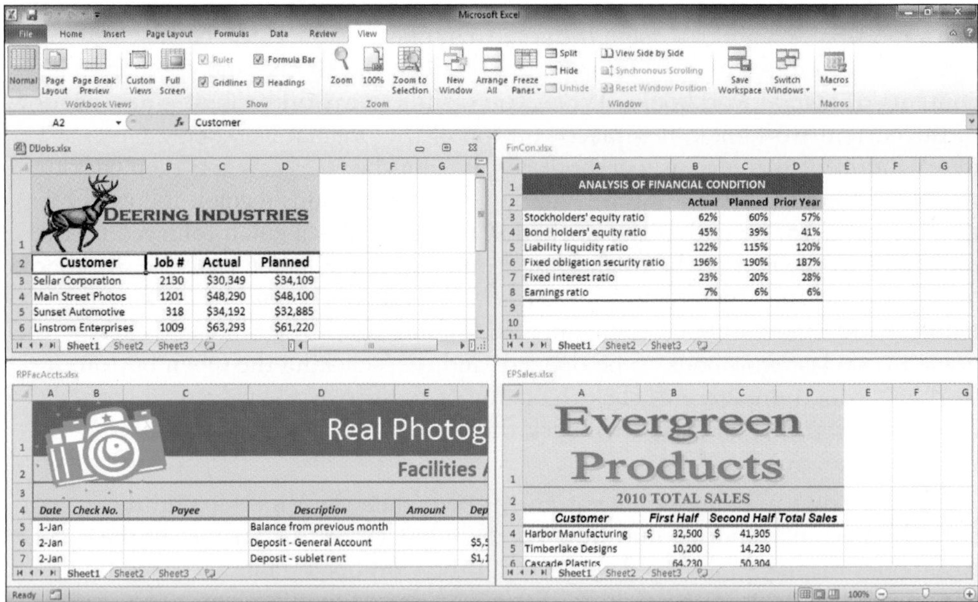

Choose the *Horizontal* option at the Arrange Windows dialog box and the open workbooks display across the screen. The *Vertical* option displays the open workbooks up and down the screen. The last option, *Cascade*, displays the Title bar of each open workbook. Figure 5.9 shows four cascaded workbooks.

The option you select for displaying multiple workbooks depends on which part of the workbooks is most important to view simultaneously. For example, the tiled workbooks in Figure 5.8 allow you to view the company logos and the first few rows and columns of each workbook.

Figure 5.9 Cascaded Workbooks

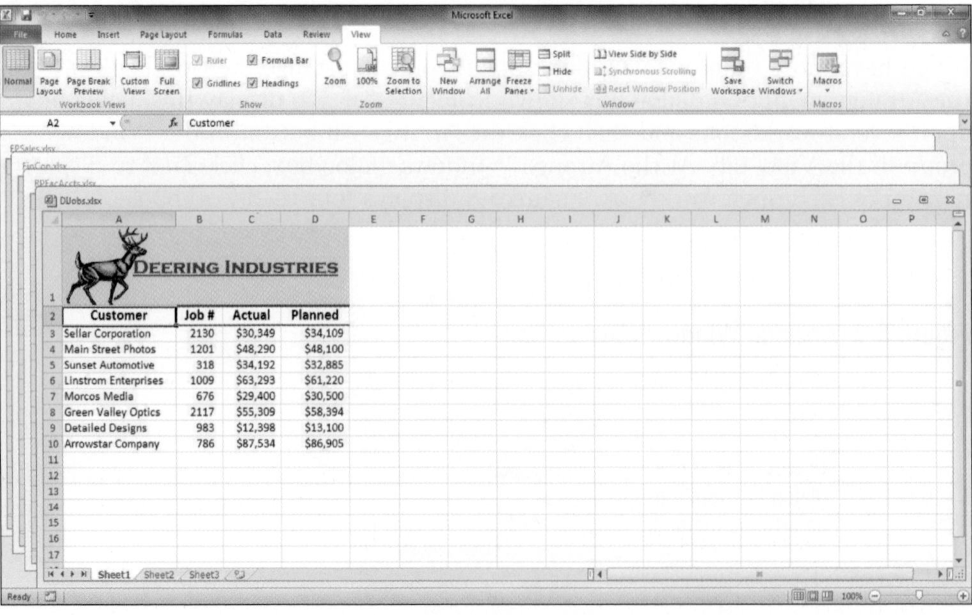

Hiding/Unhiding Workbooks

Hide

Unhide

With the Hide button in the Window group in the View tab, you can hide the active workbook. If a workbook has been hidden, redisplay the workbook by clicking the Unhide button in the Window group in the View tab. At the Unhide dialog box, make sure the desired workbook is selected in the list box and then click OK.

Project 3a Opening, Arranging, and Hiding/Unhiding Workbooks

Part 1 of 3

1. Open several workbooks at the same time by completing the following steps:
   a. Display the Open dialog box.
   b. Click the workbook named ***DIJobs.xlsx***.
   c. Hold down the Ctrl key, click ***EPSales.xlsx***, click ***FinCon.xlsx***, and click ***RPFacAccts.xlsx***.
   d. Release the Ctrl key and then click the Open button in the dialog box.
2. Make **DIJobs.xlsx** the active workbook by clicking the View tab, clicking the Switch Windows button, and then clicking ***DIJobs.xlsx*** at the drop-down list.

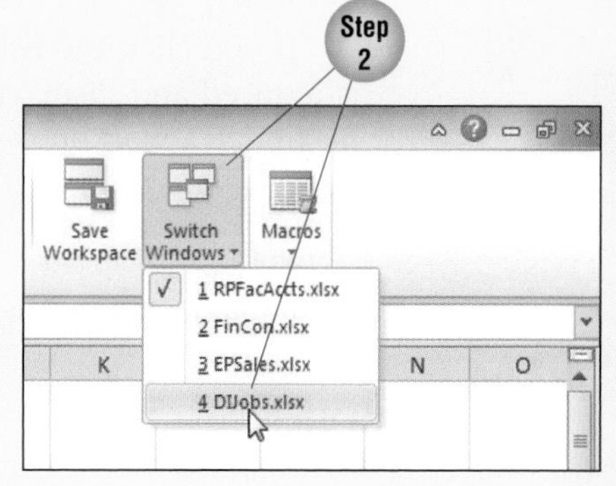

3. Tile the workbooks by completing the following steps:
   a. Click the Arrange All button in the Window group in the View tab.
   b. At the Arrange Windows dialog box, make sure *Tiled* is selected and then click OK.

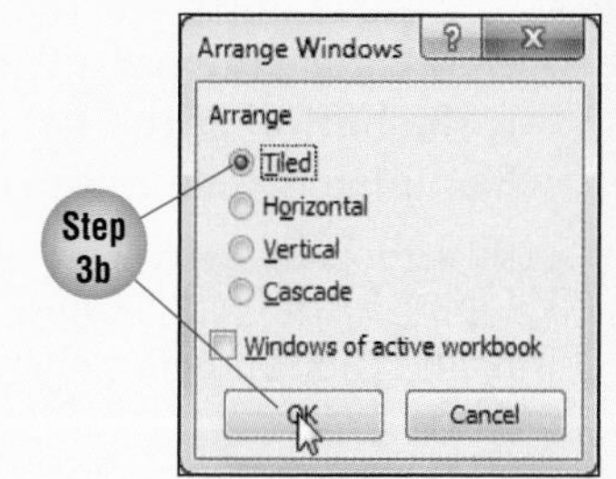

4. Tile the workbooks horizontally by completing the following steps:
   a. Click the Arrange All button.
   b. At the Arrange Windows dialog box, click *Horizontal*.
   c. Click OK.
5. Cascade the workbooks by completing the following steps:
   a. Click the Arrange All button.
   b. At the Arrange Windows dialog box, click *Cascade*.
   c. Click OK.
6. Hide and unhide workbooks by completing the following steps:
   a. Make sure **DIJobs.xlsx** is the active workbook (displays on top of the other workbooks).
   b. Click the Hide button in the Window group in the View tab.
   c. Make sure **RPFacAccts.xlsx** is the active workbook (displays on top of the other workbooks).
   d. Click the Hide button.
   e. Click the Unhide button.
   f. At the Unhide dialog box, click ***RPFacAccts.xlsx*** in the list box, and then click OK.
   g. Click the Unhide button.
   h. At the Unhide dialog box, make sure **DIJobs.xlsx** is selected in the list box and then click OK.

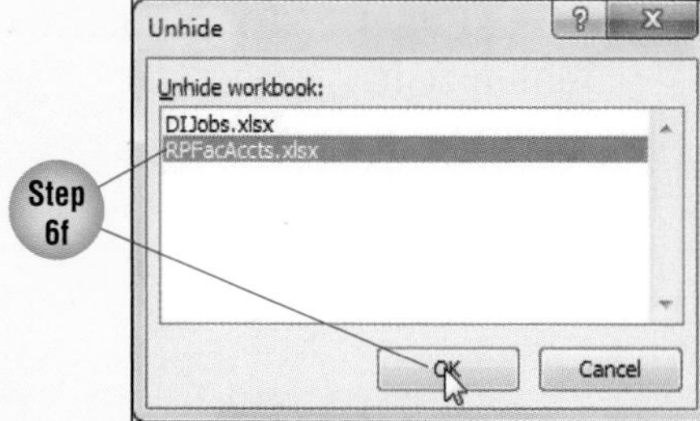

7. Close all of the open workbooks (without saving changes) except **DIJobs.xlsx**.
8. Open a new window with the current workbook by clicking the View tab and then clicking the New Window button in the Window group. (Notice that the new window contains the workbook name followed by a colon and the number 2.)
9. Switch back and forth between the two versions of the workbook.
10. Make **DIJobs.xlsx:2** the active window and then close the workbook.

Sizing and Moving Workbooks

Maximize

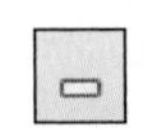
Minimize

Close

Restore Down

You can use the Maximize and Minimize buttons located in the upper right corner of the active workbook to change the size of the window. The Maximize button is the button in the upper right corner of the active workbook immediately to the left of the Close button. (The Close button is the button containing the *X*.) The Minimize button is located immediately to the left of the Maximize button.

If you arrange all open workbooks and then click the Maximize button in the active workbook, the active workbook expands to fill the screen. In addition, the Maximize button changes to the Restore Down button. To return the active workbook back to its size before it was maximized, click the Restore Down button.

If you click the Minimize button in the active workbook, the workbook is reduced and displays as a layer behind the Excel button on the Taskbar. To maximize a workbook that has been minimized, click the Excel button on the Taskbar and then click the thumbnail representing the workbook.

Project 3b **Minimizing, Maximizing, and Restoring Workbooks** Part 2 of 3

1. Make sure **DIJobs.xlsx** is open.
2. Maximize **DIJobs.xlsx** by clicking the Maximize button at the right side of the workbook Title bar. (The Maximize button is the button at the right side of the Title bar, immediately to the left of the Close button.)
3. Open **EPSales.xlsx** and **FinCon.xlsx**.
4. Make the following changes to the open workbooks:
   a. Tile the workbooks.
   b. Make **DIJobs.xlsx** the active workbook. (Title bar displays with a light gray background [the background color may vary depending on how Windows is customized]).
   c. Minimize **DIJobs.xlsx** by clicking the Minimize button that displays at the right side of the Title bar.
   d. Make **EPSales.xlsx** the active workbook and then minimize it.
   e. Minimize **FinCon.xlsx**.
5. Close all workbooks.

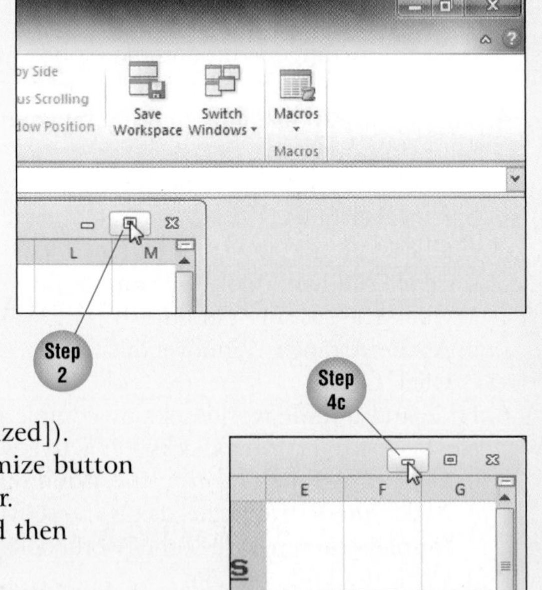

Moving, Copying, and Pasting Data

With more than one workbook open, you can move, copy, and/or paste data from one workbook to another. To move, copy, and/or paste data between workbooks, use the cutting and pasting options you learned earlier in this chapter, together with the information about windows in this chapter.

Project 3c Copying Selected Cells from One Open Worksheet to Another

Part 3 of 3

1. Open **DIFebJobs.xlsx**.
2. If you just completed Project 3b, click the Maximize button so the worksheet fills the entire worksheet window.
3. Save the workbook with Save As and name it **EL1-C5-P3-DIFebJobs**.
4. With **EL1-C5-P3-DIFebJobs.xlsx** open, open **DIJobs.xlsx**.
5. Select and then copy text from **DIJobs.xlsx** to **EL1-C5-P3-DIFebJobs.xlsx** by completing the following steps:
   a. With **DIJobs.xlsx** the active workbook, select cells A3 through D10.
   b. Click the Copy button in the Clipboard group in the Home tab.
   c. Click the Excel button on the Taskbar and then click the **EL1-C5-P3-DIFebJobs.xlsx** thumbnail.

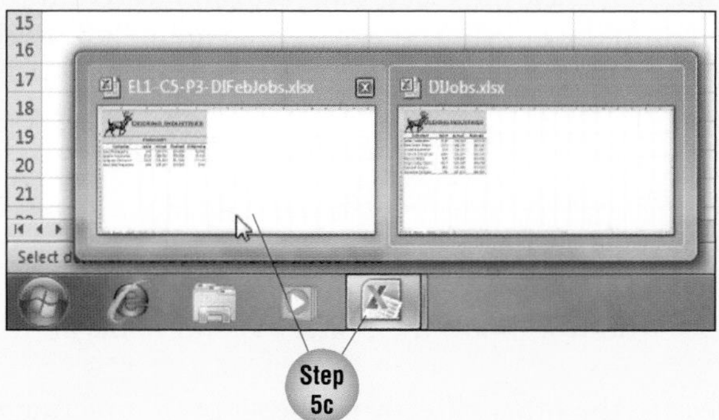

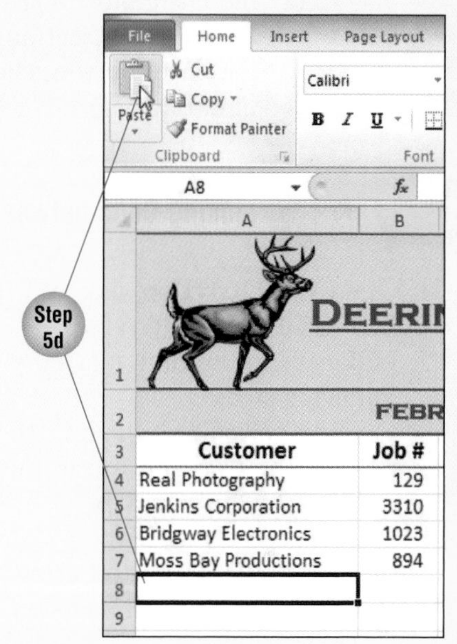

   d. Make cell A8 the active cell and then click the Paste button in the Clipboard group in the Home tab.
   e. Make cell E7 active and then drag the fill handle down to cell E15.
6. Print **EL1-C5-P3-DIFebJobs.xlsx** horizontally and vertically centered on the page.
7. Save and then close **EL1-C5-P3-DIFebJobs.xlsx**.
8. Close **DIJobs.xlsx**.

Project 4 Linking and Copying Data within and between Worksheets and Word

2 Parts

You will open a workbook containing four worksheets with quarterly expenses data, copy and then link cells between the worksheets, and then copy and paste the worksheets into Word as picture objects.

Moving Data

You can move or copy data within a worksheet, between worksheets, and also between workbooks and other programs such as Word, PowerPoint, or Access. The Paste Options button provides a variety of options for pasting data in a worksheet, another workbook, or another program. In addition to pasting data, you can also link data and paste data as an object or a picture object.

Linking Data

In some situations, you may want to copy and link data within or between worksheets or workbooks rather than copy and paste data. Linking data is useful in worksheets or workbooks where you need to maintain consistency and control over critical data. When data is linked, a change made in a linked cell is automatically made to the other cells in the link. You can make links with individual cells or with a range of cells. When linking data, the worksheet that contains the original data is called the ***source worksheet*** and the worksheet relying on the source worksheet for the data in the link is called the ***dependent worksheet***.

Quick Steps

Link Data between Worksheets

1. Select cells.
2. Click Copy button.
3. Click desired worksheet tab.
4. Click in desired cell.
5. Click Paste button arrow.
6. Click *Paste Link* at drop-down list.

To create a link, make active the cell containing the data to be linked (or select the cells) and then click the Copy button in the Clipboard group in the Home tab. Make active the worksheet where you want to paste the cells, click the Paste button arrow, and then click the Paste Link button located in the *Other Paste Options* section in the drop-down list. You can also create a link by clicking the Paste button, clicking the Paste Options button, and then clicking the Paste Link button.

Project 4a **Linking Cells between Worksheets** Part 1 of 2

1. Open **DWQtrlyExp.xlsx** and then save the workbook with Save As and name it **EL1-C5-P4-DWQtrlyExp**.
2. Link cells in the first quarter worksheet to the other three worksheets by completing the following steps:
   a. Select cells C4 through C10.
   b. Click the Copy button in the Clipboard group in the Home tab.
   c. Click the 2nd Qtr tab.
   d. Make cell C4 active.
   e. Click the Paste button arrow and then click the Paste Link button located in the *Other Paste Options* section in the drop-down list.
   f. Click the 3rd Qtr tab and then make cell C4 active.
   g. Click the Paste button arrow and then click the Paste Link button.
   h. Click the 4th Qtr tab and then make cell C4 active.
   i. Click the Paste button.
   j. Click the Paste Options button and then click the Paste Link button in the *Other Paste Options* section in the drop-down list.

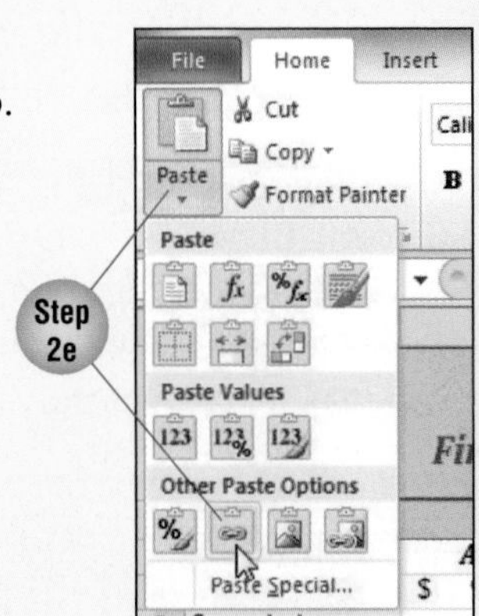

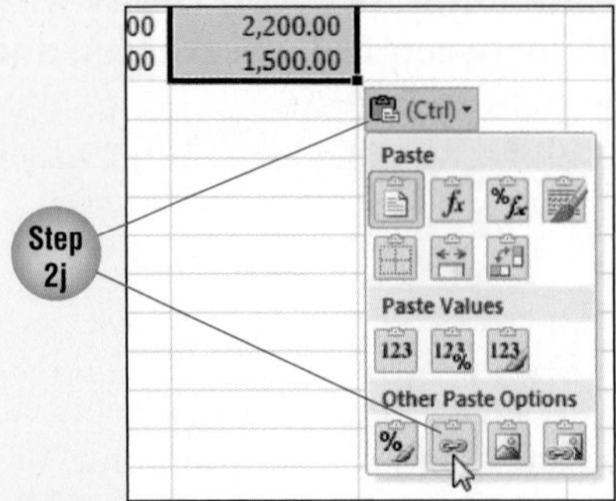

3. Click the 1st Qtr tab and then press the Esc key to remove the moving marquee.
4. Insert a formula in all worksheets that subtracts the Budget amount from the Variance amount by completing the following steps:
   a. Make sure the first quarter worksheet displays.
   b. Hold down the Shift key and then click the 4th Qtr tab. (This selects all four tabs.)
   c. Make cell D4 active and then type the formula =C4-B4 and press Enter.
   d. Copy the formula in cell D4 down to cells D5 through D10.
   e. Make cell D4 active and then click the Accounting Number Format button.
   f. Click the 2nd Qtr tab and notice that the formula was inserted and copied in this worksheet.
   g. Click the other worksheet tabs and notice the amounts in column D.
   h. Click the 1st Qtr tab.

C	D
Wise Services	
arter	
Budget	*Variance*
$ 126,000.00	4,000.00
54,500.00	(3,500.00)
10,100.00	1,850.00
6,000.00	(350.00)
4,500.00	360.00
2,200.00	(230.00)
1,500.00	50.00

Step 4d

5. With the first quarter worksheet active, make the following changes to some of the linked cells:
   C4: Change *$126,000* to *$128,000*
   C5: Change *54,500* to *56,000*
   C9: Change *2,200* to *2,400* 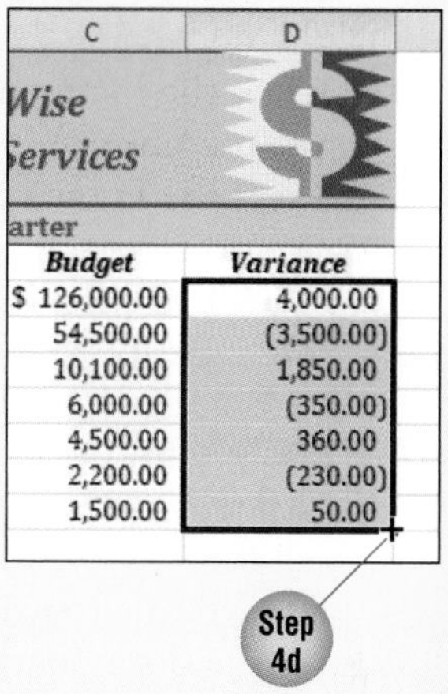
6. Click the 2nd Qtr tab and notice that the values in cells C4, C5, and C9 automatically changed (because they were linked to the first quarter worksheet).
7. Click the other tabs and notice that the values changed.
8. Save **EL1-C5-P4-DWQtrlyExp.xlsx** and then print all four worksheets in the workbook.

Copying and Pasting Data between Programs

Microsoft Office is a suite that allows integration, which is the combining of data from two or more programs into one file. Integration can occur by copying and pasting data between programs. For example, you can create a worksheet in Excel, select specific data in the worksheet, and then copy it to a Word document. When pasting Excel data in a Word document, you can choose to keep the source formatting, use destination styles, link the data, insert the data as a picture, or keep the text only.

Project 4b Copying and Pasting Excel Data into a Word Document — Part 2 of 2

1. With **EL1-C5-P4-DWQtrlyExp.xlsx** open, open the Word program.
2. In Word, open the document named **DWQtrlyRpt.docx** located in the Excel2010L1C5 folder on your storage medium.
3. Save the Word document with Save As and name it **EL1-C5-P4-DWQtrlyRpt**.
4. Click the Excel button on the Taskbar.
5. Copy the first quarter data into the Word document by completing the following steps:
   a. Click the 1st Qtr tab.
   b. Select cells A2 through D10.
   c. Click the Copy button in the Clipboard group in the Home tab.
   d. Click the Word button on the Taskbar.

e. In the **EL1-C5-P4-DWQtrlyRpt.docx** document, press Ctrl + End to move the insertion point below the heading.
f. Click the Paste button arrow. (This displays a drop-down list of paste option buttons.)
g. Move your mouse over the various buttons in the drop-down list to see how each option will insert the data in the document.
h. Click the Picture button. (This inserts the data as a picture object.)
i. Press the Enter key twice. (This moves the insertion point below the data.)
j. Click the Excel button on the Taskbar.

Step 5f

Step 5h

6. Click the 2nd Qtr tab and then complete steps similar to those in Step 5 to copy and paste the second quarter data to the Word document.
7. Click the 3rd Qtr tab and then complete steps similar to those in Step 5 to copy and paste the third quarter data to the Word document.
8. Click the 4th Qtr tab and then complete steps similar to those in Step 5 to copy and paste the fourth quarter data to the Word document. (The data should fit on one page.)
9. Print the document by clicking the File tab, clicking the Print tab, and then clicking the Print button at the Print tab Backstage view.
10. Save and then close **EL1-C5-P4-DWQtrlyRpt.docx** and then exit Word.
11. In Excel, press the Esc key to remove the moving marquee and then make cell A1 active.
12. Save and then close **EL1-C5-P4-DWQtrlyExp.xlsx**.

Chapter Summary

- An Excel workbook, by default, contains three worksheets. Click a worksheet tab to display the worksheet.
- Move selected cells and cell contents in and between worksheets using the Cut, Copy, and Paste buttons in the Clipboard group in the Home tab or by dragging with the mouse.
- Move selected cells with the mouse by dragging the outline of the selected cells to the desired position.
- Copy selected cells with the mouse by holding down the Ctrl key and the left mouse button, dragging the outline of the selected cells to the desired location, releasing the left mouse button, and then releasing the Ctrl key.
- When pasting data, use the Paste Options button to specify what you want pasted. Click the Paste Options button and a drop-down list of buttons displays with options to specify how you want the data posted.
- Use the Clipboard task pane to collect and paste data within and between worksheets and workbooks. Display the Clipboard task pane by clicking the Clipboard group dialog box launcher.
- Insert a worksheet in a workbook by clicking the Insert Worksheet tab located to the right of the Sheet3 tab or pressing Shift + F11.

- Perform maintenance activities, such as deleting and renaming, on worksheets within a workbook by clicking the right mouse button on a sheet tab and then clicking the desired option at the shortcut menu.
- You can use the mouse to move or copy worksheets. To move a worksheet, drag the worksheet tab with the mouse. To copy a worksheet hold down the Ctrl key and then drag the worksheet tab with the mouse.
- Use the *Tab Color* option at the sheet tab shortcut menu to apply a color to a worksheet tab.
- Hide and unhide a worksheet by clicking the Format button in the Cells group and then clicking the desired option at the drop-down list or by right-clicking the worksheet tab and then clicking the desired option at the shortcut menu.
- Manage more than one worksheet at a time by first selecting the worksheets. Use the mouse together with the Shift key to select adjacent worksheet tabs and use the mouse together with the Ctrl key to select nonadjacent worksheet tabs.
- If you want formatting to apply to multiple worksheets in a workbook, select the tabs of the desired worksheets and then apply the formatting.
- To print all worksheets in a workbook, display the Print tab Backstage view, click the first gallery in the Settings category, and then click *Print Entire Workbook* at the drop-down list. You can also print specific worksheets by selecting the tabs of the worksheets you want to print.
- Split the worksheet window into panes with the Split button in the Window group in the View tab or with the split bars on the horizontal and vertical scroll bars.
- To remove a split from a worksheet, click the Split button to deactivate it or drag the split bars to the upper left corner of the worksheet.
- Freeze window panes by clicking the Freeze Panes button in the Window group in the View tab and then clicking *Freeze Panes* at the drop-down list. Unfreeze window panes by clicking the Freeze Panes button and then clicking *Unfreeze Panes* at the drop-down list.
- A selected group of cells is referred to as a range. A range can be named and used in a formula. Name a range by typing the name in the Name Box located to the left of the Formula bar or at the New Name dialog box.
- To open multiple workbooks that are adjacent, display the Open dialog box, click the first workbook, hold down the Shift key, click the last workbook, and then click the Open button. If workbooks are nonadjacent, click the first workbook, hold down the Ctrl key, click the desired workbooks, and then click the Open button.
- To see a list of open workbooks, click the View tab and then click the Switch Windows button in the Window group.
- Arrange multiple workbooks in a window with options at the Arrange Windows dialog box.
- Hide the active workbook by clicking the Hide button and unhide a workbook by clicking the Unhide button in the Window group in the View tab.
- Click the Maximize button located in the upper right corner of the active workbook to make the workbook fill the entire window area. Click the Minimize button to shrink the active workbook to a button on the Taskbar. Click the Restore Down button to return the workbook to its previous size.
- You can move, copy, and/or paste data between workbooks.

Commands Review

FEATURE	RIBBON TAB, GROUP	BUTTON, OPTION	KEYBOARD SHORTCUT
Cut selected cells	Home, Clipboard		Ctrl + X
Copy selected cells	Home, Clipboard		Ctrl + C
Paste selected cells	Home, Clipboard		Ctrl + V
Clipboard task pane	Home, Clipboard		
Insert worksheet			Shift + F11
Hide worksheet	Home, Cells	, Hide & Unhide, Hide Sheet	
Unhide worksheet	Home, Cells	, Hide & Unhide, Unhide Sheet	
Split window into pane	View, Window		
Freeze window panes	View, Window	, Freeze Panes	
Unfreeze window panes	View, Window	, Unfreeze Panes	
New Name dialog box	Formulas, Defined Names		
Arrange Windows dialog box	View, Window		
Maximize window			
Restore Down			
Minimize window			

Concepts Check Test Your Knowledge

Completion: In the space provided at the right, indicate the correct term, symbol, or command.

1. By default, a workbook contains this number of worksheets. ____________________
2. The Cut, Copy, and Paste buttons are located in this group in the Home tab. ____________________
3. To copy selected cells with the mouse, hold down this key while dragging the outline of the selected cells to the desired location. ____________________

4. This button displays in the lower right corner of pasted cells. ____________

5. Use this task pane to collect and paste multiple items. ____________

6. Click this tab to insert a new worksheet. ____________

7. Click this option at the sheet tab shortcut menu to apply a color to a worksheet tab. ____________

8. To select adjacent worksheet tabs, click the first tab, hold down this key, and then click the last tab. ____________

9. To select nonadjacent worksheet tabs, click the first tab, hold down this key, and then click any other tabs you want selected. ____________

10. To print all worksheets in a workbook, display the Print tab Backstage view, click the first gallery in the Settings category, and then click this option at the drop-down list. ____________

11. The Split button is located in this tab. ____________

12. Display the Arrange Windows dialog box by clicking this button in the Window group in the View tab. ____________

13. Click this button to make the active workbook expand to fill the screen. ____________

14. Click this button to reduce the active workbook to a layer behind the Excel button on the Taskbar. ____________

15. When linking data between worksheets, the worksheet containing the original data is called this. ____________

Skills Check Assess Your Performance

Assessment 1

COPY AND PASTE DATA BETWEEN WORKSHEETS IN A SALES WORKBOOK

1. Open **EPSales.xlsx** and then save the workbook with Save As and name it **EL1-C5-A1-EPSales**.
2. Turn on the display of the Clipboard task pane, click the Clear All button to clear any content, and then complete the following steps:
   a. Select and copy cells A7 through C7.
   b. Select and copy cells A10 through C10.
   c. Select and copy cells A13 through C13.
   d. Display the second worksheet, make cell A7 active, and then paste the *Avalon Clinic* cells.
   e. Make cell A10 active and then paste the *Stealth Media* cells.

f. Make A13 active and then paste the *Danmark Contracting* cells.

g. Make the third worksheet active and then complete similar steps to paste the cells in the same location as the second worksheet.

h. Clear the contents of the Clipboard task pane and then close the task pane.

3. Change the name of the Sheet1 tab to *2010 Sales*, the name of the Sheet2 tab to *2011 Sales*, and the name of the Sheet3 tab to *2012 Sales*.
4. Change the color of the 2010 Sales tab to blue, the color of the 2011 Sales tab to green, and the color of the 2012 Sales tab to yellow.
5. Display the 2010 Sales worksheet, select all three tabs, and then insert a formula in cell D4 that sums the amounts in cells B4 and C4. Copy the formula in cell D4 down to cells D5 through D14.
6. Make cell D15 active and then insert a formula that sums the amounts in cells D4 through D14.
7. Apply the Accounting Number Format style with no decimal places to cell D4 (on all three worksheets).
8. Insert a footer on all three worksheets that prints your name at the left side and the current date at the right.
9. Save **EL1-C5-A1-EPSales.xlsx**.
10. Print all three worksheets and then close **EL1-C5-A1-EPSales.xlsx**.

Assessment 2

COPY, PASTE, AND FORMAT WORKSHEETS IN AN INCOME STATEMENT WORKBOOK

1. Open **CMJanIncome.xlsx** and then save the workbook with Save As and name it **EL1-C5-A2-CMJanIncome**.
2. Copy cells A1 through B17 in Sheet1 and paste them into Sheet2. (Click the Paste Options button and then click the Keep Source Column Widths button at the drop-down list.)
3. Make the following changes to the Sheet2 worksheet:
   a. Adjust the row heights so they match the heights in the Sheet1 worksheet.
   b. Change the month from *January* to *February*.
   c. Change the amount in B4 to *97,655*.
   d. Change the amount in B5 to *39,558*.
   e. Change the amount in B11 to *1,105*.
4. Select both sheet tabs and then insert the following formulas:
   a. Insert a formula in B6 that subtracts the *Cost of Sales* from the *Sales Revenue* (*=B4-B5*).
   b. Insert a formula in B16 that sums the amounts in B8 through B15.
   c. Insert a formula in B17 that subtracts the *Total Expenses* from the *Gross Profit* (*=B6-B16*).
5. Change the name of the Sheet1 tab to *January* and the name of the Sheet2 tab to *February*.
6. Change the color of the January tab to blue and the color of the February tab to red.
7. Insert a custom header on both worksheets that prints your name at the left side, the date in the middle, and the file name at the right side.
8. Save, print, and then close **EL1-C5-A2-CMJanIncome.xlsx**.

Assessment

3 FREEZE AND UNFREEZE WINDOW PANES IN A TEST SCORES WORKBOOK

1. Open **CMCertTests.xlsx** and then save the workbook with Save As and name it **EL1-C5-A3-CertTests**.
2. Make cell A1 active and then split the window by clicking the View tab and then clicking the Split button in the Window group. (This causes the window to split into four panes.)
3. Drag both the horizontal and vertical gray lines up and to the left until the horizontal gray line is immediately below the second row and the vertical gray line is immediately to the right of the first column.
4. Freeze the window panes.
5. Add two rows immediately above row 18 and then type the following text in the specified cells:

A18	=	Nauer, Sheryl	A19	=	Nunez, James
B18	=	75	B19	=	98
C18	=	83	C19	=	96
D18	=	85	D19	=	100
E18	=	78	E19	=	90
F18	=	82	F19	=	95
G18	=	80	G19	=	93
H18	=	79	H19	=	88
I18	=	82	I19	=	91
J18	=	92	J19	=	89
K18	=	90	K19	=	100
L18	=	86	L19	=	96
M18	=	84	M19	=	98

6. Insert a formula in cell N3 that averages the percentages in cells B3 through M3 and then copy the formula down to cells N4 through N22.
7. Unfreeze the window panes.
8. Remove the split.
9. Change the orientation to *Landscape* and then scale the worksheet to print on one page. ***Hint: Do this with the* Width *option in the Scale to Fit group in the Page Layout tab.***
10. Save, print, and then close **EL1-C5-A3-CertTests.xlsx**.

Assessment

CREATE, COPY, PASTE, AND FORMAT CELLS IN AN EQUIPMENT USAGE WORKBOOK

1. Create the worksheet shown in Figure 5.10. (Change the width of column A to 21.00.)
2. Save the workbook and name it **EL1-C5-A4-HCMachRpt**.
3. With **EL1-C5-A4-HCMachRpt.xlsx** open, open **HCEqpRpt.xlsx**.
4. Select and copy the following cells from **HCEqpRpt.xlsx** to **EL1-C5-A4-HCMachRpt.xlsx**:
   a. Copy cells A4 through G4 in **HCEqpRpt.xlsx** and paste them into **EL1-C5-A4-HCMachRpt.xlsx** beginning with cell A12.

b. Copy cells A10 through G10 in **HCEqpRpt.xlsx** and paste them into **EL1-C5-A4-HCMachRpt.xlsx** beginning with cell A13.

5. With **EL1-C5-A4-HCMachRpt.xlsx** the active workbook, make cell A1 active and then apply the following formatting:
   a. Change the height of row 1 to 25.50.
   b. Change the font size of the text in cell A1 to 14 points.
   c. Insert Olive Green, Accent 3, Lighter 60% fill color to cell A1.
6. Select cells A2 through G2 and then insert Olive Green, Accent 3, Darker 50% fill color.
7. Select cells B2 through G2, change the text color to white, and turn on italics. (Make sure the text in the cells is right aligned.)
8. Select cells A3 through G3 and then insert Olive Green, Accent 3, Lighter 80% fill color.
9. Select cells A7 through G7 and then insert Olive Green, Accent 3, Lighter 80% fill color.
10. Select cells A11 through G11 and then insert Olive Green, Accent 3, Lighter 80% fill color.
11. Print the worksheet centered horizontally and vertically on the page.
12. Save and then close **EL1-C5-A4-HCMachRpt.xlsx**.
13. Close **HCEqpRpt.xlsx** without saving the changes.

Figure 5.10 Assessment 4

	A	B	C	D	E	F	G	H
1			EQUIPMENT USAGE REPORT					
2		January	February	March	April	May	June	
3	Machine #12							
4	Total hours available	2300	2430	2530	2400	2440	2240	
5	In use	2040	2105	2320	2180	2050	1995	
6								
7	Machine #25							
8	Total hours available	2100	2240	2450	2105	2390	1950	
9	In use	1800	1935	2110	1750	2215	1645	
10								
11	Machine #30							
12								

Assessment 5

COPYING AND LINKING DATA IN A WORD DOCUMENT

1. In this chapter you learned how to link data in cells between worksheets. You can also copy data in an Excel worksheet and then paste and link the data in a file in another program such as Word. Use buttons in the Paste Options button drop-down list to link data or use options at the Paste Special dialog box. Open Word and then open the document named **DWLtr.docx** located in the Excel2010L1C5 folder on your storage medium. Save the document with Save As and name it **EL1-C5-A5-DWLtr**.
2. Click the Excel button on the Taskbar, open **DWMortgages.xlsx** and then save the workbook with Save As and name it **EL1-C5-A5-DWMortgages**.
3. In column G, insert a formula using the PMT function. Automatically adjust the width of column G.

4. Select cells A2 through G10 and then click the Copy button.
5. Click the Word button on the Taskbar. (This displays **EL1-C5-A5-DWLtr.docx**.)
6. Move the insertion point between the two paragraphs of text.
7. Click the Paste button arrow and then click *Paste Special* at the drop-down list.
8. At the Paste Special dialog box, look at the options available and then click the *Paste link* option, click *Microsoft Excel Worksheet Object* in the *As* list box, and then click OK.
9. Click the Center button in the Paragraph group in the Home tab. (This enters the cells between the left and right margins.)
10. Save, print, and then close **EL1-C5-A5-DWLtr.docx**.
11. Click the Excel button on the Taskbar.
12. Make cell A3 active and then change the number from $300,000 to $400,000. Copy the number in cell A3 down to cells A4 through A10. (Cells A3 through A10 should now contain the amount $400,000.)
13. Save, print, and then close **EL1-C5-A5-DWMortgages.xlsx**.
14. Click the Word button on the Taskbar.
15. Open **EL1-C5-A5-DWLtr.docx**. At the message that displays asking if you want to update the data from the linked files, click Yes.
16. Save, print, and then close **EL1-C5-A5-DWLtr.docx**.
17. Exit Word.

Visual Benchmark Demonstrate Your Proficiency

CREATE AND FORMAT A SALES WORKSHEET USING FORMULAS

1. At a blank workbook, create the worksheet shown in Figure 5.11 with the following specifications:
   - Do not type the data in cells D4 through D9; instead enter a formula that totals the first-half and second-half yearly sales.
   - Apply the formatting shown in the figure including changing font sizes, column widths, and row heights; and inserting shading and border lines.
   - Rename the sheet tab and change the tab color as shown in the figure.
2. Copy cells A1 through D9 and then paste the cells in Sheet2.
3. Edit the cells and apply formatting so your worksheet matches the worksheet shown in Figure 5.12. Rename the sheet tab and change the tab color as shown in the figure.
4. Save the completed workbook and name it **EL1-C5-VB-CMSemiSales**.
5. Print both worksheets.
6. Close **EL1-C5-VB-CMSemiSales.xlsx**.

Figure 5.11 Sales 2011 Worksheet

	A	B	C	D	E
1	Clearline Manufacturing				
2	SEMIANNUAL SALES - 2011				
3	Customer	1st Half	2nd Half	Total	
4	Lakeside Trucking	$ 84,300	$ 73,500	$ 157,800	
5	Gresham Machines	33,000	40,500	73,500	
6	Real Photography	30,890	35,465	66,355	
7	Genesis Productions	72,190	75,390	147,580	
8	Landower Company	22,000	15,000	37,000	
9	Jewell Enterprises	19,764	50,801	70,565	
10					
11					
12					
13					
14					
15					
16					
17					
18					
19					
20					
21					
22					
23					
24					

Sales 2011 | Sales 2012

Figure 5.12 Sales 2012 Worksheet

	A	B	C	D	E
1	Clearline Manufacturing				
2	SEMIANNUAL SALES - 2012				
3	Customer	1st Half	2nd Half	Total	
4	Lakeside Trucking	$ 84,300	$ 73,500	$ 157,800	
5	Gresham Machines	33,000	40,500	73,500	
6	Real Photography	20,750	15,790	36,540	
7	Genesis Productions	51,270	68,195	119,465	
8	Landower Company	22,000	15,000	37,000	
9	Jewell Enterprises	14,470	33,770	48,240	
10					
11					
12					
13					
14					
15					
16					
17					
18					
19					
20					
21					
22					
23					

Sales 2011 | Sales 2012

Case Study Apply Your Skills

Part 1

You are an administrator for Gateway Global, an electronics manufacturing corporation. You are gathering information on money spent on supplies and equipment purchases. You have gathered information for the first quarter of the year and decide to create a workbook containing worksheets for monthly information. To do this, create a worksheet that contains the following information:

- Company name is Gateway Global.
- Create the title *January Expenditures*.
- Create the following columns:

Department	**Supplies**	**Equipment**	**Total**
Production	$25,425	$135,500	
Research and Development	$50,000	$125,000	
Technical Support	$14,500	$65,000	
Finance	$5,790	$22,000	
Sales and Marketing	$35,425	$8,525	
Facilities	$6,000	$1,200	
Total			

- Insert a formula in the *Total* column that sums the amounts in the *supplies* and *equipment* columns and insert a formula in the *total* row that sums the supplies amounts, equipment amounts, and total amounts.
- Apply formatting such as fill color, borders, font color, and shading to enhance the visual appeal of the worksheet.

After creating and formatting the worksheet, complete the following:

- Copy the worksheet data to Sheet2 and then to Sheet3.
- Make the following changes to data in Sheet2:
    - Change *January Expenditures* to *February Expenditures*.
    - Change the Production department supplies amount to *$38,550* and the equipment amount to *$88,500*.
    - Change the Technical Support department equipment amount to *$44,250*.
    - Change the Finance department supplies amount to *$7,500*.
- Make the following changes to data in Sheet3:
    - Change *January Expenditures* to *March Expenditures*.
    - Change the Research and Development department supplies amount to *$65,000* and the equipment amount to *$150,000*.
    - Change the Technical Support department supplies amount to *$21,750* and the equipment amount to *$43,525*.
    - Change the Facilities department equipment amount to *$18,450*.

Create a new worksheet that summarizes the supplies and equipment totals for January, February, and March. Apply the same formatting to the worksheet as applied to the other three. Change the tab name for Sheet1 to *Jan. Expenditures*, the tab name for Sheet2 to *Feb. Expenditures*, the tab name for Sheet3 to *Mar. Expenditures*, and the tab name for Sheet4 to *Qtr. Summary*. Change the color of each tab. (You determine the colors.)

Insert a header that prints your name at the left side of each worksheet and the current date at the right side of each worksheet. Save the workbook and name it **EL1-C5-CS-GGExp**. Print all the worksheets in the workbook and then close the workbook.

Part 2

Employees of Gateway Global have formed two intramural co-ed softball teams and you have volunteered to keep statistics for the players. Open **GGStats.xlsx** and then make the following changes to both worksheets in the workbook:

- Insert a formula that calculates a player's batting average (Hits ÷ At Bats).
- Insert a formula that calculates a player's on-base percentage: (Walks + Hits) ÷ (At Bats + Walks). Select E5 through F15 and then specify that you want three decimal places displayed.
- Insert the company name.
- Apply formatting to enhance the visual appeal of the worksheets.
- Horizontally and vertically center the worksheets.
- Insert a footer that prints on both worksheets and prints your name at the left side of the worksheet and the date at the right of the worksheet.

Use the Help feature to learn about applying cell styles or click the Cells Styles button in the Styles group in the Home tab and then experiment with applying different styles. Apply the *Good* cell style to any cell in the *Batting Average* column with an average over .400. Apply this style to cells in both worksheets. Save the workbook and name it **EL1-C5-CS-GGStats**. Print both worksheets and then close **EL1-C5-CS-GGStats.xlsx**.

Part 3

Many of the suppliers for Gateway Global are international and use different length, weight, and volume measurements. The purchasing manager has asked you to prepare a conversion chart in Excel that displays conversion tables for length, weight, volume, and temperature. Use the Internet to locate conversion tables for length, weight, and volume. When preparing the workbook, create a worksheet with the following information:

- Include the following length conversions:
  - 1 inch to centimeters
  - 1 foot to centimeters
  - 1 yard to meters
  - 1 mile to kilometers
- Include the following weight conversions:
  - 1 ounce to grams
  - 1 pound to kilograms
  - 1 ton to metric tons
- Include the following volume conversions:
  - 1 fluid ounce to milliliters
  - 1 pint to liters
  - 1 quart to liters
  - 1 gallon to liters

Locate a site on the Internet that provides the formula for converting Fahrenheit temperatures to Celsius temperatures and then create another worksheet in the workbook with the following information:

- Insert Fahrenheit temperatures beginning with zero, continuing to 100, and incrementing by 5 (for example, 0, 5, 10, 15, and so on).
- Insert a formula that converts the Fahrenheit temperature to a Celsius temperature.

Include the company name, Gateway Global, in both worksheets. Apply additional formatting to improve the visual appeal of both worksheets. Rename both sheet names and apply a color to each tab (you determine the names and colors). Save the workbook and name it **EL1-C5-CS-GGConv**. Print both worksheets centered horizontally and vertically on the page and then close **EL1-C5-CS-GGConv.xlsx**.

Part 4

Open Microsoft Word and then create a letterhead document that contains the company name *Gateway Global*, the address (you decide the address including street address, city, state, and ZIP code or street address, city, province, and postal code), and the telephone number (you determine the telephone number). Apply formatting to improve the visual appeal of the letterhead. Save the document and name it **EL1-C5-CS-GGLtrhd**. Save the document again and name it **EL1-C5-CS-GGConvLtr**.

In Excel, open **EL1-C5-CS-GGConv.xlsx** (the workbook you created in Part 3). In the first worksheet, copy the cells containing data and then paste the cells in **EL1-C5-CS-GGConvLtr.docx** as a picture object. Center the cells (picture object) between the left and right margins. Save, print, and then close **EL1-C5-CS-GGConvLtr.docx**. Exit Microsoft Word and then, in Excel, close **EL1-C5-CS-GGConv.xlsx**.

Microsoft® Excel®

CHAPTER 6

Maintaining Workbooks

PERFORMANCE OBJECTIVES

Upon successful completion of Chapter 6, you will be able to:

- **Create and rename a folder**
- **Delete workbooks and folders**
- **Copy and move workbooks within and between folders**
- **Copy and move worksheets between workbooks**
- **Maintain consistent formatting with styles**
- **Insert, modify, and remove hyperlinks**
- **Create financial forms using templates**

Tutorials

6.1 Maintaining Workbooks
6.2 Managing Folders
6.3 Managing the Recent List
6.4 Managing Worksheets
6.5 Formatting with Cell Styles
6.6 Inserting Hyperlinks
6.7 Using Templates

Once you have been working with Excel for a period of time you will have accumulated several workbook files. Workbooks should be organized into folders to facilitate fast retrieval of information. Occasionally you should perform file maintenance activities such as copying, moving, renaming, and deleting workbooks to ensure the workbook list in your various folders is manageable. You will learn these file management tasks in this chapter along with creating and applying styles, inserting hyperlinks in a workbook, and using Excel templates to create a workbook. Model answers for this chapter's projects appear on the following pages.

Excel2010L1C6

Note: Before beginning the projects, copy to your storage medium the Excel2010L1C6 subfolder from the Excel2010L1 folder on the CD that accompanies this textbook and then make Excel2010L1C6 the active folder.

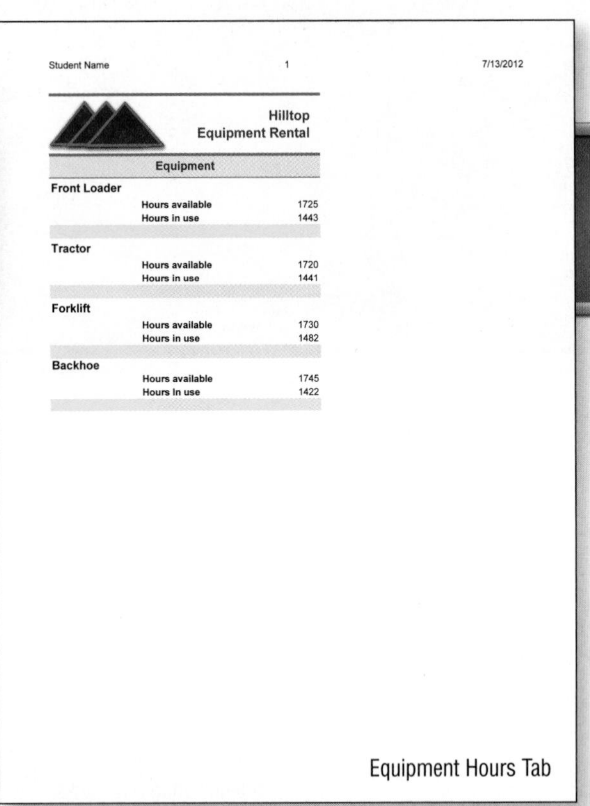

Student Name 1 7/13/2012

Hilltop
Equipment Rental

Equipment		
Front Loader		
	Hours available	1725
	Hours in use	1443
Tractor		
	Hours available	1720
	Hours in use	1441
Forklift		
	Hours available	1730
	Hours in use	1482
Backhoe		
	Hours available	1745
	Hours In use	1422

Equipment Hours Tab

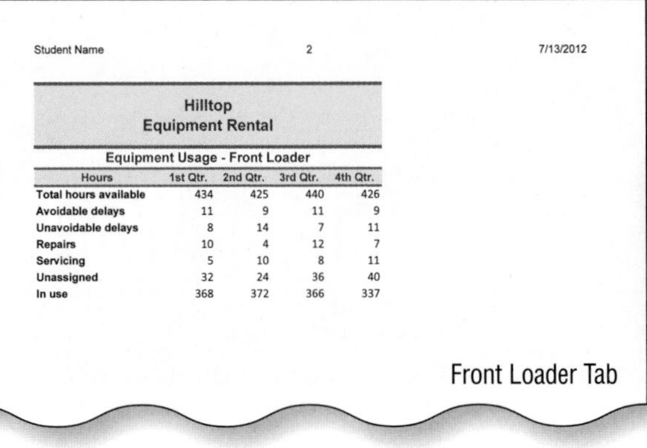

Student Name 2 7/13/2012

Hilltop
Equipment Rental

Equipment Usage - Front Loader

Hours	1st Qtr.	2nd Qtr.	3rd Qtr.	4th Qtr.
Total hours available	434	425	440	426
Avoidable delays	11	9	11	9
Unavoidable delays	8	14	7	11
Repairs	10	4	12	7
Servicing	5	10	8	11
Unassigned	32	24	36	40
In use	368	372	366	337

Front Loader Tab

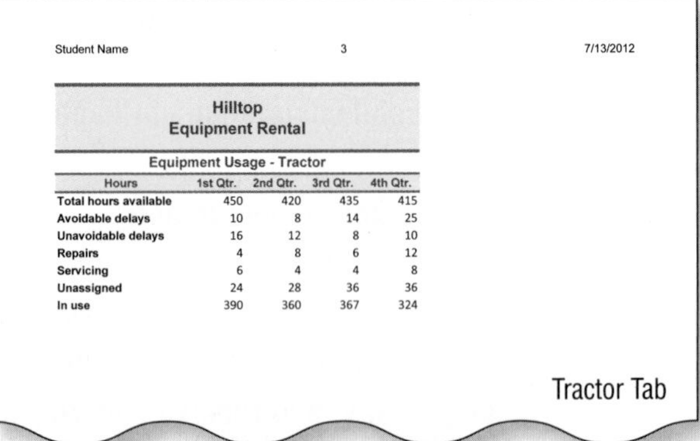

Student Name 3 7/13/2012

Hilltop
Equipment Rental

Equipment Usage - Tractor

Hours	1st Qtr.	2nd Qtr.	3rd Qtr.	4th Qtr.
Total hours available	450	420	435	415
Avoidable delays	10	8	14	25
Unavoidable delays	16	12	8	10
Repairs	4	8	6	12
Servicing	6	4	4	8
Unassigned	24	28	36	36
In use	390	360	367	324

Tractor Tab

Project 2 Copy and Move Worksheets into an Equipment Rental Workbook EL1-C6-P2-HEREquip.xlsx

Student Name 4 7/13/2012

Hilltop
Equipment Rental

Equipment Usage - Forklift

Hours	1st Qtr.	2nd Qtr.	3rd Qtr.	4th Qtr.
Total hours available	436	440	428	426
Avoidable delays	12	8	5	8
Unavoidable delays	7	10	10	5
Repairs	4	9	12	3
Servicing	12	6	12	8
Unassigned	32	21	32	29
In use	369	386	365	362

Forklift Tab

Student Name 5 7/13/2012

Hilltop
Equipment Rental

Equipment Usage - Backhoe

Hours	1st Qtr.	2nd Qtr.	3rd Qtr.	4th Qtr.
Total hours available	450	435	440	420
Avoidable delays	14	10	8	15
Unavoidable delays	12	8	12	12
Repairs	8	5	14	8
Servicing	10	8	10	4
Unassigned	62	32	26	45
In use	344	372	370	336

Backhoe Tab

O'Rourke Enterprises

Maintenance Department - Weekly Payroll

Employee	Hrly. Rate	Hours	Gross	W/H Tax	SS Tax	Net
Williams, Pamela	$ 43.00	40	$ 1,720.00	$ 481.60	$ 131.58	$ 1,106.82
Ternes, Reynaldo	41.50	40	1,660.00	464.80	126.99	1,068.21
Sinclair, Jason	38.00	30	1,140.00	319.20	87.21	733.59
Pierson, Rhea	38.00	40	1,520.00	425.60	116.28	978.12
Nyegaard, James	25.00	25	625.00	175.00	47.81	402.19
Lunde, Beverly	21.00	40	840.00	235.20	64.26	540.54

Withholding rate	28%
Social Security rate	7.65%

Weekly Payroll Tab

O'Rourke Enterprises

Invoices

Invoice #	Customer #	Date	Amount	Tax	Amount Due
1001	34002	4/2/2012	$ 450.00	8.50%	$ 488.25
1002	12034	4/4/2012	1,075.00	8.80%	1,169.60
1003	40059	4/6/2012	225.00	0.00%	225.00
1004	23002	4/10/2012	750.00	8.50%	813.75
1005	59403	4/10/2012	350.00	0.00%	350.00
1006	80958	4/11/2012	875.00	8.50%	949.38
1007	23494	4/13/2012	750.00	8.50%	813.75
1008	45232	4/17/2012	560.00	8.80%	609.28
1009	76490	4/18/2012	400.00	0.00%	400.00
1010	45466	4/19/2012	600.00	8.50%	651.00
1011	34094	4/23/2012	95.00	0.00%	95.00
1012	45450	4/25/2012	2,250.00	8.50%	2,441.25
1013	23044	4/26/2012	225.00	8.80%	244.80
1014	48933	4/30/2012	140.00	0.00%	140.00

Invoices Tab

Project 3 Create and Apply Styles to a Payroll Workbook
EL1-C6-P3-OEPayroll.xlsx

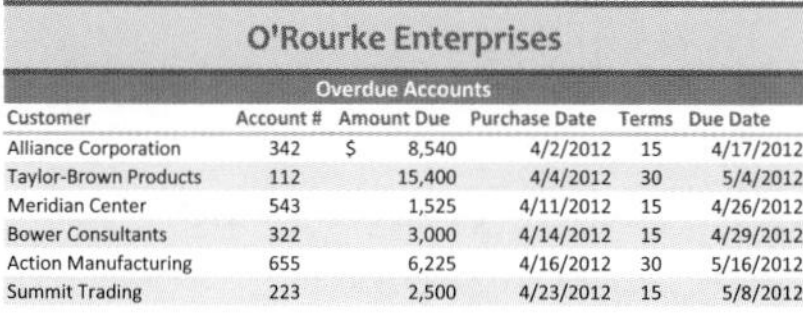

O'Rourke Enterprises					
Overdue Accounts					
Customer	Account #	Amount Due	Purchase Date	Terms	Due Date
Alliance Corporation	342	$ 8,540	4/2/2012	15	4/17/2012
Taylor-Brown Products	112	15,400	4/4/2012	30	5/4/2012
Meridian Center	543	1,525	4/11/2012	15	4/26/2012
Bower Consultants	322	3,000	4/14/2012	15	4/29/2012
Action Manufacturing	655	6,225	4/16/2012	30	5/16/2012
Summit Trading	223	2,500	4/23/2012	15	5/8/2012

Overdue Accounts Tab

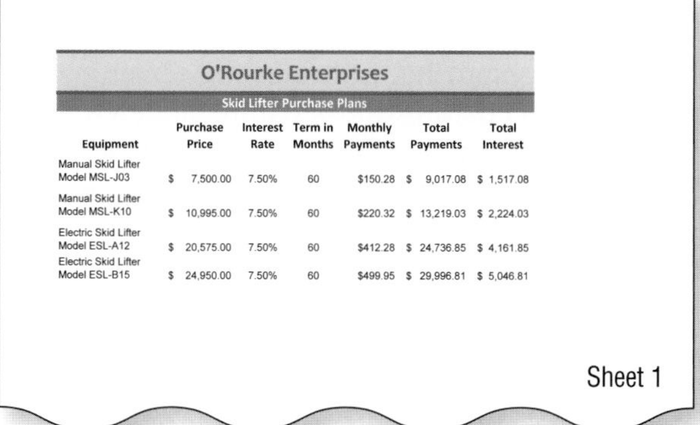

O'Rourke Enterprises						
Skid Lifter Purchase Plans						
Equipment	Purchase Price	Interest Rate	Term in Months	Monthly Payments	Total Payments	Total Interest
Manual Skid Lifter Model MSL-J03	$ 7,500.00	7.50%	60	$150.28	$ 9,017.08	$ 1,517.08
Manual Skid Lifter Model MSL-K10	$ 10,995.00	7.50%	60	$220.32	$ 13,219.03	$ 2,224.03
Electric Skid Lifter Model ESL-A12	$ 20,575.00	7.50%	60	$412.28	$ 24,736.85	$ 4,161.85
Electric Skid Lifter Model ESL-B15	$ 24,950.00	7.50%	60	$499.95	$ 29,996.81	$ 5,046.81

Sheet 1

EL1-C6-P3-OEPlans.xlsx

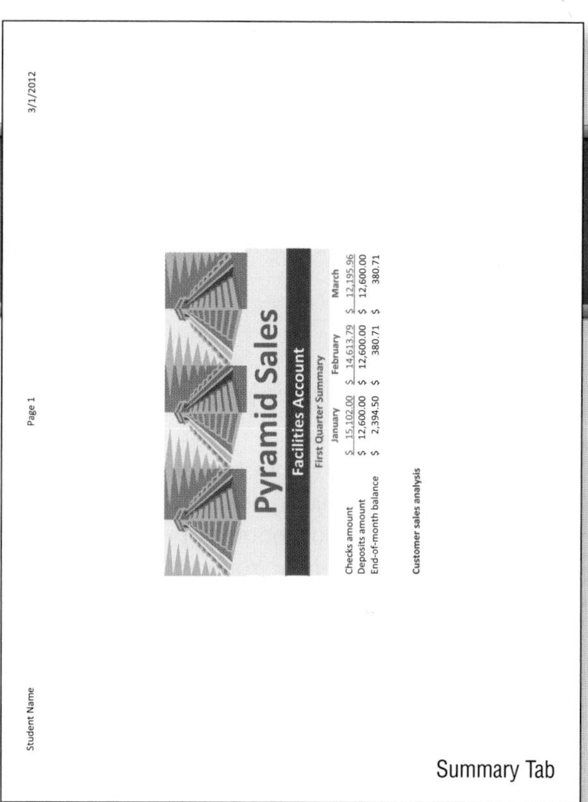

3/1/2012

Page 1

Student Name

Pyramid Sales

Facilities Account

First Quarter Summary

	January	February	March
Checks amount	$ 15,102.00	$ 14,613.79	$ 12,195.96
Deposits amount	$ 12,600.00	$ 12,600.00	$ 12,600.00
End-of-month balance	$ 2,394.50	$ 380.71	$ 380.71

Customer sales analysis

Summary Tab

Project 4 Insert, Modify, and Remove Hyperlinks

EL1-C6-P4-PSAccts.xlsx

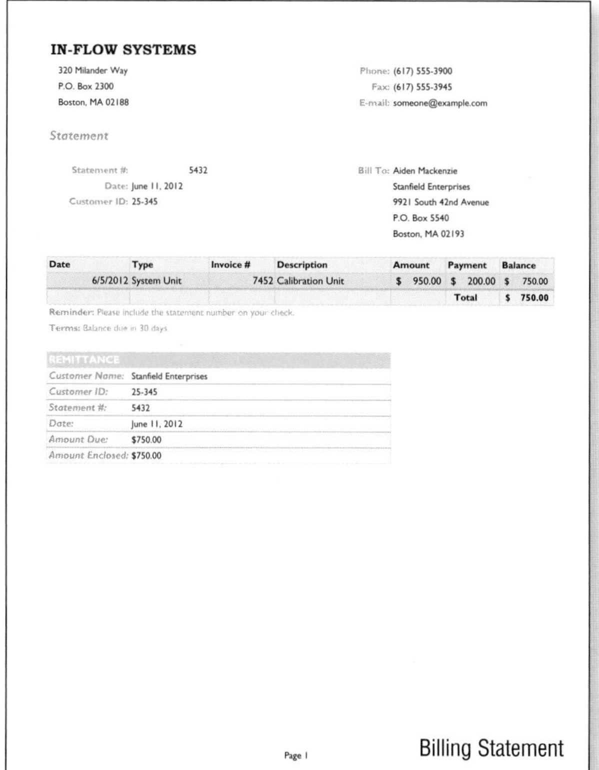

IN-FLOW SYSTEMS

320 Milander Way
P.O. Box 2300
Boston, MA 02188

Phone: (617) 555-3900
Fax: (617) 555-3945
E-mail: someone@example.com

Statement

Statement #: 5432
Date: June 11, 2012
Customer ID: 25-345

Bill To: Aiden Mackenzie
Stanfield Enterprises
9921 South 42nd Avenue
P.O. Box 5540
Boston, MA 02193

Date	Type	Invoice #	Description	Amount	Payment	Balance
6/5/2012	System Unit	7452	Calibration Unit	$ 950.00	$ 200.00	$ 750.00
					Total	$ 750.00

Reminder: Please include the statement number on your check.

Terms: Balance due in 30 days

REMITTANCE	
Customer Name:	Stanfield Enterprises
Customer ID:	25-345
Statement #:	5432
Date:	June 11, 2012
Amount Due:	$750.00
Amount Enclosed:	$750.00

Page 1

Billing Statement

Project 5 Create a Billing Statement Workbook Using a Template

EL1-C6-P5-Billing.xlsx

Project 1 Manage Workbooks 8 Parts

You will perform a variety of file management tasks including creating and renaming a folder; selecting and then deleting, copying, cutting, pasting, and renaming workbooks; deleting a folder; and opening, printing, and closing a workbook.

Maintaining Workbooks

You can complete many workbook management tasks at the Open and Save As dialog boxes. These tasks can include copying, moving, printing, and renaming workbooks; opening multiple workbooks; and creating and renaming a new folder. You can perform some file maintenance tasks such as creating a folder and deleting files with options from the Organize button drop-down list or a shortcut menu and navigate to folders using the Address bar. The elements of the Open dialog box are identified in Figure 6.1.

Figure 6.1 Open Dialog Box

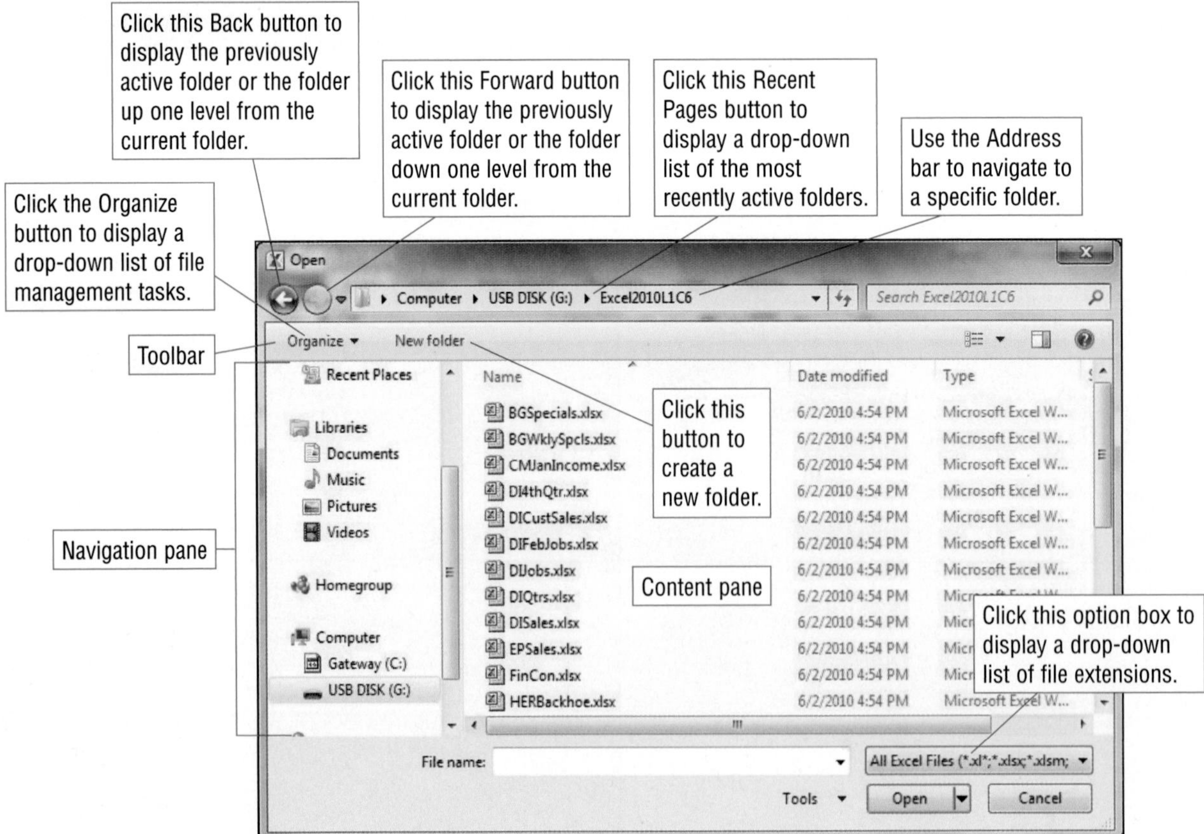

Creating a Folder

In Excel, you should logically group and store workbooks in folders. For example, you could store all of the workbooks related to one department in one folder with the department name being the folder name. You can create a folder within a folder (called a ***subfolder***). If you create workbooks for a department by individuals, each individual name could have a subfolder within the department folder. The main folder on a disk or drive is called the root folder. You create additional folders as branches of this root folder.

At the Open or Save As dialog boxes, workbook file names display in the Content pane preceded by a workbook icon and a folder name displays preceded by a folder icon. Create a new folder by clicking the New folder button located in the toolbar at the Open dialog box or Save As dialog box. This inserts a new folder in the Content pane. Type the name for the folder and then press Enter.

A folder name can contain a maximum of 255 characters. Numbers, spaces, and symbols can be used in the folder name, except those symbols explained in Chapter 1 in the "Saving a Workbook" section.

Quick Steps

Create a Folder
1. Click File tab, Open button.
2. Click New folder button.
3. Type folder name.
4. Press Enter.

HINT

Change the default folder with the *Default file location* option at the Excel Options dialog box with *Save* selected.

New folder

New Folder

Project 1a **Creating a Folder** Part 1 of 8

1. Create a folder named *Payroll* on your storage medium. To begin, display the Open dialog box.
2. Double-click the *Excel2010L1C6* folder name to make it the active folder.
3. Click the New folder button on the toolbar.
4. Type Payroll and then press Enter.
5. Close the Open dialog box.

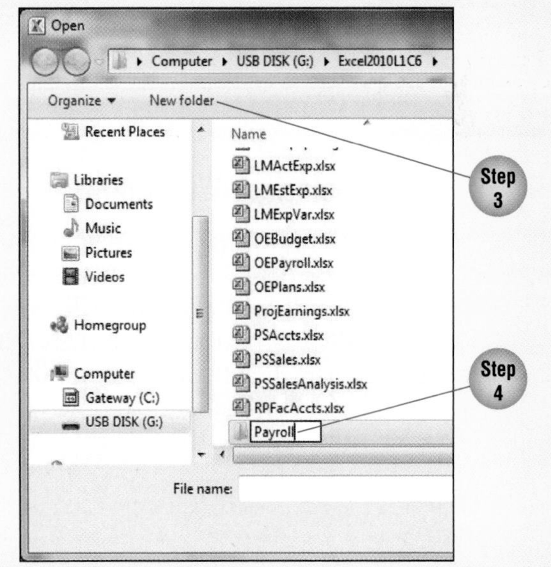

Quick Steps

Rename a Folder

1. Click File tab, Open button.
2. Click desired folder.
3. Click Organize button, *Rename*.
4. Type new name.
5. Press Enter.

OR

1. Click File tab, Open button.
2. Right-click folder name.
3. Click *Rename*.
4. Type new name.
5. Press Enter.

Renaming a Folder

As you organize your files and folders, you may decide to rename a folder. Rename a folder using the Organize button in the Open dialog box or using a shortcut menu. To rename a folder using the Organize button, display the Open dialog box, click in the Content pane the folder you want to rename, click the Organize button located on the toolbar, and then click *Rename* at the drop-down list. This selects the folder name and inserts a border around the name. Type the new name for the folder and then press Enter. To rename a folder using a shortcut menu, display the Open dialog box, right-click the folder name in the Content pane, and then click *Rename* at the shortcut menu. Type a new name for the folder and then press Enter.

A tip to remember when you are organizing files and folders is to be sure that your system is set up to display all of the files in a particular folder and not just the Excel files, for example. You can display all files in a folder by clicking the button to the right of the *File name* text box and then clicking *All Files (*.*)* at the drop-down list.

Project 1b **Renaming a Folder** Part 2 of 8

1. Display the Open dialog box.
2. Right-click the *Payroll* folder name in the Content pane.
3. Click *Rename* at the shortcut menu.
4. Type Finances and then press Enter.

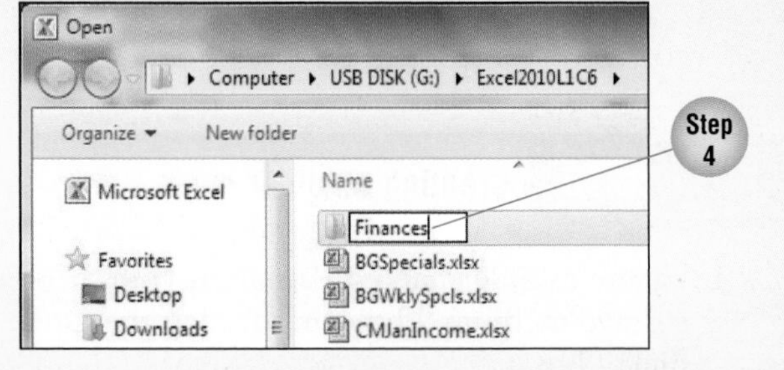

Selecting Workbooks

You can complete workbook management tasks on one workbook or selected workbooks. To select one workbook, display the Open dialog box and then click the desired workbook. To select several adjacent workbooks (workbooks that display next to each other), click the first workbook, hold down the Shift key, and then click the last workbook. To select workbooks that are not adjacent, click the first workbook, hold down the Ctrl key, click any other desired workbooks, and then release the Ctrl key.

Deleting Workbooks and Folders

At some point, you may want to delete certain workbooks from your storage medium or any other drive or folder in which you may be working. To delete a workbook, display the Open or Save As dialog box, click the workbook in the Content pane, click the Organize button, and then click *Delete* at the drop-down list. At the dialog box asking you to confirm the deletion, click Yes. To delete a workbook using a shortcut menu, display the Open dialog box, right-click the workbook name in the Content pane, and then click *Delete* at the shortcut menu. Click Yes at the confirmation dialog box.

Quick Steps

Delete Workbook/ Folder

1. Click File tab, Open button.
2. Right-click workbook or folder name.
3. Click *Delete.*
4. Click Yes.

Deleting to the Recycle Bin

Workbooks deleted from the hard drive are automatically sent to the Windows Recycle Bin. You can easily restore a deleted workbook from the Recycle Bin. To free space on the drive, empty the Recycle Bin on a periodic basis. Restoring a workbook from or emptying the contents of the Recycle Bin is completed at the Windows desktop (not in Excel). To display the Recycle Bin, minimize the Excel window and then double-click the Recycle Bin icon located on the Windows desktop. At the Recycle Bin, you can restore file(s) and empty the Recycle Bin.

Project 1c **Selecting and Deleting Workbooks** Part 3 of 8

1. At the Open dialog box, open **RPFacAccts.xlsx** (located in the Excel2010L1C6 folder).
2. Save the workbook with Save As and name it **EL1-C6-P1-RPFacAccts**.
3. Close **EL1-C6-P1-RPFacAccts.xlsx**.
4. Delete **EL1-C6-P1-RPFacAccts.xlsx** by completing the following steps:
   a. Display the Open dialog box with Excel2010L1C6 the active folder.
   b. Click ***EL1-C6-P1-RPFacAccts.xlsx*** to select it.
   c. Click the Organize button and then click *Delete* at the drop-down list.
   d. At the question asking if you are sure you want to delete the worksheet, click Yes.

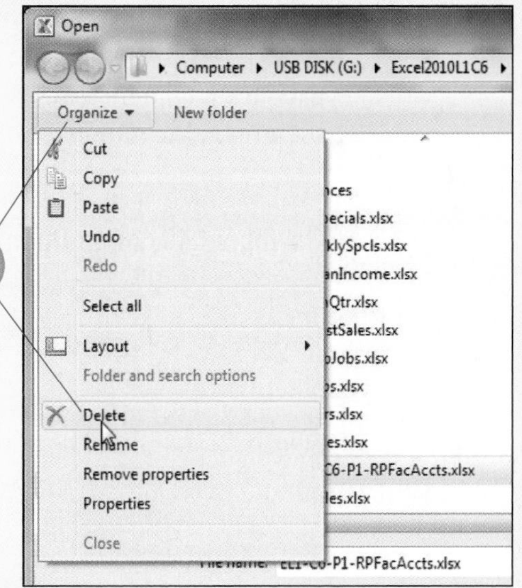

5. Delete selected workbooks by completing the following steps:
   a. Click ***DICustSales.xlsx*** in the Content pane.
   b. Hold down the Shift key and then click ***DIJobs.xlsx***.
   c. Position the mouse pointer on one of the selected workbooks and then click the right mouse button.
   d. At the shortcut menu that displays, click *Delete*.
   e. At the question asking if you are sure you want to delete the items, click Yes.
6. Close the Open dialog box.

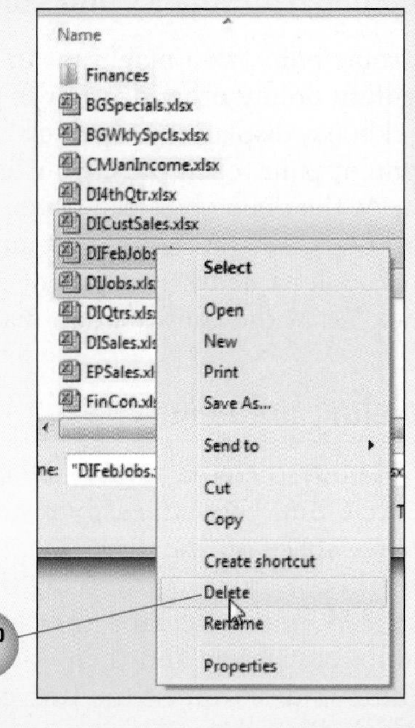

Copying Workbooks

In previous chapters, you have been opening a workbook from your storage medium and saving it with a new name in the same location. This process makes an exact copy of the workbook, leaving the original on your storage medium. You have been copying workbooks and saving the new workbook in the same folder as the original workbook. You can also copy a workbook into another folder.

Project 1d Saving a Copy of an Open Workbook

Part 4 of 8

1. Open **EPSales.xlsx**.
2. Save the workbook with Save As and name it **TotalSales**. (Make sure Excel2010L1C6 is the active folder.)
3. Save a copy of the **TotalSales.xlsx** workbook in the Finances folder you created in Project 1a (and renamed in Project 1b) by completing the following steps:
   a. With **TotalSales.xlsx** open, display the Save As dialog box.
   b. At the Save As dialog box, change to the Finances folder. To do this, double-click *Finances* at the beginning of the Content pane. (Folders are listed before workbooks.)
   c. Click the Save button located in the lower right corner of the dialog box.
4. Close **TotalSales.xlsx**.
5. Change back to the Excel2010L1C6 folder by completing the following steps:
   a. Display the Open dialog box.
   b. Click *Excel2010L1C6* that displays in the Address bar.
6. Close the Open dialog box.

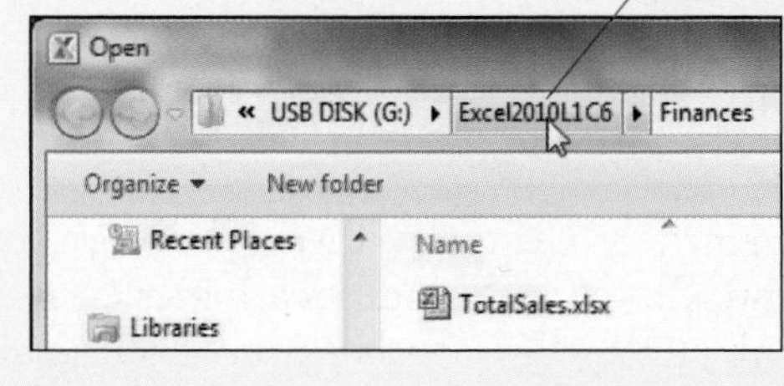

You can copy a workbook to another folder without opening the workbook first. To do this, use the *Copy* and *Paste* options from a shortcut menu at the Open (or Save As) dialog box. You can also copy a workbook or selected workbooks into the same folder. When you do this, Excel adds a hyphen followed by the word *Copy* to the end of the document name. You can copy one workbook or selected workbooks into the same folder.

Quick Steps

Copy a Workbook
1. Click File tab, Open button.
2. Right-click workbook name.
3. Click *Copy*.
4. Navigate to desired folder.
5. Right-click blank area in Content pane.
6. Click *Paste*.

Project 1e **Copying a Workbook at the Open Dialog Box** Part 5 of 8

1. Copy **CMJanIncome.xlsx** to the Finances folder. To begin, display the Open dialog box with the Excel2010L1C6 folder active.
2. Position the arrow pointer on **CMJanIncome.xlsx**, click the right mouse button, and then click *Copy* at the shortcut menu.
3. Change to the Finances folder by double-clicking *Finances* at the beginning of the Content pane.
4. Position the arrow pointer in any blank area in the Content pane, click the right mouse button, and then click *Paste* at the shortcut menu.
5. Change back to the Excel2010L1C6 folder by clicking *Excel2010L1C6* that displays in the Address bar.
6. Close the Open dialog box.

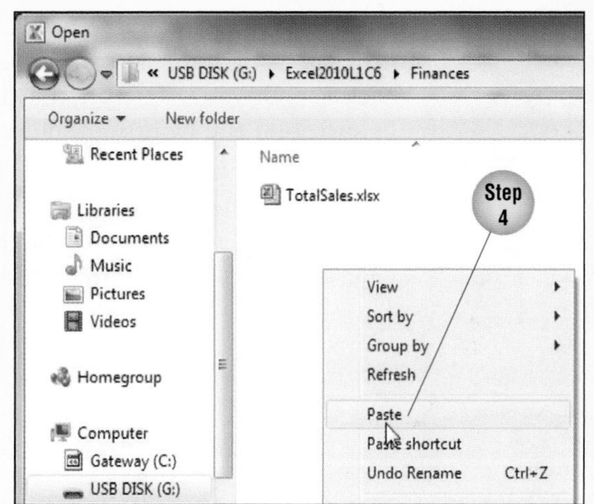

Sending Workbooks to a Different Drive or Folder

Copy workbooks to another folder or drive with the *Copy* and *Paste* options from the shortcut menu at the Open or Save As dialog box. With the *Send To* option, you can send a copy of a workbook to another drive or folder. To use this option, position the arrow pointer on the workbook you want copied, click the right mouse button, point to *Send To* (this causes a side menu to display), and then click the desired drive or folder.

Quick Steps

Move a Workbook
1. Click File tab, Open button.
2. Right-click workbook name.
3. Click *Cut*.
4. Navigate to desired folder.
5. Right-click blank area in Content pane.
6. Click *Paste*.

Cutting and Pasting a Workbook

You can remove a workbook from one folder and insert it in another folder using the *Cut* and *Paste* options from the shortcut menu at the Open dialog box. To do this, display the Open dialog box, position the arrow pointer on the workbook to be removed (cut), click the right mouse button, and then click *Cut* at the shortcut menu. Change to the desired folder or drive, position the arrow pointer in any blank area in the Content pane, click the right mouse button, and then click *Paste* at the shortcut menu.

Project 1f Cutting and Pasting a Workbook

Part 6 of 8

1. Move a workbook to a different folder. To begin, display the Open dialog box with the Excel2010L1C6 folder active.
2. Position the arrow pointer on **FinCon.xlsx**, click the right mouse button, and then click *Cut* at the shortcut menu.
3. Double-click *Finances* to make it the active folder.
4. Position the arrow pointer in any blank area in the Content pane, click the right mouse button, and then click *Paste* at the shortcut menu.
5. Click *Excel2010L1C6* that displays in the Address bar.

Quick Steps

Rename Workbook

1. Click File tab, Open button.
2. Click desired workbook.
3. Click Organize button, *Rename.*
4. Type new name.
5. Press Enter.

OR

1. Click File tab, Open button.
2. Right-click workbook name.
3. Click *Rename.*
4. Type new name.
5. Press Enter.

Renaming Workbooks

At the Open dialog box, use the *Rename* option from the Organize button drop-down list or the shortcut menu to give a workbook a different name. The *Rename* option changes the name of the workbook and keeps it in the same folder. To use *Rename*, display the Open dialog box, click once on the workbook to be renamed, click the Organize button, and then click *Rename*. This causes a thin black border to surround the workbook name and the name to be selected. Type the new name and then press Enter.

You can also rename a workbook by right-clicking the workbook name at the Open dialog box and then clicking *Rename* at the shortcut menu. Type the new name for the workbook and then press the Enter key.

Project 1g Renaming a Workbook

Part 7 of 8

1. Rename a workbook located in the Finances folder. To begin, make sure the Open dialog box displays with Excel2010L1C6 the active folder.
2. Double-click *Finances* to make it the active folder.
3. Click once on ***FinCon.xlsx*** to select it.
4. Click the Organize button on the toolbar.
5. Click *Rename* at the drop-down list.
6. Type Analysis and then press the Enter key.
7. Complete steps similar to those in Steps 3 through 6 to rename **CMJanIncome.xlsx** to *CMJanProfits*.

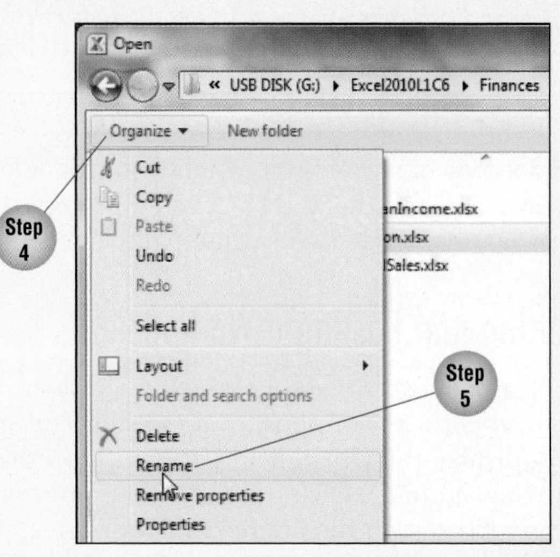

8. Click the Back button (displays as *Back to Excel2010L1C6*) at the left side of the Address bar.

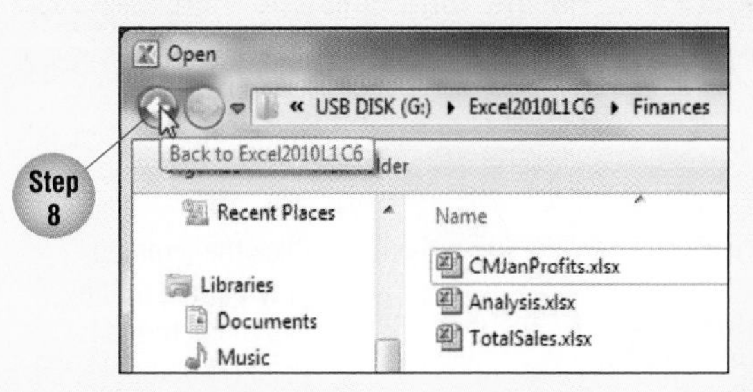

Deleting a Folder and Its Contents

As you learned earlier in this chapter, you can delete a workbook or selected workbooks. In addition to workbooks, you can delete a folder and all of its contents. Delete a folder in the same manner as you delete a workbook.

Deleting a Folder and Its Contents Part 8 of 8

1. Delete the Finances folder and its contents. To begin, make sure the Open dialog box displays with the Excel2010L1C6 folder active.
2. Right-click on the *Finances* folder.
3. Click *Delete* at the shortcut menu.
4. At the Delete Folder dialog box, click Yes.
5. Close the Open dialog box.

Copy and Move Worksheets into an Equipment Rental Workbook **3 Parts**

You will manage workbooks at the Recent tab Backstage view and then open multiple workbooks and copy and move worksheets between the workbooks.

Managing the Recent List

When you open and close workbooks, Excel keeps a list of the most recently opened workbooks. To view this list, click the File tab and then click the Recent tab. This displays the Recent tab Backstage view similar to what you see in Figure 6.2. (Your workbook names and recent places may vary from what you see in the figure.) The most recently opened workbook names display in the *Recent Workbooks* list and the most recently accessed folder names display in the *Recent Places* list. Generally, the 20 most recently opened workbook names display in the *Recent Workbooks* list. To open a workbook, scroll down the list and then click the desired workbook name.

Figure 6.2 Recent Tab Backstage View

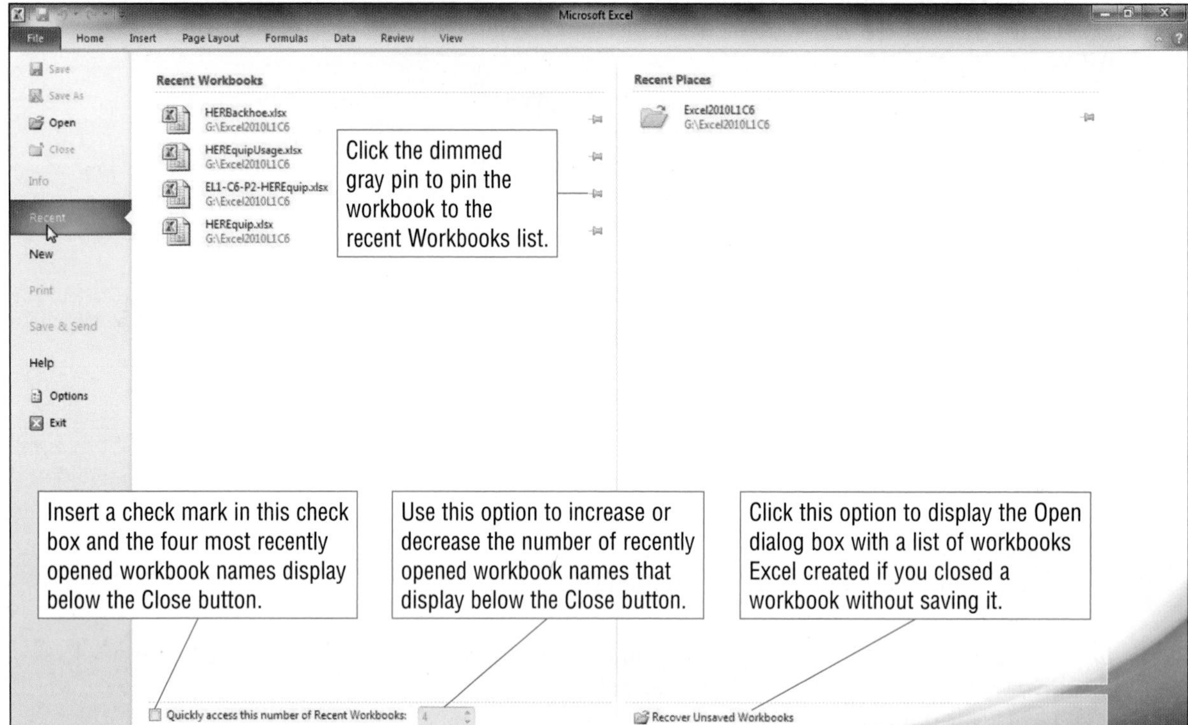

Displaying a Quick List

The Recent tab Backstage view contains the option *Quickly access this number of Recent Workbooks* located below the *Recent Workbooks* list. Insert a check mark in this option and the names of the four most recently opened workbooks display in the Backstage navigation bar (the panel at the left) below the Close button. You can increase or decrease the number of displayed workbook names by increasing or decreasing the number that displays at the right side of the *Quickly access this number of Recent Workbooks* option. To remove the list of most recently opened workbooks from the navigation bar, click the *Quickly access this number of Recent Workbooks* option to remove the check mark.

Pinning a Workbook

If you want a workbook name to remain at the top of the *Recent Workbooks* list, pin the workbook name. To do this, click the dimmed, gray pin that displays at the right side of the workbook name. This changes the dimmed, gray pin to a blue pin. The next time you display the Recent tab Backstage view, the workbook name you pinned displays at the top of the list. To unpin a workbook name, click the blue pin to change it to a dimmed, gray pin. You can also pin a workbook name to the Recent Workbooks list by right-clicking the workbook name and then clicking *Pin to list* at the shortcut menu. To unpin the workbook name, right-click the workbook name and then click *Unpin from list* at the shortcut menu.

Recovering an Unsaved Workbook

If you close a workbook without saving it, you can recover it with the *Recover Unsaved Workbooks* option located below the *Recent Places* list. Click this option and the Open dialog box displays with workbook names that Excel automatically saved. At this dialog box, double-click the desired workbook name to open the workbook.

Clearing the Recent Workbooks List

You can clear the contents (except pinned workbooks) of the *Recent Workbooks* list by right-clicking a workbook name in the list and then clicking *Clear unpinned Workbooks* at the shortcut menu. At the message asking if you are sure you want to remove the items, click the Yes button. To clear the *Recent Places* list, right-click a folder in the list and then click *Clear unpinned Places* at the shortcut menu. Click Yes at the message asking if you are sure you want to remove the items.

Project 2a Managing Workbooks at the Recent Tab Backstage View — Part 1 of 3

1. Close any open workbooks.
2. Click the File tab. (This displays the Recent tab Backstage view.)
3. Notice the workbook names that display in the *Recent Workbooks* list and the folders that display in the *Recent Places* list.
4. Open **HEREquip.xlsx** and then save the workbook with Save As and name it **EL1-C6-P2-HEREquip**.
5. Close **EL1-C6-P2-HEREquip.xlsx**.
6. Open **HEREquipUsage.xlsx** and then close it.
7. Open **HERBackhoe.xlsx** and then close it.
8. You will use the three workbooks you just opened in Project 2b, so you decide to pin them to the *Recent Workbooks* list and display the three most recently opened workbook names below the Close button. To do this, complete the following steps:
   a. Click the File tab. (This should display the Recent tab Backstage view. If it does not display, click the Recent tab.)
   b. Click the dimmed gray pin that displays at the right side of **EL1-C6-P2-HEREquip.xlsx**. (This changes the gray pin to a blue pin.)

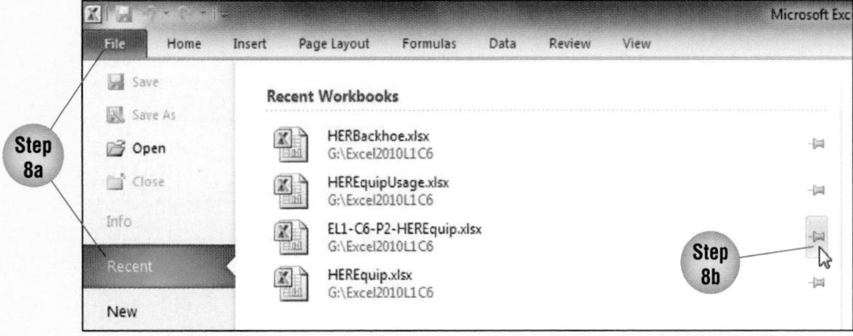

   c. Click the dimmed gray pin that displays at the right side of **HEREquipUsage.xlsx**.

d. Right-click **HERBackhoe.xlsx** and then click *Pin to list* at the shortcut menu.

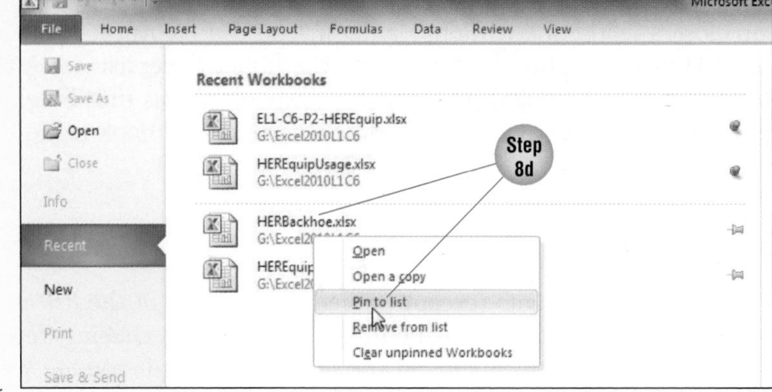

e. Click the *Quickly access this number of Recent Workbooks* option located at the bottom of the Recent tab Backstage view to insert a check mark.

f. Click the down-pointing arrow at the right side of the number *4*. (This changes *4* to *3*.)

g. Click the File tab to remove the Recent tab Backstage view.

9. Open **EL1-C6-P2-HEREquip.xlsx** by clicking the File tab (this displays the Recent tab Backstage view) and then clicking ***EL1-C6-P2-HEREquip.xlsx*** in the *Recent Workbooks* list.

Managing Worksheets

Quick Steps

Copy a Worksheet to Another Workbook

1. Right-click desired sheet tab.
2. Click *Move or Copy*.
3. Select desired destination workbook.
4. Select desired worksheet location.
5. Click *Create a copy* check box.
6. Click OK.

You can move or copy individual worksheets within the same workbook or to another existing workbook. Exercise caution when moving sheets since calculations or charts based on data on a worksheet might become inaccurate if you move the worksheet. To make a duplicate of a worksheet in the same workbook, hold down the Ctrl key and then drag the worksheet tab to the desired position.

Copying a Worksheet to Another Workbook

To copy a worksheet to another existing workbook, open both the source and the destination workbooks. Right-click the sheet tab and then click *Move or Copy* at the shortcut menu. At the Move or Copy dialog box shown in Figure 6.3, select the destination workbook name from the *To book* drop-down list, select the worksheet that you want the copied worksheet placed before in the *Before sheet* list box, click the *Create a copy* check box, and then click OK.

Figure 6.3 Move or Copy Dialog Box

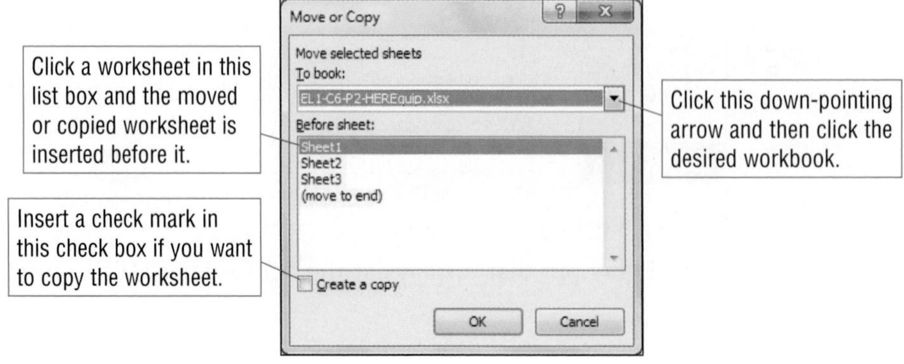

Project 2b Copying a Worksheet to Another Workbook

Part 2 of 3

1. With **EL1-C6-P2-HEREquip.xlsx** open, open **HEREquipUsage.xlsx**.
2. Copy the Front Loader worksheet by completing the following steps:
   a. With **HEREquipUsage.xlsx** the active workbook, right-click the Front Loader tab and then click *Move or Copy* at the shortcut menu.
   b. Click the down-pointing arrow next to the *To book* option box and then click ***EL1-C6-P2-HEREqip.xlsx*** at the drop-down list.
   c. Click *Sheet2* in the *Before sheet* list box.
   d. Click the *Create a copy* check box to insert a check mark.
   e. Click OK. (Excel switches to the **EL1-C6-P2-HEREquip.xlsx** workbook and inserts the copied Front Loader worksheet between Sheet1 and Sheet2.)
3. Complete steps similar to those in Step 2 to copy the Tractor worksheet to the **EL1-C6-P2-HEREquip.xlsx** workbook. (Insert the Tractor worksheet between Front Loader and Sheet2.)
4. Complete steps similar to those in Step 2 to copy the Forklift worksheet to the **EL1-C6-P2-HEREquip.xlsx** workbook. (Insert the Forklift worksheet between Tractor and Sheet2.)
5. Save **EL1-C6-P2-HEREquip.xlsx**.
6. Make **HEREquipUsage.xlsx** the active workbook and then close it.

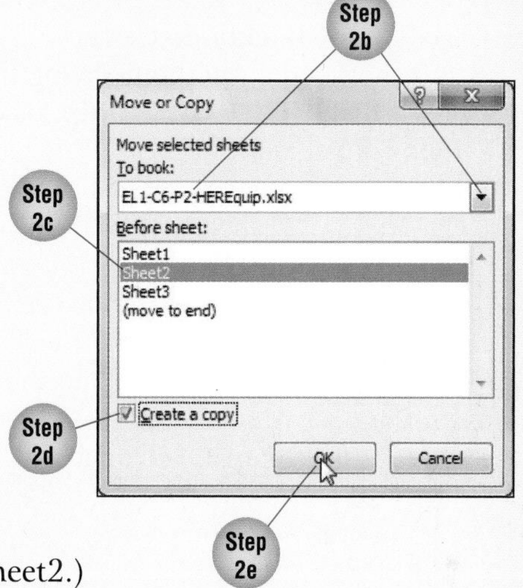

Moving a Worksheet to Another Workbook

To move a worksheet to another existing workbook, open both the source and the destination workbooks. Make active the sheet you want to move in the source workbook, right-click the sheet tab and then click *Move or Copy* at the shortcut menu. At the Move or Copy dialog box shown in Figure 6.3, select the destination workbook name from the *To book* drop-down list, select the worksheet that you want the worksheet placed before in the *Before sheet* list box, and then click OK. If you need to reposition a worksheet tab, drag the tab to the desired position.

Be careful when moving a worksheet to another workbook file. If formulas exist in the workbook that depend on the contents of the cells in the worksheet that is moved, they will no longer calculate properly.

Quick Steps

Move a Worksheet to Another Workbook
1. Right-click desired sheet tab.
2. Click *Move or Copy*.
3. Select desired destination workbook.
4. Select desired worksheet location.
5. Click OK.

Project 2c Moving a Worksheet to Another Workbook

1. With **EL1-C6-P2-HEREquip.xlsx** open, open **HERBackhoe.xlsx**.
2. Move Sheet1 from **HERBackhoe.xlsx** to **EL1-C6-P2-HEREquip.xlsx** by completing the following steps:
   a. With **HERBackhoe.xlsx** the active workbook, right-click the Sheet1 tab and then click *Move or Copy* at the shortcut menu.
   b. Click the down-pointing arrow next to the *To book* option box and then click ***EL1-C6-P2-HEREquip.xlsx*** at the drop-down list.
   c. Click *Sheet2* in the *Before sheet* list box.
   d. Click OK.

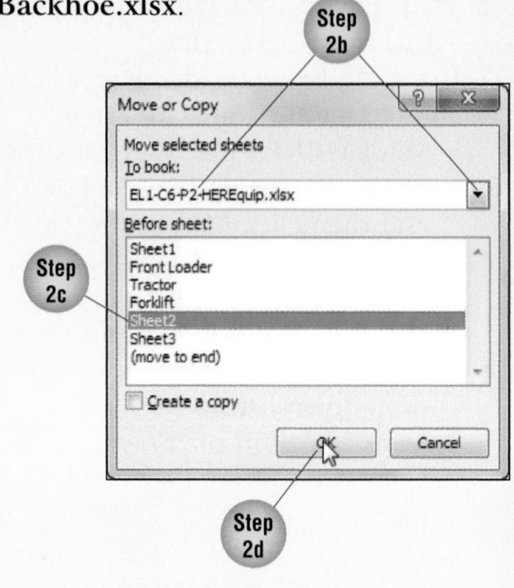

3. Make **HERBackhoe.xlsx** the active workbook and then close it without saving the changes.
4. With **EL1-C6-P2-HEREquip.xlsx** open, make the following changes:
   a. Delete the Sheet2 and Sheet3 tabs. (These worksheets are blank.)
   b. Rename Sheet1 to *Equipment Hours*.
   c. Rename Sheet1 (2) to *Backhoe*.
5. Create a range for the front loader total hours available by completing the following steps:
   a. Click the Front Loader tab.
   b. Select cells B4 through E4.
   c. Click in the Name Box.
   d. Type FrontLoaderHours.
   e. Press Enter.

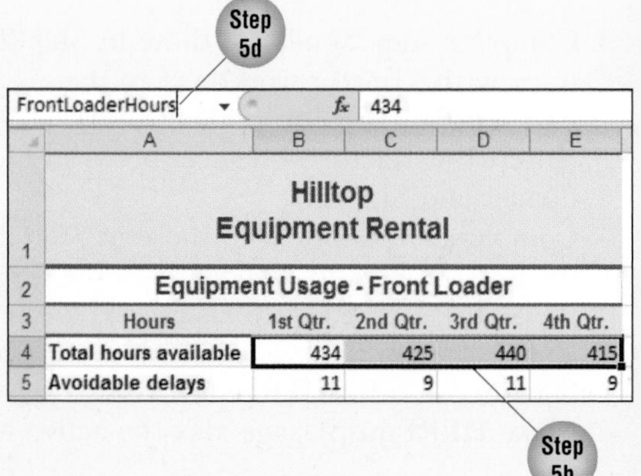

6. Complete steps similar to those in Step 5 to create the following ranges:
   a. In the Front Loader worksheet, create a range with cells B10 through E10 and name it *FrontLoaderHoursInUse*.
   b. Click the Tractor tab and then create a range with cells B4 through E4 and name it *TractorHours* and create a range with cells B10 through E10 and name it *TractorHoursInUse*.
   c. Click the Forklift tab and then create a range with cells B4 through E4 and name it *ForkliftHours* and create a range with cells B10 through E10 and name it *ForkliftHoursInUse*.
   d. Click the Backhoe tab and then create a range with cells B4 through E4 and name it *BackhoeHours* and create a range with cells B10 through E10 and name it *BackhoeHoursInUse*.
7. Click the EquipmentHours tab to make it the active worksheet and then insert a formula that inserts the total hours for the front loader by completing the following steps:
   a. Make cell C4 active.
   b. Type =SUM(Fr.
   c. When you type *Fr* a drop-down list displays with the front loader ranges. Double-click *FrontLoaderHours*.

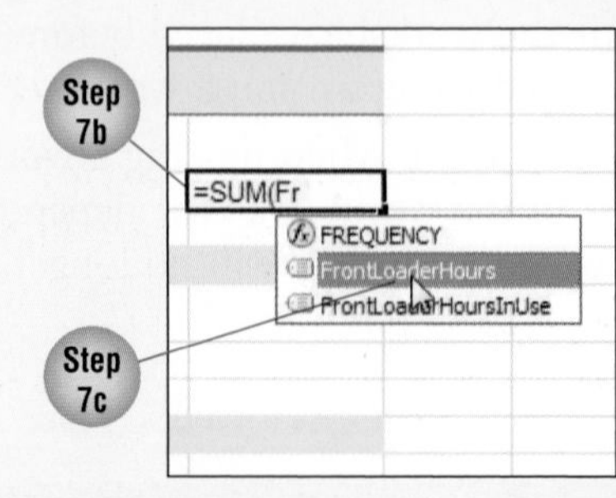

d. Type) (the closing parenthesis).

e. Press Enter.

8. Complete steps similar to those in Step 7 to insert ranges in the following cells:
   a. Make cell C5 active and then insert a formula that inserts the total in-use hours for the front loader.
   b. Make cell C8 active and then insert a formula that inserts the total hours available for the tractor.
   c. Make cell C9 active and then insert a formula that inserts the total in-use hours for the tractor.
   d. Make cell C12 active and then insert a formula that inserts the total hours available for the forklift.
   e. Make cell C13 active and then insert a formula that inserts the total in-use hours for the forklift.
   f. Make cell C16 active and then insert a formula that inserts the total hours available for the backhoe.
   g. Make cell C17 active and then insert a formula that inserts the total in-use hours for the backhoe.
9. Make the following changes to specific worksheets:
   a. Click the Front Loader tab and then change the number in cell E4 from *415* to *426* and change the number in cell C6 from *6* to *14*.
   b. Click the Forklift tab and then change the number in cells E4 from *415* to *426* and change the number in cell D8 from *4* to *12*.
10. Select all of the worksheet tabs and then create a header that prints your name at the left side of each worksheet, the page number in the middle, and the current date at the right side of each worksheet.
11. Save and then print all of the worksheets in **EL1-C6-P2-HEREquip.xlsx**.
12. Close the workbook.
13. Make the following changes to the Recent tab Backstage view.
    a. Click the File tab.
    b. Change the number to the right of *Quickly access this number of Recent Workbooks* from *3* to *4*.
    c. Click the *Quickly access this number of Recent Workbooks* option to remove the check mark.
    d. Unpin the **EL1-C6-P2-HEREquip.xlsx** workbook name from the *Recent Workbooks* list by clicking the blue pin that displays at the right side of **EL1-C6-P2-HEREquip.xlsx**. (This changes the blue pin to a dimmed, gray pin and moves the file down the list.)
    e. Unpin the **HERBackhoe.xlsx** workbook and the **HEREquip.xlsx** workbook.
    f. Click the File tab to remove the Recent tab Backstage view.

Project 3 Create and Apply Styles to a Payroll Workbook 5 Parts

You will open a payroll workbook, define and apply styles, and then modify the styles. You will also copy the styles to another workbook and then apply the styles in the new workbook.

Formatting with Cell Styles

Quick Steps

Apply Cell Style
1. Select desired cell(s).
2. Click Cell Styles button.
3. Click desired style option.

Cell Styles

In some worksheets, you may want to apply formatting to highlight or accentuate certain cells. You can apply formatting to a cell or selected cells with a cell style. A ***style*** is a predefined set of formatting attributes such as font, font size, alignment, borders, shading, and so forth. You can use one of the predesigned styles from the Cell Styles drop-down gallery or create your own style.

Applying a Style

To apply a style, select the desired cell(s), click the Cell Styles button in the Styles group in the Home tab and then click the desired option at the drop-down gallery shown in Figure 6.4. If you hover your mouse pointer over a style option in the drop-down gallery, the cell or selected cells display with the formatting applied.

Figure 6.4 Cell Styles Drop-Down Gallery

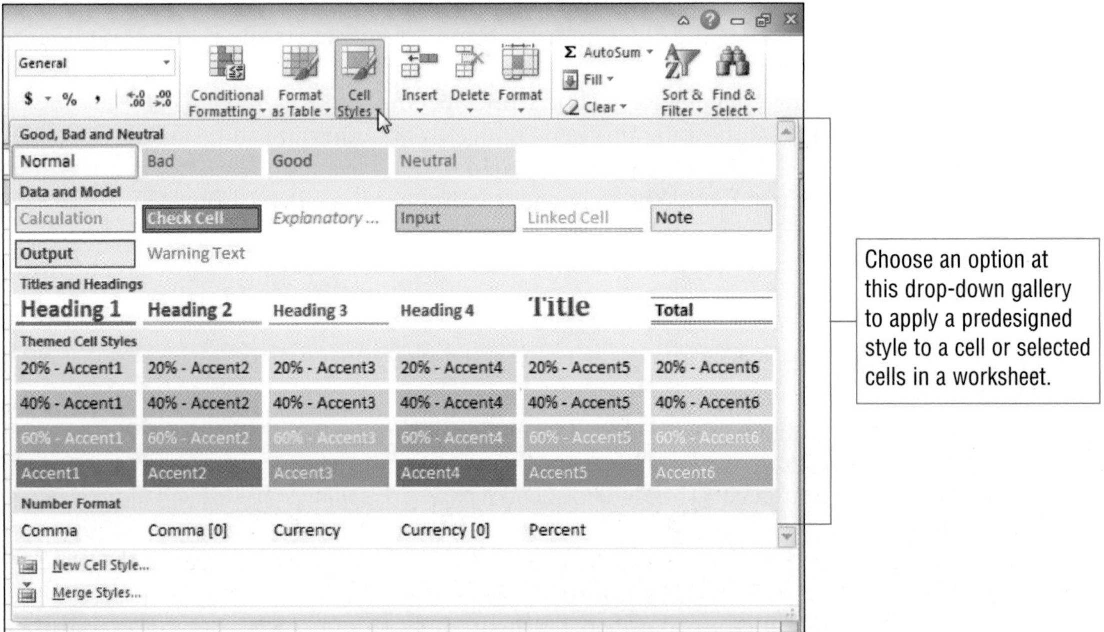

Project 3a **Formatting with Cell Styles** Part 1 of 5

1. Open **OEPayroll.xlsx** and then save the workbook with Save As and name it **EL1-C6-P3-OEPayroll**.
2. With Sheet1 the active worksheet, insert the necessary formulas to calculate gross pay, withholding tax amount, Social Security tax amount, and net pay. ***Hint: Refer to Project 5c in Chapter 2 for assistance***. Apply the Accounting Number Format style to cells D4 through G4.
3. Make Sheet2 active and then insert a formula that calculates the amount due. Apply the Accounting Number Format style to cell F4.

4. Make Sheet3 active and then insert a formula in the *Due Date* column that calculates the purchase date plus the number of days in the *Terms* column. ***Hint: Refer to Project 3c in Chapter 2 for assistance.***
5. Apply cell styles to cells by completing the following steps:
   a. Make Sheet1 active and then select cells A11 and A12.
   b. Click the Cell Styles button in the Styles group in the Home tab.
   c. At the drop-down gallery, hover your mouse over style options to see how the style formatting affects the selected cells.
   d. Click the *Check Cell* option in the *Data and Model* section.
6. Select cells B11 and B12, click the Cell Styles button, and then click the *Output* option in the *Data and Model* section (first option from the left in the second row in the *Data and Model* section).

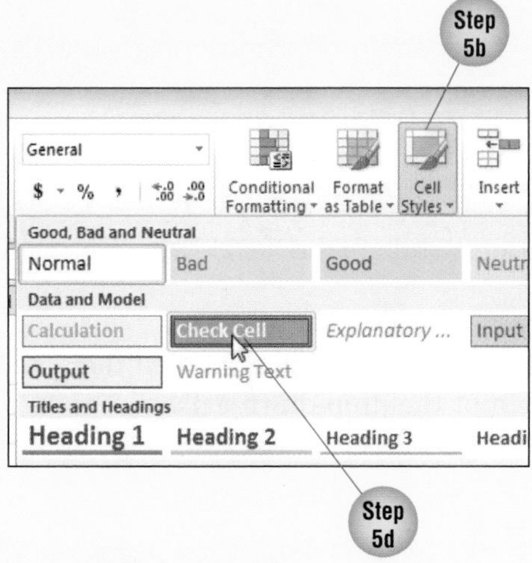

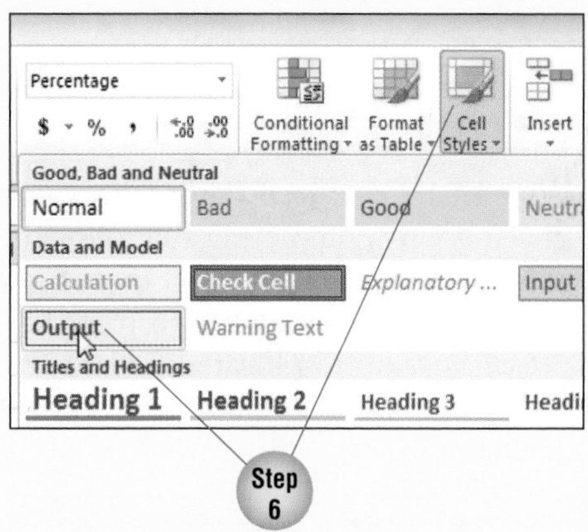

7. Save **EL1-C6-P3-OEPayroll.xlsx**.

Defining a Cell Style

You can apply styles from the Cell Styles drop-down gallery or you can create your own style. Using a style to apply formatting has several advantages. A style helps to ensure consistent formatting from one worksheet to another. Once you define all attributes for a particular style, you do not have to redefine them again. If you need to change the formatting, change the style and all cells formatted with that style automatically reflect the change.

Two basic methods are available for defining your own cell style. You can define a style with formats already applied to a cell or you can display the Style dialog box, click the Format button, and then choose formatting options at the Format Cells dialog box. Styles you create are only available in the workbook in which they are created. To define a style with existing formatting, select the cell or cells containing the desired formatting, click the Cell Styles button in the Styles group in the Home tab, and then click the *New Cell Style* option located toward the bottom of the drop-down gallery. At the Style dialog box, shown in Figure 6.5, type a name for the new style in the *Style name* text box and then click OK to close the dialog box. The styles you create display at the top of the drop-down gallery in the *Custom* section when you click the Cell Styles button.

Quick Steps

Define a Cell Style with Existing Formatting

1. Select cell containing formatting.
2. Click Cell Styles button.
3. Click *New Cell Style*.
4. Type name for new style.
5. Click OK.

Cell styles are based on the workbook theme.

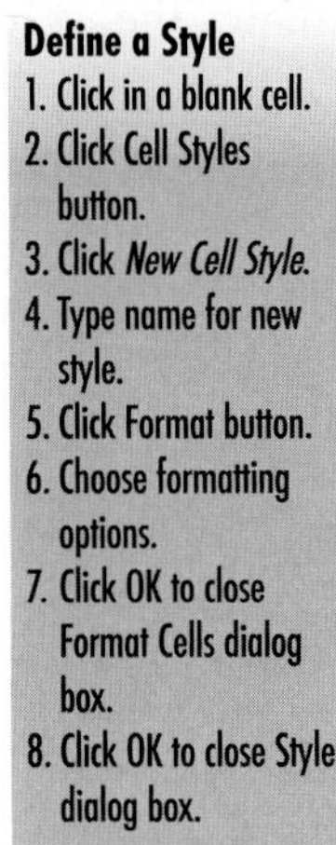

Quick Steps

Define a Style
1. Click in a blank cell.
2. Click Cell Styles button.
3. Click *New Cell Style*.
4. Type name for new style.
5. Click Format button.
6. Choose formatting options.
7. Click OK to close Format Cells dialog box.
8. Click OK to close Style dialog box.

Figure 6.5 Style Dialog Box

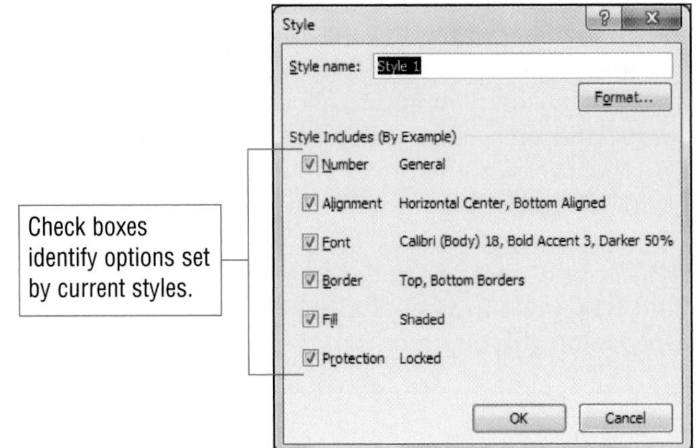

Project 3b Defining and Applying a Style

Part 2 of 5

1. With **EL1-C6-P3-OEPayroll.xlsx** open, define a style named *C06Title* with the formatting in cell A1 by completing the following steps:
   a. Make Sheet 1 active and then make cell A1 active.
   b. Click the Cell Styles button in the Styles group in the Home tab and then click the *New Cell Style* option located toward the bottom of the drop-down gallery.
   c. At the Style dialog box, type C06Title in the *Style name* text box.
   d. Click OK.

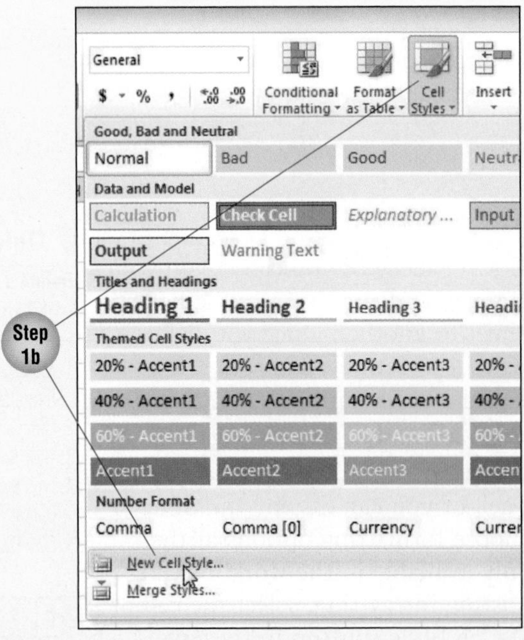

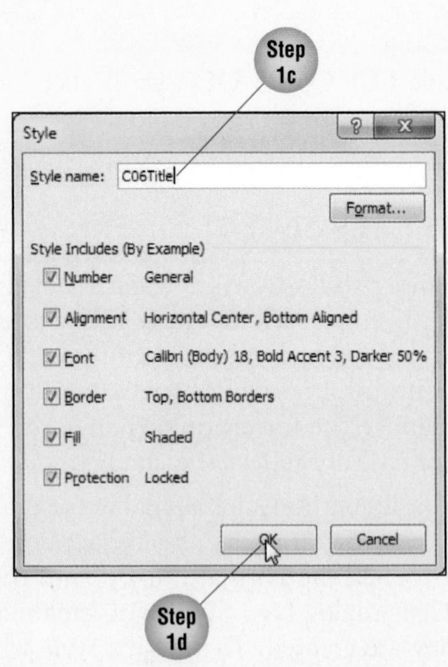

2. Even though cell A1 is already formatted, the style has not been applied to it. Later, you will modify the style and the style must be applied to the cell for the change to affect it. Apply the C06Title style to cell A1 by completing the following steps:
   a. Make sure cell A1 is the active cell.

b. Click the Cell Styles button in the Styles group in the Home tab.
c. Click the *C06Title* style in the *Custom* section located toward the top of the drop-down gallery.

3. Apply the C06Title style to other cells by completing the following steps:
   a. Click the Sheet2 tab.
   b. Make cell A1 active.
   c. Click the Cell Styles button in the Styles group and then click the *C06Title* style at the drop-down gallery. (Notice that the style did not apply the row height formatting. The style applies only cell formatting.)
   d. Click the Sheet3 tab.
   e. Make cell A1 active.
   f. Click the Cell Styles button and then click the *C06Title* style at the drop-down gallery.
   g. Click the Sheet1 tab.
4. Save **EL1-C6-P3-OEPayroll.xlsx**.

In addition to defining a style based on cell formatting, you can also define a new style without first applying the formatting. To do this, you would display the Style dialog box, type a name for the new style, and then click the Format button. At the Format Cells dialog box, apply any desired formatting and then click OK to close the dialog box. At the Style dialog box, remove the check mark from any formatting that you do not want included in the style and then click OK to close the Style dialog box.

Project 3c Defining a Style without First Applying Formatting

Part 3 of 5

1. With **EL1-C6-P3-OEPayroll.xlsx** open, define a new style named *C06Subtitle* without first applying the formatting by completing the following steps:
   a. With Sheet1 active, click in any empty cell.
   b. Click the Cell Styles button in the Styles group and then click *New Cell Style* at the drop-down gallery.
   c. At the Style dialog box, type C06Subtitle in the *Style name* text box.
   d. Click the Format button in the Style dialog box.
   e. At the Format Cells dialog box, click the Font tab.
   f. At the Format Cells dialog box with the Font tab selected, change the font to Candara, the font style to bold, the size to 12, and the color to white.

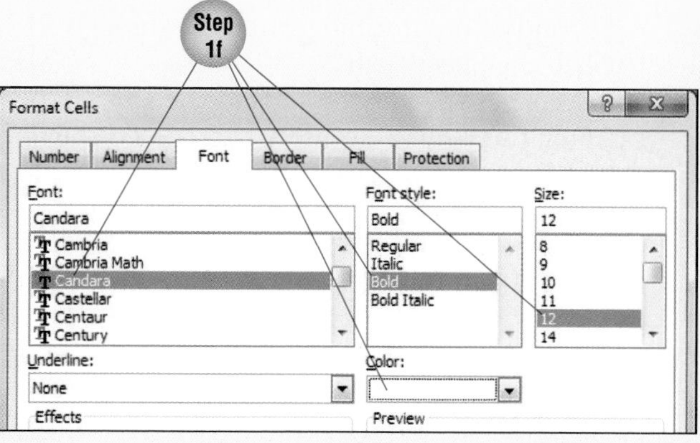

g. Click the Fill tab.
h. Click the bottom color in the green column as shown at the right.
i. Click the Alignment tab.
j. Change the Horizontal alignment to Center.
k. Click OK to close the Format Cells dialog box.
l. Click OK to close the Style dialog box.

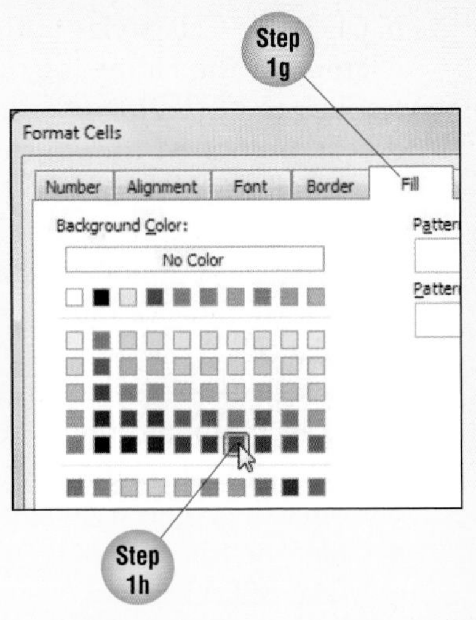

2. Apply the C06Subtitle style by completing the following steps:
   a. Make cell A2 active.
   b. Click the Cell Styles button and then click the C06Subtitle style located toward the top of the drop-down gallery in the *Custom* section.
   c. Click the Sheet2 tab.
   d. Make cell A2 active.
   e. Click the Cell Styles button and then click the C06Subtitle style.
   f. Click the Sheet3 tab.
   g. Make cell A2 active.
   h. Click the Cell Styles button and then click the C06Subtitle style.
   i. Click the Sheet1 tab.
3. Apply the following predesigned cell styles:
   a. Select cells A3 through G3.
   b. Click the Cell Styles button and then click the Heading 3 style at the drop-down gallery.
   c. Select cells A5 through G5.
   d. Click the Cell Styles button and then click the 20% - Accent3 style.
   e. Apply the 20% - Accent3 style to cells A7 through G7 and cells A9 through G9.
   f. Click the Sheet2 tab.
   g. Select cells A3 through F3 and then apply the Heading 3 style.
   h. Select cells A5 through F5 and then apply the 20% - Accent3 style.
   i. Apply the 20% - Accent3 style to every other row of cells (A7 through F7, A9 through F9, and so on, finishing with A17 through F17).
   j. Click the Sheet3 tab.
   k. Select cells A3 through F3 and then apply the Heading 3 style.
   l. Apply the 20% - Accent3 style to A5 through F5, A7 through F7, and A9 through F9.
4. With Sheet3 active, change the height of row 1 to 36.00 (48 pixels).
5. Make Sheet2 active and then change the height of row 1 to 36.00 (48 pixels).
6. Make Sheet1 active.
7. Save **EL1-C6-P3-OEPayroll.xlsx** and then print only the first worksheet.

Modifying a Style

One of the advantages to formatting with a style is that you can modify the formatting of the style and all cells formatted with that style automatically reflect the change. You can modify a style you create or one of the predesigned styles provided by Word. When you modify a predesigned style, only the style in the current workbook is affected. If you open a blank workbook, the cell styles available are the default styles.

To modify a style, click the Cell Styles button in the Styles group in the Home tab and then right-click the desired style at the drop-down gallery. At the shortcut menu that displays, click *Modify*. At the Style dialog box, click the Format button. Make the desired formatting changes at the Format Cells dialog box and then click OK. Click OK to close the Style dialog box and any cells formatted with the specific style are automatically updated.

Quick Steps

Modify a Style
1. Click Cell Styles button.
2. Right-click desired style at drop-down gallery.
3. Click *Modify*.
4. Click Format button.
5. Make desired formatting changes.
6. Click OK to close Format Cells dialog box.
7. Click OK to close Style dialog box.

Project 3d **Modifying Styles** Part 4 of 5

1. With **EL1-C6-P3-OEPayroll.xlsx** open, modify the C06Title style by completing the following steps:
   a. Click in any empty cell.
   b. Click the Cell Styles button in the Styles group.
   c. At the drop-down gallery, right-click on the C06Title style located toward the top of the gallery in the *Custom* section, and then click *Modify*.
   d. At the Style dialog box, click the Format button.
   e. At the Format Cells dialog box, click the Font tab, and then change the font to Candara.
   f. Click the Alignment tab.
   g. Click the down-pointing arrow to the right of the *Vertical* option box, and then click *Center* at the drop-down list.
   h. Click the Fill tab.
   i. Click the light turquoise fill color as shown at the right.
   j. Click OK to close the Format Cells dialog box.
   k. Click OK to close the Style dialog box.

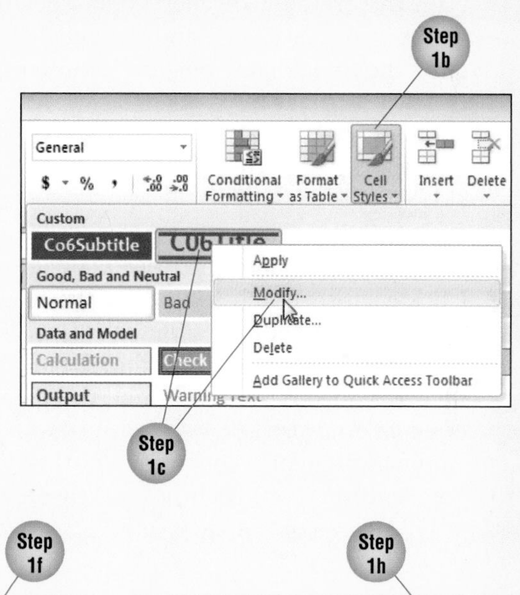

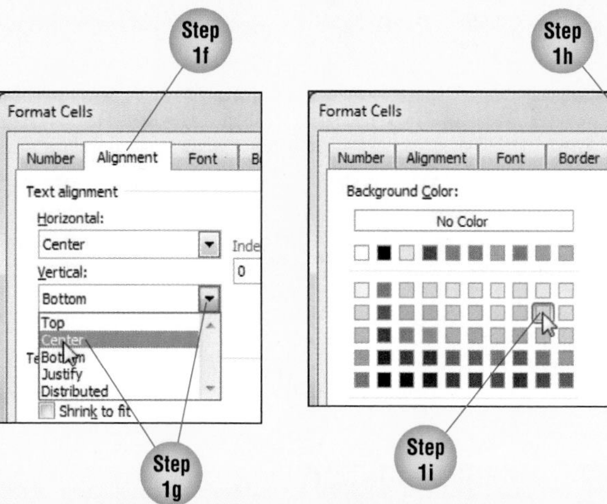

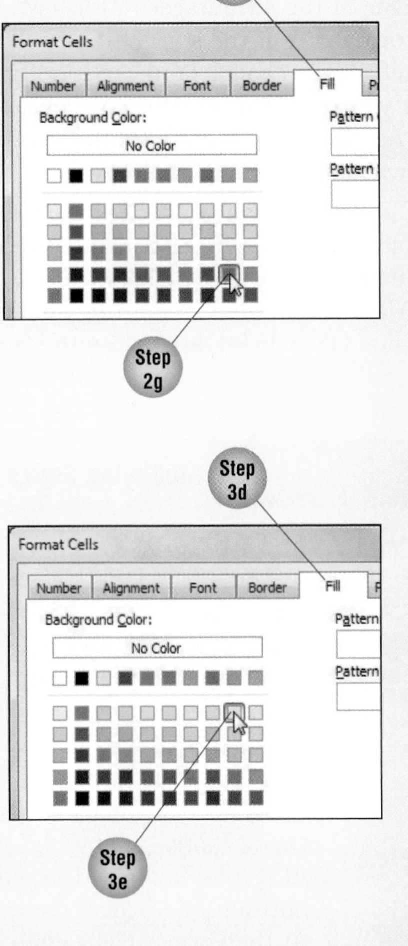

2. Modify the C06Subtitle style by completing the following steps:
   a. Click in any empty cell.
   b. Click the Cell Styles button in the Styles group.
   c. At the drop-down gallery, right-click on the C06Subtitle style located toward the top of the gallery in the *Custom* section, and then click *Modify*.
   d. At the Style dialog box, click the Format button.
   e. At the Format Cells dialog box, click the Font tab, and then change the font to Calibri.
   f. Click the Fill tab.
   g. Click the dark turquoise fill color as shown at the right.
   h. Click OK to close the Format Cells dialog box.
   i. Click OK to close the Style dialog box.
3. Modify the predefined 20% - Accent3 style by completing the following steps:
   a. Click the Cell Styles button in the Styles group.
   b. At the drop-down gallery, right-click on the 20% - Accent3 style and then click *Modify*.
   c. At the Style dialog box, click the Format button.
   d. At the Format Cells dialog box, make sure the Fill tab is active.
   e. Click the light turquoise fill color as shown at the right.
   f. Click OK to close the Format Cells dialog box.
   g. Click OK to close the Style dialog box.
4. Click each sheet tab and notice the formatting changes made by the modified styles.
5. Change the name of Sheet1 to *Weekly Payroll*, the name of Sheet2 to *Invoices*, and the name of Sheet3 to *Overdue Accounts*.
6. Apply a different color to each of the three worksheet tabs.
7. Save and then print all the worksheets in **EL1-C6-P3-OEPayroll.xlsx**.

Quick Steps

Copy Styles to Another Workbook
1. Open workbook containing desired styles.
2. Open workbook you want to modify.
3. Click Cell Styles button.
4. Click *Merge Styles* option.
5. Double-click name of workbook that contains styles you want to copy.

Copying Styles to Another Workbook

Styles you define are saved with the workbook in which they are created. You can, however, copy styles from one workbook to another. To do this, open the workbook containing the styles you want to copy and open the workbook into which you want to copy the styles. Click the Cell Styles button in the Styles group in the Home tab and then click the *Merge Styles* option located at the bottom of the drop-down gallery. At the Merge Styles dialog box shown in Figure 6.6, double-click the name of the workbook that contains the styles you want to copy and then click OK.

Removing a Style

If you apply a style to text and then decide you do not want the formatting applied, return the formatting to Normal, which is the default formatting. To do this, select the cells formatted with the style you want to remove, click the Cell Styles button, and then click *Normal* at the drop-down gallery.

Figure 6.6 Merge Styles Dialog Box

Quick Steps

Remove a Style
1. Select cells formatted with style you want removed.
2. Click Cell Styles button.
3. Click *Normal* at drop-down gallery.

Delete a Style
1. Click Cell Styles button.
2. Right-click desired style to delete.
3. Click *Delete* at shortcut menu.

You cannot delete the Normal style.

The Undo command will not reverse the effects of the Merge Styles dialog box.

Deleting a Style

To delete a style, click the Cell Styles button in the Styles group in the Home tab. At the drop-down gallery that displays, right-click the style you want to delete and then click *Delete* at the shortcut menu. Formatting applied by the deleted style is removed from cells in the workbook.

Project 3e Copying Styles

Part 5 of 5

1. With **EL1-C6-P3-OEPayroll.xlsx** open, open **OEPlans.xlsx**.
2. Save the workbook with Save As and name it **EL1-C6-P3-OEPlans**.
3. Copy the styles in **EL1-C6-P3-Payroll.xlsx** into **EL1-C6-P3-OEPlans.xlsx** by completing the following steps:
   a. Click the Cell Styles button in the Styles group in the Home tab.
   b. Click the *Merge Styles* option located toward the bottom of the drop-down gallery.
   c. At the Merge Styles dialog box, double-click ***EL1-C6-P3-OEPayroll.xlsx*** in the *Merge styles from* list box.
   d. At the message that displays asking if you want to merge styles that have the same names, click Yes.
4. Apply the C06Title style to cell A1 and the C06Subtitle style to cell A2.
5. Increase the height of row 1 to 36.00 (48 pixels).
6. Insert the required formulas in the workbook. ***Hint: Refer to Project 3a in Chapter 2 for assistance.***
7. If neccessary, adjust column widths so all text is visible in cells.
8. Save, print, and then close **EL1-C6-P3-OEPlans.xlsx**.
9. Close **EL1-C6-P3-OEPayroll.xlsx**.

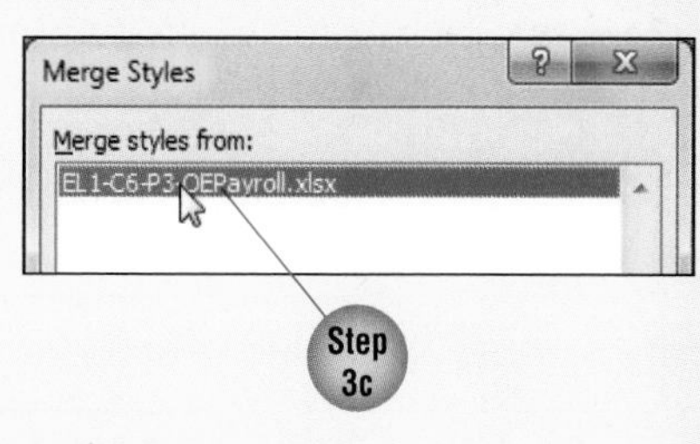

Project 4 Insert, Modify, and Remove Hyperlinks

3 Parts

You will open a facilities account workbook and then insert hyperlinks to a website, to cells in other worksheets in the workbook, and to another workbook. You will modify and edit hyperlinks and then remove a hyperlink from the workbook.

Inserting Hyperlinks

Quick Steps

Insert Hyperlink
1. Click Insert tab.
2. Click Hyperlink button.
3. Make desired changes at Insert Hyperlink dialog box.
4. Click OK.

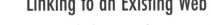

A hyperlink in a workbook can serve a number of purposes: Click it to navigate to a web page on the Internet or a specific location in the workbook, to display a different workbook, to open a file in a different program, to create a new document, or to link to an email address. You can create a customized hyperlink by clicking the desired cell in a workbook, clicking the Insert tab, and then clicking the Hyperlink button in the Links group. This displays the Insert Hyperlink dialog box, shown in Figure 6.7. At this dialog box, identify what you want to link to and the location of the link. Click the ScreenTip button to customize the hyperlink ScreenTip.

Linking to an Existing Web Page or File

Hyperlink

You can link to a web page on the Internet by typing a web address or with the Existing File or Web Page button in the *Link to* group. To link to an existing web page, type the address of the web page such as *www.emcp.com*. By default, the automatic formatting of hyperlinks is turned on and the web address is formatted as a hyperlink (text is underlined and the color changes to blue). You can turn off the automatic formatting of hyperlinks at the AutoCorrect dialog box. Display this dialog box by clicking the File tab, clicking the Options button, and then clicking *Proofing* in the left panel of the Excel Options dialog box. Click the AutoCorrect Options button to display the AutoCorrect dialog box. At this dialog

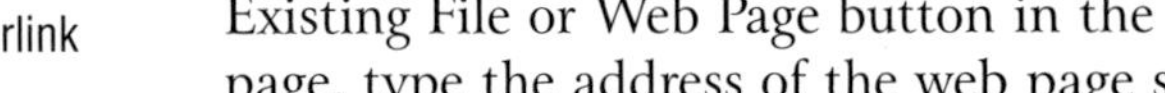

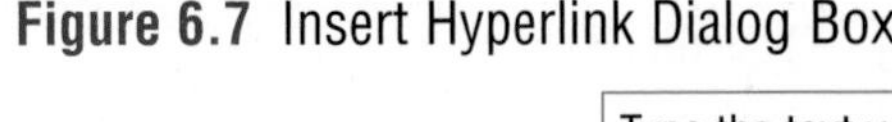

Figure 6.7 Insert Hyperlink Dialog Box

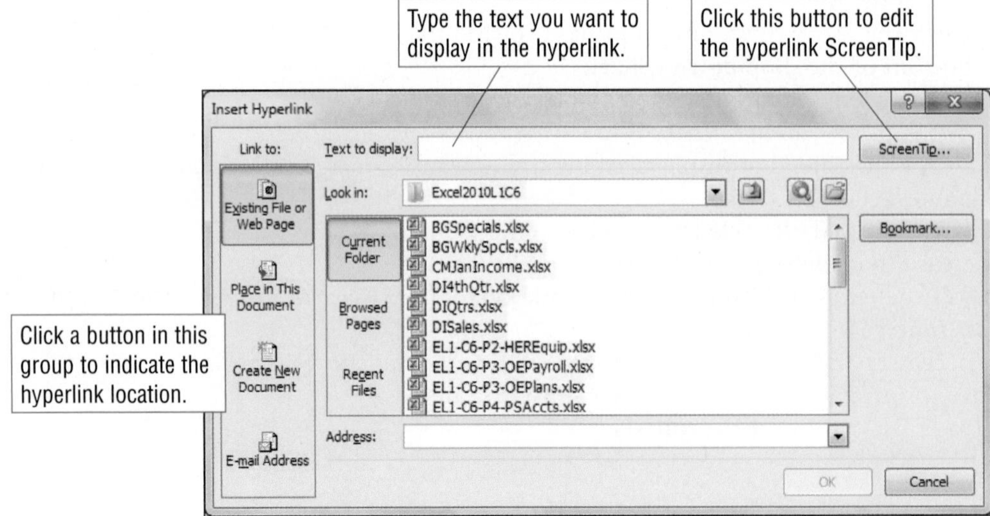

box, click the AutoFormat As You Type tab and then remove the check mark from the *Internet and network paths with hyperlinks* check box. To link to a web page at the Insert Hyperlink dialog box, display the dialog box, click the Existing File or Web Page button in the *Link to* group and then type the web address in the *Address* text box.

In some situations, you may want to provide information to your readers from a variety of sources. You may want to provide additional information in an Excel workbook, a Word document, or a PowerPoint presentation. To link an Excel workbook to a workbook or a file in another application, display the Insert Hyperlink dialog box and then click the Existing File or Web Page button in the *Link to* group. Use the *Look in* option to navigate to the folder containing the desired file and then click the file. Make other changes in the Insert Hyperlink dialog box as needed and then click OK.

Navigating Using Hyperlinks

Navigate to a hyperlink by clicking the hyperlink in the worksheet. Hover the mouse over the hyperlink and a ScreenTip displays with the hyperlink. If you want specific information to display in the ScreenTip, click the ScreenTip button in the Insert Hyperlink dialog box, type the desired text in the Set Hyperlink ScreenTip dialog box, and then click OK.

Project 4a **Linking to a Website and Another Workbook** Part 1 of 3

1. Open **PSAccts.xlsx** and then save the workbook with Save As and name it **EL1-C6-P4-PSAccts**.
2. Insert a hyperlink to company information (since Pyramid Sales is a fictitious company, you will hyperlink to the publishing company website) by completing the following steps:
   a. Make cell A13 active.
   b. Click the Insert tab and then click the Hyperlink button in the Links group.
   c. At the Insert Hyperlink dialog box, if necessary, click the Existing File or Web Page button in the *Link to* group.
   d. Type www.emcp.com in the *Address* text box.
   e. Select the text that displays in the *Text to display* text box and then type Company information.
   f. Click the ScreenTip button located in the upper right corner of the dialog box.

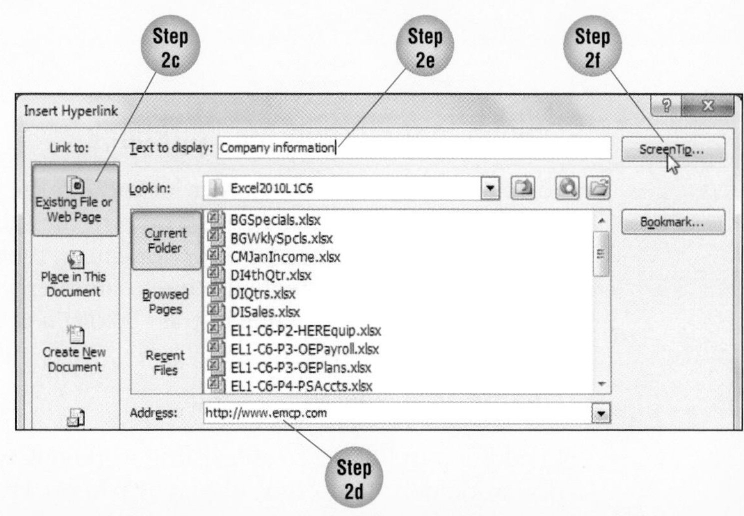

g. At the Set Hyperlink ScreenTip dialog box, type View the company website. and then click OK.
h. Click OK to close the Insert Hyperlink dialog box.
3. Navigate to the company website (in this case, the publishing company website) by clicking the Company information hyperlink in cell A13.
4. Close the Web browser.
5. Create a link to another workbook by completing the following steps:
   a. Make cell A11 active, type Semiannual sales, and then press the Enter key.
   b. Make cell A11 active and then click the Hyperlink button in the Links group in the Insert tab.
   c. At the Insert Hyperlink dialog box, make sure the Existing File or Web Page button is selected.
   d. If necessary, click the down-pointing arrow at the right side of the *Look in* option and then navigate to the Excel2010L1C6 folder on your storage medium.
   e. Double-click ***PSSalesAnalysis.xlsx***.
6. Click the Semiannual sales hyperlink to open the **PSSalesAnalysis.xlsx** workbook.
7. Look at the information in the workbook and then close the workbook.
8. Save **EL1-C6-P4-PSAccts.xlsx**.

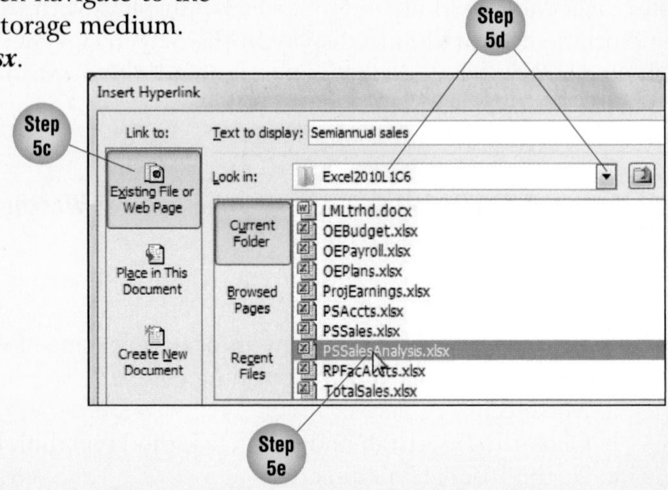

Linking to a Place in the Workbook

To create a hyperlink to another location in the workbook, click the Place in This Document button in the *Link to* group in the Edit Hyperlink dialog box. If you are linking to a cell within the same worksheet, type the cell name in the *Type the cell reference* text box. If you are linking to another worksheet in the workbook, click the desired worksheet name in the *Or select a place in this document* list box.

Linking to a New Workbook

In addition to linking to an existing workbook, you can create a hyperlink to a new workbook. To do this, display the Insert Hyperlink dialog box and then click the Create New Document button in the *Link to* group. Type a name for the new workbook in the *Name of new document* text box and then specify if you want to edit the workbook now or later.

Linking Using a Graphic

You can use a graphic such as a clip art image, picture, or text box to hyperlink to a file or website. To hyperlink with a graphic, select the graphic, click the Insert tab, and then click the Hyperlink button. You can also right-click the graphic and then click *Hyperlink* at the shortcut menu. At the Insert Hyperlink dialog box, specify where you want to link to and text you want to display in the hyperlink.

Linking to an Email Address

You can insert a hyperlink to an email address at the Insert Hyperlink dialog box. To do this, click the E-Mail Address button in the *Link to* group, type the desired address in the *E-mail address* text box, and type a subject for the email in the *Subject* text box. Click in the *Text to display* text box and then type the text you want to display in the document. To use this feature, the email address you use must be set up in Outlook 2010.

Project 4b **Linking to Place in a Workbook, to Another Workbook, and Using a Graphic** Part 2 of 3

1. With **EL1-C6-P4-PSAccts.xlsx** open, create a link from the checks amount in cell B6 to the check amount in cell G20 in the January worksheet by completing the following steps:
   a. Make cell B6 active.
   b. Click the Insert tab and then click the Hyperlink button in the Links group.
   c. At the Insert Hyperlink dialog box, click the Place in This Document button in the *Link to* group.
   d. Select the text in the *Type the cell reference* text box and then type G20.
   e. Click *January* in the *Or select a place in this document* list box.
   f. Click OK to close the Insert Hyperlink dialog box.

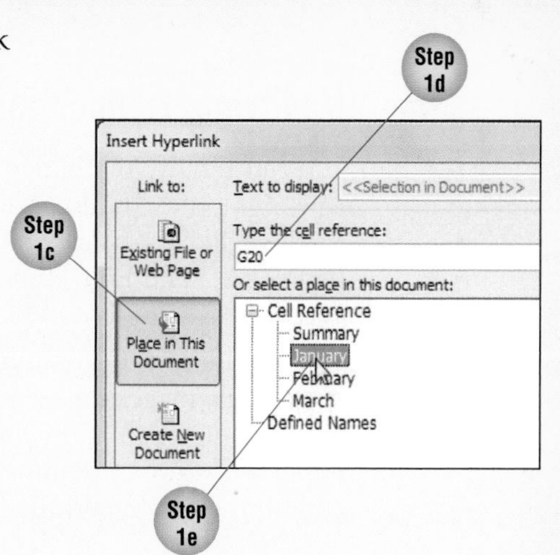

2. Make cell C6 active and then complete steps similar to those in Steps 1b through 1f except click *February* in the *Or select a place in this document* list box.
3. Make cell D6 active and then complete steps similar to those in Steps 1b through 1f except click *March* in the *Or select a place in this document* list box.
4. Click the hyperlinked amount in cell B6. (This makes cell G20 active in the January worksheet.)
5. Click the Summary worksheet tab.
6. Click the hyperlinked amount in cell C6. (This makes cell G20 active in the February worksheet.)
7. Click the Summary worksheet tab.
8. Click the hyperlinked amount in cell D6. (This makes cell G20 active in the March worksheet.)
9. Click the Summary worksheet tab.

10. Use the first pyramid graphic image in cell A1 to create a link to the company web page by completing the following steps:
    a. Right-click the first pyramid graphic image in cell A1 and then click *Hyperlink* at the shortcut menu.
    b. At the Insert Hyperlink dialog box, if necessary, click the Existing File or Web Page button in the *Link to* group.
    c. Type www.emcp.com in the *Address* text box.
    d. Click the ScreenTip button located in the upper right corner of the dialog box.
    e. At the Set Hyperlink ScreenTip dialog box, type View the company website. and then click OK.
    f. Click OK to close the Insert Hyperlink dialog box.

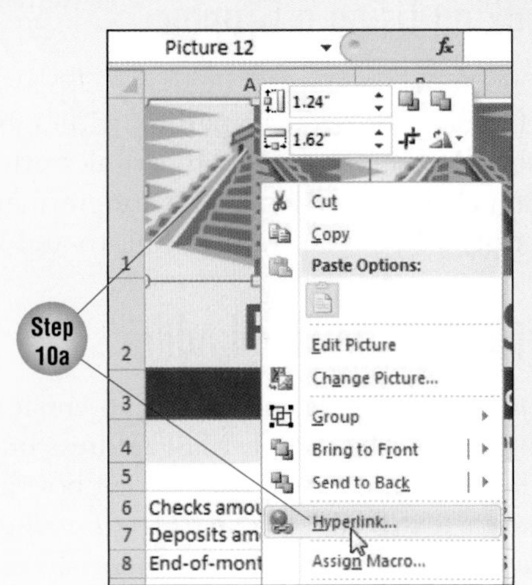

11. Make cell A5 active.
12. Navigate to the company website (the publishing company website) by clicking the first pyramid graphic image.
13. Close the Web browser.
14. Save **EL1-C6-P4-PSAccts.xlsx**.

Modifying, Editing, and Removing a Hyperlink

You can modify or change hyperlink text or the hyperlink destination. To do this, right-click the hyperlink and then click *Edit Hyperlink* at the shortcut menu. At the Edit Hyperlink dialog box, make any desired changes and then close the dialog box. The Edit Hyperlink dialog box contains the same options as the Insert Hyperlink dialog box.

In addition to modifying the hyperlink, you can edit hyperlink text in a cell. To do this, make the cell active and then make the desired editing changes. For example, you can apply a different font or font size, change the text color, and apply a text effect. Remove a hyperlink from a workbook by right-clicking the cell containing the hyperlink and then clicking *Remove Hyperlink* at the shortcut menu.

Project 4c Modifying, Editing, and Removing a Hyperlink

Part 3 of 3

1. With **EL1-C6-P4-PSAccts.xlsx** open, modify the Semiannual sales hyperlink by completing the following steps:
    a. Position the mouse pointer on the Semiannual sales hyperlink in cell A11, click the right mouse button, and then click *Edit Hyperlink* at the shortcut menu.
    b. At the Edit Hyperlink dialog box, select the text *Semiannual sales* in the *Text to display* text box and then type Customer sales analysis.

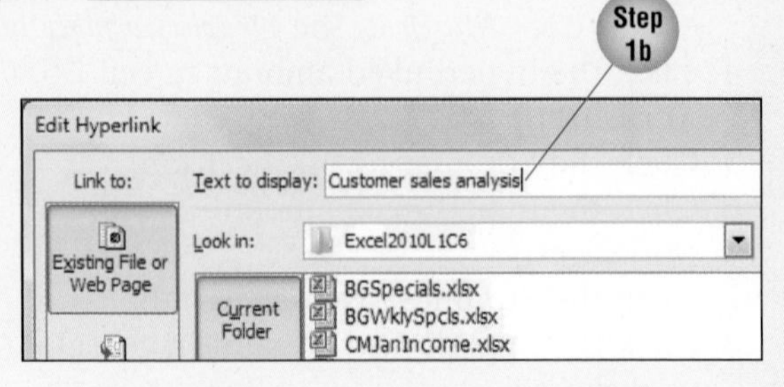

    c. Click the ScreenTip button located in the upper right corner of the dialog box.
    d. At the Set Hyperlink ScreenTip dialog box, type Click this hyperlink to display workbook containing customer sales analysis.

e. Click OK to close the Set Hyperlink ScreenTip dialog box.
f. Click OK to close the Edit Hyperlink dialog box.
2. Click the Customer sales analysis hyperlink.
3. After looking at the **PSSalesAnalysis.xlsx** workbook, close the workbook.
4. With cell A11 active, edit the Customer sales analysis hyperlink text by completing the following steps:
a. Click the Home tab.
b. Click the Font Color button arrow in the Font group and then click the *Red, Accent 2, Darker 50%* color (located toward the bottom of the sixth column).
c. Click the Bold button.
d. Click the Underline button. (This removes underlining from the text.)
5. Remove the Company information hyperlink by right-clicking in cell A13 and then clicking *Remove Hyperlink* at the shortcut menu.
6. Press the Delete key to remove the contents of cell A13.
7. Save, print only the first worksheet (the Summary worksheet), and then close **EL1-C6-P4-PSAccts.xlsx**.

Create a Billing Statement Workbook Using a Template

1 Part

You will open a Billing Statement template provided by Excel, add data, save it as an Excel workbook, and then print the workbook.

Using Excel Templates

Excel includes a number of template worksheet forms formatted for specific uses. With Excel templates you can create a variety of worksheets with specialized formatting such as balance sheets, billing statements, loan amortizations, sales invoices, and time cards. Display installed templates by clicking the File tab and then clicking the New tab. This displays the New tab Backstage view as shown in Figure 6.8.

Quick Steps

Use an Excel Template
1. Click File tab.
2. Click New tab.
3. Click Sample templates button.
4. Double-click desired template.

Click the Sample templates button in the *Available Templates* category and installed templates display. Click the desired template in the Sample templates list box and a preview of the template displays at the right side of the screen. Click the Create button that displays below the template preview and the template opens and displays on the screen. Locations for personalized text display in placeholders in the template worksheet. To enter information in the worksheet, position the mouse pointer (white plus sign) in the location where you want to type data and then click the left mouse button. After typing the data, click the next location. You can also move the insertion point to another cell using the commands learned in Chapter 1. For example, press the Tab key to make the next cell active or press Shift + Tab to make the previous cell active.

If you are connected to the Internet, you can download a number of predesigned templates that Microsoft offers. Templates are grouped into categories and the category names display in the *Office.com Templates* section of the New tab Backstage view. Click the desired template category and available templates display. Click the desired template and then click the Download button.

Figure 6.8 New Tab Backstage View

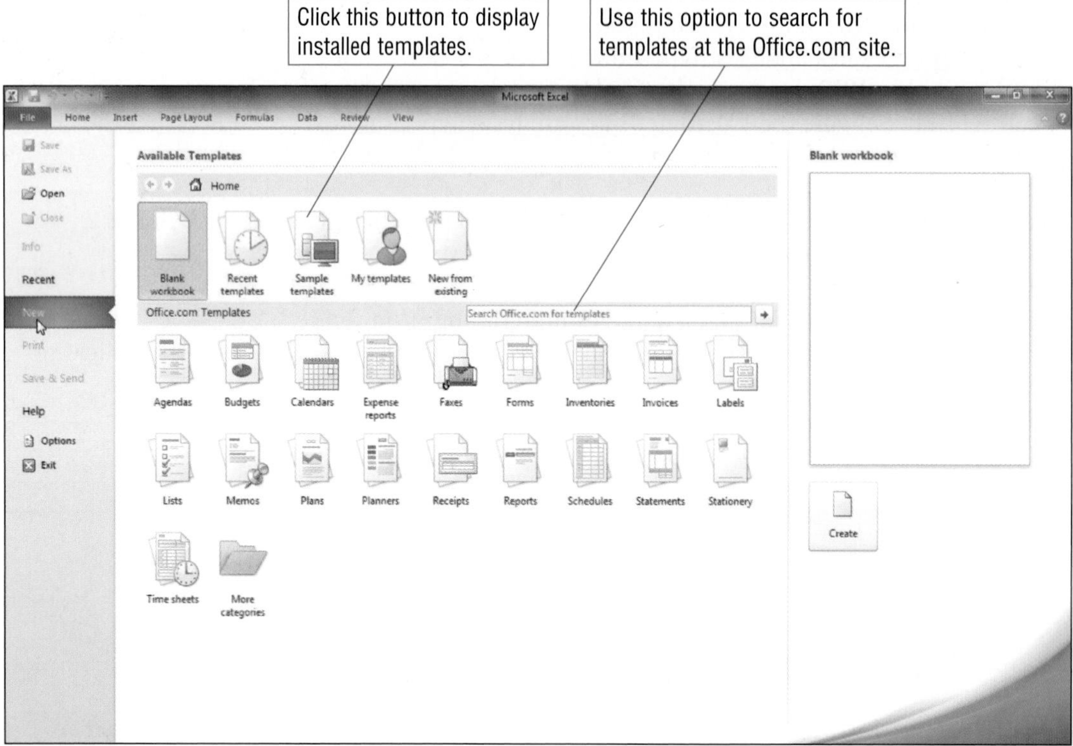

Project 5 Preparing a Billing Statement Using a Template

1 Part

1. Click the File tab and then click the New tab.
2. At the New tab Backstage view, click the Sample templates button in the *Available Templates* category.
3. Double-click the *Billing Statement* template in the *Available Templates* category of the dialog box.
4. Click the Normal button in the view area on the Status bar.
5. With cell B1 active, type IN-FLOW SYSTEMS.
6. Click the text *Street Address* (cell B2) and then type 320 Milander Way.

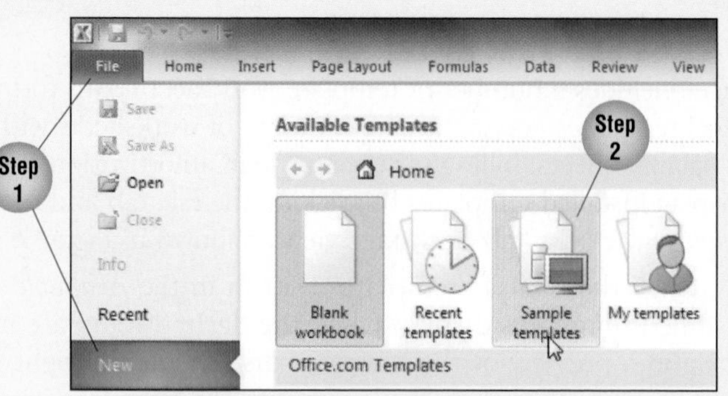

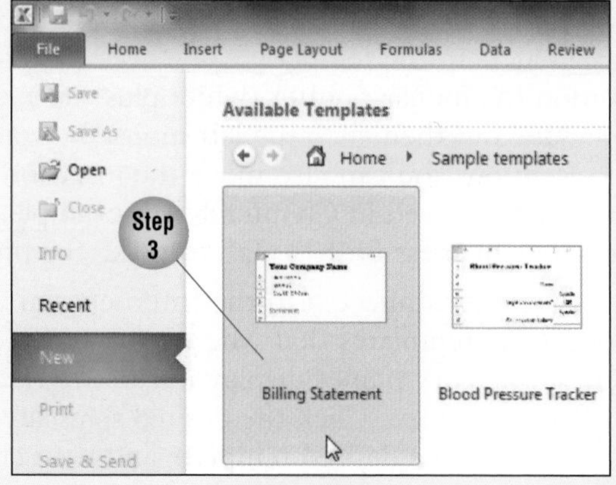

7. Click in the specified location (cell) and then type the text indicated:
   Address 2 (cell B3) = P.O. Box 2300
   City, ST ZIP Code (cell B4) = Boston, MA 02188
   Phone (cell F2) = (617) 555-3900
   Fax (cell F3) = (617) 555-3945
   Statement # (cell C8) = 5432
   Customer ID (cell C10) = 25-345
   Name (cell F8) = Aidan Mackenzie
   Company Name (cell F9) = Stanfield Enterprises
   Street Address (cell F10) = 9921 South 42nd Avenue
   Address 2 (cell F11) = P.O. Box 5540
   City, ST ZIP Code (cell F12) = Boston, MA 02193
   Date (cell B15) = (insert current date in numbers as ##/##/####)
   Type (cell C15) = System Unit
   Invoice # (cell D15) = 7452
   Description (cell E15) = Calibration Unit
   Amount (cell F15) = 950
   Payment (cell G15) = 200
   Customer Name (cell C21) = Stanfield Enterprises
   Amount Enclosed (C26) = 750

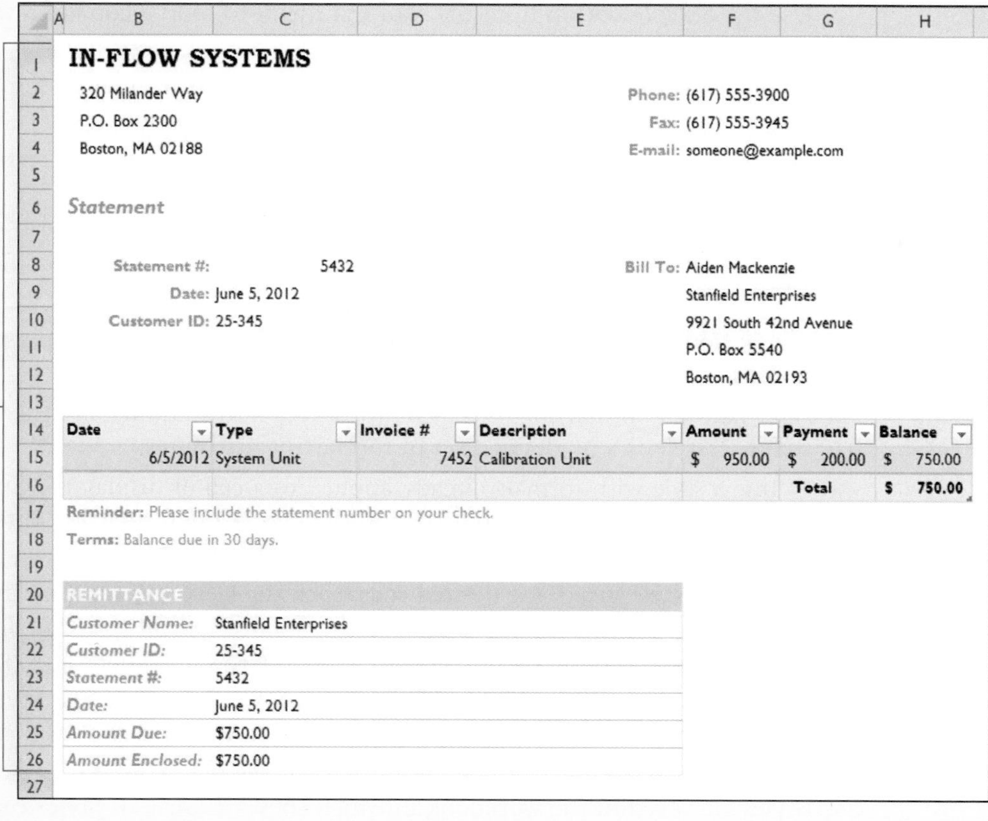

8. Save the completed invoice and name it **EL1-C6-P5-Billing**.
9. Print and then close **EL1-C6-P5-Billing.xlsx**.

Chapter Summary

- Perform file management tasks such as copying, moving, printing, and renaming workbooks and creating a new folder and renaming a folder at the Open or Save As dialog boxes.
- Create a new folder by clicking the New folder button located on the toolbar at the Open dialog box or Save As dialog box.
- Rename a folder with the *Rename* option from the Organize button drop-down list or with a shortcut menu.
- Use the Shift key to select adjacent workbooks in the Open dialog box and use the Ctrl key to select nonadjacent workbooks.
- To delete a workbook, use the *Delete* option from the Organize button drop-down list or with a shortcut menu option. Workbooks deleted from the hard drive are automatically sent to the Windows Recycle Bin where they can be restored or permanently deleted.
- Use the *Copy* and *Paste* options from the shortcut menu at the Open (or Save As) dialog box to copy a workbook from one folder to another folder or drive.
- Use the *Send To* option from the shortcut menu to send a copy of a workbook to another drive or folder.
- Remove a workbook from a folder or drive and insert it in another folder or drive using the *Cut* and *Paste* options from the shortcut menu.
- Use the *Rename* option from the Organize button drop-down list or the shortcut menu to give a workbook a different name.
- To move or copy a worksheet to another existing workbook, open both the source and the destination workbook and then open the Move or Copy dialog box.
- Use options from the Cell Styles button drop-down gallery to apply predesigned styles to a cell or selected cells.
- Automate the formatting of cells in a workbook by defining and then applying styles. A style is a predefined set of formatting attributes.
- Define a style with formats already applied to a cell or display the Style dialog box by clicking the Format button and then choosing formatting options at the Format Cells dialog box.
- To apply a style, select the desired cells, click the Cell Styles button in the Styles group in the Home tab, and then click the desired style at the drop-down gallery.
- Modify a style and all cells to which the style is applied automatically reflect the change. To modify a style, click the Cell Styles button in the Styles group in the Home tab, right-click the desired style, and then click *Modify* at the shortcut menu.
- Styles are saved in the workbook in which they are created. Styles can be copied, however, to another workbook. Do this with options at the Merge Styles dialog box.
- With options at the Insert Hyperlink dialog box, you can create a hyperlink to a web page, another workbook, a location within a workbook, a new workbook, or to an email. You can also create a hyperlink using a graphic.

- You can modify, edit, and remove hyperlinks.
- Excel provides preformatted templates for creating forms. Display the available templates by clicking the Sample templates button in the New tab Backstage view.
- Templates contain unique areas where information is entered at the keyboard. These areas vary depending on the template.

Commands Review

FEATURE	RIBBON TAB, GROUP	BUTTON, OPTION	KEYBOARD SHORTCUT
Open dialog box	File	Open	Ctrl + O
Save As dialog box	File	Save As	Ctrl + S
Cell Styles drop-down gallery	Home, Styles		
Style dialog box	Home, Styles	, New Cell Style	
Merge Styles dialog box	Home, Styles	, Merge Styles	
Insert Hyperlink dialog box	Insert, Links		
New tab Backstage view	File	New	
New folder	File	Open, New folder	

Concepts Check Test Your Knowledge

Completion: In the space provided at the right, indicate the correct term, symbol, or command.

1. Perform file management tasks such as copying, moving, or deleting workbooks with options at the Open dialog box or this dialog box. ____________________
2. At the Open dialog box, a list of folders and files displays in this pane. ____________________
3. Rename a folder or file at the Open dialog box using a shortcut menu or this button. ____________________
4. At the Open dialog box, hold down this key while selecting nonadjacent workbooks. ____________________

5. Workbooks deleted from the hard drive are automatically sent to this location. ________________

6. Insert a check mark in this check box at the Recent tab Backstage view and the four most recently opened workbook names display in the Backstage navigation bar. ________________

7. Do this to a workbook name you want to remain at the top of the *Recent Workbooks* list at the Recent tab Backstage view. ________________

8. If you close a workbook without saving it, you can recover it with this option at the Recent tab Backstage view. ________________

9. The Cell Styles button is located in this group in the Home tab. ________________

10. Click the *New Cell Style* option at the Cell Styles button drop-down gallery and this dialog box displays. ________________

11. A style you create displays in this section of the Cell Styles button drop-down gallery. ________________

12. Copy styles from one workbook to another with options at this dialog box. ________________

13. To link a workbook to another workbook, click this button in the *Link to* group in the Insert Hyperlink dialog box. ________________

14. Display installed templates by clicking this button in the *Available Templates* category at the New tab Backstage view. ________________

Skills Check Assess Your Performance

Assessment

1 MANAGE WORKBOOKS

1. Display the Open dialog box with Excel2010L1C6 the active folder.
2. Create a new folder named *O'Rourke* in the Excel2010L1C6 folder.
3. Copy **OEBudget.xlsx**, **OEPayroll.xlsx**, and **OEPlans.xlsx** to the O'Rourke folder.
4. Display the contents of the O'Rourke folder and then rename **OEBudget.xlsx** to **OEEquipBudget.xlsx**.
5. Rename **OEPlans.xlsx** to **OEPurchasePlans.xlsx** in the O'Rourke folder.
6. Change the active folder back to Excel2010L1C6.
7. Close the Open dialog box.

Assessment 2

MOVE AND COPY WORKSHEETS BETWEEN SALES ANALYSIS WORKBOOKS

1. Open **DISales.xlsx** and then save the workbook with Save As and name it **EL1-C6-A2-DISales**.
2. Rename Sheet1 to *1st Qtr*.
3. Open **DIQtrs.xlsx**.
4. Rename Sheet1 to *2nd Qtr* and then copy it to **EL1-C6-A2-DISales.xlsx** following the 1st Qtr worksheet. (When copying the worksheet, make sure you insert a check mark in the *Create a copy* check box in the Move or Copy dialog box.)
5. Make **DIQtrs.xlsx** active, rename Sheet 2 to *3rd Qtr* and then copy it to **EL1-C6-A2-DISales.xlsx** following the 2nd Qtr tab. (Make sure you insert a check mark in the *Create a copy* check box.)
6. Make **DIQtrs.xlsx** active and then close it without saving the changes.
7. Open **DI4thQtr.xlsx**.
8. Rename Sheet1 to *4th Qtr* and then move it to **EL1-C6-A2-DISales.xlsx** following the 3rd Qtr worksheet.
9. Make **DI4thQtr.xlsx** active and then close it without saving the changes.
10. With **EL1-C6-A2-DISales.xlsx** open, make the following changes to all four quarterly worksheets at the same time:
    a. Make 1st Qtr the active worksheet.
    b. Hold down the Shift key and then click the 4th Qtr tab. (This selects the four quarterly worksheet tabs.)
    c. Insert in cell E4 a formula to calculate average of cells B4 through D4 and then copy the formula down to cells E5 through E9.
    d. Insert in cell B10 a formula to calculate the sum of cells B4 through B9 and then copy the formula across to cells C10 through E10.
    e. Make cell E4 active and apply the Accounting Number Format with no decimal places.
11. Insert a footer on all worksheets that prints your name at the left, the page number in the middle, and the current date at the right.
12. Horizontally and vertically center all of the worksheets.
13. Click the Sheet2 tab and then delete it. Click the Sheet3 tab and then delete it.
14. Save and then print all four worksheets.
15. Close **EL1-C6-A2-DISales.xlsx**.

Assessment 3

DEFINE AND APPLY STYLES TO A PROJECTED EARNINGS WORKBOOK

1. At a blank worksheet, define a style named *C06Heading* that contains the following formatting:
    a. 14-point Cambria bold in dark blue color
    b. Horizontal alignment of Center
    c. Top and bottom border in a dark red color
    d. Light purple fill
2. Define a style named *C06Subheading* that contains the following formatting:
    a. 12-point Cambria bold in dark blue color
    b. Horizontal alignment of Center
    c. Top and bottom border in dark red color
    d. Light purple fill

3. Define a style named *C06Column* that contains the following formatting:
   a. At the Style dialog box, click the *Number* check box to remove the check mark.
   b. 12-point Cambria in dark blue color
   c. Light purple fill
4. Save the workbook and name it **EL1-C6-A3-Styles**.
5. With **EL1-C6-A3-Styles.xlsx** open, open **ProjEarnings.xlsx**.
6. Save the workbook with Save As and name it **EL1-C6-A3-ProjEarnings**.
7. Make cell C6 active and then insert a formula that multiplies the content of cell B6 with the amount in cell B3. (When writing the formula, identify cell B3 as an absolute reference.) Copy the formula down to cells C7 through C17.
8. Make cell C6 active and then click the Accounting Number Format button.
9. Copy the styles from **EL1-C6-A3-Styles.xlsx** into **EL1-C6-A3-ProjEarnings.xlsx**. ***Hint: Do this at the Merge Styles dialog box.***
10. Apply the following styles:
    a. Select cells A1 and A2 and then apply the C06Heading style.
    b. Select cells A5 through C5 and then apply the C06Subheading style.
    c. Select cells A6 through A17 and then apply the C06Column style.
11. Save the workbook again and then print **EL1-C6-A3-ProjEarnings.xlsx**.
12. With **EL1-C6-A3-ProjEarnings.xlsx** open, modify the following styles:
    a. Modify the C06Heading style so it changes the font color to dark purple (instead of dark blue), changes the vertical alignment to Center, and inserts a top and bottom border in dark purple (instead of dark red).
    b. Modify the C06Subheading style so it changes the font color to dark purple (instead of dark blue) and inserts a top and bottom border in dark purple (instead of dark red).
    c. Modify the C06Column style so it changes the font color to dark purple (instead of dark blue). Leave all of the other formatting attributes.
13. Save and then print the workbook.
14. Close **EL1-C6-A3-ProjEarnings.xlsx** and then close **EL1-C6-A3-Styles.xlsx** without saving the changes.

Assessment 4

INSERT HYPERLINKS IN A BOOK STORE WORKBOOK

1. Open **BGSpecials.xlsx** and then save the workbook with Save As and name it **EL1-C6-A4-BGSpecials.xlsx**.
2. Make cell E3 active and then hyperlink it to the www.microsoft.com website.
3. Make cell E4 active and then hyperlink it to the www.symantec.com website.
4. Make cell E5 active and then hyperlink it to the www.nasa.gov website.
5. Make cell E6 active and then hyperlink it to the www.cnn.com website.
6. Make cell A8 active, type Weekly specials!, and then create a hyperlink to the workbook named **BGWklySpcls.xlsx**.
7. Click the hyperlink to the Microsoft website, explore the site, and then close the web browser.
8. Click the hyperlink to the NASA website, explore the site, and then close the web browser.
9. Click the Weekly specials! hyperlink, view the workbook, and then close the workbook.
10. Save, print, and then close **EL1-C6-A4-BGSpecials.xlsx**.

Assessment

5 APPLY CONDITIONAL FORMATTING TO A SALES WORKBOOK

1. Use Excel Help files or experiment with the options at the Conditional Formatting button drop-down gallery to learn about conditional formatting.
2. Open **PSSales.xlsx** and then save the workbook with Save As and name it **EL1-C6-A5-PSSales**.
3. Select cells D5 through D19 and then use conditional formatting to display the amounts as data bars.
4. Insert a header that prints your name, a page number, and the current date.
5. Save, print, and then close **EL1-C6-A5-PSSales.xlsx**.

Visual Benchmark Demonstrate Your Proficiency

FILL IN AN EXPENSE REPORT FORM

1. Display the New tab Backstage view, click the Sample templates button, and then double-click the *Expense Report* template.
2. With the expense report open, apply the Paper theme.
3. Select cells J1 through L1 and then apply the Note cell style.
4. Type the information in the cells as indicated in Figure 6.9.
5. Make cell L18 active and apply the Bad cell style.
6. Save the completed workbook and name it **EL1-C6-VB-OEExpRpt**.
7. Print and then close **EL1-C6-VB-OEExpRpt.xlsx**.

Figure 6.9 Visual Benchmark

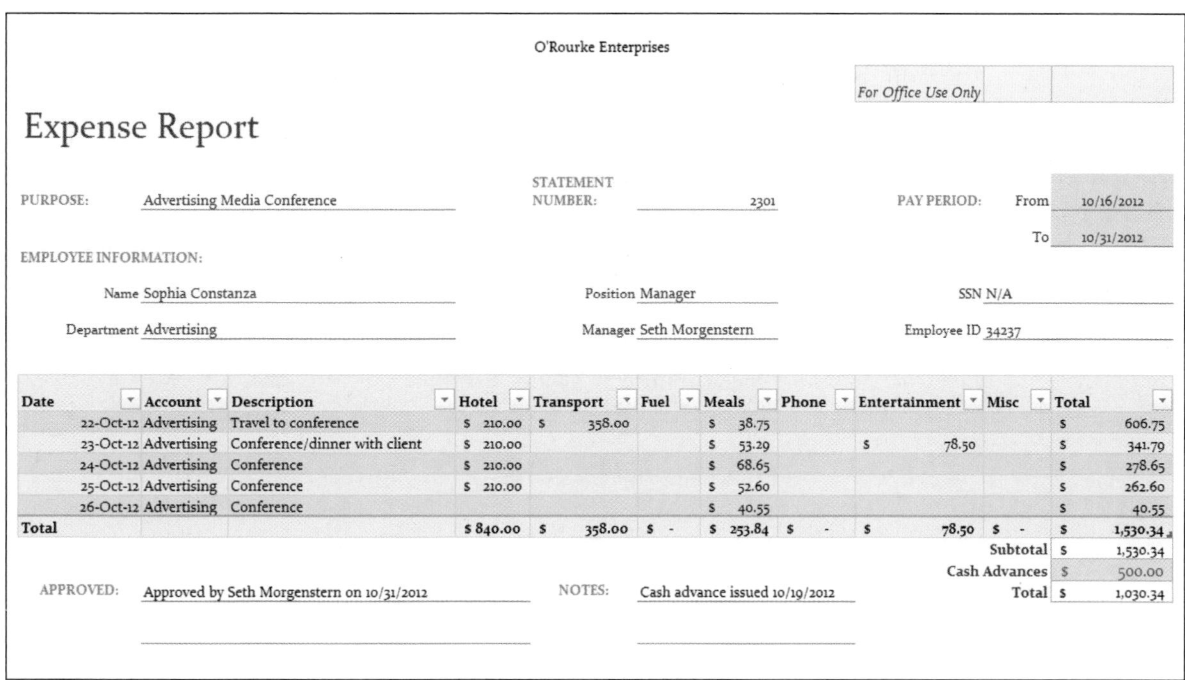

O'Rourke Enterprises

For Office Use Only

Expense Report

PURPOSE: Advertising Media Conference

STATEMENT NUMBER: 2301

PAY PERIOD: From 10/16/2012 To 10/31/2012

EMPLOYEE INFORMATION:

Name Sophia Constanza

Position Manager

SSN N/A

Department Advertising

Manager Seth Morgenstern

Employee ID 34237

Date	Account	Description	Hotel	Transport	Fuel	Meals	Phone	Entertainment	Misc	Total
22-Oct-12	Advertising	Travel to conference	$ 210.00	$ 358.00		$ 38.75				$ 606.75
23-Oct-12	Advertising	Conference/dinner with client	$ 210.00			$ 53.29		$ 78.50		$ 341.79
24-Oct-12	Advertising	Conference	$ 210.00			$ 68.65				$ 278.65
25-Oct-12	Advertising	Conference	$ 210.00			$ 52.60				$ 262.60
26-Oct-12	Advertising	Conference				$ 40.55				$ 40.55
Total			$ 840.00	$ 358.00	$ -	$ 253.84	$ -	$ 78.50	$ -	$ 1,530.34
									Subtotal	$ 1,530.34
									Cash Advances	$ 500.00
									Total	$ 1,030.34

APPROVED: Approved by Seth Morgenstern on 10/31/2012

NOTES: Cash advance issued 10/19/2012

Case Study Apply Your Skills

Part 1

You are the office manager for Leeward Marine and you decide to consolidate into one workbook worksheets containing information on expenses. Open **LMEstExp.xlsx** and then save the workbook and name it **EL1-C6-CS-LMExpSummary**. Open **LMActExp.xlsx**, copy the worksheet into **EL1-C6-CS-LMExpSummary.xlsx**, make **LMActExp.xlsx** the active workbook, and then close it. Apply appropriate formatting to numbers and insert necessary formulas in each worksheet. (Use the Clear button in the Home tab to clear the contents of cells N8, N9, M13, and M14 in both worksheets.) Include the company name, Leeward Marine, in each worksheet. Create styles and apply the styles to cells in each worksheet to maintain consistent formatting. Automatically adjust the widths of the columns to accommodate the longest entry. Save **EL1-C6-CS-LMExpSummary.xlsx**.

Part 2

You decide that you want to include another worksheet that displays the yearly estimated expenses, the actual expenses, and the variances (differences) between the expenses. With **EL1-C6-CS-LMExpSummary.xlsx** open, open **LMExpVar.xlsx**. Copy the worksheet into **EL1-C6-CS-LMExpSummary.xlsx**, make **LMExpVar.xlsx** the active workbook, and then close it. Rename the sheet tab containing the estimated expenses to *Estimated Exp*, rename the sheet tab containing the actual expenses to *Actual Exp*, and rename the sheet tab containing the variances to *Summary*. Recolor the three sheet tabs you just renamed.

Select the yearly estimated expense amounts (column N) in the Estimated Exp worksheet and then paste the amounts in the appropriate cells in the Summary worksheet. Click the Paste Options button and then click the Values & Number Formatting button in the *Paste Values* section of the drop-down list. (This pastes the value and the cell formatting rather than the formula.) Select the yearly actual expense amounts (column N) in the Actual Exp worksheet and then paste the amounts in the appropriate cells in the Summary worksheet. Click the Paste Options button and then click the Values & Number Formatting button in the *Paste Values* section of the drop-down list. Apply appropriate formatting to numbers and insert a formula to insert the variances (differences) of estimated and actual expenses. Clear the contents of cells D8, D9, D13, and D14. Apply styles to the Summary worksheet so it appears with formatting similar to the Estimated Exp and Actual Exp worksheets.

Insert an appropriate header or footer in each worksheet. Scale the worksheets so each prints on one page. Save, print all of the worksheets, and then close **EL1-C6-CS-LMExpSummary.xlsx**.

Part 3

You are not happy with the current product list form, so you decide to look at template forms available at Office.com. Display the New tab Backstage view, click the *Lists* option in the *Office.com Templates* section, click the *Business* folder, and then double-click the *Product price list* template. (These steps may vary.) Use the information below to fill in the form in the appropriate locations:

Leeward Marine
4500 Shoreline Drive
Ketchikan, AK 99901
(907) 555-2200
(907) 555-2595 (fax)
www.emcp.com/lmarine

Insert the following information in the appropriate columns:

Product Number	Name	Description	Retail Price Per Unit	Bulk Price Per Unit*
210-19	Ring Buoy	19-inch, white, solid plastic	$49.95	$42.00
210-20	Ring Buoy	20-inch, white, solid plastic	$52.95	$49.50
210-24	Ring Buoy	24-inch, white, solid plastic	$59.95	$52.00
320-05	Horseshoe Buoy	Vinyl fabric over plastic core	$83.95	$78.50
225-01	Ring Buoy Holder	Aluminum holder	$6.50	$5.75
234-24	Ring Buoy Bracket	Stainless steel bracket	$7.25	$6.50

Save the completed products list form and name it **EL1-C6-CS-LMProdList**. Print and then close the workbook.

Part 4

You need to print a number of copies of the product list and you want the company letterhead to print at the top of the page. You decide to use the letterhead you created in Word and copy the product list information from Excel into the Word letterhead document. To do this, open Word and then open the document named **LMLtrd.docx**. Press the Enter key four times. Make Excel the active program and then open **EL1-C6-CS-LMProdList.xlsx**. Copy cells A2 through E11 and then paste them into the **LMLtrhd.docx** Word document as a picture object (click the Paste Options button and then click the Picture button). Save the document with Save As and name it **EL1-C6-CS-LMProducts**. Print and then close **EL1-C6-CS-LMProducts.docx** and then exit Word. In Excel, close **EL1-C6-CS-ProdList.xlsx**.

Microsoft® Excel®

Creating a Chart in Excel

CHAPTER

PERFORMANCE OBJECTIVES

Upon successful completion of Chapter 7, you will be able to:

- **Create a chart with data in an Excel worksheet**
- **Size, move, and delete charts**
- **Print a selected chart and print a worksheet containing a chart**
- **Choose a chart style, layout, and formatting**
- **Change chart location**
- **Insert, move, size, and delete chart labels, shapes, and pictures**

Tutorials

7.1 Creating Charts in Excel
7.2 Editing Chart Data
7.3 Changing the Chart Design
7.4 Changing a Chart Type
7.5 Inserting Shapes and Images
7.6 Changing the Chart Formatting

In the previous Excel chapters, you learned to create data in worksheets. While a worksheet does an adequate job of representing data, you can present some data more visually by charting the data. A ***chart*** is sometimes referred to as a ***graph*** and is a picture of numeric data. In this chapter, you will learn to create and customize charts in Excel. Model answers for this chapter's projects appear on the following pages.

Excel2010L1C7

Note: Before beginning the projects, copy to your storage medium the Excel2010L1C7 subfolder from the Excel2010L1 folder on the CD that accompanies this textbook and then make Excel2010L1C7 the active folder.

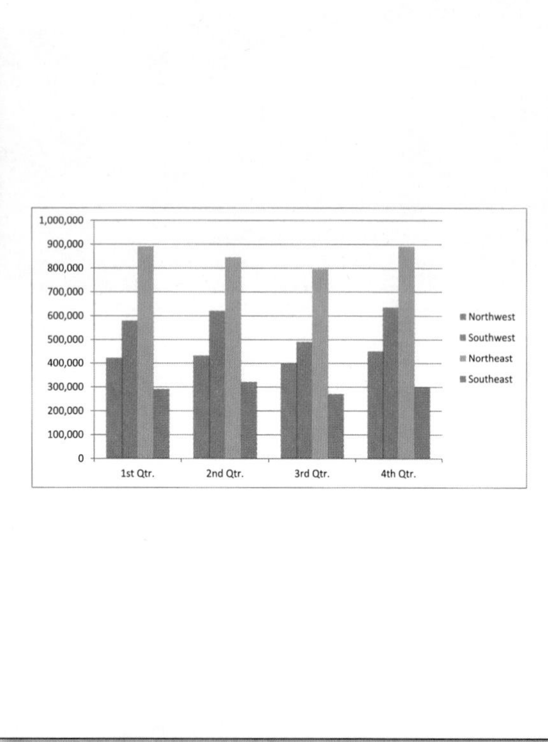

Project 1 Create a Quarterly Sales Column Chart
EL1-C7-P1-SalesChart.xlsx

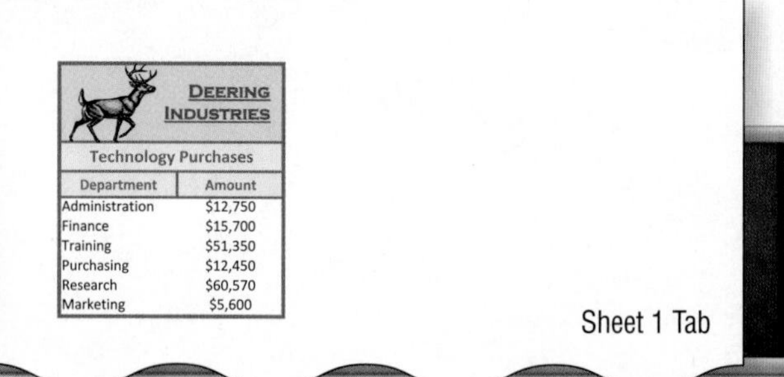

DEERING INDUSTRIES

Technology Purchases

Department	Amount
Administration	$12,750
Finance	$15,700
Training	$51,350
Purchasing	$12,450
Research	$60,570
Marketing	$5,600

Sheet 1 Tab

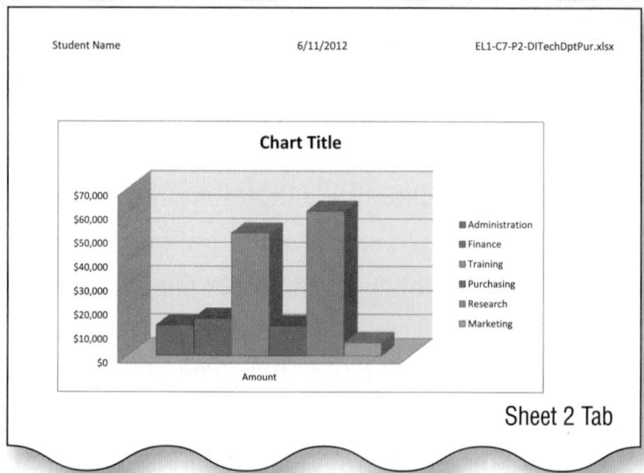

Sheet 2 Tab

Project 2 Create a Technology Purchases Bar Chart and Column Chart
EL1-C7-P2-DITechDptPur.xlsx

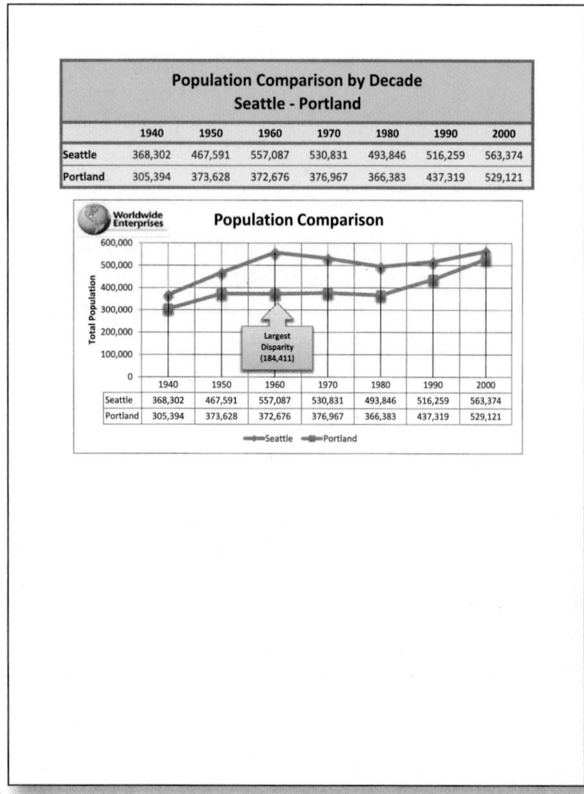

Population Comparison by Decade
Seattle - Portland

	1940	1950	1960	1970	1980	1990	2000
Seattle	368,302	467,591	557,087	530,831	493,846	516,259	563,374
Portland	305,394	373,628	372,676	376,967	366,383	437,319	529,121

Project 3 Create a Population Comparison Bar Chart
EL1-C7-P3-PopComp.xlsx

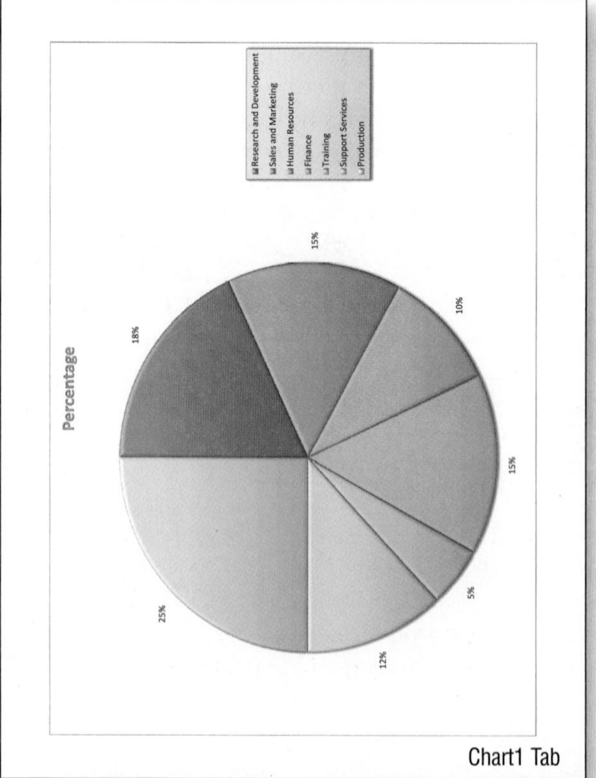

Chart1 Tab

Project 4 Create a Costs Percentage Pie Chart
EL1-C7-P4-DIDptCosts.xlsx

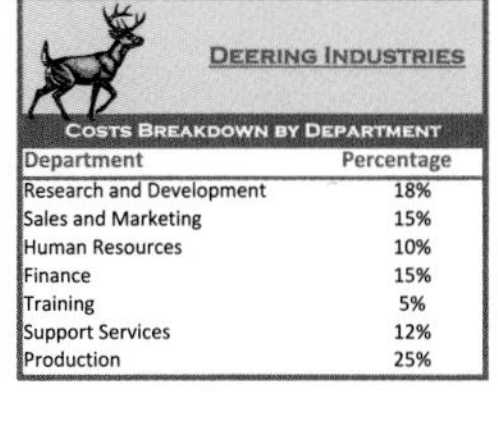

DEERING INDUSTRIES

COSTS BREAKDOWN BY DEPARTMENT

Department	Percentage
Research and Development	18%
Sales and Marketing	15%
Human Resources	10%
Finance	15%
Training	5%
Support Services	12%
Production	25%

Sheet 1 Tab

Deering Industries

Northeast Regional Sales

Salesperson	Sales
Rehberg, Robin	$1,120,500
Hutchinson, Lee	$1,500,750
Ludlow, William	$890,525
Newman, Jared	$735,400
Ortega, Cecilia	$1,250,770

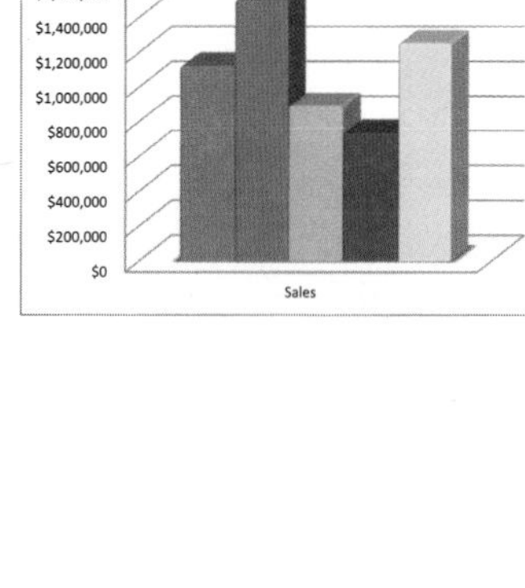

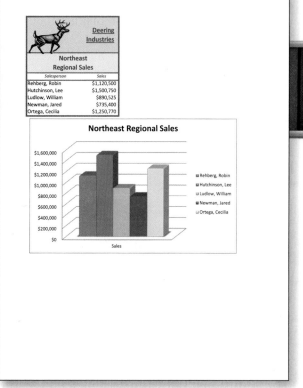

Project 5 Create a Regional Sales Column Chart

EL1-C7-P5-DIRegSales.xlsx

Project 1 Create a Quarterly Sales Column Chart — 2 Parts

You will open a workbook containing quarterly sales data and then use the data to create a column chart. You will decrease the size of the chart, move it to a different location in the worksheet, and then make changes to sales numbers.

Creating a Chart

In Excel, create a chart with buttons in the Charts group in the Insert tab as shown in Figure 7.1. With buttons in the Charts group you can create a variety of charts such as a column chart, line chart, pie chart, and much more. Excel provides 11 basic chart types as described in Table 7.1. To create a chart, select cells in a worksheet that you want to chart, click the Insert tab, and then click the desired chart button in the Charts group. At the drop-down gallery that displays, click the desired chart style. You can also create a chart by selecting the desired cells and then pressing Alt + F1. This keyboard shortcut, by default, inserts the data in a 2-D column chart (unless the default chart type has been changed).

Quick Steps

Create a Chart
1. Select cells.
2. Click Insert tab.
3. Click desired chart button.
4. Click desired chart style at drop-down list.

Create Chart as Default Chart Type
1. Select cells.
2. Press Alt + F1.

Figure 7.1 Charts Group Buttons

These buttons display in the Insert tab and you can use them to create a variety of charts.

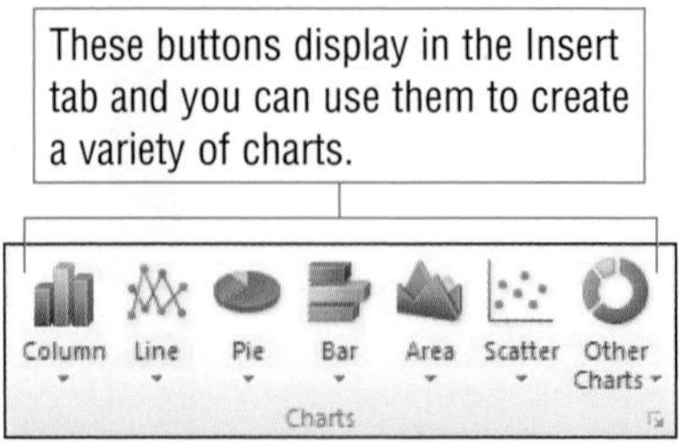

Table 7.1 Type of Charts

Chart	*Description*
Area	Emphasizes the magnitude of change, rather than time and the rate of change. It also shows the relationship of parts to a whole by displaying the sum of the plotted values.
Bar	Shows individual figures at a specific time, or shows variations between components but not in relationship to the whole.
Bubble	Compares sets of three values in a manner similar to a scatter chart, with the third value displayed as the size of the bubble marker.
Column	Compares separate (noncontinuous) items as they vary over time.
Doughnut	Shows the relationship of parts of the whole.
Line	Shows trends and change over time at even intervals. It emphasizes the rate of change over time rather than the magnitude of change.
Pie	Shows proportions and relationships of parts to the whole.
Radar	Emphasizes differences and amounts of change over time and variations and trends. Each category has its own value axis radiating from the center point. Lines connect all values in the same series.
Stock	Shows four values for a stock—open, high, low, and close.
Surface	Shows trends in values across two dimensions in a continuous curve.
XY (Scatter)	Shows the relationships among numeric values in several data series or plots the interception points between x and y values. It shows uneven intervals of data and is commonly used in scientific data.

Sizing, Moving, and Deleting a Chart

When you create a chart, the chart is inserted in the same worksheet as the selected cells. Figure 7.2 displays the worksheet and chart you will create in Project 1a. The chart is inserted in a box which you can size and/or move in the worksheet.

To size the worksheet, position the mouse pointer on the four dots located in the middle of the border you want to size until the pointer turns into a two-headed arrow, hold down the left mouse button, and then drag to increase or decrease the size of the chart. To increase or decrease the height and width of

Figure 7.2 Project 1a Chart

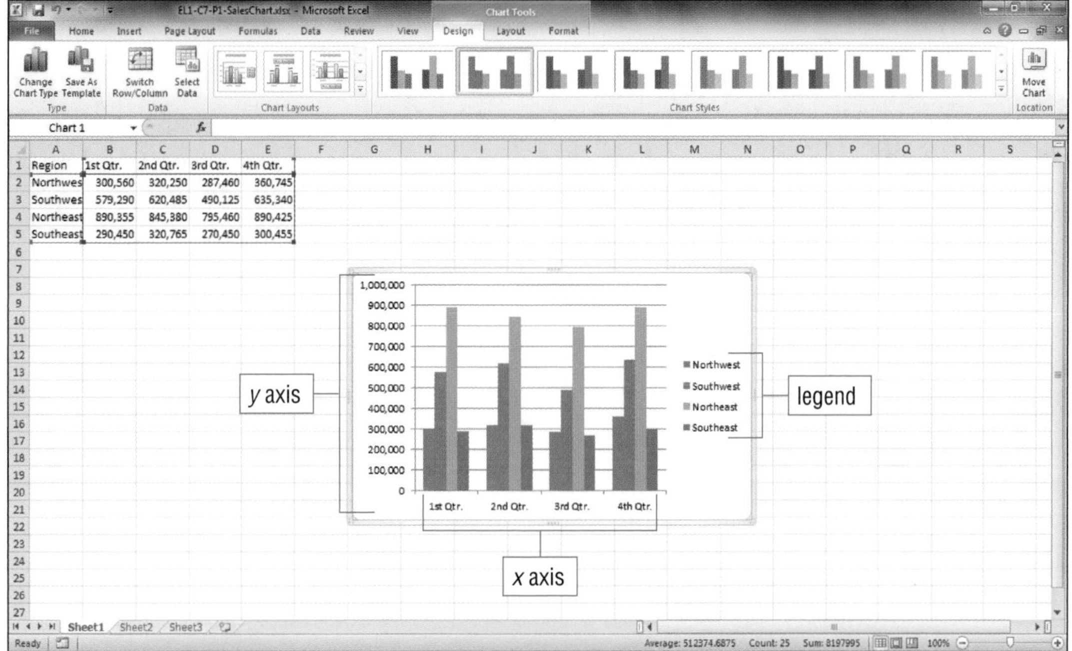

the chart at the same time, position the mouse pointer on the three dots that display in a chart border corner until the pointer displays as a two-headed arrow, hold down the left mouse button, and then drag to the desired size. To increase or decrease the size of the chart and maintain the proportions of the chart, hold down the Shift key while dragging a chart corner border.

To move the chart, make sure the chart is selected (light gray border displays around the chart), position the mouse pointer on a border until it turns into a four-headed arrow, hold down the left mouse button, and then drag to the desired position.

Editing Data

Hide rows or columns that you do not want to chart.

The cells you select to create the chart are linked to the chart. If you need to change data for a chart, edit the data in the desired cell and the corresponding section of the chart is automatically updated.

Project 1a Creating a Chart

Part 1 of 2

1. Open **SalesChart.xlsx** and then save the workbook with Save As and name it **EL1-C7-P1-SalesChart**.
2. Select cells A1 through E5.
3. Press Alt + F1.
4. Slightly increase the size of the chart and maintain the proportions of the chart by completing the following steps:
   a. Position the mouse pointer on the bottom right corner of the chart border until the pointer turns into a two-headed arrow pointing diagonally.
   b. Hold down the Shift key and then hold down the left mouse button.

c. Drag out approximately one-half inch and then release the mouse button and then the Shift key.

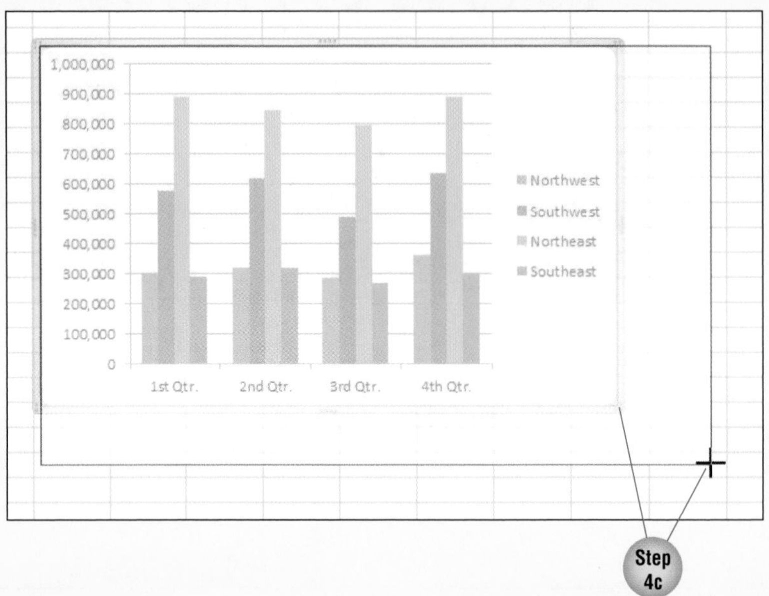

5. Move the chart below the cells containing data by completing the following steps:
   a. Make sure the chart is selected (light gray border surrounds the chart).
   b. Position the mouse pointer on the chart border until the pointer turns into a four-headed arrow.
   c. Hold down the left mouse button, drag the chart so it is positioned below the cells containing data, and then release the mouse button.

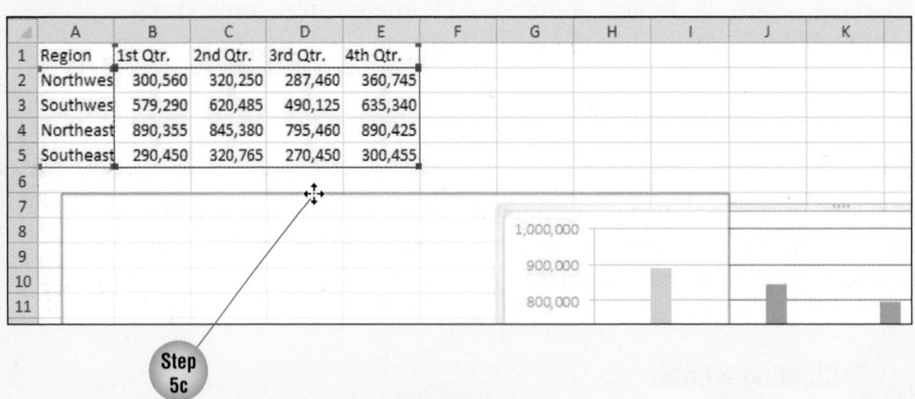

	A	B	C	D	E
1	Region	1st Qtr.	2nd Qtr.	3rd Qtr.	4th Qtr.
2	Northwes	300,560	320,250	287,460	360,745
3	Southwes	579,290	620,485	490,125	635,340
4	Northeast	890,355	845,380	795,460	890,425
5	Southeast	290,450	320,765	270,450	300,455

6. Make the following changes to the specified cells:
   a. Make cell B2 active and then change *300,560* to *421,720*.
   b. Make cell C2 active and then change *320,250* to *433,050*.
   c. Make cell D2 active and then change *287,460* to *397,460*.
   d. Make cell E2 active and then change *360,745* to *451,390*.
7. Save **EL1-C7-P1-SalesChart.xlsx**.

Printing a Chart

In a worksheet containing data in cells as well as a chart, you can print only the chart. To do this, select the chart, display the Print tab Backstage view, and then click the Print button. With a chart selected, the first gallery in the *Settings* category is automatically changed to *Print Selected Chart*. A preview of the chart displays at the right side of the Print tab Backstage view.

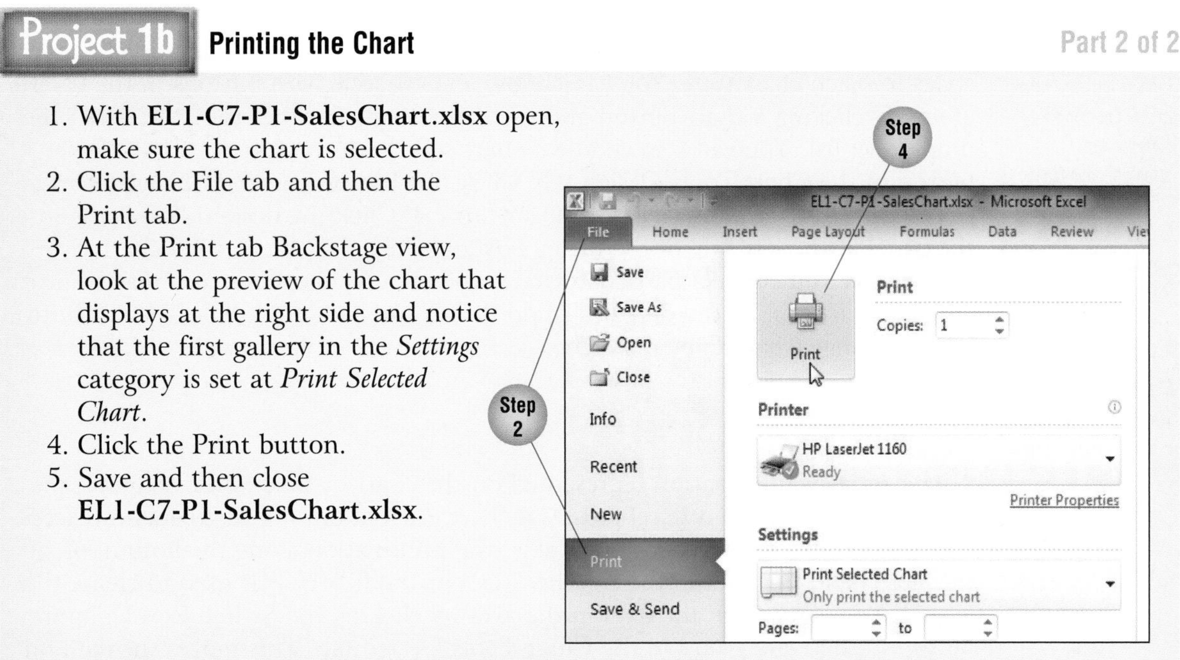

1. With **EL1-C7-P1-SalesChart.xlsx** open, make sure the chart is selected.
2. Click the File tab and then the Print tab.
3. At the Print tab Backstage view, look at the preview of the chart that displays at the right side and notice that the first gallery in the *Settings* category is set at *Print Selected Chart*.
4. Click the Print button.
5. Save and then close **EL1-C7-P1-SalesChart.xlsx**.

Project 2 Create a Technology Purchases Bar Chart and Column Chart — 2 Parts

You will open a workbook containing technology purchases data by department and then create a bar chart with the data. You will then change the chart type, layout, and style and move the chart to a new sheet.

Changing the Chart Design

When you insert a chart in a worksheet, the Chart Tools Design tab displays as shown in Figure 7.3. With options in this tab, you can change the chart type, specify a different layout or style for the chart, and change the location of the chart so it displays in a separate worksheet.

Figure 7.3 Chart Tools Design Tab

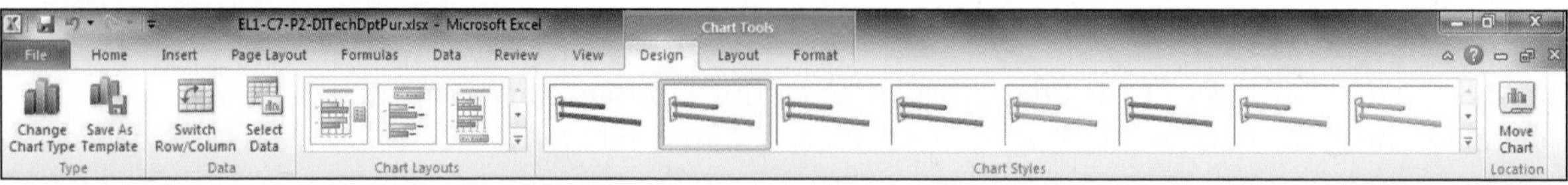

Choosing a Custom Chart Style

The chart feature offers a variety of preformatted custom charts and offers varying styles for each chart type. You can choose a chart style with buttons in the Charts group by clicking a chart button and then choosing from the styles offered at the drop-down list. You can also choose a chart style with the Change Chart Type button in the Chart Tools Design tab. Click this button and the Change Chart Type dialog box displays as shown in Figure 7.4. Click the desired chart type in the panel at the left side of the dialog box and then click the desired chart style at the right. If you create a particular chart type on a regular basis, you may want to set that chart type as the default. To do this, click the Set as Default Chart button in the Change Chart Type dialog box.

Quick Steps

Change Chart Type and Style
1. Make the chart active.
2. Click Chart Tools Design tab.
3. Click Change Chart Type button.
4. Click desired chart type.
5. Click desired chart style.
6. Click OK.

Change Chart Data Series
1. Make the chart active.
2. Click Chart Tools Design tab.
3. Click Switch Row/Column button.

Change Chart Type

Switch Row/Column

Changing the Data Series

A data series is information represented on the chart by bars, lines, columns, pie slices, and so on. When Excel creates a chart, the data in the first column (except the first cell) is used to create the *x* axis (the information along the bottom of the chart) and the data in the first row (except the first cell) is used to create the legend. You can switch the data in the axes by clicking the Switch Row/Column button in the Data group in the Chart Tools Design tab. This moves the data on the *x* axis to the *y* axis and the *y* axis data to the *x* axis.

Figure 7.4 Change Chart Type Dialog Box

Choose a custom chart type in this list box.

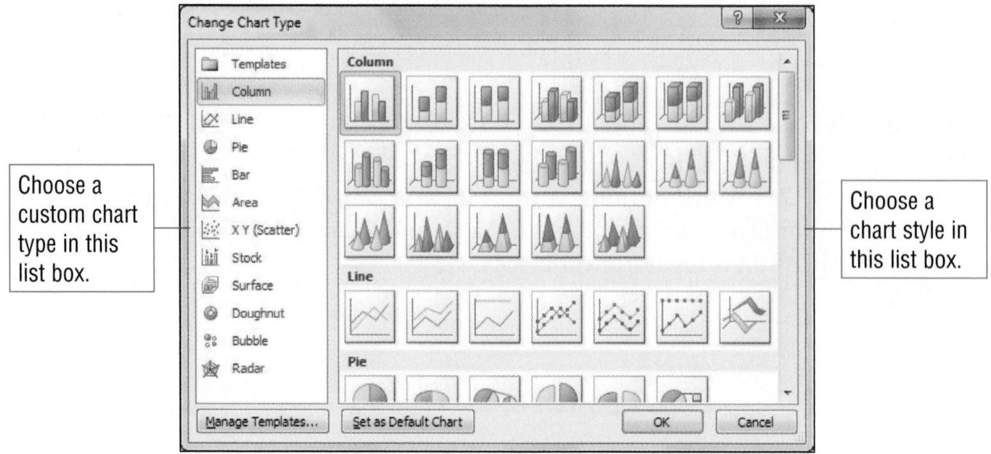

Choose a chart style in this list box.

Project 2a Creating a Chart and Changing the Design

Part 1 of 2

1. Open **DITechDptPur.xlsx** and then save the workbook with Save As and name it **EL1-C7-P2-DITechDptPur**.
2. Create a bar chart by completing the following steps:
   a. Select cells A3 through B9.
   b. Click the Insert tab.
   c. Click the Bar button in the Charts group.
   d. Click the first option from the left in the *Cylinder* section (*Clustered Horizontal Cylinder*).
3. With the chart selected and the Chart Tools Design tab displayed, change the data series by clicking the Switch Row/Column button located in the Data group.

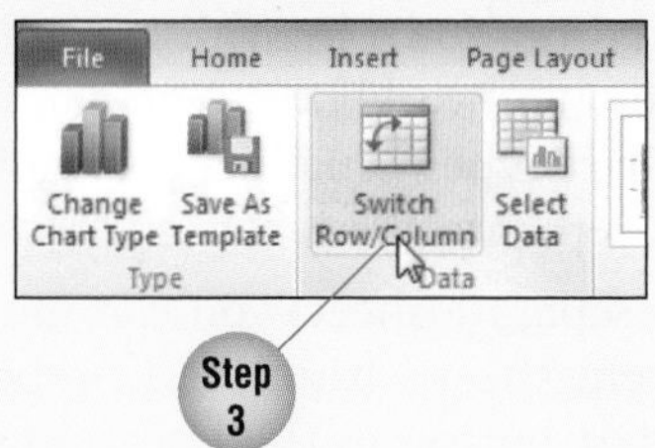

Step 2c

Step 2d

4. Change the chart type and style by completing the following steps:
   a. Click the Change Chart Type button located in the Type group.
   b. At the Change Chart Type dialog box, click the *Column* option in the left panel.
   c. Click the *3-D Cylinder* option in the *Column* section (fourth chart style from the left in the second row of the *Column* section).
   d. Click OK to close the Change Chart Type dialog box.
5. Save **EL1-C7-P2-DITechDptPur.xlsx**.

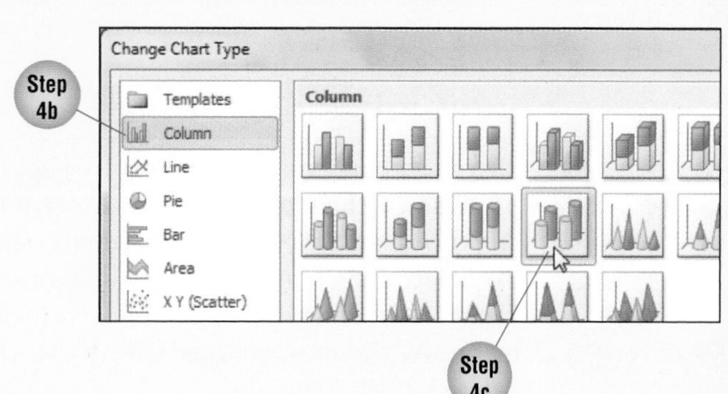

Changing Chart Layout and Style

Click the Save As Template button in the Type group in the Chart Tools Design tab to save the formatting and layout of the current chart as a template you can use to create future charts.

The Chart Tools Design tab contains options for changing the chart layout and style. The Chart Layouts group in the tab contains preformatted chart layout options. Click the More button (contains an underline and a down-pointing arrow) to display a drop-down list of layout options. Hover the mouse pointer over an option and a ScreenTip displays with the option name. You can also scroll through layout options by clicking the up-pointing arrow or the down-pointing arrow located at the right side of the Chart Layouts group.

Use options in the Chart Styles group to apply a particular style of formatting to a chart. Click the More button located at the right side of the Chart Styles group to display a drop-down list with all the style options or click the up-pointing or down-pointing arrow at the right of the group to scroll through the options.

Changing Chart Location

Quick Steps

Change Chart Location

1. Make the chart active.
2. Click Chart Tools Design tab.
3. Click Move Chart button.
4. Click *New Sheet* option.
5. Click OK.

Move Chart

Create a chart and the chart is inserted in the currently open worksheet as an embedded object. You can change the location of a chart with the Move Chart button in the Location group. Click this button and the Move Chart dialog box displays as shown in Figure 7.5. Click the *New sheet* option to move the chart to a new sheet within the workbook. Excel automatically names the sheet *Chart1*. Click the down-pointing arrow at the right side of the *Object in* option box and then click the desired location. The drop-down list will generally display the names of the worksheets within the open workbook. You can use the keyboard shortcut, F11, to create a default chart type (usually a column chart) and Excel automatically inserts the chart in a separate sheet.

If you have moved a chart to a separate sheet, you can move it back to the original sheet or move it to a different sheet within the workbook. To move a chart to a sheet, click the Move Chart button in the Location group in the Chart Tools Design tab. At the Move Chart dialog box, click the down-pointing arrow at the right side of the *Object in* option and then click the desired sheet at the drop-down list. Click OK and the chart is inserted in the specified sheet as an object that you can move, size, and format.

Deleting a Chart

Quick Steps

Delete a Chart

1. Click once in chart.
2. Press Delete key.

OR

1. Right-click chart tab.
2. Click Cut.

Delete a chart created in Excel by clicking once in the chart to select it and then pressing the Delete key. If you move a chart to a different worksheet in the workbook and then delete the chart, the chart is deleted but not the worksheet. To delete the chart as well as the worksheet, position the mouse pointer on the Chart1 tab, click the right mouse button, and then click *Delete* at the shortcut menu. At the message box telling you that selected sheets will be permanently deleted, click Delete.

Figure 7.5 Move Chart Dialog Box

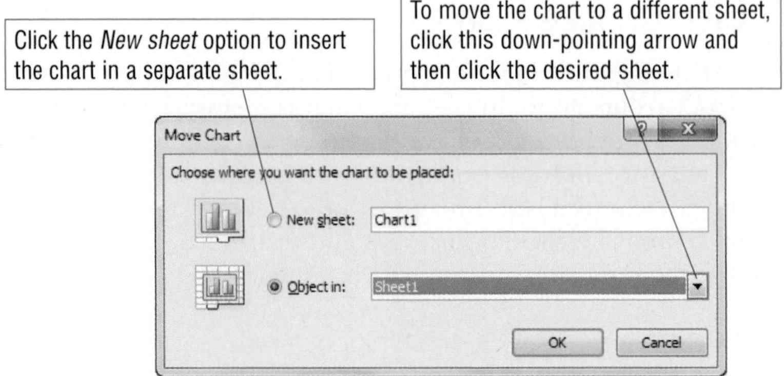
Click the *New sheet* option to insert the chart in a separate sheet.
To move the chart to a different sheet, click this down-pointing arrow and then click the desired sheet.
Move Chart
Choose where you want the chart to be placed:
New sheet:
Chart1
Object in:
Sheet1
OK
Cancel

Project 2b Changing Chart Layout, Style, and Location

Part 2 of 2

1. With **EL1-C7-P2-DITechDeptPur.xlsx** open, make sure the Chart Tools Design tab displays. (If it does not, make sure the chart is selected and then click the Chart Tools Design tab.)
2. Change the chart type by completing the following steps:
   a. Click the Change Chart Type button in the Type tab.
   b. Click *3-D Clustered Column* (fourth column style from the left in the top row).
   c. Click OK to close the dialog box.

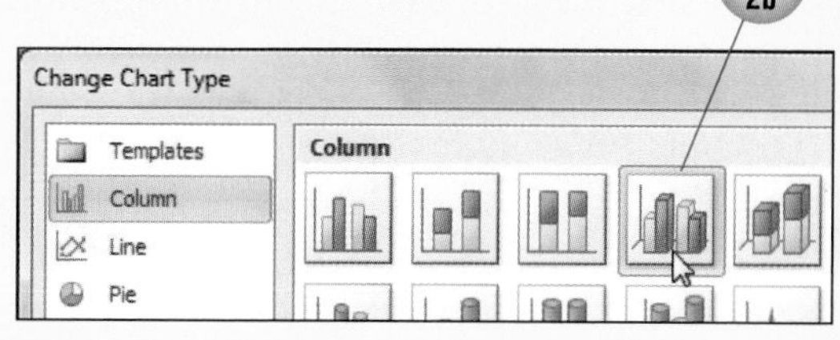

3. Change the chart layout by clicking the *Layout 1* option in the Chart Layouts group (first option from the left). This layout inserts the words *Chart Title* at the top of the chart.

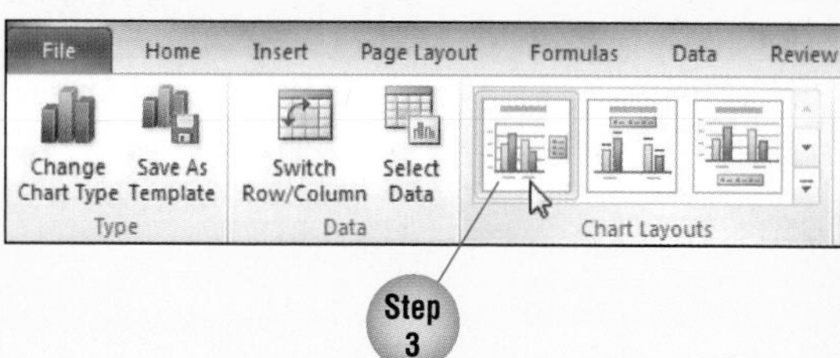

4. Change the chart style by clicking the More button located at the right side of the Chart Styles group and then clicking *Style 34* (second option from the left in the fifth row).

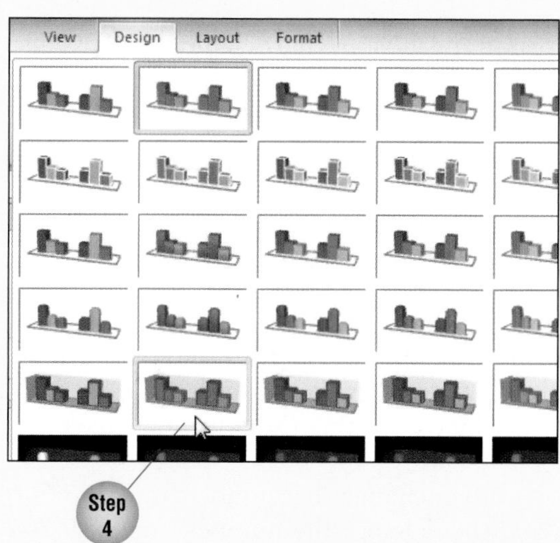

5. Move the chart to a new location by completing the following steps:
   a. Click the Move Chart button in the Location group.
   b. At the Move Chart dialog box, click the *New sheet* option and then click OK. (The chart is inserted in a worksheet named *Chart1*.)
6. Save **EL1-C7-P2-DITechDptPur.xlsx**.
7. Print the Chart1 worksheet containing the chart.

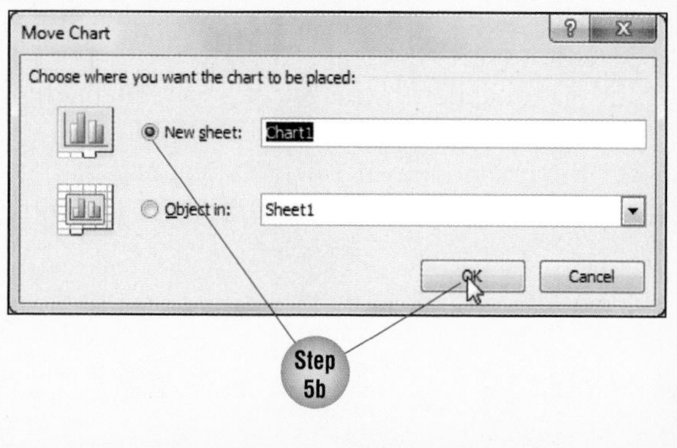

8. Move the chart from Chart1 to Sheet2 by completing the following steps:
   a. Make sure Chart1 is the active sheet and that the chart is selected (not an element in the chart).
   b. Make sure the Chart Tools Design tab is active.
   c. Click the Move Chart button in the Location group.
   d. At the Move Chart dialog box, click the down-pointing arrow at the right side of the *Object in* option and then click *Sheet2* at the drop-down list.

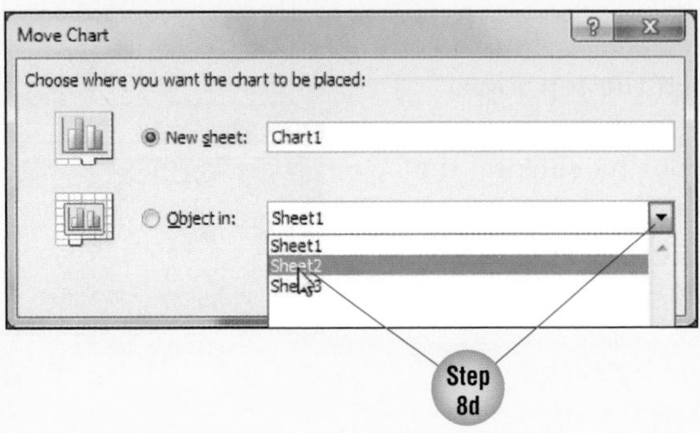

   e. Click OK.
9. Increase the size of the chart and maintain the proportions by completing the following steps:
   a. Click inside the chart but outside any chart elements. (This displays a light gray border around the chart. Make sure the entire chart is selected and not a specific chart element.)
   b. Hold down the Shift key.
   c. Position the mouse pointer on the upper left border corner until the pointer turns into a double-headed arrow pointing diagonally.
   d. Hold down the left mouse button, drag left approximately one inch and then release the mouse button and then the Shift key.
   e. Click outside the chart to deslect it.
   f. Display the Print tab Backstage view to determine if the chart will print on one page. If the chart does not fit on the page, return to the worksheet and then move and/or decrease the size of the chart until it fits on one page.
10. Change amounts in Sheet1 by completing the following steps:
    a. Click Sheet1.
    b. Make cell B4 active and then change the number from *$33,500* to *$12,750*.
    c. Make cell B9 active and then change the number from *$19,200* to *$5,600*.
    d. Make cell A2 active.
    e. Click the Sheet2 tab and notice that the chart displays the updated amounts.
11. Click outside the chart to deselect it.
12. Insert a header in the Sheet2 worksheet that prints your name at the left, the current date in the middle, and the workbook file name at the right.
13. Print the active worksheet (Sheet2).
14. Save and then close **EL1-C7-P2-DITechDptPur.xlsx**.

Create a Population Comparison Bar Chart 3 Parts

You will open a workbook containing population comparison data for Seattle and Portland and then create a bar chart with the data. You will also add chart labels and shapes and move, size, and delete labels and shapes.

Changing the Chart Layout

Customize the layout of labels in a chart with options in the Chart Tools Layout tab as shown in Figure 7.6. With buttons in this tab, you can change the layout and/or insert additional chart labels. Certain chart labels are automatically inserted in a chart including a chart legend and labels for the *x* axis and *y* axis. Add chart labels to an existing chart with options in the Labels group in the Chart Tools Layout tab. In addition to chart labels, you can also insert shapes, pictures, and/or clip art and change the layout of 3-D chart labels.

Inserting, Moving, and Deleting Chart Labels

Certain chart labels are automatically inserted in a chart, including a chart legend and labels for the *x* axis and *y* axis. The legend identifies which data series is represented by which data marker. Insert additional chart labels with options in the Labels group in the Chart Tools Layout tab. For example, click the Chart Title button in the Labels group and a drop-down list displays with options for inserting a chart title in a specific location in the chart.

You can move and/or size a chart label. To move a chart label, click the label to select it and then move the mouse pointer over the border line until the pointer turns into a four-headed arrow. Hold down the left mouse button, drag the label to the desired location, and then release the mouse button. To size a chart label, use the sizing handles that display around the selected label to increase or decrease the size. To delete a chart label, click the label to select it and then press the Delete key. You can also delete a label by right-clicking the label and then clicking *Delete* at the shortcut menu.

Quick Steps

Add Chart Labels
1. Make the chart active.
2. Click Chart Tools Layout tab.
3. Click desired chart labels button.
4. Choose desired option at drop-down list.

Chart Title

Figure 7.6 Chart Tools Layout Tab

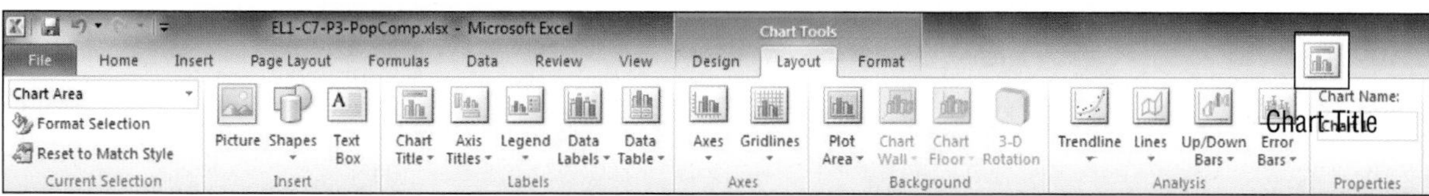

Project 3a Creating a Chart and Changing Layout of Chart Labels

1. Open **PopComp.xlsx** and then save the workbook with Save As and name it **EL1-C7-P3-PopComp**.
2. Create a Bar chart by completing the following steps:
   a. Select cells A2 through H4.
   b. Click the Insert tab.
   c. Click the Bar button in the Charts group and then click the *Clustered Horizontal Cylinder* option in the *Cylinder* section.
3. Change to a Line chart by completing the following steps:
   a. Click the Change Chart Type button in the Type group.
   b. At the Change Chart Type dialog box, click *Line* located at the left side of the dialog box.
   c. Click the *Line with Markers* option in the *Line* section (fourth option from the left).

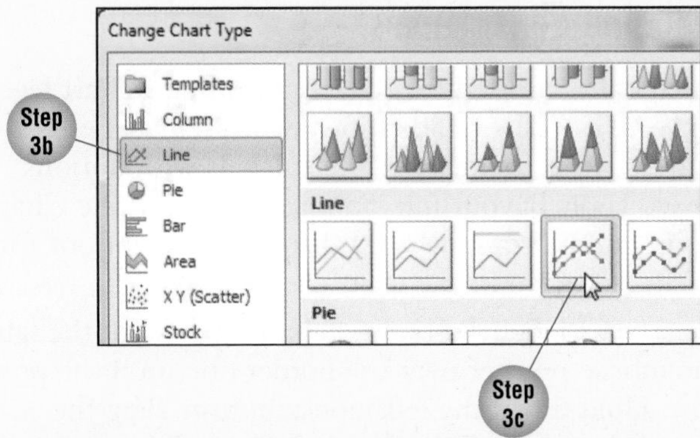

   d. Click OK to close the Change Chart Type dialog box.
4. Click the More button in the Chart Styles group in the Chart Tools Design tab and then click *Style 18* at the drop-down gallery (second option from left in the third row).

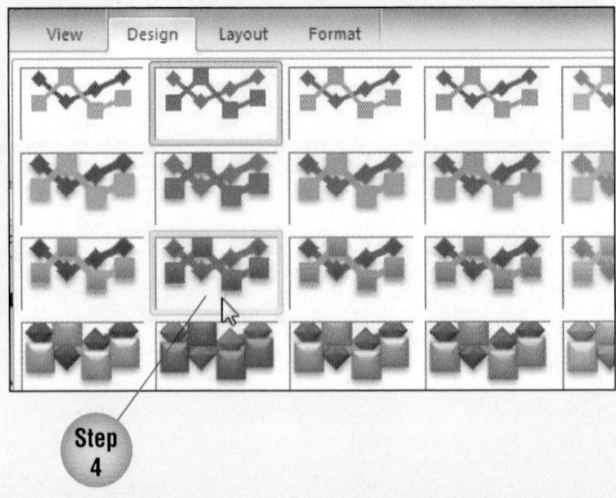

5. Change the layout of the chart by completing the following steps:
   a. Click the Chart Tools Layout tab.
   b. Click the Legend button in the Labels group.
   c. At the drop-down list, click the *Show Legend at Bottom* option.
   d. Click the Chart Title button in the Labels group.
   e. At the drop-down list, click the *Above Chart* option.

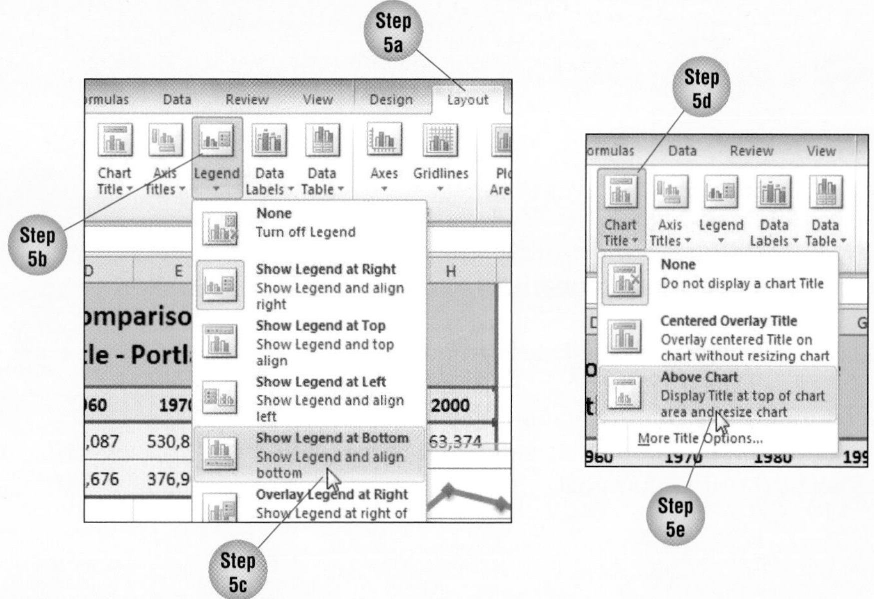

   f. Select the text *Chart Title* located in the chart title text box and then type Population Comparison.
6. Insert an *x*-axis title by completing the following steps:
   a. Click the Axis Titles button, point to the *Primary Horizontal Axis Title* option at the drop-down list, and then click *Title Below Axis* at the side menu.
   b. Select the text *Axis Title* located in the title text box and then type Decades.

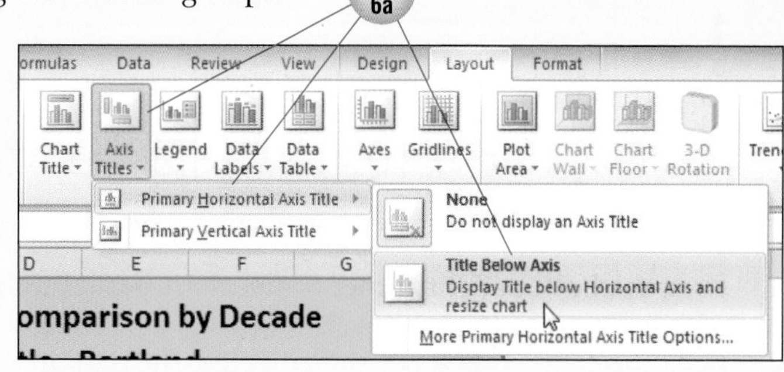

7. Insert a *y*-axis title by completing the following steps:
   a. Click the Axis Titles button, point to the *Primary Vertical Axis Title* option at the drop-down list, and then click *Rotated Title* at the side menu. (This inserts a rotated title at the left side of the chart containing the text *Axis Title*).
   b. Select the text *Axis Title* located in the axis title text box and then type Total Population.

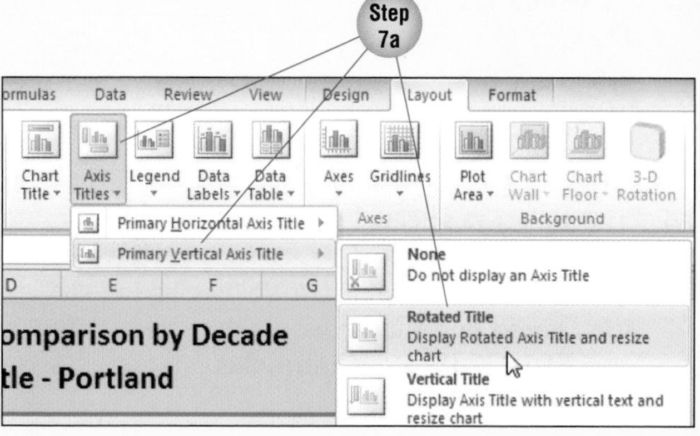

8. Click the Gridlines button in the Axes group, point to *Primary Vertical Gridlines*, and then click the *Major & Minor Gridlines* option at the side menu.

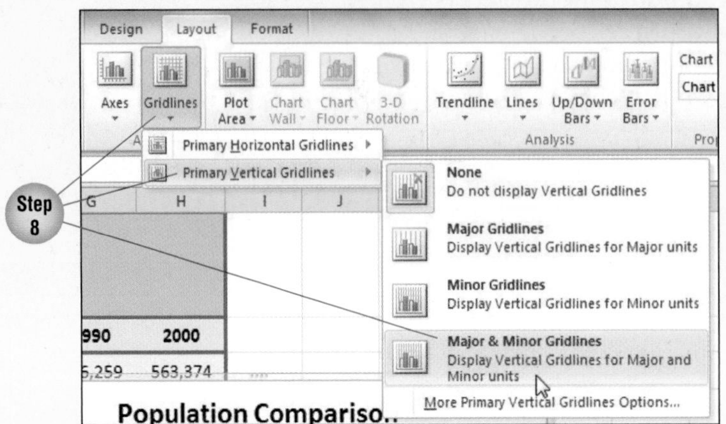

9. Click the Data Table button in the Labels group and then click the *Show Data Table* option. (This inserts cells toward the bottom of the chart containing cell data.)
10. Click the Lines button in the Analysis group and then click *Drop Lines* at the drop-down list.

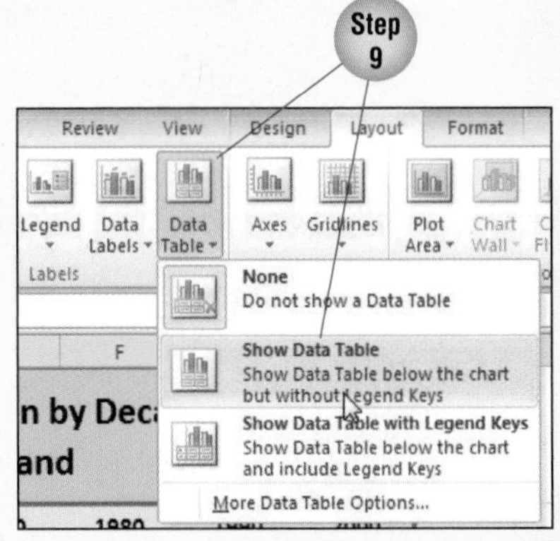

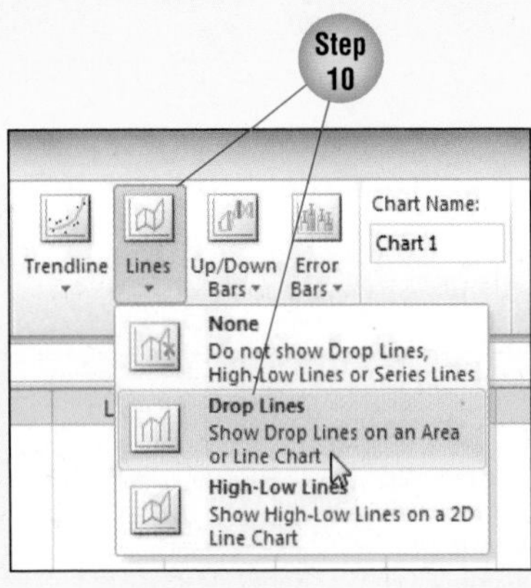

11. Drag the bottom right corner of the chart border to increase the size by approximately one inch.
12. Drag the chart so it is positioned below the data in cells but not overlapping the data.
13. Click the *x*-axis title (*Decades*) to select the title text box and then drag the box so it is positioned as shown at right.
14. Print only the selected chart.
15. Delete the horizontal axis title by clicking the axis title *Decades* and then pressing the Delete key.
16. Save **EL1-C7-P3-PopComp.xlsx**.

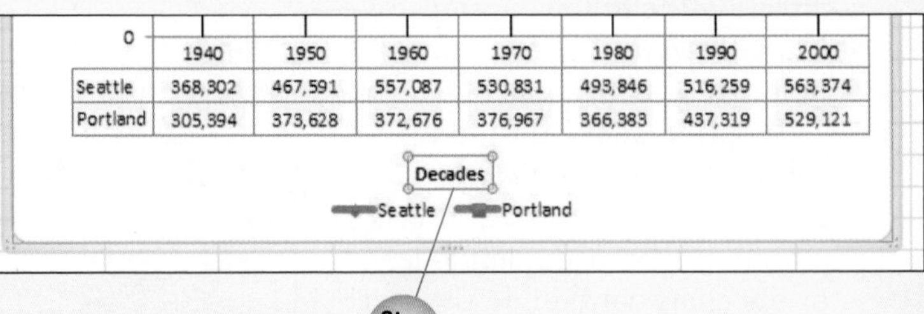

Inserting Shapes

The Insert group in the Chart Tools Layout tab contains three buttons with options for inserting shapes or images in a chart. Click the Shapes button in the Insert group and a drop-down list displays with a variety of shape options as shown in Figure 7.7. Click the desired shape at the drop-down list and the mouse pointer turns into a thin, black plus symbol. Drag with this pointer symbol to create the shape in the chart. The shape is inserted in the chart with default formatting. You can change this formatting with options in the Drawing Tools Format tab. This tab contains many of the same options as the Chart Tools Format tab. For example, you can insert a shape, apply a shape or WordArt style, and arrange and size the shape.

Quick Steps

Insert Shape
1. Make the chart active.
2. Click Chart Tools Layout tab.
3. Click Shapes button.
4. Click desired shape at drop-down list.
5. Drag pointer symbol to create shape in chart.

Shapes

Moving, Sizing, and Deleting Shapes

Move, size, and delete shapes in the same manner as moving, sizing, and deleting chart elements. To move a shape, select the shape, position the mouse pointer over the border line until the pointer turns into a four-headed arrow. Hold down the left mouse button, drag the shape to the desired location, and then release the mouse button. To size a shape, select the shape and then use the sizing handles that display around the shape to increase or decrease the size. Delete a selected shape by clicking the Delete key or right-clicking the shape and then clicking *Cut* at the shortcut menu.

Chart elements can be repositioned for easier viewing.

Figure 7.7 Shapes Button Drop-down List

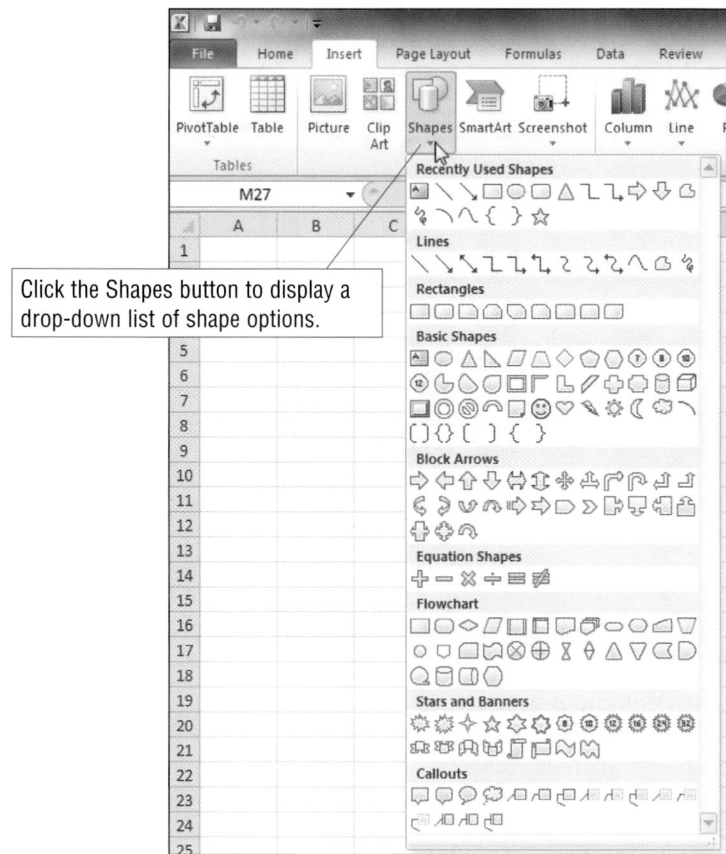

Project 3b Inserting and Customizing a Shape Part 2 of 3

1. With **EL1-C7-P3-PopComp.xlsx** open, make sure the Chart Tools Layout tab displays.
2. Create a shape similar to the shape shown in Figure 7.8. Begin by clicking the Shapes button in the Insert group.
3. Click the *Up Arrow Callout* shape in the *Block Arrows* section (last shape in the second row).

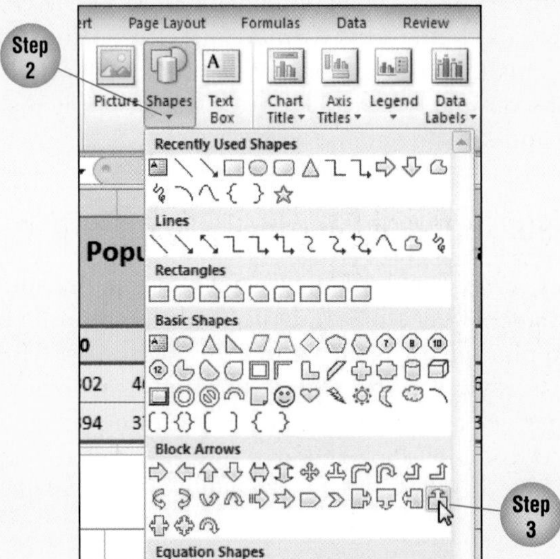

4. Drag in the chart to create the shape. To do this, position the mouse pointer in the chart, hold down the left mouse button, drag to create the shape, and then release the mouse button.
5. Click the More button located to the right of the shape style thumbnails in the Shapes Styles group and then click *Subtle Effect - Blue, Accent 1* at the drop-down gallery.

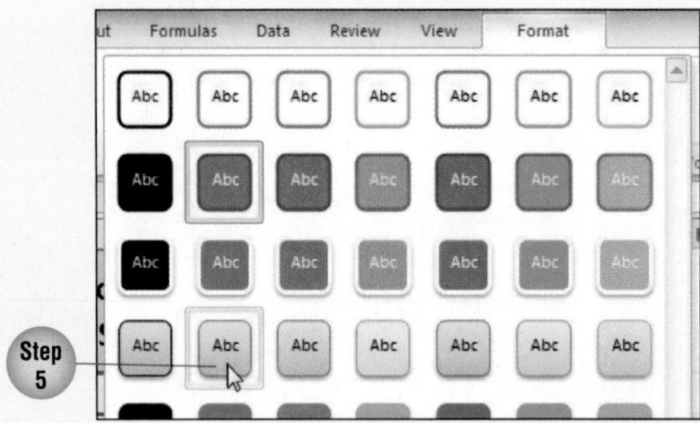

6. With the shape selected, use the sizing handles around the shape to increase and/or decrease the size so it displays as shown in Figure 7.8.
7. With the shape still selected, type Largest Disparity in the shape box, press Enter, and then type (184,411).
8. Select the text you just typed and then complete the following steps:
   a. Click the Home tab.
   b. Click the Center button in the Alignment group.
   c. Click the Bold button in the Font group.
   d. Click the Font Size button arrow and then click *9*.
9. With the shape selected, drag the shape so it is positioned as shown in Figure 7.8.
10. Save **EL1-C7-P3-PopComp.xlsx**.

Figure 7.8 Project 3b Chart

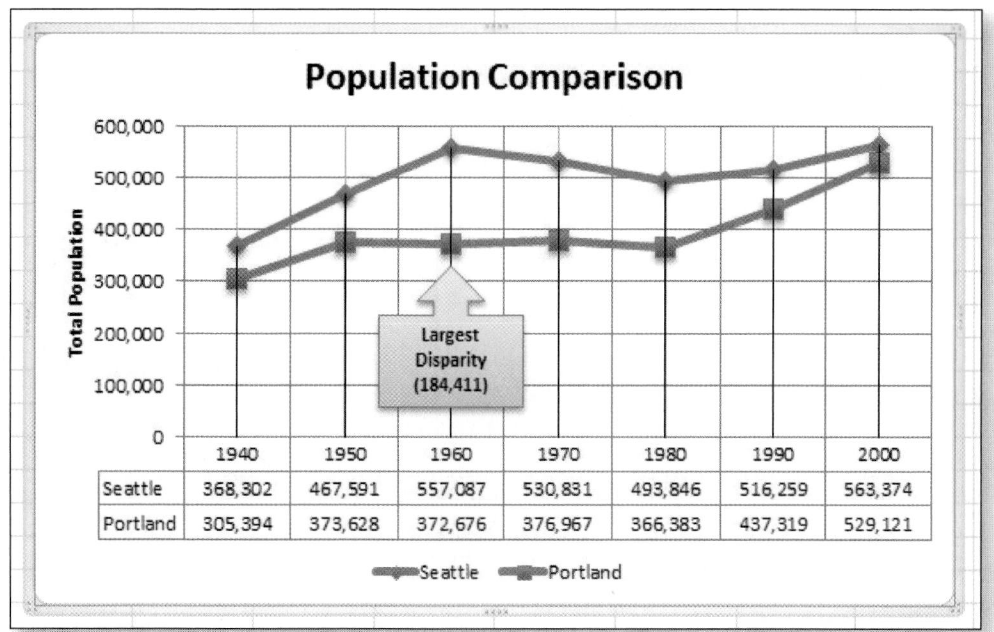

Inserting Images

Click the Picture button in the Insert group in the Chart Tools Layout tab and the Insert Picture dialog box displays. If you have a picture or image file saved in a folder, navigate to the desired folder and then double-click the file name. This inserts the picture or image in the chart. Drag the picture or image to the desired position in the chart and use the sizing handles to change the size.

Quick Steps

Insert Image
1. Make the chart active.
2. Click Chart Tools Layout tab.
3. Click Picture button.
4. Double-click desired file name.

Project 3c **Inserting a Picture in a Chart** Part 3 of 3

1. With **EL1-C7-P3-PopComp.xlsx** open, make sure the chart is selected and then click the Chart Tools Layout tab.
2. Insert the company logo by completing the following steps:
   a. Click the Picture button in the Insert group.
   b. At the Insert Picture dialog box, navigate to the Excel2010L1C7 folder on your storage medium and then double-click ***WELogo.jpg*** in the list box.

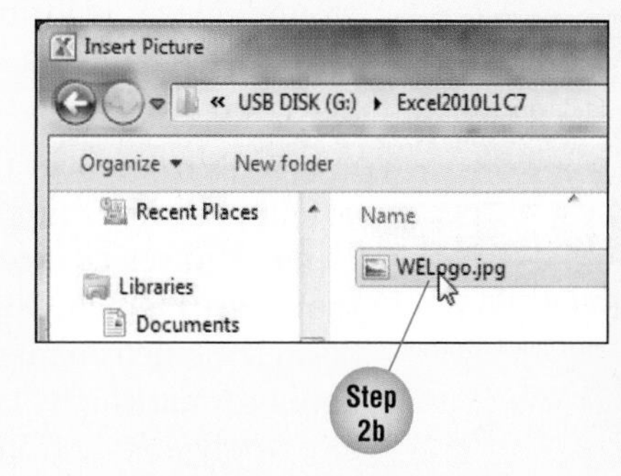

3. With the logo image inserted in the chart, use the sizing handles to decrease the size of the image and then move the image so it displays in the upper left corner of the chart area as shown in Figure 7.9.
4. Print only the selected chart.
5. Save and then close **EL1-C7-P3-PopComp.xlsx**.

Figure 7.9 Project 3c Chart

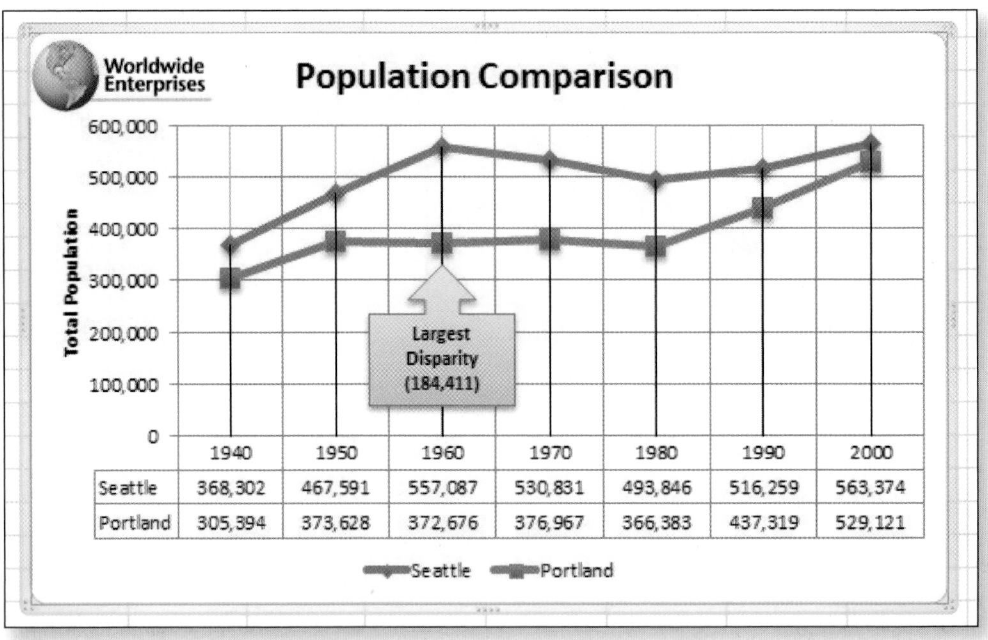

Project 4 Create a Costs Percentage Pie Chart

1 Part

You will open a workbook containing percentage of costs for company departments and then create a pie chart with the data. You will apply formatting to the chart and then move the chart to a new worksheet.

Reset to Match Style

Chart Elements

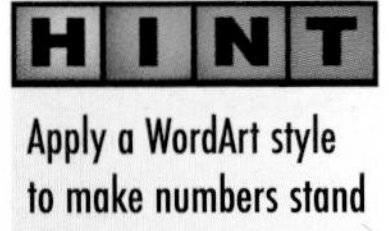

Apply a WordArt style to make numbers stand out.

Changing the Chart Formatting

Customize the format of the chart and chart elements with options in the Chart Tools Format tab as shown in Figure 7.10. With buttons in the Current Selection group you can identify a specific element in the chart and then apply formatting to that element. You can also click the Reset to Match Style button in the Current Selection group to return the formatting of the chart back to the original layout.

With options in the Shape Styles group, you can apply formatting styles to specific elements in a chart. Identify the desired element either by clicking the element to select it or by clicking the down-pointing arrow at the right side of the Chart Elements button in the Current Selection group and then clicking the desired element name at the drop-down list. With the chart element specified, apply formatting by clicking a style button in the Shape Styles group. You can also apply a style from a drop-down gallery. Display this gallery by clicking the

Figure 7.10 Chart Tools Format Tab

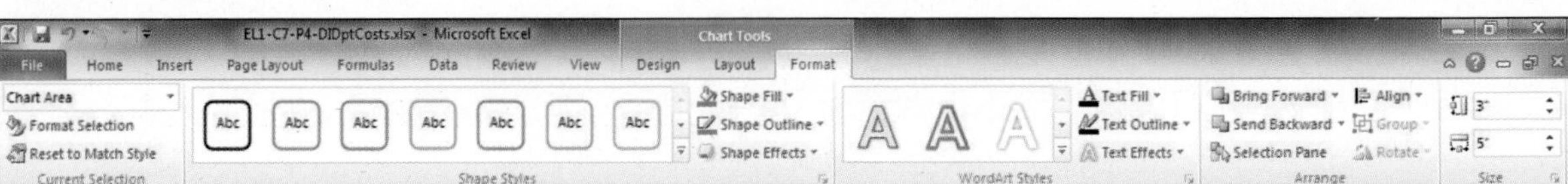

More button located at the right side of the shape styles. Click the up-pointing or the down-pointing arrow at the right of the shape styles to cycle through the available style options.

Project 4 Creating and Formatting a Pie Chart

Part 1 of 1

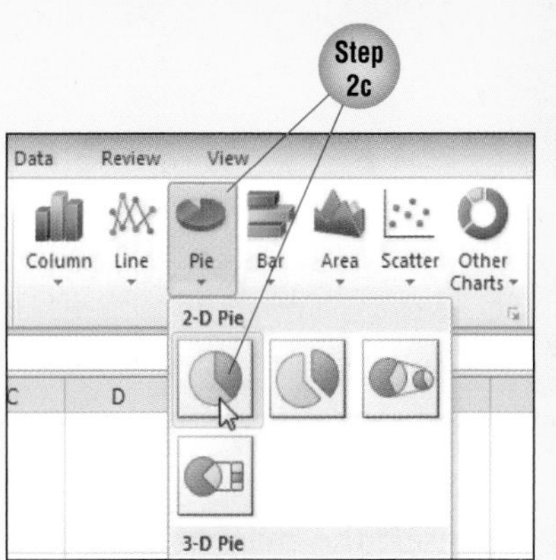

1. Open **DIDptCosts.xlsx** and then save the workbook with Save As and name it **EL1-C7-P4-DIDptCosts.**
2. Create the pie chart as shown in Figure 7.11 by completing the following steps:
   a. Select cells A3 through B10.
   b. Click the Insert tab.
   c. Click the Pie button in the Charts group and then click the first pie option in the *2-D Pie* section.
3. Click the More button located at the right side of the Chart Styles group.
4. At the drop-down gallery, click the *Style 32* option (last option in the fourth row).

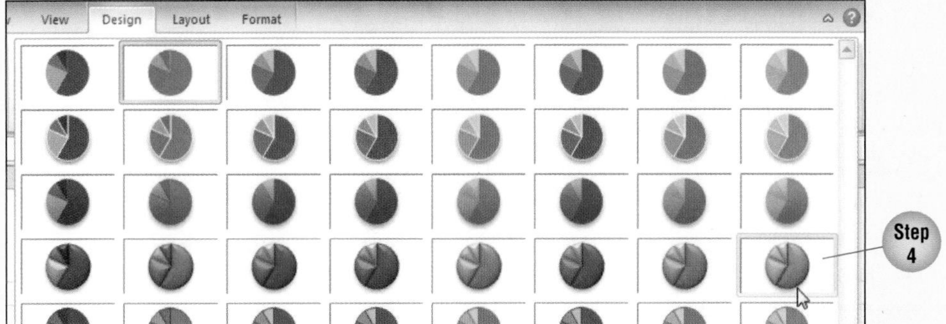

5. Click the Chart Tools Layout tab.
6. Insert data labels by clicking the Data Labels button in the Labels group and then clicking *Outside End* at the drop-down list.
7. Format chart elements by completing the following steps:
   a. Click the Chart Tools Format tab.
   b. Click the down-pointing arrow at the right side of the Chart Elements button in the Current Selection group and then click *Legend* at the drop-down list.
   c. Click the More button at the right of the shape style thumbnails in the Shape Styles group and then click the last option in the fourth row (*Subtle Effect - Orange, Accent 6*).
   d. Click the down-pointing arrow at the right side of the Chart Elements button in the Current Selection group and then click *Chart Title*.

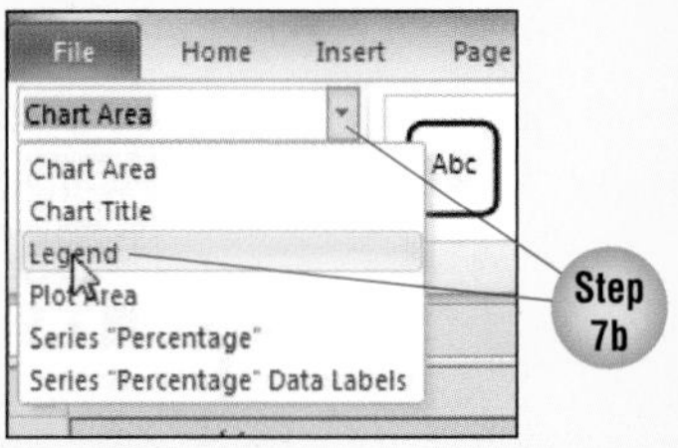

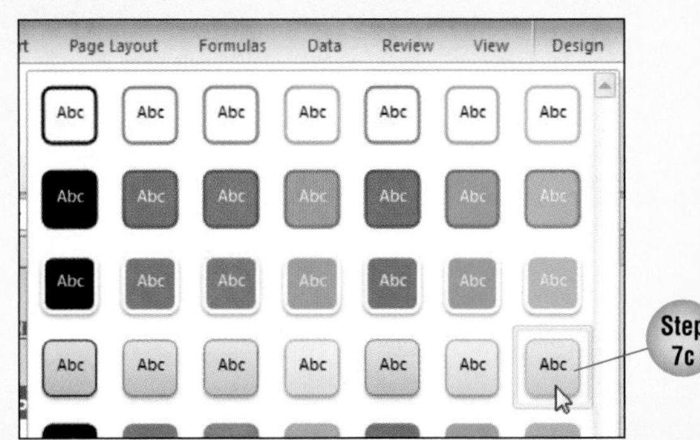

e. Click the More button at the right side of the WordArt style thumbnails in the WordArt Styles group and then click the *Gradient Fill - Orange, Accent 6, Inner Shadow* (second option from the left in the fourth row).

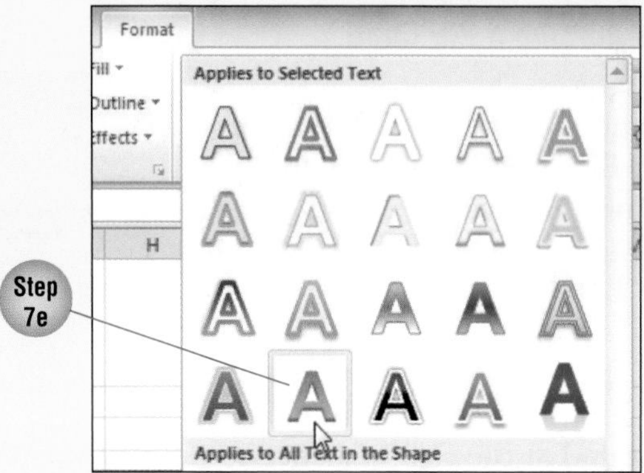

f. Deselect the chart title.

8. Insert the chart in a new sheet by completing the following steps:
   a. With the chart selected, click the Chart Tools Design tab.
   b. Click the Move Chart button in the Location group.
   c. At the Move Chart dialog box, click the *New sheet* option.
   d. Click OK.
9. Print only the worksheet containing the chart.
10. Save and then close **EL1-C7-P4-DIDptCosts.xlsx**.

Figure 7.11 Project 4

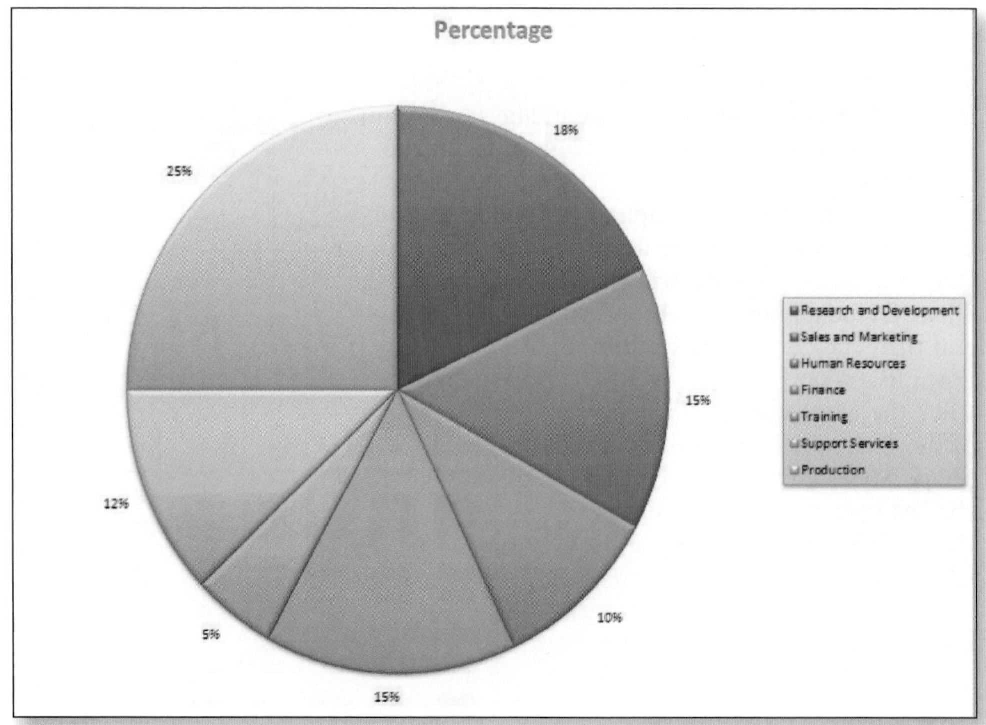

Project 5 Create a Regional Sales Column Chart 1 Part

You will create a column chart using regional sales data, change the layout of the chart, apply formatting, and change the height and width of the chart.

Quick Steps

Change Chart Height and/or Width
1. Make the chart active.
2. Click Chart Tools Format tab.
3. Insert desired height and/or width with *Shape Height* and/or *Shape Width* text boxes.

You can size a chart by selecting the chart and then dragging a sizing handle. You can also size a chart to specific measurements with the *Shape Height* and *Shape Width* measurement boxes in the Size group in the Chart Tools Format tab. Change the height or width by clicking the up- or down-pointing arrows that display at the right side of the button or select the current measurement in the measurement box and then type a specific measurement.

Project 5 Changing the Height and Width of a Chart

Part 1 of 1

1. Open **DIRegSales.xlsx**.
2. Save the workbook with Save As and name it **EL1-C7-P5-DIRegSales**.
3. Create a Column chart by completing the following steps:
   a. Select cells A3 through B8.
   b. Click the Insert tab.
   c. Click the Column button in the Charts group.
   d. Click the *3-D Clustered Column* option (first option in the *3-D Column* section).
   e. Click the Switch Row/Column button located in the Data group to change the data series.
   f. Click the *Layout 1* option in the Chart Layouts group (first option from the left in the group).
   g. Select the text *Chart Title* and then type Northeast Regional Sales.
   h. Click the More button located at the right side of the thumbnails in the Chart Styles group and then click *Style 32* at the drop-down gallery (last option in fourth row).

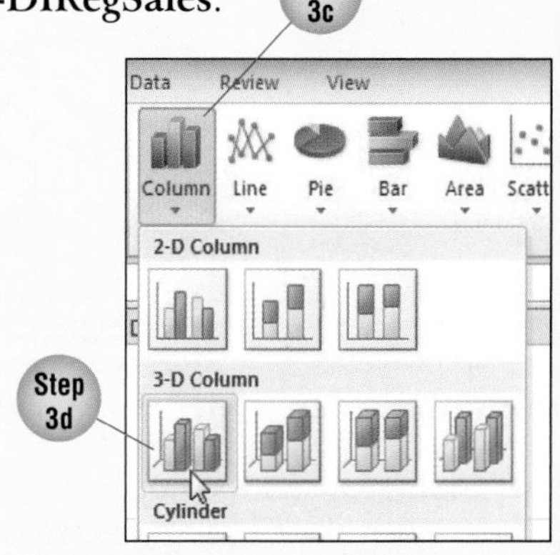

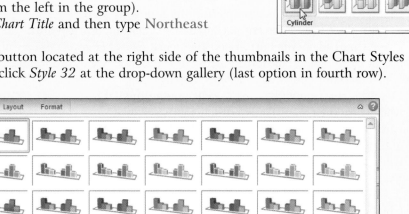

4. Change a series color by completing the following steps:
   a. Click the Chart Tools Format tab.
   b. Click the down-pointing arrow at the right side of the Chart Elements button in the Current Selection group and then click *Series "Newman, Jared"* at the drop-down list.

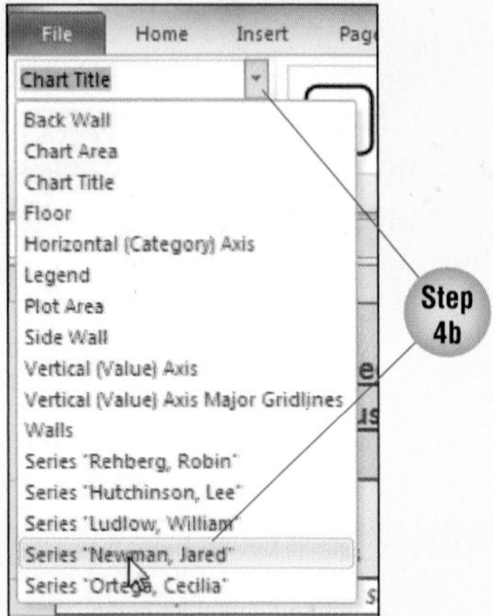

   c. Click the Shape Fill button arrow in the Shape Styles group and then click the dark red color *Red, Accent 2, Darker 25%*.

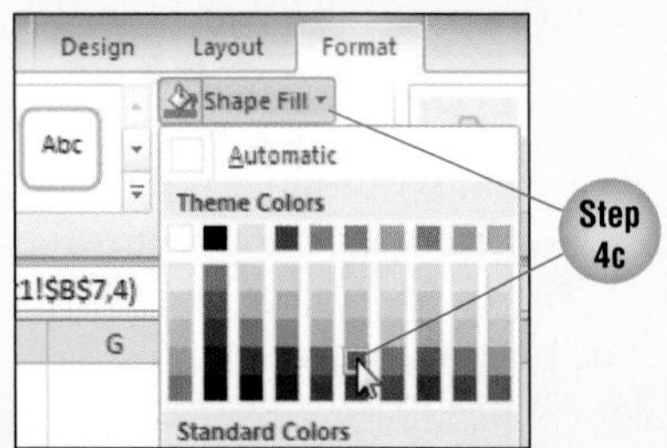

5. Change a series color by completing the following steps:
   a. With the Chart Tools Format tab active, click the down-pointing arrow at the right side of the Chart Elements button and then click *Series "Hutchinson, Lee"* at the drop-down list.
   b. Click the Shape Fill button arrow in the Shape Styles group and then click the dark green color *Olive Green, Accent 3, Darker 25%*.
6. Drag the chart down below the cells containing data.
7. Make sure the Chart Tools Format tab is selected.
8. Click in the *Shape Height* measurement box in the Size group and then type 3.8.
9. Click the up-pointing arrow at the right side of the *Shape Width* measurement box in the Size group until *5.5* displays in the text box.
10. Click outside the chart to deselect it.
11. Make sure the chart fits on one page and then print the worksheet (cells containing data and the chart).
12. Save and then close **EL1-C7-P5-DIRegSales.xlsx**.

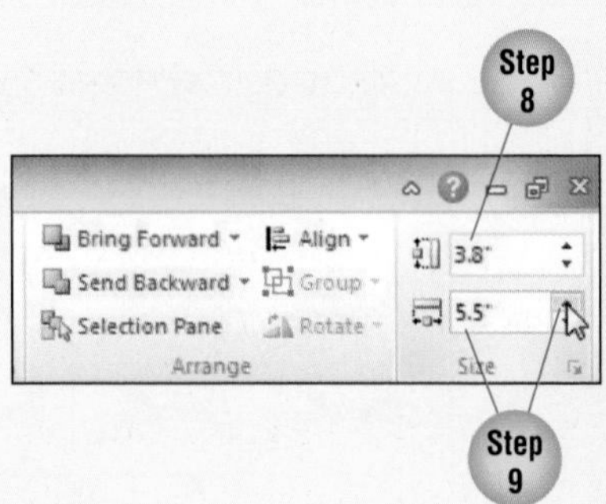

Chapter Summary

- A chart is a visual presentation of data. Excel provides 11 basic chart types: Area, Bar, Bubble, Column, Doughnut, Line, Pyramid, Radar, Stock, Surface, and XY (Scatter).
- To create a chart, select cells containing data you want to chart, click the Insert tab, and then click the desired chart button in the Charts group.
- A chart you create is inserted in the same worksheet as the selected cells.
- You can increase or decrease the size of a chart by positioning the mouse pointer on the four dots located in the middle of each border line or the three dots at each corner, and then dragging to the desired size.
- Move a chart by positioning the mouse pointer on the chart border until it turns into a four-headed arrow and then dragging with the mouse.
- Data in cells used to create the chart are linked to the chart. If you change the data in cells, the chart reflects the changes.
- Print by selecting the chart, displaying the Print tab Backstage view, and then clicking the Print button.
- When you insert a chart in a worksheet, the Chart Tools Design tab is active. Use options in this tab to change the chart type, specify a different layout or style, and change the location of the chart.
- Choose a chart style with buttons in the Charts group in the Insert tab or at the Change Chart Type dialog box.
- The Chart Layouts group in the Chart Tools Design tab contains preformatted chart layout options. Use options in the Chart Styles group to apply a particular style of formatting to a chart.
- By default, a chart is inserted in the active worksheet. You can move the chart to a new sheet within the workbook with the *New sheet* option at the Move Chart dialog box.
- To delete a chart in a worksheet, click the chart to select it, and then press the Delete key. To delete a chart created in a separate sheet, position the mouse pointer on the chart tab, click the right mouse button, and then click Delete.
- Use options in the Chart Tools Layout tab to change the layout and/or insert additional chart labels, shapes, pictures, or clip art images.
- Insert additional chart labels with options in the Labels group in the Chart Tools Layout tab.
- Use buttons in the Insert group in the Chart Tools Layout tab to insert shapes, pictures, or text boxes.
- To move a chart label, click the label to select it and then drag the label with the mouse. To delete a label, click the label and then press the Delete key.
- Use options in the Chart Tools Format tab to customize the format of the chart and chart elements.
- Change the chart size by dragging the chart sizing handles or by entering a measurement in the *Shape Height* and *Shape Width* measurement boxes in the Size group in the Chart Tools Format tab.

Commands Review

FEATURE	RIBBON TAB, GROUP	BUTTON, OPTION	KEYBOARD SHORTCUT
Default chart in worksheet			Alt + F1
Default chart in separate sheet			F11
Change Chart Type dialog box	Chart Tools Design, Type		
Move Chart dialog box	Chart Tools Design, Location		
Shapes button drop-down list	Chart Tools Layout, Insert		
Insert Picture dialog box	Chart Tools Layout, Insert		

Concepts Check Test Your Knowledge

Completion: In the space provided at the right, indicate the correct term, symbol, or command.

1. This is the keyboard shortcut to create a chart with the default chart type in the active worksheet. ____________________
2. The Charts group contains buttons for creating charts and is located in this tab. ____________________
3. This type of chart shows proportions and relationships of parts to the whole. ____________________
4. When you create a chart, the chart is inserted in this location by default. ____________________
5. Select a chart in a worksheet, display the Print tab Backstage view, and the first gallery in the Settings category is automatically changed to this option. ____________________
6. Use buttons in the Insert group in this tab to insert shapes or pictures. ____________________
7. When Excel creates a chart, the data in the first row (except the first cell) is used to create this. ____________________
8. Click this option at the Move Chart dialog box to move the chart to a separate sheet. ____________________

9. Click the Picture button in the Chart Tools Layout tab and this dialog box displays. ____________

10. Change the chart size by entering measurements in these measurement boxes in the Size group in the Chart Tools Format tab. ____________

Skills Check Assess Your Performance

Assessment 1

CREATE A COMPANY SALES COLUMN CHART

1. Open **CMSales.xlsx** and then save the workbook with Save As and name it **EL1-C7-A1-CMSales**.
2. Select cells A3 through C15 and then create a Column chart with the following specifications:
   a. Choose the *3-D Clustered Column* chart at the Chart button drop-down list.
   b. At the Chart Tools Design tab, click the *Layout 3* option in the Chart Layouts group.
   c. Change the chart style to *Style 26*.
   d. Select the text *Chart Title* and then type Company Sales.
   e. Move the location of the chart to a new sheet.
3. Print only the worksheet containing the chart.
4. Save and then close **EL1-C7-A1-CMSales.xlsx**.

Assessment 2

CREATE QUARTERLY DOMESTIC AND FOREIGN SALES BAR CHART

1. Open **CMPQtrlySales.xlsx** and then save the workbook with Save As and name it **EL1-C7-A2-CMPQtrlySales**.
2. Select cells A3 through E5 and then create a Bar chart with the following specifications:
   a. Click the *Clustered Bar in 3-D* option at the Bar button drop-down list.
   b. At the Chart Tools Design tab choose the *Layout 2* option in the Chart Layouts group.
   c. Choose the *Style 23* option in the Chart Styles group.
   d. Select the text *Chart Title*, type Quarterly Sales, and then click in the chart but outside any chart elements.
   e. Display the Chart Tools Layout tab and then insert primary vertical minor gridlines. (Do this with the Gridlines button.)
   f. Display the Chart Tools Format tab and then apply to the chart the *Subtle Effect - Olive Green, Accent 3* option in the Shape Styles group.
   g. Select the *Domestic* series (using the Chart Elements button) and then apply a purple fill (*Purple, Accent 4, Darker 25%*) using the Shape Fill button in the Shape Styles group.
   h. Select the Foreign series and then apply a dark aqua fill (*Aqua, Accent 5, Darker 25%*) using the Shape Fill button in the Shape Styles group.

i. Select the chart title and then apply the *Gradient Fill - Purple, Accent 4, Reflection* option with the WordArt Styles button.
j. Increase the height of the chart to 4 inches and the width to 6 inches.
k. Move the chart below the cells containing data and make sure the chart fits on the page with the data.

3. Print only the worksheet.
4. Save and then close **EL1-C7-A2-CMPQtrlySales.xlsx**.

Assessment 3

CREATE AND FORMAT A CORPORATE SALES COLUMN CHART

1. Open **CorpSales.xlsx** and then save the workbook with Save As and name it **EL1-C7-A3-CorpSales**.
2. Create a column chart and format the chart so it displays as shown in Figure 7.12.
3. Save, print, and then close **EL1-C7-A3-CorpSales.xlsx**.

Figure 7.12 Assessment 3

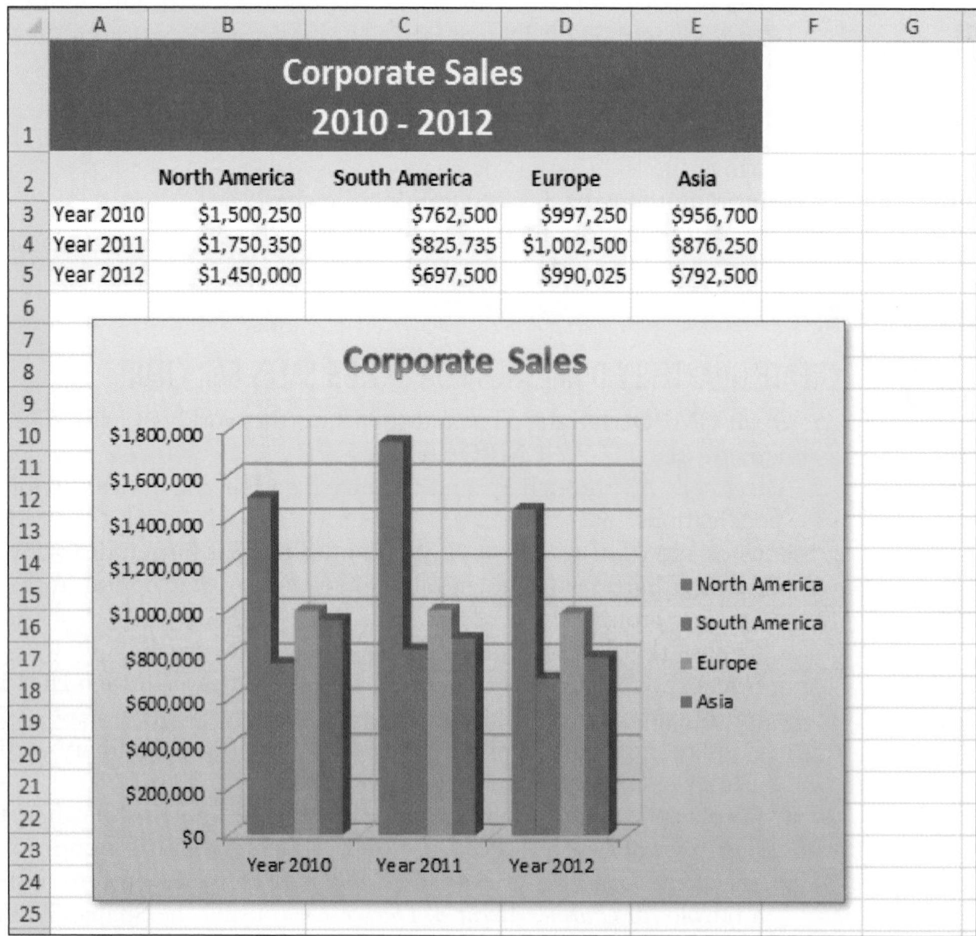

Assessment 4

CREATE A FUND ALLOCATIONS PIE CHART

1. At a blank worksheet, create a worksheet with the following data:

Fund Allocations	
Fund	Percentage
Annuities	23%
Stocks	42%
Bonds	15%
Money Market	20%

2. Using the data above, create a pie chart as a separate worksheet with the following specifications:
   a. Create a title for the pie chart.
   b. Add data labels to the chart.
   c. Add any other enhancements that will improve the visual presentation of the data.
3. Save the workbook and name it **EL1-C7-A4-Funds**.
4. Print only the worksheet containing the chart.
5. Close **EL1-C7-A4-Funds.xlsx**.

Assessment 5

CREATE AN ACTUAL AND PROJECTED SALES CHART

1. Open **StateSales.xlsx** and then save the workbook with Save As and name it **EL1-C7-A5-StateSales**.
2. Look at the data in the worksheet and then create a chart to represent the data. Add a title to the chart and add any other enhancements to improve the visual display of the chart.
3. Save the workbook and then print the chart.
4. Close **EL1-C7-A5-StateSales.xlsx**.

Assessment

CREATE A STACKED CYLINDER CHART

1. Use Excel's help feature to learn more about chart types and specifically about stacked 3-D column charts and then create a worksheet with the data shown in Figure 7.13. Create with the data a 100% stacked cylinder chart in a separate sheet. Create an appropriate title for the chart and apply any other formatting to enhance the appearance of the chart.
2. Save the completed workbook and name it **EL1-C7-A6-CMPerSales**.
3. Print both sheets of the workbook (the sheet containing the data in cells and the sheet containing the chart).
4. Close **EL1-C7-A6-CMPerSales.xlsx**.

Figure 7.13 Assessment 6

Clearline Manufacturing Regional Sales Percentages				
	Region 1	Region 2	Region 3	Region 4
Jan-June	12%	20%	41%	27%
July-Dec	16%	27%	35%	22%

Visual Benchmark Demonstrate Your Proficiency

CREATE AND FORMAT A PIE CHART

1. At a blank workbook, enter data and then create a pie chart in a separate sheet as shown in Figure 7.14. Use the information shown in the pie chart to create the data. Format the pie chart so it appears similar to what you see in Figure 7.14.
2. Save the completed workbook and name it **EL1-C7-VB-CMFebExp**.
3. Print both worksheets in the workbook.
4. Close **EL1-C7-VB-CMFebExp.xlsx**

Figure 7.14 Visual Benchmark

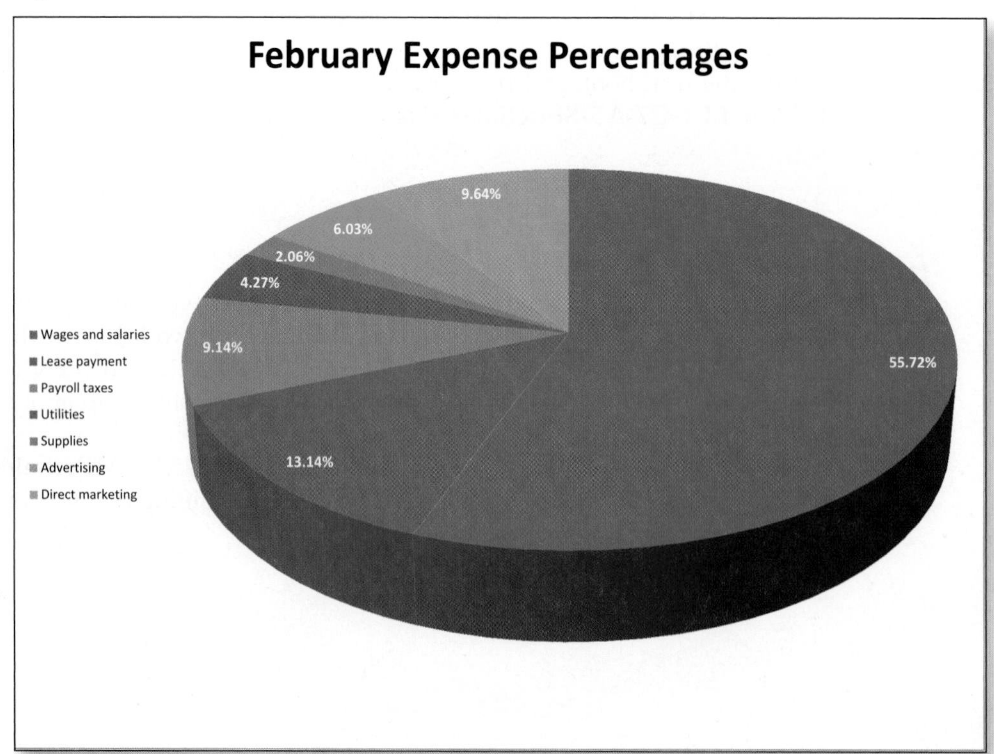

Case Study Apply Your Skills

Part 1

You are an administrator for Dollar Wise Financial Services and you need to prepare charts indicating home loan and commercial loan amounts for the past year. Use the information below to prepare a chart in Excel. You determine the type and style of chart and the layout and formatting of the chart. Insert a shape in the Commercial Loans chart that contains the text *All-time High* and points to the second quarter amount (*$6,785,250*).

Home Loans
1st Qtr. = $2,675,025
2nd Qtr. = $3,125,750
3rd Qtr. = $1,975,425
4th Qtr. = $875,650

Commercial Loans
1st Qtr. = $5,750,980
2nd Qtr. = $6,785,250
3rd Qtr. = $4,890,625
4th Qtr. = $2,975,900

Save the workbook and name it **EL1-C7-CS-DWQtrSales**. Print only the chart and then close **EL1-C7-CS-DWQtrSales.xlsx**.

Part 2

You need to present information on the budget for the company. You have the dollar amounts and need to convert the amounts to a percentage of the entire budget. Use the information below to calculate the percentage of the budget for each item and then create a pie chart with the information. You determine the chart style, layout, and formatting.

Total Budget: $6,000,000

Building Costs	=	$720,000
Salaries	=	$2,340,000
Benefits	=	$480,000
Advertising	=	$840,000
Marketing	=	$600,000
Client Expenses	=	$480,000
Equipment	=	$420,000
Supplies	=	$120,000

Save the workbook containing the pie chart and name it **EL1-C7-CS-DWBudgetPercentages**. Print only the chart and then close **EL1-C7-CS-DWBudgetPercentages.xlsx**.

Part 3

One of your clients owns a number of stocks and you would like to prepare a daily chart of the stocks' high, low, and close price. Use the Help feature to learn about stock charts and then create a stock chart with the following information (the company stock symbols are fictitious):

	IDE	POE	QRR
High	$23.75	$18.55	$34.30
Low	$18.45	$15.00	$31.70
Close	$19.65	$17.30	$33.50

Save the workbook containing the stock chart and name it **EL1-C7-CS-DWStocks**. Print only the chart and then close **EL1-C7-CS-DWStocks.xlsx**.

Part 4

You need to prepare information on mortgage rates for a community presentation. You decide to include the information on mortgage rates in a chart for easy viewing. Use the Internet to search for historical data on the national average for mortgage rates. Determine the average mortgage rate for a 30-year FRM (fixed-rate mortgage) for each January and July beginning with the year 2008 and continuing to the current year. Also include the current average rate. Use this information to create the chart. Save the workbook and name it **EL1-C7-CS-DWRates**. Print only the chart and then close **EL1-C7-CS-DWRates.xlsx**.

Microsoft® Excel®

Adding Visual Interest to Workbooks

PERFORMANCE OBJECTIVES

Upon successful completion of Chapter 8, you will be able to:

- **Insert symbols and special characters**
- **Insert, size, move, and format a clip art image**
- **Insert a screenshot**
- **Draw, format, and copy shapes**
- **Insert, size, move, and format a picture image**
- **Insert, format, and type text in a text box**
- **Insert a picture image as a watermark**
- **Insert and format SmartArt diagrams**
- **Insert and format WordArt**

Tutorials

8.1 Inserting Symbols and Special Characters

8.2 Inserting Pictures and Clip Art

8.3 Creating Screenshots

8.4 Inserting a Picture as a Watermark

8.5 Inserting and Formatting a SmartArt Diagram

8.6 Creating WordArt

Microsoft Excel includes a variety of features that you can use to enhance the visual appeal of a workbook. Some methods for adding visual appeal that you will learn in this chapter include inserting and modifying clip art images, screenshots, shapes, pictures, text boxes, SmartArt, and WordArt. Model answers for this chapter's projects appear on the following pages.

Excel2010L1C8

Note: Before beginning the projects, copy to your storage medium the Excel2010L1C8 subfolder from the Excel2010L1 folder on the CD that accompanies this textbook and make Excel2010L1C8 the active folder.

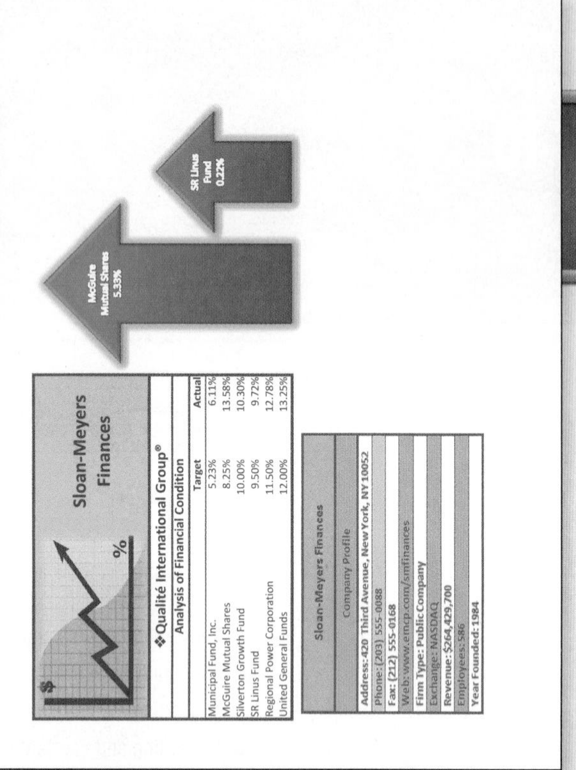

❖ Qualité International Group®

Analysis of Financial Condition

	Target	Actual
Municipal Fund, Inc.	5.23%	6.11%
McGuire Mutual Shares	8.25%	13.58%
Silverton Growth Fund	10.00%	10.30%
SR Linus Fund	9.50%	9.72%
Regional Power Corporation	11.50%	12.78%
United General Funds	12.00%	13.25%

Sloan-Meyers Finances

Company Profile

Address: 420 Third Avenue, New York, NY 10052
Phone: (203) 555-0088
Fax: (212) 555-0168
Web: www.emcp.com/smfinances
Firm Type: Public Company
Exchange: NASDAQ
Revenue: $264,429,700
Employees: 586
Year Founded: 1984

Project 1 Insert a Clip Art Image and Shapes in a Financial Analysis Workbook EL1-C8-P1-SFFinCon.xlsx

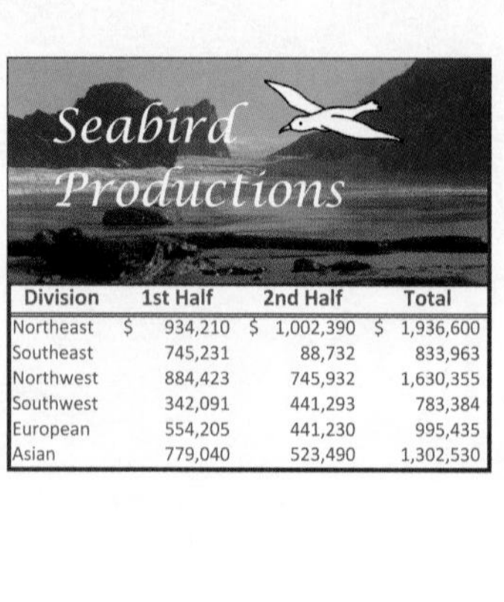

Division	1st Half	2nd Half	Total
Northeast	$ 934,210	$ 1,002,390	$ 1,936,600
Southeast	745,231	88,732	833,963
Northwest	884,423	745,932	1,630,355
Southwest	342,091	441,293	783,384
European	554,205	441,230	995,435
Asian	779,040	523,490	1,302,530

Project 2 Insert a Picture and Text Box in a Division Sales Workbook EL1-C8-P2-SPDivSales.xlsx

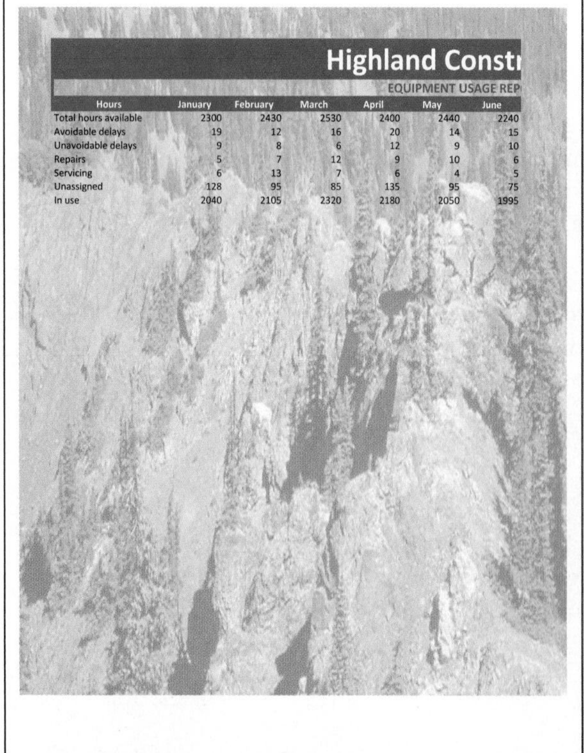

Highland Constr

EQUIPMENT USAGE REP

Hours	January	February	March	April	May	June
Total hours available	2300	2430	2530	2400	2440	2240
Avoidable delays	19	12	16	20	14	15
Unavoidable delays	9	8	6	12	9	10
Repairs	5	7	12	9	10	6
Servicing	6	13	7	6	4	5
Unassigned	128	95	85	135	95	75
In use	2040	2105	2320	2180	2050	1995

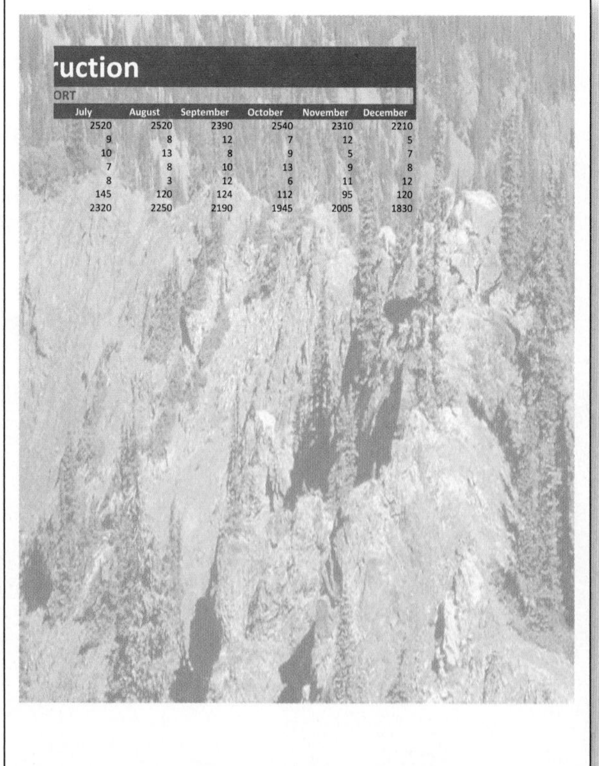

uction

ORT

July	August	September	October	November	December
2520	2520	2390	2540	2310	2210
9	8	12	7	12	5
10	13	8	9	5	7
7	8	10	13	9	8
8	3	12	6	11	12
145	120	124	112	95	120
2320	2250	2190	1945	2005	1830

Project 3 Insert a Watermark in an Equipment Usage Workbook EL1-C8-P3-HCEqpRpt.xlsx

Division	First Half	Second Half	Total Sales
Seattle	$ 1,250,360	$ 1,345,200	$ 2,595,560
Spokane	$ 905,250	$ 987,550	$ 1,892,800
Portland	$ 1,125,000	$ 1,200,500	$ 2,325,500
Olympia	$ 705,610	$ 789,450	$ 1,495,060
Total	$ 3,986,220	$ 4,322,700	$ 8,308,920

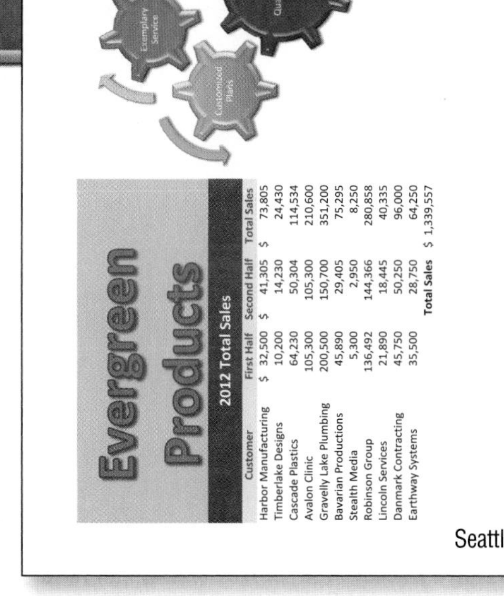

Customer	First Half	Second Half	Total Sales
Harbor Manufacturing	$ 32,500	$ 41,305	$ 73,805
Timberlake Designs	10,200	14,230	24,430
Cascade Plastics	64,230	50,304	114,534
Avalon Clinic	105,300	105,300	210,600
Gravelly Lake Plumbing	200,500	150,700	351,200
Bavarian Productions	45,890	29,405	75,295
Stealth Media	5,300	2,950	8,250
Robinson Group	136,492	144,366	280,858
Lincoln Services	21,890	18,445	40,335
Danmark Contracting	45,750	50,250	96,000
Earthway Systems	35,500	28,750	64,250
		Total Sales	$ 1,339,557

Project 4 Insert and Format Diagrams in a Company Sales Workbook EL1-C8-P4-EPSales.xlsx

Project 1 Insert a Clip Art Image and Shapes in a Financial Analysis Workbook — 5 Parts

You will open a financial analysis workbook and then insert, move, size, and format a clip art image in the workbook. You will also insert an arrow shape, type and format text in the shape, and then copy the shape.

Inserting Symbols and Special Characters

You can use the Symbol button in the Insert tab to insert special symbols in a worksheet. Click the Symbol button in the Symbols group in the Insert tab and the Symbol dialog box displays as shown in Figure 8.1. At the Symbol dialog box, double-click the desired symbol and then click Close; or click the desired symbol, click the Insert button, and then click Close. At the Symbol dialog box with the Symbols tab selected, you can change the font with the *Font* option. When you change the font, different symbols display in the dialog box. Click the Special Characters tab at the Symbol dialog box and a list of special characters displays along with keyboard shortcuts to create the special character.

Quick Steps

Insert Symbol
1. Click in desired cell.
2. Click the Insert tab.
3. Click Symbol button.
4. Double-click desired symbol.
5. Click Close.

Symbol

Quick Steps

Insert Special Character
1. Click in desired cell.
2. Click Insert tab.
3. Click Symbol button.
4. Click Special Characters tab.
5. Double-click desired special character.
6. Click Close.

HINT

You can increase or decrease the size of the Symbol dialog box by positioning the mouse pointer on the lower right corner until the pointer displays as a two-headed arrow and then dragging with the mouse.

Figure 8.1 Symbol Dialog Box with Symbols Tab Selected

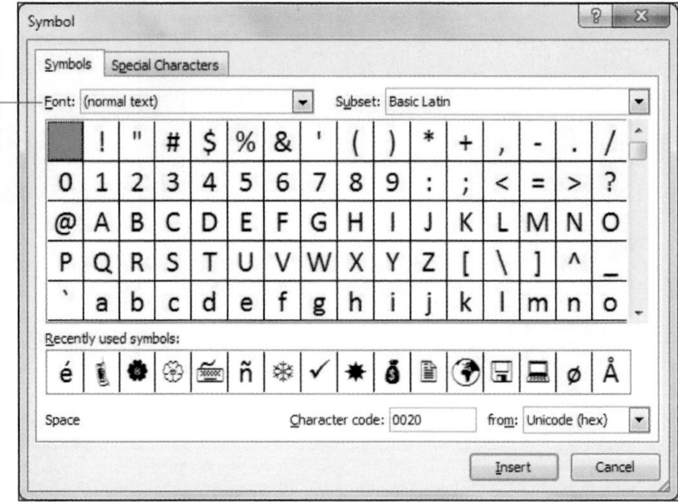

Project 1a Inserting Symbols and Special Characters

Part 1 of 5

1. Open **SFFinCon.xlsx** and then save the workbook with Save As and name it **EL1-C8-P1-SFFinCon**.
2. Insert a symbol by completing the following steps:
   a. Double-click cell A2.
   b. Delete the *e* that displays at the end of *Qualite*.
   c. With the insertion point positioned immediately right of the *t* in *Qualit*, click the Insert tab.
   d. Click the Symbol button in the Symbols group.
   e. At the Symbol dialog box, scroll down the list box and then click the *é* symbol (located in approximately the tenth or eleventh row).
   f. Click the Insert button and then click the Close button.

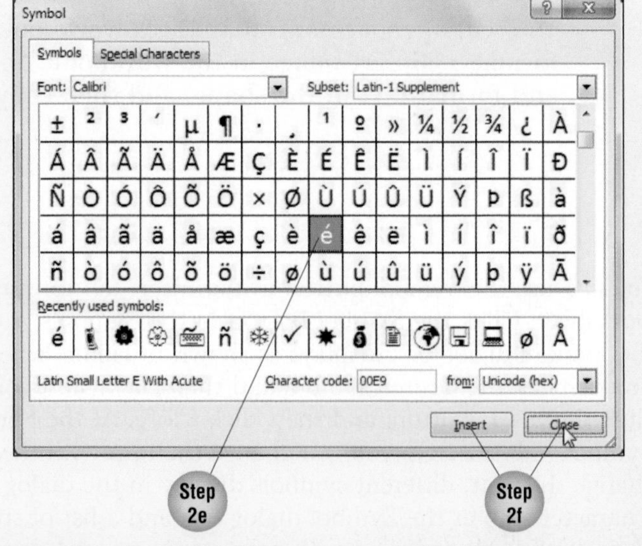

3. Insert a special character by completing the following steps:
   a. With cell A2 selected and in Edit mode, move the insertion point so it is positioned immediately right of *Group*.
   b. Click the Symbol button in the Symbols group.
   c. At the Symbol dialog box, click the Special Characters tab.
   d. Double-click the ® symbol (tenth option from the top).
   e. Click the Close button.
4. Insert a symbol by completing the following steps:
   a. With cell A2 selected and in Edit mode, move the insertion point so it is positioned immediately left of the *Q* in *Qualité*.
   b. Click the Symbol button in the Symbols group.
   c. At the Symbol dialog box, click the down-pointing arrow at the right side of the *Font* option box and then click *Wingdings* at the drop-down list. (You will need to scroll down the list to display this option.)
   d. Click the ❖ symbol (located in approximately the sixth row).
   e. Click the Insert button and then click the Close button.
5. Click in cell A3.
6. Save **EL1-C8-P1-SFFinCon.xlsx**.

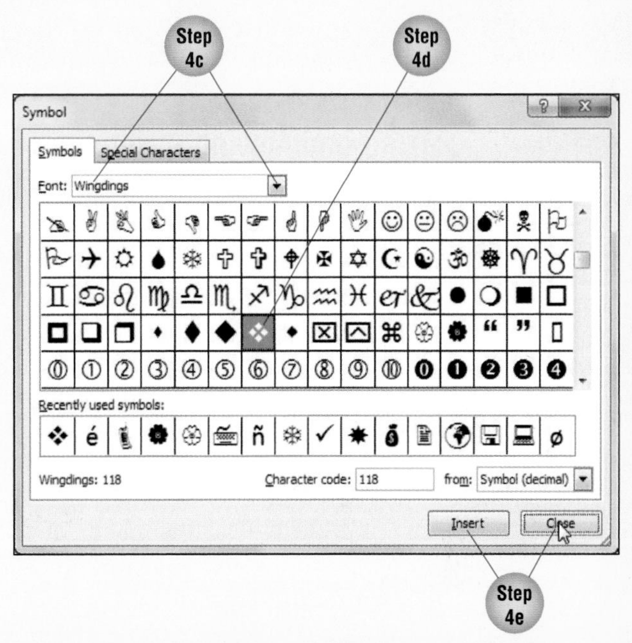

Inserting an Image

You can insert an image such as a picture or clip art in an Excel workbook with buttons in the Illustrations group in the Insert tab. Click the Picture button to display the Insert Picture dialog box where you can specify the desired picture file, or click the Clip Art button and then choose from a variety of images available at the Clip Art task pane. When you insert a picture or a clip art image in a worksheet, the Picture Tools Format tab displays as shown in Figure 8.2.

Picture

Figure 8.2 Picture Tools Format Tab

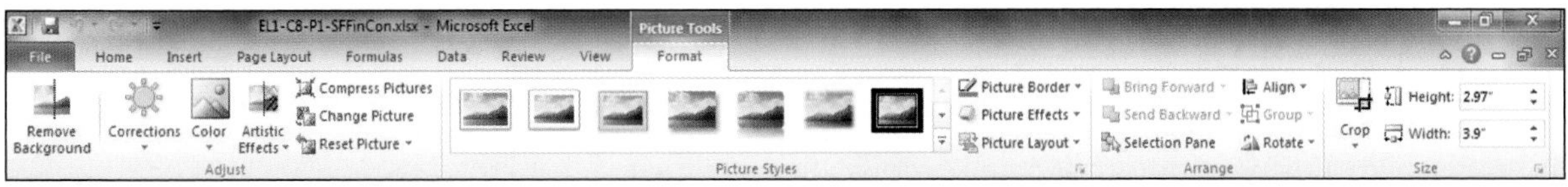

Customizing and Formatting an Image

With buttons in the Adjust group in the Picture Tools Format tab you can recolor the picture or clip art image, correct its brightness and contrast, and apply artistic effects. Use the Remove Background button to remove unwanted portions of the image. You can reset the picture or clip art back to its original color or change to a different image. You can also compress the size of the image file with the Compress Pictures button. Compressing the size of an image is a good idea because it reduces the amount of space the image requires on your storage medium.

Compress Pictures

Crop

With buttons in the Picture Styles group, you can apply a predesigned style to your image, change the image border, or apply other effects to the image. With options in the Arrange group, you can position the image in the worksheet, specify how text will wrap around it, align the image with other elements in the worksheet, and rotate the image. With the Crop button in the Size group, you can remove any unnecessary parts of the image and specify the image size with the *Shape Height* and *Shape Width* measurement boxes.

Sizing and Moving an Image

You can change the size of an image with the *Shape Height* and *Shape Width* measurement boxes in the Size group in the Picture Tools Format tab or with the sizing handles that display around the selected image. To change size with a sizing handle, position the mouse pointer on a sizing handle until the pointer turns into a double-headed arrow and then hold down the left mouse button. Drag the sizing handle in or out to decrease or increase the size of the image and then release the mouse button. Use the middle sizing handles at the left or right side of the image to make the image wider or thinner. Use the middle sizing handles at the top or bottom of the image to make the image taller or shorter. Use the sizing handles at the corners of the image to change both the width and height at the same time. Hold down the Shift key while dragging a sizing handle to maintain the proportions of the image.

HINT

You can use arrow keys on the keyboard to move a selected object. To move the image in small increments, hold down the Ctrl key while pressing one of the arrow keys.

Move an image by positioning the mouse pointer on the image border until the pointer displays with a four-headed arrow attached. Hold down the left mouse button, drag the image to the desired position, and then release the mouse button. Rotate the image by positioning the mouse pointer on the green, round rotation handle until the pointer displays as a circular arrow. Hold down the left mouse button, drag in the desired direction, and then release the mouse button.

Project 1b Formatting an Image — Part 2 of 5

1. With **EL1-C8-P1-SFFinCon.xlsx** open, scroll down the worksheet and then click the Wall Street image to select it. (This image is located below the cells containing data.)
2. Remove the yellow background from the image by completing the following steps:
   a. Click the Picture Tools Format tab.
   b. Click the Remove Background button in the Adjust group in the Picture Tools Format tab.

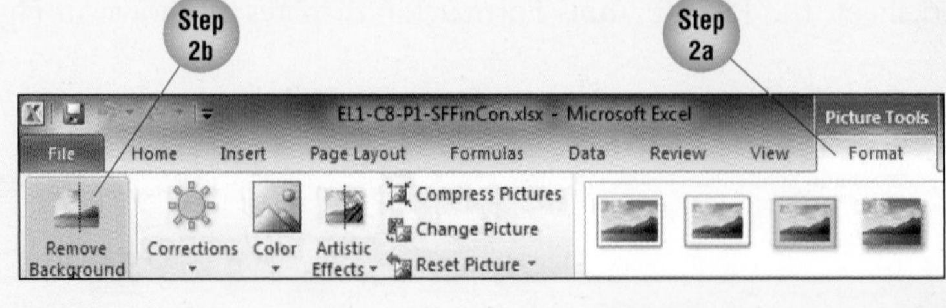

c. Position the mouse pointer on the middle sizing handle at the top of the image until the pointer displays as a two-headed arrow pointing up and down.

d. Hold down the left mouse button, drag the border up to the top of the image, and then release the mouse.

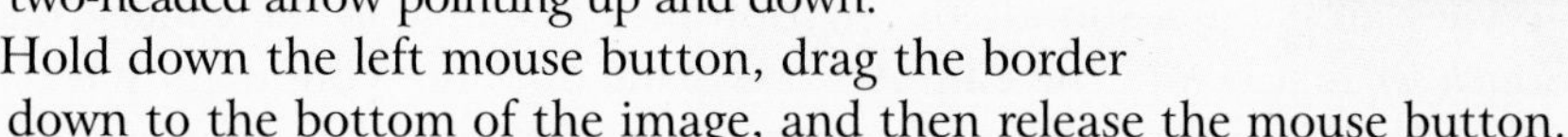

e. Position the mouse pointer on the middle sizing handle at the bottom of the image until the pointer displays as a two-headed arrow pointing up and down.

f. Hold down the left mouse button, drag the border down to the bottom of the image, and then release the mouse button.

g. Click the Keep Changes button in the Close group in the Background Removal tab.

3. Change the color by clicking the Color button in the Adjust group and then clicking the *Blue, Accent color 1 Light* color (second color from the left in the third row of the *Recolor* section).
4. Apply a correction by clicking the Corrections button and then clicking the *Brightness: +20% Contrast: +20%* option (fourth option from the left in the fourth row in the *Brightness and Contrast* section).

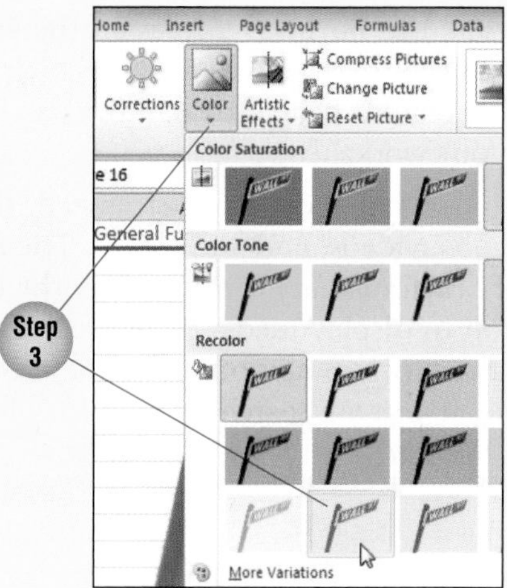

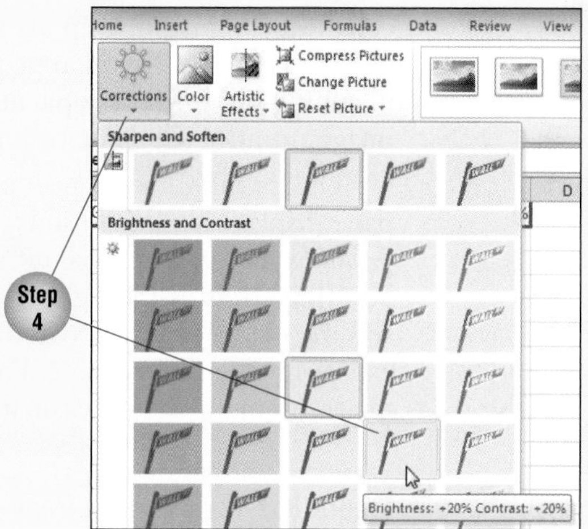

5. Apply an artistic effect by clicking the Artistic Effects button and then clicking the Glow Edges option (last option in the drop-down gallery).
6. Click in the *Height* measurement box in the Size group, type 2, and then press Enter.
7. Move the image by completing the following steps:

a. Position the mouse pointer on the image (displays with a four-headed arrow attached).

b. Hold down the left mouse button, drag the image to the upper left corner of the worksheet, and then release the mouse button.

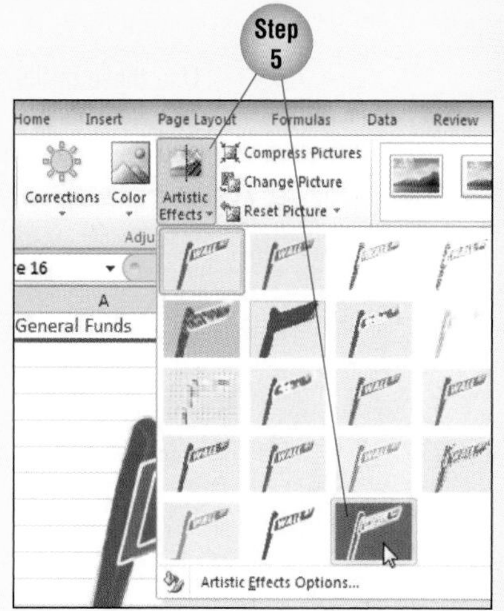

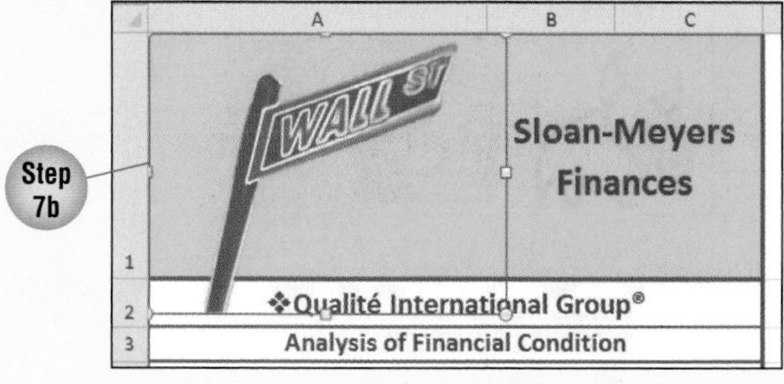

8. Save and then print **EL1-C8-P1-SFFinCon.xlsx**.

Inserting a Clip Art Image

Quick Steps

Insert Clip Art Image
1. Click Insert tab.
2. Click Clip Art button.
3. Type desired word or topic in *Search for* text box.
4. Click Go button or press Enter.
5. Click desired image.

Clip Art

Microsoft Office includes a gallery of media images you can insert in a worksheet. The gallery includes clip art, photographs, and movie images, as well as sound clips. To insert an image, click the Insert tab and then click the Clip Art button in the Illustrations group. This displays the Clip Art task pane at the right side of the screen, as shown in Figure 8.3.

To view all picture, sound, and motion files available in the gallery, make sure the *Search for* text box in the Clip Art task pane does not contain any text and then click the Go button. Scroll through the images that display until you find one you want to use and then click the image to insert it in the worksheet. Use buttons in the Picture Tools Format tab (see Figure 8.2 on page 275) to format and customize the clip art image.

If you are searching for a specific type of image, click in the *Search for* text box, type a category and then click the Go button. For example, if you want to find images related to business, click in the *Search for* text box, type *business*, and then click the Go button. Clip art images related to business display in the viewing area of the task pane. If you are connected to the Internet, Word will search for images matching the word or topic at the Office.com website. You can drag a clip art image from the Clip Art task pane to your worksheet.

Unless the Clip Art task pane default setting has been customized, the task pane displays all illustrations, photographs, videos, and audio files. The *Results should be* option has a default setting of *Selected media file types*. Click the down-pointing arrow at the right of this option to display media types. To search for a specific media type, remove the check mark before all options at the drop-down list except for the desired type. For example, if you are searching only for photograph images, remove the check mark before *Illustrations*, *Videos*, and *Audio*.

Figure 8.3 Clip Art Task Pane

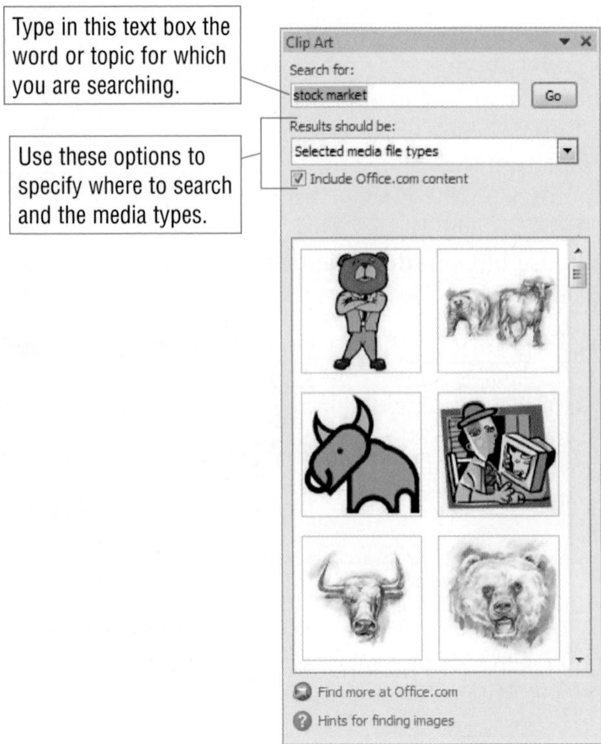

Project 1c Inserting and Formatting a Clip Art Image

Part 3 of 5

1. With **EL1-C8-P1-SFFinCon.xlsx** open, delete the Wall Street sign image by clicking the image and then pressing the Delete key.
2. Insert a clip art image by completing the following steps:
   a. Make cell A1 active.
   b. Click the Insert tab and then click the Clip Art button in the Illustrations group.
   c. At the Clip Art task pane, click the down-pointing arrow at the right of the *Results should be* option box and then click in the *Photographs*, *Videos*, and *Audio* check boxes to remove the check marks. (The *Illustrations* check box should be the only one with a check mark.)

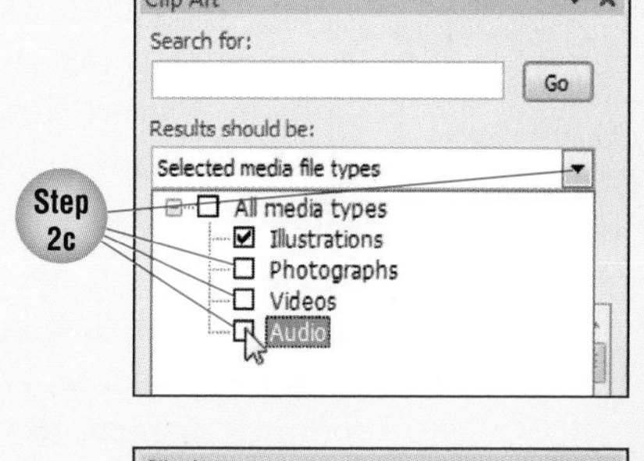

   d. Select any text that displays in the *Search for* text box, type stock market, and then press the Enter key.
   e. Click the image in the list box as shown at the right. (You will need to scroll down the list box to display the image. If this image is not available, click a similar image.)

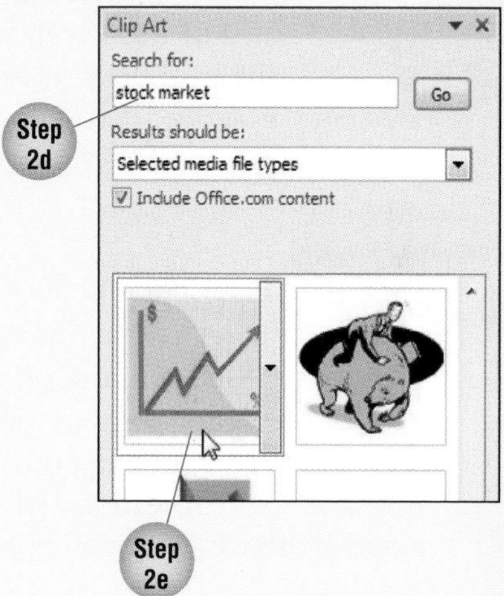

   f. Click the down-pointing arrow at the right of the *Results should be* option box and then click in the *All media types* check box to insert check marks in all of the check boxes.
   g. Close the Clip Art task pane by clicking the Close button (contains an X) located in the upper right corner of the task pane.
3. Apply a correction by clicking the Corrections button in the Adjust group in the Picture Tools Format tab and then clicking the *Brightness: -20% Contrast: +40%* option (second option from the left in the bottom row of the drop-down gallery).
4. Apply a picture style by clicking the More button that displays at the right side of the thumbnails in the Picture Styles group and then clicking the *Soft Edge Rectangle* option.

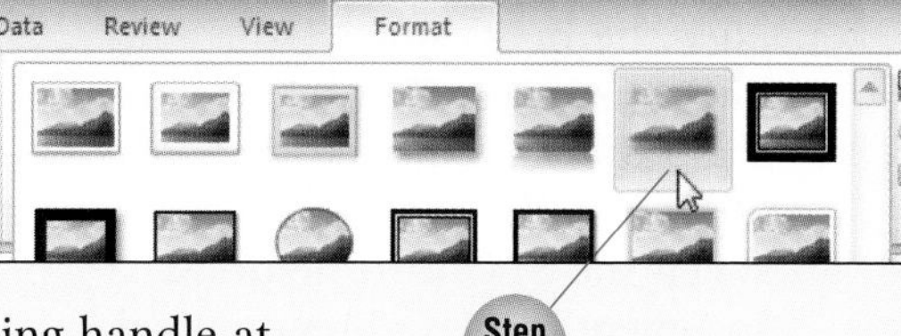

5. Increase the width of the image by completing the following steps:
   a. Position the mouse pointer on the middle sizing handle at the right side of the image until the pointer displays as a two-headed arrow pointing left and right.
   b. Hold down the left mouse button, drag to the right until the right edge of the image border aligns with the right edge of column A, and then release the mouse button.
6. Click outside the clip art image to deselect it.
7. Save **EL1-C8-P1-SFFinCon.xlsx**.

Creating Screenshots

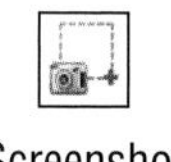
Screenshot

The Illustrations group in the Insert tab contains a Screenshot button you can use to capture the contents of a screen as an image or capture a portion of a screen. This is useful for capturing information from a web page or from a file in

Quick Steps

Insert Screenshot
1. Open workbook.
2. Open another file.
3. Display desired information.
4. Make workbook active.
5. Click Insert tab.
6. Click Screenshot button.
7. Click desired window at drop-down list.

OR

6. Click Screenshot button, Screen Clipping.
7. Drag to specify capture area.

another program. If you want to capture the entire screen, display the desired web page or open the desired file from a program, make Excel active, and then open a workbook or a blank workbook. Click the Insert tab, click the Screenshot button, and then click the desired screen thumbnail at the drop-down list. The currently active worksheet does not display as a thumbnail at the drop-down list, only any other file or program you have open. If you do not have another file or program open, the Windows desktop displays. When you click the desired thumbnail, the screenshot is inserted as an image in the open workbook, the image is selected, and the Picture Tools Format tab is active. Use buttons in this tab to customize the screenshot image.

In addition to making a screenshot of an entire screen, you can make a screenshot of a specific portion of the screen by clicking the *Screen Clipping* option at the Screenshot button drop-down list. When you click this option, the open web page, file, or Windows desktop displays in a dimmed manner and the mouse pointer displays as crosshairs. Using the mouse, draw a border around the specific area of the screen you want to capture. The specific area you identify is inserted in the workbook as an image, the image is selected, and the Picture Tools Format tab is active. If you have only one workbook or file open when you click the Screenshot tab, clicking the *Screen Clipping* option will cause the Windows desktop to display.

Project 1d Inserting and Formatting a Screenshot

Part 4 of 5

1. With **EL1-C8-P1-SFFinCon.xlsx** open, make sure that no other programs are open.
2. Open Word and then open the document named **SFCoProfile.docx** from the Excel2010L1C8 folder on your storage medium.
3. Click the Excel button on the Taskbar.
4. Insert a screenshot of the table in the Word document by completing the following steps:
   a. Click the Insert tab.
   b. Click the Screenshot button in the Illustrations group and then click *Screen Clipping* at the drop-down list.
   c. When the **SFCoProfile.docx** document displays in a dimmed manner, position the mouse crosshairs in the upper left corner of the table, hold down the left mouse button, drag down to the lower right corner of the table, and then release the mouse button. (See image at the right.)
5. With the screenshot image inserted in the **EL1-C8-P1-SFFinCon.xlsx** workbook, make the following changes:
   a. Click in the *Width* measurement box in the Size group in the Picture Tools Format tab, type 3.7, and then press Enter.

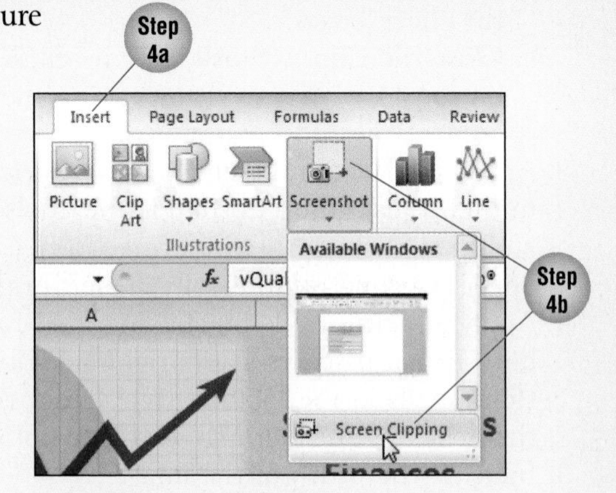

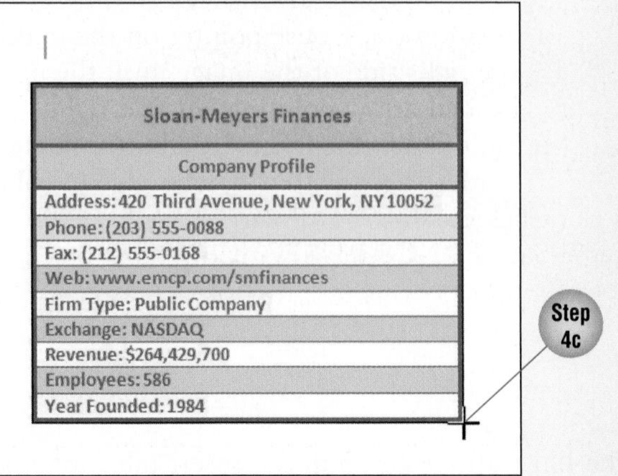

b. Click the Corrections button and then click the *Sharpen 25%* option (fourth option from the left in the *Sharpen and Soften* section).

c. Click the Corrections button and then click the *Brightness: 0% (Normal) Contrast: -40%* (third option from the left in the top row in the *Brightness and Contrast* section).

d. Using the mouse, drag the screenshot image one row below the data in row 10.

6. Make cell A4 active.
7. Save **EL1-C8-P1-SFFinCon.xlsx**.
8. Click the Word button, close **SFCoProfile.docx**, and then exit Word.

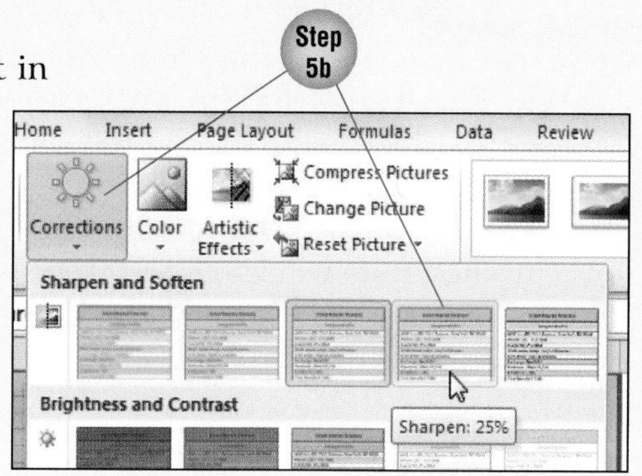

Inserting and Copying Shapes

Quick Steps

Insert Shape
1. Click Insert tab.
2. Click Shapes button.
3. Click desired shape at drop-down list.
4. Drag in worksheet to create shape.

Copy Shape
1. Select shape.
2. Click Copy button.
3. Position insertion point in desired location.
4. Click Paste button.

OR
1. Select shape.
2. Hold down Ctrl key.
3. Drag shape to desired location.

Shapes

In Chapter 7, you learned how to insert shapes in a chart. With the Shapes button in the Illustrations group in the Insert tab, you can also insert shapes in a worksheet. Use the Shapes button in the Insert tab to draw shapes in a worksheet including lines, basic shapes, block arrows, flow chart shapes, callouts, stars, and banners. Click a shape and the mouse pointer displays as crosshairs (plus sign). Position the crosshairs where you want the shape to begin, hold down the left mouse button, drag to create the shape, and then release the mouse button. This inserts the shape in the worksheet and also displays the Drawing Tools Format tab shown in Figure 8.4. Use buttons in this tab to change the shape, apply a style to the shape, arrange the shape, and change the size of the shape.

If you choose a shape in the *Lines* section of the Shapes button drop-down list, the shape you draw is considered a line drawing. If you choose an option in the other sections of the drop-down list, the shape you draw is considered an enclosed object. When drawing an enclosed object, you can maintain the proportions of the shape by holding down the Shift key while dragging with the mouse to create the shape. You can type text in an enclosed object and then use buttons in the WordArt Styles group to format the text.

If you have drawn or inserted a shape, you may want to copy it to other locations in the worksheet. To copy a shape, select the shape and then click the Copy button in the Clipboard group in the Home tab. Position the insertion point at the location where you want the copied image and then click the Paste button. You can also copy a selected shape by holding down the Ctrl key while dragging the shape to the desired location.

Figure 8.4 Drawing Tools Format Tab

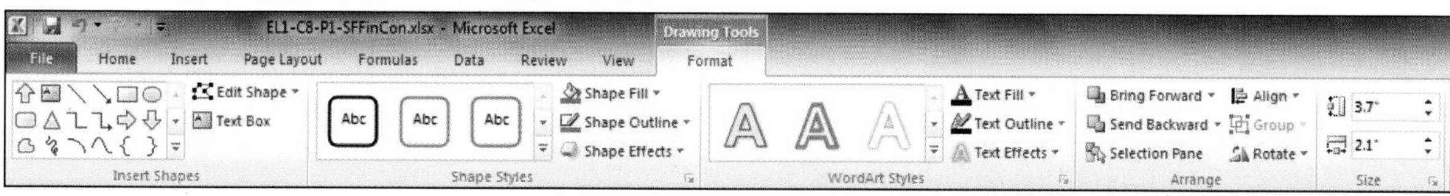

Drawing Arrow Shapes

Part 5 of 5

1. With **EL1-C8-P1-SFFinCon.xlsx** open, create the tallest arrow shown in Figure 8.5 on page 284 by completing the following steps:
   a. Click the Insert tab.
   b. Click the Shapes button and then click the *Up Arrow* shape (third option from the left in the top row of the *Block Arrows* section).

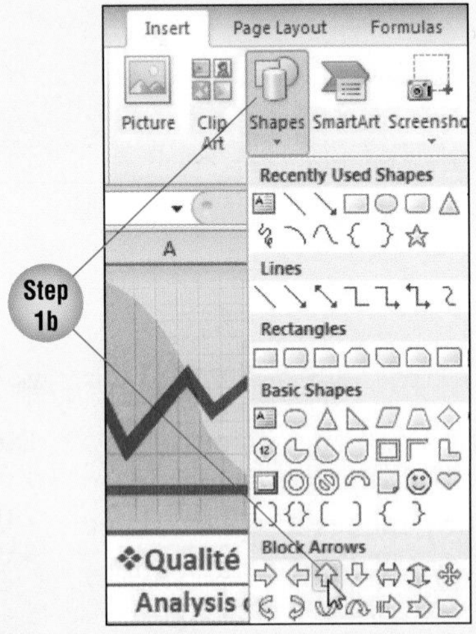

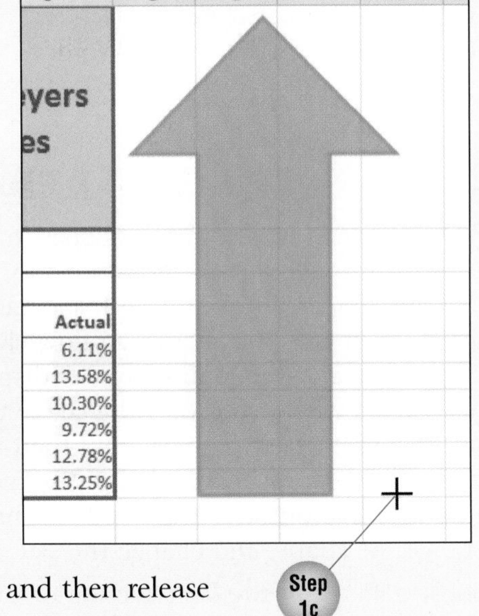

   c. Position the mouse pointer (displays as a thin, black cross) near the upper left corner of cell D1, hold down the left mouse button, drag down and to the right to create the shape as shown below, and then release the mouse button.
   d. Click in the *Shape Height* measurement box and then type 3.7.
   e. Click in the *Shape Width* measurement box, type 2.1, and then press Enter.
   f. If necessary, drag the arrow so it is positioned as shown in Figure 8.5. (To drag the arrow, position the mouse pointer on the border of the selected arrow until the pointer turns into a four-headed arrow, hold down the left mouse button, drag the arrow to the desired position, and then release the mouse button.)
   g. Click the More button at the right side of the thumbnails in the Shape Styles group in the Drawing Tools Format tab and then click the *Intense Effect - Blue, Accent 1* option (second option from the left in the bottom row).

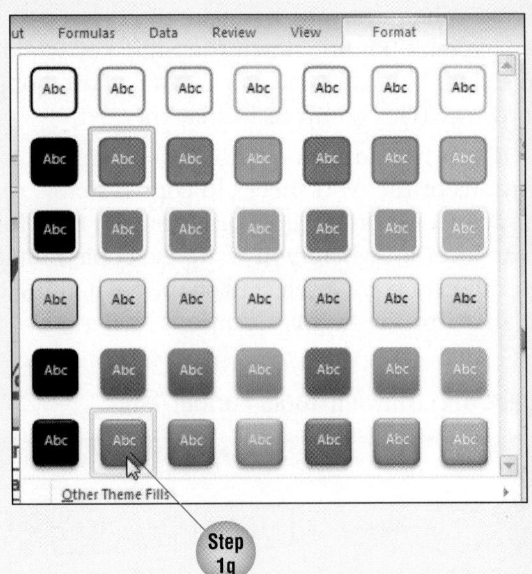

h. Click the Shape Effects button in the Shape Styles group, point to *Glow*, and then click the last option in the third row in the *Glow Variations* section (*Orange, 11 pt glow, Accent color 6*).

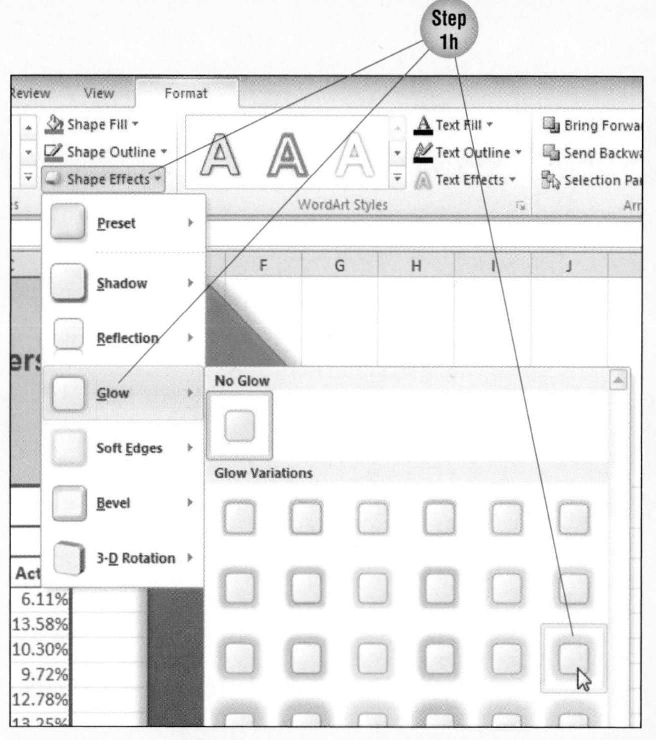

2. Insert text in the arrow shape by completing the following steps:
   a. With the arrow shape selected, type McGuire Mutual Shares 5.33%.
   b. Select the text you just typed (*McGuire Mutual Shares 5.33%*).
   c. Click the More button at the right side of the thumbnails in the WordArt Styles group and then click the third option from the left in the top row (*Fill - White, Drop Shadow*).
   d. Click the Home tab.
   e. Click the Center button in the Alignment group.

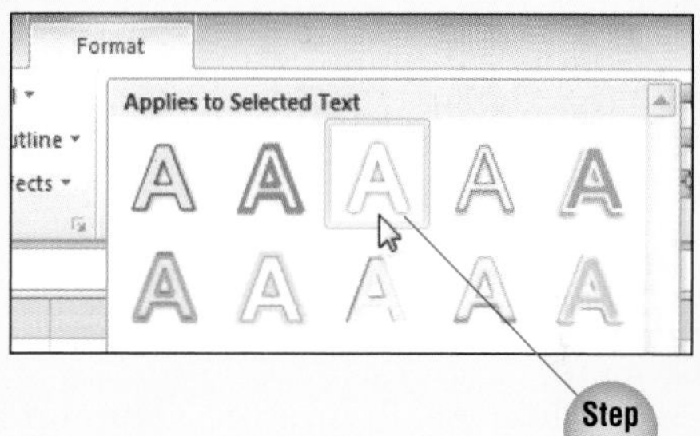

3. With the arrow selected, copy the arrow by completing the following steps:
   a. Hold down the Ctrl key.
   b. Position the mouse pointer on the arrow border until the pointer displays with a square box and plus symbol attached.
   c. Hold down the left mouse button and drag to the right so the outline of the arrow is positioned at the right side of the existing arrow.
   d. Release the mouse button and then release the Ctrl key.
4. Format the second arrow by completing the following steps:
   a. With the second arrow selected, click the Drawing Tools Format tab.
   b. Click in the *Shape Height* measurement box and then type 2.
   c. Click in the *Shape Width* measurement box, type 1.6, and then press Enter
   d. Select the text *McGuire Mutual Shares 5.33%* and then type SR Linus Fund 0.22%.
   e. Drag the arrow so it is positioned as shown in Figure 8.5.
5. Change the orientation to landscape. (Make sure the cells containing data, the screenshot image, and the arrows will print on the same page.)
6. Save, print, and then close **EL1-C8-P1-SFFinCon.xlsx**.

Figure 8.5 Project 1e

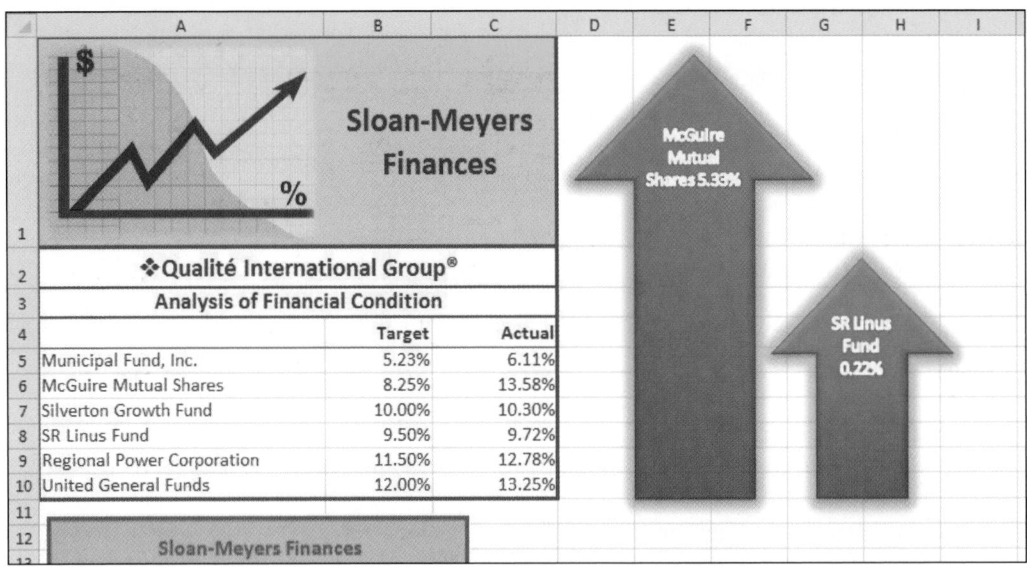

Project 2 Insert a Picture and Text Box in a Division Sales Workbook

2 Parts

You will open a division sales workbook and then insert, move, and size a picture. You will also insert a text box and then format the text.

Quick Steps

Insert Picture
1. Click Insert tab.
2. Click Picture button.
3. Navigate to desired folder.
4. Double-click desired picture.

Pictures

Inserting a Picture

To insert a picture in a worksheet, click the Insert tab and then click the Picture button in the Illustrations group. At the Insert Picture dialog box, navigate to the folder containing the desired picture and then double-click the picture. Use buttons in the Picture Tools Format tab to format and customize the picture.

Project 2a Inserting and Customizing a Picture

Part 1 of 2

1. Open **SPDivSales.xlsx** and then save the workbook with Save As and name it **EL1-C8-P2-SPDivSales**.
2. Make the following changes to the bird clip art image:
   a. Click the bird clip art image to select it.
   b. Click the Picture Tools Format tab.
   c. Click the Rotate button in the Arrange group and then click *Flip Horizontal* at the drop-down list.

Step 2c

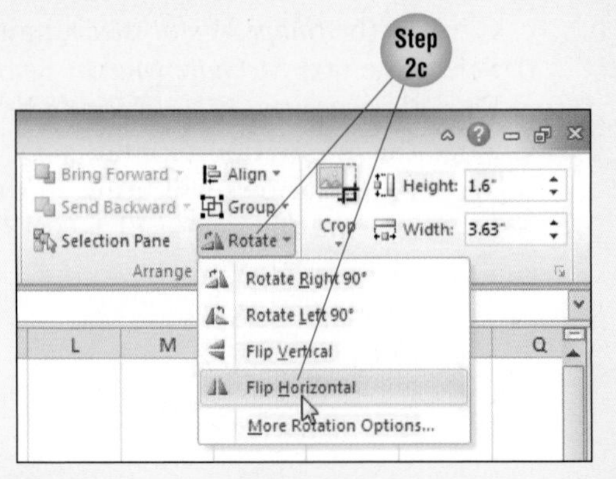

d. Click the Color button in the Adjust group and then click the *Black and White: 75%* option in the *Recolor* section (last option in the top row).

e. Click in the *Shape Height* measurement box, type 0.6, and then press Enter.

3. Insert and format a picture by completing the following steps:
   a. Click in cell A1 outside of the bird image.
   b. Click the Insert tab.
   c. Click the Picture button in the Illustrations group.
   d. At the Insert Picture dialog box, navigate to the Excel2010L1C8 folder on your storage medium and then double-click ***Ocean.jpg***.
   e. With the picture selected, click the Send Backward button in the Arrange group in the Picture Tools Format tab.
   f. Use the sizing handles that display around the picture image to move and size it so it fills cell A1 as shown in Figure 8.6.
   g. Click the bird clip art image and then drag the image so it is positioned as shown in Figure 8.6.
4. Save **EL1-C8-P2-SPDivSales.xlsx**.

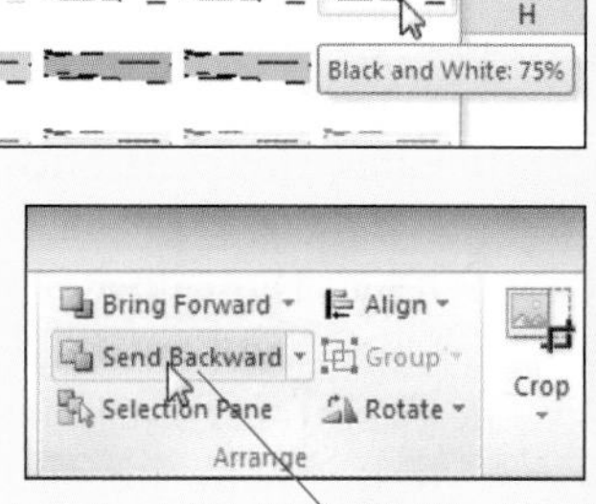

Drawing and Formatting a Text Box

Use the Text Box button in the Insert tab to draw a text box in a worksheet. To draw a text box, click the Insert tab and then click the Text Box button in the Text group. This causes the mouse pointer to display as a long, thin, cross-like pointer. Position the pointer in the worksheet and then drag to create the text box. When a text box is selected, the Drawing Tools Format tab displays with options for customizing the text box.

Click a text box to select it and a dashed border and sizing handles display around the text box. If you want to delete the text box, click the text box border again to change the dashed border lines to solid border lines and then press the Delete key.

Quick Steps

Draw Text Box
1. Click Insert tab.
2. Click Text Box button.
3. Drag in worksheet to create text box.

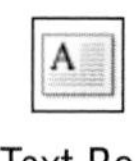

Text Box

Project 2b **Inserting and Formatting a Text Box** Part 2 of 2

1. With **EL1-C8-P2-SPDivSales.xlsx** open, draw a text box by completing the following steps:
   a. Click the Insert tab.
   b. Click the Text Box button in the Text group.
   c. Drag in cell A1 to draw a text box the approximate size and shape shown at the right.

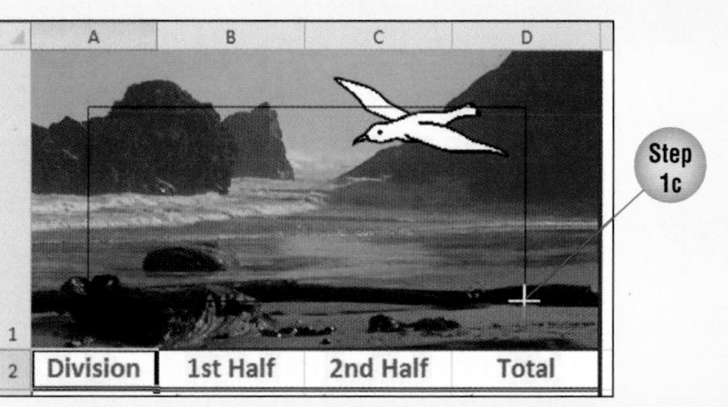

2. Format the text box by completing the following steps:
   a. Click the Drawing Tools Format tab.
   b. Click the Shape Fill button arrow in the Shape Styles group and then click *No Fill* at the drop-down gallery.
   c. Click the Shape Outline button arrow in the Shape Styles group and then click *No Outline* at the drop-down gallery.
3. Insert text in the text box by completing the following steps:
   a. With the text box selected, click the Home tab.
   b. Click the Font button arrow and then click *Lucida Calligraphy* at the drop-down gallery. (You will need to scroll down the gallery to display this font.)
   c. Click the Font Size button arrow and then click *32* at the drop-down gallery.
   d. Click the Font Color button arrow and then click *White, Background 1* (first option in the first row in the *Theme Colors* section).
   e. Type **Seabird Productions**.
4. Move the text box so the text is positioned in cell A1 as shown in Figure 8.6. If necessary, move the bird clip art image. (To move the bird image, you may need to move the text box so you can select the image. Move the text box back to the desired location after moving the bird image.)
5. Save, print, and then close **EL1-C8-P2-SPDivSales.xlsx**.

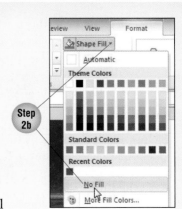

Figure 8.6 Projects 2a and 2b

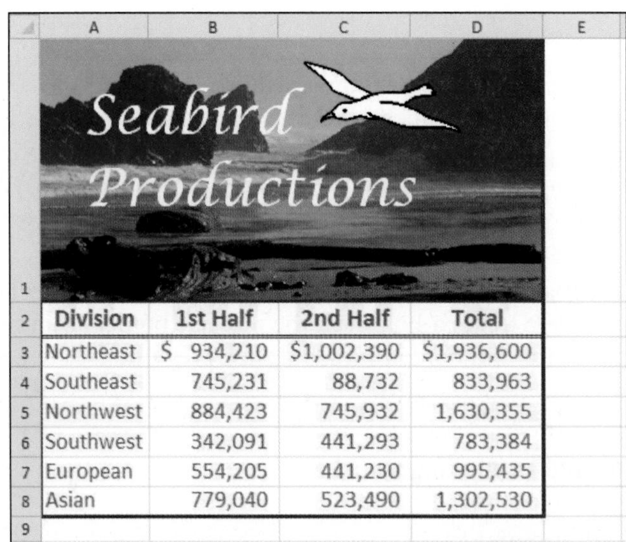

Division	1st Half	2nd Half	Total
Northeast	$ 934,210	$1,002,390	$1,936,600
Southeast	745,231	88,732	833,963
Northwest	884,423	745,932	1,630,355
Southwest	342,091	441,293	783,384
European	554,205	441,230	995,435
Asian	779,040	523,490	1,302,530

Project 3 Insert a Watermark in an Equipment Usage Workbook — 1 Part

You will open an equipment usage report workbook and then insert a picture as a watermark that prints on both pages of the worksheet.

Inserting a Picture as a Watermark

A ***watermark*** is a lightened image that displays behind data in a file. You can create a watermark in a Word document but the watermark functionality is not available in Excel. You can, however, insert a picture in a header or footer and then resize and format the picture to display behind each page of the worksheet.

To create a picture watermark in a worksheet, click the Insert tab and then click the Header & Footer button in the Text group. With the worksheet in Print Layout view, click the Picture button in the Header & Footer Elements group in the Header & Footer Tools Design tab. At the Insert Picture dialog box, navigate to the desired folder and then double-click the desired picture. This inserts *&[Picture]* in the header. Resize and format the picture by clicking the Format Picture button in the Header & Footer Elements group. Use options at the Format Picture dialog box with the Size tab selected to specify the size of the picture and use options in the dialog box with the Picture tab selected to specify brightness and contrast.

Quick Steps

Insert Picture as Watermark

1. Click Insert tab.
2. Click Header & Footer button.
3. Click Picture button.
4. Navigate to desired folder.
5. Double-click desired picture.

Format Picture

Project 3 Inserting a Picture as a Watermark

Part 1 of 1

1. Open **HCEqpRpt.xlsx** and then save the workbook with Save As and name it **EL1-C8-P3-HCEqpRpt**.
2. Insert a picture as a watermark by completing the following steps:
   a. Click the Insert tab.
   b. Click the Header & Footer button in the Text group.
   c. Click the Picture button in the Header & Footer Elements group in the Header & Footer Tools Design tab.
   d. At the Insert Picture dialog box, navigate to the Excel2010L1C8 folder on your storage medium and then double-click ***Olympics.jpg***.
   e. Click the Format Picture button in the Header & Footer Elements group.
   f. At the Format Picture dialog box with the Size tab selected, click the *Lock aspect ratio* check box in the *Scale* section to remove the check mark.
   g. Select the current measurement in the *Height* measurement box in the *Size and rotate* section and then type 10.
   h. Select the current measurement in the *Width* measurement box in the *Size and rotate* section and then type 7.5.
   i. Click the Picture tab.
   j. At the Format Picture dialog box with the Picture tab selected, select the current percentage number in the *Brightness* option box in the *Image control* section and then type 75.
   k. Select the current percentage number in the *Contrast* option box and then type 25.
   l. Click OK to close the Format Picture dialog box.

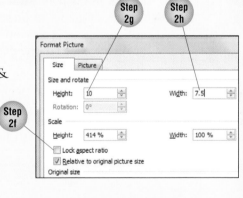

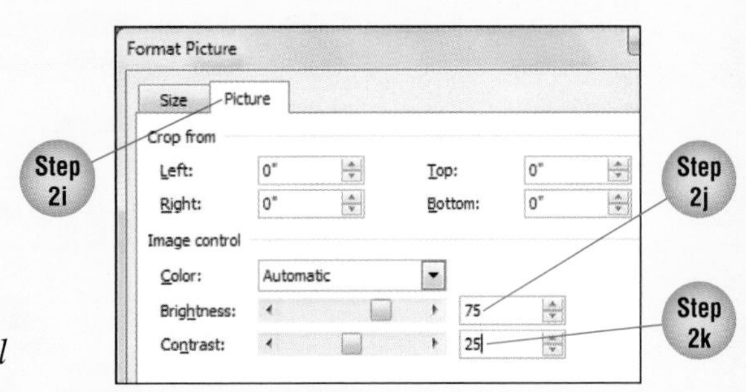

3. Click in the worksheet.
4. Display the worksheet in the Print tab Backstage view to view how the image will print on page 1 and page 2 and then print the worksheet.
5. Save and then close **EL1-C8-P3-HCEqpRpt.xlsx**.

Insert and Format Diagrams in a Company Sales Workbook — 4 Parts

You will open a workbook that contains two company sales worksheets. You will insert and format a cycle diagram in one worksheet and insert and format a relationship diagram in the other. You will also create and format WordArt text.

Inserting a SmartArt Diagram

Quick Steps

Insert SmartArt Diagram
1. Click Insert tab.
2. Click SmartArt button.
3. Double-click desired diagram.

SmartArt

Excel includes the SmartArt feature you can use to insert diagrams and organizational charts in a worksheet. SmartArt offers a variety of predesigned diagrams and organizational charts that are available at the Choose a SmartArt Graphic dialog box shown in Figure 8.7. Display this dialog box by clicking the Insert tab and then clicking the SmartArt button in the Illustrations group. At the dialog box, *All* is selected in the left panel and all available predesigned diagrams display in the middle panel. Use the scroll bar at the right side of the middle panel to scroll down the list of diagram choices. Click a diagram in the middle panel and the name of the diagram displays in the right panel along with a description of the diagram type. SmartArt includes diagrams for presenting a list of data; showing data processes, cycles, and relationships; and presenting data in a matrix or pyramid. Double-click a diagram in the middle panel of the dialog box and the diagram is inserted in the worksheet.

Figure 8.7 Choose a SmartArt Graphic Dialog Box

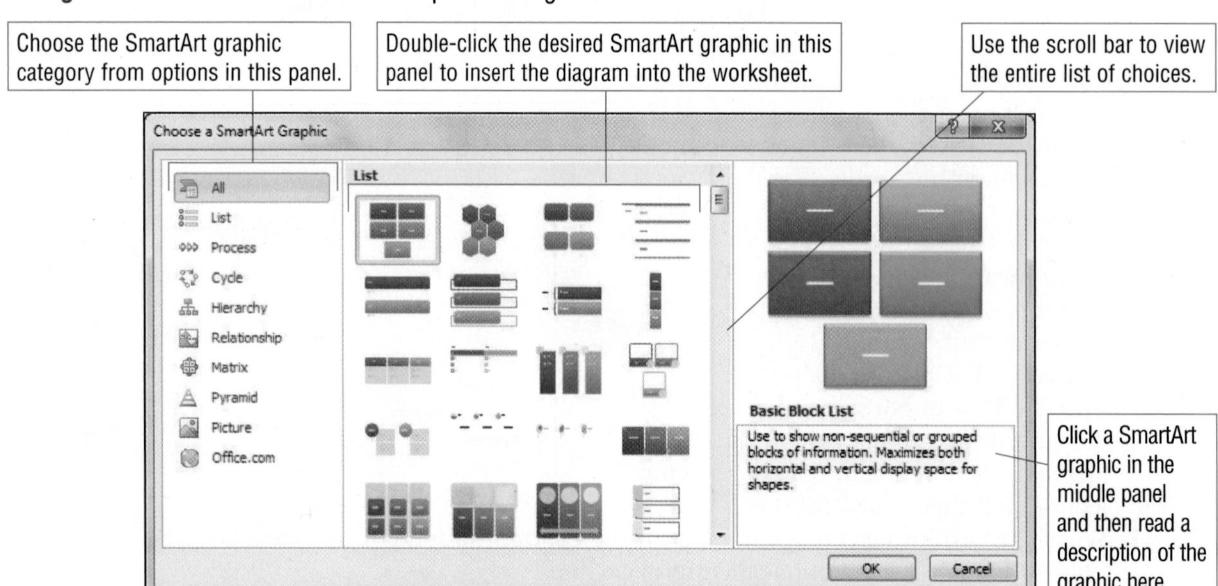
Choose the SmartArt graphic category from options in this panel.
Double-click the desired SmartArt graphic in this panel to insert the diagram into the worksheet.
Use the scroll bar to view the entire list of choices.
Choose a SmartArt Graphic
All
List
Process
Cycle
Hierarchy
Relationship
Matrix
Pyramid
Picture
Office.com
List
Basic Block List
Use to show non-sequential or grouped blocks of information. Maximizes both horizontal and vertical display space for shapes.
OK
Cancel
Click a SmartArt graphic in the middle panel and then read a description of the graphic here.

Entering Data in a Diagram

Some diagrams are designed to include text. You can type text in a diagram by selecting the shape and then typing text in the shape or you can display a text pane and then type text in the pane. Display the text pane by clicking the Text Pane button in the Create Graphic group in the SmartArt Tools Design tab. Turn off the display of the pane by clicking the Text Pane button or by clicking the Close button that displays in the upper right corner of the text pane.

HINT

Generally, you would use a SmartArt diagram to represent text and a chart to represent numbers.

Text Pane

Sizing, Moving, and Deleting a Diagram

Increase or decrease the size of a diagram by dragging the diagram border. Increase or decrease the width of the diagram by positioning the mouse pointer on the set of four dots that displays in the middle of the left and right borders until the pointer turns into a left- and right-pointing arrow, hold down the left mouse button and then drag the border to the desired size. Increase or decrease the height of the diagram in a similar manner using the set of four dots that displays in the middle of the top and bottom borders. To increase or decrease both the height and the width of the diagram, drag one of the sets of three dots that displays in each corner of the border.

To move a diagram, select the diagram and then position the mouse pointer on the diagram border until the pointer turns into a four-headed arrow. Hold down the left mouse button, drag the diagram to the desired position, and then release the mouse button. Delete a diagram by selecting the diagram and then pressing the Delete key.

Project 4a **Inserting a Diagram in a Worksheet** Part 1 of 4

1. Open **EPSales.xlsx** and then save the workbook with Save As and name it **EL1-C8-P4-EPSales**.
2. Create the diagram shown in Figure 8.8 on page 291. To begin, click the Insert tab.
3. Click the SmartArt button in the Illustrations group.
4. At the Choose a SmartArt Graphic dialog box, click *Cycle* in the left panel.
5. Double-click *Radial Cycle* as shown at the right.
6. If the text pane is not open, click the Text Pane button in the Create Graphic group. (The text pane will display at the left side of the diagram.)
7. With the insertion point positioned after the top bullet in the text pane, type Evergreen Products.
8. Click the *[Text]* box below *Evergreen Products* and then type Seattle.
9. Click the next *[Text]* box and then type Olympia.

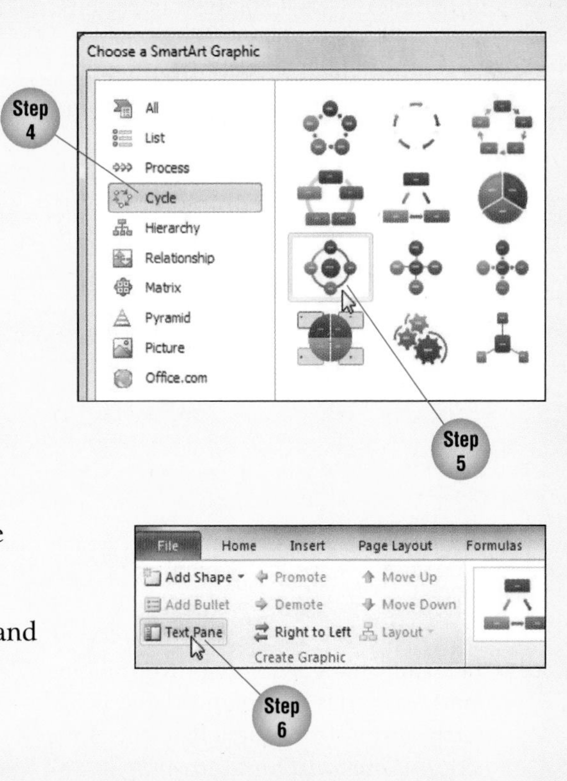

10. Click the next *[Text]* box and then type Portland.
11. Click the next *[Text]* box and then type Spokane.
12. Click the Text Pane button to turn off the display of the text pane.
13. Drag the diagram so it is positioned as shown in Figure 8.8. To drag the diagram, position the mouse pointer on the diagram border until the pointer turns into a four-headed arrow. Hold down the left mouse button, drag the diagram to the desired position, and then release the mouse button.
14. Increase or decrease the size of the diagram so it displays as shown in Figure 8.8. Use the sets of dots on the diagram border to drag the border to the desired size.
15. Save **EL1-C8-P4-EPSales.xlsx**.

Changing the Diagram Design

HINT

To restore the SmartArt default layout and color, click the Reset Graphic button in the Reset group in the SmartArt Tools Design tab.

When you double-click a diagram at the dialog box, the diagram is inserted in the worksheet and the SmartArt Tools Design tab is active. With options and buttons in this tab, you can add objects, change the diagram layout, apply a style to the diagram, and reset the diagram back to the original formatting.

Project 4b Changing the Diagram Design

Part 2 of 4

1. With **EL1-C8-P4-EPSales.xlsx** open, make sure the SmartArt Tools Design tab is active and the *Spokane* circle shape is selected.
2. Click the Right to Left button in the Create Graphic group. (This switches *Olympia* and *Spokane*.)
3. Click the More button located at the right side of the SmartArt Styles group and then click the *Polished* option at the drop-down list (first option from the left in the top row of the *3-D* section).

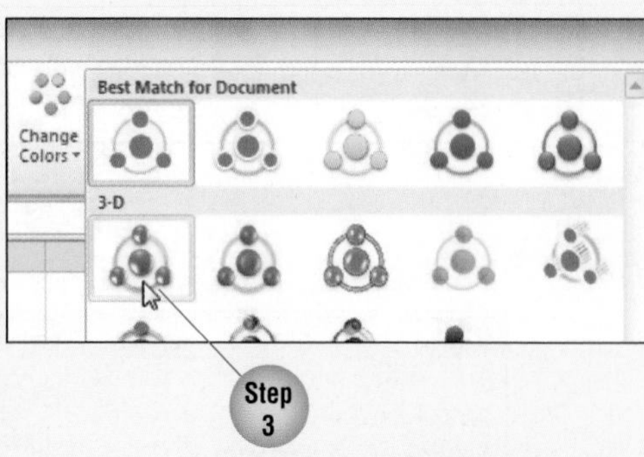

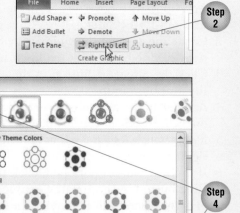

4. Click the Change Colors button in the SmartArt Styles group and then click the fourth option from the left in the *Accent 3* section (*Gradient Loop - Accent 3*).

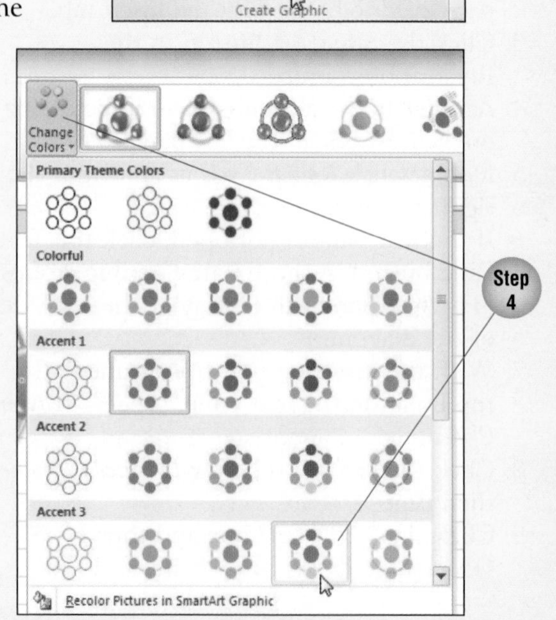

5. Click outside the diagram to deselect it.
6. Change the orientation to landscape. (Make sure the diagram fits on the first page.)
7. Save **EL1-C8-P4-EPSales.xlsx** and then print the Total Sales worksheet.

Figure 8.8 Projects 4a and 4b

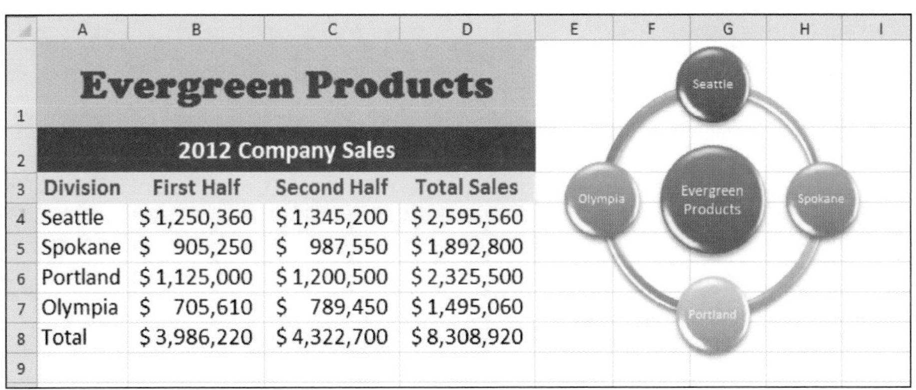

	A	B	C	D
1	**Evergreen Products**			
2	2012 Company Sales			
3	Division	First Half	Second Half	Total Sales
4	Seattle	$ 1,250,360	$ 1,345,200	$ 2,595,560
5	Spokane	$ 905,250	$ 987,550	$ 1,892,800
6	Portland	$ 1,125,000	$ 1,200,500	$ 2,325,500
7	Olympia	$ 705,610	$ 789,450	$ 1,495,060
8	Total	$ 3,986,220	$ 4,322,700	$ 8,308,920
9				

Changing the Diagram Formatting

Click the SmartArt Tools Format tab and options display for formatting a diagram. Use buttons in this tab to insert and customize shapes; apply a shape quick style; customize shapes; insert WordArt quick styles; and specify the position, alignment, rotation, wrapping style, height, and width of the diagram.

Project 4c Changing the Diagram Formatting — Part 3 of 4

1. With **EL1-C8-P4-EPSales.xlsx** open, click the Seattle Sales worksheet tab.
2. Create the diagram shown in Figure 8.9. To begin, click the Insert tab and then click the SmartArt button in the Illustrations group.
3. At the Choose a SmartArt Graphic dialog box, click *Relationship* in the left panel and then double-click *Gear* in the middle panel.
4. Click *[Text]* that appears in the bottom gear and then type Quality Products.
5. Click *[Text]* that appears in the left gear and then type Customized Plans.
6. Click *[Text]* that appears in the top gear and then type Exemplary Service.
7. Click inside the diagram border but outside any diagram element.
8. Click the More button that displays at the right side of the SmartArt Styles group and then click the *Inset* option (second option from the left in the top row of the *3-D* section).

Step 3

Choose a SmartArt Graphic
All
List
Process
Cycle
Hierarchy
Relationship
Matrix

9. Click the Change Colors button in the SmartArt Styles group and then click the third option from the left in the *Accent 3* section (*Gradient Range - Accent 3*).
10. Click the SmartArt Tools Format tab.
11. Click in the *Height* text box in the Size group and then type 3.75.
12. Click in the *Width* text box, type 5.25, and then press Enter.

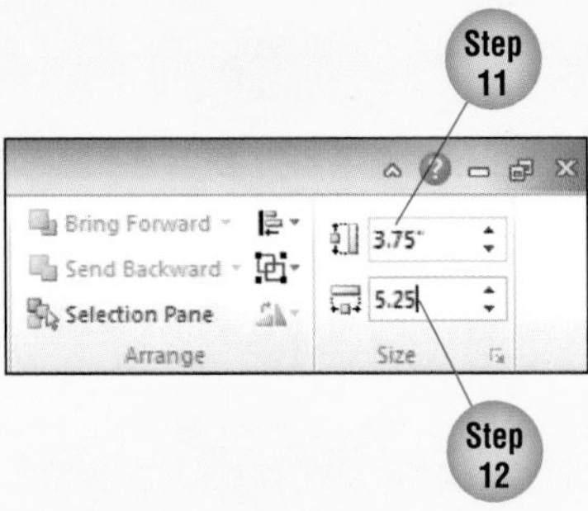

13. Click the bottom gear to select it.
14. Click the Shape Fill button arrow in the Shape Styles group and then click the bottom dark green color (*Olive Green, Accent 3, Darker 50%*) that displays in the *Theme Colors* section.
15. Click the top gear to select it.
16. Click the Shape Fill button arrow and then click the dark green color (*Olive Green, Accent 3, Darker 25%*) that displays in the *Theme Colors* section.
17. Change the orientation to landscape.
18. Move the diagram so it fits on the first page and displays as shown in Figure 8.9.
19. Click outside the chart to deselect it.
20. Save **EL1-C8-P4-EPSales.xlsx** and then print the Seattle Sales worksheet.

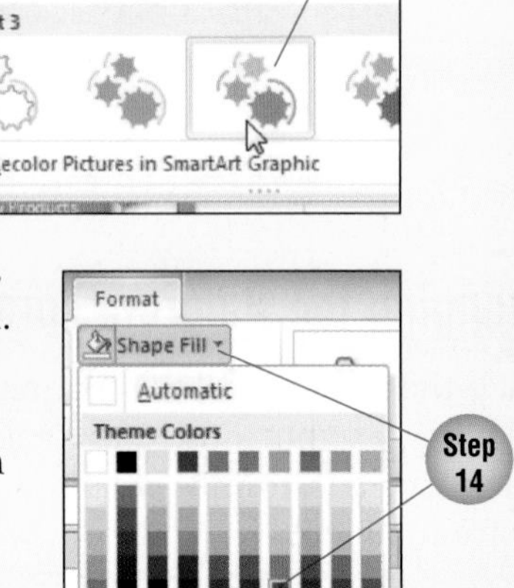

Figure 8.9 Project 4c

	A	B	C	D
1	**Evergreen Products**			
2	2012 Total Sales			
3	Customer	First Half	Second Half	Total Sales
4	Harbor Manufacturing	$ 32,500	$ 41,305	$ 73,805
5	Timberlake Designs	10,200	14,230	24,430
6	Cascade Plastics	64,230	50,304	114,534
7	Avalon Clinic	105,300	105,300	210,600
8	Gravelly Lake Plumbing	200,500	150,700	351,200
9	Bavarian Productions	45,890	29,405	75,295
10	Stealth Media	5,300	2,950	8,250
11	Robinson Group	136,492	144,366	280,858
12	Lincoln Services	21,890	18,445	40,335
13	Danmark Contracting	45,750	50,250	96,000
14	Earthway Systems	35,500	28,750	64,250
15			**Total Sales**	$1,339,557
16				

Creating WordArt

Create WordArt
1. Click Insert tab.
2. Click WordArt button.
3. Click desired WordArt style at drop-down list.
4. Type desired text.

With the WordArt application, you can distort or modify text to conform to a variety of shapes. This is useful for creating company logos and headings. With WordArt, you can change the font, style, and alignment of text. You can also use different fill patterns and colors, customize border lines, and add shadow and three-dimensional effects.

To insert WordArt in an Excel worksheet, click the Insert tab, click the WordArt button in the Text group, and then click the desired option at the drop-down list. This displays *Your Text Here* inserted in the worksheet in the WordArt option you selected at the gallery. Type the desired text and then use the buttons on the Drawing Tools Format tab to format the WordArt.

HINT

To remove WordArt style from text and retain the text, click the More button in the WordArt Styles group in the Drawing Tools Format tab and then click *Clear WordArt*.

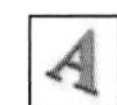

WordArt

Sizing and Moving WordArt

WordArt text inserted in a worksheet is surrounded by white sizing handles. Use the white sizing handles to change the height and width of the WordArt text. To move WordArt text, position the arrow pointer on the border of the WordArt until the pointer displays with a four-headed arrow attached. Hold down the left mouse button, drag the outline of the WordArt text box to the desired position, and then release the mouse button. When you change the shape of the WordArt text, the WordArt border displays with a purple diamond shape. Use this shape to change the slant of the WordArt text.

Project 4d **Inserting and Formatting WordArt** Part 4 of 4

1. With **EL1-C8-P4-EPSales.xlsx** open, click the Total Sales worksheet tab.
2. Make cell A1 active and then press the Delete key. (This removes the text from the cell.)
3. Increase the height of row 1 to 136.50.
4. Click the Insert tab.
5. Click the WordArt button in the Text group and then click the last option in the top row (*Fill - Olive Green, Accent 3, Outline - Text 2*).

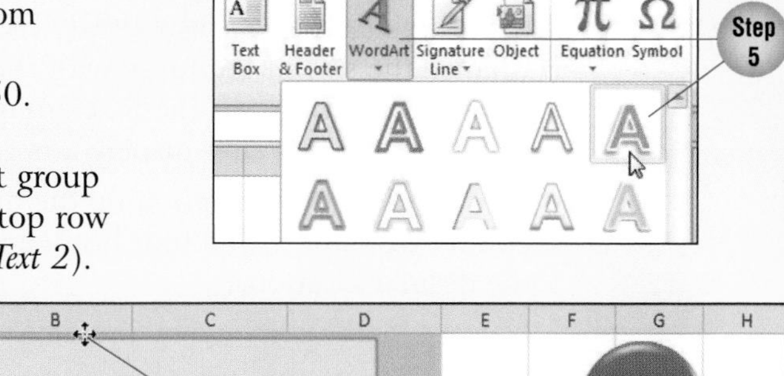

6. Type **Evergreen**, press the Enter key, and then type **Products**.
7. Position the mouse pointer on the WordArt border until the pointer displays with a four-headed arrow attached and then drag the WordArt inside cell A1.

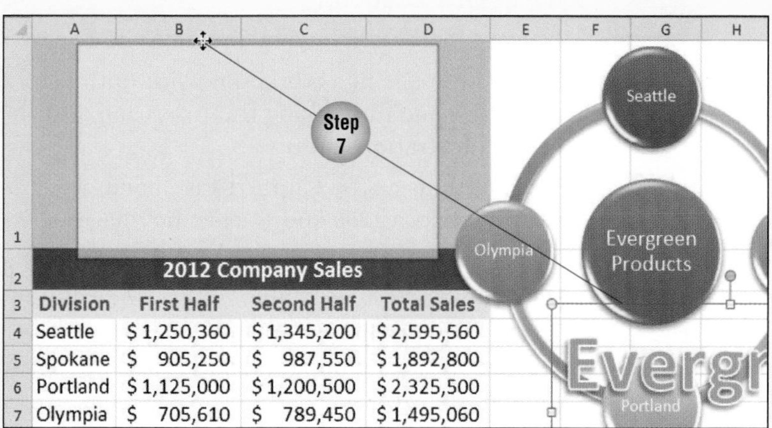

8. Click the Text Fill button arrow in the WordArt Styles group and then click the dark green color (*Olive Green, Accent 3, Darker 25%*).
9. Click the Text Outline button arrow in the WordArt Styles group and then click the dark green color (*Olive Green, Accent 3, Darker 50%*).
10. If necessary, resize the diagram and position it so it prints on one page with the data.
11. Click the Seattle Sales worksheet tab and then complete steps similar to those in Steps 2 through 9 to insert *Evergreen Products* as WordArt.

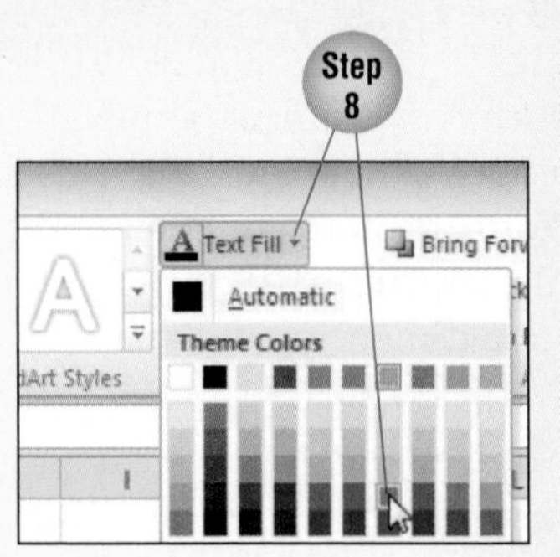

12. Make sure the SmartArt diagram fits on the page with the data. If necessary, decrease the size of the diagram.
13. Save **EL1-C8-P4-EPSales.xlsx** and then print both worksheets.
14. Close **EL1-C8-P4-EPSales.xlsx**.

Chapter Summary

- Insert symbols with options at the Symbol dialog box with the Symbols tab or the Special Characters tab selected.
- With buttons in the Illustrations group in the Insert tab, you can insert a picture, clip art image, shape, or a SmartArt diagram.
- When you insert a picture or clip art image in a worksheet, the Picture Tools Format tab is active and includes options for adjusting the image, applying preformatted styles, and arranging and sizing the image.
- Change the size of an image with the *Shape Height* and *Shape Width* measurement boxes in the Size group in the Picture Tools Format tab or with the sizing handles that display around the selected image.
- Move an image by positioning the mouse pointer on the image border until the pointer displays with a four-headed arrow attached and then drag the image to the desired location.
- Delete a selected image by pressing the Delete key.
- Insert an image in a workbook with options at the Clip Art task pane. Display this task pane by clicking the Insert tab and then clicking the Clip Art button in the Illustrations group.
- With options at the Clip Art task pane, you can narrow the search for images to specific locations and to specific images.
- Use the Screenshot button in the Illustrations group in the Insert tab to capture the contents of a screen or capture a portion of a screen.
- To draw shapes in a workbook, click the Insert tab, click the Shapes button in the Illustrations group, and then click the desired shape at the drop-down list. Drag in the worksheet to draw the shape. To maintain the proportions of the shape, hold down the Shift key while dragging in the worksheet.

- Copy a shape with the Copy and Paste buttons in the Clipboard group in the Home tab or by holding down the Ctrl key while dragging the shape.
- You can type text in an enclosed drawn object.
- To insert a picture in a worksheet, click the Insert tab and then click the Picture button in the Illustrations group. At the Insert Picture dialog box, navigate to the desired folder and then double-click the file name.
- Draw a text box in a worksheet by clicking the Insert tab, clicking the Text Box button in the Text group and then dragging in the worksheet. Use options at the Drawing Tools Format tab to format and customize the text box.
- A watermark is a lightened image that displays behind data in a file. You can create a picture watermark in a worksheet by inserting a picture in a header or footer and then changing the size and formatting of the picture.
- Insert a SmartArt diagram in a worksheet by clicking the Insert tab, clicking the SmartArt button in the Illustrations group, and then double-clicking the desired diagram at the Choose a SmartArt Graphic dialog box. Customize a diagram with options in the SmartArt Tools Design tab or the SmartArt Tools Format tab.
- Use WordArt to create, distort, modify, and/or conform text to a variety of shapes. Insert WordArt in a worksheet with the WordArt button in the Text group in the Insert tab. Customize WordArt text with options in the Drawing Tools Format tab.

Commands Review

FEATURE	RIBBON TAB, GROUP	BUTTON
Symbol dialog box	Insert, Symbols	Ω
Clip Art task pane	Insert, Illustrations	
Screenshot	Insert, Illustrations	
Shapes drop-down list	Insert, Illustrations	
Insert Picture dialog box	Insert, Illustrations	
Text box	Insert, Text	
Choose a SmartArt Graphic dialog box	Insert, Illustrations	
WordArt drop-down list	Insert, Text	

Concepts Check Test Your Knowledge

Completion: In the space provided at the right, indicate the correct term, symbol, or command.

1. The Symbol button is located in this tab. ____________________
2. The *Font* option is available at the Symbol dialog box with this tab selected. ____________________
3. Insert a picture, clip art image, screenshot, shape, or SmartArt diagram with buttons in this group in the Insert tab. ____________________
4. When you insert a picture or clip art image in a worksheet, this tab is active. ____________________
5. Maintain the proportions of the image by holding down this key while dragging a sizing handle. ____________________
6. To move an image, position the mouse pointer on the image border until the mouse pointer displays with this attached and then drag the image to the desired location. ____________________
7. To capture a portion of a screen, click the Screenshot button and then click this option at the drop-down list. ____________________
8. To copy a shape, hold down this key while dragging the shape. ____________________
9. When you draw a text box in a worksheet and then release the mouse button, this tab is active. ____________________
10. This term refers to a lightened image that displays behind data in a file. ____________________
11. Click the SmartArt button in the Illustrations group in the Insert tab and this dialog box displays. ____________________

Skills Check Assess Your Performance

Assessment 1

INSERT A CLIP ART IMAGE AND WORDART IN AN EQUIPMENT PURCHASE WORKBOOK

1. Open **ASPurPlans.xlsx** and then save the workbook with Save As and name it **EL1-C8-A1-ASPurPlans**.
2. Insert a formula in cell E4 using the PMT function that calculates monthly payments. ***Hint: Refer to Chapter 2, Project 3a.***
3. Copy the formula in cell E4 down to cells E5 and E6.
4. Insert a formula in cell F4 that calculates the total amount of the payments. ***Hint: Refer to Chapter 2, Project 3a.***
5. Copy the formula in cell F4 down to cells F5 and F6.
6. Insert a formula in cell G4 that calculates the total amount of interest paid. ***Hint: Refer to Chapter 2, Project 3a.***
7. Copy the formula in cell G4 down to cells G5 and G6.
8. Insert the clip art image shown in Figure 8.10 with the following specifications:
   - Search for the clip art image using the search word *movies*. (The colors of the original clip art image are yellow and black.)
   - Change the clip art image color to *Blue, Accent color 1 Light*.
   - Apply the *Brightness: 0% (normal) Contrast: +40%* correction.
   - Apply the *Reflected Rounded Rectangle* picture style.
   - Size and move the image so it is positioned as shown in Figure 8.10.
9. Insert the company name *Azure Studios* in cell A1 as WordArt. Use the *Fill - Blue, Accent 1, Metal Bevel, Reflection* option to create the WordArt.
10. Change the worksheet orientation to landscape.
11. Save, print, and then close **EL1-C8-A1-ASPurPlans.xlsx**.

Figure 8.10 Assessment 1

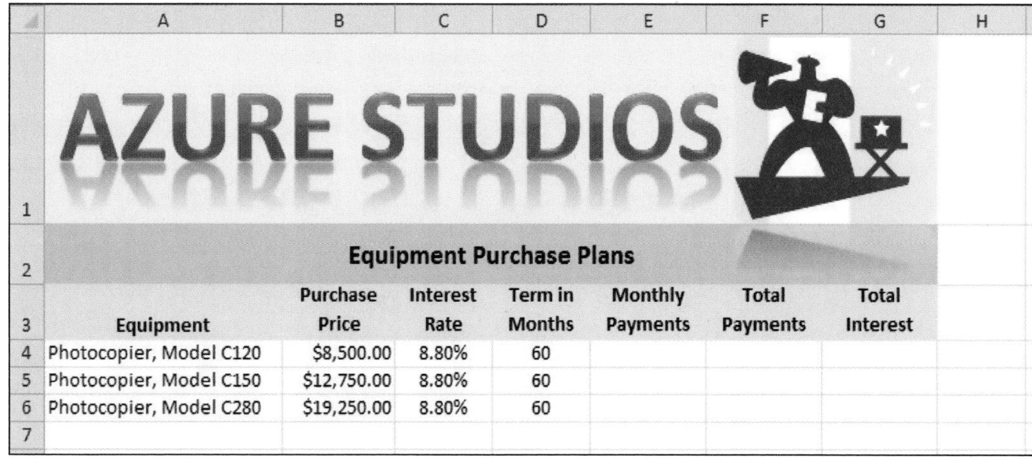

Assessment 2

INSERT FORMULAS AND FORMAT A TRAVEL COMPANY WORKBOOK

1. Open **TSGEVacs.xlsx** and then save the workbook with Save As and name it **EL1-C8-A2-TSGEVacs**.
2. Apply the shading to data in cells as shown in Figure 8.11. (Use shading options in the Aqua column.)
3. Insert appropriate formulas to calculate the prices based on a 10 percent and 20 percent discount and apply the appropriate number formatting. ***Hint: For the 10% discount column, multiply the price per person by .90 (this determines 90 percent of the price) and multiply the price per person by .80 for the 20% discount column.***
4. Format the image of the airplane and position as shown in Figure 8.11 with the following specifications:
   a. Use the Remove Background button in the Picture Tools Format tab to remove a portion of the yellow background so your image displays similar to what you see in the figure.
   b. Rotate the image.
   c. Apply the *Brightness: +20% Contrast: +20%* correction.
   d. Position the image as shown in the figure.
5. Open Word and then open the document named **TSAirfare.docx** located in the Excel2010L1C8 folder on your storage medium. Click the Excel button on the Taskbar and then use the Screenshot button (use the *Screen Clipping* option) to select and then insert the airfare information in **EL1-C8-A2-TSGEVacs.xlsx**. Position the information at the right side of the data in the worksheet.
6. Change the orientation to landscape.
7. Make sure the data and the airfare information display on one page and then print the worksheet.
8. Save and then close **EL1-C8-A2-TSGEVacs.xslx**.
9. Click the Word button on the Taskbar and then exit Word.

Figure 8.11 Assessment 2

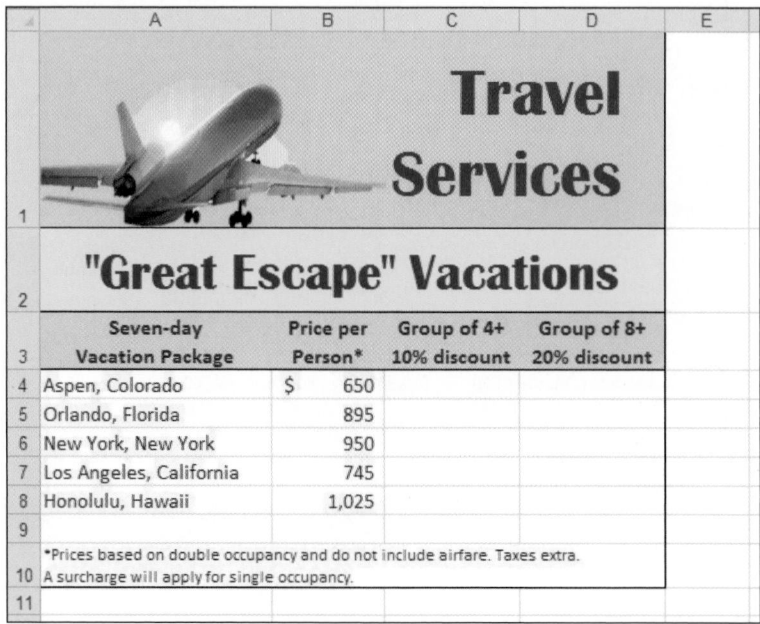

	A	B	C	D	E
1	Travel Services				
2	"Great Escape" Vacations				
3	Seven-day Vacation Package	Price per Person*	Group of 4+ 10% discount	Group of 8+ 20% discount	
4	Aspen, Colorado	$ 650			
5	Orlando, Florida	895			
6	New York, New York	950			
7	Los Angeles, California	745			
8	Honolulu, Hawaii	1,025			
9					
10	*Prices based on double occupancy and do not include airfare. Taxes extra. A surcharge will apply for single occupancy.				
11					

Assessment

3 INSERT AND FORMAT SHAPES IN A COMPANY SALES WORKBOOK

1. Open **MSSales.xlsx** and then save the workbook with Save As and name it **EL1-C8-A3-MSSales**.
2. In cell A1, type Mountain, press Alt + Enter, and then type Systems.
3. Select *Mountain Systems* and then change the font to 26-point Calibri bold.
4. Change the horizontal alignment of cell A1 to left and the vertical alignment to middle.
5. Display the Format Cells dialog box with the Alignment tab selected and then change the *Indent* measurement to *2*. ***Hint: Display the Format Cells dialog box by clicking the Alignment group dialog box launcher in the Home tab.***
6. Click outside cell A1.
7. Use the *Isosceles Triangle* shape located in the *Basic Shapes* section of the Shapes drop-down palette to draw a triangle as shown in Figure 8.12.
8. Copy the triangle three times. Add olive green fill and dark olive green outline color of your choosing to the triangles so they appear in a similar manner to the triangles in Figure 8.12. Position the triangles as shown in the figure.
9. Apply shading to cells as shown in the figure (use colors in the Olive Green column).
10. Insert the total amounts in cells B10 through D10.
11. Insert the arrow pointing to $97,549 using the left arrow shape. Apply olive green fill to the shape and remove the shape outline. Set the text in 10-point Calibri bold. Position the arrow as shown in the figure.
12. Save, print, and then close **EL1-C8-A3-MSSales.xlsx**.

Figure 8.12 Assessment 3

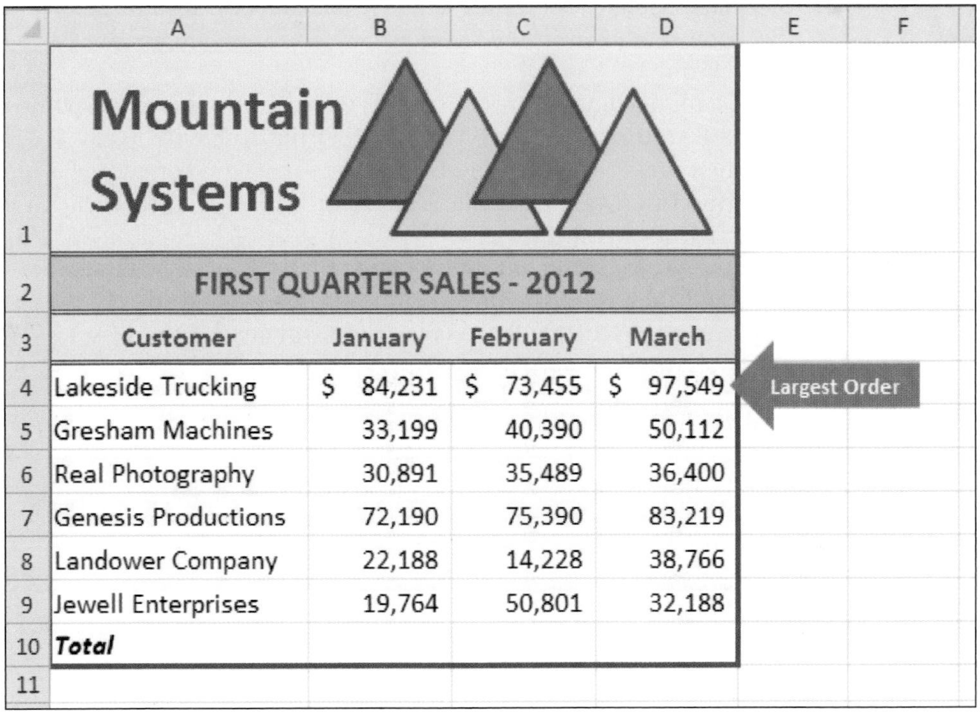

	A	B	C	D	E	F
1	Mountain Systems					
2	FIRST QUARTER SALES - 2012					
3	Customer	January	February	March		
4	Lakeside Trucking	$ 84,231	$ 73,455	$ 97,549	Largest Order	
5	Gresham Machines	33,199	40,390	50,112		
6	Real Photography	30,891	35,489	36,400		
7	Genesis Productions	72,190	75,390	83,219		
8	Landower Company	22,188	14,228	38,766		
9	Jewell Enterprises	19,764	50,801	32,188		
10	***Total***					
11						

Assessment

4 INSERT AND FORMAT A SMARTART DIAGRAM IN A SALES WORKBOOK

1. Open **PS2ndQtrSales.xlsx** and then save the workbook with Save As and name it **EL1-C8-A4-PS2ndQtrSales**.
2. Change the orientation to landscape.
3. Insert a pyramid shape at the right side of the worksheet data using the *Pyramid List* diagram with the following specifications:
   a. Change the color to *Gradient Loop - Accent 3*.
   b. Apply the *Cartoon* SmartArt style.
   c. In the bottom text box, type Red Level, press Enter, and then type $25,000 to $49,999.
   d. In the middle text box, type Blue Level, press Enter, and then type $50,000 to $99,999.
   e. In the top text box, type Gold Level, press Enter, and then type $100,000+.
   f. Apply fill to each of the text boxes to match the level color.
4. Size and/or move the diagram so it displays attractively at the right side of the worksheet data. (Make sure the entire diagram will print on the same page as the worksheet data.)
5. Save, print, and then close **EL1-C8-A4-PS2ndQtrSales.xlsx**.

Assessment

5 CREATE AND INSERT A SCREENSHOT

1. Open **RPRefiPlan.xlsx** and then display formulas by pressing Ctrl + `.
2. Insert the arrow shape shown in Figure 8.13. Add fill to the shape, remove the shape outline, bold the text in the shape, and then figure out how to rotate the shape using the rotation handle (green circle). Rotate, size, and position the arrow as shown in the figure.
3. Open Word.
4. At a blank document, press Ctrl + E to center the insertion point, press Ctrl + B to turn on bold, type Excel Worksheet with PMT Formula, and then press the Enter key twice.
5. Click the Insert tab, click the Screenshot button, and then click the thumbnail of the Excel worksheet.
6. Save the Word document and name it **EL1-C8-A5-PMTFormula**.
7. Print and then close the document and then exit Word.
8. In Excel, close **RPRefiPlan.xlsx** without saving the changes.

Figure 8.13 Assessment 5

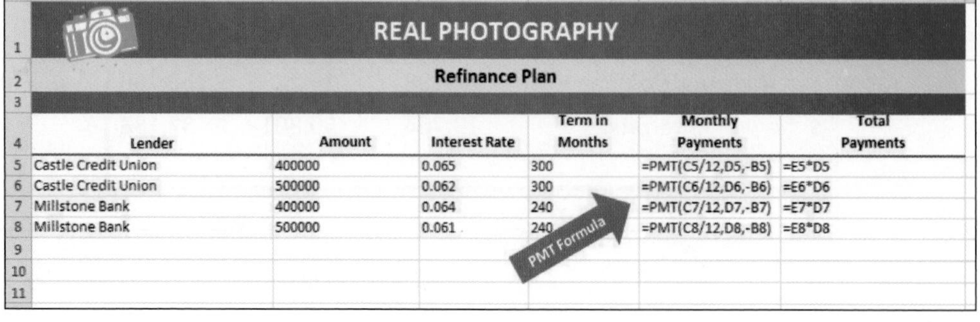

	A	B	C	D	E	F
1	REAL PHOTOGRAPHY					
2	Refinance Plan					
3						
4	Lender	Amount	Interest Rate	Term in Months	Monthly Payments	Total Payments
5	Castle Credit Union	400000	0.065	300	=PMT(C5/12,D5,-B5)	=E5*D5
6	Castle Credit Union	500000	0.062	300	=PMT(C6/12,D6,-B6)	=E6*D6
7	Millstone Bank	400000	0.064	240	=PMT(C7/12,D7,-B7)	=E7*D7
8	Millstone Bank	500000	0.061	240	=PMT(C8/12,D8,-B8)	=E8*D8
9						
10						
11						

PMT Formula

Visual Benchmark Demonstrate Your Proficiency

INSERT FORMULAS, WORDART, AND CLIP ART IN A WORKSHEET

1. Open **TSYrlySales.xlsx** and then save the workbook with Save As and name it **EL1-C8-VB-TSYrlySales**.
2. Insert the following formulas in the worksheet shown in Figure 8.14: (***Do not*** type the data in the following cells—instead insert the formulas as indicated. The results of your formulas should match the results you see in the figure.)
    - Cells C4 through C14: Insert a formula with an IF function that inserts *5%* if the amount in the cell in column B is greater than $249,999 and inserts *2%* if the amount is not greater than $249,999.
    - Cells D4 through D14: Insert a formula that multiplies the amount in column B with the amount in column C.
3. Insert the company name *Target Supplies* as WordArt with the following specifications:
    - Use the *Gradient Fill - Black, Outline - White, Outer Shadow* WordArt option.
    - To type the WordArt text, press Ctrl + L (this changes to left text alignment), type Target, press Enter, and then type Supplies.
    - Change the text outline color to *Orange, Accent 6, Darker 25%*.
    - Move the WordArt so it is positioned as shown in Figure 8.14.
4. Insert the target clip art image (use the word *target* to search for this clip art image) with the following specifications:
    - Change the color to *Red, Accent color 2 Dark*.
    - Change the correction to *Brightness: 0% (Normal) Contrast: +40%*.
    - Apply the *Drop Shadow Rectangle* picture style.
    - Size and position the clip art image as shown in the figure.
5. Draw the shape that displays below the data with the following specifications:
    - Use the *Bevel* shape (located in the *Basic Shapes* section).
    - Type the text in the shape, apply bold formatting, and change to center and middle alignment.
    - Change the shape fill color to *Red, Accent 2, Darker 50%*.
    - Change the shape outline color to *Orange, Accent 6, Darker 25%*.
6. Save and then print the worksheet.
7. Press Ctrl + ` to turn on the display of formulas and then print the worksheet again.
8. Turn off the display of formulas and then close the workbook.

Figure 8.14 Visual Benchmark

	A	B	C	D	E
1	Target Supplies				
2	ANNUAL CUSTOMER SALES ANALYSIS				
3	*Salesperson*	*Sales*	*Bonus*	*Bonus Amount*	
4	Barclay, Richard	$ 350,182	5%	$ 17,509	
5	Carolus, Lisa	203,485	2%	4,070	
6	Ehrlich, Arnold	150,274	2%	3,005	
7	Hale, Rebecca	363,740	5%	18,187	
8	Kinyon, Christopher	257,954	5%	12,898	
9	Martinez, Michelle	274,655	5%	13,733	
10	Oswald, Jeffery	109,485	2%	2,190	
11	Parente, Heather	200,455	2%	4,009	
12	Rios, Douglas	149,304	2%	2,986	
13	Uznay, Grace	302,938	5%	15,147	
14	Walden, Albert	177,439	2%	3,549	
15					
16					
17		Top Sales			
18		Rebecca Hale			
19					
20					

Case Study Apply Your Skills

Part 1

You are the office manager for Ocean Truck Sales and are responsible for maintaining a spreadsheet of the truck and SUV inventory. Open **OTSales.xlsx** and then save the workbook and name it **EL1-C8-CS-OTSales**. Apply formatting to improve the appearance of the worksheet and insert at least one clip art image (related to "truck" or "ocean"). Save **EL1-C8-CS-OTSales.xlsx** and then print the worksheet.

Part 2

With **EL1-C8-CS-OTSales.xlsx** open, save the workbook with Save As and name it **EL1-C8-CS-OTSalesF&C**. You make the inventory workbook available to each salesperson at the beginning of the week. For easier viewing, you decide to divide the workbook into two worksheets with one worksheet containing all Ford vehicles and the other worksheet containing all Chevrolet vehicles. Rename the worksheet tabs to reflect the contents. Sort each worksheet by price from the most expensive to the least expensive. The owner offers incentives each week to help motivate the sales force. Insert in the first worksheet a SmartArt diagram of your choosing that contains the following information:

Small-sized truck = $100

2WD Regular Cab = $75

SUV 4x4 = $50

Copy the diagram in the first worksheet and then paste it into the second worksheet. Change the orientation to landscape and then save, print, and close **EL1-C8-CS-OTSalesF&C.xlsx**.

Part 3

You have been asked to save the inventory worksheet as a web page for viewing online. Open **EL1-C8-CS-OTSales.xlsx**, display the Save As dialog box, click the *Save as type* option, and then determine how to save the workbook as a single file web page (*.mht, *.mhtml). Save the workbook as a single file web page with the name **EL1-CS-OTSales-WebPage**. Open your Internet browser and then open the web page. Look at the information in the file and then close the Internet browser.

Part 4

As part of your weekly duties, you need to post the incentive diagram in various locations throughout the company. You decide to insert the diagram in PowerPoint for easy printing. Open **EL1-C8-CS-OTSalesF&C.xlsx** and then open PowerPoint. Change the slide layout in PowerPoint to Blank. Copy the diagram in the first worksheet and paste it into the PowerPoint blank slide. Increase and/or move the diagram so it better fills the slide. Print the slide and then close PowerPoint without saving the presentation. Close **EL1-C8-CS-OTSalesF&C.xlsx**.

Microsoft® Excel®

UNIT 2

Performance Assessment

Note: Before beginning unit assessments, copy to your storage medium the Excel2010L1U2 subfolder from the Excel2010L1 folder on the CD that accompanies this textbook and then make Excel2010L1U2 the active folder.

Assessing Proficiency

In this unit, you have learned how to work with multiple windows; move, copy, link, and paste data between workbooks and applications; create and customize charts with data in a worksheet; save a workbook as a web page; insert hyperlinks; and insert and customize pictures, clip art images, shapes, SmartArt diagrams, and WordArt.

Assessment 1 Copy and Paste Data and Insert WordArt in a Training Scores Workbook

1. Open **RLTraining.xlsx** and then save the workbook with Save As and name it **EL1-U2-A1-RLTraining**.
2. Delete row 15 (the row for *Kwieciak, Kathleen*).
3. Insert a formula in cell D4 that averages the percentages in cells B4 and C4.
4. Copy the formula in cell D4 down to cells D5 through D20.
5. Make cell A22 active, turn on bold, and then type Highest Averages.
6. Display the Clipboard task pane and make sure it is empty.
7. Select and then copy each of the following rows (individually): row 7, 10, 14, 16, and 18.
8. Make cell A23 active and then paste row 14 (the row for *Jewett, Troy*).
9. Make cell A24 active and then paste row 7 (the row for *Cumpston, Kurt*).
10. Make cell A25 active and then paste row 10 (the row for *Fisher-Edwards, Theresa*).
11. Make cell A26 active and then paste row 16 (the row for *Mathias, Caleb*).
12. Make cell A27 active and then paste row 18 (the row for *Nyegaard, Curtis*).
13. Click the Clear All button in the Clipboard task pane and then close the task pane.
14. Insert in cell A1 the text *Roseland* as WordArt. Format the WordArt text to add visual appeal to the worksheet.
15. Save, print, and then close **EL1-U2-A1-RLTraining.xlsx**.

Assessment 2 Manage Multiple Worksheets in a Projected Earnings Workbook

1. Open **RLProjEarnings.xlsx** and then save the workbook with Save As and name it **EL1-U2-A2-RLProjEarnings**.
2. Delete *Roseland* in cell A1. Open **EL1-U2-A1-RLTraining.xlsx** and then copy the *Roseland* WordArt text and paste it into cell A1 in **EL1-U2-A2-RLProjEarnings.xlsx**. If necessary, increase the height of row 1 to accommodate the WordArt text.
3. Notice the fill color in cells in **EL1-U2-A1-RLTraining.xlsx** and then apply the same fill color to cells of data in **EL1-U2-A2-RLProjEarnings.xlsx**. Close **EL1-U2-A1-RLTraining.xlsx**.
4. Select cells A1 through C11 and then copy and paste the cells to Sheet2 keeping the source column widths.
5. With Sheet2 displayed, make the following changes:
   a. Increase the height of row 1 to accommodate the WordArt text.
   b. Delete the contents of cell B2.
   c. Change the contents of the following cells:
      A6: Change *January* to *July*
      A7: Change *February* to *August*
      A8: Change *March* to *September*
      A9: Change *April* to *October*
      A10: Change *May* to *November*
      A11: Change *June* to *December*
      B6: Change *8.30%* to *8.10%*
      B8: Change *9.30%* to *8.70%*
6. Make Sheet1 active and then copy cell B2 and paste link it to cell B2 in Sheet2.
7. Rename Sheet1 to *First Half* and rename Sheet2 to *Second Half*.
8. Make the First Half worksheet active and then determine the effect on projected monthly earnings if the projected yearly income is increased by 10% by changing the number in cell B2 to *$1,480,380*.
9. Horizontally and vertically center both worksheets in the workbook and insert a custom header that prints your name at the left, the current date in the center, and the sheet name (click the Sheet Name button in the Header & Footer Elements group in the Header & Footer Tools Design tab) at the right.
10. Print both worksheets.
11. Determine the effect on projected monthly earnings if the projected yearly income is increased by 20% by changing the number in cell B2 to *$1,614,960*.
12. Save the workbook again and then print both worksheets.
13. Close **EL1-U2-A2-RLProjEarnings.xlsx**.

Assessment 3 Create Charts in Worksheets in a Sales Totals Workbook

1. Open **EPYrlySales.xlsx** and then save the workbook with Save As and name it **EL1-U2-A3-EPYrlySales**.
2. Rename Sheet1 to *2010 Sales*, rename Sheet2 to *2011 Sales*, and rename Sheet3 to *2012 Sales*.
3. Select all three sheet tabs, make cell A12 active, click the Bold button, and then type Total. Make cell B12 active and then insert a formula to total the amounts in cells B4 through B11. Make cell C12 active and then insert a formula to total the amounts in cells C4 through C11.
4. Make the 2010 Sales worksheet active, select cells A3 through C11 (make sure you do not select the totals in row 12) and create a column chart. Click the Switch Row/Column button at the Chart Tools Design tab. Apply formatting to increase the visual appeal of the chart. Drag the chart below the worksheet data. (Make sure the chart fits on the page.)
5. Make the 2011 Sales worksheet active and then create the same type of chart you created in Step 4.
6. Make the 2012 Sales worksheet active and then create the same type of chart you created in Step 4.
7. Save the workbook and then print the entire workbook.
8. Close **EL1-U2-A3-EPYrlySales.xlsx**.

Assessment 4 Create and Format a Line Chart

1. Type the following information in a worksheet:

Country	**Total Sales**
Denmark	$85,345
Finland	$71,450
Norway	$135,230
Sweden	$118,895

2. Using the data just entered in the worksheet, create a line chart with the following specifications:
   a. Apply a chart style of your choosing.
   b. Insert major and minor primary vertical gridlines.
   c. Insert drop lines. (Do this with the Lines button in the Analysis group in the Chart Tools Layout tab.)
   d. Apply any other formatting to improve the visual appeal of the chart.
   e. Move the chart to a new sheet.
3. Save the workbook and name it **EL1-U2-A4-CtrySales**.
4. Print only the sheet containing the chart.
5. Change the line chart to a bar chart of your choosing.
6. Save the workbook and then print only the sheet containing the chart.
7. Close **EL1-U2-A4-CtrySales.xlsx**.

Assessment 5 Create and Format a Pie Chart

1. Open **EPProdDept.xlsx** and then save the workbook with Save As and name it **EL1-U2-A5-EPProdDept**.
2. Create a pie chart as a separate sheet with the data in cells A3 through B10. You determine the type of pie. Include an appropriate title for the chart and include percentage labels.
3. Print only the sheet containing the chart.
4. Save and then close **EL1-U2-A5-EPProdDept.xlsx**.

Assessment 6 Insert a Text Box in and Save a Travel Workbook as a Web Page

1. Open **TravDest.xlsx** and then save the workbook with Save As and name it **EL1-U2-A6-TravDest**.
2. Insert a text box in the workbook with the following specifications:
   a. Draw the text box at the right side of the clip art image.
   b. Remove the fill in the text box and the outline around the text box.
   c. Type **Call 1-888-555-1288 for last-minute vacation specials!**
   d. Select the text and then change the font to 24-point Forte in a blue color.
   e. Size and position the text box so it appears visually balanced with the travel clip art image.
3. Make sure you are connected to the Internet and then search for sites that might be of interest to tourists for each of the cities in the worksheet. Write down the web address for the best web page you find for each city.
4. Create a hyperlink for each city to the web address you wrote down in Step 3. (Select the hyperlink text in each cell and change the font size to 18 points.)
5. Test the hyperlinks to make sure you entered the web addresses correctly by clicking each hyperlink and then closing the web browser.
6. Save, print, and then close **EL1-U2-A6-TravDest.xlsx**.

Assessment 7 Insert Clip Art Image and SmartArt Diagram in a Projected Quotas Workbook

1. Open **SalesQuotas.xlsx** and then save the workbook with Save As and name it **EL1-U2-A7-SalesQuotas**.
2. Insert a formula in cell C3 using an absolute reference to determine the projected quotas at a 10% increase of the current quotas.
3. Copy the formula in cell C3 down to cells C4 through C12. Apply the Accounting Number Format style to cell C3.
4. Insert a clip art image in row 1 related to money. You determine the size and position of the clip art image. If necessary, increase the height of the row.
5. Insert a SmartArt diagram at the right side of the data that contains three shapes. Insert the following quota ranges in the shapes and apply the specified fill color:
   $50,000 to $99,999 (apply green color)
   $100,000 to $149,999 (apply blue color)
   $150,000 to $200,000 (apply red color)
6. Apply formatting to the SmartArt diagram to improve the visual appeal.
7. Insert a custom header that prints your name at the left, the current date in the middle, and the file name at the right.
8. Change the orientation to landscape and make sure the diagram fits on the page.
9. Save, print, and then close **EL1-U2-A7-SalesQuotas.xlsx**.

Assessment 8 Insert Symbol, Clip Art, and Comments in a Sales Workbook

1. Open **CISales.xlsx** and then save the workbook with Save As and name it **EL1-U2-A8-CISales**.
2. Delete the text *Landower Company* in cell A7 and then type **Económico** in the cell. (Use the Symbol dialog box to insert *ó*.)
3. Insert a new row at the beginning of the worksheet.
4. Select and then merge cells A1 through D1.
5. Increase the height of row 1 to approximately 141.00.
6. Insert the text *Custom Interiors* as WordArt in cell A1. You determine the formatting of the WordArt. Move and size the WordArt so it fits in cell A1.
7. Open Word and then open **CICustomers.docx** located in the Excel2010L1U2 folder on your storage medium. Click the Excel button and with **EL1-U2-A8-CISales.xlsx** open, make a screenshot (use the *Screen Clipping* option) of the customer information in the Word document. Position the screenshot image below the data in the cells.
8. Insert a custom footer that prints your name at the left and the file name at the right.
9. Make sure the data in cells and the screenshot display on the same page and then print the worksheet.
10. Save and then close **EL1-U2-A8-CISales.xlsx**.

Assessment 9 Insert and Format a Shape in a Budget Workbook

1. Open **SEExpenses.xlsx** and then save the workbook with Save As and name it **EL1-U2-A9-SEExpenses**.
2. Make the following changes to the worksheet so it displays as shown in Figure U2.1:
   a. Select and then merge cells A1 through D1.
   b. Add fill to the cells as shown in Figure U2.1.
   c. Increase the height of row 1 to the approximate size shown in Figure U2.1.
   d. Type the text **SOLAR ENTERPRISES** in cell A1 set in 20-point Calibri bold, center and middle aligned, and set in aqua (*Aqua, Accent 5, Darker 25%*).
   e. Insert the sun shape (located in the *Basic Shapes* section of the Shapes button drop-down list). Apply orange shape fill and change the shape outline to aqua (*Aqua, Accent 5, Darker 25%*)
3. Save, print, and then close **EL1-U2-A9-SEExpenses.xlsx**.

Figure U2.1 Assessment 9

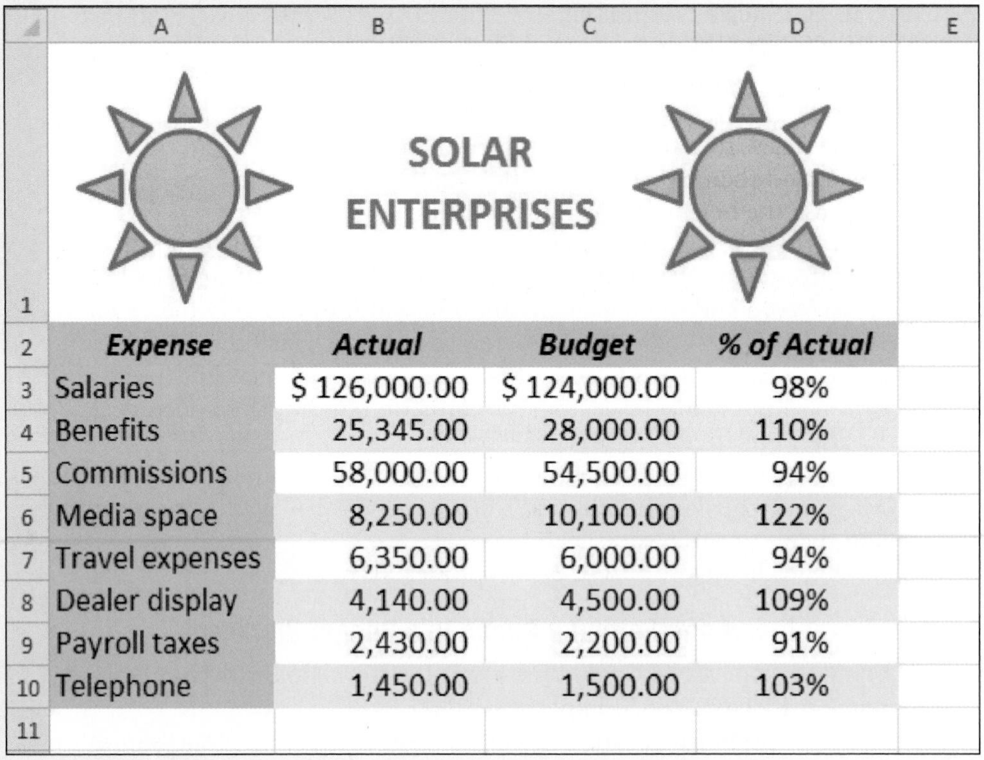

	A	B	C	D	E
1	SOLAR ENTERPRISES				
2	*Expense*	*Actual*	*Budget*	*% of Actual*	
3	Salaries	$ 126,000.00	$ 124,000.00	98%	
4	Benefits	25,345.00	28,000.00	110%	
5	Commissions	58,000.00	54,500.00	94%	
6	Media space	8,250.00	10,100.00	122%	
7	Travel expenses	6,350.00	6,000.00	94%	
8	Dealer display	4,140.00	4,500.00	109%	
9	Payroll taxes	2,430.00	2,200.00	91%	
10	Telephone	1,450.00	1,500.00	103%	
11					

Writing Activities

The following activities give you the opportunity to practice your writing skills along with demonstrating an understanding of some of the important Excel features you have mastered in this unit. Use correct grammar, appropriate word choices, and clear sentence constructions.

Activity 1 Prepare a Projected Budget

You are the accounting assistant in the financial department of McCormack Funds and you have been asked to prepare a yearly proposed department budget. The total amount for the department is $1,450,000. You are given the percentages for the proposed budget items, which are: Salaries, 45%; Benefits, 12%; Training, 14%; Administrative Costs, 10%; Equipment, 11%; and Supplies, 8%. Create a worksheet with this information that shows the projected yearly budget, the budget items in the department, the percentage of the budget, and the amount for each item. After the worksheet is completed, save the workbook and name it **EL1-U2-Act1-MFBudget**. Print and then close the workbook.

Optional: Using Word 2010, write a memo to the McCormack Funds Finance Department explaining that the proposed annual department budget is attached for their review. Comments and suggestions are to be sent to you within one week. Save the file and name it **EL1-U2-Act1-MFMemo**. Print and then close the file.

Activity 2 Create a Travel Tours Bar Chart

Prepare a worksheet in Excel for Carefree Travels that includes the following information:

Scandinavian Tours	
Country	**Tours Booked**
Norway	52
Sweden	62
Finland	29
Denmark	38

Use the information in the worksheet to create and format a bar chart as a separate sheet. Save the workbook and name it **EL1-U2-Act2-CTTours**. Print only the sheet containing the chart and then close **EL1-U2-Act2-CTTours.xlsx**.

Activity 3 Prepare a Ski Vacation Worksheet

Prepare a worksheet for Carefree Travels that advertises a snow skiing trip. Include the following information in the announcement:

- At the beginning of the worksheet, create a company logo that includes the company name *Carefree Travels* and a clip art image related to travel.
- Include the heading *Whistler Ski Vacation Package* in the worksheet.
- Include the following below the heading:
    - Round-trip air transportation: $395
    - Seven nights' hotel accommodations: $1,550
    - Four all-day ski passes: $425
    - Compact rental car with unlimited mileage: $250
    - Total price of the ski package: (calculate the total price)
- Include the following information somewhere in the worksheet:
    - Book your vacation today at special discount prices.
    - Two-for-one discount at many of the local ski resorts.

Save the workbook and name it **EL1-U2-Act3-CTSkiTrips**. Print and then close **EL1-U2-Act3-CTSkiTrips.xlsx**.

Internet Research

Find Information on Excel Books and Present the Data in a Worksheet

Locate two companies on the Internet that sell new books. At the first new book company site, locate three books on Microsoft Excel. Record the title, author, and price for each book. At the second new book company site, locate the same three books and record the prices. Create an Excel worksheet that includes the following information:

- Name of each new book company
- Title and author of the three books
- Prices for each book from the two book company sites

Create a hyperlink for each book company to the website on the Internet. Then save the completed workbook and name it **EL1-U2-DR-Books**. Print and then close the workbook.

Job Study

Create a Customized Time Card for a Landscaping Company

You are the manager of a landscaping company and are responsible for employee time cards. Locate the time card template that is available with *Sample templates* selected at the New tab Backstage view. Use the template to create a customized time card for your company. With the template open, insert additional blank rows to increase the spacing above the Employee row. Insert a clip art image related to landscaping or gardening and position and size it attractively in the form. Include a text box with the text Lawn and Landscaping Specialists inside the box. Format, size, and position the text attractively in the form. Fill in the form for the current week with the following employee information:

Employee = Jonathan Holder
Address = 12332 South 152nd Street, Baton Rouge, LA 70804
Manager = (Your name)
Employee phone = (225) 555-3092
Employee email = None
Regular hours = 8 hours for Monday, Tuesday, Wednesday, and Thursday
Overtime = 2 hours on Wednesday
Sick hours = None
Vacation = 8 hours on Friday
Rate per hour = $20.00
Overtime pay = $30.00

Save the completed form and name it **EL1-U2-JS-TimeCard**. Print and then close **EL1-U2-JS-TimeCard.xlsx**.

Index

D

I

K

L

M

N

O

X

Y

Excel 2010 Feature	Ribbon Tab, Group	Button	Shortcut
Accounting number format	Home, Number		
Align text left	Home, Alignment		
Align text right	Home, Alignment		
Bold	Home, Font		Ctrl + B
Borders	Home, Font		
Bottom align	Home, Alignment		
Cell styles	Home, Styles		
Center	Home, Alignment		
Change file type	File, Save & Send		
Clip Art	Insert, Illustrations		
Close workbook	File		Ctrl + F4
Comma style	Home, Number		
Comments	Review, Comments		
Conditional Formatting	Home, Styles		
Consolidate	Data, Consolidate		
Convert Text to Columns	Table Tools Design, Tools		
Copy	Home, Clipboard		Ctrl + C
Custom number format	Home, Number		
Cut	Home, Clipboard		Ctrl + X
Data Table	Data, Data Tools		
Data Validation	Data, Data Tools		

Excel 2010 Feature	Ribbon Tab, Group	Button	Shortcut
Decrease decimal	Home, Number		
Decrease indent	Home, Alignment		Ctrl + Alt + Shift + Tab
Delete cells	Home, Cells		
Document Inspector	File, Info		
Fill color	Home, Editing		
Financial functions	Formulas, Function Library		
Find & Select	Home, Editing		
Font color	Home, Font		
Format Painter	Home, Clipboard		
Goal Seek	Data, Data Tools		
Group and Ungroup	Data, Outline		Shift + Alt + Right Arrow key, Shift + Alt + Left Arrow key
Header & Footer	Insert, Text		
Help			F1
Hyperlink	Insert, Links		Ctrl + K
Import from Access, web page, or text file	Data, Get External Data		
Increase decimal	Home, Number		
Increase indent	Home, Alignment		Ctrl + Shift + Tab
Insert cells	Home, Cells		
Insert Chart dialog box	Insert, Charts		
Insert function dialog box	Formulas, Function Library		
Italic	Home, Font		Ctrl + I

Excel 2010 Feature	Ribbon Tab, Group	Button	Shortcut
Logical functions	Formulas, Function Library		
Lookup & Reference functions	Formulas, Function Library		
Macros	View, Macros		Alt + F8
Mark workbook as final	File, Info		
Math & Trigonometry functions	Formulas, Function Library		
Merge & Center	Home, Alignment		
Middle align	Home, Alignment		
Name Manager dialog box	Formulas, Defined Names		
New workbook	File, New		Ctrl + N
Number format	Home, Number	General	
Open dialog box	File	Open	Ctrl + O
Orientation	Home, Alignment		
Page orientation	Page Layout, Page Setup		
Paste	Home, Clipboard		Ctrl + V
Percent style	Home, Number	%	Ctrl + Shift + %
PivotTable or PivotChart	Insert, Tables or PivotTable Tools Options, Tools		
Print tab Backstage view	File, Print		Ctrl + P
Protect Worksheet	Review, Changes		
Remove Duplicates	Data, Data Tools or Table Tools Design, Tools		
Save or Save As	File	Save As	Ctrl + S, F12
Save as PDF/XPS	File, Save & Send		

Excel 2010 Feature	Ribbon Tab, Group	Button	Shortcut
Scenario Manager	Data, Data Tools		
Screenshot	Insert, Illustrations		
Share workbook	Review, Changes		
SmartArt	Insert, Illustrations		
Sort & Filter	Home, Editing		
Sparklines	Insert, Sparklines		
Spelling	Review, Proofing		
Statistical functions	Formulas, Function Library		
Subtotals	Data, Outline		
Sum	Home, Editing	Σ	Alt + =
Symbol dialog box	Insert, Symbols	Ω	
Text box	Insert, Text		
Text functions	Formulas, Function Library		
Themes	Page Layout, Themes		
Top align	Home, Alignment		
Trace Dependents or Trace Precedents	Formulas, Auditing		
Track Changes	Review, Changes		
Underline	Home, Font	U	Ctrl + U
Unlock cells	Home, Cells		
Wrap text	Home, Alignment		